From Hunters to Farmers

FROM HUNTERS TO FARMERS

**The Causes and Consequences
of Food Production
in Africa**

EDITED BY

J. Desmond Clark
AND *Steven A. Brandt*

*University of California Press
Berkeley, Los Angeles, London*

University of California Press
Berkeley and Los Angeles, California
University of California Press, Ltd.
London, England
© 1984 by
The Regents of the University of California
Printed in the United States of America
1 2 3 4 5 6 7 8 9

Library of Congress Cataloging in Publication Data
Main entry under title:

From hunters to farmers.

Bibliography: p.
Includes index.
1. Agriculture, Primitive—Africa—Addresses,
essays, lectures. 2. Agriculture—Origin—Addresses,
essays, lectures. 3. Neolithic period—Africa—Addresses,
essays, lectures. 4. Africa—Antiquities—Addresses, essays,
lectures. I. Clark, J. Desmond (John Desmond), 1916–
II. Brandt, Steven A.
GN861.F73 1983   307.7'2'096   82–20004
ISBN 0–520–04574–2

Contents

List of Figures

An Introduction to an Introduction

J. DESMOND CLARK AND
STEVEN A. BRANDT

On November 17, 1978, a symposium entitled
"The Causes and Consequences of Food Production in Africa" was held in Los Angeles as part of
the Seventy-Seventh Annual Meeting of the American Anthropological Association. The main purpose of the symposium was to present to a broad,
anthropologically oriented audience the current
state of research into Late Quaternary human/
plant/animal relationships and the processes leading to food production in Africa. An overriding
concern of the session was to consider what advances over the last decade had been made in our
understanding of *why*, and not just of *how*, food
production came about and what avenues of research still remained open for future investigations.

Upon moving west or south of Egypt, many
anthropologists may be somewhat unfamiliar with
the modern food production systems in Africa and
this, to a certain extent, is understandable, since
many of the indigenously domesticated plants such
as sorghum, *noog*, *enset*, finger millet, oil palm and
African rice, to mention only a few, are not exactly
common fare on our Western dinner-table! Nevertheless, these and other more familiar plants, as
well as animals, are of vital importance to the hundreds of millions of Africans dependent upon such

foods, not only for their daily meal but for life itself.

Now that archaeologists are concentrating their efforts upon elucidation of the processes leading to food production (and on the results of these processes), it has become necessary to expand our geographical horizons in search of models of culture change that are applicable not only to one specific region but are also relevant to an understanding of the more global question of why humans first took to domesticating plants and animals, the consequences of which have largely shaped the world in which we live. The participants of the symposium shared the belief that Africa represented one of the most important laboratories for investigating this question, for it is in that continent that traditional forms of agriculture still persist and can be used to compare and contrast the ever-growing evidence of such traditional systems provided by the archaeological record. Moreover, most of the remaining hunters and gatherers who still inhabit tropical and subtropical latitudes are found in Africa. Many of these people are now in the process of changing their subsistence strategies from hunting/gathering to food-producing, and it is from these people that we may expect to gain insights into the reasons behind such a significant shift and its social and economic ramifications.

The papers presented at the symposium dealt with a diverse yet cohesive set of topics which included (1) the climatic and human impact on the physical environment; (2) the development of pre-adaptive strategies for domestication; (3) the transition from food-collecting to food-producing and its social, economic, and technological consequences; (4) dietary studies from faunal assemblages; (5) the relatively late introduction of domesticates into southern Africa; and (6) ethnographic and ethnoarchaeological investigations into the transition from hunting and gathering to food production. The encouraging reception the symposium received and the interest it aroused have prompted us to publish the papers that were presented and, where regional or conceptual gaps needed to be filled, to solicit some additional chapters in order to produce a more balanced coverage, as far as possible in a single volume.

More than eight years have elapsed since the

first conference on the origins of African agriculture, sponsored by the Wenner-Gren Foundation for Anthropological Research, was held in Austria in 1972. This first interdisciplinary conference represents a milestone in the study of agricultural origins but it, nevertheless, was concerned almost exclusively with the evidence for plant domestication; the results were published in 1976 (*Origins of African Plant Domestication*, edited by J. R. Harlan et al., 1976a). The Los Angeles symposium, therefore, represents the first time that specialists engaged in the study of both African plant *and* animal domesticates had met. Ethnography shows the intimate relationship existing in the traditional patterns of African agriculture between the human populations and their stock and food plants. This is hardly surprising, since a similar inseparable bond is present between the hunter/gatherers and the game and plants and, indeed, all the natural features of the environment in which they live. When *nagana* or other diseases do not preclude the keeping of stock, it is usually the animals, especially cattle and camels, that determine how the society is organized. When the larger animal domesticates are absent, one or more staple food plants are the basis of the economy and the lives of those relying on them are controlled by the seasonal activities relating to their cultivation and storage. Where mixed farming is possible, many different kinds of behavioral adjustments are found. These have their origins in the relative genetic suitability and yields of the different resources in the varied tropical and subtropical environments where they are used; in the traditional behavior of the farmers; and in the extent to which the availability of both plants and animals can serve as insurance against disasters that periodically result from reliance on herding or cultivating alone. These are patterns that archaeology, the historical record (where available) and the evidence from historical linguistics and oral tradition show to be deeply rooted in the past, representing continuities that can be seen to stretch back in some cases for several millennia.

Archaeologists in Africa have in general adopted an empirical approach to their material and this has resulted in some significant inductive models. In full context, the archaeological evidence will always be the basis for understanding the sequence of events and activities at any particular site, besides showing how groups of sites may be interrelated, and it is this that generates the hypotheses on which the specific site interpretations are made. The part played by each site in the general subsistence pattern will be understood better by adopting a broad, systemic view of prehistoric economy, as some of the contributors to this volume demonstrate, and thereby making possible a more realistic comprehension of the changes that had to be made in the transition from one land-use pattern to another and so of the chain of events and processes leading ultimately to the village-farming way of life. Although we are never likely and, indeed, have no way yet to know the precise course this may have taken in any one region or population, the improved methods now in use for recovery and interpretation of the archaeological evidence are greatly increasing the amount of information that a site can provide. And now that archaeologists are beginning to study their material with the eyes and perception of the anthropologist and the ecologist, some notable advances have already been made, as this volume demonstrates, but shows also where these new strategies and concepts still remain to be applied. The increasing interest in the African evidence for what it can contribute to a better understanding of the problems facing specialists in many other fields besides archaeology—animal and plant geneticists, ecologists, epidemiologists, nutritionists, pathologists, linguists, and many others—and most especially also of the problems of the African peoples themselves, is attracting new resources and expertise that will narrow down the possible alternative pathways and so bring about a more realistic appreciation of the causes of the adoption of food production and of the consequent adaptations necessitated in any one region and that are antecedant to the indigenous pastoral and agricultural economies of Africa today.

If the wild cattle of northern Africa are now seen as the most likely ancestors of the indigenous humpless domestic stock, the origins of the sheep, goats, as also of the camel, must be sought outside the continent, as no wild ancestors of these are known to have been present in Africa in the late Pleistocene or early Holocene. Although the Egyptians experimented with a number of indigenous animals and birds, the only other important animal domesticate of African origin is the donkey. The significance of the donkey, however, is not so much for food as for transport, especially where mobility was an essential part of the economic pattern. If Africa is deficient in successful, indigenous, domesticated food animals, this is not so where the plants are concerned and more than forty genera and species of plants have been domesticated, of which a number are still very important, or even staple, crops for the peoples who first brought them under cultivation.

This diversity of cultigens and paucity of animal domesticates is examined in this book against the background of the climatic and environmental events that preceded and accompanied the change to pastoralism and agriculture. Some significant new evidence has become available over the last few years that has made it necessary to revise the views expressed in some of the papers given at the 1976 symposium so that the present volume is concerned with presenting some of this new evidence and the new hypotheses and models generated from it. Of special importance also are the studies being carried out on the causes and effects of the adoption of domestic stock and cultivating by the San of the Kalahari. These show how some San were able to remain independent and to continue in their hunting and gathering way of life by establishing a viable, symbiotic relationship with the surrounding agriculturalists and pastoralists. Other groups provide examples of how, when the pressures or incentives are strong enough, stock-keeping and cultivation can be successfully incorporated into the economy without having to relinquish very much of the traditional behavior. The next step, for which the Sandawe of central Tanzania might provide the model, is one in which incipient agriculture leads to efficient food production.

It must be emphasized that systematic and interdisciplinary work on the transition to agriculture in Africa is only now beginning. The archaeological evidence is minimal, that from linguistics cannot be securely tied into any chronological framework, the historical evidence is usually highly ambiguous, and the ethnographic is subject to the shortcomings arising from inability to assess the effects that past cultural interactions may have had on traditional structure and economy as these changed through time. We are, therefore, very much at the beginning but, with each new decade, we come closer to a better understanding of some of the causes and consequences of the change from hunting and gathering to food-producing. Since this volume provides a broad spectrum of information relevant to this transition, presenting new evidence, new approaches, and some new understanding, we hope it will prove useful to a wide range of anthropologists as well as to non-anthropologists.

The editors would like to acknowledge the extensive and invaluable help provided by Mrs. B. C. Clark with the subediting.

November, 1980

I

General Perspectives: Historical Critique and the Evidence from Botany and Linguistics

INTRODUCTION

If efficient subsistence agriculture is the base on which all the higher civilizations of the world were built up, it might be expected that domestic animals and plants would have spread and been adopted rapidly wherever they could be kept or cultivated. That such was not the case is only too clear from archaeology and ethnography. The change from food-gathering to food production, once looked upon as a relatively rapid transition—a revolution—can now be seen to have its roots in the late Pleistocene and to have been sporadic rather than spontaneous, in accordance with the local circumstances affecting individual populations. It was not, however, until the work of Lee, Woodburn, and others among the Kalahari San and the Hadza of Tanzania that archaeologists began to recognize the resistance to change that appears to be a characteristic of all hunting and gathering populations. By making the change to food-producing, not only is personal liberty sacrificed but drastic reorganization of the whole social system becomes essential. Also, the balanced diet enjoyed by most hunter/gatherers renders them nutritionally much better off than many subsistence farmers, so that it is not difficult to see why stock-keeping and cultivating became acceptable only after stresses on the existing system became sufficiently great or compelling to provide the incentive to balance the advantages of a change against its disadvantages.

In much of tropical Africa the great richness of the biome appears to have made the hunting/gathering way of life viable for a good deal longer than it was in the subtropical or temperate regions of the world. At least the chronology indicates that agriculture was later in coming to sub-Saharan Africa than to southwest Asia, for example, where it may well have been that domestication was the only practical way that each of the post-Pleistocene populations had of combatting stresses brought about by environmental changes and increased population pressures. In Africa other alternatives were possible besides turning to food production. Such alternatives stemmed from the degree of mobility allowed by the geography and ecosystems of the continent and from the abundance and range of different kinds of animal and plant resources available. Such broadly based economies were able to persist, sometimes up to historic times or even to the present day where symbiotic exchange relationships were successfully established with food producers. This offers one explanation as to why the late Paleolithic populations of the Nile, who were collecting, perhaps even sowing and reaping, barley and wheat 18,000 years ago in Upper Egypt during a period of severe aridity, did not make the change to farming long before the fifth millennium B.C. and why the populations of the subcontinent did not adopt agriculture until the coming of the Bantu-speaking metallurgists in the early centuries of the first millennium A.D.

The environment and biome of the higher rainfall parts of tropical Africa were less affected by the climatic fluctuations in rainfall and temperature of the late Pleistocene and earlier Holocene than was most of northern Africa, where the ecological disequilibrium caused in the fragile environments of the desert and Sahel is believed to have been an important factor in hastening the domestication process. While the effects of drought and famine on the overpopulated parts of the West African Sahel are only too obvious, it is not always easy to make any direct correlation between climatic fluctuation and economic change, and it is likely that the effects of any such change will become apparent

in the archaeological record after rather than during times of climatic adversity. Ann Stahl provides an historical synopsis of this and of the course of investigations into the origins of African plant domestication and the way in which ideas have changed—from the simple diffusionist hypothesis deriving sub-Saharan agriculture through stimulus diffusion from the Nile Valley—to that of independent centers in West Africa and Ethiopia—to the broad, systemic approach favored today.

Plant geneticists have shown that the crucial zone for the development of indigenous African crops was the Sahel, Sudan, and ecotone between the Sudan and the forest south of the Sahara, stretching from Senegambia in the west to the Ethiopian highlands in the east. It is here that the great majority of the indigenous African food plants were brought under cultivation. The development of these cereal grasses and plant cultigens appears on the present evidence to coincide in time with a period of rapid desiccation in the Sahara after 2000 B.C. While not precluding a much earlier manifestation of these plant staples, the chronology as we know it today suggests that the movement of large numbers of cattle pastoralists out of the Sahara into the Sahel and Sudan is related to the change from gathering to regular crop cultivation there, and Ann Stahl discusses some of the hypotheses and models that have been put forward to explain how this came about, why it occurred where it did, and the processes whereby complexes of crops spread into the subcontinent.

Archaeological evidence for food production is both direct, from the plants and animals themselves, and indirect, from cultural and other evidence in archaeological context. Daniel Livingstone discusses some of the botanical evidence and its shortcomings, in particular as regards pollens, showing that, in this field, the archaeologist should no longer expect much help from the palynologist where it comes to identifying cultivated and wild forms apart, while we stand much more chance of success from grains, inflorescences, and other macro-remains of plants.

It is perhaps this uncertainty, not to say disappointment, that has caused archaeologists to turn to the evidence for the spread of food production that is offered by historical and linguistic data. As

Christopher Ehret shows in his discussion, there is a wealth of evidence here if it were only possible to reconcile it with that coming from archaeology and the chronological framework established by the radiocarbon and other chronometric methods. The linguistic evidence seems to favor a long chronology, the archaeological evidence a short one, and the best promise of being able to reconcile them will come from systematic archaeological fieldwork of a regional nature at carefully selected multi-context sites with good preservation of fauna and, hopefully, also of plant remains. Good radiometrically dated sequences that might in time be tied into the Dynastic Egyptian historical chronology will provide the best framework, within which the linguistic evidence for the migrations of peoples and the spread and borrowings of domesticates and technologies will add greatly to understanding the ramifications of food-producing economies and the peoples who adopted them.

1

A History and Critique of Investigations into Early African Agriculture

ANN BROWER STAHL

The purpose of this paper is to trace the development of thought concerning early African agriculture, to assess critically the direction past research has taken, and to suggest lines for future research. *Agriculture* is defined here as a subsistence strategy that relies in whole or in part on the cultivation of crops. In some instances the terms *agriculture* and *crop cultivation* will be used interchangeably. In order to limit the scope of the paper, no consideration is given to the study of animal domestication, to the sources of domestic animals found in the African continent, or to any impact the introduction of domestic animals may have had on the transition to crop cultivation.

Three issues have proved to be of outstanding importance in the study of early African agriculture: (1) the geographic origin of African agriculture; (2) the effect of climatic change on the transition from hunting and gathering to agriculture; and (3) the spread of crop complexes in the African continent. Each of these topics and the relevant studies will be reviewed in the following sections.

Geographic Origins: Independent Invention, or Diffusion?

A major concern of researchers has been to determine whether or not an independent "invention" of agriculture took place on the African continent. Coupled with this has been an interest in the geographic origins of specific crops. To begin with, subsistence agriculture on the African continent may be divided into two categories on the basis of crop types, namely, grains or cereals and vegeculture (plant crops such as yams) (D. R. Harris, 1976).

CEREAL CROPS

The earliest studies of African agriculture were undertaken by botanists and plant geographers, whose studies were based, reasonably enough, upon distributions of present-day cultigens and their proposed wild ancestors. Vavilov (1951b: 37–39) first drew attention to the African continent as a possible early center of plant domestication when he included Ethiopia in his list of independent centers of agricultural development, attributing a total of thirty-eight species of grain crops, oil plants, vegetables, spices, and stimulants to his Ethiopian center (Ethiopia, Eritrea, and Somalia).

The French botanist Chevalier (1938) disagreed with the placement of Vavilov's center. Instead, he saw a center of cereal-crop domestication on the fringes of the Sahara. Portères, another French botanist, has suggested that two centers of domestication should be recognized in Africa, one in the east and the other in the west. It is his "West African center" which has received the most attention in the literature. From an analysis of variation of African rice (*Oryza glaberrima*), Portères concluded that its primary center of domestication was along the central Niger, with a secondary center in the Senegambian region (Portères, 1950; 1962; 1976). Portères thought that the cultivation of African rice was associated with Senegambian megalithic sites, which he suggested might date from 1500 to 800 B.C. More recent evidence, however, indicates that the megalithic complex probably

dates between 200 B.C. and A.D. 800 (Hill, 1978: 605), although to the best of this writer's knowledge, no evidence is available regarding the subsistence base of the peoples associated with the megalithic circles.

Largely on the basis of ethnographic and linguistic evidence, G. P. Murdock (1959: 64, 67) claimed that independent development of agriculture had occurred around the headwaters of the Niger River in approximately 4500 B.C.:

> Agriculture must have been fully established in the Sudan before this region was exposed to the diffusion of southwest Asian crops from Egypt, which could not have been many centuries after 4,500 B.C., or else borrowing of cultivated plants from this source would surely have been more extensive than it has been in actual fact. Fewer than ten Negro tribes in the entire Sudan, for example, have adopted either barley or wheat.

Murdock failed to make the point, however, that both barley and wheat are crops of the temperate zone and do not grow well in tropical regions unless cultivated under irrigation or at high altitudes (Purseglove, 1972: 159, 293).

Murdock (1959: 66–67) suggested that Mande speakers had developed the "Sudanic complex" of crops. "We should expect the particular people who first advanced from a hunting and gathering economy to an agricultural one to have multiplied in number and to have expanded geographically at the expense of their more backward neighbors, with the result that the group of languages which they spoke should have spread over an unusually wide expanse of territory." Other factors could have been involved in this expansion of the Mande languages, however, and there is no evidence that agriculture played a key role. C. Wrigley (1960) argued that "the dispersion of Mande languages can more plausibly be attributed to empire-building and trading activities at a very much later date," a view shared by J. D. Fage (1961: 305).

Murdock's hypothesis has found only limited support among his colleagues (Stanton, 1962; Anderson, 1960; 1967). From an analysis of the distribution of agricultural societies displaying interest or disinterest in ornamental plants, Anderson (1960: 80) concluded that "they are concentrically arranged around two poles. The pole of non-floral, seed-crop agriculture is in central Africa. The pole of floral agriculture is in Indonesia." This geographical separation indicated to Anderson an independent origin for agriculture in each of these regions. He saw the Middle East as an area in which these two types of agriculture met and intermingled, and he welcomed Murdock's analysis as independent verification of his own ideas.

Among other researchers who have conceded the possibility of an independent development of seed-crop agriculture in Africa are Hobler and Hester (1969), Hays (1975), D. R. Harris (1976: 352), Higgs (1976: 30), T. Shaw (1978: 63–64), and Wendorf et al. (1979).

By far the most popular view of the origins of cereal-crop agriculture in sub-Saharan Africa is that it was the product of human migration or some form of culture diffusion or stimulus deriving from southwest Asia (e.g., Sutton, 1967; Aschmann, 1968: 495; Brentjes, 1968; Clark, 1976b). One such suggestion is that a group (or groups) of wheat and barley cultivators moved into the Sahara from the north and northwest during a period of climatic amelioration, taking with them crops ultimately derived from the Fertile Crescent. Later, deterioration of the Saharan climate forced some of these wheat and barley cultivators to move southward into the Sahel and Sudanic zones. As they continued their migration to the south, they found that their cultivars, which were suited to winter rains, had reached their ecological limits, and it was at this point that domestication of indigenous sorghums and "millets" occurred. Variations on this theme are put forth by Wrigley (1960), J. D. Clark (1962; 1964b; 1967a; 1967b), Doggett (1965), Fagan (1965: 43–44), and Oliver and Fagan (1975: 20). Other researchers have suggested either diffusion of Middle Eastern crops without an accompanying migration or a stimulus diffusion whereby the "idea" of agriculture was introduced to sub-Saharan Africa (Wrigley, 1960; McMaster, 1962; Oliver, 1966; Posnansky, 1966; D. R. Harris, 1967; Mauny, 1967; H. J. Hugot, 1968; Munson, n.d.; 1976; Harlan et al., 1976b; Carter, 1977).

Discussion of the geographical origins of cereal-crop cultivation has focused largely on crops of the West African savanna. Only Portères (1950, 1962, 1976) has addressed himself at length to the origins of West African rice cultivation. The domestication of two Ethiopian crops, *teff*—(*Eragrostis tef*), a grain yielding flour, fodder, and straw—and *ensete*—(*Ensete ventricosum*), a variety of banana grown for its edible stalk—has received little attention in the literature. Clark originally believed that both were domesticated in Ethiopia by wheat and barley cultivators from the Upper Nile Valley (J. D. Clark, 1967a). Later, however, Clark commented that "it would seem unlikely that any of these cereals or ensete would have been domesticated if wheat and barley and the associated plough culture were already present in Ethiopia" (1976b: 78). Clark therefore suggested a (presumably) indigenous domestication of teff and a later introduction (ca. 500 B.C.) of wheat and barley by "Semitic South Arabians." Portères, by contrast, has attributed the domestication of teff to the "Cushites" of the Ethiopian high plateau, reasoning that, had the later "Semitic" populations domesticated teff, "there is no doubt that it would also have been cultivated as far as Asia Minor and around the Persian Gulf, along East Africa" (1976: 426). According to Purseglove, contemporary cultivation of *Eragrostis tef* is restricted to Ethiopia (1972: 157).

Lwanga-Lunyiigo (1976: 285–286) has made a claim for an independent origin of agriculture in the interlacustrine area of East Africa:

> Indirect evidence suggests that during the 1st millennium B.C., there was extensive forest clearance in the Lake Victoria basin. Pollen studies show that 3,000 years ago there was a sharp decrease in forest pollens and a corresponding rise in grass pollens. . . . All this points to the importance of the interlacustrine region with regard to the beginnings of agriculture.

Such evidence, however, hardly necessitates the presence of agricultural communities. A marked decrease in forest pollens could be the result of fire, induced by either a natural or a human agent; H. T. Lewis (1972) has noted the deliberate use of fire by man in Southwest Asia as an exploitative technique prior to the advent of agriculture. Lwanga-Lun-yiigo has suggested a date in the mid-first millennium B.C. for the conjectured independent development of agriculture in East Africa, and dismisses the possibility of external connections. He also (1976: 285) does not believe the "Stone Bowl Complex," present in the Rift Valley at this time, to have possessed domesticated crops. Influences from West Africa are "also unlikely, for it is not until the 1st millennium A.D. that there is evidence of agriculture in the Zaïre basin" (Lwanga-Lunyi-igo, 1976: 285). Negative evidence is not conclusive in this case, in view of the paucity of fieldwork in central Africa to date. In all, Lwanga-Lunyiigo presents no convincing evidence in support of an independent development of crop cultivation in East Africa.

Although the majority of researchers would support diffusionist interpretations, several have allowed that African populations may have been "pre-adapted" to seed-cultural systems of agriculture (i.e., they were intensive grain collectors) (J. D. Clark, 1967b: 14–15; 1971: 39–40; 1976a: 70–72; Seddon, 1968: 490; Wendorf et al., 1970: 1161; Wendorf and Schild, 1976b: 269). The use of sickles and grinding stones is evidenced in the Nile Valley as early as 12,500 B.C. (Wendorf et al., 1970: 1161; Wendorf and Schild, 1976a: 270–71), suggesting the use of ground grain as a food source. This is "some 4000 years earlier than suggested by present evidence for the use of this food source in the Levant or elsewhere in the Near East" (Wendorf et al., 1970: 1161). In the past, Wendorf et al. (1970: 1161) and Wendorf and Schild (1976b: 269) suggested that the distribution of the wild wheats and barleys may have been significantly different at 10,000 B.C. from that witnessed today. If so, this distribution *may* have included the Nile Valley, and the inhabitants of the Nile Valley *may* have played a part in the domestication of these crops (Wendorf et al., 1970: 1161; Wendorf and Schild, 1976b: 269). Recent evidence has substantiated this viewpoint (Wendorf et al., 1979). The recovery of carbonized barley (*Hordeum vulgare*) from a late Paleolithic context at Wadi Kubbaniya, north of Aswan, is indicative of at least incipient cultivation in the Nile Valley 17,000 to 18,000 years ago (Wendorf et al., 1979: 1341, 1345–47).

J. D. Clark (1971: 39–40; 1976a: 70–72) has also commented on this early use of ground grain in the Nile Valley. Given an early orientation toward such a subsistence adaptation, Clark found it "difficult to understand why a similar manipulation of plant . . . resources leading to incipient domestication was not taking place in the Nile between 12,000 and 5000 B.C." (Clark, 1976a: 71). Nile Valley populations were, nonetheless, "pre-adapted communities that were very ready to accept food production" (Clark, 1976a: 72).

Clark implied a similar situation for West Africa (1967b: 14–15). He has suggested that populations south of the Sahara would have begun experimenting with plant resources as a result of contact with Saharan pastoralists (Clark, 1967b: 14). Sorghum and "millet" may have served as "subsidiary crops" for these Sudanic populations prior to 2000 B.C. but it was not until after 2000 B.C., with the desiccation of the Sahara, that they were fully domesticated. Their domestication was dependent upon the dispersal of the Saharan pastoralists, who were in need of summer rainfall substitutes for wheat and barley (Clark, 1967b: 15).

VEGECULTURAL COMPLEXES

The question of the geographical origin of West African forest agriculture has generally been ignored in favor of studies of the origin of seed-crop cultivation. This may result in part from the fact that the replacement of indigenous forest cultigens by American and Indonesian crops has been more complete than in the savanna zone (e.g., manioc, cocoyam, plantain, Southeast Asian yams). By colonial times, many of these nonindigenous cultigens were firmly entrenched in the diet of the humid tropical peoples. It was felt, therefore, that agriculture in the forested regions was a relatively recent phenomenon, dependent upon the arrival of these crops. Additionally, it was believed that agriculture in the forest would have been impossible before the advent of iron. Some researchers have suggested that without iron tools, man would have been unable to clear the forest (J. D. Clark, 1962: 212; 1967b: 16; David, 1976: 231).

One of the earliest researchers to speculate on

the "penetration" of the forest zone was Murdock (1959). Although he had included several indigenous species of yam (*Dioscorea* sp.) in his list of West African domesticates, Murdock did not consider these important staple foods (1959: 222). In his opinion (1959: 233, 273), the forest zone would have remained uninhabitable for the agriculturalist until the arrival of the Malaysian food crops (Asian yams: *D. alata* and *D. esculenta*; taro: *Colocasia esculenta*; and bananas: *Musa sapientum*). This view has been expressed by a number of other researchers as well (J. D. Clark, 1962: 212; 1964b: 181; 1967b: 16; Cole, 1963: 275; Fagan, 1965: 48; Oliver, 1966: 364; Posnansky, 1966: 90–91; D. R. Harris, 1967: 100; Wiesenfeld, 1967: 1135; T. Shaw, 1968: 500).

This viewpoint, as crystallized by Murdock, has met with some opposition (Wrigley, 1960: 198; Fage, 1961: 307–308; Morgan, 1962: 239; Coursey and Alexander, 1968: 1475; Coursey, 1972: 226, 227; 1976: 391–92). It has been recognized that, contrary to Murdock's opinion (1959: 222), the indigenous West African yams (*D. cayenensis* and more especially *D. rotundata*) play an important dietary role and are often distinguished linguistically as "proper yams" (Coursey and Alexander, 1968: 1474; Alexander and Coursey, 1969: 418).

Several researchers have elaborated on the question of the development of African forest agriculture (O. Davies, 1960; 1968; Coursey and Alexander, 1968; Alexander and Coursey, 1969; Coursey and Coursey, 1971; Coursey, 1972, 1976). It is interesting that, although a long tradition of the gathering of indigenous wild tubers is hypothesized, and it is suggested that such gathering led to a "proto-agricultural" stage, none of the studies listed above goes so far as to suggest the independent development of forest agriculture in West Africa. All believe that crop cultivation in the forest developed as a result of contact with seed agriculturalists from the north (O. Davies, 1967: 151–52, 206; 1968: 480; Alexander and Coursey, 1969: 421; Coursey and Coursey, 1971: 478; Coursey, 1972: 224).

It is significant that both Davies and Coursey have suggested that their "proto-agricultural" stage is of considerable antiquity (O. Davies, 1960; Coursey, 1972). Both believed that the basic equipment needed for the harvesting of wild tubers was available by early Upper Pleistocene times (O. Davies, 1968; Coursey, 1967: 13). Coursey has rejected the notion that forest clearance, and hence forest cultivation, was impossible before the advent of iron in Africa. "It has been established . . . that African Neolithic stone axes are quite effective tools for felling moderate-sized trees, while the larger areas could be cleared by firing" (Coursey, 1976: 397).

From a study of the present distribution of yam cultivation in Africa, Coursey has proposed a center of domestication "on the fringe of the West African forest belt, either within the savannah, or possibly in the Dahomey Gap" (1976: 393). He and his colleague Alexander place this center outside the forest proper, reasoning that, since it is the dormant phase of the yam's growth cycle in which man is interested, species native to regions with a short wet season would be the most likely candidates for domestication (Alexander and Coursey, 1969; Coursey, 1972). Such species would have a longer dormancy period due to the increased length of the dry season, would "tend to build up larger reserves in their tubers, and are thus better suited for use as crop plants" (Alexander and Coursey, 1969: 420).

The only researcher known to this author to have suggested a completely independent development of agriculture in the humid tropics of Africa is Lathrap, a specialist in South American archaeology. Lathrap went so far as to propose:

> Sauer was correct in focusing our attention on the alluvial food plains of tropical rivers, . . . he was probably correct in stating that all agricultural systems are historically related in deriving from a single localized pattern of neolithic experimentation, but he was probably wrong in localizing that pattern in southeastern Asia. I vote for tropical Africa. (1977: 716)

Lathrap suggested that cultivation initially arose out of man's efforts to increase supplies of "rare" or "potentially rare" useful plant species. "This concern . . . is understandable in the moist tropics where *most* species are rare in the sense that individuals of each species are widely dispersed and few in number" (1977: 723). Following the lead of

Sauer (1969), Lathrap postulated that certain species were exploited more intensively in conjunction with an increased reliance on riparian resources. These included species useful as fish poisons, cotton for netting, and bottle gourds (*Lagenaria siceraria*) employed as floats and containers. As a result of their increased reliance on these plant resources, people would have perceived a scarcity and "would have increased the supply of these plants by transplanting and tending individual specimens in the yard surrounding their now permanent residences," a development that may be related to "the rather broad cultural category, Sangoan" (1977: 725).

UNDERLYING ASSUMPTIONS

An examination of studies of the geographical origins of African agriculture reveals several fundamental assumptions. Historically, it was presumed that the hunting-and-gathering way of life was an undesirable and precarious one (Buckland, 1878; Roth, 1886; Peake, 1928: 9–10, 17; Ward, 1940; Curwen, 1946: 1–5; Helbaek, 1959; Braidwood, 1960; J. G. D. Clark, 1961: 76). The resources upon which hunters and gatherers relied were believed to be scarce and unpredictable, so foraging peoples were thought to have spent more time and energy than agriculturalists in the acquisition of food and therefore to have had little leisure in which to develop a complex culture. It was believed that the transition to agriculture allowed permanent communities to develop and provided both a more stable existence and greater leisure (Childe, 1936: 69; Braidwood, 1960).

A corollary of this was that once hunting and gathering peoples had "discovered" or had been introduced to agriculture, they would immediately make the transition to this inherently more desirable lifestyle. Only ignorance prevented man from becoming an agriculturalist (Peake, 1927; 1928: 9, 73).

Early researchers, then, felt no further need to explain the transition from hunting and gathering to agriculture, although, as has been said, a number of them suggested that, prior to the "introduction" of agriculture, certain prehistoric African groups were "pre-adapted" to agricultural techniques be-

cause they were intensive grain-collectors. However, although African populations may have been "pre-adapted" to both cereal cultivation and vegecultural systems, researchers maintained that it was contact with either fully agricultural or pastoral populations that was the stimulus leading to domestication of indigenous African crops. The implication seems to be that the concepts of domestication and agriculture were unavailable to African populations before contact with the Middle East.

The Role of Environmental Change

A number of researchers have postulated environmental change as the catalytic factor in establishing agriculture in sub-Saharan Africa. Their discussions have been confined largely to West and North Africa, and especially the Sahara. Two lines of thought have been pursued: (1) that environmental change acted as a moderating factor, permitting the diffusion of agriculture or a knowledge thereof from the Middle East into sub-Saharan Africa; or (2) that the stresses of environmental change led to the development or adoption of agricultural techniques.

Chevalier was the first to postulate climatic changes as an important factor in the emergence of agriculture in the African continent. He believed that the southern fringes of the Sahara were an independent center of plant domestication and suggested that five successive stages of man's increasing dependence on plants had occurred during the Quaternary in the Sahara. Progression through these stages was triggered, in Chevalier's opinion, by climatic deterioration (1938: 310).

Environmental change was also rated as important by those who hypothesized that African agriculture derived initially from migration or stimulus from the Middle East (O. Davies, 1960; 1968; J. D. Clark, 1962; 1964b; 1967a; 1967b; Munson, n.d.: 126, 128, 138, 144; 1976; Harlan et al., 1976b; Phillipson, 1977c: 64–65). A route of entry of the relevant crops had to be postulated, as well as a subsequent route for their dispersal. Possible entry routes were southward along the Nile Valley or west along the Mediterranean coast. Under modern environmental conditions, however, the Sahara desert would present an insuperable barrier to the spread of plant or cereal cultivation, and it is here that environmental change entered the picture. Paleoclimatic studies have demonstrated that significant climatic change occurred in the Sahara during the late Pleistocene and early Holocene. Arid conditions prevailed from 21,000 to 12,500 years B.P., giving way to a more moist period lasting until ca. 10,000 years B.P. The period of roughly 10,000–5000 years B.P. was characterized by "expansion of open water, marshes and forest" (Street and Grove, 1976: 387–388). Researchers who saw agriculture in Africa as deriving from the Middle East have suggested that it was during such moist periods that the spread of agriculture from the Nile Valley or the Mediterranean littoral into the Sahara took place.

J. D. Clark (1962, 1964b, 1967a, 1967b) has most fully developed the thesis of environmental change and the spread of agriculture. He sees the Sahara as being populated by Mesolithic populations during a period of increased rainfall (6th–3rd millennia B.C.), which would have facilitated the spread of the Near Eastern agricultural complex. "Such a favourable habitat . . . must have rendered these communities particularly receptive of and quick to adopt the new practices of cereal and crop cultivation . . . when they were diffused" (Clark, 1962: 213). The Near Eastern crop complex, with its staple cereal grains, wheat and barley, would thus have spread throughout the Sahara. With the intensification of aridity (ca. 2000 B.C.) would have come movement of populations out of the Sahara (Clark, 1967b), some of them to the south, taking with them their Middle Eastern wheat and barley. As this southward movement continued, the ecological limit of the winter rainfall cultigens would have been reached, and local sorghum and "millets" would have been domesticated in their place (Clark, 1964b).

Other researchers who have suggested an introduction of agriculture to sub-Saharan Africa due to a desiccation of the Sahara include O. Davies (1960; 1968), Posnansky (1966), and Phillipson (1977c: 65). Common to these studies is the implicit assumption that agriculture is adopted as a subsistence strategy as soon as it becomes available

through cultural diffusion. Environmental change is invoked as a stimulus to migration and diffusion.

Hobler and Hester have suggested that too much emphasis has been placed on a north-south axis of migration in the Sahara during periods of climatic fluctuation. A topographic map illustrating the position of the Saharan massifs shows a semi-circular band of elevated landforms running in a southeast-northwest direction. They believe that "because of the effects of this elevation upon temperature and rainfall this crescentic plateau must have functioned through time both as a corridor and as a refuge for migration of plants, animals and man during times of climatic fluctuation" (Hobler and Hester, 1969: 130). Munson (n.d.: 144; 1976) has suggested that this "fertile crescent," this elevated area which remained relatively unaffected by climatic fluctuation, was the most probable route of entry of agriculture into the African subcontinent. Hays (1975: 193) also sees this as an important route of migration.

Although climatic fluctuation has been seen as a means of stimulating diffusion, seldom has the question arisen as to *why* Saharan post-Pleistocene populations would have adopted agricultural techniques in the first place. In recent years, however, the need for an explanation of why nonagricultural populations would adopt an agricultural mode of subsistence has become evident (Harlan et al., 1976b). Studies of modern-day hunters and gatherers have demonstrated that theirs is not in fact a precarious and undesirable lifestyle. Lee's (1968, 1969) studies of the !Kung Bushmen and Woodburn's (1968b) work with the Hadza of Tanzania found that the subsistence base of these hunting and gathering groups was surprisingly abundant and predictable. Although they had to make subsistence efforts throughout the year, both the Bushmen and the Hadza enjoyed considerable leisure. M. D. Sahlins has, in fact, been inspired to label the Paleolithic as "the original affluent society" (1968: 85).

If hunters and gatherers actually spent fewer hours in subsistence activities than did agriculturalists and apparently did not suffer from food shortages, why would they change to a more time-consuming mode of subsistence?

Researchers were led to seek factors that would

create a disequilibrium in an otherwise stable hunting and gathering way of life. African environmental deterioration has been postulated as one such factor by those who see an external origin for Saharan agriculture (e.g., Munson, n.d.: 128; 1976), as well as those who suggest the possibility of an indigenous African development of proto-agriculture or agriculture (Coursey and Coursey, 1971; J. D. Clark, 1976a; Coursey, 1976; T. Shaw, 1978: 63–64). Several of these researchers have suggested that with the gradual desiccation of lakes in the Sahara, Epi-Paleolithic populations for whom the lakes were a primary food source would have been forced to adopt alternative subsistence strategies, whether obtained by diffusion, stimulus diffusion, or independent invention (Munson, n.d.: 137–139; 1976; J. D. Clark, 1976b; T. Shaw, 1978: 63–64).

Others have postulated demographic stress as a direct result of environmental deterioration. Contraction of vegetational zones would have led to a concentration of formerly diffuse populations, and this increased population density would have put a strain on existing food resources. Attempts to increase plant resources artificially would eventually have resulted in domestication and agriculture (Coursey and Coursey, 1971; Harlan et al., 1976b; T. Shaw, 1978: 66).

Munson has argued that cereal cultivation was introduced from the central Sahara to the Dhar Tichitt region of Mauritania about 1000 B.C. as a result of a series of climatic fluctuations that undermined the existing Epi-Paleolithic subsistence strategy (n.d.: 139–142). He thinks that cultivation was practiced in the central Sahara as early as 3000 B.C., adducing as evidence the identification of pollen grains from Meniet and Amekni, both sites in the Hoggar (n.d.: 144–145; 1976). Two pollen grains were recovered from each site. That from Amekni was identified as *Pennisetum* on the basis of size and shape; the Meniet pollen could be identified only as "Cerealia" type (T. Shaw, 1976). "Cerealia" pollens, however, include "wild species, wild ancestors of cultivated species and cultivated species" (Leroi-Gourhan, 1969: 143). Considering the small sample size from the two sites and the difficulties of identifying pollen of the Gramineae, Munson's evidence is less than conclusive (see also

Stemler: this volume). Given Munson's environmental deterioration hypothesis, why would *Saharan* populations have adopted food production techniques by 3000 B.C.? The period of 10,000–5000 B.P. was one of fluctuating but still generally moist conditions (Street and Grove, 1976: 387–388). One would think that aquatic resources would have been adequate, so that no incentive would have existed for these populations to become food producers.

A problem with such environmental-stress hypotheses is that although a period of climatic fluctuation may coincide with the origin or adoption of agriculture south of the Sahara, such climatic change may or may not have been a sufficient or necessary cause for the transition (Wagner, 1977). Even a high degree of correlation of particular climatic conditions with a transition to agriculture would not explain *why* such a shift occurred (D. R. Harris, 1977). In just what way such changes caused a stress or disequilibrium and how they affected particular subsistence strategies must be explained.

The Spread of Crop Complexes: East and South Africa

Interest in the domestication of African crop plants has focused on West Africa and, to a lesser extent, Ethiopia. Only Portères (1950: 489) and Lwanga-Lunyiigo (1976: 285–286) have hypothesized a center of domestication in East Africa. Current archaeological evidence suggests that agriculture was a relatively late development in East and South Africa (Seddon, 1968: 491; Phillipson, 1977c). The literature on early agriculture in these regions has therefore focused on the spread of crop complexes, both indigenous and nonindigenous, into the area. The outstanding feature of these discussions is the repeated association of crop complexes and their movements with particular linguistic and/or "racial" groups (Murdock, 1959: 196–203, 271–274; McMaster, 1962; Cole, 1963: 302; J. D. Clark, 1964b; 1967a; 1967b; 1970: 208–210; 1976b; Doggett, 1965; Oliver, 1966; Sutton, 1966; 1967; 1968; 1969; 1971; Ehret,

1968b; 1974a; Fagan, 1968; Seddon, 1968; Purseglove, 1972: 263–265; Hiernaux, 1974: 98, 140, 178; Stemler et al., 1975). Two linguistic groups (also sometimes associated with "racial" types) have been of particular interest: the Bantu and the Cushites.

It was, once again, Murdock who first discussed the introduction of crop complexes into East and South Africa. His thesis was that a "Megalithic Cushite" population had moved south into East Africa, bringing with them an intensive form of agriculture based on finger millet and durra sorghum (1959: 197–199). This "Caucasoid" population settled in dispersed, elevated regions, leaving the intervening lower areas to the indigenous "Bushmanoid" hunting and gathering groups. Murdock believed these Cushites to be associated with the "Stone Bowl Complex" of East Africa.

A second aspect of Murdock's thesis of crop dispersal concerned the Bantu. Prior to their expansion into the southern half of the African continent, he believed that they had been confined to a homeland near the Cameroon-Nigeria border (1959: 271, after Greenberg, 1949). Their expansion to the south and east was triggered by the adoption of Malaysian food crops—banana, taro, and yam (p. 273)—that had arrived in Africa in the centuries immediately preceding the Christian era (p. 222). Once introduced to the East African coast by the ancestors of the Malagasy, these crops had reached the Bantu homeland by overland diffusion. "The Megalithic Cushites, of course, carried the Malaysian complex on the first leg of its westward journey, providing the necessary corridor through otherwise Bushmanoid territory" (p. 225). The Central Sudanic speakers, who were already cultivating crops of the indigenous Sudanic complex (e.g., sorghum) adopted these Malaysian crops from the "Megalithic Cushites" and passed them on to the west along the savanna belt, by which route they eventually reached the Bantu homeland. Thus the Bantu, who had formerly cultivated Sudanic crops (p. 273), were, with the aid of the Malaysian crops, able to penetrate the equatorial forest. They eventually emerged from the forest into savanna country in the area of Uganda. Here they directly encountered the Cushites, "whom they were ultimately to absorb but not until

they had borrowed from them the elements of East African agriculture" (p. 279).

Murdock's thesis is based entirely on modern distribution of crops and ethnographic traits. His conclusions concerning the role of the Malaysian crops in the expansion of the Bantu are based on a list of food plants compiled for nine northwest Bantu groups:

> Bananas, taro and yams appear in every one of the nine, and in nearly every instance as staples, whereas no crop of the Sudanic complex except the oil palm occurs in more than one list. . . . One can scarcely conceive of stronger proof that the Northwestern Bantu could not have entered their present habitat until they received the Malaysian food plants. (p. 273)

The widespread distribution of Malaysian food crops, however, may have occurred after the hypothesized Bantu expansion and have replaced indigenous food crops (e.g., *Dioscorea rotundata, D. cayenensis*). Such replacement of indigenous food plants by nonindigenous domesticates is well documented during the colonial period (e.g., maize and cassava, both native to the New World). Various factors may have been involved in such a replacement, for example, disease resistance of the introduced plant, or higher yield. It should be noted that both D. R. Harris (1976) and Coursey (1967: 15–16) believe Asian yams to be colonial introductions.

Oliver essentially agreed with Murdock's conclusions concerning the role of the Malaysian food crops. However, he questioned Murdock's placement of the Bantu homeland and his proposed sequence of events:

> Is it not a little strange, one might ask, that the South-East Asian food plants should have reached Bantu Africa via West Africa? . . . Is it not rather an odd proposition that the Eastern Sudanic speakers living . . . immediately to the north of what was to become Bantu Africa, did nothing to penetrate southwards themselves, but merely speeded the new plants westward until they reached the apparently more enterprising speakers of the Western Sudanic languages? (1966: 365)

Oliver postulated a Bantu homeland in central Africa, an area suited to sorghum and millet cultivation:

> [The Bantu's] obvious success over against [sic] any earlier hunting, gathering and tenuously vegecultural peoples whom they found in this region would be more adequately explained by their possession of a rudimentary iron technology and a knowledge of cereal agriculture which enabled them to take over and develop with Iron Age equipment the East African varieties of sorghums and millets introduced by the neolithic Kushites. (pp. 367–368)

Oliver, then, believed the southeast Asian food crops to have been introduced directly to a Bantu population already inhabiting East Africa.

More recently, Ehret reconstructed, on the basis of linguistic analysis, the "early Bantu cultivation of yams, presumably indigenous African varieties; one bean species; one other cultigen which was either a bean or a Bambara groundnut; oil palms; and one variety of gourd" (1974a: 2), dating this planting tradition to the second millennium B.C. He attributed the spread of this planting complex into central Africa to Bantu movements and assigned the introduction of cereal-crop cultivation into East Africa to Central Sudanic speakers. From a study of loan words, he claimed that it is "possible to reconstruct proto-Central Sudanic cultivation of sorghum and other grains. . . . The evidence of Central Sudanic loan words in Bantu languages of central Africa shows that the Sudanic complex carried south by Central Sudanic speakers included in addition the cultivation of eleusine [finger millet and] pumpkins" (p. 3).

Both Dalby (1976: 24) and Phillipson have questioned Ehret's conclusions concerning the role of Central Sudanic speakers. Phillipson has noted that

> this hypothesis would involve accepting the presence over an enormous area of southern and eastern Africa of a Central Sudanic-speaking population surviving until less than a millennium ago. It is highly improbable that such a population could have existed so recently and yet left so little archaeological or

linguistic trace of its specifically Sudanic character. (1976a: 13)

Other authors who associate crop dispersal with the movement of either Cushite or Bantu peoples, or both, include McMaster (1962), Cole (1963: 302), J. D. Clark (1964b; 1970: 208–210; 1976b), Doggett (1965), Sutton (1966; 1967; 1968; 1969; 1971), Ehret (1968b), Fagan (1968), Seddon (1968), and Purseglove (1972: 263–265; 1976).

Harlan and Stemler have observed a fairly close correlation between the distribution of particular varieties of *Sorghum bicolor* and that of the major African language groups. "Guinea is a sorghum of the Niger-Congo family, kafir a Bantu sorghum. Durra follows the Afro-Asian family fairly closely and caudatum seems to be associated with the Chari-Nile family of languages" (1976: 476). The correspondence between the Chari-Nile family and caudatum sorghum has been explored in greater depth by Stemler, Harlan, and de Wet:

> The unmistakable correspondence of the distribution of caudatum sorghums and Chari-Nile speakers over such a vast area suggests that caudatum sorghums are so important a part of the agriculture and way of life of Chari-Nile-speaking peoples that they have been carried to every place Chari-Nile-speaking peoples have settled. (1975: 168)

> We might further speculate that the appearance of rouletted wares [ceramics with twisted cord decoration] and herding economies indicates an influx of Chari-Nile-speaking peoples from the north bringing caudatum to East Africa. (p. 179)

They have suggested a tentative date of around A.D. 1250 for the incursion.

Although the correspondence between language groups and particular varieties of sorghum is deserving of study, Stemler, Harlan, and de Wet have extended their conclusions well beyond the limits of the data. The association of rouletted wares with caudatum sorghum has not been demonstrated in the archaeological record; the case rests entirely on modern distributional evidence. Even if the asserted association of language group, crop variety, and ceramic style could be demonstrated (though this would be difficult in itself), it would not necessarily follow that wherever the ceramic style was found, one could then infer the language group and the crop type. The association would not be an absolute one, for any of the three traits—language, crop, or ceramic style—could have diffused without the others.

This point raises the more general problem of the association of archaeological materials with physical or linguistic groups. The three very distinct categories of language, physical "type," and archaeological remains have been treated in the past as if they were a single unit. This supposed correlation has until recently gone unquestioned. "The idea has emerged of clearly separate groups of Bushmen, Hottentots and Bantu, distinct in physical form, language, economy and technology" (Derricourt, 1976). Such a breakdown was applied rigidly to archaeological sites, with each term implying a distinctive physical and linguistic population. As Derricourt has pointed out, however, "Hunters and herders do not show language differences along the same lines as economy and technology" (p. 217).

Summary

Interest in African agricultural origins was initially generated among botanists and plant geographers, who postulated at least one independent center of origin in the African continent. Discussion on the topic appeared in the anthropological literature in the 1960s, much of it generated by the 1959 study in which Murdock put forward a number of hypotheses concerning African agriculture. Three principal issues have gained the attention of researchers: (1) the elucidation of the geographical origins of African agriculture; (2) the role of environmental change in the transition to agriculture; and (3) the spread of various crop complexes within the African continent.

The controversy over the geographical origins of African agriculture has focused on whether it was an independent development or whether it diffused from either the Middle East or Southeast

Asia. Although most African subsistence crop complexes have indigenous African domesticates as their staples, researchers have been reluctant to postulate that agriculture developed in Africa independently of influence from the Middle East. It is interesting that most of the workers who have postulated such an independent development are botanists (Chevalier, 1938; Portères, 1950, 1962, 1976; Vavilov, 1951b; Anderson, 1960, 1967) or anthropologists whose main area of interest is outside the African continent (Murdock, 1959; Lathrap, 1977). Researchers such as Wendorf et al. (1979) are an exception.

Interpretations dealing with the role of environmental change in the transition to agriculture in Africa have shifted their emphasis through time. Earlier studies postulated climatic change as a permissive factor, allowing or stimulating the diffusion of agriculture from the Near East into sub-Saharan Africa. Such an interpretation assumed a transition to agriculture as automatic, since it was thought to provide an inherently better lifestyle. Under the impact of modern studies of hunters and gatherers, however, it has become apparent that this transition could not be assumed. Hence, more recent studies have postulated climatic change as a stress factor.

The spread of crop complexes to East and South Africa has also been discussed. Most researchers connect the spread of crop complexes with movements of Bantu- or Cushitic-speaking peoples, who are believed to have been intimately involved in the introduction of agriculture to these areas.

Conclusions

Research into the origins of African agriculture lags ten to fifteen years behind studies of early agriculture elsewhere. Outside the African continent, current interest is primarily explaining the transition from hunting and gathering to agriculture, but the need to elucidate the motivating factors behind the change in mode of subsistence is only now being recognized among African researchers. They have turned to the factor of environmental stress as a means of explaining the transition to agriculture. Some believe that by demonstrating the coincidence of a change in subsistence strategy with a period of environmental deterioration, they can explain the transition in mode of subsistence. Until it has been demonstrated how such an environmental change affected the existing subsistence strategy and how this in turn led to adoption of an agricultural mode of subsistence, however, one cannot speak of a causal sequence.

In addition, an assumption has been made that stress models apply only to situations in which an independent transition from hunting and gathering to agriculture has occurred. It has been taken for granted that once agricultural techniques became available, they would then be diffused. If one is working from the premise that change in mode of subsistence results from a disequilibrium in the existing system, it must apply equally to cases of independent invention and to instances of diffusion. The conditions under which such a transition occurred must therefore be elucidated.

The conventional approach to prehistoric African agriculture has been a diffusionist one, in which the benefit of the doubt has been given to diffusion rather than to the possibility of independent invention (Flight, 1976a). Researchers have gone to great lengths to demonstrate how agriculture might have diffused from the Middle East, although there are a number of problems involved in such a derivation for sub-Saharan agriculture. With the exception of highland Ethiopia, the crops grown in sub-Saharan Africa differ from those grown in the Middle East: wheat and barley will not grow satisfactorily in the tropical summer rainfall zone. The method of cultivation also differs substantially. The plow is the main agricultural implement in the Middle East, whereas the hoe and the digging stick are the traditional tools in sub-Saharan Africa. The reason for this difference cannot lie in the presence of the tsetse fly, which admittedly would exclude the use of draft animals, for there are vast tsetse-free areas in which livestock are present but where the hoe serves as the main agricultural implement. If one postulates a diffusion of agricultural techniques from the Middle East, with or without an accompanying migration of peoples,

one must deal with the change in crop type as well as the "substitution" of the hoe for the plow.

The evidence in support of such diffusionistic hypotheses is scanty. Evidence pointing to independent invention is equally scanty, if not nonexistent, but it can no longer be assumed that diffusion is more likely than independent invention. Among those who favor the invention mode, there is a lingering tendency to identify the development of crop complexes in the African subcontinent with specific linguistic or "racial" groups. The problems of identifying "racial" type from skeletal material are manifold; indeed, the concept of "race" is a questionable one. Hypotheses regarding the racial affiliation of archaeological populations remain untestable, for it is difficult, if not impossible, to determine the genetic affiliation of skeletal remains precisely enough to identify "race."

The difficulties in determining linguistic affiliation of preliterate archaeological populations are manifest. Too often, archaeologists have attempted to use their data to test hypotheses generated by linguists. An example is the attempt to correlate the spread of iron-working, of agriculture, and of Bantu-speaking peoples. The association of these three factors has met with overwhelming and uncritical acceptance by archaeologists, an association which, so far as language is concerned, the archaeologist can never demonstrate satisfactorily. In the author's opinion, the attempt to attribute cultural remains to a particular linguistic group represents an archaeological cul-de-sac.

Available evidence bearing on the origin of African agriculture is meager. Hypotheses have most often been formulated on the basis of plant geography and on linguistic and ethnographic evidence. A striking characteristic of most of the published studies is their lack of supporting archaeological evidence; that which has been put forth is usually of an indirect nature (e.g., the presence of ceramics or of tools assumed to have been used for cultivation). Most of the direct evidence (e.g., carbonized seeds, seed impressions) has been recovered as a by-product of investigations focusing on other issues, since few research projects in Africa have been devoted specifically to the elucidation of agricultural origins. Studies investigating the transition to agriculture as an integral part of their objectives are needed if an understanding of that transition is ever to be gained, and this will not come about through chance discoveries of direct evidence.

This paper is not meant as an exhaustive review of the literature on African agriculture, but the intent has been to identify the major topics in the study of early African agriculture, and to illustrate these with selected studies. It is the author's conclusion that our knowledge of early African agriculture has made little progress since the publication of Murdock's (1959) study. Although the body of literature on the subject is growing rapidly, we have little or no understanding of the *processes* involved in the transition in the African continent from hunting and gathering to agriculture. Reassessment and reorientation of the questions being asked are needed. Murdock's study provided hypotheses concerning the origins and spread of agriculture in Africa which acted as a catalyst for other researchers. Two decades later, however, researchers are still studying the same problems. Some, such as the linguistic and "racial" affiliations of archaeological populations, are questions which, given the current state of archaeological method and technique, are unanswerable. Others, such as the geographical origins of African agriculture, are descriptive in nature and, as such, give no understanding of processes involved in the transition from a hunting-and-gathering to a food-producing economy. *Why* this transition occurred is, in the author's opinion, the most important and fundamental question, extending beyond the shift to agriculture to the more general one of why changes in subsistence strategy should occur at all.

2

Interactions of Food Production and Changing Vegetation in Africa

DANIEL A. LIVINGSTONE

The vegetational context and consequences of pre-historic agriculture were pursued first, and with great success, in northwestern Europe. The European flora is small and its pollen morphology has been well known for thirty years. Data on climate and soils are abundant, the ecology of the indigenous vegetation is well understood, and its largely wind-pollinated forest flora has left a clear record in the fossil pollen assemblages of lakes and bogs. The main features of pollen stratigraphy, and even vegetational change, for the postglacial period have been well known for fifty years. The crop plants and weeds of western Europe include some of high pollen productivity and some whose pollen is certainly, if not readily, distinguishable from grains of the wild flora. The plants were introduced in a series of sudden waves from distant source areas. The pollen signals of food production are strong and unambiguous, the noise against which they must be recognized minimal. Under such circumstances Iversen (1941) was able to demonstrate the agricultural activities of Neolithic Beaker Folk to a skeptical

The research on which this paper was based was supported by grants from the National Science Foundation and Duke University.

archaeological community, and the vegetational effects of ensuing waves of bronze- and iron-wielding agriculturists are documented in great detail in the pollen record.

Tropical African conditions are much less favorable to the success of the enterprise. The flora is some orders of magnitude larger, placing a heavier burden on the memory of the pollen analyst and making some identifications impossible. A large factor in the European success (Faegri and Iversen, 1964: 196–197) was the size difference between the pollen of wheat and barley ($>40\mu$) and the pollen of all the wild inland grasses ($<40\mu$). Cereals were identifiable solely on the basis of size. In Africa only maize is so identifiable and many wild grasses produce pollen as large (i.e., $>40\mu$) and in every other known respect identical to that of cereals (Bonnefille, n.d.: 243; Hamilton, 1972: 141; and unpublished observations). Although we work with pollen reference collections of an order of magnitude larger than those of our European colleagues, they should probably be two orders of magnitude larger still for comparable accuracy of identification. The vegetation itself is complex, and its history is equally complex. Understanding of that complexity is bedevilled by lack of data on soils, climate, and even the distribution and abundance of the constituent species.

The historical record of vegetational change is blurred by the importance in tropical vegetation of pollen that is disseminated by animals rather than the wind; the pollen productivity of many trees is for this reason low. Of the many thousands of modern pollen samples needed to comprehend the relation between pollen assemblage and vegetation under such circumstances we have only a few score, and those not from the places where we need them most.

The difficulties are many, but the workers are few, and the total number of African pollen diagrams is much less than that of Denmark or Scotland. We have a few published pollen diagrams from the Atlas to the Cape, and a scattering of isolated spectra from Southern Africa and the Sahara, but only in Kenya and Uganda are there enough carbon-dated pollen diagrams from enough laboratories to provide a satisfactory stratigraphy for the past 15,000 years. Even here the density of

investigated sites does not permit paleovegetational mapping (Bonnefille, 1968, 1969, 1970, 1973, 1976a, 1976b, n.d.; Bolick, n.d.; Coetzee, 1964, 1967; Cour and Duzer, 1976; Fredoux and Tastet, 1976; Hamilton, 1976; Hedberg, 1954; Kendall, 1969; D. A. Livingstone, 1967, 1971, 1975, 1980, in press; Livingstone and van der Hammen, 1978; A. R. H. Martin, 1968; Morrison, 1961, 1966, 1968; Morrison and Hamilton, 1974; Osmaston, 1958, n.d.; Reille, 1976, 1977; Schalke, 1973; Van Zinderen Bakker, 1962, 1964; Van Zinderen Bakker and Coetzee, 1972).

There is reasonable agreement about the nature of the main vegetational changes. Prior to 12,000 B.P., forest trees were very scarce; between 10,000 and 6,000 B.P. they were abundant. There is some suggestion of a shift from evergreen to semideciduous forest in the wetter localities in about 6,000 B.P., and during the past two or three millennia there has been a conspicuous decline in the importance of forest, although the trend has not yet reproduced the extreme treelessness of the late Pleistocene. Throughout the tree-rich Holocene the vegetation has been dynamic, with significant changes in the relative importance of various genera during most if not all millennia.

Climatic interpretation of even the major features of vegetational change is still a matter of debate, with the Bloemfontein school (Coetzee, 1967; Van Zinderen Bakker, 1962, 1964; Van Zinderen Bakker and Coetzee, 1972) professing to find an African analogue to the detailed sequence of changes in temperature and moisture that was commonly inferred from the European pollen record twenty years ago. In my own laboratory (Bolick, n.d.; Kendall, 1969; D. A. Livingstone, 1967, 1971) we have been more cautious in drawing climatic inferences, being much impressed by the critical reassessment the classic European and American interpretations have received at the hands of Danish, English, and, especially, American workers during the past decade. We do know from glacial geology that the late Pleistocene was cool, at least prior to 15,000 B.P., and from changes in lake level that the late Pleistocene was dry between 15,000 and 12,500 B.P., when there was no discharge from the Great Lakes to the White Nile. Lake levels also show that the first half of the Holocene was much wetter than the second (Butzer et al., 1972; Gasse, 1977, n.d.; Gasse, Fontes, and Rognon, 1974; Harlan, 1975; Harvey, n.d.; H. Heine, 1963; Holdship, n.d.; Kamau, 1967; Kendall, 1969; Richardson, 1972; Richardson, Harvey, and Holdship, 1978; Richardson and Richardson, 1972; Servant-Vildary, 1970, n.d.; Street and Grove, 1976).

The decline of forest during the past few millennia is compatible with food production, but in no case is the evidence of human influence as compelling as Iversen's (1941) from Neolithic Denmark. Archaeological evidence suggests an antiquity of several millennia for agriculture in East Africa and human influence is undeniable today (J. D. Clark, 1976b). Without such independent evidence it is doubtful that the forest decline would be attributed to man.

From time to time, in the archaeological literature, one encounters tentative identifications of crop plants by their pollen. When these deal with grasses other than maize, they should be treated with something between skepticism and incredulity. One would not like to deny categorically the possibility that a very experienced investigator might have some real basis for separating millet pollen from all other members of the relatively depauperate grass flora of the central Sahara, but the basis for the identification should be explained. For the most part, however, the statement that a fossil grain resembles, say, barley, is misleading, because it omits the significant information that the same grain resembles as closely a hundred or more wild species of African grasses. Much work in several laboratories, using ordinary light microscopy, phase microscopy, interference microscopy, size statistics, and scanning electron microscopy, has been devoted to the problem of identifying fossil grass pollen. Perhaps some day someone will learn how to make such identifications, but that discovery will have to be substantiated by detailed presentation of the evidence.

In the hope of ending this paper on a positive note, the writer recently went through his pollen collection with Harlan's (1975: 71–72) list of the major indigenous African crop plants in hand, to see how many might be identifiable from their pollen. Of the forty-three taxa Harlan lists, there seems good reason to hope for the certain identification of three—the baobab tree, the bottle gourd, and the bambara ground nut. Careful study of more material might lead to identification of the pollen of a few others, notably in the Leguminosae, Cucurbitaceae, and Malvaceae, but the amount of morphological work required is sobering. For many crop plants the prospects are even poorer. One despairs of ever recognizing the two cultivated species of *Solanum*, which are now identified only uncertainly to genus, among its twenty-two wild congeners listed in the *Flora of West Tropical Africa* (H. Heine, 1963). As for post-Columbian introductions from America, the potato has not yet been identified from pollen in the Holocene deposits of Ireland. Bananas, plantains, and *ensete*, those fascinating staples of so many African peoples, belong to an order of plants in which the fossilizable layer is reduced to isolated granules (D. E. Stone, pers. comm.), and their pollen is disseminated by bats. Such pollen is unlikely to be deposited in a lake, unlikely to be preserved if it were, and unlikely to be recognized by a pollen analyst if it were preserved.

To provide definitive evidence of food production, a pollen type would have to be found in usefully large numbers outside the limits of its uncultivated range. In 18 years of looking for the pollen of cultivated plants in African deposits, the present writer has found a single grain of *Basella alba* (*Enderema* in western Uganda, *Ndemra* in Luo), which might have been either cultivated or wild in the Rift Valley deposit where it occurred.

Recently, J. M. J. de Wet kindly sent samples of leaves from the important African grass plants and their wild relatives, and these have been examined by P. G. Palmer and A. E. Tucker at Duke. We are quite optimistic about the use of leaf cuticles for working out the history of the genera of African grasses (Palmer, 1976), but apparently they will not support the more stringent requirements of identification to species or cultivar. Preliminary examination of the material suggested that only the rices, African and Asian, were distinguishable from each other and their wild relatives, but when the sample was doubled, a disturbing number of intermediates turned up, and we are no longer sanguine even about the rice identification.

There are many more cultivated plants in Africa than the forty-three on Harlan's list, and some of them may produce distinctive pollen. Possibly some of them, or even some no longer cultivated, may have played a larger role in the history of food production than did the major crops of today. It will, however, be appreciated that working out the history of their use by microfossils is not going to be easy. For the foreseeable future, as at present, information about the history of food production in Africa promises to be scarce, unsatisfactory, and to come from the work of archaeologists rather than palynologists. We will be able to say more and more about the general vegetational context in which cultures have developed, including some much too old for food production to be an issue, but archaeologists seem likely to provide most of the detailed information about specific occurrences of the small part of the vegetation propagated, transported, exploited, or obliterated by man.

3

Historical/Linguistic Evidence for Early African Food Production

C. EHRET

The Antiquity of African Food-Production

The linguistic evidence from sub-Saharan Africa supports distinctly earlier dates for the invention of agriculture than archaeologists generally have yet been able to verify. The data published in Joseph Greenberg's pioneering classifications of African languages (1949–1951, 1963, etc.) first brought to light several apparently reconstructible root words for domestic animals in three of the four African language families and so gave grounds for the then-startling notion that food production might have begun as early in tropical Africa as in several other seminal locations in the Old World and in Mesoamerica. Greenberg himself made this implication explicit in an important article more than fifteen years ago (Greenberg, 1964), and even earlier Christopher Wrigley (1960), drawing both on Greenberg's evidence and on the classificatory work of Diedrich Westermann (1927), recognized its significance for agricultural history among the Niger-Congo–speaking peoples of West Africa. It is perhaps still a startling idea, since no general text on African history yet takes even implicit account of it, and archaeologists have not seen the implication as sufficiently worthy of note to embark on programs of research designed to test it. Only piece by piece has archaeology pushed the accepted dates of food production back closer to those the linguistical historians have long expected.

Linguistic evidence, of course, does more than suggest the bare existence of some sort of early agricultural practice in Africa. As we approach the present, the evidence becomes progressively fuller, and the elaborations and transformations in food-producing activities and the separate additions of new crops, animals, and procedures to the existing body of knowledge are all reflected in vocabulary change (cf. Ehret, 1968a, 1974a, 1979, in press). Just as our archaeological knowledge of Africa is often sketchy, with great informational gaps, so the linguistic sources have received very uneven attention. In some few cases the language evidence has been rather well sampled for its historical implications; in many other cases practically nothing is known. This is not the place to describe the procedures of linguistic analysis that must be undertaken before the data can be interpreted, but it is the place to attempt a summary of where the work of interpretation now stands.

For peoples of three of the language families of Africa—Afroasiatic (Hamito-Semitic), Niger-Congo, and Nilo-Saharan—a long-standing acquaintance with food production can be supposed; for the fourth family, Khoisan, only relatively recent associations with food-producing activities can be proposed from the linguistic evidence. Niger-Congo is considered by Greenberg to be related at a still more distant remove to the territorially limited Kordofanian languages of the Republic of Sudan, but the Kordofanian tongues are too little known at present to provide any useful evidence about early subsistence.

Afroasiatic Peoples

The Afroasiatic family, with six generally recognized branches—Cushitic, Omotic, Chadic, Egyptian, Berber, and Semitic—is an immensely ancient and widespread language family. The proto-Afroasiatic language may have been spoken more than 15,000 years ago (Fleming, 1974; Munson, 1977; Ehret, 1979). Its origins may surely be traced back to somewhere in northeastern Africa, and several recent studies even more narrowly locate the proto-Afroasiatic homeland in or adjoining the Ethiopian highlands (Fleming, 1969b, 1974; Bender, 1975b; Ehret, 1979, 1980d).

The proto-Afroasiatic vocabulary included, so a tentative reconstruction suggests, a goodly number of nouns whose reflexes in modern Afroasiatic languages refer specifically to domesticates. They include words for "cow" and "donkey" and for grains and foods made from grains (Ehret, 1979). But the verbs determinative of the existence of the processes of food production have not been identified. Greenberg proposed a possible proto-Afroasiatic root word for "to cultivate," *mar, based on linking proto-Semitic *mr "hoe" and a Chadic verb *mar "to cultivate" (Greenberg, 1964). The linkage looks to be a valid one, but the cognate form in the Cushitic branch of Afroasiatic, occurring as proto-Southern Cushitic *mara?—"cave, den," implies an original application of the verb root to the digging of holes rather than specifically to the digging involved in cultivation. An alternative explanation of the proto-Afroasiatic subsistence reconstructions seems for now more probable: cattle and donkeys were both wild animals of the ancient northeast African regions from which Afroasiatic languages originally came, and so would have been well known to proto-Afroasiatic speakers; and the grain terms would have been as necessary for collectors of wild grasses as for cultivators of domesticated varieties. Since the adoption of intensive grass-collecting can be traced back to northeastern Africa 15,000-plus years ago, an archaeological basis may also exist for thinking the proto-Afroasiatic people to have been pre-agricultural users of grains (Ehret, 1979).

Agricultural knowledge and practice are clearly attested, however, for the proto-languages of each of the branches of Afroasiatic except Omotic, for which the data are as yet insufficient. The proto-Semites we may leave aside as participants in or early beneficiaries of the Near Eastern invention of agriculture, as the reconstructibility of proto-Semitic roots for "barley," "wheat," and the like implies. The break-up of proto-Semitic linguistic unity in any case probably dates no earlier than about the fourth or fifth millennium B.C. (Rabin, 1975), well after Near Eastern agriculture had fully taken shape. The Berber expansion is a much more recent event, beginning probably just a little over 2,000 years ago (Strowbridge, n.d.), and so proto-Berber reconstructions tell us only about agriculture in North Africa in the last millennium B.C., 6,000 or more years after the first indications of food production there (McBurney, 1975). Egyptian, as a single language, is not susceptible to comparative reconstruction (although Egyptian data can of course be compared with those from other branches of the family). The Omotic evidence, on the other hand, may have a great deal to tell us about the origins of agriculture in Ethiopia, but is as yet incompletely investigated. We are left for the present with two very important sets of evidence, from the Cushitic and Chadic branches of Afroasiatic.

The proto-Cushitic language was spoken on the order of 7,000 years ago, more likely earlier rather than later than that date (Ehret, 1976, 1979), and it was spoken by people living probably along or near the northern fringes of the Ethiopian highlands. The language contained a complex livestock nomenclature diagnostic of livestock-raising, the animals herded being cattle, goats, and most likely sheep. Donkeys were probably also kept by the proto-Cushites, but not as sources of subsistence. From a very early time the Cushites were cultivators, although whether this cultivation was as early as the livestock-raising or of somewhat later inception cannot yet be determined. The staples were probably finger millet or teff (Ehret, 1979). Thus the linguistic evidence strongly favors the presence of agriculture in some area on or adjoining the Ethiopian plateaux by about 5000 B.C. This agricultural system would have had a herding component in which at least two animals, the goat and sheep, were probably very indirect diffusions from the Near East, and a cultivating component of indigenous inspiration.

Later in the last millennium B.C., a significant settlement of South Arabians took place in the northern Horn of Africa, eventually bringing about replacement of Cushitic by Semitic languages in large areas of northern and central Ethiopia. What is fascinating for the history of food production in northeastern Africa is that these particular Semitic languages nonetheless adopted a considerable body of agricultural terminology from their Cushitic predecessors, including even the word for "wheat," usually that for "barley," and often that for "plow," despite the fact that these were characteristic elements of the Near Eastern cultivation already long practiced by Semites. This result can only be explained by assuming a previous thoroughgoing establishment of Near Eastern grains and the plow in large parts of Ethiopia before the Semitic intrusion. Most probably these introductions diffused southward from Egypt in the fourth millennium B.C. (Ehret, 1979; Simoons, 1965).

The linguistic evidence, therefore, requires the appearance of food production somewhere in the region of the Horn of Africa by or before 5000 B.C. and the addition of wheat, barley, and the plow to the indigenous cultivating complex of the Horn sometime markedly earlier than the last millennium B.C. The poorly known archaeology of pre-Semitic Ethiopia has not yet yielded evidence of food production so early in date (see Brandt, this volume). The Near Eastern food crops dated at Lalibela Cave to the first half of the last millennium B.C. (Dombrowski, 1970) may, however, reflect pre-Semitic possession of the cultigens, since Semitic settlement had probably not yet pressed so far inland from the Red Sea littoral. Otherwise, the first Ethiopian date for finger millet and, apparently, cattle is the third-millennium-B.C. Gobedra site in the far north (Phillipson, 1977a). But the linguistic evidence is too formidable here to dismiss, and we can with some confidence expect earlier sites more in keeping with the linguistic indications to turn up in the future.

A possible entirely separate invention of cultivation based on the ensete plant may have taken place among Omotic peoples in central or southwestern Ethiopia. If so, it could have developed in the wetter portions of Ethiopia conceivably as early as grain cultivation in drier areas of the Horn (Ehret, 1979). This possibility remains to be investigated both linguistically and archaeologically (see Brandt, this volume).

The proto-Chadic language belongs to a somewhat later time period than does the proto-

Cushitic or proto-Omotic. The maximum divergence among the numerous Chadic languages of northern Nigeria, Cameroun, and Chad is not as great as within the two Ethiopian branches of Afroasiatic but is still sufficiently great to place the proto-Chadic period in the general range of about 6,000 years ago, i.e., around about 4000 B.C. As in proto-Cushitic, so in proto-Chadic a fairly complex livestock nomenclature probably existed. Even from the limited sampling of culture vocabulary so far gathered from Chadic languages, words for "sheep," "ram," "goat," and "cow" can be reconstructed, along with grain vocabulary, for example, words for "flour," "porridge," "bulrush millet," and "sorghum" (D. Saxon, n.d.; P. Newman, 1977). The linguistic analysis thus indicates the presence in the Lake Chad region no later than 4000 B.C. of people with a well-developed Sudanic seed agriculture in which sorghum and bulrush millet formed the staples and livestock was a major component.

Niger-Congo

A second language family in which early agriculture may be traceable is Niger-Congo. Pan–Niger-Congo roots for "cow," "goat," and "yam" turn up (Westermann, 1927; Greenberg, 1963), and a couple of possible widespread terms for sorghum also can be found among West African Niger-Congo languages (Westermann, 1927).

The grain terms probably do not go back to proto–Niger-Congo. One term cited by Westermann as -gi, -giu occurs only in a near-block distribution from the northern Nigerian plateau region west to Gurma and isolated in Banyun of southern coastal Senegal. The block occurrence is typical of diffusionary spread; the isolated Banyun form is thus most probably a chance resemblance. Westermann's second term, -lí, has the appearance of being a widely scattered root, with the sort of distribution indicative of ancient standing in the family. Still, the occurrences where the root specifically names sorghum all cluster in one region, the savanna gap between Nigeria and Ghana. Westermann's other, more scattered examples of this root

word all have sufficiently different meanings that it seems probable the word took on the sense imputed to it only with the beginnings of the introduction of grain crops to Niger-Congo peoples of the Dahomey gap. Both root words may reflect a fairly early spread of sorghum; nevertheless, it was a spread by diffusion, after the expansion and differentiation of Niger-Congo peoples was well underway.

It is harder to get around the evidence of the roots for "cow," "goat," and "yam." Cows and goats were certainly not native to the West African woodland savanna and forest zones in which the earliest Niger-Congo peoples lived, and they could therefore have become known only through the spread of the domestic versions of each. The old root words naming the two animals both occur across a scattered, broken distribution in languages of every branch of Niger-Congo. That is exactly the sort of distribution that roots of indisputably proto–Niger-Congo provenance could be expected to show. It is also conceivable that either or both of the animals reached Niger-Congo peoples very early in their history, but still somewhat after the proto–Niger-Congo period, and then diffused fairly rapidly through a still somewhat geographically restricted span of Niger-Congo communities, so that the names were spread almost universally with the animals.

The pan–Niger-Congo word for "yam" does not by itself in the same way require the postulation of food production, because intensive collecting of yams probably formed the prelude to their deliberate cultivation in West Africa. There is in addition, however, a possible proto–Niger-Congo root for "to cultivate," seen in Bantu *-lim- and Fulani -rim- (Greenberg, 1964). On the evidence of its known occurrences it appears to be a good candidate for that meaning, but its possible presence elsewhere in Niger-Congo needs to be explored carefully to determine whether that is its primary meaning or whether some other sort of digging might originally have been meant.

The proto–Niger-Congo period probably fell 8,000 years ago at the very least (as also Greenberg, 1964). The Mande branch is thought by some scholars (cf. Welmers, 1973) to be the first split from proto–Niger-Congo; that is, it is thought to form one primary branch of the family, with all the rest of Niger-Congo forming the second branch. Between Mande and the Bantu languages at the other geographical extreme of the family, percentages of cognation in core vocabulary appear to run at around 4–5 percent in the 100-word list; if glottochronological reckonings are taken literally, 5 percent would imply a beginning of Niger-Congo divergence at almost 10,000 years ago, or 8000 B.C. Even allowing for considerable leeway in interpreting the cognation, it would still be difficult to see how the proto–Niger-Congo period could be any more recent than 6000 B.C., and it could quite possibly be much earlier.

The location of the proto–Niger-Congo homeland cannot be guessed at yet, except that it must have been somewhere in West Africa and, until a more exact subgrouping of the recognized branches of Niger-Congo is worked out, the location will remain no better specified. By no later than the period of about the fifth through the fourth millennium B.C., however, Niger-Congo peoples must have been found throughout most of the regions of West Africa that are today Niger-Congo–speaking. This can be most clearly argued in the case of southern Nigeria (Armstrong, 1964), but seems equally true for the countries further west (cf. L. E. Wilson, n.d., for the Gold Coast region, for instance).

The comparative vocabulary evidence, despite having more blanks than spaces filled, provides good reason, then, for giving serious attention to the possibility of some food-producing activities among the Niger-Congo peoples of West Africa by 6000 B.C. or even earlier. The most surprising conclusion, given all past and recent ideas on the topic among archaeologists, is that the proto–Niger-Congo peoples had some sort of knowledge of goats and cattle. It may be possible and necessary some day to explain this linguistic evidence as remaining from a slightly later diffusion of the animals. Even then it would have to reflect a pre-4000 B.C. spread, since by that date Niger-Congo peoples had become too diverse and far-flung to allow plausibly for such wide and repeated borrowing of the same two names for the two animals.

The evidence for cultivation at the proto–Niger-Congo period is as yet less strong; if the proto–Niger-Congo people cultivated, their probable staple was the yam, which is difficult to verify archaeologically. Sorghum also spread among the Niger-Congo peoples some thousands of years ago but almost certainly after the proto–Niger-Congo threshold. As for African rice, this crop may be an old collected grain in some parts of West Africa such as the Guinea coast and the interior delta of the Niger. But its domestication, surely by Niger-Congo peoples, probably took place well after the Niger-Congo expansion was underway, because its distribution is much narrower than climate and Niger-Congo language spread would allow. In the whole of eastern Africa and most of equatorial Africa the naming evidence shows rice—presumably Asiatic varieties—to have been introduced via the Portuguese and Swahili, not reaching some areas, e.g., northeastern Zaire, until the close of the nineteenth century (Ehret, in press). As in the Horn, the agricultural remains positively identified in West Africa do not go back nearly so far in time as the linguistic evidence suggests that they must.

Nilo-Saharan Farmers

The third family of African languages among which linguistic traces of early cultivation and herding have been studied is Nilo-Saharan. The difference between this case and those of Niger-Congo and Cushitic is that here archaeology and linguistics seem, at least for now, more in step in their dating of the inception of food production.

The Nilo-Saharan family is another, like the Afroasiatic, of apparently very great internal diversity. Some stages of expansion and diversification within the family probably indeed correlate, as J. E. G. Sutton (1974) suggests, with the spread of the "Aquatic Civilization," but the earliest stages may belong to even more remote times. There are at least two very widespread old root words for cattle in Nilo-Saharan languages (Greenberg, 1963); neither by itself requires domestication, since early Nilo-Saharans very possibly lived in areas which had wild cattle of some kind. Greenberg also cites a sheep term in his Nilo-Saharan evidence, but it is not at all clear whether his citations reflect a single root or two distinct but phonetically similar roots. In either case his citations are limited to the eastern Sudan and so could reflect the routes of initial diffusion of this non-African domesticate into that region, albeit several thousand years ago, to account for the breaks in distribution and degree of phonological variation among the cited forms. The chances are, then, that the proto–Nilo-Saharan people were food collectors and not yet farmers—nor, for that matter, intensive utilizers of aquatic resources.

The relationships between the various recognized subfamilies of Nilo-Saharan remain to be worked out, and the working out itself will probably take many years. But reconstruction of several of the narrower and even of some of the not-so-narrow subgroups of the family is progressing, through the efforts of a number of scholars, and within a relatively few years this current work should lead to elucidation of still deeper levels of relationships. For now, the two earliest reconstructions are of proto-Nilotic and proto-Central Sudanic. A provisional consonantal reconstruction of Nilotic has existed for over ten years (as implied in Ehret, n.d.a; see also Ehret, 1980c), though not yet properly published, and a Central Sudanic reconstruction has taken shape more recently (Ehret and Saxon, n.d., and implied in Ehret, 1973, and Ehret et al., 1974). What these data have allowed for both language groups is the reconstruction of a considerable vocabulary pertaining to food production.

Both proto-languages were spoken probably by the third millennium B.C. at the latest (Ehret et al., 1974); proto-Nilotic apparently east of the Nile in the southern Sudan Republic and proto-Central Sudanic to the west of the river and south of the Bahr-el-Ghazal. Proto-Nilotic vocabulary clearly contained a complex array of livestock terms, including a verb root for "to herd," diagnostic of stock-raising. On the other hand, it has proven difficult to find any solidly reconstructible proto-Nilotic cultivation terms. In contrast, using the often much less complete data available for Central Sudanic languages, it was still possible to reconstruct vocabulary both of cultivation of grains and of herding for proto-Central Sudanic, including verbs for "to weed," "to cultivate," and "to milk."

What can be suggested is that both proto-Nilotes and proto-Central Sudanic peoples already had a well-developed reliance on food production by 3000–2000 B.C., but that subsistence emphasis varied in different areas. The proto-Nilotes were pastoralists, to perhaps a greater extent than any of their descendants today except some Maasai, whereas the Central Sudanic people were mixed farmers. The proto-Nilotes may provide an instance of the spread of herding before that of cultivation.

In both cases an earlier history of food production is required, but just how much earlier remains to be seen. The Central Sudanic group seems only rather distantly related to other Nilo-Saharan languages, so its nearest point of connection to other members of the family is probably several thousand years earlier than the proto-Central Sudanic period, and could pre-date food production altogether. Nilotic seems to belong to a somewhat more closely related subfamily within Nilo-Saharan, called Eastern Sudanic. The limits of Eastern Sudanic are in dispute today, but it appears probable that a reconstituted Eastern Sudanic containing Nilotic and some of the other members of Greenberg's Eastern Sudanic—those with a unique grammatical innovation, the addition of -ŋ singular and -*k* plural to the older Nilo-Saharan root *te or *ti, "cow"—will eventually be recognized. The use of this innovation distinguishes five of Greenberg's subgroups of Eastern Sudanic—Nilotic, Surma (Didinga, Murle, etc.), Ingessana, Temein, and Daju—from two others, Nubian and Tama-Merarit. The proto-Eastern Sudanic period has a good probability of belonging to the earliest eras in which food production of some kind was practiced in the eastern Sudan region. It may well be that the force impelling the break-up and expansion of such an Eastern Sudanic grouping as that postulated here was the adoption of livestock. The differences between the Nilotic subgroup and its nearest related languages is such that this period of change would probably have to be placed another two thousand years or so before proto-Nilotic times, in other words, about the fifth millennium B.C. (Ehret, 1974b) or possibly even earlier. Verification of this speculation will require the working out of a solid basis for Eastern Sudanic subclassification, followed by systematic reconstruction of vocabulary including subsistence lexicon; and that is a task not yet truly begun.

Archaeological data bearing on the period of agricultural beginnings in the Sudan belt are few. The Kadero site in the Republic of Sudan (Krzyzaniak, 1978), with a calibrated date of ca. 4000 B.C., has yielded cattle, sheep, and goat bones as well as sorghum and (bulrush?) millet seed impressions. Apparently, agriculture was sufficiently evolved by that time to postulate that a period of development toward food production had preceded it, perhaps putting agricultural beginnings in the eastern Sudan back to the early fifth millennium. Such a timespan more than accounts for the solid linguistic evidence so far available for early Sudanic agriculture, namely, that of proto-Nilotic, proto-Central Sudanic and, much farther west, proto-Chadic, all dating to 3000 B.C. or before by linguistic reckoning. It also fits the as yet more speculative association of food production with the Eastern Sudanic-speaking ancestors of the Nilotes and related peoples of the eastern portions of the Sudan belt. The gaps in both linguistic and archaeological knowledge are enormous, but the convergent indications of the two sources of historical evidence should encourage us to believe that the endeavor to explore linguistics as well as archaeology in the Sudan is going to be well worth while.

Overview

What the linguistic arguments depict overall is the emergence of several systems of food production in different parts of sub-Saharan Africa well before 3000 B.C. One development of grain cultivation by Cushites probably took place in the northern Horn by about 5000 B.C.; its invention preceded the diffusion of Near Eastern cultigens to the region. A possible second, separate form of cultivation, involving the *enset* plant, may have originated among Omotic peoples in southern Ethiopia at almost as early a date, but the confirmatory linguistic evidence is as yet lacking. A third kind of early cultivation, based on sorghum and/or bulrush millet, can be discerned in the eastern Sudan and as

far west as northern Nigeria. Its practitioners by about 3000 B.C. included the proto-Central Sudanic and proto-Chadic peoples and it may have been slightly later in inception than Cushitic agriculture. A fourth African form of cultivation, a planting tradition based on the yam, can be proposed as the contribution of Niger-Congo peoples of West Africa. Domestication of the yam may go back to the proto–Niger-Congo period, no more recently than 6000 B.C., although the proto–Niger-Congo people could alternatively have begun as intensive collectors of yams and their descendants only in somewhat later times have become true cultivators.

Each of these agricultural systems had a livestock component of some sort. Cattle were apparently known to peoples of each of the traditions. Goats are clearly attested for early Niger-Congo, Chadic, and Cushitic populations, while sheep seem to have been the commoner animal in the eastern Sudan. On the whole, the linguistic evidence implies that the livestock components became established earlier than the archaeology can yet verify—notably among the Niger-Congo peoples, where the most probable explanation of the lexical distributions is that cows and goats were known in some parts of West Africa as early or almost as early as they appear in North African archaeology. In some cases adoption of livestock can be supposed to have preceded the beginnings of actual cultivation, as possibly among Cushites and Nilotes.

Further Spread of Food Production

By 3000 B.C., so the various types of linguistic evidence conjoin in implying, most of Africa down to about 5° North Latitude had become the domain of societies increasingly dependent on food production for survival. Between then and the middle of the last millennium B.C., agriculture in various forms seems to have been carried across the equator as far as about 5° South Latitude.

In western equatorial Africa it is in the period 3000–500 B.C. that the first stages of Bantu expansion must, on linguistic grounds, be placed (Ehret,

1972, 1973, 1974a; Meeussen, 1956). That Bantu expansion began in the northwest of the vast present-day Bantu speech area and well pre-dates the Iron Age is now beginning to receive general recognition (Ehret, 1972; de Maret and Nsuka, 1977; and even Oliver, 1979). Validly reconstructible proto-Bantu subsistence vocabulary (for the relevant criteria, see Ehret, 1972, 1974a) includes root words for "yam" (the pan–Niger-Congo root word, in fact), three seed crops—a gourd, a pulse, and one other, possibly the Voandzeia nut—and "goat." Another word, *-cangu, has been thought by some to name a grain species, but it was probably instead a generic term for "small seeds," narrowed in some Bantu areas during the past two thousand years to apply to newly introduced grain crops (Ehret, 1974a). The proto–Niger-Congo word for "cow" also lasted into proto-Bantu but was shifted in application to the buffalo in a few forest Bantu languages and was dropped entirely by the Bantu groups who eventually expanded through and beyond the equatorial rain forest. Apparently, the early stages of Bantu expansion south and eastward into the forest zones brought an agriculture with yams as the staple but also with a few seed crops that had already diffused south from the Sudanic centers of plant domestication by the third millennium B.C. What knowledge the earliest Bantu may have had of cattle was lost because the animals could not live in the forest. Goats, however, remained a significant element in Bantu subsistence. Sheep apparently did not spread to Bantu peoples until later (Ehret, 1974a).

Far to the east, between Lake Victoria and the Indian Ocean, contemporaneous introduction of food production can be laid to the agency of Southern Cushites entering Kenya from the north in the third millennium and spreading to northcentral Tanzania by the second millennium B.C. (Ehret, 1974b). Archaeological confirmation for this linguistically attested extension of food production southward is now beginning to appear (Ambrose, this volume). The Southern Cushites cultivated grains, it can be argued from vocabulary reconstruction, and kept cattle, goats, donkeys, and probably sheep. Their agriculture may have combined elements of Sudanic origin with an Ethiopian highland agricultural base. Finger millet is one

likely early Southern Cushitic crop; two others, of Sudanic background, were sorghum (Ehret, 1974b) and possibly Voandzeia groundnuts (Ehret, unpublished data).

For the areas between the equatorial rain forest and Lake Victoria, still a third agency of the spread of food production can be proposed, the expansion of Central Sudanic-speaking peoples. Loanwords in western Tanzanian Bantu languages and modern Lacustrine Bantu languages (Ganda, Nyoro, Rwanda, etc.) of Uganda and the Western Rift show a quite clear earlier Central Sudanic presence in those regions. The loanwords include subsistence terms, e.g., proto-Lacustrine *-te "cow" from Central Sudanic *ti (one of the old Nilo-Saharan roots discussed above); and in any case the Central Sudanic peoples, as we have seen, were already food producers by about 3000 B.C. The archaeological identification of this strongly attested substratum in the lake region has not met with general agreement. The Kansyore tradition has the best distributional fit with linguistically postulated Central Sudanic locations, but we need better evidence to show that most of the makers of Kansyore ware were true food producers.

Last Stages of the Spread of Food Production

Between about 500 B.C. and A.D. 500 African modes of food production were spread to the far southern tip of the continent. The agents generally recognized in this process have been the Early Iron Age Bantu, who by the mid-first millennium A.D. had expanded eastward from Zaire as far as the East African coasts, settling in southern Uganda, western Tanzania, and parts of highland Kenya and northeastern Tanzania; they also expanded southward to Malawi, Zambia, Angola, Zimbabwe, Mozambique, Natal, and the Transvaal. D. W. Phillipson (cf 1977c) has proposed an almost equally vast Later Iron Age expansion replacing the Early Iron Age settlement and accounting for the modern Bantu languages. However, the linguistic evidence rules out this interpretation. It requires only one large Eastern Bantu expansion beginning at least 2,000 years ago and probably some centuries earlier—certainly nowhere near as recently as 1,000 years ago, as Phillipson's Later Iron Age spread would necessitate. On the other hand, the linguistic evidence points to several later expansions, in various parts of southern and eastern Africa, of Bantu groups established during the earlier great expansion, all at about the time generally thought of as marking the inception of the Later Iron Age (Ehret, 1980, 1981b). Thus the Early Iron Age seems, linguistically, to have indeed been one related set of expansions, while the Later Iron Age Bantu societies arose from a series of lesser and more regional population readjustments.

The kinds of agricultural systems spread by the Early Iron Age Bantu expansion in eastern and southern Africa frequently contained elements from the older Niger-Congo planting agriculture, but the staples tended to be African grain crops: sorghum from the Sudanic background and, in the very driest situations, bulrush millet, with finger millet a common crop accompanying sorghum in the wetter areas of settlement. The evidence of early Eastern Bantu vocabulary transformations indicates a generally Central Sudanic source for those new kinds of Bantu cultivation better suited to eastern and southern African climates, with the crucial changes developing just before Early Iron Age expansion, probably in or near the areas of the Great Lakes and the Western Rift. The reacquaintance of Bantu with cattle probably began in those same areas, but full adoption of cattle-raising by Bantu-speaking communities probably generally took place only over the course of the first millennium A.D. and had several local sources in the suitable areas of Bantu settlement—Southern Nilotes and Southern Cushites generally in Tanzania and Kenya and Central Sudanic peoples in the lake region and perhaps elsewhere (Ehret, 1974a, 1980a).

The Early Iron Age Bantu expansion does not, however, entirely account for the final spread of food production to the southern tip of the continent. Archaeological discoveries of the past decade have revealed quite different sorts of food-producing populations in the southwestern Cape of South Africa. As early as the beginning of the first millennium these people were tending sheep and, not long after, cattle as well; an equally early presence of shepherd folk in Namibia is now also attested.

The linguistic indications seem to coincide nicely with the still meager and uneven archaeology. They reveal two sets of Khoisan societies that had acquired sheep sufficiently long ago to correlate with the material remains so far recovered. The sheep-raisers of the Cape can be understood as the cultural and linguistic ancestors of the later Khoikhoi pastoralists of the Cape and the Orange River regions. A second Khoisan herding population of recent centuries were the Kwadi of far southern coastal Angola; it can be proposed that the proto-Kwadi expansion, of which the later Kwadi were the last remnant, brought sheep pastoralism to Namibia and presumably to adjoining areas of southern Angola, as yet archaeologically unexplored (Ehret, 1982). That the Kwadi and Khoikhoi obtained their sheep from a common source is clear from their retention of a common generic term for the animal (*gu), and since the several closest linguistic relatives of both their languages are all spoken in the limited region of northern and northeastern Botswana, it is there or near there that the source of the common factor in their subsistence history should most probably be sought. The linguistic arguments, then, favor some region in or close to northern Botswana as the area in which knowledge of pastoral pursuits was transferred to a few southern African Khoisan communities who, with this new addition to their collecting pursuits, then expanded fairly rapidly through suitable grazing lands westward toward the Atlantic and southward to the Cape.

Where did this stock-raising knowledge come from? The linguistic evidence does not indicate a Bantu source, and in any case the earliest known Bantu settlements south of the Zambezi are too late in time to account for the change-over. By the early centuries A.D., when Bantu-speaking immigrants were pressing into southeastern Africa, the Khoisan herding way of life had not only become well established but had been spread hundreds of miles west and south from the area of its probable inception to the farthest edges of the continent. The modern Southwest Bantu (Herero, Kwanyama, Nyaneka, etc.) and Southeast Bantu (Sotho,

Nguni, etc.) both have the same root word for sheep (*gu) as the Kwadi and Khoikhoi, as, in an altered form (*kuai), do the Shona; but in each case it appears to be an early Kwadi or Khoikhoi loanword showing Bantu adoption of sheep from their Khoisan-speaking predecessors (Ehret et al., 1972; Ehret, 1981).

The evidence of subsistence vocabulary in Khoikhoi does allow proposal of a Central Sudanic source for this knowledge. (Adequate data on Kwadi are unfortunately lacking at present.) Not only can apparent Central Sudanic loanwords for "ram," "milk ewe," and "cow" be identified in the Khoikhoi lexicons, but also loanwords for "broth," "porridge," and "grain" (Ehret, 1973). The latter two loans do not necessarily imply Khoikhoi adoption of grain-growing along with stock-raising, but only that they knew of such foods through contacts with cultivators. The linguistic indications thus favor the adoption first of sheep-raising and secondarily of cattle-raising by Khoisan hunter-gatherers from Central Sudanic mixed farmers. The most probable setting for the adoption was far northern Botswana or some nearby area in the centuries preceding Bantu arrival. Archaeological evidence for a Central Sudanic people in or near the region is lacking, but so is such evidence for *any* kind of food production before the spread of the Bantu in the wide gap between eastern Africa and the Cape. Yet, unless sheep were introduced by sea to far southern Africa—a highly improbable alternative—some sort of spread of food production across that gap, however sparse and scattered the settlements of its bearers may have been, must have taken place prior to Bantu settlement. Other linguistic evidence exists suggesting the pre-Bantu presence of Central Sudanic food-producers in portions of that gap, specifically in the corridor between lakes Tanganyika and Malawi and in southern Zambia (Ehret, 1968a, 1973), so that archaeological corroboration may eventually be found.

Diversification of African Food-Production

Even as agriculture was first being introduced to southern Africa, more complex and diversified forms of food production were emerging through the spread of cultigens from certain African centers of domestication to other regions, for instance, Sudanic crops such as gourds and sorghum had spread to Niger-Congo–speaking regions probably by the third millennium B.C., and animals had spread even earlier, especially in northern Africa and the Horn; crops had also entered from outside the continent, mainly from the Near East. Of course, African crops like cotton, sorghum, and sesame were already spreading, even 4,000 or 5,000 years ago, beyond the confines of the continent to enrich the agriculture of non-African peoples. During the past 2,000 years, further diversification of African food-production came via the introduction of two major new sets of food crops: from Indonesia and Southeast Asia apparently in the first millennium A.D. and from the Americas after 1500. Linguistic traces of these introductions frequently remain in the modern distributions of names for the domesticates, and these data can be used to infer eras and places of introduction and directions of spread (cf. Ehret, in press, for the East African adoption of American crops). In the same way it is possible to develop evidence for the spread of the introduced domestic animals—the pig, chicken, camel, and horse.

These are matters that await the future attention of linguistical historians, as do the great and numerous gaps in the general knowledge of subsistence vocabulary all across the span of African languages. Even though a number of important inferences about the history of African food-production can be made from the available linguistic evidence, development of this approach and correlation of its findings with those of archaeology are tasks still barely begun.

II

Paleoenvironments and
Ecological Adaptations

INTRODUCTION

This section of the volume is divided on a regional basis into four parts—northern Africa and the Sahara, west, eastern and southern Africa. This is also to some extent a chronological division, since radiometric dating indicates that the earliest evidences of domestication are manifest in the north and some of the latest in the south.

The appearance of food-producing strategies in northern Africa is related to the time of climatic and ecological amelioration in the early Holocene between ca. 8000 and 5000 B.P. This is the period of the earliest village farming in the Nile Valley and the Western Desert of Egypt, in Cyrenaica and the Maghreb, and the increasing rate of desiccation that followed, in the Sahara perhaps in large part man-induced, resulted in movements of large numbers of people and animals. The pattern of transhumant subsistence described by David Lubell for the Epi-Paleolithic hunter/gatherers in the Maghreb is, with local variations, a likely model for much of the northern part of the continent and the Nile Valley immediately prior to the adoption of domesticated animals and plants. The very special nature of the environment of the seasonally flooded Nile Valley permitted the development of a viable system of animal domestication and crop production which may be as old as any in the continent. The field program initiating reexamination of the Egyptian Predynastic is now producing the first understanding of the internal organization of habitation sites at this time as well as of the spatial distribution of settlements and of the seasonal use of land and resources in the valley. Major discoveries and advances in understanding the changes in the socioeconomic system leading to a unified kingdom and dynastic rule can be expected to follow from the initial researches described here by Hassan and Hays, who also show that the chronology established on Petrie's sequence-dating now requires to be revised in the light of the suite of radiocarbon dates obtained from the main Predynastic sites.

If there are some who doubt the effect of drought or other adverse climatic conditions on prehistoric human economy, Karl Butzer provides ample evidence for this and the effect the Nile flood variation had on the political continuity of the Dynastic kingdom. Similarly, Martin Williams' synthesis of fluctuating climate and environment in the Sahara serves as an essential base for understanding the events leading to domestication—the advantages and consequences accruing from the regular use of aquatic foods by the populations round the Sahara lakes and along the Nile and, in particular, the adoption of nomadic pastoralism in the desert. Fred Wendorf and Romuald Schild, Andrew Smith and Desmond Clark present regional studies of the changing prehistoric economies in the Sahara and on the Upper Nile showing how similar habitats and the exploitation of similar resources have produced generally similar lifestyles based on a system of regular seasonal movement and exchange relationships.

The cereal crops of northern Africa are the winter rainfall ones (wheat and barley) but these do not do well in the summer rainfall areas south of the desert, so that here crops had to be developed from wild staples. Ann Stemler discusses what is involved in the domestication of two of these— sorghum and bullrush millet—both of which are still major crop plants for large numbers of people and which spread widely throughout southern Africa with the first agriculturalists.

Researches by George Armelagos and his collaborators into the biological changes in the prehistoric populations of Nubia show how the robust Mesolithic population became modified after the introduction of food production and the authors discuss some of the effects of the nutritional deficiencies that accompanied this economic change. Their important conclusions invite further studies of a similar nature on other archaeological populations.

Much has been written about the origins of West African agriculture and the greater part of the 1976 volume *Origins of African Plant Domestication* was devoted to it, in particular to the evidence coming from the plants themselves, and there is little new to report in this direction. The three papers on this region are devoted to the archaeology, to reports on new evidence and to position papers for future research. Although the West African savanna and Sahel was clearly a crucial region for indigenous plant cultivation, it is surprising how little is known about it archaeologically outside Ghana. Now, with the new work at Jenné, there are high hopes of learning something about the origins of African rice cultivation in the Niger bend and of the towns and cities in the Sahel.

An important hypothesis to be investigated is why the pastoralists coming into the savanna from the Sahara in the third and second millennia B.C. did not themselves turn to cultivating rather than leave this to the indigenous peoples. A number of alternative hypotheses could be presented—that, in their homeland, they had not cultivated but had collected wild grain in the same way that the majority of the Sahara nomads still do today; or that the tropical grasses were so unlike those they were accustomed to that they were without an efficient technology with which to deal with them. It is, however, possible that some of the savanna farmers today are descended from pastoralists who did, in fact, turn to cultivation. Perhaps the most cogent reason why the indigenous hunter/gatherers turned to cultivating and were not absorbed by or made subservient to the pastoralists, as resulted in most cases of interaction and conflict between hunters and herders, was because the presence of tsetse fly carrying *nagana* permitted the pastoral nomads only seasonal incursions into much of the savanna, thereby providing the indigenous people with the time and opportunity to establish successful cultigens, permanent village settlement, and mutually beneficial exchange relationships.

Only in the last few years have archaeologists turned again to studying the later prehistoric cultures of eastern Africa and the origins there of indigenous agriculture. We still have little solid evidence to report from Ethiopia but great potential can be seen to exist there for learning more about why and how such peculiarly Ethiopian domesticates as *teff* and *enset* were first cultivated. The position in East Africa has now become clearer due to the work of physical anthropologists and archaeologists studying the settlements and faunal remains associated with them. The new evidence from the Lake Turkana basin not only shows some kind of relationship between the early Holocene hunting, fishing and gathering economies of the peoples living along the upper Nile and round the Saharan and Western Rift lakes, but the oldest evidence for domestic stock is found there also in relation to assemblages which may have northern connections with Ethiopia. Archaeologists working in East Africa have probably made better use of the linguistic evidence than have those in other areas, except for the study of the spread of Bantu. The archaeological sequence and possible linguistic associations during the time of the Pastoral Neolithic in the highlands of East Africa are largely unpublished or still in press and are well summarized by Stanley Ambrose. Diane Gifford's paper analyzing the faunal assemblage associated with a late Pastoral Neolithic site in the Kenya Rift is an example of the kind of inductive model that follows from detailed analysis studied against a background of game ecology and pastoral systems. The last paper in this section describes the use of ethnography and archaeology for establishing alternative models of behavior for the prehistoric pastoral cultures of East Africa; models which can, in most cases, be tested in the field.

A great deal has been written about the Early Iron Age food producers and metallurgists who introduced the African food plants and livestock into southern Africa in the first few centuries A.D. and this is summarized and discussed, following the latest research there, by David Phillipson. Previously it appeared that the incoming agricultural Negroes speaking Bantu languages overran and eliminated the existing hunter/gatherer populations. Now, however, physical anthropology is showing that this Central African population was by no means always of Khoisan stock but also showed affinities with the present-day Negroes. There is, therefore, now good reason to modify the original view and to allow that a proportion of the population was able to make the change from hunting to farming without any significant displacement by immigrant groups.

The remainder of the section is concerned with the Khoisan peoples of the southwestern parts of the continent and their acquisition of stock. Biological changes in the Khoisan populations attendant upon the adoption of the herding economy are discussed, as is the relationship between the Khoikhoi (Hottentot) and San (Bushmen). Sheep (and also pottery) are associated with the Khoisan peoples from at least the first century B.C. but the origin of these sheep and, later, of cattle and other cultural traits remains uncertain. It will require future research to show whether the stone-using Khoikhoi once inhabited parts of eastern Africa, moving south with their herds at a period somewhat before the coming of the first Iron Age farmers to Zimbabwe and the Transvaal, or whether they were an autochthonous Stone Age people who acquired their stock from early Iron Age groups somewhere south of the Zaire basin or, alternatively, on the high veld in the northern part of South Africa.

4

A. NORTH AFRICA

Paleoenvironments and Epi-Paleolithic Economies in the Maghreb (ca. 20,000 to 5000 B.P.)

DAVID LUBELL

Situated midway between Europe and both sub-Saharan Africa and the Near East, the Maghreb has long been prime territory for colonizing movements, and this has affected the way in which prehistorians have viewed the region. While strictly diffusion-migration explanations for Maghreb prehistory can no longer be accepted, it is a fact that there are strong, if generalized, similarities

This paper is based largely on research funded by the Canada Council and the Social Sciences and Humanities Research Council. Fieldwork was authorized by the Ministry of Higher Education and Scientific Research and the Ministry of Information and Culture, Museums and Monuments Division, in Algiers. Acknowledgment is made to the Director of the Centre de Recherches Anthropologiques, Préhistoriques et Ethnographiques and the Director of Museums and Monuments for facilitating our research. Thanks are also due to co-workers J. L. Ballais, I. A. N. Cambell, W. R. Farrand, A. Gautier, F. A. Hassan, M. .K. Jackes, J. C. Ritchie, and P. J. Sheppard. If borrowing from their ideas has been too indiscriminate, perhaps they will forgive even though they may disagree with the interpretations proposed. Farrand, and especially Antonio Gilman, suggested changes to an earlier draft which were most helpful. Mary Jackes has shared the burden of preparing this version. Figures 1 and 3 were drawn by I. Wilson, Cartographic Services, Department of Geography, University of Alberta.

throughout the circum-Mediterranean during the late Pleistocene and early to mid-Holocene. These similarities cover the full range of archaeological data and interpretations, yet in the Maghreb the situation appears distinctive. The Neolithic mode of production, apparently so well-documented elsewhere in the circum-Mediterranean (or are we still, unconsciously, overwhelmed by the developments in southwestern Asia?), cannot be shown to have arrived in the Maghreb until a late date and probably from an external source. Why not? Some interpret this as evidence for cultural stagnation or, at least, a lower level of cultural development. This writer, on the contrary, sees it as evidence that the Epi-Paleolithic populations of the Maghreb had, from an early date, achieved an effective, successful, and, above all, flexible subsistence adaptation to their environment(s) that obviated the "necessity" of introducing a new mode of production, despite declining environmental productivity, until later than elsewhere in North Africa specifically or the circum-Mediterranean in general. It should, however, be borne in mind that the data available are neither complete nor conclusive, and that the writer will, therefore, rely heavily on his own research, which covers a limited timespan (the Capsian, 10,000 to 6000 B.P.) and a restricted area (the Chéria and Télidjène basins in eastern Algeria).

Paleoenvironments

The climatic history of the Maghreb during the last 18,000 to 20,000 years is not well documented. The available data are of uneven quality, are from widely dispersed localities, and are poorly calibrated. No detailed palynological studies cover this period. Most interpretations rest on the study of alluvial and colluvial deposits which have all too often been dated by the archaeological remains they contain (Coque, 1962; Vita-Finzi, 1967; Ballais, 1976), archaeological faunal assemblages (Higgs, 1967b; E. C. Saxon, 1976; Lubell et al., 1975), or charcoal from archaeological deposits (Hassan in Lubell et al., 1975); we seem to know a great deal more about other parts of the Mediterra-

nean and the Sahara than we do about the Maghreb (e.g., Rognon, 1976; Thunell, 1979); and the Maghreb data are not always consistent. Thus, the outline presented here is very tentative.

The CLIMAP model (CLIMAP, 1976) suggests that at 18,000 B.P. the Maghreb was cooler than it is today. July surface air temperatures are estimated to have been between 13° C. (northwest) and 3° C. (northeast) lower than at present (Gates, 1976: 1142). The average temperature depression seems to have been about 6° C., which is in agreement with the estimate of Peterson et al. (1979) based on terrestrial data. Higher elevations in the Moroccan Atlas are reconstructed as snow-covered (Gates, 1976: 1139), while the coastal plain and high inland plateaux are said to have been covered by forest or other dense vegetation (CLIMAP, 1976: 1132). Sea-surface temperatures off the northwest coast of Africa were apparently about 2° C. colder than today, while in the western Mediterranean they were more than 4° colder. The western Mediterranean was apparently 10° cooler than the eastern Mediterranean, whereas the difference today is only 1° to 2° (CLIMAP, 1976: 1135). A low-pressure cell over the western central Sahara (Gates, 1976: 1141) probably brought increased precipitation to this region, and the depression of the westerlies (in combination with other factors) may have brought more precipitation to the Maghreb as well (Peterson et al., 1979). The latter is, however, far from certain; Rognon (1976) argues for an inverse relationship between the Sahara and the Maghreb, that is, one being wet while the other was dry and vice versa.

The available data are not entirely in agreement with this general model. Charcoal from archaeological sites (Couvert, 1972, 1976) suggests that the period from about 20,000 to 12,000 B.P. was cool and relatively dry. Sheet-flood erosion resulting in widespread erosional surfaces (pediment formation) was common (cf. Coque, 1962), with concurrent sedimentation occurring downslope, i.e., toward the centers of basins. In some areas these surfaces may have formed over a long period, and the downslope portion of a pediment-sediment surface may be younger than its upslope portion. Despite the uncertainty surrounding the term, these surfaces are often called Soltanian (Lubell et al., 1976: n. 16). In eastern Algeria they frequently appear to have been truncated by erosion and to have been overlain unconformably by Holocene deposits. In several instances we have observed Capsian sites resting directly on such surfaces. At the site of Ain Misteheyia this emplacement can be dated no earlier than 10,000 B.P., while 5 km down-

Locale	Lab. No.	Provenience		Material	B.P. (T½ 5568)
	I–9833	± 10 m upstream from Ballais's section and 2.1 m, below Roman age deposits		snail shell	2270 ± 80
Wadi Mezeraa	I–9834	marsh deposits ± 50 m downstream from Ballais's section		snail shell	4685 ± 95
	I–7693	marsh deposits at Ballais's section		snail shell	5830 ± 95
	SMU 655 (temp.)	*in situ* hearth ± 200 m upstream from Ballais's section in higher (older) terrace		charcoal	11,619 ± 109
Wadi Oussif	SMU 688 (temp.)	Marsh deposits exposed in tributary to Wadi Télidjène		snail shell	6957 ± 69
Oued Télidjène A	I–9832	Escargotière—middle of deposits: 120–125 cm		snail shell	7280 ± 120
	I–9835	Capsien supérieur levels (within shelter):	90–95 cm	charcoal	5965 ± 115
	I–9836		125–130 cm	charcoal	6485 ± 125
Kef Zoura D	I–9837		145–150 cm	charcoal	6505 ± 125
	I–9838		165–170 cm	charcoal	6575 ± 170
	SMU 704 (temp.)	Capsien typique levels (in front of shelter): 260 (hearth)		charcoal	8607 ± 161
	SMU 712 (temp.)		280–290 cm	charcoal	9213 ± 158
	I–7690	Upper assemblage:	J9 40–45 cm	snail shell	7280 ± 115
	I–9782		L9N 48–55 cm	snail shell	7640 ± 115
	I–9781		K10W 50–60 cm	snail shell	7725 ± 120
	I–8378	Lower assemblages:	J9 80–90 cm (disturbed)	snail shell	8835 ± 140
	I–9783		M8E/N 90–100 cm	snail shell	7990 ± 125
Ain Misteheyia	I–9784		L11N 95–105 cm	snail shell	8125 ± 125
	I–7691		J9 125–135 cm	snail shell	9280 ± 135
	I–9785		M10S 130–140 cm	snail shell	9430 ± 150
	I–9786		K9 140–145 cm	snail shell	9615 ± 155
	I–9826		K8 140–150 cm (burial)	snail shell	9130 ± 150
	I–9824		K12 145–150 cm	snail shell	9805 ± 160
	I–9825		K10N 150–155 cm	snail shell	9590 ± 155

TABLE 1. **Radiocarbon Dates from the Chéria/Télidjène Region**

All depths for archaeological deposits are below datum.

slope, at the site of Oued Télidjène A, the emplacement appears to be no earlier than about 8000 B.P. (see Table 1).

It has been suggested that somewhat to the west, in Algeria, the Soltanian *glacis* can be dated to about 19,000 B.P. (Guiraud, n.d.). However, given the probability that such surfaces are time-transgressive, such a date does not necessarily refer to the end of their formation. It is, of course, possible that a hiatus is present, especially considering the truncated nature of many of these surfaces.

It is also far from clear that such surfaces formed continuously throughout the late Pleistocene and early Holocene. There are several alluvial sections (located both in basin centers and on basin margins) in which deposits suggestive of marshy conditions have been observed. We have obtained a provisional radiocarbon date of 6957 ± 69 B.P. (SMU 688) for one such deposit in the Télidjène basin. These observations may, of course, be indicative of local rather than regional conditions, and additional research in several areas must be done before a more accurate picture can be drawn.

Some additional data are available now which permit a partial (and tentative) reconstruction of paleoenvironments during the early Holocene in a restricted part of eastern Algeria. The region is near the modern town of Chéria, some 40 km southwest of Tébessa (Fig. 1). Working in this area since 1972, we have collected data that bear on paleoenvironments.

The Wadi Mezeraa drains the Chéria basin, passing through a narrow gorge just west of the Télidjène basin. A 6-meter section in this gorge was studied by Ballais (1976; and in Lubell et al., 1975), who defined the "Chéria formation" on the basis of his observations. Subsequent work by the present writer and Achilles Gautier (1979) and by W. R. Farrand suggests that Ballais's conclusions were premature. The section he studied (cf. Lubell et al., 1975: fig. 3) does not span the entire Holocene but, rather, at most the last 5000 years (see Table 1). Furthermore, just upstream from his type section there is a 10 m exposure of generally fine-grained sediments that underlie a terrace that is at least 5 m higher than at Ballais's section and that do not contain the sort of dark-colored organic facies

present in the section he studied. In addition, toward the base of the higher section, we observed two *in situ* hearths. Charcoal from one of these has been provisionally dated to 11,619 ± 109 B.P. (SMU 655). Thus, the "Chéria formation" must be abandoned as a formal unit (Lubell and Gautier, 1979). The deposits used to define it appear to represent a mid to late Holocene series of short periods of marshy sedimentation interrupted by deposition of stream gravels in shallow channels cut into the marsh sediments, perhaps during flood spates (W. R. Farrand, *in litt.*, 1978).

These data appear to suggest an earlier period (first half of the Holocene?) of slower alluvial deposition and more complete weathering with little colluviation (i.e., greater vegetation cover on the slopes), followed by a period of more irregular deposition in which colluvial, alluvial, and marshy depositional environments were all present—though not necessarily at the same time. This period seems to have begun by at least 5000 B.P. and has probably continued through the Roman period and into the present, both here and elsewhere in the Maghreb (e.g., Vita-Finzi, 1967: 211–213).

How much of the difference is due to climatic change and how much to human interference cannot be accurately determined. Certainly the Roman colonization of the Maghreb had some effect. Urban population densities during the Roman and Byzantine eras were as great as or greater than today. When the Third Augustan Legion was stationed at Tébessa during the reign of Vespasian (A.D. 69–79), the population of the town is estimated to have been at least 40,000, 25 percent larger than now (Pierre, 1977).

Rural densities were, in some areas at least, also apparently higher than at present, though little is known about these settlements. It seems that some were farms of indigenous people, while others belonged to discharged Legionnaires. Olive cultivation on valley sides was certainly an important part of the economic pattern in eastern Algeria—a practice almost obsolete today, since the slopes now are likely to be bedrock (cf. Leveau, 1978).

Many Roman wells of up to 20 m deep are dry today. It is clear that in North Africa (Le Houerou, 1970), as elsewhere in the Mediterranean (e.g.,

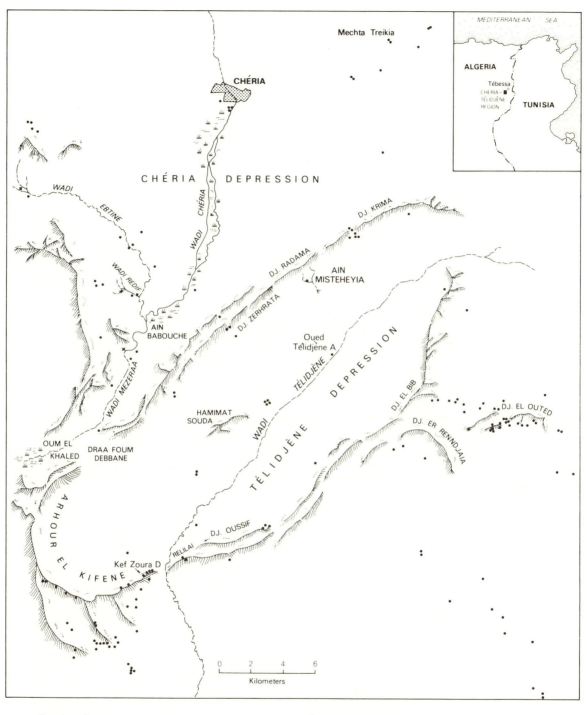

Figure 1. Chéria/Télidjène region.

MEDITERRANEAN SEA

ALGERIA

Tébessa

CHÉRIA-
TÉLIDJÈNE
REGION

TUNISIA

Mechta Treikia

CHÉRIA

CHÉRIA DEPRESSION

WADI EBTINE

WADI CHÉRIA

WADI REDIF

DJ. KRIMA

DJ. RADAMA

AIN
MISTEHEYIA

DJ. ZERHRATA

AIN
BABOUCHE

Oued
Télidjène A

TÉLIDJÈNE DEPRESSION

WADI MEZERAA

HAMIMAT
SOUDA

WADI TÉLIDJÈNE

DJ. EL BIB

DJ. EL OUTED

DJ. ER RENNDJAIA

OUM EL
KHALED

DRAA FOUM
DEBBANE

ARHOUR EL KIFENE

DJ. OUSSIF

RELILAI

Kef Zoura D

0   2   4   6

Kilometers

•   Capsian sites

----   Wadi (intermittent watercourse)

✕   Geological section

Fresh water marsh

Ridge

Naveh and Dan, 1973), environmental degradation resulting in lowered water tables has been extensive during the last 2,000 years. As a result, there has been both destruction and masking of evidence for earlier environments and settlements. This makes it all the more difficult to comprehend fully the nature of late Pleistocene and early Holocene paleoenvironments and paleoeconomies.

Using charcoal from archaeological deposits, Couvert (1972) has proposed a tentative reconstruction of variations in temperature and precipitation for the past 14,000 years in Algeria. He suggests a warming trend with more or less modern precipitation values from about 13,000 to 8000 B.P., interrupted by two periods of lower temperatures and higher precipitation about 10,500–10,000 and again about 8,500 years ago. Following this and until about 4000 B.P., temperature declined while precipitation increased.

While his conclusions can be criticized (he does not control for elevation; the charcoal was brought into the sites by people and does not, therefore, necessarily represent an accurate picture of the regional climate), his reconstruction does agree, in general terms, with what one might expect (cf. CLIMAP, 1976; Rognon, 1976). Couvert is aware of these problems and has attempted to resolve them (Couvert, 1976), trying to reconstruct the phytogeography of the Télidjène basin during the mid-Holocene occupation at Relilai. If he is correct, the area was much more heavily covered by forests than it is at present. However, Couvert's methods are not quantitative in the same way as are palynological studies, and these latter will be required before his reconstruction can be confirmed.[1]

Further suggestions for higher plant (and animal) biomass during the early and mid-Holocene come from the study of prehistoric site distributions and the faunal remains from those sites. Even

given that many sites have been destroyed (cf. Grébénart, 1976; Lubell et al., 1976), their present numbers argue for (at least seasonally) higher population densities than one might expect for hunting-gathering populations in a semiarid environment. Furthermore, the apparent abundance of large herbivores (*Bos, Equus, Alcelaphus*) in many Capsian sites (ca. 10,000 to at least 6000 B.P.) argues for more productive grassland than is presently the case.

Geoarchaeological analyses (Hassan in Lubell et al., 1975) suggest that a decline in the abundance of these larger herbivores, and their replacement by *Gazella* and other small mammals such as lagomorphs, may have been due in part to change in environmental conditions just before 8000 B.P. (Lubell et al., 1976; Lubell and Gautier, 1979; in press). This is the period during which Couvert (1972) indicates rapid oscillation between cold-wet and warm-dry climatic conditions. While our reconstruction here is based on data from only two sites (Ain Misteheyia and Kef Zoura D) in a restricted area (the Télidjène basin), there do appear to be parallels at one other site (Medjez II) located several hundred kilometers to the northwest near Setif (see Bouchud in Camps-Fabrer, 1975).

The suggestion that forest cover may have been more common at higher elevations and along the coast (cf. CLIMAP, 1976) also receives some confirmation from the archaeozoological data. At Medjez II, *Ammotragus lervia* (the Barbary sheep) is far more common than it is further south, suggesting the presence of more forested biotopes to the north. At Tamar Hat on the coast near Bejaia, *A. lervia* is the most common animal in the deposits throughout the period of occupation, which spans ca. 20,000 to 16,000 B.P. (Saxon et al., 1974).

In sum, the available data suggest that during the late Pleistocene and early to mid-Holocene the Maghreb was a rather more lush environment than it is today. It seems to have been cooler, less arid, more heavily vegetated, and more densely populated by large herbivores—all conditions that would have made it attractive to hunter/gatherer populations. Local differences certainly existed, as they do today, but we do not yet have sufficient information to determine their importance.

There are a number of questions that cannot

---

1. In 1978, J. C. Ritchie obtained a preliminary 2.5 auger sample from the Oum el Khaled marsh, just northwest of Draa Foum Debbane (see Fig. 1). Pollen are well preserved in the sediments and stratigraphic changes are present. Since the basin contains at least 5 m of sediment and is within the Wadi Mezeraa drainage, additional coring (November 1979) should recover a record for, at least, the Holocene (cf. Table 1).

be answered adequately until we have more information. Why, for example, does it seem that coastal and inland regions were occupied during different periods by groups producing distinctive stone tools (earlier Iberomaurusian on the coast and later Capsian inland)? Why do there appear to be no immediate successors to the former and no immediate predecessors to the latter in their respective areas? Finally, what was the character of the economies that sustained these groups and why does it appear that a Neolithic mode of production was never established autochthonously in the Maghreb but instead was introduced at a late date, apparently from outside the region? An attempt will be made below to deal with these questions.

Epi-Paleolithic Economies

Until recently, most investigations into the prehistory of the Maghreb were not primarily concerned with the collection and study of data on prehistoric economies. While Pond and his colleagues (Pond et al., 1938) attempted this, their example was not followed by subsequent investigators. Vaufrey (1955) concluded that all Epi-Paleolithic groups (i.e., Capsian and Iberomaurusian) were hunter/gatherers. Balout (1955) concurred, although he did mention the possibility that some Capsian groups might have practiced a rudimentary form of agriculture (p. 431) and even discussed the idea of their having raised snails (p. 392). Gobert (1938) insisted that snails were never a major source of food among Capsian groups, and Morel (1974) argued that snails could only have been a seasonal resource. The latter point is particularly important in that (a) we have come to the same conclusion on independent grounds (Lubell et al., 1975, 1976) and (b) some investigators continue to argue that Capsian groups were sedentary (e.g., Grébénart, 1978).

A number of recent studies have added more in the way of speculation than useful data. While Camps (1974) sees no evidence of either domestic animals or cultivated plants among Capsian and Iberomaurusian groups, E. C. Saxon (1976; Saxon et al., 1974) has argued that the latter domesticated

the Barbary sheep (*Ammotragus lervia*) and the former the hartebeest (*Alcelaphus buselaphus*) and possibly snails. The presence of domestic sheep and goat in the Neolithic levels at Haua Fteah appears well attested (Higgs, 1967b), while domestic pigs and sheep seem to have been present during the Neolithic in Morocco (Gilman, 1976). Roubet (1978) claims the presence of domestic sheep and goat during the Neolithic of Capsian Tradition in eastern Algeria by about 6,500 years ago, in association with a transhumant pastoral economy without domestic plants or cultivation. Further to the south in the Sahara, a widespread pastoral economy with domestic cattle seems to have been in evidence by about 8000 B.P. (e.g., Wendorf et al., 1977), but the pattern is apparently far from uniform. At Amekni, Camps (1969, 1979) suggests that millet was cultivated but that no domestic animals were present. The existence of a Neolithic economy (with ceramics) might be earlier in the Sahara proper than further to the north in the Maghreb. However, along the Atlantic coast of the Sahara, hunting/gathering and shellfish collection seem to have been the main subsistence adaptations throughout the past 10,000 years. No evidence is yet available for cultivated plants and domestic animals, although some of the archaeological evidence (heavy and fragile artifacts) has suggested to investigators that sedentary occupation was not unknown (cf. Petit-Maire, 1979a).

There is, thus, a diversity of opinions based, in the writer's view, on largely inadequate data. A critical review of these data seems appropriate.

THE REFUGIUM HYPOTHESIS AND PLANT DOMESTICATION

H. E. Wright (1976) has hypothesized that parts of the Maghreb were a refugium for wild wheats and barley during the late Pleistocene. While the distribution of barley may have been wider, and its domestication earlier, than was once believed (Wendorf et al., this volume), there is simply no evidence that these grains existed in the

Maghreb before a very late date.[2] Moreover, since wild wheats and barley are absent from the modern Algerian flora (Quézel and Santa, 1962) and do not seem to be present elsewhere in the Maghreb (Quézel, 1978), it seems most logical to conclude that the domestic forms were imported. It seems unlikely that their modern absence can be explained by habitat destruction: elsewhere in the circum-Mediterranean these grasses grow well in secondary (disturbed) habitats. Furthermore, if cereals (including millet, sorghum, and oats) were an important part of prehistoric subsistence in the Maghreb, we should have some evidence for them even though recovery of botanical remains has not normally been a focus of archaeological research in the region (cf. P. E. L. Smith, 1976). In addition, one would expect evidence for the sort of artifacts and settlement patterns we know were a part of those subsistence adaptations that utilized both wild and domestic grains in the Nile Valley (Wendorf, and Schild, 1976b; Wendorf and Schild, this volume) and the Near East (Flannery, 1972; P. E. L. Smith, 1976; Kraybill, 1977; Reed, 1977).

True, there is some evidence for grinding stones, "sickles," and artifacts with silica gloss in both Iberomaurusian and Capsian sites (cf. Camps-Fabrer, 1966; Clarke, 1976). However, there is no reason to assume *a priori* that these were used to harvest or process either wild or domestic grains. The only good evidence available for prehistoric use of plant foods in the Maghreb (Roubet, 1978) comes from the Neolithic of Capsian Tradition. The range of plants includes fruits, seeds, bulbs, nuts, and grasses, but not cereal grains.

Thus, Wright's hypothesis cannot be substantiated with the data at present available. Palynological work is required. A start has been made on this in both Tunisia (Van Zeist, *in litt.*, 1978) and Algeria (research begun by J. C. Ritchie in 1978 and continuing).

2. Included is only that part of the Maghreb north of the Saharan boundary, i.e., north of 34° N and with average elevations of 1000 m above msl.

ANIMAL DOMESTICATION

There do not appear to be any convincing data that argue *on strictly morphological grounds* for prehistoric animal domestication in the Maghreb. The evidence rests primarily on the interpretation of age and mortality curves and sex ratios; osteometric data are inconclusive. Evidence for morphological changes associated with domestication is not yet to hand, and the basis for Roubet's (1978) identification of domestic sheep and goat during the Neolithic of Capsian Tradition is not explained.

The best evidence comes from the Neolithic levels at Haua Fteah in Cyrenaica (not strictly within the Maghreb), where Higgs (1967b) argues that domestic caprines were present by about 6800 years ago. Gilman's (1976) evidence for domestic pigs and caprines during the Mediterranean Neolithic at Ashakar in northern Morocco by about the seventh millennium B.P. seems plausible. It is interesting that he interprets the mortality curve of the (imported) caprines as suggesting that they were treated as "feral" while the pigs were not. It is difficult to assess Roubet's data prior to full publication, but given the dates for the Neolithic of Capsian Tradition (ca. 6500 to at least 4500 B.P.: cf. Roubet, 1971, 1978) and the evidence from Haua Fteah and Morocco, her interpretation seems plausible.

E. C. Saxon's argument (1976; Saxon et al., 1974) for domestication of Barbary sheep (*Ammotragus lervia*) by Iberomaurusian groups as early as 20,000 B.P. is not very convincing, and even less so is his suggestion that Capsian groups had domesticated the hartebeest (*Alcelaphus buselaphus*). Saxon's data suggest that Barbary sheep are the most frequent mammals in the Iberomaurusian deposits at Tamar Hat, as seems to be the case at other Iberomaurusian sites. He argues that since the sample from Tamar Hat differs in certain osteometric, mortality-curve, and sex-ratio characteristics from modern wild populations, and that modern populations are difficult to hunt even with firearms, a special man-animal relationship existed during the Iberomaurusian which was not one of intensive and selective hunting of an abundant resource. His data are open to different interpretations, notably one of seasonal hunting.[3]

Shackleton (in Saxon et al., 1974) analyzed the o^{16}/o^{18} ratio of twenty-five *Monodonta turbinata* shells from layers 7–14 (ca. 16,000 to 17,000 B.P.) at Tamar Hat. He concludes (p. 70) that "the oxygen isotope analysis provides positive evidence for a winter occupation and no indication of a summer occupation." Saxon (Saxon et al., 1974: 71) appears to accept a hypothesis of only winter occupation throughout the entire Iberomaursian period at Tamar Hat. Thus, there seems to be no necessity to explain the characteristics of the *Ammotragus* remains as due to anything other than season of kill, and there seems every reason to assume that the site was not occupied throughout the year. Even though the oxygen isotope results from lower levels are not yet available, the invertebrate assemblage is relatively uniform over the entire depth of the deposits and there does not seem to be any reason to question the premise of strictly seasonal occupation.[4]

Saxon also implies (Saxon et al., 1974: 81) that Capsian groups may have domesticated both the hartebeest and the land snail. He develops his speculation about the former at some length in a later paper (1976) in which he defines three types of domestication, all dependent on varying degrees of control by people over an animal species. He suggests that two of these types are "evident in the Capsian economy" and that "a marked degree of control (possibly including artificial pens) was established by Man over the hartebeest" (p. 211).

This suggestion seems to have no foundation. First, no such structures (implying a system of *parcage*) have been found in association with a Capsian site. Second, the sample of juvenile hartebeest teeth from Dra-Mta-El-Ma-El-Abiod (Morel, 1974) on which Saxon bases his suggestion have been reexamined by Gautier, who disagrees with Morel's interpretation (A. Gautier, *in litt.*, 1978). Morel has accepted this revision and, furthermore, does not agree with Saxon's interpretation of the data (J. Morel, 1978b: 77 and *in litt.*, 1977).

While it is possible to accept that Capsian groups depended heavily on hartebeest and that land snails were less important as sources of food, to suggest that domestication in any sense of the term (cf. Brothwell, 1975) was involved does not accord with our data. On the contrary, our information suggests that variability in Capsian faunal assemblages is best explained by season of occupation, an idea first suggested by Romer (1938: 166) and which Saxon (1976: 210) also entertains. In fact, our reconstruction of the Capsian economy in eastern Algeria (Lubell et al., 1975, 1976) seems to fit neatly with Roubet's (1978) interpretation of the succeeding Neolithic of Capsian Tradition. We think Capsian groups were very mobile and that occupation of any one site was of short duration. We suspect this may have involved movement between the Sahara (winter), the high plateaus (summer), and intervening areas (such as the Télidjène valley) in either spring or fall, or both. Roubet suggests a short-distance (altitudinal) transhumant pattern for Neolithic pastoralist-gatherers in the Aurès, and this can be interpreted as supporting evidence for a hypothesis of long-term continuity in the subsistence adaptations of prehistoric people in the Maghreb.

---

3. Much of this writer's dissatisfaction with Saxon's argument stems from a critique written by Gary Nurkin when he was a graduate student in anthropology at the University of Toronto. Nurkin points out that Saxon's osteometric data are not always accurate and that his interpretation of them can be questioned. See also Morel (n.d.).

4. If the CLIMAP estimates for Mediterranean sea-surface temperatures are correct, Shckleton's interpretation may require revision. Thus, the case for strictly seasonal occupation at Tamar Hat might be open to question. Nonetheless, Saxon's reconstruction (cf. n. 3 above) is unconvincing.

Continuity Versus Change

Can this hypothesis be confirmed or refuted with the data now available? Although this is doubtful, the evidence will be discussed here.

If continuity existed it should be manifested in many aspects of the archaeological record. Yet, at the present time, the two main archaeological "cultures" in the Maghreb, the Iberomaurusian and the Capsian, are said to be completely distinctive in time, distribution, the typology and, to some extent, the technology of stone tools, and the biology of the human populations who produced those artifacts. It is sometimes argued that Capsian peoples were "invaders" (Balout, 1955: 398) from the Near East (Chamla, 1978: 397).

Iberomaurusian sites are, in general, older than Capsian ones. Furthermore, with probably only two exceptions, they are found in different geographical regions: Iberomaurusian along the modern Maghreb coast, and Capsian south of the Tell and extending into the northern fringe of the Sahara. The exceptions are the site of El Hamel near Bou Saâda (Tixier, 1954), which is technically within Capsian territory, and El Haouita-versant near Laghouat in the Saharan Atlas (Estorges, Aumassip, and Dagorne, 1969). In both instances Iberomaurusian assemblages are said to be present.

The question of chronology is clear. The earliest dates for the Iberomaurusian are from Tamar Hat, where Saxon (Saxon et al., 1974) has an internally consistent series beginning at ca. 20,000 B.P. The latest dates for the Iberomaurusian cluster around 10,000 B.P., although there are one or two in the 8000 B.P. range (Camps, 1975). The oldest Capsian date is ca. 9800 B.P. from the base of Ain Misteheyia (see Table 1), and numerous dates suggest that the industry lasted until at least 6000 B.P. It no longer seems necessary to envisage a hiatus between the Iberomaurusian and the Capsian (cf. Tixier, 1963). There does, however, seem to be clear spatial separation, which is curious, in that the Capsian follows the Iberomaurusian.

On typological grounds (and less so, perhaps, on technological ones) the two industries are distinct. This has been satisfactorily demonstrated by applying a cluster analysis using both average linkage and Ward's method (CLUSTAN 1C in Wishart, 1978) to 122 Iberomaurusian and Capsian assemblages. The sample includes most of the assemblages published by Camps (1974), as well as those from Tamar Hat (Close in Saxon et al., 1974), Ain Dokkara (Tixier, 1976), Dra-Mta-El-Ma-El-Abiod (Morel, 1978a) and the writer's own unpublished figures for Ain Misteheyia and Kef Zoura D. Both clustering procedures clearly distinguish between the two industries, on the basis of the percentages of the eight major tool classes present (see Appendix). Other characteristics

(metrical data, stylistic attributes, etc.) might well give different results. Unfortunately, the data necessary for such procedures are not available.[5]

What about the people? Chamla (1978) continues to argue that Iberomaurusian populations belonged to the Mechta-Afalou and Mechtoid types and that these were distinct from the proto-Mediterranean type of the Capsian. She uses Penrose's C^2H distance coefficient to construct matrices which purport to show the degree of similarity among all Maghreb populations from the Epi-Paleolithic to the present; her data are selected measurements of the skull and mandible. It is important to note here that Penrose's coefficient is calculated from the means of previously determined groups and thus tends to reinforce the idea of separation. In fact, and Chamla does not discuss this, the distance between Iberomaurusian populations is frequently greater than the distance between Iberomaurusian and Capsian populations.[6] Table 2 has been constructed from her data (Chamla, 1978: 42, table 15).

Furthermore, Chamla points out that there are now several instances in which Mechtoid individuals are known from Capsian sites and proto-Mediterranean individuals from Iberomaurusian sites. At Medjez II (Camps-Fabrer, 1975), a site with a Capsien supérieur assemblage, both types are present. Chamla (1978: 393) states that "le type de Mechta-Afalou est loin d'être rare dans les gisements capsiens."

Meiklejohn and Molgat (n.d.) have used Chamla's data together with data of their own to perform a cluster analysis with CLUSTAN. Their results do not substantiate the typological division advocated by Chamla. The various human types are distributed throughout the array, and there is great variability within each type, as well as overlap between them. Thus, there is reason to question any division between the two human populations

5. Peter Sheppard is writing his Ph.D. dissertation at the University of Toronto on stylistic criteria for distinguishing variability in Capsian stone tool assemblages. He is largely responsible for the attempt to use cluster analysis in this paper. We are preparing a more detailed analysis, which we hope to publish shortly.

6. The writer is indebted to Mary Jackes for pointing out this inconsistency in Chamla's data and for explaining Penrose's coefficient.

TABLE 2. **Penrose's distance coefficient for selected Maghreb populations. Data from Chamla (1978).**

	Western Iberomaurusian		Eastern Capsian	
	Males	Females	Males	Females
Eastern Iberomaurusian				
Males	0.497		0.438	
Females		0.475		0.386
Western Iberomaurusian				
Males	0.0		0.821	
Females		0.0		0.564

and, by inference, between the cultural remains they produced.

The following points should be noted.

1. The apparent geographical separation of the two industries could be a result of pre-Holocene erosion producing the erosion surfaces discussed earlier. In other words, is it possible that almost all the pre-Capsian Epi-Paleolithic sites south of the Tell were destroyed? This seems improbable, but the idea warrants close examination.[7]

2. There seems to be a hiatus at many Iberomaurusian sites. Epi-Paleolithic levels are usually followed by Neolithic levels that are several thousand years younger.

3. Capsian sites frequently seem to have been established on bare ground. There is almost no evidence for immediately pre-Capsian occupation at any site, so far as is known, with the possible exception of Haua Fteah (which seems to be exceptional in many ways).

What happened? Is it possible that post-

Glacial sea levels rose sufficiently to make the coastal plain unattractive and thus initiated movement to the south? Are there post-Iberomaurusian sites now beneath the sea? Did the inland regions suddenly become more attractive for other reasons? These questions cannot be answered at present, but they clearly deserve investigation.

It at least seems clear that there is more variability in Capsian lithic assemblages than in Iberomaurusian ones. Could it be that a move to the interior plateaux required more and different tool kits? Certainly, Capsian assemblages occur in what one can only interpret as having been a wide range of habitats—savanna, parkland, lakeside, perhaps even desert. Movement, probably seasonal, between such habitats seems a likely possibility.

There are two main kinds of Capsian: the Capsien typique, in which burins and larger tools are frequent, and the Capsien supérieur, in which geometric microliths, backed bladelets, and notched or denticulated tools are more common. Radiocarbon dates suggest that the two were contemporaneous (Camps, 1975). However, the known geographical extent of the typique is more restricted (Camps, 1974: 110).

In only a few instances have both kinds of Capsian been identified in a single site. With the possible exception of Relilai (Grébénart, 1976), the typique appears to lie beneath the supérieur. The question is complex, for we now know that horizontal variation within a single site can be great and that neighboring sites which appear to be more or less contemporaneous may contain very different assemblages (Grébénart, 1976; Morel, 1978a; and personal observations). An analogous situation

---

7. This idea may not be all that farfetched. Numerous surface finds in the Télidjène basin have a Middle Paleolithic character. Some are clearly Levallois cores and flakes which could be derived from Aterian assemblages. There is one Aterian site in the area (Grébénart, 1976). All the examples seen were heavily patinated. Moreover, we have some evidence at Kef Zoura D (see Fig. 1) for an erosional break between the Capsien typique and Capsien supérieur levels. This needs to be confirmed by additional excavation. Furthermore, we have observed several destroyed Capsian sites in wadi sections. Taken together, these data suggest that many sites have been destroyed; whether by one or several periods of erosion, and at what date, is not yet known.

may occur in the Nile Valley (Lubell, 1974; Wendorf and Schild, 1976b).

Camps and Camps-Fabrer (1972; Camps, 1974) have proposed a division of the Capsien typique into two facies (one with a high frequency of burins, the other with a low frequency) and a subdivision of the Capsien supérieur into three phases spread over five regional facies. These are distinguished by the differential frequencies of certain classes of tools (e.g., endscrapers, burins), as well as by the frequency of certain, supposedly diagnostic, types in Tixier's (1963) typology. Can these subdivisions be considered valid? As a check, the CLUSTAN program has been used to analyze 81 Capsian and other Epi-Paleolithic assemblages, using both average linkage and Ward's method (see Appendix). The data were the percentage frequencies of eight major tool classes; in each case the percentages were recalculated on the total of the eight classes used.

Both clustering methods distinguish typique from supérieur assemblages and confirm a subdivision within the typique. Six southern Tunisian assemblages always cluster as a group and one Keremian assemblage (Bois des Pins) is always isolated. There are no clear divisions among the Capsien supérieur assemblages: the different facies and phases are spread, more or less indiscriminately, across the entire array. Only the cluster diagram for the average linkage procedure is reproduced here (Fig. 2). Figure 3 shows the percentage occurrence of each previously defined assemblage group in the various clusters distinguished by both the average linkage and Ward's method analyses.

If this method of analysis is valid, one is led to the conclusion that the proposed subdivisions of the Capsien supérieur cannot be substantiated. Furthermore, while different levels of a single site often cluster, sites of the same facies do not. The analysis thus produced almost no clear geographical groupings. Therefore, if the assemblages represent distinctive Capsian populations, they must have been quite mobile—a clear refutation of the idea that Capsians had a sedentary lifestyle (cf. Grébénart, 1978).

Many Capsian assemblages seem to have rather individual styles—in other words, both inter- and intra-assemblage variability is high. Yet, it is sug-

gested that one group would have habitually returned to the same area, even to the same site. While direct archaeological evidence for this is slight, we know that modern hunter/gatherer populations do have habitual rounds and that man, in general, does not wander at random but moves along familiar routes.

How, then, can we explain the diversity of Capsian assemblages? One part of the answer must lie with the diversity of habitats in which the sites occurred. This may answer the question of regional diversity, but can it bear at all on the problem of change over time? Probably, so long as we realize that the environmental changes which occurred were likely to have been localized but, nonetheless, marked enough to require short-term adaptive changes. Thus, if we interpret the variations in stone-tool assemblages as methods of dealing with varying environmental conditions, we may have an explanation for both inter- and intra-assemblage variability.

A full explanation along these lines will require many more data than we now have. Specifically, questions of function and style will become paramount. The former will necessitate coordinated analyses of lithic, faunal, and paleobotanical assemblages from a number of sites. The latter can build upon these using additional techniques of analysis.

We already have two sets of data from the Télidjène basin that suggest that an explanation along these lines may be possible. At Ain Misteheyia there are two major assemblages. The lower one (9805 ± 160 to 7990 ± 125 B.P.) contains large artifacts, among which are many burins and a number of geometric microliths. The mammals in these levels are predominantly large herbivores (*Bos, Equus, Alcelaphus*). The upper assemblage (with a terminal date of 7280 ± 115 B.P.) contains smaller artifacts, few burins or geometrics, and large numbers of notched or denticulated pieces, as well as backed bladelets. The associated fauna still contains numerous *Alcelaphus*, but there are also many lagomorphs and *Gazella*. The upper assemblage is certainly Capsien supérieur; the lower assemblage may belong within the Capsien typique— the data are equivocal.

At Kef Zoura D the situation is clear. A Capsien typique assemblage is found in the deposits in

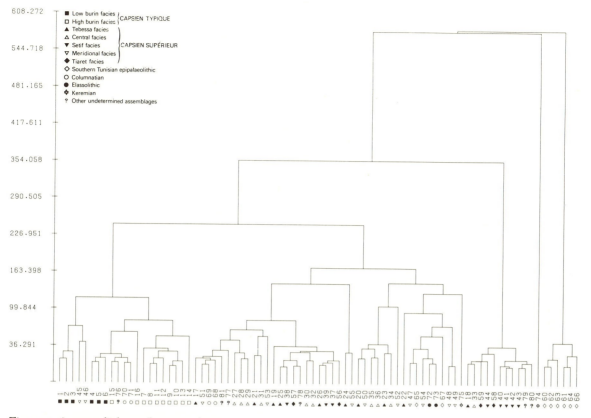

Figure 2. Average linkage cluster analysis.

front of the shelter (No. 76 in Fig. 2) in association with a faunal assemblage composed of large herbivores. The stone tools bear certain resemblances to the lower assemblage at Ain Misteheyia. Two provisional radiocarbon dates for these deposits of 8607 ± 161 B.P. (higher) and 9213 ± 158 B.P. (lower) (Table 1) place them in the time range of the lower Ain Misteheyia deposits.

Within the shelter (No. 79 in Fig. 2), in levels which appear to overlie those in front of the shelter and for which four radiocarbon dates are available (6575 ± 170 to 5965 ± 115 B.P.), we have recovered a Capsien supérieur assemblage with a mammalian fauna consisting almost exclusively of *Gazella* and lagomorphs.

Thus, within the Télidjène basin, we have two sites at which the Capsien typique is associated with a fauna composed predominantly of large mammals, and the Capsien supérieur is associated with a fauna composed predominantly of small mammals.

A similar situation may be present at Medjez II both in regard to change in the fauna (Bouchud in Camps-Fabrer, 1975) and the stone-tool assemblages (Camps-Fabrer, 1975).

The archaeozoological and geoarchaeological evidence from Ain Misteheyia indicates a short period of increased aridity and reduced grassland between about 8000 and 7500 B.P. (Lubell et al., 1976; Lubell and Gautier, in press). Yet, so far as we can determine, the subsistence practices of Capsian groups living at the site did not change in any fundamental way. The larger vertebrates and invertebrates they had hunted and gathered previously were replaced by more but smaller animals. The ratio between mammal and snail meat does not change very much over time (Lubell and Gautier, in press). It is too early to say whether a similarly flexible and adaptable set of subsistence practices is evidenced at Kef Zoura.

Several lines of evidence convince us that nei-

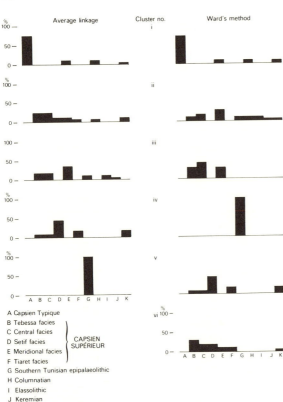

A Capsien Typique
B Tebessa facies
C Central facies
D Setif facies } CAPSIEN SUPÉRIEUR
E Meridional facies
F Tiaret facies
G Southern Tunisian epipalaeolithic
H Columnatian
I Elassolithic
J Keremian
K Other undetermined assemblages

Figure 3. Frequency of assemblages by clusters.

ther Ain Misteheyia nor Kef Zoura was ever occupied for more than a few months at a time (Lubell and Gautier, in press) and that this pattern of occupation reflects a seasonal round involving movement over substantial distances. Short-distance seasonal movements seem to have been an adjustment made to this pattern by certain groups, belonging to the Neolithic of Capsian Tradition, who

acquired domestic animals about 6500 years ago. Colette Roubet (1978) interprets the subsistence adaptation of one such group in the Aurès as a pastoralist/gathering economy in which short-distance transhumance was practiced. A sense of continuity is furthered by the lack of difference between Capsien supérieur and Neolithic of Capsian Tradition artifact assemblages. There seems no reason to argue that the two were culturally distinct.

All the evidence suggests that certain elements of a Neolithic economy were introduced into the Maghreb and not developed there independently. Part of the explanation for this possibly lies in the absence of native plants and animals suitable for domestication (although the exception of *Bos primigenius* is curious), but it seems certain that a greater part of the answer has to do with the very successful nature of the Capsian subsistence adaptation. Capsian groups were able to adjust their way of life to a number of habitats, as well as to changing environmental conditions. Some of this flexibility no doubt involved collection of numerous kinds of plants, as Clarke (1976) suggested should be and as Roubet (1978) has demonstrated was indeed the case. Among populations with such a flexible pattern of adaptation there was simply no need (or desire?) to change to a different mode of production before a date which is rather late by comparison with the rest of the circum-Mediterranean.[8]

8. Many of the points made in this paper, written in 1978, are treated at greater length and with new information in a paper by Lubell, Sheppard, and Jackes which will be published in Volume 3 of *Advances in World Archaeology*.

Appendix: Key to the Sites in Figure 2
(Data used for cluster analysis of Capsian and other assemblages)

A. Tool classes

1. endscrapers	4. backed flakes and blades	6. notches and denticulates
2. perforators	5. backed bladelets,	7. truncations
3. burins	including Ouchtata bladelets	8. geometric microliths

B. Assemblages

No.	Name	Affiliation	Source
1.	Redeyef table sud inférieur	Capsien typique, low burin facies	Camps, 1974
2.	El Mekta grande tranchée	Capsien typique, low burin facies	Camps, 1974
3.	Abri 402	Capsien typique, low burin facies	Camps, 1974
4.	Relilai Phase I	Capsien typique, low burin facies	Grébénart, 1976
5.	Relilai Phase III	Capsien typique, low burin facies	Grébénart, 1976
6.	El Outed Niveau I	Capsien typique, low burin facies	Grébénart, 1976
7.	Ain Zannouch	Capsien typique, high burin facies	Camps, 1974
8.	Ain Sendes	Capsien typique, high burin facies	Camps, 1974
9.	Bortal Fakher talus	Capsien typique, high burin facies	Camps, 1974
10.	Bortal Fakher abri	Capsien typique, high burin facies	Camps, 1974
11.	Relilai (Vaufrey excav.)	Capsien typique, high burin facies	Camps, 1974
12.	Relilai Phase II	Capsien typique, high burin facies	Grébénart, 1976
13.	Relilai Phase IV	Capsien typique, high burin facies	Grébénart, 1976
14.	El Outed Niveau II	Capsien typique, high burin facies	Grébénart, 1976
15.	El Outed Niveau III	Capsien typique, high burin facies	Grébénart, 1976
16.	Bir Hammairia II	Capsien typique, high burin facies	Grébénart, 1976
17.	El Mekta	Capsien supérieur, Tébessa facies	Camps, 1974
18.	Nechiou	Capsien supérieur, Tébessa facies	Camps, 1974
19.	Lalla	Capsien supérieur, Tébessa facies	Camps, 1974
20.	Hamda	Capsien supérieur, Tébessa facies	Camps, 1974
21.	Bir Hammairia	Capsien supérieur, Tébessa facies	Camps, 1974
22.	Relilai	Capsien supérieur, Tébessa facies	Camps, 1974
23.	Khanguet el Mouhâad	Capsien supérieur, Tébessa facies	Camps, 1974
24.	Bekkaria	Capsien supérieur, Tébessa facies	Camps, 1974
25.	R'Fana inférieur	Capsien supérieur, Tébessa facies	Camps, 1974
26.	R'Fana supérieur	Capsien supérieur, Tébessa facies	Camps, 1974
27.	Bou Nouara	Capsien supérieur, Central facies	Camps, 1974
28.	Koudiat Kifène Lahda supérieur B	Capsien supérieur, Central facies	Camps, 1974
29.	Koudiat Kifène Lahda supérieur A	Capsien supérieur, Central facies	Camps, 1974
30.	Site 51 inférieur	Capsien supérieur, Central facies	Camps, 1974
31.	Site 51 supérieur	Capsien supérieur, Central facies	Camps, 1974
32.	Kef Fenteria inférieur	Capsien supérieur, Central facies	Camps, 1974
33.	Kef Fenteria supérieur	Capsien supérieur, Central facies	Camps, 1974
34.	Faid Souar inférieur	Capsien supérieur, Central facies	Camps, 1974
35.	Faid Souar moyen	Capsien supérieur, Central facies	Camps, 1974
36.	Faid Souar supérieur	Capsien supérieur, Central facies	Camps, 1974
37.	Medjez II phase 1	Capsien supérieur, Sétif facies	Camps, 1974
38.	Medjez II phase 2	Capsien supérieur, Sétif facies	Camps, 1974
39.	Medjez II phase 3	Capsien supérieur, Sétif facies	Camps, 1974
40.	Medjez II phase 4	Capsien supérieur, Sétif facies	Camps, 1974

41.	Ain Boucherit inférieur	Capsien supérieur, Sétif facies	Camps, 1974
42.	Ain Boucherit moyen	Capsien supérieur, Sétif facies	Camps, 1974
43.	Ain Boucherit supérieur	Capsien supérieur, Sétif facies	Camps, 1974
44.	MacDonald II	Capsien supérieur, Sétif facies	Camps, 1974
45.	Rabah I	Capsien supérieur, Meridional facies	Camps, 1974
46.	Rabah II	Capsien supérieur, Meridional facies	Camps, 1974
47.	Rabah III	Capsien supérieur, Meridional facies	Camps, 1974
48.	Rabah IV	Capsien supérieur, Meridional facies	Camps, 1974
49.	Rabah V	Capsien supérieur, Meridional facies	Camps, 1974
50.	El Mermouta	Capsien supérieur, Meridional facies	Camps, 1974
51.	Dakhlat es Sâadane inférieur	Capsien supérieur, Meridional facies	Camps, 1974
52.	Dakhlat es Sâadane supérieur	Capsien supérieur, Meridional facies	Camps, 1974
53.	Rocher des Pigeons	Capsien supérieur, Meridional facies	Camps, 1974
54.	Ain Naga	Capsien supérieur, Meridional facies	Camps, 1974
55.	El Haouita versant	Capsien supérieur, Meridional facies	Camps, 1974
56.	Ain Keda	Capsien supérieur, Tiaret facies	Camps, 1974
57.	Ain Cherita	Capsien supérieur, Tiaret facies	Camps, 1974
58.	Côte de la Fontaine Noire	Capsien supérieur, Tiaret facies	Camps, 1974
59.	Kef Torad	Capsien supérieur, Tiaret facies	Camps, 1974
60.	Sidi Mansour	S. Tunisian bladelet industries	Camps, 1974
61.	Lalla	S. Tunisian bladelet industries	Camps, 1974
62.	Menchia	S. Tunisian bladelet industries	Camps, 1974
63.	Ain el Atrouss	S. Tunisian bladelet industries	Camps, 1974
64.	Mareth	S. Tunisian bladelet industries	Camps, 1974
65.	Oued Akarit Station C	S. Tunisian bladelet industries	Camps, 1974
66.	Oued Akarit Station A	S. Tunisian bladelet industries	Camps, 1974
67.	Oued Akarit Station B	S. Tunisian bladelet industries	Camps, 1974
68.	Columnata "sous abri"	Columnatian	Camps, 1974
69.	Cubitus niveau inférieur	Columnatian	Camps, 1974
70.	Cubitus niveau moyen	Columnatian	Camps, 1974
71.	Cubitus niveau supérieur	Columnatian	Camps, 1974
72.	El Hamel couche A	Elassolithic	Camps, 1974
73.	Koudiat Kifène Lahda supérieur	Elassolithic	Camps, 1974
74.	Bois des Pins	Keremian	Camps, 1974
75.	Bou Aichem	Keremian	Camps, 1974
76.	Kef Zoura D—T/20–5	Capsien typique	Lubell, unpub.
77.	Ain Misteheyia lower	?	Lubell, unpub.
78.	Ain Misteheyia upper	Capsien supérieur	Lubell, unpub.
79.	Kef Zoura D—main excavations	Capsien supérieur	Lubell, unpub.
80.	Ain Dokkara	Capsien supérieur, Ain Aachena type	Tixier, 1976
81.	Dra-Mta-El-Ma-El-Abiod	Capsien supérieur	Morel, 1978a

5

Environment and Subsistence in Predynastic Egypt

FEKRI A. HASSAN

Early Food Production in the Nile Valley

Egypt is the gift of the Nile and the fellah (Ghorbal, n.d.). This is as true of Egypt today as it was for Predynastic Egypt. By the fifth millennium B.C., Egypt was beginning to undergo a profound transformation. The beginning was modest: farming and animal herding were added to hunting, fishing, fowling, and gathering activities. Within the span of about two millennia, however, Egypt had become unified from south to north.

This paper is an attempt to outline briefly the environment and subsistence of Predynastic Egypt up to the emergence of the Egyptian civilization.

The writer wishes to express his thanks to Professor F. Wendorf, Professor K. W. Butzer, Dr. T. R. Hays, Professor W. Fairservis, Dr. M. Hoffman, Mr. Zahi Hawwass, Dr. J. Gallagher, and Professor J. D. Clark. Funding for the research in Egypt was provided by grants nos. BN578–08177 from the National Science Foundation and FC8–066–2700 from the Smithsonian Institution.

CHRONOLOGY

The Predynastic period in Egypt, characterized by food-producing communities, comes immediately before the First Dynasty (Fig. 1). It
commences in about 5000 B.C. and lasts until about
3150 B.C. In dealing with the Predynastic it has
been traditional to speak of three major cultural
stages: the Badarian, Amratian (Nagada I), and
Gerzean (Nagada II). It also has been traditional
to speak of a separate "Merimda Neolithic" and a
"Fayum A. Neolithic," since these were difficult to
fit into that developmental scheme. The three-
stage system was engineered by Sir Flinders Petrie
on the basis of seriating ceramics into Sequence
Dates (Brunton, 1928: 78; Kaiser, 1957; Baumgartel, 1965: 4, 14). Radiocarbon dates, however, show
that the Badarian, Amratian, and Gerzean are at
least in part co-equal (Arnold and Libby, 1955;
Libby, 1955; Hays, this volume), while the Fayum
and Merimda Neolithic are older (Olsson, 1959;
Wendorf et al., 1970; Flight, 1973).

THE ENVIRONMENTAL SETTING

After 10,000 B.C. the Nile flood levels dropped
below those of the Terminal Pleistocene Nile.
Many of the Predynastic sites, e.g., at Merimda,
Nagada, and Hierakonpolis, are located on Terminal Pleistocene Nilotic silt (Butzer, 1960).

The Nile levels at the Fayum as recorded on
the banks of Lake Qarun (Fig. 2) indicate that the
Nile floods, which were low at ca. 4500 uncalibrated $C14$ years B.C., began to rise and were at 15
and 17 m above sea level at 3910 ± 115 years and
3860 ± 115 years B.C., respectively (Wendorf and
Schild, 1976a). It was during that time that the
settlements at Fayum and Merimda were established. At ca. 3350 uncalibrated $C14$ years B.C., the
Nile levels were dropping as recorded in Nubia by
the Qadrus recession (Heinzelin, 1968: 48), and in
the Fayum (Wendorf and Schild, 1976a: 223). According to Wendorf and Schild (1976a: 226), the
drop in the Nile level was short-lived. The level of
Lake Qarun at the Fayum was rising during the late
Predynastic, reachinag a maximum of 23 m above
sea level during the Old Kingdom (Fourth Dynasty). According to J. A. Wilson (1963: 319), the

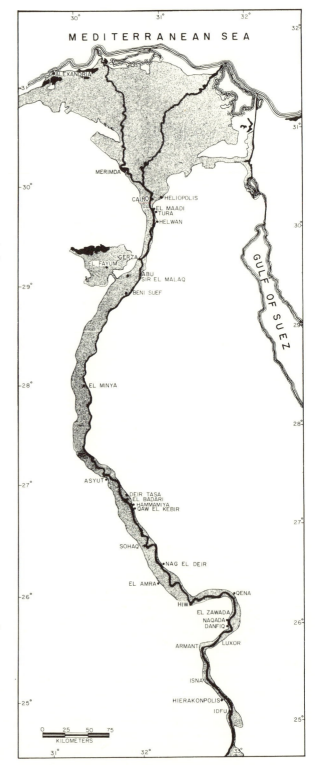

Figure 1. Predynastic sites in Egypt.

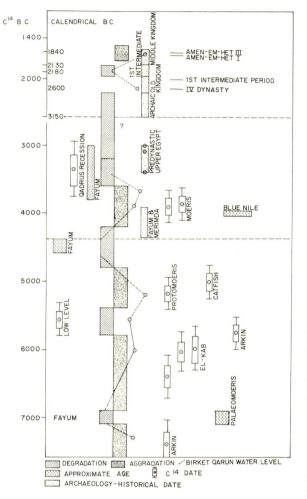

Figure 2. Changes in the pattern of riverine alluviation in the Nile Valley. The levels of the Birket Qarun Lake are from Wendorf and Schild (1976a). The Arkin aggradation and the Qadrus recession were recognized and dated by Heinzelin (1968). The El-Kab aggradation was reported and dated by Vermeersch (1970); the high Nile stand at Catfish was noted by Wendt (1966). The high Blue Nile level corresponding to the high stand of the Moeris stage of Birket Qarun is from Arkell (1953). For the period ca. 3000–2000 uncalibrated radiocarbon years B.C., Wendorf and Schild (1976a) suggest a rising lake level at Birket Qarun, in contradiction to Nilometer records interpreted by Pollard (1968) and B. Bell (1970) to indicate a falling of the Nile level at the same period. Historical Nile levels are after Butzer (1959a, 1976). The dates for historical periods are after J. A. Wilson (1963).

beginning of the Fourth Dynasty is 2650 B.C. (equivalent to ca. 2200 uncalibrated C14 years B.C.). Pollard (1968) and B. Bell (1970: 572), however, have determined, on the basis of the oldest historical records of Nile flood levels, that after the First Dynasty the Nile flood declined in height.

The moist phase in the Egyptian deserts, during the period from ca. 7500 to 4600 uncalibrated C14 years B.C., was ending by the beginning of the Predynastic (Wendorf and Hassan, 1980). Deflation and movements of dune sand were rapidly changing the desert landscape. Climatic conditions continued to be dry all during the Predynastic. This is documented by the writer's sedimentological studies of stratigraphic sections from Hierakonpolis, Nagada-Khattara, and Merimda Beni Salama; the sediments consist of aeolian sand mixed with anthropogenic (cultural) materials.

Caton-Thompson observed a layer of cemented scree breccia above a Badarian level, which (Brunton and Caton-Thompson, 1928) she thought might indicate a moist interval, but this seems unlikely. Scree lenses were found at Khattara, but they represent gravel imported by the people to floor their houses. Water derived from human and animal sources under such a dry climate could easily explain the cementation of the scree.

The climate was perhaps not as hyperdry as it is today. Scant rainfall, perhaps no more than 10 mm on the average, was sufficient to sustain some vegetation around the desert wadis draining toward the Nile. The cutting of wood for fuel, building, and tools, and grazing by cattle, sheep, and goats must have contributed to the creation of the modern bleak desert landscape in the proximity of the Nile Valley. The presence of many species of animals in the Egyptian deserts during the Predynastic is indicated both by faunal remains and by animal motifs on ceramics. It may be noted that gazelle, hare, and ibex may still be found there today.

SUBSISTENCE AND DIET

Data on the subsistence base of Predynastic communities in Egypt are available from Fayum, Merimda, Omari, and Badari. There is sufficient evidence of the cultivation of wheat and barley and the exploitation of domestic sheep and perhaps goats, cattle, and pigs. Unfortunately, no quantitative data are yet available, but initial results from analysis of the faunal remains from Khattara indicate that ewes were predominant among mammals (Hays, 1976 and this volume).

The cultivated wheat was emmer wheat at the Fayum (Caton-Thompson and Gardner, 1934; Täckholm, 1941), although club wheat is reported from El-Omari (Debono, 1956). Barley was identified as both two-row barley (*H. vulgare*) and six-row barley (57 percent). Wheat and barley have been also identified in botanical samples from Tasa, Mostagedda, Qau, and Badari in upper Egypt (Brunton, 1937; Brunton and Caton-Thompson, 1928; Brunton et al., 1927–30).

Wild plant sources exploited are represented by the remains of *Panicum* grasses, which now grow wild in the wadis along the Nile, *Manisurus* grass, which grows now along the Mediterranean coast, *Echinochloa colonum* grass and dom palm (*Hyphaena thebaica*), *Cyperus esculentus*, wild sugarcane (*Saccharum spontaneum*), castor (*Ricinus communis*), the herb *Asphodelus fistulosus*, Acadia trees, date palm, and sycamore figs (Caton-Thompson and Gardner, 1934; Debono, 1956; Hays, 1976). Gautier (1976), who recently examined a faunal collection from the Fayum Neolithic, reports domestic cattle and notes that the domestic sheep belong to a breed with outward-directed horns twisted in a corkscrew fashion. This is the breed called *Ovis longipes palaeoaegypticus*, commonly represented in drawings from Ancient Egypt.

Hunting was widely practiced during the Predynastic period. Game animals include hippopotamus, crocodile, and antelope. The faunal evidence is reported from Badari and Qau, Fayum, Merimda, Omari, and Maadi (Brunton et al., 1927–1930; Brunton and Caton-Thompson, 1928; Caton-Thompson and Gardner, 1934; Junker, 1929–1940; Menghin and Amer, 1932, 1936; Debono, 1956; Täckholm, 1941). There is also evidence in the Fayum for the hunting of pig, gazelle, and elephant (*Loxodonta africana*). The presence of arrowheads indicates that bows and arrows were used in hunting; an arrowhead was even found embedded in an elephant carcass (Caton-Thompson and Gardner, 1934). Wooden throwing sticks (boomer-

angs?) were found in a Badarian context and might have been used in fowling, as in Dynastic times (Baumgartel, 1965).

The Annual Ecologic Cycle and Economic Scheduling

In the Nile Valley during the terminal Pleistocene, before the beginning of farming and animal herding, people must have been bound to the ebb and rise of the flood and the changes of the seasons (Hassan, 1974). By the end of June, the Nile started to rise, and the floodplain lowlands were the first to be flooded (Fig. 3). As the flood advanced, the shallow basins of the upland, the main part of the floodplain, became progressively submerged. The hillocks and ancient levees with their groves of trees dotted the surface of the water-covered plain. During most of the inundation the lands close to the plateau usually remained dry, only to be reached by exceptionally high floods. The hillocks and levees, mixed with dunes in some localities, provided a dry area protected from the rising water of the flood (Butzer, 1960). During this season, rainfall was scant, the wadis were dry, and the vegetation on the hills was thin and scarce. Game animals, both those that inhabited the floodplain and those that descended from the desert steppe to obtain water and food, congregated along the edge of the floodplain.

Following the high flood during October, the flood water receded rapidly. During that season, fish became abundant and easy to catch from the lagoons and streams being drained by the receding flood (Sadek, 1916: 50). This is still the pattern in Nuerland (Evans-Pritchard, 1940). A variety of plants then grew. These plants—grasses, brush, young shoots, bulrush, and papyrus—formed a lush vegetation cover that provided ample resources both for pasture and for food-collecting (Butzer, 1959a). The swamps and marshes became filled with both indigenous and migratory waterfowl. Birds were in fact so numerous that the ancient Egyptians used to liken a crowd to "a bird-pond at the time of the inundation" (Kees, 1961: 93). This season, which lasted approximately from

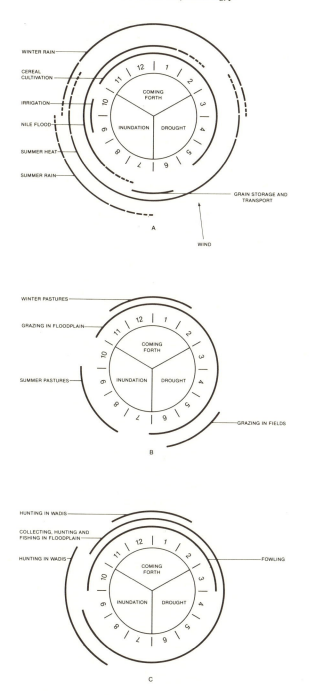

Figure 3. The annual ecological cycle in the Nile Valley and the probable scheduling of subsistence activities: (a) agricultural activities; (b) pastoral activities; (c) hunting.

November to March, coincided with the local season of winter rain. On the hills vegetation appeared almost overnight after the rain and the dry streams started intermittently to flow. The herds of hartebeest, wild ass, and gazelle could then move into the hills to take advantage of the ephemeral luxury of that short season. This must have been indeed the time of abundance. Resources included plenty of fish from the stagnant pools, young shoots, fruits, and vegetables from the floodplain, birds from the ponds, grasses from the hills, and wild game. One can postulate that during this period, settlements would have accommodated a greater number of people. This season was perhaps marked with ceremonial gatherings and feasting.

By April, as the Nile approached its low level and continued to shrink, the water-table fell and the vegetation started to diminish. During this time the wadi vegetation became scarce and the game either moved southward or started to scatter. Fishing became limited to the permanent pools, the side channels, and the river. The seasonal water pools dried up and exploitation of the wooded gallery near the river and the permanent swamps intensified. Turtles, rodents, and Nile clams were probably collected in large amounts. Hippopotami from the river, as well as stray individuals in the swamps, would have provided a sufficient amount of meat for many days. During the drought, one may suspect, the populations split into small groups that scattered to make the most of the sparse resources. Small transient encampments were probably constructed in several places on the floodplain during that period. By June, the Nile again started to rise and the cycle was repeated.

With the beginning of the Predynastic, cultivation and herding were combined with hunting, fishing, and collecting. Hassan (1974) and Butzer (1976) have presented a seasonal model of these activities.

Cereals were most probably cultivated, since they are winter crops which make use of natural irrigation and spring warmth. The moment for sowing wheat in basin lands depends on the timing of the flood (Foaden and Fletcher, 1910: 432–435): as soon as the water recedes, the seed is sown. In Upper Egypt this falls anywhere between the middle of October and the end of November, but it is best to sow the seed during the period from the first to the third week of November (Beliquini, 1946: 61). Nothing more is done—expect weeding, in rare cases—until the harvest. The crop ripens about six months (165–185 days) after sowing (Beliquini, 1946: 106).

Barley seed is also sown following the recession of flood water, from about October 20 to the end of November (Beliquini, 1946: 140). In basin lands there is no need for watering. Barley ripens after 150–170 days, about 15 days more quickly than wheat.

During the period following the recession of the floodwaters and before the decimation of grasses by summer heat, herd animals can be allowed to graze on wild grasses in the floodplain. During the period of inundation, if summer rains are active, the herd animals may graze near the wadis, and they may also be allowed to graze in the fields after the harvest. Winter rain may support grasses in the wadis, but at that time the more plentiful floodplain grasses become available. It is very likely that *golobban* (*Vicia sativa*) was grown as an animal feed and that the straw from barley and wheat crops was stored and also used as fodder during the period of inundation.

It is interesting to note here that as long as the floodplain was not intensively cultivated, animals could be allowed to graze there. However, as more land was brought under cultivation, either the size of the herds had to be reduced or a transhumant pastoral pattern might emerge. This was evidently the case in Dynastic Egypt when specialized herdsmen drove their cattle to the marshes of the Delta (Erman, 1971: 439); even today the herds of sheep and goats may be sent to the oases. Pigs were herded in Dynastic times and possibly in Predynastic times. The extensive cultivation of the floodplain, the best habitat for pigs, must have discouraged any large-scale pig-herding. The rearing of pigs would also have been complicated by their inability to metabolize straw (M. Harris, 1978a: 197).

It may be also noted here that shipping was widely used as a means of transport in Predynastic Egypt, as is indicated by designs on Gerzean ceramics. It seems very likely that a great deal of shipping was concerned with the internal trade in grain, which would have taken place after the harvest, during the summer. At that time, the need for grain by some communities would have been high and those who had had a good harvest could afford to dispense with a part of their yield. At that time also, the velocity of the Nile is 1.5 km/hr, accelerating to 5 km/hr during the flood, and as the breeze is generally from the northwest and the current flows northward, northbound transport is facilitated. At low Nile, navigation may be hindered but, between Aswan and Cairo, boats drawing less than 1 m of water can ply during the summer, except in years of very low water level (Willcocks, 1889: 19–20).

The Ecospace: Subsistence, Catchment Areas, and Carrying Capacity

It is important when dealing with prehistoric economies to relate subsistence activities both to the temporal and the spatial attributes of the environment. Vita-Finzi and Higgs (1970) have developed the concept of *catchment territory*, defined as a distance of 5 km for agricultural groups and 10 km for hunter/gatherers (later this was modified to the equivalent of 1 and 2 hours of walking around the base camp). Their methodology consisted of drawing a circle with a 5 or 10 km radius and determining the resource availability within the area enclosed by the circle.

This delimitation of a catchment territory, however, needs modification. The distance from a settlement covered during subsistence activities in any direction will be a function of the yield to the labor input in that direction. People will tend to exploit those resources that provide the highest yield at the lowest cost, unless they are forced to do otherwise (Jochim, 1976). In any case, the distance that can be covered during daily activities from a base camp cannot be greater than a one-day round trip (cf. Yellen, 1977b) Finally, the minimum area covered during subsistence activities will tend to be no less than the area that can support the local population. The minimal size of a group is a function of the size of the cooperative economic unit and the minimal viable, reproductive unit (about 20 persons). The maximum size of a group is a function of the maximum amount of yield that can be obtained from the catchment area, within the range of daily mobility, and the level of social integration. For hunter/gatherers, group size usually ranges from 15 to 50 persons; early farming settlements may range from 50 to 1,000 persons (Hassan, 1974: 140 with references; 1979).

At present underway is a study of the ecospace of Predynastic subsistence activities. Final results are not yet available for publication, but the following preliminary remarks can be made. The maximum catchment territory (area within a one-day return trip) is not likely to be circular. This is a result of differences in transport cost as energy input along the Nile and from the channel to the desert plateau, and also of the richness of natural resources in the Nile floodplain compared to those of the desert margin. The resources along the wadi courses are attractive only when there is enough rain to support plant and game-animal communities that can reward the effort expended in collecting and hunting.

Under hunting/gathering conditions, a potential population density of 0.9 to 2.1 persons/km^2 has been estimated (Hassan, 1974). This indicates that a band of 25 persons can be supported by an area about 2.3 km in radius. The model constructed for estimating this population density is static; the area required may have been greater for seasonal and periodic variations in resource yield, but the figure represents at least an order of magnitude—the Nilotic groups were not forced to roam over areas of vast extent.

Agricultural communities during the Predynastic period seem to have been clustered in several regions. One of the clusters is at Nagada, Upper Egypt. Hays (1976) located 9 sites, in addition to South Town, which was first excavated by Petrie (1895). Two exploratory seasons by Hays in 1976 and 1977 (see Hays, this volume) and a season of extensive surveying and excavation by Hassan in 1978 have begun to clarify some of the key problems of the Predynastic. One interesting observation relates to the spacing of the sites in that region. The spacing between adjacent sites is about 2 km. Thus, each site seems to dominate 1 km of land on either side. The sites appear to have been

contemporaneous, spanning a period of perhaps no more than 200 years. The outer part of the floodplain, the part most likely to have been used for cultivation during the early Predynastic, is about 2 km × 1.5 km, or approximately 715 feddans (1 feddan = 4200 m^2). If we assume that only 25 percent of that acreage was land suitable for cultivation each year, each settlement would have possessed 178.5 feddans. The yield per feddan of wheat and barley is estimated by Audebeau (1919) at 4–6.6 ardeb/feddan between Luxor and Cairo. Maquirizi (1854) provides an estimate of 2–3 ardebs of wheat/feddan during the Fatimid period (A.D. 969–1171). Maquirizi thus provides a figure of 260 kg/feddan and Audebeau an estimate of 560–924 kg. Kees (1961) provides an estimate of 748 kg/acre for wheat and 721 kg/acre for barley during Pharaonic times. It is difficult to determine the yield during the Predynastic period, but it must have been on the lower side of all the above-mentioned figures, since agricultural improvements tended to increase the yield throughout the historical period. In 1945, for example, the yield of barley was 8–10 ardeb/feddan, or 960–1200 kg/feddan (in 1977 good soil yields were said to be between 19 and 12 ardebs).

The yield in Predynastic times was perhaps no more than the 2 ardebs/feddan obtained during the Fatimid period. Thus, 178.5 feddans would have produced 46,410 kg. From this figure must be subtracted the amount used for seed (0.5 ardebs, or 65 kg/feddan) and about 10 percent for storage loss. This leaves 31,325 kg. Assuming that the consumption rate was 450 grams/day (1. lb., personal ethnographic inquiry), the cultivated crop could have supported about 190 persons. Considering the range of fluctuation in the Nile level, the carrying capacity was perhaps closer to 76–114 persons.

The utility of this exercise does not lie in the significance of the absolute figures but in the range of population size indicated and the implications of agrarian change for the carrying capacity. First, the availability of good arable land could be increased by tree-cutting, removing grasses, and construction of dikes. Close to the Nile, where floodwater was retained beyond the time appropriate for sowing, the digging of drainage canals would have opened up large tracts of prime agricultural land.

The arable land could thus have been increased four or even eight times, and as many as 760 to 1,520 persons could have been supported. Towns with large populations could thus have emerged as more land was brought into cultivation and as part of the harvest was diverted from consumption by the food-producers to the town-dwellers working as craft specialists or in the administrative cadre.

Summary

The Predynastic sites have traditionally been grouped into "cultures" on the basis of their ceramic content. The cultures include the Merimda "Neolithic" and the Fayum "Neolithic" A, the Badarian, the Amratian, and the Gerzean.

The Predynastic archaeological units (cultures) were arranged according to Sequence Dating of ceramics into three stages, which are, from oldest to youngest, Badarian, Amratian (Nagada I), and Gerzean (Nagada II). This sequence is highly questionable. The chronology of the Fayum A and Merimda Neolithic date back to ca. 5100–4500 years B.C. (tree-ring–corrected radiocarbon years). The majority of Badarian, Amratian, and Gerzean sites date to between 4100 and 3500 B.C. (corrected radiocarbon years).

Early Predynastic occupations coincided with a period of declining Nile level. Local climate was perhaps slightly moist at the onset of Predynastic occupation but drier conditions seem to have prevailed during most of the period of Predynastic development. The desert landscape, however, was not as bleak as it is at present, either because today's climate is more arid or, perhaps, because the land now suffers more overgrazing by goats and the cutting of trees for fuel and other purposes.

Predynastic settlements were established in many places on desert spurs and terraces both adjacent to the floodplain and, presumably, along its edge. A settlement evaluation (geokistic) map of the landscape shows that these locations were apparently of prime value for economic reasons and for shelter.

The subsistence base of Predynastic peoples was varied, consisting of cultivating six-row barley and emmer wheat, raising of goats, sheep, cattle, and pigs, hunting, fishing, and plant-gathering. The catchment territory from sites located at the edge of the floodplain or the desert pediments and abandoned Nile terraces provided access to several biotopes. Cultivation could have been undertaken at the outer edge of the floodplain; hunting was practiced in the floodplain and along the Nile channel.

The Nile flooding governed subsistence activities, resulting in three economic seasons which coincided with the inundation, the drought, and the period between the two.

6

A Reappraisal of the Egyptian Predynastic

T. R. HAYS

Ancient Egyptian civilization is generally thought to have developed from local Predynastic cultures. The Predynastic period saw the advent of food-producing settlements along the Nile River prior to the political unification of Upper and Lower Egypt around 3100 B.C. This change in subsistence economy was apparently accompanied by demographic and sociopolitical adjustments that culminated in the beginnings of Egyptian civilization. An understanding of the nature of the Egyptian Predynastic is important for an elucidation of the processes involved in the subsequent florescence of culture in Egypt.

The best-known Predynastic sequence has been recovered in Upper Egypt. Work conducted several decades ago (Petrie, 1895; Brunton and

The author wishes to express his gratitude to all those who have contributed to the successful completion of this research and, in particular, the staffs of the American Research Center in Egypt, the Egyptian Geological Survey, and the American Embassy in Cairo. Funding is acknowledged from the National Science Foundation, the Smithsonian Institution, and North Texas State University.

Caton-Thompson, 1928; Brunton, 1937) resulted in an evolutionary sequence of cultures; the earliest was called the "Badarian," followed by the "Amratian" and "Gerzean." These Predynastic Egyptian cultures were dated at approximately 4000–3000 B.C. and were characterized by "Neolithic" traits (ground stone, pottery, and domesticated plants and animals).

Unfortunately, however, the proposed cultural evolution of the early Predynastic is not clearly understood. Even though the overall configuration of cultural history has been outlined, numerous inconsistencies have become apparent regarding economy, chronology, and cultural descriptions. The serious deficiencies in current knowledge of the prehistoric origins of Egyptian civilization have been attributed to the lack of well-excavated sites (Arkell and Ucko, 1965; Trigger, 1968). Most of the recent studies have consisted merely of reworking of old excavation data rather than actual field excavations (Arkell, 1975; Krzyzaniak, 1977). Consequently, new excavations using modern interdisciplinary archaeological techniques were needed

to refine our knowledge of the Egyptian Predynastic.

This paper presents the results of recent field research in Upper Egypt the purpose of which was to elucidate the processes involved in the Predynastic beginnings of Egyptian civilization. Exploratory excavations provided new data for interdisciplinary investigations and allowed initiation of a reappraisal of earlier models of Predynastic Egyptian cultural chronology, subsistence patterns, and sociopolitical affinities.

Results of the Research

GEOMORPHOLOGICAL SETTING

The Nile Valley in Upper Egypt is bordered on the east and west by imposing limestone cliffs. The cliffs are now totally barren and the streams that once flowed toward the Nile are devoid of any pronounced vegetation. The valley watered by the Nile River presents a tamed landscape of lush green which contrasts markedly with the low desert,

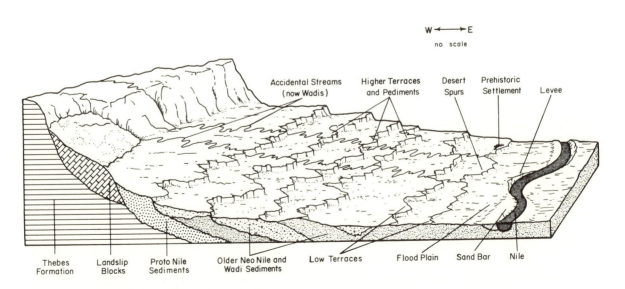

Figure 1. Geomorphological setting of Predynastic sites in Upper Egypt.

cliffs, and plateaux that confine its course. Near
Luxor, on the west bank, the Nile is very close to
the Lower Eocene limestone cliffs, which rise 400
meters above the floodplain. The stretch from
Luxor to Qina is characterized by massive landslip
blocks that were dislodged during the excavation of
the Nile canyon. On the east bank, the cliffs are
lower in elevation and the slope is much more gradual, as a result of the Wadi Hamammat and Wadi
Qina.

The deposits that accumulated during the
Pleistocene by successive wadi aggradations and
higher Nile levels beyond the modern floodplain
now form a low desert that rises above the modern
floodplain in a series of terraces and pediments.
Between Luxor and Qina, this low desert forms an
irregular flat surface dissected by dry wadis, forming what has often been referred to as "desert
spurs." The oldest Nile terrace exposed in the area
is the 45 m terrace of the Proto-Nile, followed by a
constructional terrace of the Dandara formation at
30 m. The landscape, however, is dominated by the
lower terraces, the highest of which stands at about
8 m above the floodplain. This represents an erosional terrace of Wadi and Nile deposits. Lower terraces stand at 5, 3.5, 2.5, and 1.5 m above the floodplain. The Predynastic occupations were situated
on top of the 8 m and the 3.5 m terraces (Fig. 1).

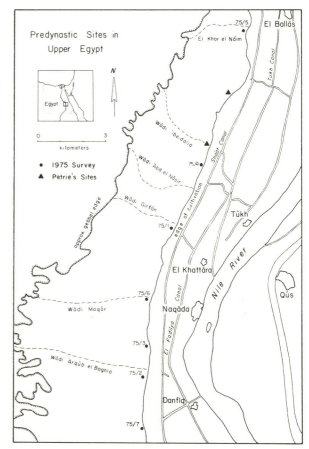

Figure 2. Map of 1975 survey area.

SURVEY AND TESTING

During two field seasons (1975, 1977) site survey and test excavations were conducted near El
Khattara, located about 30 km north of Luxor on
the west bank of the Nile River. In order to maximize the chance of site discovery, the survey was
concentrated along the margins of the desert near
the edge of cultivation. Unexpectedly, a large number of unreported Predynastic sites were identified
in the 18-km-long survey area (Fig. 2). Most of the
sites were quite large and consisted of several
mounds of midden deposits (Hays, 1976). These
sites were easily distinguished from a site such as
Petrie's South Town, which has a completely different suite of artifacts on its surface.

Controlled test excavations were conducted at
five sites (75/1, 75/2, 75/3, 75/6, and 75/7). Site

75/3 was the most intensively investigated, since it
was the least disturbed (Fig. 3). The excavations
revealed some of the mounds to be over one meter
deep. The areas between mounds contained midden material which may have been derived. The
mounds were composed of many-layered deposits
of fine sand, ash, charcoal, lithic and ceramic artifacts, animal dung, bone, and plant remains. Organic preservation was quite good, although the
desiccation had made some of the bone friable.
None of the midden deposits exhibited a break in
the sequence of deposition. Sterile lenses were not
noticed in any of the tests, but differential horizontal deposition was evident. During the second season, evidence of mud-brick construction was found
at Site 3.

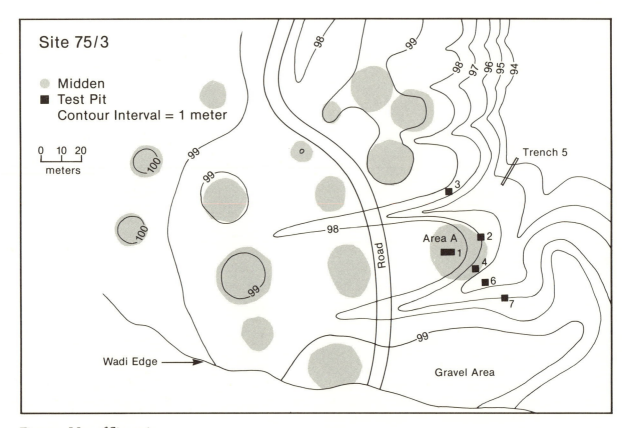

Figure 3. Map of Site 75/3.

CULTURAL REMAINS

Structures

Since small circular house patterns had been reported for the Amratian (Brunton and Caton-Thompson, 1928), it was thought that the circular mounds at the Predynastic sites might represent old structures that had been filled in with cultural refuse. During excavations at Site 3 in 1977, evidence for the use of unfired mud-bricks was discovered. The blocky rectangular bricks were easily defined and clearly overlie one another. The bricks, fairly homogeneous in composition, probably represent decomposing bricks similar to the hand-molded mud bricks used in Egypt today.

Adjacent to the mound containing the mud bricks was a large area of compressed animal dung (primarily sheep/goat). It is interesting to note that a depositional analog can be found today. Investigation of a recently abandoned Bedouin house indi-

cated mud-brick construction with an adjacent animal pen. The fallen walls of the house were partially covered with wind-deposited refuse and sand. The possible implications for the prehistoric sites were striking. (Further investigation of the ethnoarchaeology of the El Khattara area was conducted in 1978 by Fekri Hassan and will be reported elsewhere.)

Fauna

As indicated by a preliminary survey of the faunal samples (A. Gautier, pers. comm.), hornless domesticated sheep (ewes) predominated among the mammals. Other, much less frequent domesticated forms are pig, possibly goat, and medium-sized canid (dog?). Wild mammals include numerous gazelle. Lower vertebrates are represented by at least two bird species and by several species of fish. Nile perch and catfish occur most often, and appear similar in size to those of today (P. H. Greenwood, pers. comm.). Freshwater molluscs in the samples include large bivalves (*Aspatharia rubens*) which may have been brought to the site as food.

Plants

Numerous small pieces of plant remains were collected during the excavations. Preliminary identification of these items indicated the presence of domesticated emmer wheat and barley (R. B. Stewart, pers. comm.). Other commonly occurring varieties of grasses are *manisuris* and *panicum*. *Panicum* has been reported as a source of food in certain areas of the sub-Sahara (J. D. Clark, 1971). Other plant remains include specimens of flowering grasses, rushes, and Acacia thorns.

Charcoal

Large amounts of charcoal were collected from all levels of the midden deposit. Several samples were submitted to the radiocarbon laboratories at the University of Texas and Southern Methodist University, from which seven dates are now available. Both laboratories commented on the good quality of the charcoal samples and the dates are considered to be technically reliable. In addition, sherds were dated at Oxford by thermoluminescence (Table 1).

Lithic Artifacts

Artifacts excavated from the Predynastic sites show a high degree of similarity. Stone tools include bifacially flaked axes, planes, large numbers of burins (especially dihedral), scrapers, notches, truncations, perforators, and denticulates. All sites contained the same tool types, but in somewhat different frequencies. Statistical testing, however, indicated that there was no significance in the occurrence of different frequencies at each site (Figs. 4, 5).

The lithic raw material for the chipped stone tools consisted of flint nodules. These nodules are derived from the Eocene limestone gebels to the west, but are easily available in the wadi bottoms adjacent to the sites. The Badarians were reported to have utilized the flint nodules rather than the tabular flint (which must be quarried from the limestone gebels) used by later groups (Baumgartel, 1960). Our collections from Petrie's South Town indicate that the lithic raw material at that site also was flint nodules.

TABLE 1. **Radiometric Dates**

	Site Number	Laboratory Number	Radiocarbon Age
	75/6–A	SMU–303	5005 ± 69 B.P.
	75/1–A	SMU–351	4930 ± 70 B.P.
	75/3–A	SMU–353	4780 ± 70 B.P.
	75/6–A	SMU–355	4810 ± 80 B.P.
	75/1–A	SMU–360	5030 ± 100 B.P.
	75/3–B	SMU–493	5214 ± 54 B.P.
	75/3–A	TX–2340	4970 ± 70 B.P.
			Thermoluminescence Age
	75/1–A	OX206 a2	5750 ± 400 B.P.
	75/3–A	OX206 b4	5300 ± 550 B.P.

DISTRIBUTION OF LITHIC TOOL TYPES

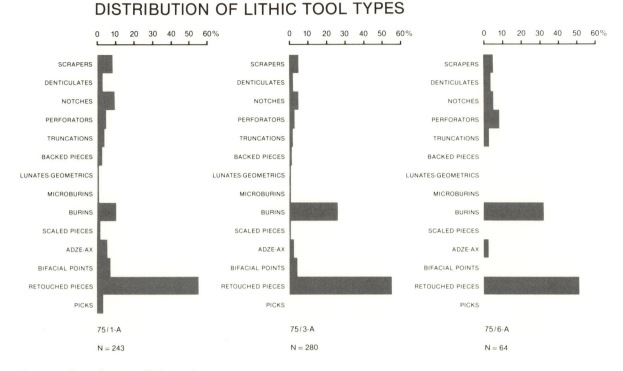

Figure 4. Distribution of lithic tool types.

The major problem in comparing lithic assemblages is the lack of previous data. Baumgartel (1960: 26) emphasized this problem for the Badarian and, especially, the Amratian period. None of the published excavation reports clearly divides the Amratian flint industry from others. The material from graves is somewhat better dated, but there is not much of it and it is not always comparable with that from the settlements. The tool list from Badarian living sites is quite limited, coming mostly from the site of Hemamieh (Brunton and Caton-Thompson, 1928). Consequently, the differences between the cultures may be due to sampling error.

The El Khattara tool typology shows great similarity with the later Gerzean. In the rather good description of the Gerzean lithic industry (Baumgartel, 1960), one can find a number of similarities with El Khattara tool types. The flaked flint axes, which are oval in shape, are considered to be the most common tool from Gerzean settlements. Many were found on the surface at El Khattara,

showing the characteristic resharpening technique of detaching a single large flake from the side. These tools accounted for less than 5 percent of the total excavated tools, however, and they are made from flint nodules. No pecked and ground stone axes were found at El Khattara. Chisel-headed or transverse arrowheads did occur but were not bifacially retouched. These tools are really double-truncated bladelets forming a triangular shape. None of the ripple-flaked and polished flint knives characteristic of the Amratian and Gerzean grave goods was found. Gravers, made by a single blow at the tip of a flake, were supposedly unknown in Badarian and Amratian context. These tools are burins, most often dihedral, and form the largest class of tool types at El Khattara sites.

The Gerzeans supposedly added the manufacture of blades to the previous tool-making technology. Many small blades (3–8 cm long and very narrow), often with the bulb thinned, occur in Gerzean graves. None is thought to be attributed to the

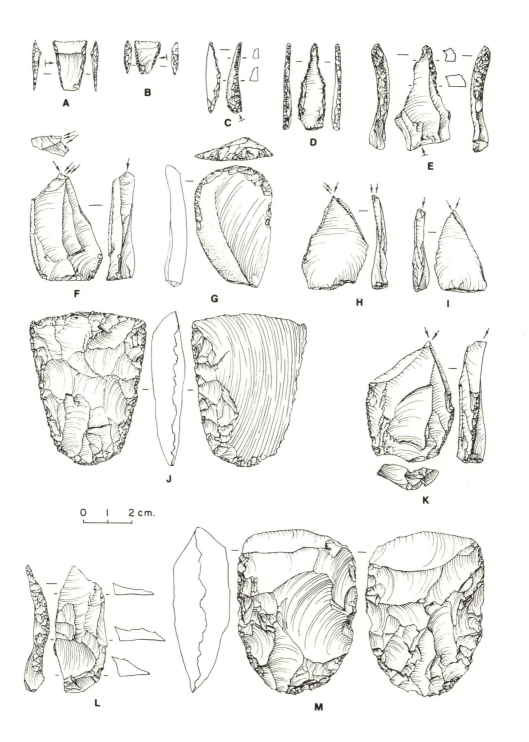

Figure 5. El Khattara lithic tool types: (A, B) "Transverse arrows," "chisel-head arrows" (double truncations). (C, D, E) Perforators. (F, H, I, K) "Groovers" (dihedral burins). (G) Endscraper. (J) "Plane" on a flake. (L) "Axe" resharpening flake. (M) Bifacial "axe" showing transverse resharpening flake scars.

earlier Amratian or Badarian (Baumgartel, 1960). Similar small (2–7 cm) blades account for about 10 percent of the debitage at the El Khattara sites. Thus, while certain aspects of the El Khattara tool typology and technology appear similar to the Gerzean, others (e.g., raw materials) do not.

Ceramic Artifacts

Because of the lack of comparable data pertaining to the Amratian and Badarian assemblages, the cultural affiliation of the El Khattara sites cannot be based on the lithic industry alone. Fortunately, the pottery found at the sites is more conclusive. Ceramics formed the basis for the earlier classifications, since some types of pottery were thought to belong exclusively to one or another temporal group: the black-top red "rippled" pottery is characteristic of the Badarian; the white-cross line ware is exclusive to the Amratian; and the Gerzean is characterized by the presence of light-colored pottery, some painted and others with "wavy" handles (Baumgartel, 1955).

It is most significant that *no* white-cross line ware or light-colored pottery, characteristic of the Amratian and Gerzean, respectively, was found at the El Khattara sites, either on the surface or in the excavations. Much of the El Khattara pottery is a brown "rough" ware. The burnished pottery is usually black-top red or, occasionally, brown ware. Although few in number, the black-top "rippled" ware sherds characteristic of the Badarian do occur. Such a sherd was found directly beneath the body of a child buried in the midden of Site 6. The child was interred in the characteristic flexed Predynastic

fashion. The body was laid on the left side, head to the south, with the legs tight against the chest and the hands in front of the face. A charcoal sample from the level above the burial was dated to 4810 B.P. ± 80 (SMU–355). If the previous ceramic schemes are correct, there is little doubt (in spite of the late date) that the El Khattara sites should be described as part of the Badarian culture.

Chronology

While the El Khattara assemblages may be attributed to the Badarian on the basis of lithic raw materials and ceramics, problems arise in accepting the radiometric dates. Previous radiocarbon dates, when tree-ring–calibrated, average approximately 4525 B.C. for the Amratian and 3670 B.C. for the Gerzean (Hassan, Hays, and Shepard, n.d.). One radiocarbon date has been published for the Badarian, of 5110 B.P. ± 150 (GrN–223). While such a late date had been rejected as relating to the Badarian, it is compatible with the dates from El Khattara (Table 2). In addition, a charcoal sample from Amratian levels at Hierakonpolis has produced a date contemporary with the Gerzean (F. A. Hassan, pers. comm.).

The dating of the Predynastic has been further complicated by a series of dates derived from thermoluminescence studies of pottery. Caton-Thompson and Whittle (1975) dated sherds from the original excavations at Hemamieh (Brunton and Caton-Thompson, 1928). The sherds were taken from museum collections and were chosen because they still retained some of the original matrix in which they were buried. This soil was important to

TABLE 2. **Radiometric Dates for Predynastic Cultures**

Culture	Samples	Average (B.C.)	MASCA Calibration (B.C.)
Badarian, El Khattara	SMU (6), TX (1)	3100 ± 30	3715 ± 25
Amratian, Nagada	C–810, C–811, C–814	3870 ± 170	4514 ± 145
Gerzean, Nagada	C–812, C–813	3070 ± 210	3665 ± 225

assess the environmental dose-rate, the main source of possible dating error (Caton-Thompson and Whittle, 1975). Heterogeneity of the burial surroundings could affect the environmental dose-rate and, therefore, the dates. Problems concerning the ages for the Amratian and Badarian levels have been discussed previously (Hays and Hassan, n.d).

The TL dates, however, are in correct stratigraphical order, and dates from the same level are similar. Furthermore, with the exception of the dates for the Badarian levels, the dates are in good agreement with the tree-ring–calibrated radiocarbon dates for the Amratian and Gerzean. On the other hand, *all* the dates are considerably older than had been expected from uncalibrated radiocarbon dates and historic correlations. The Gerzean is considered to end with the First Dynasty, ca. 3100 B.C. (H. S. Smith, 1964). Consequently, all these dates place the Gerzean several hundred years earlier than had previously been thought from historical contexts.

Conclusions

Recent field research has produced new data to apply toward an understanding of the Egyptian Predynastic. The site survey indicated the presence of numerous early Predynastic sites on the western edge of the Nile Valley in Upper Egypt. The test excavations provided data on lithic and ceramic technology, absolute dating, past environment, food resources, and settlement structure.

As is often the case, this recent fieldwork has raised new questions and underscored old problems in the study of the Egyptian Predynastic. One problem involves the relationship of the tested sites with the previous characterizations of the Predynastic cultures. As indicated above, the surface manifestations of the El Khattara sites are quite different from those of the Predynastic sites worked by Petrie and others. In addition, the excavated artifacts do not lend themselves to direct correlations with other published stone-tool industries.

A major part of the problem has been the lack of comparable data. Previous excavations were directed more to graveyards than to living areas. On the basis of the previous ceramic schemes, however, the El Khattara sites should be described as part of the Badarian culture. Finally, acceptance of the radiometric dates casts doubts on previous radiometric dating (Libby, 1955; Whittle, 1975) and necessitates a reappraisal of the long-standing evolutionary sequence of Predynastic development.

Nevertheless, the evidence gathered during two seasons of excavation in Upper Egypt strongly suggests that both the cultural affiliation and the age of the El Khattara sites are correct. The new radiometric dates indicate that the previously conceived evolutionary sequence of Predynastic development is in error. At El Khattara, at least, the Badarian was coeval with the Gerzean. Consequently, the differences in cultural materials (primarily ceramics) between Badarian and Gerzean must be explained by differences in contemporaneous political organization or social status.

7

Late Quaternary Prehistoric Environments in the Sahara

M. A. J. WILLIAMS

That the Sahara has been less arid at some periods during the Holocene is not in doubt: dry lakebeds, fossil rivers, animal bones, plant remains, diatoms, and pollen grains all bear witness to these moister interludes. The question at issue is not whether the desert was once green, but the more difficult ones of how green, and when. A related issue is the possible influence of Holocene climates upon early food production in the Sahara. The fact that herding and farming began at different times in different parts of the desert suggests that the interaction between early Neolithic man and his environment was far from simple.

Recovery in early 1970 of the nearly complete skeleton of a small domesticated shorthorn cow (*Bos brachyceros*) from Adrar Bous in the Ténéré Desert of Niger demonstrated that toward 6000 B.P. cattle could live in what is now a very dry and empty part of the southcentral Sahara (J. D. Clark et al., 1973). Some 600 km to the north, at Uan Muhuggiag in the Acacus Mountains, a *Bos brachyceros* skull and horn cores of similar age to the Adrar Bous specimen were excavated by Mori, who also unearthed cattle bones dating back to 7500

B.P. (Mori, 1978: 254). Rock art depicting cattle is dated somewhere between 6800 and 4800 B.P. in this same area (Mori, 1978).

Although wild barley is present at Wadi Kubbaniya near Aswan in Upper Egypt between 17,000 and 18,300 B.P. (Wendorf et al., 1979) (but see p. 101), domesticated barley and emmer wheat are not evident in the Nile Valley until 7000–5500 B.P., roughly 3,000 years after their initial cultivation in the Near East (Hassan, 1980). Domestication of the tougher-stemmed panicoid cereal grasses seems, on present evidence, to have been very much later: 3000 B.P. for *Pennisetum* at Dhar Tichitt in Mauritania, and 2000 B.P. for *Sorghum* at Jebel Tomat in central Sudan (Clark and Stemler, 1975; Munson, 1976; Stemler, 1980).

The impact of the Late Quaternary climatic changes on early food production depended as much upon social and technological factors as on the available soil, plant, and water resources. Early agriculturalists, like their modern counterparts, had to operate within the constraints imposed by climate, but their responses to these limitations were culturally determined. Clay soils may indeed be optimal for many species of wild sorghum, just as barley and millet fare better on lighter soils. Nevertheless, until an efficient cutting tool was available to harvest whole heads of *Sorghum* and *Pennisetum*—a prerequisite for the eventual domestication of these grasses—no major change from food-gathering to food-growing was possible (Stemler, 1980).

Prehistoric communities interacted with the biosphere in complex and subtle ways not always evident in the archaeological record. Associated with the final drying out of a Neolithic lake at Adrar Bous was a great increase in sedimentation rates along the valley floors (Williams, 1976a). Did overgrazing cause the accelerated erosion? Or did climatically induced erosion, by destroying the soil mantle, further reduce the plant cover?

On a longer time-scale, there is good circumstantial evidence in support of the view that Late Holocene climatic desiccation was associated with migration of cattle-herders from the central and southern Sahara into West Africa (A. B. Smith, 1980b). A further repercussion of this desiccation was the probable movement of pastoralists away

from the eastern Sahara toward the Nile (J. D. Clark, 1980a). More local but equally important changes were the rapid increase in wild grass-seed-collecting at Dhar Tichitt in Mauritania, soon followed by the culling of an increasing proportion of wild *Pennisetum*, leading ultimately to its cultivation (Munson, 1976; Stemler, 1980). These changes were inferred from seed impressions on dated potsherds, since direct evidence is lacking.

In order to refute or validate these and other models of early food production in the Sahara, it is necessary to reconstruct the pattern of environmental changes during the critical Holocene interval as well as during the equally long pre-adaptive times of the late Pleistocene, from about 20,000 B.P. onward. Needless to say, there are as many diverse microclimates and habitats within the Sahara as there are gaps in our present knowledge relating to them. Any generalizations put forward in this chapter should be viewed in that context, as further working hypotheses rather than as established facts.

For clarity, evidence from five broad geographical regions, starting with the Atlantic seaboard of the desert, will be reviewed. The areas in question are the western, northern, central, southern, and eastern Sahara. The latter area includes the Nile, although this river originates well outside the Sahara.

Coastal Upwelling and Littoral Aridity along the Western Sahara

The aridity of coastal deserts like the Atacama and the Namib is a function of the intensity of cold upwelling offshore and of the proximity of cold ocean currents. The western Sahara, no exception to this rule, adjoins an ocean that has been studied in some detail by marine geologists from the CLIMAP project (McIntyre et al., 1976a, b).

Both the intensity and the locus of upwelling have varied, as have the velocity and thermal structure of the cold Canary Current off the western Sahara. Analysis of the abundance and distribution of tropical, temperate, and polar planktonic foraminifera in cores taken off northwest Africa between 5°N and 35°N points to stronger upwelling and vigorous surface flow of polar water southward along the Mauritanian coast toward 18,000 B.P. (McIntyre et al., 1976b; Diester-Haass, 1980; Pflaumann, 1980).

Associated with the inferred intensification of the cold Canary Current was a marked increase in the westward movement of desert dust from the Sahara out to sea (Kolla et al., 1979; Sarnthein and Koopman, 1980). The dust export is coupled with signs of severe aridity and dune activity along the Atlantic margin of the Sahara as far south as the Senegal River (Michel, 1973, 1980).

This phase of intertropical glacial aridity toward 18,000 B.P. was not peculiar to the western Sahara but seems to have been of global importance (M. A. J. Williams, 1975; Sarnthein, 1978). Increased aridity and greater trade-wind velocities seem adequate to account for dune mobilization along the southwestern borders of the desert at this time, without any southward movement of the trades (Parkin and Shackleton, 1973; Parkin, 1974; M. R. Talbot, 1980). Earlier trade-wind displacements are of course not excluded, and quantitative estimates of sand-carrying wind vectors are consistent with a southward shift of these winds in Mauritania, Niger, and Sudan (Warren, 1970, 1972; Fryberger, 1980).

One issue on which the deep-sea record offers no clear guide is that of distinguishing wind-blown sands from water-transported sands. Inheritance of prior sediments, exemplified in fluviatile reworking of dune sands, bedevils paleoclimatic deductions based solely upon grain-size analysis. Given this limitation, Sarnthein and Koopman (1980) may be wrong to equate fluvial depostis solely with clay-sized particles. If so, the absence of river deposits between 10°N and 28°N in 18,000 B.P. offshore sediments may be more apparent than real. Diester-Haass (1980), who regards a high input of mixed coarse and fine sediments onto the sea floor as fluviatile, argues that rivers were flowing from sparsely vegetated Saharan catchments into the Atlantic at this time. An additional reason for the conflicting conclusions reached by the marine geologists may stem from the poor time-resolution of certain cores, in which the age of the 18,000 B.P. level is only accurate to within ± 3000 years (Sarnthein and Koopman, 1980).

World-wide warming of the ocean surface is apparent at a number of sites dated to 11,000 B.P. (Broeker et al., 1960). Increased evaporation from the warmer seas resulted in higher precipitation on land, especially along the western and southern margins of the Sahara. During the preceding Pleistocene glacial maximum (25,000–15,000 B.P.), evaporation was probably 70 percent lower between 10°N and 10°S than it is today (Flohn and Nicholson, 1980).

Paleoecological studies of marine foraminifera and of shallow-water marine mollusca reveal that sea-surface temperatures were warmer off Mauritania during the early to mid-Holocene (Petit-Maire, 1979a, b; Pflaumann, 1980). Tropical summer rains reached further north along the now-arid Mauritanian littoral as well as further inland (Petit-Maire, 1979b).

Previously intermittent or very much reduced rivers such as the Senegal and Niger flowed copiously during this time (Michel, 1973; Pastouret et al., 1978). Faunal, sedimentological, and stable isotope studies off the Niger delta show that Niger discharge was exceptionally high at 13,000–11,800 B.P. and 11,500–4500 B.P., reflecting high rainfall over the southwestern borders of the Sahara (Pastouret et al., 1978). Lake Chad and isolated lakes in Niger were also high at these times (Servant, n.d.).

Late Quaternary Rainfall and Runoff in the Northern Sahara

At the same time that the Atlantic coast of Morocco was being chilled by polar surface-waters offshore, the western Mediterranean was also very much colder than it is today (Thiede, 1978). During glacial maximum at 18,000 B.P., summer sea-surface temperatures were as low as 8° C. in the Bay of Biscay, increasing to over 25° C. in the eastern Mediterranean (Thiede, 1980). In winter, polar surface-water reached the Bay of Biscay, reducing sea-surface temperatures to 4° C. off Portugal and to 7°–11° C. in the western Mediterranean.

Valley glaciers formed at about this time in the western Atlas and in western Portugal (Daveau, 1977; Messerli and Winiger, 1980). Although the North African mountains were cold and inhospitable, summer meltwater from the High Atlas doubtless augmented the very high seasonal runoff evident until 14,000–15,000 B.P. in the Saoura and other rivers flowing from the Atlas into the Sahara during the Late Pleistocene (Conrad, 1969: 266, 445). Conrad's stratigraphic studies in the desert plains and dunefields between the Atlas and the Hoggar have yielded a record of fluctuations in river, lake, and dune activity between the tropic and the southern Atlas piedmont in an area the size of France.

Episodic erosion and deposition by the Saoura River reflect climatic changes in its mountain headwaters (see Fig. 1). From >40,000 B.P. until

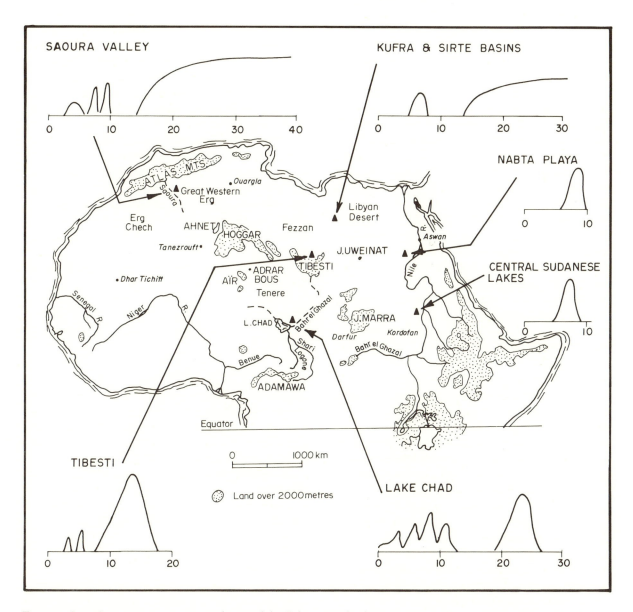

Figure 1. Late Quaternary events in and around the Sahara (peaks denote moister phases; ages in thousands of years; for sources see text).

14,500 B.P., the Saoura flowed several hundred kilometers farther south than it does today and built up a floodplain 25–30 meters thick in its middle and lower reaches. This floodplain, now the main Saoura terrace, consists chiefly of fine, well-sorted, wind-blown sand derived from the two great sand seas traversed by the Saoura on its southward journey into the desert. At intervals within the sands there are beds of lignite and shell-bearing calcareous units indicative of localized swamps and lakes sustained by ponded drainage and high water-tables. These lake deposits are severally dated between 34,000 and 16,000 B.P. (Conrad, 1969: 277).

Downcutting resumed after 14,500 B.P. and has continued since, with a brief interruption during a short-lived more humid Neolithic interval between 6500 and 3000 B.P. (Conrad, 1969: 444–446). There was a delay of several thousand years between the onset of aridity in the Saoura Valley and the fall in groundwater level, which remained high until about 2000 B.P. (ibid.: 292).

The now active dunes of the Great Western Erg overlie aeolian and fluvio-lacustrine sediments sealed by 20,000–30,000 B.P. calcareous crusts (Conrad, 1969: 263). In contrast, the dunes of Erg Chech, which lie west of the barren Tanezrouft and extend south to the tropic, were active throughout most of the Upper Pleistocene. Small lakes occupied hollows within the Erg Chech dunes toward 24,000 B.P., from 18,000 to 10,000 B.P., and again during the mid-Holocene (6500 B.P.), when watertables were once again high (ibid.: 270).

In the Ahnet depression west of the Hoggar, freshwater lakes with a *Cardium* mollusc fauna reflect wetter conditions from at least 34,000 until somewhat later than 19,000 B.P. The regional climate is unlikely to have been wetter than semiarid at this time (Conrad, 1969: 452), a conclusion consistent with recent isotopic analyses of freshwater mollusca from Upper Pleistocene lake deposits at Wadi Shati in western Libya (Hillaire-Marcel, 1979; Petit-Maire et al., 1980). The late Pleistocene interval of high runoff from the Atlas is also evident in the Soltanian deposits of Morocco (Beaudet et al., 1976). Interpreting the hillslope and alluvial fan deposits of Morocco is far more problematic (Weisrock and Rognon, 1977; Roh-

denburg and Sabelberg, 1980). Landscape response to geomorphic events involves thresholds and time-lags. Indeed, stream aggradation is notoriously time-transgressive (Vita-Finzi, 1976; M. A. J. Williams, 1976b; Hagedorn, 1980). Furthermore, radiocarbon-dated charcoal samples may be up to 1,500 years older than the alluvial unit in which they occur (Blong and Gillespie, 1978).

Along the Saharan borders of the Atlas (33°–34°N) a very dry interval during 14,000–12,000 B.P. gave way to a humid phase toward 8000–7000 B.P. that was characterized by human settlement around perennial ponds fed by streams issuing from the uplands (Aumassip, 1979).

Two early Holocene lake intervals in the Sebkha Mellala near Ouargla in northcentral Algeria have yielded ages of 9550 ± 130 and 7400 ± 110 B.P. (Boyé et al., 1978). The lake phases may reflect a more favorable rainfall/evaporation balance than today (? 100–250 mm rain as against 40 mm) but could equally be a delayed response between aquifer recharge and groundwater emergence (Rognon, 1979), as noted also by Conrad in the Touat basin during the Late Holocene (Conrad, 1969: 292).

Along the northern margin of the Sahara in both Tunisia and Algeria, the dominant trend throughout the Quaternary is one of increasing desiccation and progressive disintegration of drainage (Coque, 1962; Conrad, 1969). The slightly more humid Holocene intervals began earlier and ended later in the north than in the south. A similar reduction in the duration of moister phases is evident in the Holocene deposits of Libya and Egypt as one proceeds from north to south, as well as from west to east (McBurney, 1967; Pachur, 1975; Wendorf et al., 1977; Edmonds and Wright, 1979; Pachur and Braun, 1980: 361).

To sum up: present evidence indicates a cooler, effectively wetter climate in the northern Sahara between >40,000 to ca. 15,000 B.P., followed by very dry conditions in the very late Pleistocene. The generally dry Holocene was interrupted by minor less arid intervals toward 9500, 8000–7000, and 6500–3000 B.P. (see Fig. 1), during which tropical mammals managed to extend their range north of the tropic in Algeria and Libya (Conrad, 1969: 460; Pachur, 1975).

In the Tassili region of Algeria, the distribution of Neolithic sites coincides closely with that of present-day settlements—a sign that perennial sources of water were relatively scarce in the sandstone and limestone plateaux. Out among the dunes, Neolithic sites have a widespread distribution, suggesting that the dune biotopes were especially favorable to pastoralists (Conrad, 1969: 299). This is not surprising, for in hot, dry areas there is usually more soil water available for plant growth on sands than on clays (J. Smith, 1949).

Intermittent Groundwater Recharge in the Central Sahara

So far in this reconstruction of prehistoric environments in the Sahara the emphasis has been upon direct geological and fossil evidence of ecological change. Equally relevant is the evidence of two distinct periods of groundwater recharge in the major aquifers of the Sahara, one in the late Pleistocene, the other early in the Holocene (Klitsch et al., 1976). The respective radiocarbon ages are >50,000–20,000 B.P. and <12,000 B.P. (Sonntag et al., 1980).

In the southern Sahara the dearth of dated groundwater samples between 19,000 and 15,000 B.P. (none out of 77 samples) reflects minimal recharge and peak aridity at that time (Sonntag et al., 1980).

In the Sirte and northern Kufra basins of Libya, groundwater recharge was at a peak during 34,000–14,000 B.P. and again from 8000 to 5000 B.P. (see Fig. 1). Between 14,000 and 8000 B.P. there was no significant recharge (Edmunds and Wright, 1979). That these intervals of recharge are related to intervals of higher rainfall directly over the desert is evident from the geochemical and stable isotopic composition of the groundwater. The deuterium content of precipitation reflects the interplay of five main mechanisms (Schiegl, n.d.). The further the rain falls from the equator, the lower the deuterium content (latitude effect). Deuterium content decreases inland (continental effect); is lower in winter than in summer poleward of latitude 25°–30° (seasonal effect); decreases with increasing elevation (altitude effect); and decreases with increased precipitation (amount effect).

Sonntag et al. (1980) have demonstrated the reality of the continental effect on the stable isotope composition of late Pleistocene Saharan groundwater, for the steady eastward decrease in the deuterium and oxygen-18 content of the groundwater implies a movement of the rain-bearing air-masses from the Atlantic eastward across North Africa (Sonntag et al., 1980: fig. 3).

There is also a strong suggestion that tropical rains may have reached well north of their present limits during the times of replenishment of the Kufra and Sirte aquifers in Libya. Groundwater in these basins has a much lighter isotopic composition than the present-day winter rains. Edmunds and Wright (1979) consider that heavy monsoonal rains from the tropical south were responsible for the late Pleistocene and Holocene recharge of the Kufra and Sirte aquifers, although the Pleistocene values also suggest a cooler source area.

Although a monsoonal source cannot be excluded, the deuterium values reported by Edmunds and Wright (1979) for Libyan groundwater may also in part reflect the combined effects of lower sea-surface temperatures, heavy rains, orographic storms over Tibesti, and winter depressions. What is not in doubt is the early to mid-Holocene recharge from streams flowing north from Tibesti across the now-arid wastes of the Calanscio serir and the Rebiana sand sea (Pachur, 1975; Edmunds and Wright, 1979).

Bones of elephant and other large tropical mammals, tamarisk wood, and mollusc shells point to a final phase of wadi activity in this area toward 3500 B.P., followed by desiccation (Pachur and Braun, 1980).

The distribution of Quaternary fossil nonmarine mollusca in the Sahara is consistent with the conclusions outlined earlier, for Palearctic species reached much further south in the northwestern quadrant of the Sahara than elsewhere (Sparks and Grove, 1961). The presence of tropical Holocene faunas in southcentral Algeria and Libya (Conrad, 1969; Pachur, 1975) prompts the hypothesis that the central Sahara was akin to the modern Australian desert in being a zone of overlap between temperate and tropical rains during Epi-Paleolithic and early Neolithic times. To test this hypothesis we will now consider geological and paleobotanical evidence from the central Saharan uplands.

Late Quaternary Environments in and around the Saharan Uplands

Despite the potentially favorable habitats offered by the desert mountains, only along their margins do well-stratified archaeological sequences exist, as at Adrar Bous in the Ténéré Desert east of the main Aïr massif (J. D. Clark et al., 1973; M. A. J. Williams, 1976a). Whether the absence of evidence of much prehistoric settlement in the Hoggar, Tibesti, Jebel Marra, and the Aïr until the late Holocene really denotes evidence of absence is still open to debate. If true, it might mean that during the driest intervals, for example, 18,000–15,000 B.P., a mobile and sparse population of hunter/gatherers preferred to migrate along the vegetated river valleys leading out of the Sahara rather than up into the mountains. Periglacial solifluction deposits and nivation hollows in Tibesti and the Hoggar indicate a probable 5°–8° C. temperature lowering during glacial maximum—a further impediment to prehistoric settlement (Messerli and Winiger, 1980).

Of all the Saharan uplands, Tibesti has the most reliably dated Late Quaternary sequence (Jäkel, 1979). The sands, silts, and clays of the Middle Terrace were laid down between 16,000 and 8000 B.P. (Geyh and Jäkel, 1974; Jäkel, 1979). North of Tibesti, the onset of deposition was much later: 10,000 B.P., according to Pachur and Braun (1980: fig. 3). Diatomaceous and shell-bearing lake and marsh deposits in central Tibesti are dated to 15,000–13,000 B.P., evidence that an effectively wetter climate prevailed there at that time (Faure et al., 1963; Jäkel, 1979). According to Jäkel (1979), peak humidity toward 9500–8500 B.P. coincided with the incidence of both tropical and temperate depressions over Tibesti, a phenomenon that began about 13,000 B.P.

A short-lived interval of downcutting gave way to renewed deposition during 6000–5000 and 4000–3000 B.P. (see Fig. 1), the pollen and mollusca of which indicate somewhat less arid environments than today (Maley et al., 1970; Jäkel, 1979). It was also at these times that Neolithic pastoralists were camping at least seasonally around the groundwater- and runoff-fed lakes that were scattered around the northern, central, and southern Sahara (Conrad, 1969; J. D. Clark et al., 1973; Gabriel, 1977; Pachur and Braun, 1980).

There are still too few dates available from the Hoggar and the Aïr to allow reliable stratigraphic correlations to be made between these two massifs and Tibesti. Such dates as do exist point to a less arid Neolithic interval in and around both massifs during the mid-Holocene (6000–4000 B.P.), preceded by somewhat more humid conditions during 11,000–7000 B.P. (Rognon, 1967: 520; Conrad, 1969: 444; Commelin and Petit-Maire, 1980).

The short, sharp, dry period prior to 6000 B.P. and the final onset of desiccation after 3000 B.P. and even, in many localities, after about 4500 B.P. are evident at many sites throughout the Sahara and are reflected in changes in economy and resource use at these times (J. D. Clark, 1980a; A. B. Smith, 1980a, b; Stemler, 1980).

Tropical Lakes and Interdune Ponds of the Southern Sahara

Geological and biological investigations in the Chad basin have yielded the most detailed late Quaternary history so far available for any part of the Sahara. Accurate reconstructions of changes in the level of Lake Chad based upon stratigraphic, diatom, and pollen studies permit more thorough water-balance estimates to be made than are yet possible elsewhere in the Sahara (see Fig. 1).

Low or dry between 20,000 and 13,000 B.P., Lake Chad was high toward 11,000, 9000–8000, 6000 and 3500–3000 B.P. (Servant, 1974, n.d.). Tropical diatom associations were dominant toward 20,000–18,000 B.P. and from 7000 B.P. until the present (Servant-Vildary, 1978). Water temperatures were low during 26,000–20,000 and again, rather surprisingly, during 12,000–7000 B.P.

When inferred water temperature and salinity levels are taken into account, the various high lake phases can be ranked according to their deduced precipitation/evaporation balance (P/E). In decreasing order of importance, the wettest phases seem to have been 9000–8000 (P>E)); 6000 (P≤E); 3500–3000 and 11,000 B.P. (P<E) (Servant and Servant-Vildary, 1980). Driest times during the Holocene were ca. 10,000; 7500; 4500–4000 B.P. and the last two thousand years (Servant and Servant-Vildary, 1980: fig. 6.9).

Analysis of modern and Holocene pollen spectra from sediments collected in and around Lake Chad and Tibesti has shown that the highly seasonal, tropical summer-rainfall regime characteristic of this region today only became established after 7000 B.P. (Maley, 1977a, b). Until about 6500 B.P., tropical depressions were the main source of Holocene rainfall in the central Sahara between 27°N and 18°N. Monsoonal rains were dominant during 6500–4400 B.P., after which aridity set in (Maley, 1977a).

Further south, in the Chad basin itself, pollen spectra show dominance of a Sudano-Guinean flora during 8000–4000 B.P., after which the modern Sahelian flora took over. Even after taking due account of water transport of pollen from the Logone and Chari headwaters in the Adamawa Mountains of Cameroon, it is still clear that during the first half of the Holocene, rainfall was more abundant, more reliable, and less seasonal than is the case today (Maley, 1972, 1977a).

Fed by runoff from the equatorial mountains of Cameroon and from the more seasonal rivers flowing south from Tibesti, Lake Chad rose to a level of 320 m and covered an area of some 360,000 km² during the early to mid-Holocene (Schneider, 1967; Servant et al., 1969; Servant, n.d.). This was the time of the "Sahara des Tchads" of the French prehistorians (Balout, 1955), and of the African "aqualithic" (Sutton, 1977). Today Lake Chad is a few meters deep, with an area of roughly 20,000 km² and a surface elevation of 280 m.

From Mauritania to the Sudan, early Holocene groundwater levels were high, and innumerable lakes came into existence at the foot of plateaux and mountains, particularly in the hollows between the Late Pleistocene dunes (Faure et al., 1963; Faure, 1966; M. A. J. Williams, 1971; Chamard, 1973; M. A. J. Williams et al., 1974). To this time

(7500–9000 B.P.) belong the hunting, fishing, and gathering communities of Early Khartoum (Arkell, 1949; Adamson et al., 1974; J. D. Clark, this volume); of Adrar Bous in central Niger (J. D. Clark et al., 1973; A. B. Smith, 1976); and of Dhar Tichitt in Mauritania (G. Hugot, n.d.).

The 710 m early Holocene lake strandline at Adrar Bous is littered with hippo bones and potsherds which pre-date the 7310 ± 120 B.P. carbonate concretions that formed as the lake dried out (Faure et al., 1963; J. D. Clark et al., 1973). The lake was replenished during the time of occupation by Neolithic herders and attained a level of 700 m toward 5500–6000 B.P. (M. A. J. Williams, 1971; J. D. Clark et al., 1973).

The mollusc assemblage associated with the 700 m lake affords us some insight into the Neolithic environment at Adrar Bous. The decrease in lake size and depth relative to the earlier lake confirms that aridity was now setting in, as does the dominance of the brackish-water mollusc *Hydrobia ventrosa* (Montagu) in the assemblage recovered from the Neolithic lake margin (M. A. J. Williams, 1976a; mollusc identifications by B. W. Sparks). Sparks (*in litt.*, 3/9/71) has further suggested that the lack of land snails from the samples collected at the 700 m lake margin may indicate that precipitation was too low for a dense vegetation to have developed away from the lake. A decrease in clay content and an increase in sedimentation rates at this time are further signs of a drier, more sparsely vegetated environment.

Once the lakes and ponds around Adrar Bous had dried out, there was every incentive to move south in the wake of the retreating tsetse-fly belt. Dated lake sequences in the Ténéré suggest that the time of this Neolithic exodus would have been about 4500–4000 B.P. (J. D. Clark, 1980a; Servant and Servant-Vildary, 1980).

A return to less arid conditions toward 3000–3500 B.P., evident in southern Mauritania (Munson, 1976) as well as in the Chad basin, is associated with final replacement of the fishing and/or herding economies of the southern Sahara by ones based upon intensive collecting of wild cereal grasses and eventual harvesting of genetically modified panicoid grasses such as *Pennisetum* and *Sorghum* (Stemler, 1980).

Playa Lakes and Mountains of the Eastern Sahara

Our paleoclimatic knowledge of the driest sector of the Sahara is also the most scanty. Neolithic rock art has long been known from Jebel 'Uweinat, but despite the relative abundance of Neolithic and earlier sites around both 'Uweinat and Archenu, no published radiocarbon ages have yet appeared (Heinzelin et al., 1969).

A complex of playa lakes 500–600 km east of 'Uweinat has yielded evidence of moister conditions between 9500 and 6700 B.P. (see Fig. 1), coinciding with Neolithic occupation toward 8200–7700 B.P. (Wendorf et al., 1977; Wendorf and Hassan, 1980). Related investigations in northwestern Sudan show that early hunters and herders also benefited from the presence of the many shallow lakes in this area between 9300 and 6000 B.P. (Haynes et al., 1979).

A thousand kilometers south of 'Uweinat lies Jebel Marra volcano. Dated algal limestones associated with former high strandlines of the shallower of the two lakes inside Deriba caldera indicate high levels toward 14,000, low levels toward 17,000, and high levels before then (M. A. J. Williams et al., 1980).

Between Jebel Marra and the Nile Valley, shallow Holocene lakes scattered among the Kordofan dunes supported life between 8400 and 7000 B.P. (see Fig. 1). All these lakes seem to have remained dry since then (Williams and Adamson, 1980).

The Nile: A Trans-Saharan Link and Holocene Drought Refuge

Although the Nile originates well south of the Sahara, it has long influenced Saharan prehistory. A strongly seasonal bed-load river from 25,000 until 12,000 B.P., the unprecedented floods of 11,500–11,000 B.P. heralded the return to a more regular, suspended-load regime. This dramatic change in Nile regime was caused by a number of factors, including the overflow of Lake Victoria and of Lake Turkana into the Sudanese White Nile

basin, and slope stabilization in the Blue Nile and Atbara headwaters (Williams and Adamson, 1980; Adamson et al., 1980).

Extensive seasonal flooding and clay deposition in central Sudan and Upper Egypt during 12,000–5000 B.P. were followed by Nile incision thereafter. As downcutting continued, the area flooded each summer also diminished, and hitherto permanent swamps dried out (Williams and Adamson, 1980). The ecological and cultural changes associated with these events are described elsewhere in this volume (J. D. Clark; K. W. Butzer).

The Nile is the only river in North Africa that traverses the Sahara from one margin to the other. As such, it links tropical south and temperate north. During the late Pleistocene the Saoura penetrated deep into the northcentral Sahara, and in early Holocene times a river flowing north from Tibesti may have reached the Mediterranean Sea (Edmunds and Wright, 1979; Pachur and Braun, 1980). These rivers were important in their day, allowing Holarctic and Mediterranean plants and animals to venture south toward the southern desert margins. In similar fashion, by taking advantage of the rivers that drained the southern flanks of the central Saharan uplands and of the multitude of inter-dune lakes characteristic of the early Holocene southern Sahara, large tropical mammals could extend their grazing range well north of the tropic, moving south again in dry years.

Nevertheless, even during the wettest times of the early Holocene, annual precipitation in the Libyan Desert is unlikely to have been more than about 250–300 mm in the Fezzan, decreasing westward to <200 mm in western Egypt toward 8000 B.P. (Pachur and Braun, 1980; Sonntag et al., 1980). For plants and animals, as well as for the prehistoric peoples dependent upon them, the eastern Sahara would always have been more marginal than the better-watered west and center. For that reason alone, the proximity of a perennial river flowing through the least hospitable part of the Sahara would have been crucial to the survival of at least some of the animals and people forced to abandon the desert during the increasingly frequent and prolonged dry intervals of the latter half of the Holocene.

Conclusion

The complex pattern of environmental change in different parts of the Sahara during the Late Quaternary is bound up with worldwide changes in atmospheric and oceanic circulation, as well as in polar ice volume and temperature (Maley, 1973; Rognon and Williams, 1977; Klaus, 1980; Flohn and Nicholson, 1980; Nicholson and Flohn, 1980). It would therefore be misleading to offer an explanation of Late Quaternary climates in the Sahara based solely on an appeal to extreme fluctuations of the present climate, for the modern temperature structure of the seas adjoining the desert is not what it was in the early Holocene, let alone in the late Pleistocene.

Although the two wettest intervals in the Late Quaternary, evident in significant recharge of Saharan aquifers, were broadly synchronous in the northern, central, and southern Sahara, there were important regional differences in timing. For example, there was a lag of several thousand years in the 8000–9000 B.P. inception of the early Holocene moist phase in the northern Sahara relative to the tropical south. Conversely, aridity was evident in the Chad basin by 20,000 B.P., but not until about 14,000–16,000 B.P. in northern Libya, Tunisia, and the Saharan piedmont of Algeria.

The dated first appearance of domesticated animals and plants was equally variable. In the Western Desert of Egypt and northern Sudan, early agriculture coincides in time with the wettest conditions in that hyperarid region of the last 10,000 years. Further afield, in Niger and Mauritania, the Neolithic pastoralists appeared on the scene when lake levels were lower than previously and desiccation was well underway. Obviously, no single deterministic model of agricultural origins would be applicable in this context.

Even if climatic changes were similar over large areas, as along the southern Sahara during the early Holocene, the ecological response may have varied. There are major floristic differences between the savanna of West Africa and that of the Sudan (Wickens, 1976). Perhaps the vastly enlarged, early Holocene Lake Chad was a barrier to the free east-west movement of savanna plants between West Africa and the Sudan (ibid.: 63). At all events, the food-gatherers would need to have had a detailed knowledge of the nutritional and medicinal properties of the local plant resources, which might have been inapplicable further afield. The regional differences between the early Holocene Saharan peoples may well have been as important as the cultural similarities between them (J. D. Clark, 1980a).

Extrapolation of the present into the past demands caution. Until 6000–7000 B.P., the southern Sahara does not seem to have experienced the highly seasonal, monsoonal rainfall regime so characteristic of this region today. Prior to 11,500–12,000 B.P., the Nile was a far more seasonal river than it is today, carrying a much coarser sediment load. Until the Nile began to cut down into its floodplain, the alluvium would not have been available for sustained farming. Indeed, the late Holocene desiccation which drove pastoralists from the eastern Sahara also helped dry out hitherto uninhabitable swamps in the central Sudan.

To sum up: any late Pleistocene experiments with plant foods such as barley would have taken place in a context of cool, wet conditions in northwest Africa and somewhat less cool and less wet conditions in Libya and Egypt. During the several thousand very dry years at the end of the Pleistocene, rivers and lakes dwindled, dunes became active, and the cold, dry, and windy Sahara would have been even less conducive to agriculture than it is today.

This climatic impediment was removed during the early Holocene, when movement of tropical plants and animals into the Sahara, and widely available surface water, allowed free movement of hunters and gatherers throughout this vast region. From about 7000 B.P. onward, conditions deteriorated: lakes and rivers dried out, grasses and trees died, game migrated. Cultivation of cereal grasses, a nomadic pastoral lifestyle, more intensive use of local plant foods—all may have delayed but did not finally prevent the Neolithic exodus from the increasingly harsh environment of the world's largest desert.

8

Origins of the Neolithic in the Sahara

ANDREW B. SMITH

Before making a general statement about the origins of the Neolithic in the Sahara we should consider the geography of North Africa. On the basis of cultural data and geographical context there are three main regions of cultural evolution. Broadly speaking, these regions are the Nile Valley north of the Nubian Desert; the Maghreb, the North African littoral, and the northern Sahara; and the central and southern Sahara including the Nile Valley from Nubia south to above the confluence of the Blue and While Niles. The Sahara, thus, must be regarded not as the home of a single, homogeneous, cultural entity but as comprising at least two major culture areas which had limited contact. This geographical and cultural separation is important in considering the possible outside influences on the Saharan populations.

The Sahara is much more than the extensive dune fields and sand seas that have made it famous. It is an area of high mountains (some exceeding 3400 m), deeply dissected valleys, and flat stony plains. Within the mountain regions exist water-catchment areas that permit the growth and survival of several species of a relict flora that are indicators of a more humid past. The Sahara lies between 18°N and 33°N Lat. Climatic variables have thus affected the northern Sahara differently from the southern Sahara. These environmental conditions (e.g., precipitation, winds), coupled with geographical variations, probably resulted in use of several different exploitation patterns by the early prehistoric inhabitants.

Epi-Paleolithic economies and environments in the Maghreb will be given in detail elsewhere in this volume; the area considered in this paper will be the central and southern Sahara, with occasional reference to events further north.

Hunting and Fishing Societies, 10,000–8000 B.P.

Prior to 8000 B.P., conditions in the central and southern Sahara were attractive to human habitation. Lacustrine environments existed in areas that today support little or no vegetation. These lakes harbored a diverse aquatic fauna—hippopotamus, crocodile, and fish—all exploited by the early human inhabitants. Microlithic tools, together with bone harpoons and points, testify to a hunting and fishing economy around these former lakes. In addition, these hunters and fishers used pottery (A. B. Smith, 1976). No indication of ground-stone tools has been found at this early period, nor is there any evidence of food production.

Contemporaneous with this lacustrine exploitation there existed similar cultural groups along the Nile, around the confluence of the two rivers and south along the White Nile, who made use of both riverine and terrestrial resources in the seventh millennium B.C. The similarities include use of bone harpoons, microlithic tools, and pottery (Arkell, 1949; Adamson et al., 1974).

The ceramics are interesting. It is from Early Khartoum that Arkell first decribed the "wavy-line" and "dotted wavy-line" wares. An almost identical tradition of "dotted wavy-line" ware was discovered at Adrar Madet in the Ténéré Desert, Niger (A. B. Smith, n.d.). Although the Adrar Madet material was not dated, the sequence worked out further north from Adrar Bous suggests occupation by these lacustrine peoples prior to 7300 B.P. (J. D. Clark et al., 1973). Similar early ce-

ramics are reported from Nabta Playa in the Nubian Desert west of Abu Simbel (Wendorf and Hassan, 1980). These authors note that Early Khartoum ceramics are missing from both Kharga Oasis and Gilf Kebir (ibid., 416).

Early ceramic traditions, lacking any indication of food production, are well documented in a number of regions of the Sahara other than those mentioned above. Barich (1978; n.d.) has dated four ceramic levels at East Torha in the Acacus Mountains, Libya, from 9080 ± 70 to 7990 ± 70 B.P. The earliest dates from Amekni in southern Algeria, 8670 ± 150 and 8050 ± 80 B.P. (Camps, 1969) and from Fozzigiaren, 8072 ± 110 (Mori, 1974) also come from levels containing pottery.

From a study of comparative environmental conditions in the northern and southern Sahara by Rognon (1976) the picture that emerges is of relatively dry conditions in the north between 12,000 and 9000 B.P., while the southern area was more humid. The wetter conditions continued in the south until ca. 8000 B.P., when a distinct drying phase affected the lake levels. The area of Lake Chad diminished in size (Servant and Servant-Vildary, 1970) and the lake at Agorass n'essoui, Adrar Bous, dried up (Faure et al., 1963).

What these changes meant in human terms is at present difficult to gauge. Adrar Bous was probably abandoned and the people forced to find their livelihood elsewhere. As yet the prehistory of the central Aïr Mountains is poorly known, but since in the mountain valleys water was available in natural underground aquifers and was capable of supporting plant life, this would have been an obvious retreat area. Today, in spite of the inhospitable conditions of much of the Sahara and the effects of modern weapons, relict populations of mouflon (*Ammotragus lervia*), ostrich (*Struthio camelus*), baboons (*Papio doguera*), and Patas monkeys still survive in the Aïr Mountains.

Introduction of Pastoralism into the Sahara

Shortly after 7000 B.P., conditions in the central and southern Sahara improved once more. The lakes filled and expanded, perhaps not to their previous levels, but sufficiently to attract animal and, thus, human life to their immediate vicinity.

A new cultural feature, that of herding economies with cattle and small stock, appeared at about this time. The chronology of the early appearance of domestic animals is based on Mori's work (1965; 1974) in the Acacus mountains of southwest Libya and on that of Wendorf in the western desert (Wendorf and Schild, this volume). The earliest direct dating of *Bos* remains—5952 ± 120 B.P.—comes from the rockshelter of Uan Muhuggiag on samples from a level containing the frontal bone of a short-horned animal. From the nearby site of Uan Telocat a date of 6754 ± 290 B.P. was obtained from deposits with cultural material similar to that from Uan Muhuggiag (Krueger and Weeks, 1965: 52). Thus, though there is some uncertainty as to exactly when cattle were introduced, these dates may bracket the time of their arrival.

From Capelletti cave in the Aurès Mountains of northern Algeria, work done by Roubet (1978) supports a fifth millennium B.C. appearance of domestic cattle. Her dates of 6530 ± 250 to 4340 ± 200 B.P. span the occupation of the cave by people utilizing cattle. During this time the proportion of cattle bones in the total bone assemblage rises from 7.3 percent to 24.7 percent, and the Caprines slightly decrease, from 89.7 percent to 70 percent. This seems to reflect the proportionately increasing use of cattle through time and may be an example of domestication actually in progress. From the study of the remaining organic materials, Roubet suggests that the cave was seasonally occupied and that the transhumant pattern from the high mountains in spring, summer, and autumn to the lower foothills in winter was sufficient without moving further south into the Sahara.

By the fourth millennium B.C., pastoralism was widespread throughout the Sahara from the Nile Valley near Khartoum (Haaland, 1978; Krzyzaniak, 1978) to Niger and Mali (A. B. Smith, 1980a). Associated cultural material included grinding equipment, but other than the data from the confluence of the Blue and While Niles (Klichowska, 1978) there is as yet little evidence to support the hypothesis of early grain domestication in the Sahara until well into the second millennium B.C. (i.e., the Dhar Tichitt area of Mauretania [Munson,

1976]). A single domesticated sorghum grain was identified from a surface sherd from Adrar Bous, Niger, and since the site was abandoned ca. 4500 B.P. it hints at possible domesticates in this area. There is probably little doubt that these early Saharan pastoralists utilized wild grains such as *Panicum* spp. and *Pennisetum*, but in spite of the many grindstones found on Saharan sites the botanical evidence is sparse and further investigation is needed.

The cultural groups of pastoral peoples who inhabited the large area of the central and southern Sahara were remarkably homogeneous. Pastoralism was the common denominator, but hunting and fishing were practiced also. The cultural material over the whole area, although not identical, has many similarities. Pottery styles and decoration have strong affinities, as have a number of tool types found in the Nile Valley across to the Ténéré and Borkou and probably as far north as the Fezzan (A. B. Smith, 1980b), for example, the rocker-stamped globular pots and round-based bowls, and the flaked and polished adzes. These latter may have been used for woodworking, suggesting more extensive tree-cover than exists there today.

Hunting equipment is ubiquitous; it is predominantly hollow-based projectile points but includes many other forms ranging from tanged, foliate, and denticulate points to tranchets (see H. J. Hugot, 1957). Styles and proportions vary from area to area, suggesting local cultural preferences.

The Spread of Pastoralism into the West African Sahel

About 4500 B.P., environmental conditions began to deteriorate, putting pressure on the prehistoric herdsmen (A. B. Smith, 1979). Surface water became scarcer, due to overall desertification of the central and southern Sahara, and a general southward movement of the Intertropical Convergence Zone (ITCZ) brought rain into the interior of West Africa (see Maley, 1977a,b). With this southward movement went the northern tsetse limits of the 500–700 mm rainfall isohyet. This meant that the more southerly lands of the Sahel became free from tsetse infestation, opening up new areas for colonization by pastoral peoples. At this time the pastoralists were following the river systems draining southward to the Niger River. The Tilemsi Valley river system, which runs north/south from the Adrar des Iforas to the Niger River at Gao, had no human occupation at its southern end until ca. 4000 B.P. The sites of Karkarichinkat Nord and Sud yielded faunal remains of predominantly domestic animals, together with fish and wild plant remains (A. B. Smith, 1974, 1975c). Analysis of these finds suggests that the sites were occupied seasonally, at the end of the year, when the two mounds became virtual islands after the rains: this would explain the accumulation of cultural debris in these two areas. It is also a pattern that can be observed among present-day pastoralists, who occupy high dune areas with adequate run-off to avoid the flooding of their camp during the wet season. This results in the entire camp compressing itself into a smaller space than is usual during the drier months of the year (see S. E. Smith, 1980).

By ca. 3300 B.P. the sites had been abandoned. This date corresponds to an increase in rainfall reflected in an expanding Lake Chad (Servant and Servant-Vildary, 1970, 1980) and possibly meant a northward shift of the tsetse belt. Data from central Ghana, at Kintampo (Carter and Flight, 1972) suggest that by this time the cattle complex had expanded south into the savanna region, probably utilizing tsetse-free corridors during the dry season. This movement was probably part of a seasonal transhumant pattern similar to that practiced by the Fulani in West Africa in more recent times (Stenning, 1959). That West African cattle have been in contact with tsetse for a long time is underlined by the degree of resistance to *Trypanosomiasis* exhibited by the modern West African shorthorn and Ndama cattle found in the Sudanic belt from the northern Ivory Coast to Nigeria.

The "Neolithic" of the Sahara

From the above data it is obvious that any use of the term *Neolithic* to describe Saharan industries must be qualified. The term *Neolithic* was coined in Europe and the Middle East and used by French speakers to refer to industries using pottery and ground-stone tools and by English speakers for groups practicing food production.

Ceramic non–food-producing societies, however, existed in the Sahara for almost 2,000 years before there were any domesticated animals or plants, and many of these ceramic industries had no ground-stone tools, although grinding equipment for preparation of pigment was known in the Acacus Mountains (Mori, 1974).

Using the European criteria for the Neolithic, it may be possible to see two distinct phases in the Sahara. For this area, therefore, it would probably be desirable to abandon entirely the use of the term *Neolithic* were it not so firmly entrenched in the literature, especially in the French-speaking world. It is suggested, therefore, that the term may best be used to refer to those societies which practiced food production.

In the literature, a distinction has been made between the cultural area of the northern Sahara, where the assemblages are grouped into a complex known as the Neolithic of Capsian Tradition (Camps, 1974; Camps-Fabrer, 1966, 1970) and the central Sahara, where the contemporary assemblages are known as the Neolithic of Sudanese Tradition. This distinction appears to be a real one and to have existed from early post-Pleistocene times, as the "fossile directeur" of the lacustrine tradition in the central and southern Sahara, the bone harpoon, is almost entirely absent from the northern area (see Camps-Fabrer, 1966). In the later, food-producing era, the pottery styles of the two areas are quite different. The wares of the Neolithic of Capsian Tradition in the region of the Atlas Mountains and the littoral have distinctive pointed bases, while straight-sided forms are found in the northern Sahara. These contrast with the globular and bowl-like forms of the central Sahara (Fig. 1).

Rainfall in the Sahara prior to 6500 B.P. is believed by Maley (1977a,b) to have resulted from the depression of northern wind systems into the tropics, but this is considered by Rognon (1976, fig. 5) to have resulted in only uncertain rainfall around latitude 28°N; thus it is possible that much of this area was only marginally attractive for human

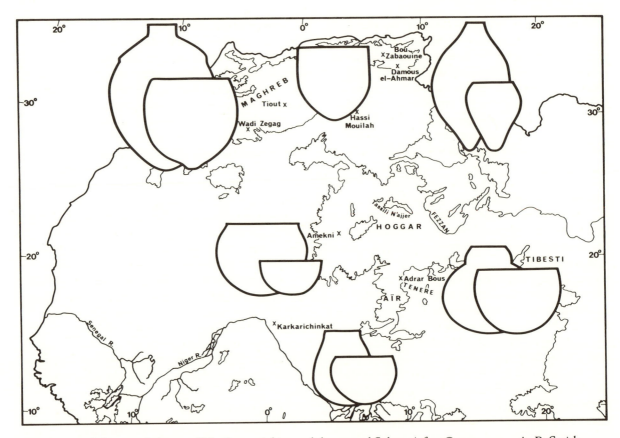

Figure 1. Neolithic vessel shapes of Northwest Africa and the central Sahara (after Camps, 1974; A. B. Smith, 1980b).

habitation and that it may to some extent have acted as a geographical barrier to cultural inter-action.

With our present knowledge it is difficult to make any statement on the causes of the beginnings of food production in the Sahara. As a result of the dry period between 8000 and 7000 B.P., many parts of the low-lying areas of the Sahara were probably abandoned. This would have resulted in an open ecological niche of extensive grasslands and open water once conditions improved again, after 7000 B.P.

Several sites have yielded reasonable faunal collections from which some of the percentages of species can be gained. The percentages of domes-tic animals in the mammalian bone analyzed from

the four levels at Capeletti range from 94.7 percent to 98.7 percent. This is consistent with the high percentages of domestic animals found further south at the site of Arlit in Niger, excavated by Henri Lhote and dated to ca. 5100 B.P. (Delibrias et al., 1974:45), where domestic animals (cattle 84.9 percent, ovicaprids 6.3 percent) represent 91.2 percent of the mammalian bones. Similarly, at Kadero, near the confluence of the Blue and White Niles and dated to ca. 5300 B.P., the domestic animals constitute 96.4 percent of the mammalian fauna (Krzyzaniak, 1980). The difference between these sites is that at Capeletti, as mentioned above, the *Bos* frequency ranges only between 7.3 percent and 24.7 percent, while at Arlit cattle remains com-prise 84.9 percent, and at Kadero, 74.3 percent.

This may reflect the way in which the sampling was done or may be a function of different environments or economies. A mountain area would be more suitable for sheep or goats, while the open plains to the west of the Aïr, or the Nile Valley, would be more suitable for cattle-herding. In comparison with both these sites, Karkarichinkat yielded only 63.2 percent of domestic animals from the mammalian fauna. There was, however, a higher percentage of *Bos* (41.4 percent) to Caprine remains (21.8 percent), which, again, may indicate a more open environment.

Where these domestic animals were obtained is as yet unknown. A number of possibilities have been outlined in A. B. Smith (1980a). The explanation that best fits the admittedly sparse data is early introduction of goats and sheep from the Near East into North Africa and along the Mediterranean littoral sometime after 8000 B.P. Domestication of cattle came slightly later, i.e., ca. 7000 B.P., and the indigenous wild cattle of the Sahara were probably the source.

The consequence of all this was rapid occupation by pastoralists of the available grassland niche and their expansion over most of the central and southern Sahara, where surface water permitted animal husbandry.

The southern limits of occupation were probably controlled by tsetse infestation which would have fluctuated, depending on rainfall conditions, seasonally. With the increasing aridity of the Sahara ca. 4500 B.P., the tsetse limits would have shifted further and further to the south, permitting colonization of more southerly latitudes, particularly along watercourses flowing from the southern Saharan highlands to the Niger River.

The earliest information on plant domestication in this area dates to ca. 3100 B.P. and comes from the southern edges of the Sahara at Dhar Tichitt in eastern Mauritania (Munson, 1976). From data based on plant impressions in potsherds Munson argues that plant domestication was an introduction from elsewhere. The evidence given above from the eastern Sudanic belt along the Nile, as well as from further north, also suggests that this may have been the case.

No direct evidence of domesticated plants has

yet been recovered from excavations at Karkarichinkat. However, impressions in surface sherds from Karkarichinkat Sud, analyzed by J. M. J. de Wet of the University of Illinois, have indicated (*in litt.*) both wild and domesticated pearl millet (*Pennisetum americanum* ssp. *monodii* (Maire) Brunken and *P. americanum* (L.) Leeke), as well as spikelets of *Brachiaria deflexa* (Schumach). Further tests are now being conducted on sherds from the excavation itself, so it may not be long before we have more evidence to confirm the presence of domesticated grains from this site.

In purely cultural evolutionary terms the Dhar Tichitt case is interesting. The trend to sedentariness there appears to have developed before the introduction of domestic cereals and, after these became important in the diet, there grew a need to fortify the settlements against incursions by outsiders (Munson, 1976: 194). It may perhaps be inferred from this that there were still some groups in the Sahara who maintained a nomadic pastoral way of life and whose preying on more sedentary neighbors forced these latter to defend themselves.

Relationship Between Animal and Plant Domestication in the Sahara

From the data outlined above it appears that animal domestication preceded any attempt to domesticate plants. Prehistoric pastoralists like those in the Saharan and Sahel zones today utilized wild grains and fruits and probably adjusted their annual transhumant cycle to coincide with the harvesting of these plants (see S. E. Smith, 1980). It is usually only under extreme duress, such as excessive drought, that a Sahelian pastoralist will consider turning to agriculture as a way of life. This, however, did not prevent development of vassalage systems in which low-caste groups would perform agricultural tasks for their higher-caste masters, as among the Tuareg today (Lhote, 1944, Nicolaisen, 1963).

That agriculture at Dhar Tichitt coincides with a period of increasing aridity in the southern Sahara may possibly be construed as being the result of pressure not only from nomadic pastoralist neighbors but also from environmental conditions that made it difficult to maintain herds large enough for subsistence. Whether the same process can be suggested as applying to other parts of the Sahara is difficult to know. Local environmental conditions along river systems such as the Nile or Niger would make sedentary agriculture easier to adopt, as floodlands would lend themselves readily to exploitation. Areas distant from the rivers would require either a dependable rainfall or underground aquifers for water storage, without which conditions there would be much greater susceptibility to yearly and/or seasonal fluctuation.

It is possible that grain cultivation in the Sahara was practiced on a strictly ad hoc basis by pastoral peoples taking advantage of an occasional particularly wet season but otherwise relying on their herds and whatever wild game they could obtain by hunting or fishing and on the wild plant foods that they collected.

Outside Influences on the Sahara

If we accept the pattern suggested here of two separate Saharan cultural areas, north and central/south, we must also consider the separate outside influences each may have received.

As mentioned previously, it is possible that the Mediterranean littoral was to some degree influenced by events in the Near East prior to 7000 B.P. Domestic goats and/or sheep have been identified from Haua Fteah, but no domestic cattle (Higgs, 1967a). The early dates for cattle at Capeletti may indicate that they were domesticated there, or they could reflect early introductions from the outside. McBurney (1967) does suggest that the cultural connections of the Haua Fteah appeared to be strongest with the Maghreb rather than with the Nile Valley, but domestic caprines could only have come out of the Near East, since the wild progenitors are not indigenous to Africa. We should, however, be careful about drawing conclusions based on faunal lists from a single site since, for various reasons, these may not be true reflections of the area as a whole. For example, at Esh Shaheinab

goats were identified but no cattle were found (Arkell, 1953), though further excavation at Esh Shaheinab (Haaland, 1979a) has produced cattle bones (Tigani el Mahi, 1979). Work by Haaland (1978) and Krzyzaniak (1978, 1980) has suggested that, at certain sites, differences in the faunal lists were the result of seasonal occupation.

As previously stated, the cultural region of the central and southern Sahara included the Nile Valley south of the Nubian Desert. As yet, there is no indication that there were domestic animals in the Egyptian Nile Valley before they appeared in the central Sahara (which, on the basis of the cultural material, also included western and southwestern Libya). It appears, from the work of Wendorf et al. (1976, and Wendorf and Schild, this volume) that domestic ovicaprids and cattle appeared in the Nubian Desert about the same time as in the central Sahara. The date from the site E−75−8 (called the Latest Neolithic) is 7150 ± 130 B.P. Here we run into confusion concerning the word *Neolithic*. Wendorf and Hassan (1980: 416) recognize Arkell's concept of a Khartoum Mesolithic—a ceramic industry with no domestic animals or plants. In this paper and in Wendorf et al. (1976) they differentiate between an Earlier and a Later Neolithic. It is not clear on what basis this distinction is made, other than C^{14} dates; however, only the Later Neolithic has domestic animals (Wendorf et al., 1976: 106). In Wendorf and Hassan (1980: 417) we are told: "The Neolithic sites also yielded a few bones of cattle, which are believed to be domestic." It is difficult to separate the concepts of a Neolithic and the associated fauna from these descriptions. From what we can deduce, it appears that Arkell's idea of a Mesolithic holds true for the Nubian Desert just as it does for the confluence of the Blue and White Niles and for the edge of the Ténéré Desert in Niger.

Unfortunately, information on the Libyan sites is sparse and, other than that from Haua Fteah, comes from surface collections. Shaheinab-type adzes and celts have been found in the Fezzan and east of Ghadames in the Hamada el-Homra; thus, it is not impossible that the desert area south of the Gulf of Sirte may have been the route whereby goats and/or sheep were introduced into the central Sahara and thence to the Nile Valley (Fig. 2).

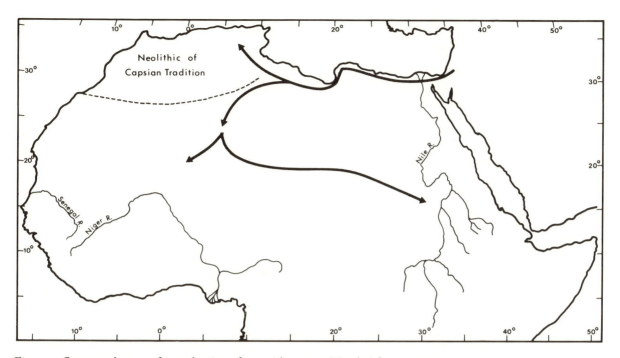

Figure 2. Suggested route of introduction of goats/sheep into North Africa ca. 8000–6500 B.P.

The Ecological Context of Early Animal Domestication in the Sahara

The argument outlined here emphasizes the ecological conditions and local environmental effects of the mid-Holocene in the Sahara and tries to place human adaptation within this context. To the early pastoralists the Sahara must always have been a marginal environment with seasonal rainfall and surface-water availability like that found in the Sahel zone of West Africa today. The introduction of ovicaprids and subsequent domestication of cattle in North Africa and the Sahara can be seen as an adaptive strategy in utilization of the grassland niche that was opened up by the amelioration of the environment ca. 7000 B.P. The impetus for the beginnings of pastoralism may well have come from the fluctuating environmental conditions that preceded introduction of domestic animals and had put serious strain on the hunter/fisher populations of the central and southern Sahara during the period 7500 to 7000 B.P.

It is probable that hunter/gatherer populations still existed in the Sahara during this period of early domestication, as they do today (Gabus, 1952); however, from the available archaeological information, the predominant way of life seems to have been pastoralism, which spread rapidly throughout the entire central and southern Sahara. So rapid was this expansion that strong cultural similarities existed as far apart as the Nile Valley at Khartoum and the Aïr Mountains of Niger. This is not unusual among pastoral peoples, as the Tuareg today occupy an area that encompasses large portions of Algeria, Niger, and Mali, while the Fulani have spread throughout the savanna zone from the Fouta Djallon of Guinea in the west to the Sudan in the east.

As the pastoralists were so closely constrained by environmental conditions, the increasing aridity of the Sahara ca. 4500 B.P. and the southward retreat of the tsetse-fly belts resulted in a general southerly movement of pastoral groups, particularly along watercourses running north/south from the Sahara. This precipitated further expansion of the "cattle complex" into both West and East Africa around 4000 B.P.

It appears probable that the seasonal harvest of wild grains in the southern Sahara led to their control and intentional planting. The tantalizing identification of domestic *Pennisetum* from Karkarichinkat adds a new dimension to our picture of the life of pastoral peoples in the second millennium B.C. and points to new skills in exploitation that were later to have ramifications for the people living in the savanna zone. Can we dare to suggest that the domestication of grains was developed by pastoral peoples in West Africa, contrary to the model (see E. Isaac, 1971) often outlined for cultural development in the Near East?

9

The Emergence of Food Production in the Egyptian Sahara

FRED WENDORF
AND ROMUALD SCHILD

The Western Desert of Egypt contains a remarkable wealth of well-preserved remains of the Terminal Paleolithic and Neolithic (Fig. 1). The sites often have deep trash accumulations, houses, and other structural features, and they have yielded convincing evidence that food production, including both domestic animals (initially cattle) and grains (barley), was known there at a very early period, certainly before 8000 B.P. and possibly 1,500 years earlier (but see p. 101). Another point of interest is that the ceramics associated with the earliest Neolithic are well made, obviously do not represent an incipient stage of pottery manufacture, are within the Saharo-Sudanese tradition known from a broad area extending from eastern Sudan across the central Sahara, and are clearly different from the earliest known (and considerably later) pottery in the adjacent Nile Valley. Finally, these localities have provided insights, in many ways unique, into a society in the process of transformation from an essentially hunting-and-gathering economy to food production.

With numerous stratigraphic trenches and bore holes and over thirty radiocarbon dates, both

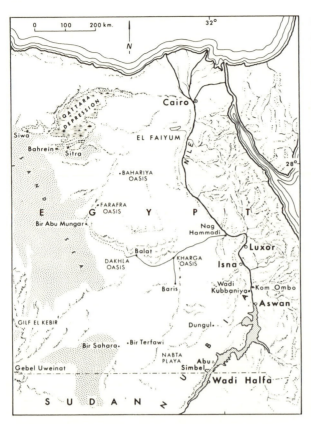

Figure 1. Map of Egypt showing locations discussed in text.

the sequence of climatic changes and the chronology of these developments are now fairly well controlled. There are, however, major limitations in the cultural data. Only one area (Nabta) has been studied in adequate detail, and only one Neolithic village has been excavated sufficiently to determine the complete structure of that settlement. The sheer size and depth of many of the Neolithic sites have limited the work at these thus far to trenches, surface mapping, and clearing of an occasional house.

Two basic geomorphic situations are known to have been used by both the Terminal Paleolithic and Neolithic groups in the Western Desert: internally drained basins, and springs. Except near Kharga, where the numerous spring pools were a favorite location, by far the more common are

those sites associated with internally drained basins. Elsewhere in the Western Desert active spring vents were extremely rare during the Holocene. Within the playa group two slightly different settings have been noted: the first is on dunes or sandy aeolian/playa sediments near the edge of the water; the second is closer to the center of the playas, within the playa silts. The fact that essentially the same settlement situations were exploited by both the Terminal Paleolithic and Neolithic has led to frequent admixture of the two entities and has caused some confusion among earlier workers (for example, the "Bedouin Microlithic" of Caton-Thompson, 1952).

The Terminal Paleolithic sites date between 9200 and 8500 B.P. and are associated with the first Holocene wet episode (Playa I). The sites of this period found in the playas on dunes near the water's edge are always characterized by the presence of several concentrations, but all of them are believed more probably to represent multiple occupations of the same locality by small groups rather than multi-unit settlements. The sites of this period within the playa sediments may be either single-unit or multi-unit occurrences, the latter always with dense and rich occupational debris. One of these sites showed traces of a circular tentlike house structure, while another had a slab-lined storage pit. The fact that these sites were located on seasonally flooded surfaces and yet contained dense debris indicates multiple reoccupations of the same spot. Presumably, these flooded areas could be occupied only in the late fall and winter, after all but the deepest pools formed by the summer rains had dried. We believe that these seasonally moist areas were of importance because it was here that the cereals or grasses being harvested would grow most abundantly.

Seven Terminal Paleolithic sites have been excavated, and in five of them the entire concentration was collected and scatter-patterned. The faunal evidence strongly indicates that these "Terminal Paleolithic" populations also had domestic cattle (as indicated by both the small size of the recovered *Bos* remains and the total absence of the megafauna expected to accompany wild cattle), although most of their food refuse consists of bones from small lagomorphs and gazelle, as does that in the early Neolithic sites. Also, the common presence in some sites of grinding stones and the occasional storage structures (the latter in one site only) may indicate some dependence on a ground grain the identity of which is not known but is suspected to be barley. Thus, the "Terminal Paleolithic" apparently was at least incipiently "food-producing," although the way the economy functioned is not yet well understood. Clearly the terms *Neolithic* and *Terminal Paleolithic* are in need of careful evaluation if we are to avoid confusion. For the moment, pending further confirmation of food production during the Terminal Paleolithic, the presence or absence of pottery is used as the diagnostic criterion. It may be more appropriate later to characterize these Terminal Paleolithic groups as a "Sudanese Pre-Pottery Neolithic."

Three taxonomic units within the Terminal Paleolithic of the southern Western Desert have been defined. They are differentiated by varying qualitative and quantitative characteristics, specifically the presence, absence, or relative frequencies of certain geometric forms, backed bladelets, stemmed points and notches, and denticulates. Two of these entities have been dated and the third is reliably placed within the defined stratigraphic sequence. The meaning of the variation is still not known; in part it may be chronological, or it may be partly geographical, or both. As yet we have no basis for evaluating the functional diversity that may be represented. Significantly, none of these entities is clearly similar to any known assemblage along the Nile except for the Arkinian at Site DIW-1, and that site is unique among known Nilotic groups. Typological studies indicate a close relationship between the Western Desert Terminal Paleolithic groups and the Arkinian and the Upper Capsian in the Maghreb, implying a broad zone of very general cultural similarity across the semiarid early Holocene Sahara.

Using the methodology developed by Close (1977), comparisons of stylistic elements have shown considerable diversity among the Terminal Paleolithic of the Western Desert. It has also been shown that there is significant stylistic overlap with the succeeding Neolithic, although the data are not yet adequate to establish a direct continuity between the two.

The assemblages of the Terminal Paleolithic

also show that considerable emphasis was given to the selection of good-quality raw material. The best-quality cherts were used almost exclusively and often transported over considerable distances, thus implying either extensive trade or high mobility of groups or both.

Settlement situations of the Neolithic playa sites are even more complex than those of the Terminal Paleolithic. Large settlements, probably of a permanent or semipermanent nature, occur on dunes at the edge of the water. Here, houses and storage structures are common features, as are large pottery storage jars and numerous superimposed hearths within deep trash accumulations. Some of these shoreline villages were formally organized. For example, the first known settlement with pottery, which is firmly dated by ten radiocarbon dates within one standard deviation of 8100 B.P., consisted of two long rows of saucer-shaped house floors each with one or more adjacent bell-shaped storage pits (see Fig. 2). Nearby was a deep walk-in well. Clearly, a complex and highly structured society is represented, and one which was strikingly different from that of the immediately preceding Terminal Paleolithic. Rare bones of cattle, morphologically within the size-range of domestic forms, indicate a herding economy, although apparently they were kept not for meat but for blood and milk, a widespread feature among modern African cattle-herders. Instead, gazelle and hare, to judge from the frequency of their bones in the refuse, were the main sources of meat. Associated floral remains include domestic six-row barley and weeds usually associated with cultivation, as well as several trees and bushes, including acacia and both dom palm and date palm.

A radically different settlement character is indicated for the sites located on the silts. Here there are two kinds of houses and two kinds of cultural accumulations. The first is represented by slab-lined houses occurring singly or in small groups and with minimal numbers of associated artifacts. The second kind of house is represented by shallow circular basins, probably tent floors, also in small groups but with relatively rich cultural debris. Because these sites within the playa settlements are situated in places that were periodically flooded, the occupations are regarded as seasonal, probably during the winter and spring months. Those sites containing rich cultural remains, however, for some reason not now evident, were particularly favored and repeatedly reoccupied. The implications of the different house forms in these situations are unknown.

Within the Neolithic there is a well-defined developmental sequence of over 2,000 years' duration, and four taxonomic units have been defined. One of these is known only from the Gilf el Kebir and will not be discussed here. The other three are well represented at several sites in the southern Western Desert. Each of these units is distinguished by a characteristic lithic assemblage.

The earliest group, represented in the organized villlage described earlier and dated around 8100 B.P. (beginning of Playa II), displays pronounced typological similarities to the preceding Terminal Paleolithic, but the tool kit has a different structure. Here, perforators are more important, followed by backed bladelets, notches, denticulates, triangles, and burins. There are numerous large, intentionally shaped grinding stones with deep oval grinding surfaces. Pottery is rare, but the impressed decorations are well within the Early Khartoum tradition.

The lithic assemblages in the second Neolithic group, associated with the next interval of increased moisture (Playa III), are very different from those of the preceding assemblages. The tool kits are dominated by retouched pieces, notches, and denticulates. Perforators are still numerous, but geometrics are almost absent and are limited to a few broad lunates with semisteep retouch. Backed bladelets are very rare. One characteristic tool group is the series of points formed by truncated bases and with either naturally pointed or retouched tips. There are also a few bifacial and stemmed points. Pecked and polished stone celts occur, as well as numerous grinding stones similar to those in the preceding group. The pottery, while still in the Saharo-Sudanese tradition, is radically different—more friable and often with smeared impressions. It is similar to some found at Amekni in the Central Sahara (Camps, 1969: 131). Ovicaprids (sheep or goat) are added to the domestic animals, and there are remains of domestic emmer wheat and barley. Radiocarbon dates indicate a range from 7500 to 6400 B.P. for this group, and their stratigraphic position correlates with the beginning through the middle of Playa III (see Fig. 3).

The third Neolithic group, known from only one site, occurs stratigraphically above the second and is similarly dominated by retouched pieces, notches, and denticulates. Geometrics, which are very rare, are limited to a few lunates and trapezes. Transverse arrowheads are also present, as are a few bifacial points. Ground and polished celts and grinding stones complete the lithic inventory. The ceramics, however, are totally outside the Saharo-Sudanese tradition and consist of a well-made, hard, buff-colored ware, sometimes red-slipped or decorated with incised straight lines parallel or diagonal to the rim. There are no painted decorations. The closest parallel is found among the Abkan ceramics in the Nile Valley, dated there after 5800 B.P. (Nordström, 1972: 58–60). The associated faunal remains include dog, in addition to the cattle and sheep noted previously, but the hunting of gazelle and hare remained important and was probably the main source of meat. This group has several radiocarbon dates between 6400 and 5800 B.P., through the later part of Playa III as it is now dated.

There are also several interesting shifts in the lithic raw material economy during the Neolithic development in the Western Desert. The earliest Neolithic is very similar to the Terminal Paleolithic, with stress placed on excellent-quality Eocene flint obtained from a considerable distance. There is, however, a significant increase in quartz and quartz crystals, which occur in the nearby basement rocks. In the second and third groups of assemblages there is a marked decline in the frequency of Eocene flint, and quartz is the major raw material, along with silicified limestone, jasper, chalcedony, and other locally available metamorphic rocks. This increase in quartz recalls the similar shift noted in the Terminal Paleolithic to Neolithic transition in the Nile Valley. It seems to accompany a changing economic structure where tools requiring the production of bladelets are less common, perhaps associated with the increasing dependence on food production. At present this seems to be the most reasonable explanation for the

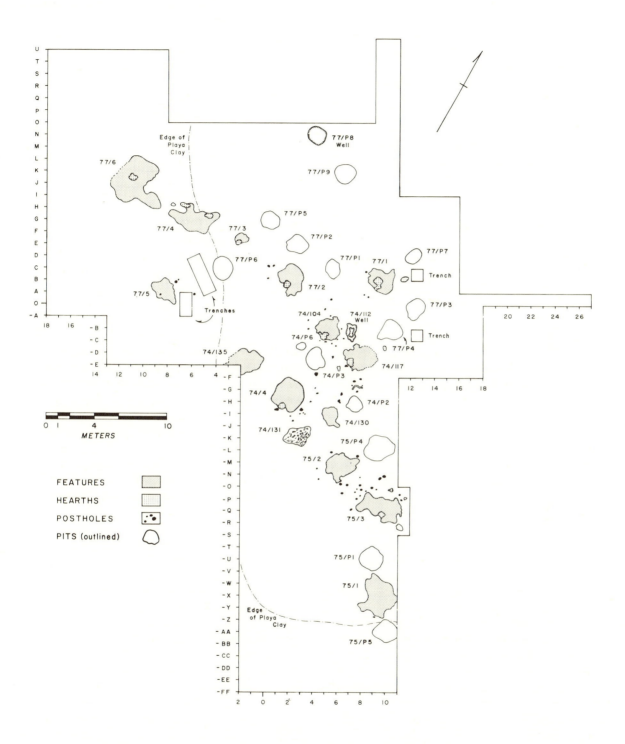

Figure 2. Map of Site E-75-6, early Neolithic settlement at Nabta Playa, dating to 8100 B.P. Note two east-west alignments of "features" (house floors) and bell-shaped storage pits.

decline in the use of flint; however, there is a possibility of reduced accessibility to the more distant Eocene quarries, or reduced social interaction between neighboring groups.

The problem of the origin of food production has been a major focus of scholarly interest for more than two decades. Most of this interest has been concentrated on the Near East, long believed to be the earliest center of domestication for both animals and grain, and a number of theories have been advanced.

One such is the "Oasis Theory" of Childe (1936), which had, in fact, been suggested by Peake in 1928. This holds that the increased aridity

during the Late Quaternary confined human groups and the as-yet-undomesticated grasses and animals together within certain moister, but limited, areas. Rather later, Braidwood (1960) proposed, in his "Hilly Flanks" theory, that the first domestication of cereals must have occurred in the area where the wild relatives of these grow today. Implicit in this theory was the assumption that there had been no significant change in the climate of the area since the early Holocene.

More recently, a number of authors have advanced slightly varying explanations for the origins of agriculture in the Near East, all of which stress population pressure as the most decisive factor

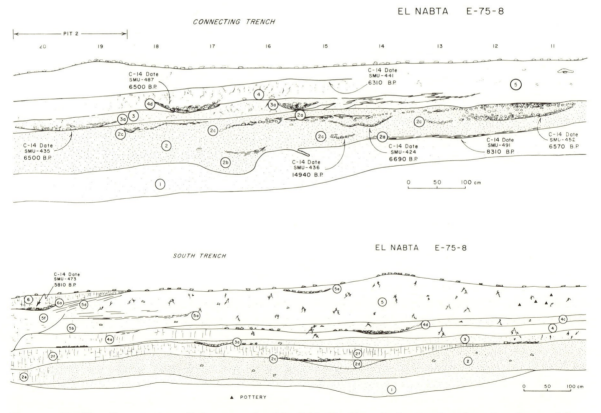

Figure 3. Profiles of two sections of a long trench at Neolithic Site E-75-8, showing interfingering playa and dune sediments. (1) Dune sand; (2) lower cultural layer; (2a) charcoal lens; (2b) pit; (2c) stone-lined hearths; (2d) lens of aeolian(?) sand; (2e) silty sand; (2f) playa silt; (3) middle cultural layer; (3a) stone-lined hearths; (4) lower portion of upper cultural layer; (4a) silty sand; (4c) charcoal-enriched upper portion of unit; (4d) stone-lined hearths; (5) upper cultural layer; (5a) charcoal lenses; (5b) silty sand; (5d) laminated sand; (5e) stone-lined hearths; (5f) pit filled with silt; (6) playa silt; (6a) stone-lined hearth.

(Binford, 1968b; Flannery, 1969; P. E. L. Smith, 1972; Smith and Young, 1972). Perhaps the most extreme presentation of this view was by Cohen (1975, 1977). All of these seem to have been stimulated by Boserup (1965), and her study of the effects of population pressure upon agricultural production (but see also Spooner, 1972; Farris, 1975). A number of criticisms have been voiced against these rather simplistic explanations, of which the most notable are those of Bronson (1972, 1975) and Polgar (1975), who advocate a complex interaction of many agencies in the origins of agriculture.

Several explanations have also been offered for the appearance of food production in northern Africa, the Nile Valley, and the Sahara (J. D. Clark, 1971, 1976a; P. E. L. Smith, 1972; B. D. Shaw, 1976; Harlan et al., 1976b; Butzer, 1976). Clark sees the domesticated plants as originating in the Nile Valley and gradually diffusing from there throughout Africa. Shaw, on the other hand, postulates the importance of population pressure due to increased aridity, a modification of the Oasis Theory of Childe. Smith has proposed that changes in population pressure resulting from fluctuations in population density in relation to resources is a causal factor. Harlan, de Wet, and Stemler postulate multiple origins for African domesticates but suggest that the desiccation of the Sahara forced hunter/gatherers to move southward into zones already intensively exploited, which resulted in stresses leading to manipulation of the plant populations (1976b: 18). Butzer (1971: 591; 1976: 9) recognizes a late date for the appearance of agriculture in the Nile Valley and suggests that it failed to develop there earlier because the broad-spectrum hunting-and-gathering economies were so well adapted to the local environment that they successfully resisted introduction of food production.

The recent discovery of possibly domestic barley and wheat, together with numerous grinding stones, associated with Late Paleolithic sites along the Nile at Wadi Kubbaniya and dating between 18,300 and 17,000 B.P. (but see p. 101) (Wendorf et al., 1979; Stemler and Falk, 1980) suggests that the process of domestication may have occurred far earlier than had previously been estimated and that

the initial steps did not occur in the Levant, as most of us had believed, but may have taken place in northeast Africa. Furthermore, at Wadi Kubbaniya there is no indication of environmental or demographic stress as causative factors of this process. The harvest grains were simply added to the foods obtained by fishing, hunting, and collecting in the already established economic system.

Even if the wheat and barley from Wadi Kubbaniya are eventually determined to be wild rather than domestic, their presence is highly significant to later events in the Sahara, for they indicate that during the late Pleistocene the plant communities in which wild wheat and barley occur had been displaced far to the south into northeast Africa, and that the late Paleolithic populations in that area were utilizing these grains as important food resources. The area in which grain utilization was important could well have extended far to the south of Kubbaniya along the Nile Valley at least into central Sudan.

The evidence accumulated from the Western Desert for the period represented by the Wadi Kubbaniya sites shows that the entire high desert of Egypt was hyperarid and almost certainly drier than today. Along the Nile, this hyperarid climate is reflected in the accumulation of massive dunefields in the embayments and wadis along the west bank from Ballana in Egyptian Nubia (see Wendorf, 1968: 829) at least to Isna, where some of the dunes were initially interpreted as beach deposits (Wendorf and Schild, 1976a: 65). This long interval of hyperaridity is believed to date from before 30,000 years ago to around 10,000 B.P. (Butzer and Hansen, 1968: 327–333).

Slightly before 9000 B.P., large areas of the Western Desert opened for new human colonization for the first time in many thousands of years. The limited summer rains which began then sustained a semiarid environment with small ruminants and lagomorphs, as well as grasses and some trees, the latter particularly near basins which collected and held the moisture. The available data indicate that human expansion into these newly opened areas was almost immediate, and from the beginning, Terminal Paleolithic sites in the desert contain evidence of domestic cattle and numerous signs of some dependence on ground grain, although we do not as yet know whether it is wild or domestic. Although the extent of dependence on these sources of produced food cannot be determined, it seems clear that the first occupants came with preexistent knowledge and technology and were already adapted to this new environment, where a combination of grain-utilization, animal husbandry, and small-mammal hunting was perhaps the most efficient exploitative strategy.

One obvious conclusion that can be drawn from these observations is that the beginning of dependence on food production in the Sahara was during a period when the territory available for human use was rapidly expanding, not contracting as is postulated by the advocates of both the Oasis Theory and demographic-pressure hypotheses. It also seems obvious that pre-adaptation in the form of existing technology and knowledge was a necessary prerequisite for this expansion. Resemblances in tool typology, subsistence pattern, settlement location, raw material economy, and technology strongly suggest a continuity between the non-pottery, "Terminal Paleolithic" societies in the Western Desert and the "Neolithic" in the same area. It is not possible to state that the same ethnic groups are represented in each, even though strong stylistic similarities are evident, but all do fall within the same technocultural complex.

Although data concerning the social structuring of the Terminal Paleolithic are not adequate for comparison, the Neolithic appears to be more highly developed. The earliest Neolithic site, E-75-6, indicates large social groups apparently composed of several families which were presumably linked together by social or kinship ties. This in turn implies large production and a more efficient division of labor that may have transcended family units.

In summary, the data from the Western Desert indicate that the first Holocene settlers arrived there immediately after the area became habitable. They brought with them the basic knowledge and technology appropriate for this very specific, semiarid environment, where animal resources were scarce but quite large areas were suitable for growing grasses or grain. They also apparently brought with them domestic or semidomestic cattle. The point of origin of the Terminal Paleolithic migrants is not known; however, a northward movement from the southeastern margin of the Sahara is a

reasonable possibility. Unfortunately, nothing is known about that portion of the Sahara during this period.

The earliest "Neolithic" is seen as a more complex society, possibly with greater stress on food production and storage, certainly using domestic grains, and perhaps more sedentary, as could be suggested by the presence of pottery. It is not seen as a basic difference in kind but, rather, as an intensification of the previous economic pattern. Nor should the development of this particular "Neolithic" be seen as the result of one cause or as limited to one area. Instead, we see it as emerging over a very broad region where the environmental situation favored trends toward increased dependence on grain and domesticates. The development of the Saharan Neolithic should, in fact, be viewed in the context of the total area of the Levant, the Sinai, and the Nile Valley: this entire area shared an early dependence on ground grain, although its intensity varied from area to area and from time to time.

It is in this general context that the emergence of food production in the Western Desert must be viewed. There are still several features of this "Neolithic" that cannot be satisfactorily explained with the data at hand, among them the history of the domestication of cattle in Africa and the early appearance of well-made, highly decorated, and well-fired pottery undoubtedly reflecting a considerable history of development. These problems may need reexamination when data are available from the southern and southeastern fringes of the Sahara. Nevertheless, the apparently sudden appearance of food production in the Sahara is no longer a mystery: we can see it as part of an adaptive process in which societies reacted swiftly to the changed environment and opening opportunities, and this reaction would not have been possible had not the basic technology already been available. This view of the prehistoric societies of northeastern Africa as complex adaptive systems successfully reacting to climatic and physiographic changes provides a better perspective for understanding prehistoric changes than do simplistic, single-cause, demographic explanations. It is also in closer accord with basic biological theory concerning colonization and adjustment in non-human societies (cf. Simon, 1969; Terell, 1977; J. M. Diamond, 1977).

Addendum

Since this article was written new information has become available which indicates that the cereals found at Wadi Kubbaniya were not associated with the Late Paleolithic occupation. This new evidence is derived from several sources, but the most critical is a series of new radiocarbon age determinations made directly on the cereal grains, using the recently developed tandem accelerator mass spectrometer at the University of Arizona at Tucson. The dated samples included six seeds of barley (one seed from each of the two clusters of barley at Site E-78-3, three of the four seeds found in the hearth in 1978 at Site E-78-4, and one seed found on the same buried floor at that site but a few meters away) and three samples of charcoal (one piece from near the cereals at Site E-78-3 and two pieces from the buried floor where the cereals were found at Site E-78-4). The charcoal samples all dated within one standard error of the other dates obtained by normal radiocarbon techniques for those horizons between 17,450 and 19,060 B.P. The cereal seeds, however, yielded much younger dates. The two seeds from Site E-78-3 dated 820 B.P. $\pm$ 500 years (AA98) and 1090 B.P. $\pm$ 500 years (AA97), while those from the buried hearth at Site E-78-4 dated 2670 B.P. $\pm$ 250 years (AA225), 133 percent $\pm$ 5 percent modern (AA227), and 239% $\pm$ 5% modern (AA226), and the isolated seed from that site dated 4850 B.P. $\pm$ 200 years (AA228).

It is very improbable that cereals of these various ages should occur together in an otherwise pure Late Paleolithic hearth, and the two post-modern readings are unusually high even for post-bomb materials. We therefore suspected that the cereals had become contaminated by carbon-14 tracers during study, and we specifically suspected the coating and the silver print paint used for SEM mounts. Our suspicions were confirmed when scrapings of the silver paint from the mounts were found to have a carbon-14 content of approximately 4,000 percent of modern.

The only seed that had not been in the laboratory where the carbon-14 tracers contamination presumably occurred and that had not been given SEM treatment was the single specimen which dated 4850 B.P. (AA228). This is probably the true age of the Kubbaniya cereals.

There are other indications that the Kubbaniya cereals were not as old as we had thought. The first such evidence came when several barley seeds from Site E-78-3 were analyzed by electron spin resonance spectroscopy to determine the maximal temperature to which they had been subjected. To survive the millennia of seasonal flooding, the seeds would have had to be somewhat charred before burial, and we were therefore surprised to learn that they have never reached a temperature above 150°C.

Shortly afterward, a large series of soil samples were examined for phytoliths. Phytoliths were present, in large quantities in some samples, but none could be positively identified as those of cereals. While this result did not prove that cereals were not grown at Kubbaniya, it made it very unlikely that they were.

Finally, we expended particular effort in the 1983 season on the recovery of plant remains, especially from Site E-78-3 and E-78-4, the two localities where cereals were found in 1978 and 1981. Extensive areas of both sites were excavated and numerous charred plant remains were recovered, from depths as great as 3.5 m below the surface. However, all the remains that could be identified were of native plants that grow in the Nile Valley today, either wild or cultivated. There were no more cereals.

Thus, all the evidence seems to converge toward the conclusion that the cereals were not associated with the Late Paleolithic occupation at Wadi Kubbaniya. Instead, the economy seems to have been one of gathering, fishing, and hunting. We cannot as yet define the structure of the economy more precisely, but so many identifiable remains of plant foods have now been recovered, in addition to the faunal remains long known from the sites, that we are confident that when the laboratory analyses are complete, Wadi Kubbaniya will still provide one of the most complete and detailed pictures from anywhere of life-ways in the Late Paleolithic.

FRED WENDORF

10

Long-Term Nile Flood Variation and Political Discontinuities in Pharaonic Egypt

KARL W. BUTZER

Egypt provides a unique physical, archaeological, and historical record of environment, technology, land use, settlement, and economic history. In effect, the Nile constitutes an oasis corridor through a thinly inhabited desert, providing a test-tube case for a society circumscribed by its environment and relatively isolated from external turmoil. Egyptian livelihood was closely linked to the waters of the river, further limiting the number of potential variables. Egyptian culture—defined by language, religion, and national consciousness—spanned some four thousand years, from late prehistoric well into Roman times. This gives an unusual time depth in which to evaluate ecological adjustments and response on various scales.

Subsistence-settlement systems of complex societies such as that of Pharaonic Egypt are in constant readjustment. They are also repeatedly modified and even transformed in response to external and internal variables. Endogenic factors in the case of Egypt include demographic trends, urbani-

This paper profited sustantially from discussion with Klaus Baer, George Cowgill, and Cynthia Bates.

zation, social and economic stratification, agricultural intensification, and spontaneous as well as governmental expansion of agriculture into marginal environments (Butzer, 1976). Exogenic factors include human variables such as repeated invasions or sustained immigration by various peoples from the Western Desert, Nubia, or western Asia and from the open Mediterranean Sea; they also include the financial and cultural impacts of the New Kingdom imperium in Asia. Epidemics related to human or environmental factors are suggested by indirect evidence, e.g., the catastrophic plague introduced to Anatolia by Egyptian prisoners of war ca. 1325 B.C. (Aldred, 1975), as well as by allegorical references in Exodus. Last but not least, pressures were exerted at the core of the human ecosystem by forces from the non-human environment, primarily reflecting climatic variability within the monsoonal rainfall belt of eastern Africa (Butzer, 1979, 1980b). The critical continuing adjustments of the agricultural system to the vicissitudes of the Nile constitute the most fundamental and most dynamic aspect of Egyptian adaptation.

In an earlier monograph this writer (1976) emphasized the continuities in Egyptian hydraulic agriculture. The present paper focuses on the discontinuities, namely, flood variation and the vulnerability of Egyptian irrigation agriculture in Pharaonic times. The potential role of environmental stress in the historical discontinuities of Egypt is outlined, but the equally important social and political processes that marked these times of turmoil can only be hinted at in a brief paper such as this. It therefore bears emphasis that the present purpose is to explore the potential co-agency of environmental variables in the historical ensemble. There are two reasons for emphasizing an ecological perspective. First, the rich corpus of historical information from Egypt has yet to be critically reviewed from such a vantage point. A number of Egyptologists tend to regard their primary source literature as metaphorical; the only "real" events were politicomilitary, and even these are considered suspect unless they are corroborated in Asiatic archives or archaeology. Second, the Egyptian case provides an unusual opportunity for examining the

role of economic limiting conditions in a complex human ecosystem.

Pharaoh and the Nile Floods

To the ancient Egyptians the Nile represented the source of life, the cosmic order, and creation itself. The annual flood reenacted creation, with the Primeval Hill rising above the receding primordial waters. The first dry land emerging from the inundation promised fresh life in the new agricultural year (J. A. Wilson, 1946). The cosmic order was identified with the cyclic, repetitive nature of events, e.g., the Nile and solar and lunar cycles. Osiris came to personify this fundamental concept of rebirth, growth, and death. The Pharaoh, by extension, was believed to cause the life-giving waters that brought fertility to Egypt and guaranteed the seasons (Frankfort, 1948: 52; Goedicke, 1960).

Pharaoh was depicted as the single representative of the entire community and sometimes described as the shepherd of his people. He was both god and man, the sole source of authority, yet Egypt was not an effectively authoritarian state. From at least the Thirteenth Dynasty (1784–1668 B.C.),[1] a vizier was responsible for actual administration, but the detailed implementation of central authority is not clear (Helck, 1954: 134ff.; 1975c). In earliest times, such direct administration may have been restricted to the royal properties scattered throughout the country (Helck, 1975a) and to such aspects as external defense and religious cult. As late as Ninetjer (ca. 2928–2884 B.C.), tribute appears to have been collected directly during periodic royal visitations to the provinces, and a complex system of taxation first began under Snefru (see Helck, 1975b). By the Sixth Dynasty (ca.

---

1. The chronology used in this paper is based on an evaluation of the radiocarbon dates (see Long, 1976, calibrated with reference to Damon et al., 1974) for the First and Second Dynasties (ca. 3170–2760 B.C.), K. Baer (n.d.) for the Old and Middle Kingdoms, and Wente and Van Siclen (1977) for the New Kingdom.

2405–2255 B.C.), the central administration appointed agents responsible for local or regional supervision of specific tasks or functions (Martin-Pardey, 1976), but such individuals served as intermediaries between the capital and the local communities rather than as components of a fully integrated bureaucratic hierarchy administering all phases of national activity.

Next to nothing is known about the emergence of artificial irrigation during late prehistoric times. The first document is the ceremonial breaching of the canal by the prehistoric Scorpion King (Butzer, 1976: 20–21), probably dating ca. 3200 B.C. Somewhat later, instances of royal canal-digging as well as tax exemption of a complex, if local, irrigation network are recorded in several Sixth Dynasty texts (Dunham, 1938; Goedicke, 1967: 72; Butzer, 1976: 45–47; Endesfelder, 1979), and an elaborate Fourth Dynasty (ca. 2680–2545 B.C.) masonry dam is preserved in one desert valley (G. W. Murray, 1947).

Flood basins would have operated as autonomous units, since they were impossible to interlink without highly elaborate technology and since, by drawing water directly from the Nile, they were unaffected by patterns of water-use upstream (see Butzer, 1976: 42–43). No regular or national appointment for irrigation and no related bureaucracy can be inferred from among almost 2,000 titles of the Old Kingdom (ca. 2760–2225 B.C.) (see K. Baer, 1960). The early record of canal-digging therefore suggests government support for expansion of artificial irrigation rather than an attempt to centralize irrigation administration; as late as 2000 B.C., the Hekanakht letters suggest that half of the valley floodplain was still traditionally used as unimproved pasture or fallow (K. Baer, 1963).

Irrigation of natural or artificial flood basins continued to be organized at the local level during the First Intermediate Period (ca. 2225–2035 B.C.), when provincial governors were first on record to cut several canals (Schenkel, 1965, 1978; Endesfelder, 1979). Middle Kingdom (2035–1668 B.C.) viziers were responsible for delegating orders for canal-digging nationwide (Endesfelder, 1979; Helck, 1975c), and during the New Kingdom (1570–1070 B.C.) new projects and possibly also maintenance were at times entrusted to ad hoc

royal appointees, although irrigation management was a local matter, judging by the handful of exclusively low-echelon officeholders on record (Endesfelder, 1979). Even so, Papyrus Wilbour (ca. 1141 B.C.) suggests that large segments of Middle Egypt were used preeminently for pastoral activities (O'Connor, 1972), implying that the irrigation network was still incomplete (Butzer, 1976: 102–103).

Competition for water was never an issue in free-flooding alluvial basins (Butzer, 1976: 109), which obviated the need for meticulous governmental regulation. Except for "new lands" in the Faiyum, the Delta, and Middle Egypt, there is no evidence of a governmental farm policy keeping the rural sector gainfully employed or distributing land, seed, and tools. Instead, community affairs, including irrigation and flood control, continued to be organized at the grassroots level by *corvée* (forced labor) under the direction of village headmen, who owed their prestige to merit as much as to wealth and who acted as first among equals. This situation persisted well into the nineteenth century A.D. (see Willcocks, 1904: 71; G. Baer, 1969: chap. 2). Government seems to have been primarily interested in agriculture as a tax base—i.e., as an end-product—contributing little to its direct organization or maintenance. Agricultural productivity, although influenced by public order and security and responsive to new technologies, was primarily a response to the Nile floods. The health of the overall economic system, overwhelmingly dependent on agriculture, was consequently controlled as much by environmental as by human variables. Ultimately, the central government was weak when the national economy was weak, although a weak government could equally well lead to a weak economy.

Limitations to Traditional Irrigation Agriculture

Spatially, the ancient Egyptians viewed their land as a flat plain of fertile alluvial soil (Black Land), sharply demarcated from a rim of mountainous desert (Red Land) inhabited by foreign peoples. Equally important was the differential productivity due to a relief variation of 1 to 3 m within the

alluvial lands (Butzer, 1976: 15–18). (1) High
levee topography along river banks provided good
settlement sites but less fertile soils which could
generally be cultivated only with lift irrigation. Tree
crops and vegetable gardens were located here. (2)
Higher parts of flood basins, next to the levees,
experienced deficient water during low flood years
and may not have been planted regularly. (3) Intermediate sectors of flood basins had both adequate
water and drainage and a rich annual increment of
fresh silt. These were the prime areas for cultivation of the single annual crop of barley, emmer
wheat, beans, chickpeas, and other vegetables
(Darby et al., 1977). (4) The lowest parts of flood
basins had excessive water during good flood years,
probably experienced long periods of fallow, and
were primarily used for seasonal pasture. (5)
Floodplain backswamps, cut-off channels, and
delta-fringe marshland were all permanently water-
logged and used for fowling and grazing. Finally,
(6) the Nile channel and its distributaries were rich
in fish and waterfowl, the former providing the major source of animal protein for the common
people.

Egyptian cultivation was implemented by
wooden hoe or plow and flint or metal-tipped
adzes. Seeds were broadcast on freshly turned soil
that was broken down with hoes and wooden mal-
lets; the seeds were then trampled into the soil by
herds of driven animals.

When the natural system of irrigation was replaced by artificial basin irrigation (Butzer, 1976:
18–20), the major difference was deliberate control
of water ingress and egress from the flood basins by
means of short canals and temporary cuts (or mud-
brick gates: see Schenkel, 1965: 71), by strengthening natural riverbank levees to form longitudinal
dikes and, eventually, by subdivision of natural basins by transverse dikes. Lift irrigation (see Butzer,
1976: 41–51) was initially limited to horticulture
by manual lifting of water, sometimes aided by
shoulder yokes with two suspended buckets. The
pole-and-lever device (*shaduf*) is first verified in
Mesopotamia on an Akkadian cylinder seal (Salonen, 1968: pl. IV.4), ca. 2370–2200 B.C. It was only
introduced to Egypt after 1500 B.C., and subsequently aided small-scale irrigation from wells or
watercourses during low water. The waterwheel

(*saqiya*), essential for large-scale and continuous-
lift irrigation, was also of Mesopotamian origin and
unknown in Egypt prior to 300 B.C. Pharaonic irrigation was then little more than a controlled version of natural basin irrigation, whereby mediocre
floods could be extended somewhat and exceptionally high floods restrained slightly. There was no
opportunity for more than one crop in the course
of the normal rhythm of the flood season.

The traditional annual cycle included three
main components: (1) Flood season or "autumn"
(beginning early August in the south, terminating
mid-November in the north), with inundation of
basins by a variable water depth averaging 1.5 m in
the fields for a duration of 6 to 10 weeks (Willcocks and Craig, 1913: 305–306); (2) Post-Flood
season or "winter" (mid-November to mid-
March), with high soil moisture and high water-
table, mild temperatures, and low evaporation,
ideal for sowing and growing of crops; (3) Pre-
Flood season or "summer" (mid-March to mid-
August), with dry soils, low water-levels, high temperatures, and periodic desiccating winds, so that
any cultivation would require lift irrigation—traditionally limited to small garden plots—with extensive grazing elsewhere.

The flood cycle was characterized by short-
term variability, i.e., year-to-year fluctuations in
flood-crest elevation and flood duration. Low or
short floods reduced the wetted area, the degree of
soil saturation, and the amount of fertile silt deposited, but increased the salt concentration of waters
reaching fields along the desert margins (Butzer,
1976: 52–54). This all reduced cultivated acreage
as well as unit productivity. The flood crest of A.D.
1877 was 2 m below average and precluded cultivation of 35 percent of the valley alluvium (see Willcocks and Craig, 1913: table 176). Unusually high
or persistent floods favored plant parasites in the
soil, while the waterlogging retarded planting, with
the harvest delayed into the parching Pre-Flood
season (Willcocks and Craig, 1913: 304). Exceptionally high floods could raze settlements, favor
epidemic disease, destroy food stores and livestock,
endanger seed stocks, and sweep away major transverse dikes (see Willcocks, 1904: 71; Ball, 1939:
231–232) that had required at least one and
often several years to construct. Overall variability

created significant year-to-year fluctuations of food supply, despite the general predictability and reliability of Nile floods.

Increased recurrence of exceptionally low or high floods (or both), from several times a century to several times a decade, could have had great impact on traditional irrigation agriculture. Long-term trends, over several generations, to overall lower or higher flood levels probably had equally important repercussions, eventually favoring geomorphic readjustments. Lower floods may eventually have favored channel incision and a floodplain of reduced size, with a lower water-table and receiving less nitrogen-rich silt; parts of the floodplain would have been incultivable, and salinization as well as dune invasion could have affected outlying areas. A systematic increase in flood height would have expanded the inundated realm and augmented fertility, but irrigation maintenance would have been more difficult, due to frequent levee-breaching and rapid siltation of canals.

The historical flood records from Egypt and geomorphic data from the upper Nile basin verify repeated changes in flood levels, in terms both of net trends and recurrence intervals (see Butzer, 1976: 27–33, 51–54). Although periodic channel incision is difficult to prove without elaborate field-work, episodes of reduced channel sinuosity are apparent in the surviving floodplain topography and, together with the tantalizingly incomplete record of rapid sediment changes from well profiles (Butzer, 1976: 15–16; Attia, 1954), suggest intervals of incision during the historical era. At the same time, various Nilometers between Aswan and the Delta refer to two successive datum levels that, in conjunction with flood reports from different periods, show an overall building-up of the Nile floodplain since the First Dynasty (Jaritz and Bietak, 1977).

Evidence for Long-Term Variation 3000 to 1000 B.C

ANOMALY I

Throughout the southern Sahara and the upper Nile drainage, hydrological trends were negative early during the third millennium, with a period of relatively moist conditions terminating 2850 ± 100 B.C. (calibrated after Damon et al., 1974; for data, see Butzer, 1976: 30–33; 1979; 1980a; 1980b). In Egypt, sixty-three annual records of Nile flood-levels are available between 3000 and 2500 B.C., and they show a net 1 m decline of flood level between the late First and mid-Second Dynasties, i.e., ca. 3000–2900 B.C. (see B. Bell, 1970; Helck, 1966). In terms of nineteenth-century criteria, 1 m implies a thirty percent reduction in discharge, comparable to the deviation of 1877, the lowest flood-year in the period A.D. 1869–1903, from that thirty-five-year mean. Year 14 of Ninetjer (ca. 2913 B.C.) experienced one of the lowest floods ever. These points require no elaboration.

ANOMALY II

Sub-Saharan lake levels remained very low until 1950 ± 50 B.C. Old Kingdom records indicate a leveling-off of the flood decline between 2900 and 2500 B.C. (B. Bell, 1970), after which we unfortunately lack information. There is no contemporary physical evidence available from Egypt proper, but a major advance of desert dunes into the western floodplain of Middle Egypt appears to have begun during this general time-range (Butzer, 1959b). Consequently, precision on Anomaly II must be derived from historical sources.

A seven-year span of low Niles is alleged for the reign of Djoser (culminating in Year 18, ca. 2720 B.C.) by the so-called Famine Stela, a Ptolemaic work based on an Old Kingdom original, probably "edited" for political purposes (Wildung, 1969: 85–91). Equally suggestive but difficult to evaluate is the sizable body of First Intermediate Period texts that record famines related to low Niles (Vandier, 1936; Schenkel, 1965; 1978: 29–51; B. Bell, 1971; Saffirio, 1975; Guglielmi, 1977). These date between the times of the Upper Egyptian governor Ankhtifi (ca. 2210–2185 B.C.) and those of the Middle Egyptian governor Ameni (ca. 1925–1895 B.C.) (K. Baer, n.d.).

The events chronicled for Ankhtifi are place- and incident-specific and consequently inspire considerable confidence. Self-congratulatory texts about feeding the hungry do appear in the earlier, royal Pyramid Texts, also once in direct reference to catastrophic famine and Nile failure ("hunger on this sand bank of Apophis [= the underworld serpent]": see Schenkel, 1965: 54), and allusions to dust storms. As B. Bell (1971) argues, this association leaves no doubt as to the intended meaning. But it is no simple copy, because a specific event is described ("all Upper Egypt was dying of hunger": Schenkel, 1965: 54) and related to cannibalism ("everyone ate his children one after the other": ibid.), an outrageous situation for Egyptian sensitivities, although patently exaggerated, and the first document of its kind. The Ankhtifi inscriptions can be faulted in terms of details of authenticity and trustworthiness but, by comparison with other ancient Near Eastern documents, their basic content is unambiguous, specific, and acceptable as a record of catastrophic Nile failure.

The second source on Nile failures is the unquestionably authentic collection of private letters by Hekanakht dating from 2002 B.C. (K. Baer, 1963). Writing to his family from one of his estates, the author describes the impact of an ongoing nationwide famine due to poor Nile flooding and his own efforts to conserve food by doling out half-rations, and notes that "they have begun to eat people here" (ibid.: 27–28).

The same confidence cannot be applied to other biographical famine inscriptions, which are highly conventional and generally date between Ankhtifi and Hekanakht. Whether or not the historicity of these other documents is accepted, an unbiased reader must be impressed by the lingering image of sociopolitical trauma illustrated in several composite or derivative works of substantially later date, each of which implies direct links between environmental and social disasters. These include the Admonitions of Ipuwer and the Prophecies of Neferti (see Fecht, 1972; Simpson, 1973; Spiegel, 1975; and Butzer, 1976: 54; contra Lichtheim, 1973: 10). The latter is a political tract dating from the accession of Amenemhet I, 1991 B.C. Previous trauma is clearly expressed by

> I will speak of what is before my eyes. . . . The river of Egypt is dry and men cross the water on foot; men will seek water for ships in order

to navigate [the river], for . . . the place of water has become a riverbank. (Simpson, 1973: 236–237)

In the present writer's view, these historical documents make a reasonable case for at least two episodes of catastrophic Nile failure ca. 2200 and 2002 B.C.

ANOMALY III

Wet conditions were abruptly reestablished in East Africa ca. 1970 B.C. Lake Rudolf was soon 75 m deeper and overflowed into the Nile system (Butzer, 1980b) and the White Nile was 2–3 m higher than at present, with a discharge 10 times greater than now (L. Berry, 1960; Williams and Adamson, 1974). In the cataracts of Sudanese Nubia there are at least twenty-seven inscriptions dating 1840–1770 B.C. that record floods 8–11 m higher than those of the present (B. Bell, 1975). These imply flood volumes three or four times greater than the maximum floods since A.D. 1869 and probably resulted in crests 2–4 m higher than normal in the northern Nile Valley, i.e., at least twice the basin-water depth of a normal year and probably comparable to the catastrophic floods of A.D. 1818–1819. Such an erratic, "wild" Nile in Egypt, with a recurrence interval of about one year in three, is not entirely unprecedented; it occurred over several centuries ca. 12,000 years ago (Butzer, 1980a). Whether catastrophically high Nile floods were common after 1770 B.C. is unknown, but an unusually high inundation is recorded ca. 1695 B.C. (Habachi, 1974).

ANOMALY IV

Lake levels fell dramatically in East Africa ca. 1260 ± 50 B.C. In Nubia, agriculture ceased almost entirely after the end of the reign of Ramesses II (i.e., after 1212 B.C.) (Trigger, 1965: 112–114). At Aksha, where floods were 1 m higher than today during Ramesses II's time, dunes spread over the floodplain and the lack of flooding allowed thick salt efflorescences to build up; cultivation only resumed ca. 300 B.C. (Heinzelin, 1964). In the Delta, discharge along the peripheral Pelusiac Nile distributary declined so much that the Ramessid residence of Avaris (Pi-Ramesse) was abandoned in favor of Tanis, on the Tanitic branch, shortly after 1200 B.C. (Bietak, 1975: 99–109). Here, once again, the physical and archaeological evidence is unequivocal, finding further support in the historical evidence discussed below.

Political Discontinuities and Nile Variation

The political history of Egypt is organized in several cycles: the Old Kingdom (ca. 2760–2225 B.C.), the Middle Kingdom (2035–1668 B.C.) and the New Kingdom (1570–1070 B.C.). Each apexed in an episode of strong central government, followed by a long period of decline. The First Dynasty, ca. 3170–2970 B.C., represents another such culmination point of a less clearly delineated protohistoric development. It appears that each phase of political devolution was accompanied by economic deterioration and at least temporary demographic setbacks. Political and economic decline coincided temporarily with long-term negative Nile behavior.

The four periods of decline are: (1) the Second Dynasty (ca. 2970–2760 B.C.), coincident with Anomaly I; (2) the Seventh and Eighth dynasties and the First Intermediate Period (ca. 2250–2035 B.C.), coincident with Anomaly II; (3) the Thirteenth Dynasty and Second Intermediate Period (1784–1560 B.C.), following Anomaly III; and (4) the Twentieth Dynasty, following the food riots of 1153 B.C. and the assassination of Ramesses III in 1151 B.C., coincident with Anomaly IV. Some aspects of each of these episodes suggest potential socioeconomic repercussions to environmental stress.

ANOMALY I

The Second Dynasty was a time of impoverishment and political confusion. The archaeological record remains ambiguous as long as the possibility exists that some Second Dynasty tombs are unidentified or undiscovered. Nonetheless, trade communications with the Near East were significantly reduced during this period and few examples of Palestinian import wares are known (Kantor, 1965). By comparison, the wealthy First Dynasty Pharaohs had magazines filled with import goods, and the resumption of international trade at the very end of the Second Dynasty is conspicuous in the archaeological record. The indisputable dynastic confusion during the Second Dynasty appears to have been heralded by a civil war during Year 13 of Ninetjer (Emery, 1961: 93). The sequence and number of the next six or so kings (Weneg, Sened, Nubnefer, Neferkasokar, Peribsen, Sekhemib) are uncertain, over a timespan of at least 43 and as much as 148 years (K. Baer, n.d.; Helck, 1956, 1974), with the calibrated radiocarbon dates (Long, 1976; see Damon et al., 1974) strongly favoring the higher figure. Records of all kinds are very scarce (Kaplony, 1965) and, significantly, no tombs are known from these kings except for the last, Sekhemib, whose burial place was not in Saqqara, Lower Egypt, but Abydos, Upper Egypt. The final ruler of the Second Dynasty, Khasekhemwy (ca. 2787–2760 B.C.), had his power base in the far south and carried only the Upper Egyptian crown on his accession (K. Baer, n.d.). The dynasty barely survived, threatened by revolt or invasion in the north, until Khasekhemwy eventually conquered his opponents in a major campaign (Kaplony, 1975; Piccione, n.d.). Persistent civil unrest or, alternatively, flimsy construction and impoverishment are implicated in the unusual circumstances that the tombs of only four of some nine or ten Second Dynasty Pharaohs have been identified (or are identifiable) so far. Finally, it may be material that, as a general index of living conditions, mean life expectancy dropped from 36 years in late prehistoric times, when Nile floods were ample, to 30 years during historical times (Masali and Chiarelli, 1972), when overall floodplain ecology was readjusted to more modest floods and population pressure was substantially greater.

ANOMALY II

Central authority markedly declined during the Sixth Dynasty, with a futile attempt to reassert this authority midway in the reign of Pepi II (ca. 2350–2260 B.C.) (K. Baer, 1960), after whose death the Old Kingdom disintegrated into regional principalities (O'Connor, 1974). An overall reduction in the size and opulence of funerary architecture, in the capital and in the provinces and among low- as well as high-echelon officials (Kanawati, 1977), documents a progressive and general economic decline during the later Sixth Dynasty. The ensuing lamentations of the First Intermediate Period causally link drought, starvation, anarchy, and political impotence. Food stores were plundered, the estates of the rich were dispossessed, and hordes of starving people roamed the countryside, threatening the foundations of the social order. The traditional Egyptian perception of the revolutionary trends of this era (Spiegel, 1975) is expressed in the admonitions of Ipuwer:

> Indeed, noblemen are in distress, while the poor man is full of joy. Every town says: "Let us suppress the powerful among us." . . . The children of princes are dashed against walls. . . . Public offices are opened and their inventories are taken away. . . . The laws of the council chamber are thrown out; indeed, men walk on them in the public places. . . . The King has been deposed by the rabble. . . . The King's storehouse is the common property of everyone, and the entire palace is without its revenues. (Simpson, 1973: 212–223)

Other textual elaborations of famine, abandoned farm lands, and dislocated people serve to illustrate the degree to which the agricultural system had lost its capacity to sustain previous levels of productivity, resulting in a mutual sharing of increased poverty. Food redistribution in times of need, as well as restoration of agricultural productivity, became key political virtues, and Ankhtifi prided himself on being the first ruler to distribute famine supplies (Schenkel, 1965: 54). The Old Kingdom temples did not store grain supplies for possible redistribution (Posener-Kriéger and Cenival, 1968), and during the famine years the governor Djehuti (ca. 2100 B.C.) was even obliged to find food to supply the temple of Amun in Thebes (Vandier, 1936: 109). In view of the national economic shortcomings apparent during the First In-

termediate Period, it seems logical that the Twelfth Dynasty kings (1991–1784 B.C.) should have begun systematic development of the Faiyum, the first example of direct government involvement in the improvement of marginal or underutilized lands (Butzer, 1976: 36–38, 92–93; Arnold, 1977).

ANOMALY III

The last kings of Dynasty Twelve were weak, and the Thirteenth Dynasty Pharaohs (1784–1668 B.C.) reigned an average of only two years each; apparently a dynasty of viziers held real control, judging by the record of over sixty-five kings and only seven viziers (K. Baer, n.d.). The steady erosion of royal power may have resulted from a disastrous economy, although the records are mute except for one curious lamentation (Kadish, 1973). By about 1720—well before the Hyksos invasion of 1668 B.C.—national unity was being threatened by petty principalities in the Delta. The decline of the Middle Kingdom remains one of the most obscure aspects of Egyptian history, so that the potential significance of the aberrant flood record can be no more than conjectural.

ANOMALY IV

The increasing political impotence of the Twentieth Dynasty is closely linked to economic stress. The Pharaoh Merneptah was still able to provide the Hittites with grain during the famine of 1210 B.C. (Faulkner, 1975), but in his sixth year, 1176 B.C., Ramesses III found it appropriate to make offerings to the Nile at Gebel Silsila, to propitiate the river and seek good floods (Stern, 1873). In 1153 the food supply failed and the workmen of Deir el-Medina rioted; the best efforts of Ramesses III's vizier to meet the crisis turned up only a bare half of the wheat needed (Faulkner, 1975). Grain prices, with respect to non-food products, had increased rapidly after 1170 B.C., to eight times and occasionally twenty-four times the standard price; the highest inflation occurred about 1130 B.C., followed by stabilization ca. 1110 B.C. and a rapid drop in food prices 1100–1070 B.C.

(Černý, 1933; Janssen, 1975: 550–558). Evidently, wheat and barley, as well as vegetable oil, were in very short supply, in response to mediocre or poor Nile floods, and the temple granaries, so important since the fifteenth century B.C. (N. de G. Davies, 1929; Butzer, 1976: 88), were applied to private gain rather than community redistribution. A succession of trials of prominent and less prominent tomb-robbers spans the period from 1154 to after 1107 B.C., reflecting on government corruption but probably also on economic hardship. The cemeteries indicate widespread impoverishment and, possibly, a declining population (B. J. Kemp, pers. comm.). Royal power withered away until, at the end of the Twentieth Dynasty (1184–1070 B.C.), the priesthood disenfranchised Pharaoh as the provider of life and safeguard of the cosmic order, declaring him a simple agent of the supreme god Amun (Černý, 1975). It is tempting to interpret this change as a reflection of Pharaoh's failure to guarantee nature and thus the livelihood of Egypt.

These potential interrelationships between long-term environmental stress and political instability range from possible to probable, and at the very least, in all instances, the co-agency of other endogenic or exogenic forces is also part of the equation. The broader context for each anomaly can now be outlined.

ANOMALY I

Quarrels about the dynastic succession are already evident during the later First Dynasty and may have been a prelude to a long era of civil strife, possibly abetted by Libyans from outside the Nile ecosystem. The power of the late Predynastic and First Dynasty rulers appears to have increased fairly steadily until the death of Dewen (ca. 3025 B.C.), who had created a rudimentary bureaucracy. But almost 250 years of devolution followed before Khasekhemwy (ca. 2775 B.C.) was able to reunite the faltering nation. Sectionalism and an inadequate administrative structure may have been primarily at fault but do not explain the probable impoverishment of the country and limited Asiatic trade even before the possible revolt of Lower

Egypt after the death of Ninetjer (ca. 2874 B.C.). It is therefore plausible that recurrent poor floods or Nile failures weakened the economy and created a periodic stress of disastrous proportions.

ANOMALY II

The Old Kingdom was in political and economic ascendancy from Khasekhemwy to the death of Cheops (ca. 2578 B.C.), and a strong, functional bureaucracy was created. But perpetual mortuary endowments were set up on an increasingly large scale, withdrawing prime agricultural lands and their produce from the revenue base to support tax-free mortuary cults (Helck, 1954). During the Fifth Dynasty (ca. 2545–2405 B.C.), the larger temples emerged as strong competitors for power, while during the mid-Sixth Dynasty the burgeoning aristocracy and upper-level bureaucracy acquired great wealth and, in part, began to create local power bases in the provinces. Thus more than two centuries of devolution preceded the political confusion that followed the death of Pepi II (ca. 2260 B.C.), which implies that Old Kingdom Egypt was hopelessly inefficient and in drastic need of socio-political reform. Political fragmentation preceded any Nile-related disasters, although these may have triggered the social unrest that ultimately led to a reassessment of traditional values. Here, again, one could argue that the case for the co-agency of environmental stress is plausible but not evidently necessary to explain the course of events.

ANOMALY III

Political ascendancy is evident with the reunification of Egypt in 2035 B.C.—despite further Nile calamities. During the Second Intermediate Period, foreign invaders, the Hyksos, took control of the Delta in 1668 B.C., but competing principalities had been set up thirty years earlier and political devolution was already apparent by the death of Amenemhet III (1794 B.C.). Why the Middle Kingdom collapsed is quite enigmatic, and recurrent, excessive high floods provide no more than a possible economic scenario.

ANOMALY IV

A new period of ascendancy began with the accession of Kamose in 1576 B.C., and major socioeconomic problems such as the growing wealth and power of the temple of Amun are patently obvious during Amenhotep III's superficially prosperous reign (1386–1349 B.C.). Ramesses II (1279–1212 B.C.) was able to delay devolution, but the real power of the Pharaoh was shrinking rapidly and corruption was rampant by the time of his death. Then, desperate struggles with major foreign invasions from land and sea shook Egypt to its roots in 1207 and 1177–1171 B.C., leading to the loss of the Asiatic empire and its monetary tribute. By the end of the century, Libyan marauders were terrorizing the countryside almost at will (Černý, 1975), while overtaxation exacerbated rural depopulation (Caminos, 1954: 389–395; 1977: 62–63, 78).

These circumstances would be adequate to explain the demise of the New Kingdom, but the significance of economic processes in the twelfth-century B.C. decline of Egypt is equally unassailable. The workers' strikes and food riots (at least six major incidents are recorded between 1153 and 1105 B.C.) are inescapably linked to the wild inflation of food prices coincident with the major, negative readjustment of Nile hydrology that forced the abandonment of the Nubian floodplain. Significantly, the loss of fiscal wealth after the destruction of Egypt's Asiatic empire in the 1170s should have led to a money, not food, shortage, and the desert gold-mines were subsequently abandoned long before they were exhausted, later kings restoring their productivity (see Gundlach, 1977a, 1977b). Furthermore, there is no correlation between the food-price spiral and either the episodes of civil war (ca. 1139 and 1089 B.C.) or the rural insecurity resulting from the Libyan infiltration after 1117 B.C. (see Černý, 1975). It is consequently highly probable that ecological stress and resulting economic deterioration were heavily implicated in the end of the New Kingdom, but as only one of several factors.

This final, lightly documented overview suggests that the major cyclic crises of Egyptian history cannot be fully explained by politically generated agrarian cycles of the type first postulated by Wittfogel (1938). Instead, one of the most consistent links in Egyptian historical trends is among water, agricultural productivity, and politicoeconomic strength. By the standards of Mesopotamian flood unpredictability or of rainfall unpredictability in many dry-farming regions of the Mediterranean Basin and southeastern Europe, Nilotic agriculture was reliable. But the simple winter-crop routine, the lack of effective lift-irrigation, and the sum of the historical insights show that this ecosystem was nonetheless fragile. It therefore becomes probable that aperiodic variability of the Nile floods had significant material consequences.

Stability and Change

The economic history of Egypt was closely dependent on the Nile and its behavior. Egypt was, after all, the gift of the river, and the river was for the cosmic order to control. Within the confined environment of a riverine oasis guaranteed by an exotic river and relatively isolated from foreign invaders, Egyptian culture evolved with unprecedented self-sufficiency and disdain for revolutionary change. Continuity and harmony—with the past, with the cosmic forces, and with the cyclic natural order—were keystones of Egyptian society. But this apparent stability was more a dynamic equilibrium in which a multitude of short- and long-term adjustments in extractive tasks and exchange patterns were made without substantially changing the basic configurations of the adaptation. Ultimately, only the spirit of the adaptation remained the same, since new domesticates, technologies, and ideas had been incorporated to create a far more complex and effective adaptive system (see Butzer, 1976: chap. 7).

Complex cultural systems are to some extent buffered from environmental variables by multiple "layers" of technology, social organization, and exchange networking. Their adaptive strategies emphasize stability—maintenance of a set of socioeconomic priorities, cultural norms, and value systems. However, interpreted in terms of their own cognitive universe, environmental catastrophes to the Ancient Egyptians or to most other complex societies were interruptions in the normal stream of events. But the system that shields both the society and the individual also suffers from an innate lack of pliancy. The instability threshold of complex cultural systems tends to be high in proportion to the number of negative-feedback mechanisms. This very multiplicity of components increases the probability of a chance concatenation of negative inputs. For example, the unexpected coincidence of poor leadership, external political stress, and environmental perturbation can trigger a catastrophic train of mutually reinforcing events which the system cannot absorb.

Viewed over a span of five millennia, Egypt, as well as Mesopotamia (see R. McC. Adams, 1978), exemplifies the inherent diachronic dynamism of an adaptive system characterized by a particular social and natural environment. The historical trajectory is marked by cyclic alternation between centuries when population and productivity increased, in apparent response to effective hierarchical control, and other centuries characterized by demographic decline and political devolution. Periodic minor and diverse crises were overcome by temporary structural shifts, whereas major crises led to reorganization of the political and economic superstructure, leaving intact the basic environmental and sociocultural components of the infrastructure. Consequently, although the social and political identities of these floodplains have repeatedly changed since the time of Old Kingdom Egypt and Sumer, the fundamental adaptive system survived in Egypt and Iraq well into the nineteenth century.

It appears, then, that elaborate cultural systems enjoy centuries of adaptive equilibrium—with or without sustained growth—followed by discontinuities. Such discontinuities have been downplayed in the organic or ontogenetic paradigms fashionable in historical and archaeological research (Butzer, 1980c), but such breaks may well be critical in understanding cultural systems. They appear to be marked by reevaluation of adaptive strategies, while the cultural system undergoes structural elaboration or changes among its fundamental components with or without a transformation of identity. In the long-range view, elaborate cultural systems are dynamic rather than stable, since structural changes are repeatedly required to ensure viability or even survival. Such systems have far too many variables for their trajectories to be predicted by a deterministic equation. On the other hand, such a plethora of interlinked variables can lead to processes and events that are to some degree stochastic. Patterns of behavior and adaptive responses should therefore be amenable to statistical evaluation in probabilistic terms. But statistical probabilities or situations are of little more than theoretical interest in the social sciences (G. Cowgill, pers. comm.), where primary concern focuses on the individual trajectory.

The Egyptian case outlined in this paper suggests strongly that environmental stress is a real— in fact, a powerful—variable among the many that make probabilistic projections difficult if not impossible. It further suggests a need for a methodology to investigate such stress in the archaeological or historical record, in particular, the identification of stress points and potential thresholds, and their systemic evaluation.

11

Prehistoric Cultural Continuity and Economic Change in the Central Sudan in the Early Holocene

J. DESMOND CLARK

This paper discusses the changing economic pattern of the prehistoric populations of the central Sudan as reconstructed from the associated cultural, plant, and animal remains on the occupation sites. These data show there to be no reason to suppose any significant change in the ethnic composition of these groups due to influx of new peoples. The technological elements that make their appearance in the fourth and again in the second to early first millennia B.C. can be shown to be related, in the first instance, to the introduction of stock, particularly cattle, and, in the second, most probably to cultivation of Sudanese food plants, especially sorghum. The model proposed is thus one of continuity punctuated by technological and economic change through long-range exchange relationships and stimulus diffusion.

Today the central Sudan (Fig. 1) between Nubia and the Ethiopian border at Kassala is a semi-arid region with a three-month rainy season and precipitation that decreases from 410 mm in the south to 164 mm at Khartoum and in the north, in Nubia, to only 1 mm. Much of the region is covered by large areas of grey-brown, cracking clays

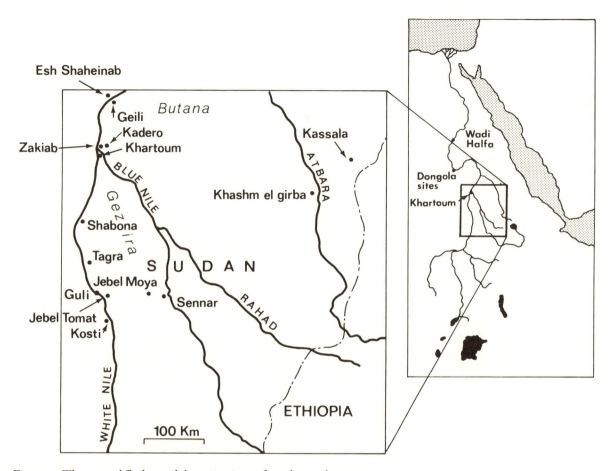

Figure 1. The central Sudan and the main sites referred to in the text.

(Gezira Formation) which make up the often featureless and flat Butana and Gezira plains. The Gezira is now an irrigated, major cotton-growing area; from antiquity it has supported vast areas of grassland of which *Sorghum*, millets (*Brachiaria* and *Digitaria*), and *Eragrostis* (the wild ancestor of *teff*) are important components. The vegetation is of woodland type, with *Acacia* and other semiarid species where the clays are overlain by areas of sand dunes (Qoz). These dunes are now considered to have formed along the edges of distributary channels of the Blue Nile when it flowed across the Gezira some 100 km south of its present confluence with the White Nile at Khartoum. In Nubia and west of the Nile, the Nubian Sandstone forms inselbergs and escarpments and the Kordofan dune

sands are encroaching upon the main river.

Geomorphology (Williams and Adamson, 1980) shows that as late as 3000 B.C. the floodplain of the main Nile was some 5 m higher than at present and that between 10,000 and 6000 B.C. it was higher still. At that time also, as the annual flood waters receded, the White Nile formed an extensive swamp or lake with many ephemeral, and some permanent, ponds or swampy areas on the clay plains between the two Niles. Paleobotanical and faunal evidence suggests that, around 6000–5000 B.C., gallery forest with much associated grassland was an important feature of the main valley and the Gezira (Arkell, 1949: 15–30). In addition, there is evidence that at about 5000 B.C. was an onset of drier conditions ending in the disappearance of the White Nile lake and the down-cutting of both the White and Blue Niles (Williams and Adamson, 1980).

During the early Holocene, therefore, the paleoenvironment in the central Sudan was one of open grass savanna with many seasonal water sources in the plains; on the dunes were forests of xerophytic species; in some places along the rivers there was gallery forest with tropical species. It is probable that before 5000 B.C. much of the southern portion would have been swampy or flooded and so unfavorable for settlement; this could account for the apparent absence of later Pleistocene occupation sites in the central Sudan. Although the Nubian section of the Nile was occupied throughout the later Pleistocene (Wendorf, 1968), there is, further south from the Dongola Reach to the Ethiopian border, an unaccountable hiatus between the Middle Paleolithic and the pre-pastoral techno-complex named from the "Early Khartoum" site. Only at Khashm el Girba is there evidence for some occupation at this time by aceramic groups with a small-blade lithic technology (Shiner, n.d.: II, 434–435).

Specialized Hunting/Fishing and Collecting Economy: The Khartoum Complex

When the Khartoum Complex makes its first appearance, around 6000 B.C.,[1] it does so in a fully developed state. That it was already widely distributed at this time is shown by dates of ± 6000 B.C. from the White Nile (Adamson et al., 1974) and the Western Desert of Egypt (Wendorf et al., 1976) and the characteristic artifact assemblages are found not only along the Nile and the Atbara but also in the plains and desert along both sides of

the river. The population at the type-site (Early Khartoum) appears to have been of ancestral Negro stock (Derry, 1949) adapted to a hunting and grain-collecting economy in which fishing also assumed special significance but with no evidence of domestic animals. The settlement itself was on the river bank and covered an area of 5600 m². Burnt fragments of clay daub with reed and grass impressions indicate that the inhabitants built mud-plastered structures, either as shelters or for storage of food (Arkell, 1949: 79). They lived by taking from the river large quantities of fish (especially catfish, lungfish, and Nile perch), as well as hippopotamus, crocodile, reed rats, python, and turtle. In the gallery forest they hunted buffalo; from the swampy backwaters they took Nile lechwe and, from the grass plains and open forest, kob, *Equus*, elephant, rhinoceros, and various medium- to small-sized antelope, among which the oribi is certainly identified. The scarcity of bird bone is of interest. Although beads of ostrich eggshell occur, it appears that the ostrich was not present locally and that fowling per se was unimportant in the economy (Arkell, 1949: 15–28). The diet was rounded off with large quantities of *Pila* (formerly *Ampullaria*) snails, the shells of which were ubiquitous on the site and sometimes occurred in concentrated pockets (ibid., pp. 28–30). Grain was also collected and upper grindstones and rubbers were comparatively numerous (358) at the site, though identifiable fragments of lower grindstones were far fewer (156).

In addition to this grinding equipment, which was used for grinding ochre as well as grain, the artifacts with which the resources were exploited comprised a number of flaked and ground stone tools. Microliths (lunates, geometrics, and *petits tranchets*) are common, as are the cores and hammerstones with which they were made and the debris resulting from their manufacture. There are also large crescent scrapers made from imported rhyolite, a rather amorphous group of other scrapers, and stone rings and grooved stones, some of which may have been net-sinkers. Local outcrops of Nubian sandstone provided the raw material for the grindstones; quartz occurred as pebbles in the Nile and the surrounding desert; and the rhyolite was transported some 80–95 km from the Sixth

---

1. The barbed bone-point from Tagra is dated to 8370 ± 350 B.P., but charcoal from the Khartoum Complex site at Sarurub II near Khartoum, yielding an assemblage similar to that from the type-site at Khartoum hospital, has been dated recently to 9370 ± 110 and 9330 ± 110 B.P., thus indicating that this complex was already present in the late tenth millennium (Abdel Rahimi Khabir, pers. comm.).

Cataract, as was the gneiss for the hammerstones. This stone industry was supplemented by numbers of characteristic barbed bone-points and a lesser number of awls. Art objects and ornaments consisted of beads of stone and shell (ostrich eggshell and *Pila*-shell), bone pendants, bone points with simple geometric engravings, and enigmatically shaped objects of modeled and fired clay.

The chief interest has generally centered on the ceramics. These are either quartz- or vegetable-tempered. The sole vessel form appears to have been a large, wide-mouthed, deepish bowl. The most common decoration with the quartz-tempered pottery was the famous Wavy-Line and Dotted Wavy-Line and motifs with rocker-stamp and mat decoration. The vegetable-tempered pottery was usually decorated with cord impressions.

The evidence from the "Early Khartoum" type-site is supplemented by that from Shabona, some 80 km south of Khartoum (J. D. Clark, 1973). This site is located on the edge of an old embayment of the Nile, with evidence for much grassland with reeds and swamp conditions close by. Radiocarbon results indicate that it dates from 7050 ± 120 B.P. or ca. 5000 B.C. The fauna at the site also suggests, on the whole, a grassland habitat close to water. As at "Early Khartoum," the largest components of the fauna were fish and tortoise. Hippopotamus, crocodile, and *Varanus* lizard are well represented, as are bovids, including buffalo, reedbuck, kob, and, perhaps, Nile lechwe and oribi. There are also remains of elephant and a suid, presumably warthog. The floor of a semisubterranean dwelling structure may be represented by an irregular, shallow depression with much pottery and worked stone. There are shallow pits containing fish bones, and *Pila* snails were collected and, apparently, stored in conical pits one meter deep.

In general the flaked stone artifacts are similar to those from "Early Khartoum" (Fig. 2), with grindstone fragments and upper handstones being among the most frequent finds. The ceramics (studied by Steven Brandt) include most of the wares and decorative motifs found at "Early Khartoum." There is, however, a suggestion at Shabona that the Wavy-Line, quartz-tempered pottery may be chronologically later than the cord-impressed, vegetable-tempered ware that is particularly common here. The carbonized and other vegetable

fragments that constitute this temper have been studied by Ann Stemler, who has concluded that it all belongs to the genus *Digitaria* and is a wild species. "This temper is *not* a domesticate or a wild relative of any imported African or Near-Eastern domestic species" (Stemler, *in litt.*).

These are the two chief sites of the Khartoum Complex along the Nile that have yielded economic evidence. Both are relatively large, riverside settlements where the population lived by hunting, fishing, and collecting wild grains. However, some evidence also exists for smaller, more compact occupation sites away from the main river, as at the possible elephant-butchery site found by us in 1972, some 20 km west of Hassa Hesa between the Blue and White Niles. Such sites suggest the possibility of seasonal movement into the plains and desert during the rains (at present July to September) when the Nile was in flood, with a return to the rivers during the winter months when the flood had receded.

The ceramic tradition from these central Sudanese sites is most likely to have had an independent origin. It can be postulated that it developed because of the need to process the fish and *Pila* snails more efficiently. The fish-processing probably followed closely that described by the classical authors for the Ichthyophagi (Budge, 1928: I, 67–68). This was not very different from that in current use among the Bozo on the interior delta of the Niger (Ligers, 1966: II, 194–203 and pl. 9), where the large pots used for boiling the fish and extracting the oil are also not dissimilar to those of the "Early Khartoum" peoples on the Nile some 7,000 years earlier. Such an economy, especially along the river, implies that larger groupings and some more permanent settlements were possible during the time of the Khartoum Complex.

The population responsible for the Khartoum Complex was spread widely along the Nile and in the plains. Localized variants of the Complex have been recognized. These include the "Khartoum Variant" industries of Nubia (Shiner, 1968) and the "Early Khartoum related group" (the Karmakol Industry) from the Dongola Reach, with pottery similar to that from "Early Khartoum" and Shabona (Hays, n.d.: 127–139). The twenty or so sites of the Saroba Industry from Khashm el Girba on the Atbara are also evidence of a spread west-

COMPARISON OF SUDANESE LITHIC INDUSTRIES

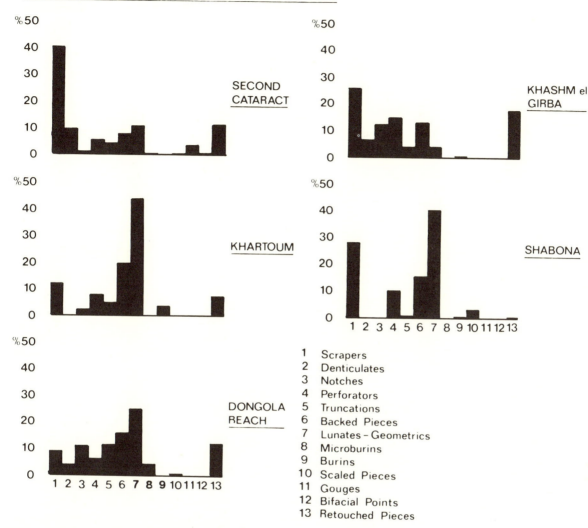

Figure 2. Comparisons of regional lithic industries of the Khartoum Complex.
Khartoun Variant: Second Cataract
Early Khartoum: Hospital site, Khartoum
Karmakol Industry: Dongola Reach
Saroba Industry: Khashm el Girba
Shabona: Fitissa District

ward to the Ethiopian foothills of what has been called the "Khartoum horizon style ceramics" (Shiner, n.d.: 317–334; Hays, 1974). It is difficult to be sure whether the resemblance is to the cultural unit exemplified by the "Early Khartoum" site or to the later entity typified by Esh Shaheinab and its contemporary variants. At least part of the "Khartoum Variant" assemblages from Nubia are likely to be contemporary with a later phase of the Khartoum Complex, and the ceramics of the Karmakol Industry from the Dongola Reach show even closer resemblances to "Early Khartoum."

The main decorative motifs of the Khartoum Complex pottery comprise Wavy and Dotted Wavy-Line, mat pattern, rocker-stamp, cord- and comb-impressed wares with various forms of "mat pattern" occurring most commonly (Hays, n.d.: 141). While these "Khartoum horizon style" ceramics are widely distributed along the Nile and in the desert, the lithic assemblages show some variability among the regions (Fig. 2). The closest comparability is among Early Khartoum, Shabona, and the Dongola Reach, where backed bladelets, lunates/geometrics, and truncations are representative, as are scrapers and drills/perforators. Denticulates are a significant feature of both the Nubian variant and the Saroba Industry from Khasm el Girba. Microburins occur in the Dongola Reach and are present also, though rarely, at the Second Cataract, while burins are a significant feature only at the "Early Khartoum" site. Scaled pieces are prominent only at Shabona, and the gouges and bifacial points at the Second Cataract are probably intrusive from later Shaheinab Complex occupation.

The Khartoum Complex appears to have no immediate antecedents in the central Sudan. However, Wavy-Line, impressed-comb, and other ceramic decorative motifs found with the Khartoum Complex are widely distributed in the eastern and central Sahara as far west as the Hoggar. In the Western Desert of Egypt adjacent to the Sudanese border and in Ennedi, this ceramic style appears at an equally early if not earlier time. At Nabta Playa recent discoveries dating to ca. 8000 B.C. show the Complex with the "Khartoum horizon style" pottery to be associated with two kinds of settlement with evidence of dwellings and storage pits. Domestic stock—ovicaprids and, perhaps, cattle—and barley, believed to have been domesticated, have been found with these occupation sites (Wendorf and Schild, 1980: 128–165). Skeletal remains in association have been provisionally identified as Negroid (Wendorf and Schild, 1980: 272). By 6000 B.C., during the early Holocene wet phase, the hunting, fishing, and grain-processing economy associated with the Khartoum Complex ceramics and other artifacts was spread not only into the central Sahara and north along the Nile into Nubia but also southeast to the foothills of the Ethiopian

escarpment and as far south as Lake Turkana (at that time connected to the Nile system), where sherds of Wavy-Line pottery are found with occupation sites of hunting/fishing communities dating to the eighth millennium and associated with a shoreline 80 m above the present level of the lake (Phillipson, 1977b; Barthelme, 1977). Whether or not the Sahara saw the first African experiments in domestication of plants and animals, groups living along the Nile and in the central Sudanese plains could have been in contact with incipient food-producers from the desert and elsewhere and so have been in a position to acquire stock even if this summer rainfall region was not conducive to growing barley or other winter rainfall crops. That they did not practice domestication until later may be a reflection of the natural wealth of the Nile Valley south of Nubia.

Mixed Food-Gathering and Food-Producing Economies: The Shaheinab Complex

The Sahara by the seventh millennium B.C., on the evidence from Nabta Playa, seems to have witnessed the beginning of those economic adjustments which, along the Nile, only became apparent some 2,000 years later in the late fifth and early fourth millennia B.C. with the beginnings of mixed farming in Egypt and herding in the Sudan. The hunting/fishing/grain-collecting economy probably continued little changed until a number of sites in the central Sudan that fall within the time range of ca. 4000 to 3000 B.C. began to show significant innovations. These sites include Esh Shaheinab, 48 km north of Khartoum and less than 1 km from the Nile; Geili, on the opposite side of the river; Kadero, 18 km north of Khartoum and 6 km east of the river; Zakiab, a smaller site in the same vicinity but nearer the Nile; and, finally, Guli, an island in the White Nile some 220 km south of Khartoum.

The site of Esh Shaheinab, dated to the second half of the fourth millennium B.C. (5446 ± 380; 5060 ± 440 B.P.), is well known from Arkell's excavations and reports (Arkell, 1953); it covered some 6000 m² on a riverbank. Although the fauna is weighted heavily (84 percent) toward hunted animals of a variety of species, some 2 percent show that the people were herding a small domestic goat and, possibly, sheep. There was also some fish bone, though not as much as at "Early Khartoum," and some bird bone. Reptilian remains were common, as were *Pila* snails and *Aetheria elliptica*, the freshwater oyster. Arkell reports at Shaheinab less than half the number of lower grindstone fragments found at "Early Khartoum" and a correspondingly smaller number of upper handstones (Arkell, 1953: 46–54), suggesting that at Shaheinab grain was not as important a food as at "Early Khartoum." This could be a circumstance of its geographical position but it may also indicate that Shaheinab was first and foremost a hunting and fishing settlement with some fowling. As such, it is to be expected that it was occupied seasonally.

This is borne out by the tool assemblage (Fig. 3). Microliths in particular are common, as are borers, and there is a small number of endscrapers; large crescent scrapers in rhyolite are also present. To the spear- and arrow-points of bone are now added harpoon-heads, also in bone, and shell and bone fishhooks, bone celts, and various other worked bone artifacts. Beads and ornaments, including lip-plugs, are common and there is much evidence for ochre-grinding. Most significant, however, is the appearance of the characteristic adze—or gouge—and percussion-flaked ground stone axes and flat-topped maceheads, these last, apparently, dating to the end of the occupation. While, therefore, the artifact assemblages show close connections with the Khartoum Complex, important new dimensions have been introduced at Esh Shaheinab, namely, heavy-duty equipment for working wood, the harpoon for hunting—most probably for hippo and large fish—and fishhooks for line fishing. This leads to the further inference that the gouges and celts, among other wood-working activities, may have been used for making dug-out canoes. The scrapers, bone celts, and awls suggest a considerable amount of skin-dressing.

The pottery at Esh Shaheinab also hints at a close connection with that of the Khartoum Complex. The vessels are deep bowls, many large and some smaller, decorated with Dotted Wavy-Line motifs. The most characteristic form, however, is one burnished on the outside. There are also im-

pressed wares with various motifs combining lines and dots, zig-zags, rocker-stamp, incised, and plain wares and some black-topped bowls and black pottery; thus to the basic Wavy-Line pottery of "Early Khartoum" other wares have been added. In general the pottery is much better made, but the vessel form suggests that the pots were put to much the same uses as were those of the Khartoum Complex.

The Kadero site (Krzyzaniak, 1978), the population of which has been described as Negroid, shows several contrasts with Esh Shaheinab. The two dates for the site—5260 ± 90 and 5030 ± 70 B.P.—suggest that it is contemporary with Esh Shaheinab. The site covers 30,000 m² and is on a low mound, nearly 2 m high, which would probably have stood above the shallow water covering the plain when the Nile was in flood. Of the mammalian bones from the site, over 88 percent are from domestic animals, with cattle the most important (>74 percent); ovicaprids represent 22 percent and domestic dog accounts for ca. 3.5 percent. The cattle are mostly shorthorn, with a few long-horned specimens. Of the wild fauna nearly 47 percent is gazelle. There is much grinding equipment, consisting of saddle quern fragments and upper handstones, the commonest artifacts on the site. Wild fruits and *Pila* snails were also collected.

The stone industry of Kadero shows a significant shift away from "Early Khartoum" and Esh Shaheinab and, compared with the latter, is rather impoverished; it also lacks the bone equipment. At Kadero, microliths are a relatively unimportant component. By contrast, scrapers, especially convex forms, become significant, as does boring equipment. Perhaps the most characteristic tool is the gouge, and there are rare tanged arrowheads, as at Esh Shaheinab. The pottery is burnished, with decoration similar to that of Esh Shaheinab except that the Dotted Wavy-Line motif is absent. Although continuity is apparent in the artifact assemblage, the new herding economy has significantly reduced the importance of some traditional forms of tool (e.g., microliths) while retaining others (e.g., gouges).

The large area covered by the site suggests that it may have been either a base camp or a seasonal collecting point for pastoral groups whose permanent settlements were elsewhere. Presumably the

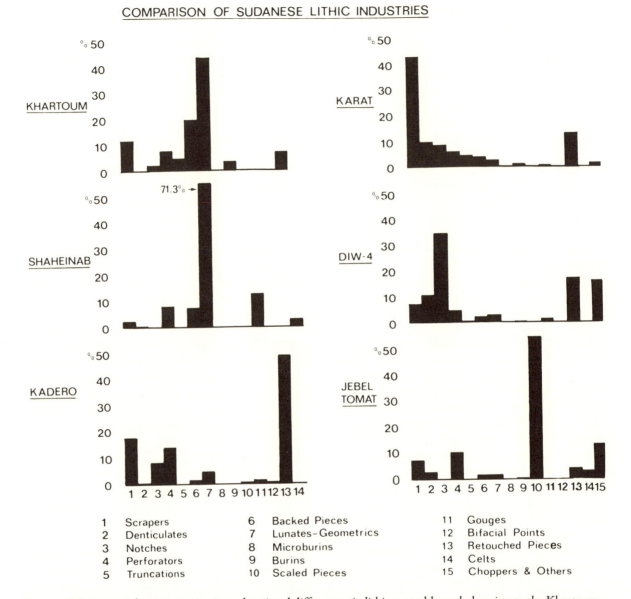

Figure 3. Histogram showing continuity and regional differences in lithic assemblages belonging to the Khartoum, Shaheinab, and Jebel Moya complexes and other contemporary groups.

site was occupied after the floodwaters had left the plain, as the emphasis is not only on herding but also on grain-grinding. Evidence for claims, based on ceramic impressions, that the grains were domestic (a range of the Sudanic cereals and barley is postulated) still has to be confirmed.

The Geili site (Caneva, n.d.) is much disturbed but appears to resemble Esh Shaheinab, with a generally similar tool inventory and an economy based on hunting, fishing, and some herding of small stock and, perhaps, of cattle. The pottery, although burnished, does not include the Dotted Wavy-Line motif and, in that respect, more nearly resembles that from Kadero.

The Zakiab site is currently being investigated by Randi Haaland (1978). It is situated near Kadero on an old Nile channel-bank 3 km from the river and dates to the same period as Kadero, but it is much smaller in area (2000 m²). The diet, as evidenced by the remains at the site, consisted of fish, molluscs, domestic cattle, and ovicaprids together with a wide range of wild animals. Grindstones are not common but the artifacts include bone points, fishhooks, and scrapers, the last presumably for hide-scraping, as at Kadero. The pottery is similar to that from Kadero.

The Guli site (Adamson et al., 1974) is situated on a former point-bar of the Nile opposite Esh Shawal. It is dated, on shell, to 5500 ± 90 B.P., or 3530 B.C., but has received only preliminary investigation. Taking into account the presence of barbed bone points and similarities in the pottery, it can be considered as a smaller-scale counterpart to Esh Shaheinab which, together probably with Geili, is closer to the Khartoum Complex (on the basis of the tool assemblages and economy) than is Kadero or Zakiab. These last two sites exhibit a significant reduction in or complete absence of certain tool forms and of the Dotted Wavy-Line motif. This, in conjunction with the dependence on domestic animals at Kadero and Zakiab, has suggested that the date for Esh Shaheinab may be too young. Fortunately, this has been resolved by two further dates on shell obtained by Haaland (1979b) from near the top and bottom of the midden; these gave ages of 5300 ± 100 B.P. and 5500 ± 100 B.P., or ca. 3400 B.C. It seems clear, therefore, since all these sites are fairly close to each other in time and space, that by the fourth millennium B.C., subsistence patterns were a good deal more varied than has previously been supposed. Esh Shaheinab, Zakiab, and Guli can be seen as the settlements and camping places along the Nile where the economy was presumably based on fishing and hunting; away from the Nile the economy was one of herding and the use of grain. The differences in the tool-kits can be expected to be reflections of these subsistence differences. Where hunting was important, so also were microlithic forms; the taking of aquatic foods necessitated barbed bone points and harpoons. These are not a feature of Kadero and other sites in the clay plains away from the river, since the main sources of food there were domestic livestock and wild grain and not game, fish, or hippopotamus. However, ceramics and adzes/gouges are common to both sorts of site, suggesting that, for all these central Sudanese communities, pottery, vessels, and other equipment of wood were essential parts of their material culture.

The Dongola Reach appears to have been occupied at this time by a people—the Karat Group (Marks and Ferring, n.d.: 187–275)—with a different kind of adaptation to the Nilotic environment from that of the Esh Shaheinab population. The two had only one ceramic ware (thin, burnished pottery with rocker-stamp decoration) in common. The lithic industry of the Karat Group (Fig. 3) is high in endscrapers (especially on cortex flakes) with low percentages of microliths, drills, and denticulate pieces and very little in the way of burins, scaled pieces, or grinding equipment. However, gouges and ground-stone axes are also represented at the Karat sites (ibid.: 225). The large number of concentrations of fire-fractured pebbles resulting from some special activity suggests that these sites may be more representative of one part of a seasonal pattern than of the full range of material culture at this time, and it appears to be necessary to look elsewhere, rather than along the Nile, for the other half of the pattern.

The Karat Group pottery also resembles that from the early A-Group sites in the Second Cataract area of Nubia (ibid.: 257). The lithic industry from one contemporary site in the same area (Dibeira West 4 [DIW4]), dated to 3,270 ± 50 B.C., shows similar primary flaking techniques and core forms, as well as a consistent but never dominant microlithic component (especially geometrics), and pecked axes and gouges. Many of the differences might be due to the use of different raw material— chert in the Karat Group and quartz at DIW4— but again, while they have common traits, a strong regional element is clearly demonstrated (ibid.: 256–268).

The site of Shaqadud (Otto, 1963) is situated in the western part of the Butana some 55 km east of the Nile at the Sixth Cataract in Upper Nubia. The site is linked to the Shaheinab Complex by the pottery and other artifacts contained in the broad terrace and the cave. The associated burials provide further information on the physical type responsible for the Complex. While unburnished

Dotted Wavy-Line pottery is present, the addition of other wares and the apparent absence of gouges suggest that the site is more likely to stand near the end rather than the beginning of the Shaheinab Complex. As yet the site remains unexcavated and undated but it is an indication that the Shaheinab Complex can be expected to be found spread widely throughout the whole area of the clay plains between the Nile and the Atbara rivers.

The Saroba Industry in the Khashm el Girba, though having traits in common with the Khartoum Complex, may in part also be contemporary with that of Shaheinab. It is as yet undated but a gouge is recorded from one of these sites. The Saroba Industry has a number of characteristics in common also with the succeeding Butana Industry (Shiner, n.d.: II, 335–394), to which it is believevd to be ancestral. Microliths, drills, denticulates, gouges, and maceheads all continue, together with new forms such as ground-stone axes, pitted stones, lip-plugs, and some grinding equipment. In general, however, the Butana Industry pottery looks to be later in age than that of the Shaheinab Complex, having more in common, in particular the large, thick-walled vessels, with the Jebel Moya Complex (see below). This would be in keeping with the single radiocarbon date from one Butana Industry site of 4410 ± 90 B.P., or 2460 B.C. This industry may therefore belong near the time when the Shaheinab Complex tradition was giving place to ceramics more characteristic of those from Jebel Moya.

Herding and Cultivation: Jebel Moya Complex

The Shaheinab Complex is contemporary with the Badarian, Amratian, and Gerzean stages of the Egyptian Predynastic (Hassan, 1980: 438) and with the Post-Shamarkian and Abkan in upper Nubia and the A-Group sites with their evidence of Egyptian contacts in lower Nubia (Trigger, 1976: 31–39). The termination of A-Group culture ca. 2800 B.C. coincided with a steady reduction in influence from early Dynastic Egypt as well as with a significant lowering of the Nile floodplain (B. Bell, 1970). Little is known about the Nubian popula-

tions during Old Kingdom times until the appearance, somewhat before 2000 B.C., of C-Group culture derived, in part at least, from A-Group origins. The C-Horizon pottery (various black-and-white incised bowl forms and red-slipped pots) is very widely distributed from Egyptian Nubia in the north, east and west of the Nile in the desert, and as far south as the highlands of Ethiopia. This may be an indication, on the one hand, of significant population movements out of the desert and the clay plains between the Blue and White Niles as desertification became more intensified, or, on the other hand, of increased population densities along the Nile itself. The C-Group populations appear to have been successful, small-scale cultivators and herders of sheep, goats, and cattle, no doubt aided in this by the high Nile floods between 1840 and 1770 B.C. (Trigger, 1976: 82). As yet, their ethnic associations have not been determined. C–Horizon-style pottery has been found at Khartoum (Omdurman Bridge Culture) but there are no certain sites of this time or association in the clay plains to the south.

Little or nothing is known concerning cultural developments in the central Sudan during the third and second millennia B.C., though it is possible that this gap may be filled by some of the later industries from the Dongola Reach (e.g., the El Malik group) and Khashm el Girba (e.g., the Butana Industry) (Shiner, n.d.: 276, 335), as well as by some of the large surface sites along the White Nile in the region of Fitissa. From these and on the evidence of classical authors, there is reason to believe that, while some groups were cultivators, others along the Nile continued into Meroitic times to depend for subsistence on hunting, fishing, and collecting, and in the Butana and Gezira plains, pastoralists had probably already adopted the transhumant pattern that persists to this day. Two sites in the Gezira Plain between the White and Blue Niles north of Kosti—Jebel Moya (Addison, 1942) and Jebel et Tomat (J. D. Clark, 1973)— have given dates between 2500 and 2000 B.C. for the basal levels, and it seems that the pottery believed to be the oldest at Jebel Moya—the unburnished and burnished Impressed Ware—dates to this time (ibid.). In vessel form and overall decoration, including rare Wavy-Line motifs, this pottery shows resemblances to that with the Shaheinab Complex while being, nevertheless, distinct. At Jebel et Tomat a disc macehead belongs to this early horizon. The large numbers of burials from Jebel Moya show the inhabitants to have been Sudanese Negroes (Mukherjee et al., 1955).

The ceramics of the Jebel Moya Complex combined shapes and motifs resembling those of C-Group and Meroitic pottery with those of the Butana Industry and from sites such as Kadero; it is, nonetheless, a distinctive ceramic tradition. The lithic technology also shows persistence of the old Neolithic tradition, with ground-stone axes, maceheads, microliths, drills, and other flaked-stone equipment, and grindstone fragments and handstones are among the commonest artifacts on the sites (Fig. 3). Some of the grindstones are now deeply dished and there is an abundance of spherical grindstone "sharpeners." The indication is that the staple cereal was cultivated sorghum of the *bicolor* race which was stored in pits after reaping (Clark and Stemler, 1975). Dates from carbonized remains fall between 80 B.C. and A.D. 350 but it could well have been cultivated earlier.[2] It would have been grown in plots in the plains during the rainy season when the group moved away from the flood area to take advantage of the abundant grazing. At Jebel et Tomat, some 10 km from the Nile, the pottery throughout the sequence shows an increasing use of sponge spicule obtained from the river as temper (D. A. Adamson, pers. comm.). It is understood that such sponge–spicule-tempered pottery has now been found to occur at Meroe also. At Jebel et Tomat this indicates that pottery made on the Nile was being increasingly brought onto the plains and may be evidence of a regular exchange system between the two areas or of a relatively rigid transhumance system. Such a system persists today, except that the modern irrigation scheme in the Gezira has reversed the season at which the move is made. Modern semipastoral cultivators along the Nile, instead of moving into the plains in the summer and rainy season and then back to the river in the dry winter when the floods recede, move into the Gezira in the winter to harvest the cotton in the irrigated plains.

The "luxury" items found at Jebel et Tomat

and Jebel Moya—imported stone beads, faience, and very rare copper and iron—show that the main part of the occupation was contemporary with the Meroitic civilization along the Nubian Nile, and this is confirmed by the radiocarbon dates. At Jebel Moya, however, Napatan imports suggest that the contacts with Nubian civilization may have begun somewhat earlier—though, as yet, this cannot be confirmed by radiocarbon dates, as the samples collected from the upper part of the midden proved insufficient.

The food waste found in our excavations at Jebel et Tomat suggests a population of seminomadic pastoralists using the abundant grazing of the plains and combining herding with hunting and fishing activities and the cultivation of sorghum gardens during the rains. Of the mammalian bones, domestic stock accounted for almost 83 percent (A. B. Smith, pers. comm.), of which 47.2 percent were from cattle and 35.7 percent from ovicaprids. The wild animals eaten comprised gazelle, oribi, klipspringer, a reedbuck, bushpig, cane rat, hare, and *Varanus* lizard. The people were also fowlers, since bones of rock pidgeon, Egyptian goose, and guineafowl occur in the food waste. A significant amount of fish was eaten, probably obtained partly from ponds filling depressions in the plains and partly brought in, perhaps dried, from the Nile. Everything at the site—the stratigraphy, the absence of any indication of permanent dwellings or other structures, and the climatic regimen (probably much the same as that of today)—suggests a well-established system of transhumance between the plains and the Nile. Movement into the Gezira would have taken place when the Nile flooded— between July and December, during the rains— when the extensive grasslands provided grazing for stock and plots of sorghum could have been grown by *hariq* cultivation. Some hunting was also carried out, and fish were taken in the shallow ponds or *maiyas*. In the dry winter months—January to July—when the Nile was low, it can be expected that the population returned to established "villages" near the river. Some of the extensive sites we found north of Fitissa probably represent such settlements. Fishing may have been of greater importance at this time and, at least in the northern Gezira, it is possible that temperatures would have permitted a winter crop of wheat or barley to be

---

2. *Sorghum bicolor* has also been found at Meroe in horizons dating to 200 B.C. (P. L. Shinnie, pers. comm.).

grown on the floodplain. This would also probably have been the time of the year when craftsmen and craftswomen carried on their work.

It can certainly be presumed that the "bright lights" of Meroe itself and of the other Meroitic centers and markets would have been regular seasonal attractions for pastoralists in the northern Butana, but the general way of life and technology of the population, especially in the southern Butana and Gezira, appears to have been largely unaffected by this civilization along the Nile. In the northern Butana, however, the building of earth dams (*hafirs*) and the Meroitic settlements there appear to have made for a greater degree of sedentariness among the local population (Ali, 1972).

Conclusion

This paper has been an attempt to show how, in the seventh and sixth millennia B.C., an early Holocene population practicing a balanced hunting-and-fishing economy with some wild-grain collecting became established in much of the central Sudan between the White and Blue Niles and the Atbara and north to Nubia. In later times their lifestyle underwent various modifications as domesticates became increasingly available and technological adjustments became a necessity. Small stock and cattle were introduced by the latter half of the fourth millennium B.C.; wheat, barley, and legumes appear to have been cultivated by the A-Group people in lower Nubia by ca. 2800 B.C. (Trigger, 1976: 35), and knowledge of these and the advantages of cultivation may have spread up the Nile to the later "Khartoum Variant" and Post-Shamarkian groups around the Second Cataract; it can also be speculated that sorghum became domesticated sometime between the early third millennium and the mid-first millennium B.C. in Meroitic times.

At first glance it is not easy to see much in common between the material culture of the sixth and the first millennia in the central Sudan (Fig. 3). If, however, those of the intervening time-ranges are studied, a pattern emerges of long-persisting traits in stone and bone tools and pottery, seeming to indicate a cultural continuity that characterizes

this region throughout prehistoric and historic times, if not, indeed, to the present day. If the human remains are considered, there is evidence for an ethnic continuity also. Figure 3 shows this well for the sites in the Khartoum area and Jebel et Tomat. "Early Khartoum" and Esh Shaheinab show the closest resemblance—as might be expected, because of their similar economies. The most significant change occurs between these two sites and Kadero which, in turn, while it differs, does bear a general resemblance to Jebel et Tomat. Significantly different are the Karat Industry from the Dongola Reach and that at Dibeira West 4 from the Second Cataract, emphasizing again the regional variability that is observable in the lithic but not the ceramic elements of the Khartoum and Shaheinab complexes. Within this cultural continuum can be seen the extent to which the introduction of herding and, later, of cultivation made necessary major readjustments in technology, land use, and social organization, though less modification was required by those communities who were able to maintain for a time their hunting-and-fishing way of life along the Nile. Within this continuity can also be seen the extent of regional variability that is manifest through time in the products of contemporary populations.

At the present time any definitive interpretation of prehistoric economic development in the central Sudan is made impossible by two factors. First, there is a scarcity of good quantitative data on the diet of the inhabitants of the sites we have been considering. Second, there is a lack of any land-use studies that would help to identify the place and relationship of the various kinds of sites within the total annual procurement system. The variability in these apparent contemporary patterns that date to the fourth and third millennia B.C. suggests that, as domestic stock became available, the relatively fluid or open system of food-gatherers was gradually superseded by a more rigidly structured, hierarchical social organization founded on the wealth that small stock and later cattle can provide. Haaland (1978) has suggested that sites such as Kadero and Zakiab formed part of an annual subsistence pattern, the former being a base camp on which the subgroups converged with their stock from cattle camps which they are considered to have occupied at a distance from the river during the rainy season; possibly Shaqadud is one such camp. Zakiab is representative of one of the more temporary dry-season camps on the Nile to which the subgroups dispersed again in winter and where they depended on aquatic foods and the hunting of terrestrial animals. The short distance separating the two sites renders it unlikely that they belonged to the same population, but some such model of seasonal transhumance is to be expected in a generally dry habitat subject to annual flooding but with a short rainy season and rapid lowering of the water-table in the dry season. Such a model could be tested by a systematic survey of prehistoric land-use patterns. In addition, it is probable that the time of the Shaheinab Complex also saw

the beginnings of more specialized behavior that resulted in some groups' concentrating on the aquatic foods and others on pastoralism and grain-collecting, with a resulting symbiotic relationship in which essential food supplies and commodities were exchanged. Such a pattern is unlikely to have been a very rigid one, in view of the arid to semiarid environment of the central Sudan. As drought or high floods dictated, these groups would make the most advantageous adjustments to their economy. The fourth and third millennia B.C. would, then, have been a time of experimentation as a result of which there evolved the more circumscribed pastoral and cultivating subsistence pattern of the first millennium B.C.

Thus, the simple model in Fig. 4 shows the

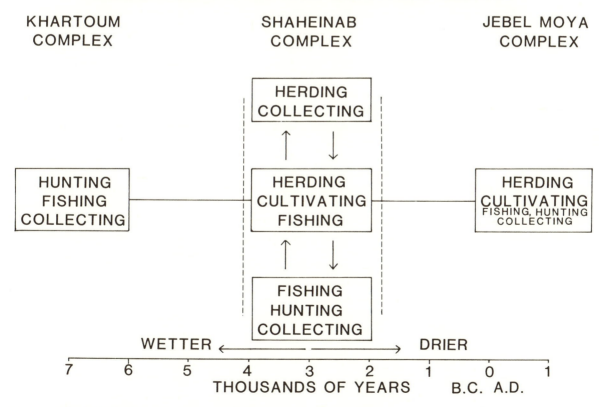

Figure 4. Model for Holocene economic adjustments in the central Sudan.

traditional Khartoum Complex giving place to several experimental adaptations (the Shaheinab Complex) based on the extent to which new resources were added to, or took the place of, the traditional ones. Along the Blue and White Niles, fishing, hunting, and collecting continued to be very important, while in the clay plains, herding, collecting, and cultivating assumed a larger role. At first, no doubt, the traditional open structure of food-gatherers, allowing freedom of movement between groups, probably maintained some fluidity in the human composition of the various communities and in their relationships with adjacent peoples. Later, however, this would have been replaced by a more closed system and more rigid seasonal transhumance such as is usually associated with predominantly pastoral populations. Later still, as the less efficient and less attractive of the adaptations were abandoned, the economy appears to have crystallized into the pattern of cattle-herding and cultivating (the Jebel Moya Complex) that prevailed in Meroitic times and also survives in some places up to the present day.

12

The Transition from Food Collecting to Food Production in Northern Africa

ANN STEMLER

Most of the presentations for this symposium are based on archaeological fieldwork done in Africa. This one is based instead on several summers of work done halfway around the world from Africa, in central Illinois. The object of the work was to learn something about gene flow among wild, weedy, and domesticated sorghums of Africa. An unexpected outcome of the study was the great respect that it instilled in this investigator for the physical strength and endurance of the sorghum plant.

The purpose of the paper is to discuss the process of cereal domestication and some characteristics of sorghum and *Pennisetum* (not necessarily shared by other, less robust tropical African cereals) that may be important in understanding the relatively late appearance of domesticated cereals in the archaeological record of tropical Africa compared to the appearance of domesticated cereals in Egypt and neighboring southwest Asia. One of the more perplexing aspects of African prehistory is the difference in the time of appearance of well-documented evidence of agriculture in Egypt and in sub-Saharan Africa. In Egypt there is good evidence of domesticated barley and wheat as early as 6250 B.C. at the site of Nabta Playa (Wendorf et al., 1976; Stemler and Falk, botanical appendix to site report, in preparation). We find no clearly documented archaeological evidence of domesticated cereals in sub-Saharan Africa until many millennia later. The earliest evidence of sorghum documented with a photograph dates to about A.D. 300 (Clark and Stemler, 1975). (In the light of the abundant examples of misidentifications of plants from archaeological sites, this investigator limits discussion to those plant specimens that have been documented with photographs or have been examined and identified unequivocally by more than one authority.)

The puzzle has become even more perplexing with presentation of evidence that people were using barley in Egypt as early as 18,000 B.P. (but see p. 101) (Wendorf and Schild, this volume; Wendorf et al., 1979). A scanning-electron-microscope study of these specimens confirmed the identification of barley but could not establish with certainty whether the cereal was domesticated (Stemler and Falk, 1981). More specimens are needed, but in the meantime, it is enough to ponder the fact that people were using barley in Egypt in 17,000 B.P. Yet we find no abundant evidence of agriculture in sub-Saharan Africa until around 1500 B.P. A study of plant impressions in pottery at the site of Dhar Tichitt in Mauritania by Jacques-Félix (n.d.) presents evidence of domesticated *Pennisetum* around 1000 B.C. (Munson, 1976), but for earlier time-levels, claims of domesticated cereals are based on fragmentary or undocumented evidence.

The information at our disposal thus suggests that early agriculture in Egypt resulted in little or no discernible influence on surrounding parts of Africa. The limited nature of cultural interaction apparent even in late historic times is probably important in explaining how two neighboring regions could have such radically different economies. There are also important ecological and physiological reasons why cereals grown in Egypt could not have been adopted in sub-Saharan Africa (Stemler, 1980). There are undoubtedly many diversities in the situations in Egypt and sub-Saharan Africa that contributed to the very different courses of agricultural development. This paper will be limited to an exploration of some of the physical characteristics of the most important tropical African cereal domesticates and will relate these to the process of cereal domestication. It will consider the idea that sorghum may have been domesticated relatively late in African prehistory because it is not easily harvested with simple stone tools.

The Sorghum Plant

From a tiny grain (100 grains weigh only 0.4–0.7 gm), the wild sorghum plant grows to a height of two meters or more. It tolerates a wide range of environmental conditions and thrives on intense heat and drought after its extensive root system is established. A single grain creates an incredible amount of biomass. In a single growing season each plant produces many grain-bearing inflorescences. A primary inflorescence may be up to 50 cm long and, in a season with abundant rain, will produce several secondary inflorescences below the primary that yield grain through the latter part of the growing season. The flower-bearing stalk (the peduncle, in botanical terminology), is a remarkably sturdy, tough, and stubborn mass of plant tissue. The width of the peduncle of wild sorghum is 0.3–0.6 cm. Harvesting large numbers of wild sorghum inflorescences, even with metal shears, is an exhausting task.

Several growing seasons spent working with this plant have resulted in firsthand experience with the difficulties involved in harvesting wild sorghum and have suggested the hypothesis that one of the reasons for the apparently late domestication of sorghum and other robust tropical African cereals may have been the difficulty in harvesting the plant in a way that would ultimately lead to domestication.

The Role of Harvesting Techniques in the Process of Cereal Domestication

There are basically two ways to harvest the grain of wild grasses. One is to pull or beat the grain off the inflorescence; grain may then be deposited by hand in receptacles or swept off the ground and gathered. Many variations of the technique exist. This basic method of harvesting does not alter the course of evolution of the wild grass population, because the people harvesting the grain are affecting the population in exactly the same way as does a natural force such as wind, which blows grains of grass away from the parent plant. Species of grasses that have been gathered in this way for thousands of years are still wild grasses, not a single step closer to domestication (Wilke et al., 1972; Harlan et al., 1976b). About sixty species of grasses are harvested regularly by this method in Africa alone (Busson et al., 1965; Jardin, 1967), but of these no more than five ever became domesticates of economic importance.

Crop evolutionists believe that domesticated cereals were developed when people began sowing wild cereals and harvesting their crop in a significantly different way, by reaping entire inflorescences rather than stripping or beating grain off the plants. Harvesting by reaping entire fruiting cobs of grain requires effective harvesting tools.

Differences in Adaptations and Structure of Wild and Domesticated Cereals

The importance of harvesting techniques in the domestication process may be clearer if we consider the important differences in structure and adaptations of wild versus domesticated cereals. The success of wild cereals depends largely on the ability of parent plants to release their grain so that natural forces such as wind and water can carry the grain away from the parent plant to open habitats where it can germinate relatively free of competition (from the parent plant and other members of the species) for sunlight, water, and nutrients. Hence, in wild cereal populations, as in all wild plants, there has been very strong selection for genetically controlled mechanisms that facilitate release of seed from the parent plant. Plants that readily release propagules are selectively favored in wild populations.

In populations sown and reaped by man, selection pressures are significantly different. (Henceforth, assume that harvesting by reaping means cutting off the entire fruiting cob or inflorescence rather than gathering grain by stripping or beating it off the parent plant.) Success of the population no longer depends on the ability of the parent plants to release their grain. In fact the opposite is true. Since man will plant the future generations, the parent plants that are selectively favored are those that contribute most to the harvest carried away from the field and stored by the cultivator for food and for seed stock for the next year's planting. Thus the plant type favored now is the cob or inflorescence that does *not* release its grain. Cobs that hold on to their grain remain intact through the processes of reaping and transporting the harvest to the storage facilities. Plants that do not release their grain are selectively favored among populations sown and reaped by man because these contribute most significantly to the seed stock for the next generation.

Plants that do not release their grain are found in very low frequencies in wild grass populations, because genes that contol seed-release mechanisms mutate, and mutants for these characters cannot shed their grain. Mutants that cannot disperse their grain are rare in wild populations because they are not selectively favored. Such mutants in populations sown and reaped by man would be selectively favored and would increase in frequency with each generation until the whole population would consist of plants that hold on to their grain throughout the reaping process. This is the character that distinguished fully domesticated cereals from their wild relatives.

Conditions Necessary for Domestication

Two points should be emphasized. First, in order for the domestication process to proceed, it is essential that seed stock for the next year's planting always be taken from the harvest of the previous year. In this way, each year's harvest and seed stock would contain a greater proportion of plants that hold on to their grain. Each time people sowed their crops using seed gathered from wild cereal populations, the domestication process was set back to the beginning because the population sown consisted almost entirely of plants that shed their grain. This is the reason why some think that domestication of cereals may have occurred in areas some distance away from those where the wild cereal grew in abundance (Harlan and Zohary, 1966). In areas outside the zone of distribution of the wild cereal, it was less likely that the domestication process would be set back by planting crops using seed stock gathered from the wild.

Second, it was essential that people harvest their crops by reaping entire fruiting cobs and carrying these to a storage area. This condition requires a harvesting tool sufficiently effective to allow people to reap the harvest within a reasonable amount of time. Without such a tool it would be more efficient to gather the grain by stripping or beating it off the plants as hunter/gatherers do.

Consideration of these factors may help us understand why domesticated cereals appear relatively late in the archaeological record of tropical Africa. With regard to the first condition, it has already been suggested that the abundance of wild game in Africa offered little incentive to early post-Pleistocene hunter/gatherers to assume more labor-intensive, food-procuring practices (J. D. Clark, 1976a). It was probably not until the periods of desiccation in Africa around 2500 B.C. and again around 1200 B.C. that wild fish and game resources may have become scarce enough to encourage the use of such labor-intensive, food-procuring practices as the sowing of wild cereals. There is good evidence that as fish and game resources decreased, some groups of people used increased amounts of wild cereals for food (Munson, 1976). People probably began sowing and harvesting wild grasses to increase food supplies at exactly the time we would expect that populations of wild grasses must have been decreasing in extent and abundance. It is under precisely such circumstances that the first condition for the process of domestication was most probably met. In dry periods, when wild fish and game supplies decreased, many groups of people undoubtedly were sowing and harvesting many different species of wild cereals. Furthermore, if indeed stands of wild cereals were less extensive and also less abundant, there was less chance at this time that the process of cereal domestication, once

begun, would have been interrupted by the use of wild seed stock for planting.

The second very important condition for domestication is that whole fruiting cobs of grain had to be reaped from the parent plants in the process of harvesting. It was in the process of reaping and transport of the harvest that a new kind of selection was exerted, favoring cobs that held on to their grain rather than releasing it. This condition may have been difficult to meet until late in sub-Saharan African history. If we now find that wild sorghum is difficult to harvest even with metal tools, what sorts of tools might have been available in prehistoric times that would have been effective enough to allow efficient reaping of wild sorghum? In Africa at the present time, individual stalks of cultivated sorghum are reaped one at a time, using a metal knife. The reaping technique is quite different from the use of a sickle to reap many stalks at a time of less robust cereal plants such as wheat, barley, and oats.

In order to evaluate the hypothesis that tool technology was an important factor in making possible the domestication of tropical African cereals, it would be necessary to reconsider the evidence of change in tool assemblages in relationship to the appearance of plant domesticates. Is there evidence of tools that might have been used to reap wild grasses as stout as sorghum in post-Pleistocene tool assemblages? Is there any evidence that new tools were developed or introduced around the periods of desiccation that appear to be related to shifts in subsistence patterns? What is the significance of stone "sickle blades" in the Maghreb (Camps-Fabrer, 1966) and in Tunisia (Camps, 1974) and the rock picture in Tassili that seems to portray a cereal harvest (Lhote, 1958)? Is it possible that herder-collectors from the Sahara may have introduced the idea of reaping whole cobs of wild grain (and possibly the tool technology as well) to sub-Saharan Africa and that this interaction and diffusion of ideas was important in setting the stage for the domestication of tropical African cereals? The spread of agriculture throughout central and southern Africa seems to coincide with the spread of iron tools. Is it possible that really effective agricultural economies were not possible in Africa until iron tools were available, not only to clear vegetation for planting but also to harvest tropical African cereals?

In conclusion: the origin of African plant domesticates appears to have come much later in time than the origin of plant domesticates in other regions. The reasons for this difference are probably many and complex. This paper is an attempt to add to the other factors discussed and considered that of the physical characteristics of the wild sorghum plant. The reaping of wild sorghum and other robust tropical African grasses such as *Pennisetum* may have presented an especially difficult challenge and may have required a more advanced harvesting tool than was needed to facilitate the process of domestication of less robust cereals native to other regions of the world.

13

Effects of Nutritional Change on the Skeletal Biology of Northeast African (Sudanese Nubian) Populations

GEORGE J. ARMELAGOS

DENNIS P. VAN GERVEN

DEBRA L. MARTIN

REBECCA HUSS-ASHMORE

Archaeologists interested in understanding the consequences of food production usually restrict their analysis to the impact on the cultural system. Specifically, these scientists have considered the relationship of agricultural development to changes in technology, social organization, and ideology. While we have accumulated considerable knowledge concerning the cultural consequences of food production, we are only beginning to understand the full impact of agricultural subsistence on human population biology. Methodological developments in skeletal biology now enable us to determine diseases of bone that reflect nutritional stress. Retardation in long bone growth, enamel hypoplasia (Goodman et al., 1980), porotic hyperostosis (Carlson et al., 1974) periosteal reactions, Harris lines, and premature osteoporosis (Martin and Armelagos, 1979) are pathological conditions indica-

Research was supported in part by the National Science Foundation, National Institute of Health Grant No. NIH–I–R01–02271–01, and University of Massachusetts Biomedical Grant No. Pr07048. We would like to thank Larry Gallant, Robin Macks, and Nancy Handler for technical assistance.

tive of nutritional and infectious disease stress (see Huss-Ashmore et al., 1981).

The shift to food production has long been thought to herald an era of improved nutrition and health. The ability of agriculturalists to increase food production is considered one of the most important factors in the adaptation of these groups. In fact, the increase in size in human populations following the development of food production is frequently used to support the assumption of improved health in the Neolithic. However, there is theoretical and empirical evidence that suggests that improved health is not a necessary consequence of food production. The development of primary food production often leads to changes in the environment which can increase the potential for nutritional and infectious disease. Degradation of the environment, increased population size and density, and the accumulation of human waste increases the possibility of infectious disease (Armelagos and McArdle, 1975). The shift to agriculture in West Africa followed by the rise of malaria there is a classic example of how changes in subsistence can alter the disease patterns (F. B. Livingstone, 1958; Wiesenfeld, 1967). The potential for nutritional deficiency also increases with food production. The reliance on single subsistence-crops combined with crop failure from drought or blight can lead to serious nutritional stress.

The biological significance of shifts in subsistence is illustrated for the New World by changes in health of the population at Dickson Mounds. During the course of 350 years (A.D. 950–A.D. 1300), the Dickson Mound population experienced a shift from gathering/hunting to intensive agricul-

ture. During this shift there was a threefold increase in infectious disease (Lallo, Rose, and Armelagos, 1978), and a fourfold increase in nutritional diseases (Lallo, Armelagos, and Mensforth, 1977). There is also a synergistic relationship between nutritional and infectious disease. Individuals afflicted with both infectious and nutritional deficiencies have a more serious manifestation of both conditions (Mensforth et al., 1978).

In this paper we will examine the effect of subsistence changes on the skeletal biology of Sudanese Nubian populations during the last 12,000 years. Specifically, we will show that the shift to primary food production resulted in facial reduction and significant related changes in craniofacial morphology. In addition, adaptation to intensive agriculture created the potential for nutritional deficiencies in later Nubian populations.

Consequence of Food Production on Craniofacial Morphology

Populations used in the study of the evolution of craniofacial morphology include materials from the Mesolithic (ca. 12,000 B.P.), A-Group (3400–2400 B.C.), C-Group (2400–100 B.C.), Meroitic (350 B.C.–A.D. 350), X-Group or Ballana (A.D. 350–550), and Christian (A.D. 550–1100) periods (see Table 1). The archaeological evidence indicates that the Mesolithic population relied on exploitation of large game, fishing, and seed-collecting. The A-Group through C-Group represents a

TABLE 1. **Samples of Nubian Crania from Scandinavian and Colorado Nubian Excavations.**

	Dates	Scandinavian Sample (Carlson, 1976a, b)	Colorado Sample (Van Gerven et al., 1973)
Christian	(A.D. 550–1500)	39	36
X-Group	(A.D. 350–550)	67	94
Meroitic	(0–A.D. 350)	57	44
C-Group	(2400–1200 B.C.)	40	
A-Group	(3400–2400 B.C.)	12	
Mesolithic	(ca. 12,000 B.P.)		39

transition from gathering/hunting to primary food production (Adams, 1970), while the Meroitic, X-Group (or Ballana), and Christian groups subsisted fully on agriculture.

Traditionally, interpretations of prehistoric cultures of Lower Nubia have relied on racial models that emphasize invasion and racial admixture to explain cultural change. Biological and cultural change during the late Pleistocene period was thought to result from the admixture of "pure" Caucasoids to the north and Negroids from the south (Dzierzykray-Rogalski, 1977; Morant, 1925, 1935; Burnor and Harris, 1968; Crichton, 1966; Billy, 1976; Strouhal, 1968, 1971a, b, c). Changes during the last 5,000 years were explained by successive migrations of alien peoples. While these models have been used extensively, there is little evidence to support the "racial admixture hypothe-

sis" of biocultural change during the Paleolithic-Mesolithic transition or the "multiple migration hypothesis" to explain change during the last 5,000 years. Evidence now suggests that evolutionary changes may account for the cultural and biological changes since the Mesolithic period (W. Y. Adams, 1967, 1970; Greene, 1966, 1972, n.d.; Van Gerven et al., 1973; Carlson, 1976a, n.d.; Armelagos and Greene, 1978).

Greene's (1966) analysis of sixteen discrete dental traits in Meroitic, X-Group, and Christian populations shows no significant biological differences. Dental traits such as complexity of molar cusp patterns are under strict genetic control and continuity of those traits between Nubian populations suggests that there have been no major displacements of populations. Green notes that unusual features such as split hypocone are found in

TABLE 2. **Comparison of Morphological Complexity of Dentition from Sudanese Nubian Mesolithic Population (6-B-36) and Meroitic Population (from Greene et al., 1967: 46)**

		Maxilla						Mandible			
		6-B-36		Meroitic				6-B-36		Meroitic	
		%	n	%	n			%	n	%	n
I	Shoveled	88	(9)	31	(22)			25	(2)	—	—
	Normal	12	(2)	69	(48)			75	(6)	—	—
M^1	4	100	(10)	69	(33)	M_1	6	54	(6)	8	(3)
	4 −			31	(15)		5	46	(5)	80	(29)
							4			12	(4)
M^2	4	11	(1)	18	(10)	M_2	6	18	(2)		
	4 −	55	(5)	46	(26)		5	27	(3)	15	(7)
	3 +	34	(3)	21	(12)		4	55	(6)	85	(41)
	3			15	(9)						
M^3	4 −	17	(2)	22	(8)	M_3	6	30	(3)	3	(1)
	3 + +	58	(7)	6	(2)		5	20	(2)	50	(17)
	3 +	17	(2)	33	(12)		4	50	(5)	47	(16)
	3	8	(1)	39	(14)						

n = number of individuals with a specific trait

Meroitic, X-Group, and Christian populations as well as in the Mesolithic group and are indicative of continuity. Similarly, Berry, Berry, and Ucko (1967), using discrete traits of the skull, did not discover any discontinuities that would indicate large-scale population displacements. These studies suggest that there have been evolutionary trends which can explain changes in skeletal morphology since the Mesolithic period.

The Mesolithic population possess large flattened faces, bun-shaped skulls, massive brow ridges, sloping foreheads, large teeth, and other features that suggest heavy musculature related to extensive use of masticatory apparatus. Mandibles display pronounced eversion of the rear (gonial) angles, massive mandibular bodies, thick mandibular symphyses, and broad ascending rami which indicate heavy chewing. Greene, Ewing, and Armelagos (1967) and Greene and Armelagos (1972) describe the large and morphologically complex dentition of the Mesolithic population, which, they hypothesize, was selected for resistance to extreme attrition.

The complexity of Mesolithic dentition is reflected in their morphology and their large size (Greene et al., 1967). The maxillary incisors are shoveled, molars often have a hypocone, and supernumerary cusps are frequently found. Over 50 percent of lower second molars have distally located third cusps and a similar percentage of third molars have an extra cusp. Thirty percent of mandibular molars have a sixth cusp (see Table 2). Shovel-shaped incisors and supernumerary cusps increase the enamel surface area, providing resistance to attrition. The overall dimensions (summed mean buccolingual and mesiodistal diameters) of Mesolithic dentition are larger than the Skūhl teeth from Mount Carmel and almost as large as the teeth of modern Australian aborigines (see Table 3).

Enamel attrition is very rapid in the Mesolithic population. In one child (age 6–9) there was stage 4 attrition (exposure of dentin linking cusps) of the deciduous molars which developed in a little over five years. Seventy percent of the adults (few of whom were aged over 40 years) show stage 4 or greater attrition on their molar teeth. The attrition in the Nubian Mesolithic is greater than that found among the Eskimo and nearly equivalent to the rate in Australian aborigines.

Carlson (n.d.; 1976a, b), Carlson and Van Gerven (1977), and Van Gerven, Armelagos, and Rohr (1977) have undertaken the most systematic analyses to date of changes in craniofacial morphology of prehistoric Nubians during the last 12,000 years. Carlson and Van Gerven (1977) divide the post-Mesolithic population into two segments. The A-Group and C-Group (A-C Group) are considered a transitional agricultural group, while the Meroitic, X-Group, and Christian population (M-X-C Group) rely on intensive agriculture.

TABLE 3. **Ranked Metric Comparison of Summed Mean Buccolingual and Mesiodistal Diameters from Mesolithic Population with Other Selected Populations (from Greene et al., 1967: 48)**

Population	Maxillary Incisor	Mandibular Incisor	Maxillary Premolars	Mandibular Premolars	Maxillary Molars	Mandibular Molars	Sum
White	28.4	23.7	31.9	29.9	61.9	62.8	238.6
Pecos	29.5	23.6	33.5	30.9	63.4	65.8	246.7
Bantu	29.6	23.9	32.3	30.6	63.3	64.3	244.0
Skūhl	32.2	26.0	36.0	31.6	65.7	65.3	256.8
6-B-36	31.5	24.8	34.8	33.0	68.2	70.2	262.5
Australian	31.9	25.6	35.4	33.0	70.5	71.4	267.8
Sinanthropus	34.7	27.1	39.4	37.2	68.4	72.3	279.1

Comparison of sixteen measurements of antero-posterior craniofacial dimensions taken from radiographs of complete skulls originally recovered by the Scandinavian expedition suggest reduction in the size of many craniofacial features (Table 4) during the last 12,000 years. Carlson and Van Gerven provide a graphic method for presenting the changes in morphology by examining the percent change in craniofacial morphology (Table 5) as a logarithmic function of time (Fig. 1). In their analysis they consider changes which seem to cluster in three groups (Table 6). Cluster I, traits related to height of cranial vault, shows an increase over time. Features related to craniofacial length and mandibular height (Cluster II) increase slightly or moderately. Cluster III, which includes measurements related to masticatory robusticity, greatly decreases over time.

The pattern of craniofacial evolution since the Mesolithic can be characterized by:

(1) decrease in robusticity of the entire cranio-facial complex, with changes most evident in features associated with mastication;

(2) trend for the midface and lower face to become positioned more inferoposteriorly to the anterior cranial vault;

(3) relative increase in cranial height and decrease in cranial length (Fig. 2).

The size and position of muscles of mastication (determined by their site of bony attachment) underwent a reduction, causing a reorientation of cranial vault/face relationship. The subsequent effect of alteration of masticatory function results in a pattern of change in craniofacial morphology in which there is a "rotation" of the cranial vault and face so that the vault becomes shorter and higher, "moving" more anterosuperiorly relative to the face. The midface and lower face underwent a concomitant change, becoming more inferoposteriorly located (Fig. 3).

While Carlson and Van Gerven combine Meroitic, X-Group, and Christian populations in their

TABLE 4. **Means and Standard Deviations for Sixteen Variables Describing Metric Variables of Three Nubian Populations (in cm) (from Carlson and Van Gerven, 1977: 497)**

Variable	Mesolithic		A-C Group		M-X-C Group	
	x̄	S.D.	x̄	S.D.	x̄	S.D.
1. Cranial length	18.58	0.32	18.18	0.64	18.27	0.82
2. Cranial height	12.75	0.56	13.91	0.66	13.64	0.64
3. Frontal chord	10.57	0.29	11.70	0.45	11.47	0.55
4. Parietal chord	11.32	0.35	0.48	0.49	12.35	0.70
5. Facial length	10.36	0.35	10.00	0.47	10.28	0.57
6. Upper face height	6.63	0.33	6.68	0.40	6.66	0.43
7. Cheek height	2.57	0.23	2.42	0.26	2.37	0.27
8. Masseter origin length	4.31	0.52	3.38	0.34	3.18	0.32
9. Ramus height	4.75	0.62	4.51	0.42	4.55	0.45
10. Corpus length	9.25	0.41	7.37	0.57	7.20	0.50
11. Symphysis height	3.35	0.22	3.19	0.38	3.28	0.37
12. Symphysis thickness	1.69	0.17	1.48	0.14	1.44	0.18
13. Ramal width	4.29	0.37	3.70	0.38	3.73	0.30
14. Sigmoid notch height	4.67	0.64	4.40	0.40	4.28	0.37
15. Coronoid process height	6.14	0.54	5.98	0.53	5.95	0.53
16. Total face height	10.92	0.60	11.55	0.60	11.46	0.65

analysis, Carlson (1976a) and Van Gerven, Armelagos, and Rohr (1977) analyze changes in the later groups. Carlson's analysis suggests that facial reduction and compensatory changes in the cranial vault continued during the Meroitic, X-Group, and Christian period.

Van Gerven, Armelagos, and Rohr (1977) used a different sample (material excavated by the University of Colorado Nubian Expedition) and a different methodology (direct measurement of crania rather than use of radiographs) to support Carlson's conclusions. Using canonical analysis, Van Gerven and co-workers noted that the pattern of reduction in facial dimensions and cranial length with an increase in cranial height and breadth occurred through Meroitic, X-Group, and Christian periods. However, they did find evidence of an increase in palate length during the X-Group period that may be related to admixture or selection.

Two alternative models have been offered to explain the reduction in facial morphology. Carlson (1976b) and Carlson and Van Gerven (1977) have developed the masticatory function hypothesis

(Fig. 4), which suggests that changes in diet from the Mesolithic through the Christian period brought about a reduction in neuromuscular activity and decrease in stress placed on jaws and teeth (Carlson and Van Gerven, 1979: 574). Carlson and Van Gerven propose two mechanisms that resulted in alteration in craniofacial growth patterns. Initially, there is a decreased mechanical stimulation of periosteal membrane of the craniofacial skeleton which leads to a reduction in robustness of craniofacial complex. The second mechanism involves progressive alteration of maxillomandibular growth resulting in a midface and lower face that are smaller and more inferoposteriorly located. Cranial vault and base compensate for these facial changes with more globular vault and more acute basal angle.

A second hypothesis, the dental reduction hypothesis (Greene and Armelagos, 1972), suggests that changes in diet (reduction of dental attrition and increase in cariogenic foods such as carbohydrates) led to selection for smaller and morphologically less complex teeth. Reduction in tooth size

TABLE 5. **Percent Change in Craniofacial Dimensions from Mesolithic through A-Group/C-Group and Meroitic/X-Group/Christian Periods (from Carlson and Van Gerven, 1977: 500)**

Variable	Mesolithic/A-C Group	A-C Group/M-X-C Group	Total
1. Cranial length	−2.2	0.05	−2.15
2. Cranial height	8.4	−2.0	6.4
3. Frontal chord	9.7	−2.0	7.7
4. Parietal chord	9.3	−1.1	8.2
5. Facial length	−3.5	2.8	0.7
6. Upper face height	0.8	−0.3	0.5
7. Cheek height	−5.9	−2.1	−8.0
8. Masseter origin length	−21.6	−6.0	−27.6
9. Ramus height	−3.8	−0.5	−4.3
10. Corpus length	−20.4	−2.4	−22.8
11. Symphysis height	−4.8	2.8	−2.0
12. Symphysis thickness	−12.5	−2.8	−15.3
13. Ramal width	−13.8	0.9	−12.9
14. Sigmoid notch height	−5.8	−2.8	−8.6
15. Coronoid process height	−2.7	−0.6	−3.3
16. Total face height	5.5	−0.8	4.7

TABLE 6. **Changes in Craniofacial Morphology that Cluster in Three Groups**

CLUSTER I	CLUSTER II	CLUSTER III
Parietal chord	Upper facial height	Ramal width
Frontal chord	Facial length	Symphyseal thickness
Cranial height	Cranial length	Corpus length
Total facial height	Symphyseal height	Masseter length
	Coronoid height	
	Ramus height	
	Cheek height	
	Sigmoid height	

and concomitant changes in supporting structures would have led to facial reduction and the compensatory changes in the vault and base of the skull. While these hypotheses provide alternative pathways for explaining facial reduction, both accept change in diet as the primary factor which led to changes in facial morphology.

The reduction in craniofacial dimension with changes in diet reflects the impact of culture on the biology of prehistoric Nubians. The adaptation to agriculture affected the craniofacial morphology by selection for smaller chewing apparatus. The subsequent intensification of agriculture continued to select for facial reduction and also resulted in more serious problems affecting the health and disease of these groups. The reliance on intensive agriculture increased the frequency and severity of nutritional deficiencies. This interpretation is supported by the combined analysis of retardation in long bone growth and development, premature osteoporosis (bone loss) in children and young adult females, occurrence of porotic hyperostosis (iron-deficiency

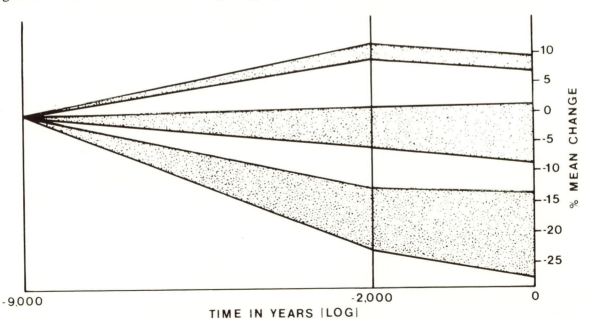

Figure 1. Mean changes in percent of craniofacial dimensions from the Mesolithic through A-C periods (A-Group and C-Group, −2000 years), and M-X-C (Meroitic, X-Group, and Christian periods, 0) plotted as a logarithmic function of time (modified from Carlson and Van Gerven, 1977: 501).

anemia), and microdefects in the enamel of the dentition which reflect growth cessation. A population analysis of these biological indicators of nutritional stress, in conjunction with archaeological evidence, strongly supports the assertion that Nubian agriculturalists suffered from nutritional deficiencies.

Long Bone Growth and Premature Osteoporosis in Children

Growth is one of the most widely used indicators of nutritional status in children. Long bone growth, an easily quantifiable feature, has been shown to be very sensitive to nutritional deficiencies. While growth has been frequently used in assessing the nutritional status in contemporary populations, the methods have not been widely used or rigorously applied to archaeological material. However, investigations by Johnston (1962, 1968), Mahler (n.d.), Armelagos et al. (1972), Sundick (n.d.), Ubelaker (1978), and Huss-Ash-more et al. (1982) have successfully used growth patterns to describe the developmental trends in prehistoric populations. For such populations, dental age can be used as an approximation of developmental age, and growth curves and relative rates of growth can be computed. With proper application, growth rates in archaeological skeletal populations can be useful in understanding patterns of development. These patterns can be further analyzed in terms of growth retardation resulting from stress.

Growth curves for the combined Meroitic, X-Group, and Christian Nubian populations (based on measurements of the femur, tibia, clavicle, humerus, and ulna) for 115 individuals aged 6 months to 31 years have been analyzed (Mahler, n.d.; Armelagos et al., 1972). The continuous growth of the long bones does not suggest any major evidence of growth retardation. However, a comparison of Nubian growth velocity (relative percent growth) with a sample of American boys (Maresh, 1955: 728–729) reveals differences in the overall patterns of growth (Fig. 5). The pattern of growth in American boys shows accelerated growth in the first few

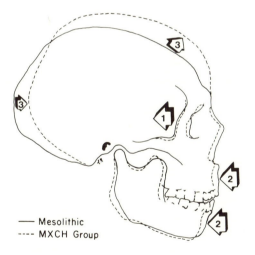

Figure 2. Changes in crania of prehistoric Nubians from the Mesolithic through M-X-C. Changes involve (1) reduction in size of the muscles of mastication; (2) reduced growth of maxillomandibular complex; and (3) reduction in cranial length and increase in cranial height (modified from Carlson and Van Gerven, 1977: 502).

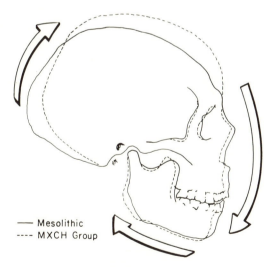

Figure 3. "Rotation" of the skull, in which a smaller face becomes located more inferoposteriorly.

years of life and decelerated growth thereafter. Further, the same sample shows a second period of acceleration in mid-childhood that reaches a peak during the adolescent growth spurt. The Nubian sample follows the same pattern of growth as the American sample. However, the relative percentage increase is not as great, and the Nubians show evidence of deceleration from the second year until the seventh year. Although the pattern of Nubian long-bone growth is not grossly abnormal, there are several phases of development that deserve to be examined more closely. The rapid deceleration of growth during early childhood and the cessation of growth around age 6 may be indications of stress during these periods of physical development.

In order more fully to examine these trends in

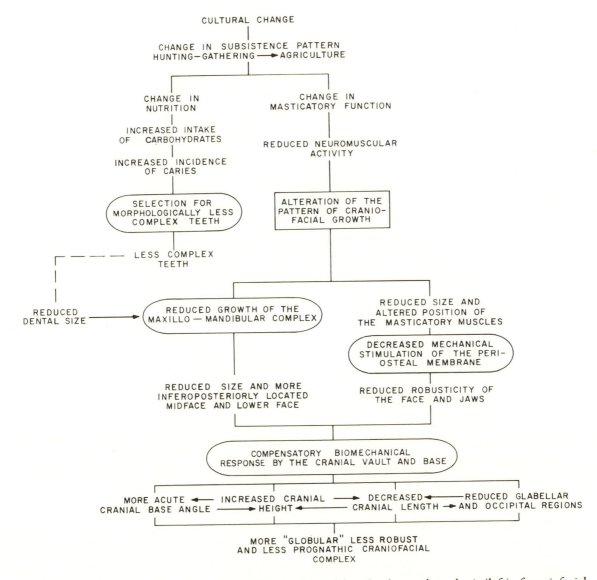

Figure 4. Model of masticatory-functional hypothesis (right) and dental reduction hypothesis (left) of craniofacial change in post-Pleistocene Nubia, from the Mesolithic period (ca. 12,000 B.P.) through the Christian period (modified from Carlson and Van Gerven, 1979: 575).

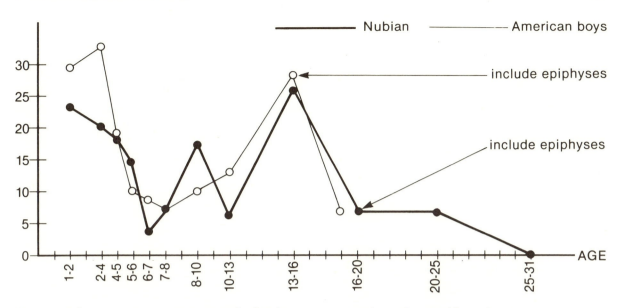

Figure 5. Relative percent increase in growth of Nubian vs. American boys (from Mahler, n.d.: 28).

overall bone growth, bone width and thickness were analyzed to determine the relative amount of bone present. While osteoporosis (relative decrease in bone volume) is a normal feature of advanced aging, its occurrence at younger ages is an important indicator of stress. Juvenile osteoporosis (a term coined by Garn et al., 1966), in particular, has been observed to result from protein-energy malnutrition.

In experimental studies, malnourished rats (Frandson et al., 1954), piglets, and cockerels (Dickerson and McCance, 1961) displayed reduced but proportional growth in length and total width of long bones. However, growth in cortical thickness of these bones was dramatically and disproportionately reduced. A similar phenomenon has been radiographically documented among modern human populations. Children hospitalized for protein-energy malnutrition show marked thinning and radiolucency of both the long bones and the flat bones of the skull (Garn et al., 1966).

This juvenile osteoporosis has also been observed in the Nubian skeletal populations. In an analysis of femoral growth patterns, Huss-Ashmore (1978) compared length, breadth, and cross-sectional development for seventy-five Nubian ju-

veniles, aged from birth to 14 years. The results indicate a discrepancy between rates of overall growth and increases in thickness of cortical bone.[1] When long-bone growth is measured for this population by the femur length plotted against dental age, the pattern is typical of a generalized somatic growth curve (Fig. 6). Growth proceeds rapidly for the first two years and slows somewhat afterward. The development of femoral midshaft width, a direct measurement of femoral diameter (Fig. 7) and of femoral cross-section area (Fig. 8), which includes the cortical and medullary area (Fig. 9), shows similar trends.

The comparison of cortical thickness with total midshaft diameter indicates growth retardation (Fig. 7). Cortical thickness not only fails to increase but shows evidence of decrease after age 10. The severity of growth retardation is also evidenced by changes in percent cortical area. This is the percentage of the total cross-sectional area

1. This represents a reanalysis of the growth patterns in the sample used by Mahler (n.d.) and Armelagos et al. (1972). These seventy-five individuals represent those individuals in the earlier study for which microradiographs are available. Age in this sample was determined in yearly increments.

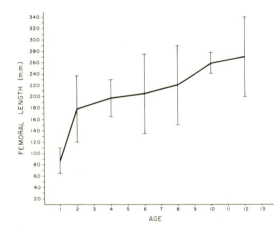

Figure 6. Growth in femoral length of Nubian juveniles (vertical lines represent variation within one standard deviation).

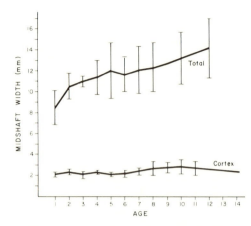

Figure 7. Growth in midshaft diameter for Nubian juveniles.

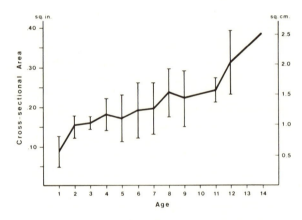

Figure 8. Growth in cross-sectional area for Nubian juveniles.

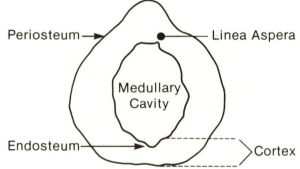

Figure 9. Diagram of a cross-section of a long bone. The cortex or cortical area is that part of the bone which is a solid bony matrix; the medullary cavity is devoid of bone.

actually occupied by bone. Cortical area is a more accurate indicator of cortical development than cortical thickness, which can vary considerably at different locations. The percent cortical area in the Nubian juveniles increases during the first two years and then declines sharply (Fig. 10). Despite fluctuations, it is maintained at a relatively low level throughout childhood. Comparison with a modern, well-nourished population (Garn, 1970) illustrates important differences. Garn's sample showed a

steady increase in percent cortical area from birth. The decrease in percent cortical area in the Nubian samples suggests that long-bone growth in juveniles was maintained at the expense of cortical bone growth.

In order to understand the biological processes that underlie these changes it is necessary to extend our analysis beyond the macroscopic level. An analysis of microstructure has been undertaken for the Nubian sample, in which individuals near the

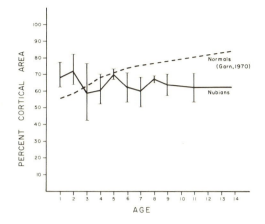

Figure 10. Percent cortical area to age in normal development (from Garn, 1970) compared with the Nubian sample.

mean for cortical area were compared with those at least one standard deviation below the mean. The group below the mean showed marked differences at the endosteal portion of the cortex. The most salient feature of this area was the presence of large, active resorption spaces, identified by rough, high-density edges with a scalloped appearance (Howship's lacunae). Apposition of circumferential lamellar bone was maintained in almost all cases. In a number of specimens, this represented the only cortical bone present. A preliminary study of a small subsample of each group indicated that for normals, the ratio of formation spaces exceeded resorption, while for those below the mean, the opposite trend was found. This is consistent with the observation by Garn et al. (1966) of bone loss in nutritionally related juvenile osteoporosis.

Thus, cortical thickness in conjunction with long-bone length provides a measure of nutritional status. Clearly, the Nubian juveniles show patterns suggestive of nutritional stress. However, the significance of nutritional stress cannot be fully understood and interpreted by these findings alone, since growth requires high inputs of energy and nutrients, and any factor that affects energy and nutrient requirements can alter growth. For example, retardation in growth can result from a decreased nutrient intake or an increase in the nutrient requirement. In the Nubian sample, long-bone

growth combined with the occurrence of nutritional anemia supports our contention that the Nubian children were experiencing stress from nutritional deficiencies.

Porotic Hyperostosis

The occurrence of porotic hyperostosis (an indicator of iron-deficiency anemia) in the Nubian population is additional evidence that nutritional stress may have been the cause of growth retardation (Lallo et al., 1977; El-Najjar et al., 1976; Mensforth et al., 1978). The physiological response to anemia results in an increase in the production of red blood cells, which causes an expansion of the marrow cavity of the thin bones of the skeleton. The diploe (marrow portion) of the skull is especially responsive to these changes. Rapid expansion of the diploe results in the outer layer's becoming very thin, exposing the porous-appearing trabecular bone.

Any anemia (hereditary anemias such as sickle-cell anemia or thalassemia and nutritional anemia) may cause porotic hyperostosis. Moseley (1965, 1966) and Steinbock (1976: 213–292) discuss the methods for distinguishing among anemias, noting that nutritional anemias are usually less severe and more limited in distribution. Eng (1958) was one of the first to argue that iron-deficiency anemia could result in skeletal changes similar to hereditary anemias, and Hengen (1971) discusses the etiology of the condition in prehistoric populations.

While porotic hyperostosis is not by itself diagnostic of a specific anemia, it is a useful tool for investigating stress. The use of such an indicator for nutritional inference should be undertaken within the context of ecological analysis of a group's total adaptation. Distribution and severity of the lesion, occurrence with respect to age and sex, and reconstruction of the group's subsistence pattern should facilitate identification of nutritional anemias.

Carlson et al. (1974) noted that one-fifth of the Nubians studied showed evidence of porotic hyperostosis. The restriction of the lesions to the superior border of the orbits and the high frequency (32 percent) among those aged 0–6 suggest a nutritional cause. Hereditary anemias are unlikely, as they would have caused severe lesions affecting other portions of the crania and postcranial skeletons. The Nubian reliance on iron-poor cereal grains, such as millet, and such factors as weaning practices and parasitic infections are likely precipitating or causal factors in nutritional anemias.

Microdefects of the Dental Enamel

Dental enamel is also extremely sensitive to physiological stresses. Stress-induced cessation of growth in enamel causes changes which cannot be remodeled and are therefore indelible markers. In a sense, these growth-disruption markers provide a "memory" of earlier metabolic events. Researchers have used gross indicators such as enamel hypoplasia (Schulz and McHenry, 1975; Swärdstedt, 1966; and Goodman et al., 1980) as well as microdefects (Rose et al., 1978) to evaluate growth disruption.

Recently, Rudney (1979) analyzed microdefects in the enamel of adult Meroitic Nubians. Rudney examined abnormal striae of Retzius (a microdefect that indicates growth disruption) in etched thin sections of molar teeth. By measuring abnormal striae in relation to the development of the enamel, he was able to determine the peak frequency of growth disruption in the Meroitic group. The greatest disruption in growth occurs during early childhood (between 1.5 and 2.4 years). Growth disruption as reflected in dental enamel is similar to patterns noted in long-bone growth and the occurrence of porotic hyperostosis. Growth retardation occurs during the most critical phase of rapid growth, when children are beginning to be weaned.

Premature Osteoporosis in Young Adults

The occurrence of premature osteoporosis in young adults is a difficult phenomenon to interpret. The age at which bone loss begins is frequently obscured by the lack of sufficient adolescent mate-

rial to establish a juvenile-adult continuum. However, despite small sample sizes and individual variability, macroscopic analysis of osteoporosis in conjunction with histological analysis reveals an early onset of bone loss in populations undergoing dietary change.

Osteoporosis has been studied extensively in contemporary and prehistoric populations (Armelagos et al., 1972; Carlson et al., 1976; Dewey et al., 1969; Garn, 1970; Erickson, 1976; Ortner, 1975; Perzigian, 1973; Stout and Teitelbaum, 1976a, b). While the studies of contemporary and prehistoric populations suggest that bone loss is a normal feature of the aging process, there have been some attempts to relate bone loss to differences in dietary pattern (Perzigian, 1973; Albanese, 1977).

Perzigian (1973) tested the hypothesis that changes in diet of prehistoric groups may affect the rate of bone loss. Although he found an increase in the size of the medullary or marrow cavity (a measure of a decrease in the amount of bone) in agriculturalists compared to gatherer/hunters, he did not believe these changes were related to diet. Perzigian reasoned that agricultural populations have a more adequate nutritional intake, and therefore the changes in diet could not explain increase in osteoporosis. However, the assumption that intensive agriculture leads to improvement of diet may not be warranted. There is abundant evidence that suggests that intensive agriculture may result in a deterioration of diet.

Building on the data derived from macroscopic studies, the microscopic study of Nubian bone demonstrates the process by which environmental disturbances alter the configuration of the skeleton. Bone, as a tissue, is an open living system and changes constantly throughout life. Both the patterns and the rates of this change have been studied histologically for normal and diseased individuals (Jowsey, 1963; Frost, 1966; Ortner, 1975; Stout and Teitelbaum, 1976a, b). The departure of Nubian populations from the expected normal pattern of bone growth is of particular interest in this research.

Evidence of premature osteoporosis in adult Nubians has been supported in a study by Martin and Armelagos (1979). A microradiographic

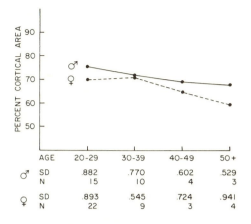

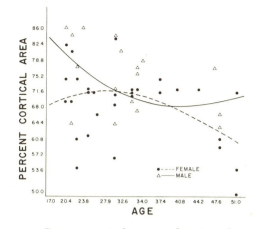

Figure 11. Relationship between percent cortical area of bone and age (SD = standard deviation, N = sample size).

Figure 12. Percent cortical area as a function of age (males and females), using regression analysis of the resultant scatterdiagram.

analysis of 74 adult femora (aged 20–50) from the Ballana (X-Group) population from Sudanese Nubia (A.D. 350–550) demonstrated the usefulness of a combined macroscopic and microscopic approach. On a gross level, males and females exhibit significant difference in osteoporotic bone-loss (Anova p. <.05) as measured by percent cortical area (Fig. 11). Measured from the third decade to the sixth decade, females lose 10.7 percent cortical area while males experience a 4.9 percent loss. This pattern is similar to that reported in other prehistoric populations. However, there is evidence that females gain bone between the third and fourth decade and then begin to show a loss following the fourth decade. Regression analysis (Fig. 12) indicates that the female pattern of increase, then decrease, in cortical area is not an artifact of the age groups used in our analysis. Because individual ages are used for this comparison, lack of bone due to immaturity cannot affect the figures reported for older individuals. Microscopic evidence of active loss of endosteal bone, even in young individuals, further supports an interpretation of stress rather than of delayed female maturation. However, the factors responsible for this pattern of cortical bone development are difficult to isolate definitely.

Actual processes underlying growth in cortical bone cannot be established from macroscopic analysis. To interpret more fully the trends found for Nubian bone loss, a microscopic study was undertaken in conjunction with the macroscopic examination.

The configuration of a given bone results from the activity of two types of specialized cell, osteoblasts (bone-forming cells) and osteoclasts (bone-resorbing cells). These cells work together in units called osteons, which together make up cortical bone. Throughout life, the laying down of new bone and the resorption of mature bone is an ongoing process.

The balance between the processes of bone formation and resorption determines the amount of bone present at any given time. During childhood, formation normally exceeds resorption, with a resultant gain in bone mass. In the young adult, the processes are in equilibrium, and bone mass is maintained at a relatively constant level. Beginning in middle age, however, resorption exceeds formation, and bone is lost. Cortices gradually become thinner throughout old age, frequently resulting in senile osteoporosis. Quantification of the ratio between osteoblastic deposition and osteoclastic resorption provides the means for the Nubian adults. Forming osteons and resorption spaces are easily recognized and quantified using the methodology of Ortner (1975) and Martin and Armelagos (1979).

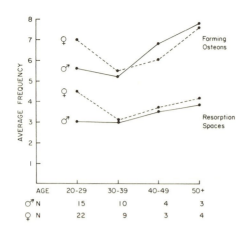

Figure 13. Combined average frequencies per microscopic field of resorption spaces and forming osteons for males and females.

Morphometric analysis of the Nubian sample indicates extreme variation between males and females in the 20–29 age range (Fig. 13). The normal ratio between forming osteons and resorption spaces approximates 2:1. This trend is seen for both males and females in all age classes except in the 20–29-year class. Females exhibit a more rapid turnover of bone, as is reflected in the increase in number of both forming osteons and resorption spaces. Recent research by Stout (1979) suggests that metabolic disturbances brought on by nutritional deficiencies are often reflected in significantly increased bone remodeling such as that seen in the young Nubian females. The finding of such a stress during the peak reproductive period suggests the possibility of nutritional involvement. Multiparous females are especially at risk, since their reserves of calcium and energy are likely to become depleted. Lactation alone requires up to 300 mg of calcium and 1,000 kilocalories per day (Worthington et al., 1977). Grain diets are normally low in both calcium and iron and high in phosphorus. Further, the outer husks of cereal grains contain phytic acid, a substance that combines with phosphorus to form phytates. These compounds can be broken down during processing by the action of yeast or cooking. Where such practices are absent or inefficient, phytate phosphorus may interfere with the absorption of calcium and, to a lesser degree, iron (Rodale, 1959). Thus, a diet already low in essential nutrients, combined with pregnancy, lactation, and high workload, may have produced the marked bone loss in this sample of Nubian females.

While osteoporosis does not result simply from a lack of dietary calcium, bone cannot be normally produced without an adequate supply. Albanese (1977) states that the magnitude of bone loss is related to dietary habits, which act in a synergistic manner with other components of osteoporosis such as genetics and diseases. In this study, the underlying processes of increased bone turnover aid in elucidating the trends in bone growth. The evidence supports an interpretation of nutritional stress specifically affecting the young female segment of the population.

Conclusion

The shift in subsistence pattern had a significant impact on the biological adaptation of prehistoric Nubians. The development of agriculture resulted in a reduction in facial dimensions and concomitant changes in cranial morphology. In addition, the intensification of agriculture led to nutritional deprivation. The pattern of bone growth and development, the occurrence of iron-deficiency anemia (as evidenced by porotic hyperostosis), microdefects in dentition, and premature osteoporosis in juveniles and young adult females all suggest that later Nubian populations involved in intensive agriculture were experiencing nutritional deficiencies. The ability to interpret the biological consequences of nutritional changes should increase our potential for understanding the full impact of the shift to agriculture.

14

B. WEST AFRICA

Early Agricultural Societies in Ghana

MERRICK POSNANSKY

The archaeological evidence for Ghana's earliest agricultural societies has been published by Colin Flight (1976b) and the story, largely of the Kintampo Industry, was amplified by Joanne Dombrowski (1976). Basically, there is circumstantial evidence of agriculture in the form of village communities mainly situated north of the forest, particularly in the Begho and Kintampo areas, where most of the research has been undertaken (Fig. 1). Other Kintampo sites are also found in areas in the forest such as Boyasi near Kumasi (Anquandah, 1976) where clearings may be of a substantial age, and on the grasslands of the Ghanaian coast. The diagnostic artifact of the Kintampo Industry is the object first called a "terracotta cigar" by O. Davies (1962) and now thought to have been used as a potting tool (Anquandah, 1965). It is associated at Ntereso with harpoons and arrowheads reminiscent of those found in the Sahel (O. Davies, 1966) and at Boyasi with stone beads and polished stone arrowheads (Anquandah, 1976). At several sites some terracotta "art" objects (Posnansky, 1979) occur, two of which appear to depict domestic animals. There is a suspicion of dwarf cattle at two

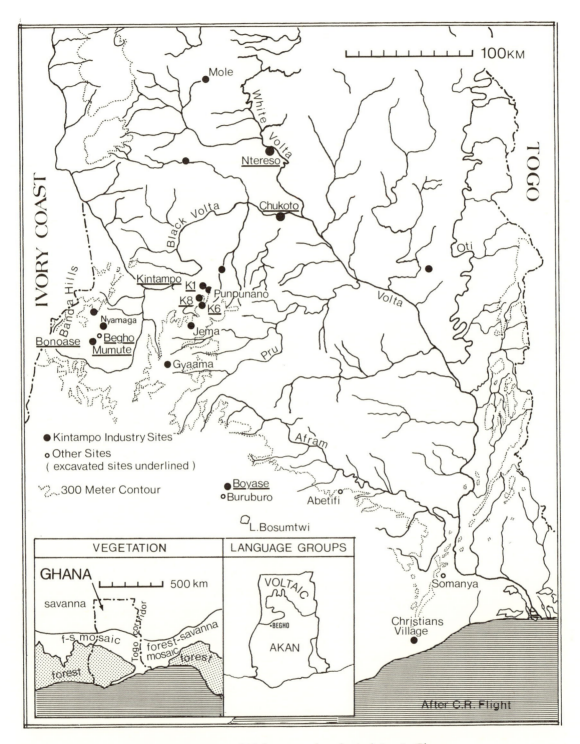

Figure 1. Language groups, vegetation, and Holocene archaeological sites in Ghana.

sites and a probability of their presence at Kintampo, while a dwarf goat occurs at Ntereso and Kintampo (Carter and Flight, 1972). The available radiocarbon dates for settlement sites, as opposed to stray finds, cluster in the middle and latter half of the second millennium B.C. (Posnansky, 1976: 60). At various sites, particularly in the Begho area, there is evidence of small wattle-and-daub houses. At Mumute the settlement covers an area of some 2,100 m² and includes at least one well or cistern. At Bonoase, huts of about 4–5 m² occur; the outline is picked out by a rough square of laterite boulders. There is an indication that oleaginous forest trees such as oil palms and *Canarium schwein-furthii*, as well as cowpeas, were being exploited or perhaps even managed (Flight, 1976b).

What is striking about the Kintampo material is, first, its relative abundance: new material is being found every year practically everywhere archaeologists dig north of the forest (most recently in 1978, by Peter Shinnie at Daboya). Second, though the artifacts are distinctive there has yet been no indication of the Kintampo Industry outside Ghana. Third and more significant, though there is a chronological gap in the evidence between the Kintampo material and the early Iron Age, several of the sites are located close to major Iron Age sites, and in areas associated in the oral traditions with the origins of some of the later Akan peoples of Ghana. One such tradition refers to the founders of Begho (a town that developed around A.D. 1000), who are said to have emerged from a hole in the ground within a grassy plain. The historians called these stories myths, but archaeological investigation revealed an area in which Kintampo sites occurred. Excavation revealed that the holes were man-made, rock-cut water cisterns designed to capture the runoff from the thinly vegetated plain in an area otherwise devoid of surface water (Agorsah, n.d.). Caves associated with the origins of the Bono Manso State to the east similarly turned out to be early sites (Effah-Gyamfi, 1974).

An approach that is perhaps more rewarding than initially anticipated is a study of the collecting and trapping activities of the people who now live in the area of Begho and several of the principal Kintampo sites. What is perhaps significant about our study, which has been repeated at different seasons to get an idea of annual subsistence patterns, is the importance attached to certain collecting activities. Seeds, leaves, roots, or bark of over 200 species are used for food, for medicinal purposes, for soapmaking, for building and as craft materials. In an area in which protein from domestic animals is scarce, the trapping of creatures like the grasscutter (cane rat) *Thryonomys swinderianus* becomes more than a pastime. Its occurrence in present-day diets and in rubbish heaps back to Kintampo contexts emphasizes the importance of continuity in collecting practices. The similar present importance of the various oleaginous nuts and fruits such as palm oil (*Elais guineensis*), shea butter (*Butyrospermum parkii*), and *Canarium schweinfurthii* and the mystique that surrounds the alleged efficacy of several of the rarer forest fringe plants as cure-alls indicate the significance of the collecting base. Many of the plants are species that do best in forest environments, particularly in secondary, more open forest areas. This is typical of Boyasi which, though within the forest, is basically a savanna inlier in which savanna species like the Borassus palm and the ground orchid are present with birds such as the Standard-winged Night-jar (Woodel and Newton, 1975).

The geomorphological and botanical data recently described by Hall, Swaine, and Talbot (1978) from Bosumtwi Crater Lake provide evidence that the forest was more open up to 6000–7000 B.C. They also provide evidence of the abundance of leaf impressions of *Canarium*, a tree that is not particularly abundant naturally. This abundance may, therefore, be the result of human activity in which the selective pressures resulting from human preference led to an increase of *Canarium* (and, presumably, other species not surviving in the record) at the expense of other, less useful species. It is of course possible that most of the leaves they found derived from a single tree (D. A. Livingstone, pers. comm.). They cite further evidence that this tree, which is rare in mature forests, is also heavily represented in the seed flora from excavated rock shelter sites in Ghana (A. B. Smith, 1975b; Musonda, n.d.) dating from the fourth millennium B.C., a period when Lake Bosumtwi was in a regressed state. This suggests that the collection of the nuts of oleaginous trees was begun before the forest became fully established. These collecting activities kept areas, albeit small and dispersed, open during the advance of the forest and the nuts formed part of the subsistence base for the later Kintampo villages. The nutritional and material-resource value of the collecting activities ensured that they continued throughout agricultural times up to the present. What now needs to be added to this multidisciplinary approach is a much more detailed linguistic analysis of the terms used to describe the collecting and trapping activities, for the items collected or for the processed end-products, to see if a pre-Akan underlay can be found, to add to our knowledge of Ghana's earliest agricultural societies.

In a detailed study of hunting and trapping activities in the village of Hani, the modern successor of the medieval town of Begho, which forms the subject of another paper (Posnansky, in press), it was discovered that some 76 percent of the households surveyed hunt with guns, 65 percent employ dogs in hunting, eighty-eight collect snails, and all, except those consisting solely of women and children, trap and collect oil-palm grubs. The net protein input from small bush animals such as grass-cutter, giant forest rat (*Cricetomys gambianus*), Royal antelope (*Neotragus pygmaeus*), and birds averages as much as 250 grams per capita each week. This, combined with fish, snails, grubs, and other wild protein sources, is more substantial than had previously been thought and was presumably even higher in the past when big game were available in addition to the varieties presently hunted and trapped. Fifty-six percent of the households collected honey, with the leading hunters often being the most successful honey-gatherers because of their more intimate knowledge of the wild environment. Our study clearly indicated the traditional importance of hunting in the southern savanna of Ghana, an importance reinforced by an analysis of folk-tales and a study of the ritual status of the hunter in certain Akan societies. In the traditions, hunters are intimately associated with the founding of villages and, in the folklore, with those same forest fringe plants, such as yams and oil palms, that occupy a place of fundamental importance in the diet and ritual life of most Akan communities.

The specialized and extensive etymology of these plants is highly suggestive of their antiquity as well as of their overall importance.

The model that emerges from the ethnoarchaeological evidence and the oral history is of small, scattered Later Stone Age populations of hunter/gatherers in the forest fringe areas gaining an appreciation of the excellent nutritional qualities and reliability of oil-palm nuts and other oleaginous plants as well as yams. During the dry period before 7000 B.C., the relatively open nature of much of central Ghana, presumably similar to conditions in the present southern savanna, would have provided ideal circumstances for both yam and oil-palm management and collection, which explains the scattered nature of Kintampo sites in areas that are now thick forest. We have no evidence of actual cultivation, though certain stone tools have been suggested as hoes by both Rattray, who looked to elongated, parallel-sided, thick-sectioned, ground-stone axes (Rattray, 1923: 322–331), and O. Davies (1960), who preferred flaked-stone tools. Both are possible, but neither suggestion is as yet provable and the chronological parameters of neither artifact have been demonstrated. Both have attractions because of their forest context, which suggested to Davies a very definite vegecultural stage in the forest. By vegecultural he had in mind periodic use of tubers, such as yams, followed by a more systematic collection, perhaps on a regular seasonal basis, which gradually led to intentional planting of yams and simple cultivation. What is more readily provable is that increased desiccation in the Sahel caused populations to move south, bringing with them dwarf cows (A. B. Smith, 1975a), cereals (sorghum and millet), and a highly distinctive lithic technology. These new groups were integrated with the existing societies in differing degrees, an integration that is reflected in the regional variations of the Kintampo industry. In the forest fringes, where, on present evidence, settlement seems to have been more widespread, the indigenous crops proved to be more productive than the exotic cereals. The arrival of iron technology about 2,000 years ago allowed populations previously relatively restricted to the forest fringes and savanna inliers within the forest to expand into the forest itself. This expansion from the southern savanna is reflected in the chronology of the Akan languages, in which Brong on the northern fringe of the forest is regarded as being earlier than forest Akan languages such as the Asante and Fante (Dolphyne, 1979: 115–116). After the middle of the second millennium A.D. the arrival of American crops displaced many of the indigenous plants as actively cultivated crops, but the latter are still used as relishes, as famine foods, as soaps, or for other valuable, though not necessarily food, purposes. The fact that, as new crops were introduced and agriculture became more productive, the hunting ethic still remained strong, even to this day at a time of decidedly diminishing returns, suggests that there is a strong element of continuity among Akan agriculturalists. If this is so it tends to support an *in situ* development of at least part of the agricultural way of life, particularly that relating to the all-important forest fringe crops such as yams, shea-butter nuts, and oil palms.

The problems that remain to be tackled are: first, to discover what grains, if any, were actually cultivated by the Kintampo settlers—the oral traditions of the founders of Begho suggest millets; second, to discover whether yam cultivation in the forest fringes is actually as old as the Kintampo sites. Unfortunately, we have very few leads on yam cultivation (Posnansky, 1969). The yam plant is noticeably difficult to detect in the archaeological record because it decays totally and is processed for food with organic implements such as wooden mortars and pestles. One hope is to discover yam mounds, which are normally up to 70 cm in height and 1.50 m in diameter, in section, or (even more remotely) in plan, in our excavations. As this would require knowing the exact location of ancient yam plots, for which no surface material indications exist, the possibilities for such discoveries, using our present retrieval capabilities, are extremely slight.

It seems perfectly feasible, however, to posit a strong collecting base, combined with trapping, for Ghana's first mixed farmers. Such activities are much more amenable to archaeological detection than either yam or millet cultivation. The oral traditions suggest that the importance of such practices has declined very rapidly in the last seventy-five years. In the course of the past ten years, for instance, during which this writer has monitored the area, both barkcloth making and dyeing using vegetable substances have almost disappeared, an indication of the speed with which collecting habits and the processing of indigenous raw materials can change. It is also an indication of the urgency of ethnoarchaeological fieldwork if we are to appreciate the development of agricultural practices in West Africa and gain insights into the general awareness traditional farmers had of the natural environment's potential as both food and raw materials.

Postscript

Discoveries made since 1980 indicate that the distribution pattern of the Kintampo Industry extends into immediately adjacent areas of the Ivory Coast and Togo (T. Garrard and P. de Barros, pers. comm.), while new excavations at Daboya (F. J. Kense, pers. comm.) give indications of a temporal continuity into the late first millennium B.C.

15

Archaeological Evidence and Effects of Food-Producing in Nigeria

THURSTAN SHAW

Archaeological Evidence

Nigeria has so far produced scant direct evidence for early food-production. Bad conditions of preservation are widespread: they are worst in the extreme south, where bone may only survive for a few decades, and best in the extreme north, which has produced the earliest evidence we have. Flotation methods have not been widely employed, but where they have been, results have been disappointing.

Domestic cattle are attested from the lowest levels of the occupation-mound site of Daima, not far south of Lake Chad, dated to ca. 600 B.C. (Connah, 1976), and they dominate the mammalian remains throughout the history of the mound (whose occupation came to an end ca. A.D. 1100). Wild game and small stock, probably goats, were more numerous in the upper part of the mound than in the lower. This apparently decreasing emphasis on cattle pastoralism is also reflected in the fact that clay figurines of cows are commonest in the lower parts of the mound and those of sheep and goats only appear in the upper. It has been suggested that this change, with the accompanying increase of grinding equipment, indicates a greater dependence on cereal-growing, especially of sorghum. It is only at these upper levels that actual remains of sorghum have been preserved. One would have expected sorghum and bulrush millet to have been grown in northern Nigeria long before this, but at present there is no direct evidence for it. It seems most likely that the site of "Bornu 38," beginning half a millennium earlier than Daima, was also food-producing, but bone material from there appears not to have been analyzed, and there were no carbonized cereal remains.

Excavation of Later Stone Age deposits at four rock shelters in Nigeria has failed to produce any direct evidence of food production. Mejiro Cave, in the woodland savanna between the northern margin of the rain forest and the river Niger above the confluence, produced a microlithic industry in quartz but no pottery or ground-stone axes (Willett, 1962). Three excavations have been carried out in the Rop rock shelter, on the Jos Plateau, and there has been disagreement over the interpretation of the stratigraphy in general and, in particular, on the associations of a skeleton found at a shallow depth at the back of the shelter (Fagg, 1944, 1972; Eyo, 1972; David, n.d.a, n.d.b). It seems that in part of the shelter there was an aceramic microlithic layer underlying one containing pottery, but in other parts of the shelter this overlying layer was absent. A radiocarbon date of 25 ± 100 B.C. was obtained from the skeleton (Fagg, 1965), whose teeth are said to show a wear pattern likely to result from subsistence based on agriculture rather than on hunting and gathering (Gaherty, 1968).

At Dutsen Kongba, a few miles from Rop, excavation revealed an aceramic microlithic layer at the bottom, overlain by one with pottery; many ground-stone axes had been collected as surface finds from the site, but none was found stratified. Radiocarbon dates suggest a date early in the fourth millennium B.C. for the first appearance of ceramics (York, 1974).

At the rock shelter site of Iwo Eleru, in the rain forest of southwestern Nigeria but only 50 km from the savanna boundary, excavation showed the lowest levels to contain an aceramic microlithic industry going back to the tenth millennium B.C.

Ground-stone axes and pottery make their appearance in the fourth millennium B.C. (T. Shaw, 1969b).

It has sometimes been supposed that introduction of food-producing practices accompanied the advent of pottery and ground-stone axes in Nigeria, but at present this remains a guess. What is of interest is the occurrence at Iwo Eleru, a little later in time than the first pottery, of trapezoids showing marked areas of gloss behind the cutting edge; they are invariably made of chalcedony, and this may account for their never having been recorded at any other site, since they would be far harder to recognize in the more generally used quartz (T. Shaw, 1973a). They certainly recall "sickle flints," but while it is a reasonable conjecture that they were slotted into some sickle-like implement, one cannot be sure whether they were used for cutting grass, reeds, or cereal stalks: gloss has been produced experimentally by slicing ripe sorghum (Shiner, 1973) but other substances can also produce gloss (Tringham et al., 1974).

If we exclude crops known to have been imported into Africa from Asia or the New World, traditional agriculture in the wet, southern part of Nigeria is seen to have been heavily dependent upon yams and oil palms, but there is at present no direct evidence about anything that can be called a process of domestication. The botanical evidence declares that there are at least seven species of wild African yam, of which four (*Dioscorea dumetorum, D. bulbifera, D. sansibarensis,* and *D. preussii*) are toxic and require special treatment to make them edible; the first two are indeed eaten in time of need. Of the remainder, *D. abyssinica* and *D. praehensilis* are southern savanna forms, *D. cayanensis* the forest form. From the latter the domesticated yellow yam was developed, while the white yam, *D. rotundata,* was developed from a cross between the wild *cayanensis* and wild *praehensilis.* Southern Nigeria is suggested as the place where the process is most likely to have taken place, and while there is no hard dating on when yam cultivation began, there is speculation that this may have occurred as much as four or five thousand years ago (Coursey, 1967, 1976; Posnansky, 1969). No other indigenous tuberous crop has the same importance as the yam, but the Hausa potato (*Plectranthus* spp.) is a cultivated crop, although the locale of its domestication is uncertain (Dalziel, 1955: 459; O. Davies, 1968; Purseglove, 1976). Just as it is likely that many tropical grasses were at one time grown for their grain, so it is likely that a number of African tubers were formerly much more widely cultivated than now (Busson et al., 1965: 405) and have come to be displaced by more successful ones such as cassava, sweet potato, and cocoyam, introduced from America by Europeans.

Just because root crops are at present invisible in the archaeological record it does not mean that we should abandon efforts to trace their presence. At one time the hope was entertained that the wing-cases of yam beetles might be recovered by flotation methods—but, unfortunately, this will not work. Yam beetles (*Heteroligus meles*) infest wild and cultivated yams equally, and their life-cycle is such that, although it is the adult beetle and not the larva which makes the holes in yams, the beetle is never found in a harvested yam, since it will have abandoned the tuber well before that time (H. Caswell, pers. comm.). However, there are two lines of investigation which should be explored further even though they may prove disappointing. One is to ascertain whether the starch grains in yams and other tuberous crops have recognizable "signatures" and can be recovered from archaeological sites (Martins, n.d.), and the other is whether such crops produce recognizable phytoliths; the allegation that such silica skeletons, better known from grasses and cereals, do not survive under tropical conditions (Goodyear, 1971: 144) is shown to be not universally the case by at least one set of finds in coastal Ecuador (Pearsall, 1978). However, since yam phytoliths would be derived from the leaves of yam vines and not from the tubers, it might not be of much archaeological use even if the method were found to work.

There may be other means of inferring the cultivation of archaeologically invisible crops. A recent study of prehistoric economy and culture in the Niger Delta has utilized column-sampling in shell-middens and made a calculation of the calorie and protein contributions from the fish, shellfish, and mammalian resources thus measured. Setting these against the timespan derived from radiocarbon dates, it has been inferred that the delta environment was only settled and exploited, by people predominantly engaged in fishing and utilizing the resources peculiar to the delta, in a system of exchange symbiosis with yam cultivators inland. This appears not to have got underway until the first millennium A.D., long after the probable date of earliest yam cultivation in the hinterland; the arrival of the Asiatic crops of banana/plantain and cocoyam (*Colocoasia* spp.) after their overland journey across Africa during the millennium may have further helped to establish the system (Nzewunwa, n.d.).

Since the evidence concerning the beginnings and early development of food-producing is so scanty in Nigeria, very little of any use can be said concerning the "causes" mentioned in the title of this book. One is on dangerous ground to speak of "causes" when one is ignorant of the relevant sequence of events and sequence of conditions, both ecological and demographic. That there were environmental changes and population changes over the relevant timespan there is no doubt, but at present we know too little about them. Various models have been put forward for the development of cereal domestication south of the Sahara (J. D. Clark, 1976b: 94; T. Shaw, 1977: 111–114), and the extreme north of Nigeria can be considered as falling within the non-center stretching from the Atlantic to the Nile (Harlan, 1971; Brunken et al., 1977), but the models proposed still need to be tested in the relevant areas by field research designed for the purpose. In the case of the population-pressure models it is extremely hard to obtain the quantitative demographic data needed to demonstrate a relationship with available food sources (Cohen, 1977: 71–84; D. R. Harris, 1978), and in any case the basis for such models has been queried (Cowgill, 1975).

Since domestic cattle are an introduced animal in Nigeria and since, unlike the situation in North Africa, there is no potential wild ancestor available for domestication, one can assume that they were introduced from north of the country's present boundaries. The cattle at Daima were small (Fagan, n.d.), and may well have belonged to the same stock that gave rise to the West African Dwarf Shorthorn.

What is not clear is how the "yam and oil-palm" agriculture of southern Nigeria came about. It has usually been assumed that it was as a result of a stimulus from cereal growers to the north (Portères, 1962; Alexander and Coursey, 1969: 421) but it could have been an independent process (T. Shaw, 1976: 129–130; Posnansky, this volume). The present state of knowledge does not give the opportunity to choose between these different hypotheses, and future research should be designed to test them.

Effects

Many effects or consequences must have flowed, directly and immediately or indirectly and after the passage of time, from the change to food production. The effect on population figures does not always seem to have been the same in all parts of the world when this change was made—there are too many other variables in the particular circumstances and manner in which the change occurred. The picture of an immediate population explosion following the "Neolithic revolution" is now seen to be false, and in Nigeria there could have been negative feedback effects through the operation of trypanosomiasis (Lambrecht, 1964) and malaria (F. B. Livingstone, 1958; Wiesenfeld, 1967). In some parts of the world great population increase is said only to have come with the application of hydraulic-control methods in the major river valleys (Tosi, 1973), while on the other side of the Atlantic, in an environment of tropical forest comparable to that of southern Nigeria, the spread of food production seems to have been along the river valleys (Lathrap, 1970: 45–83). In Africa, on the other hand, attempts to maximize on riverain environments for food production may have had disastrous results as a consequence of "river blindness," onchocerciasis, which is known historically to have caused inhabited river valleys to become depopulated (Hunter, 1966). Perhaps this is where oil-palm products may have been important in enabling human populations to maintain themselves in areas where the disease was endemic, along the river valleys and streams where the *Simulium damnosum* fly, the vector of onchocerciasis, is accus-

tomed to breed; for the vitamin A in palm oil gives a large measure of immunity to the disease. This was an additional, but very important, benefit derived from a basic diet of yams and palm oil; necessary small quantities of protein were supplied by fish, goat-meat, and wild game, supplemented by a whole range of products culled from trees, bushes, and herbs to add sauce and variety and which also provided a well-balanced nutritional intake. The plentiful supply of calories from yams would have made possible maximum utilization of the small supply of protein, which would therefore have been adequate. Such a diet, further supplemented by palm-wine, could well help to account for the build-up to great densities of population in southern Nigeria, contrasting so sharply with the sparsity of population in the Middle Belt, where the oil palm grows with difficulty if at all and where calories may have been harder to come by from cereals than from yams.

One other long-term effect of the change to food production is connected with the development of dense populations in southern Nigeria. It concerns the progression toward centralization of economic and political power and the beginnings of urbanization and state formation, without influence from the Sudanic zone and before Europeans arrived on the coast. This applies particularly to the area of southern Nigeria west of the river Niger, where the origin of Yoruba urbanism has puzzled many sociologists, historians, and social anthropologists (Bascom, 1955; Krapf-Askari, 1969: 154; Mabogunje, 1968: 74–79). This is not the place to go into this question, but it is appropriate in the present context to point out that the city of Ife arose at the center of an area of some ecological diversity, after agriculture had been practiced with iron implements for over a thousand years. This period is likely to have seen the pay-off from the build-up of the sickle-cell gene and from a plentiful, balanced diet, resulting in a lowering of the mortality rate; this would produce an increase in population, with larger and more closely spaced villages.

At present, that picture is largely speculative. One of the great needs of Yoruba archaeology is to find, map, and date the earliest village settlements—not an easy task: the evidence either lies

underneath existing settlements or under forest—
but much of the forest is periodically cleared for
agricultural purposes and the evidence should be
systematically sought. Yoruba urbanism will never
be properly understood until we have a much
clearer picture of the peasant communities peo-
pling the land before the towns arose—the matrix
in which urbanism grew (assuming that that was the
pattern). The only archaeological evidence we have
at the moment belonging to such a formative period is charcoal from pits, otherwise devoid of finds,
at the site of Orun Oba Ado in Ife, which has
yielded five radiocarbon dates from the sixth to the
tenth century A.D. (Willett, 1971: 366).

In western Nigeria, the northern boundary of
the forest takes a great sweep northward, running
northwest from the coast near Porto Novo on the
eastern side of the Dahomey Gap to within 50 km
of the river Niger downstream from Jebba, before
swinging southeast again to cross the Niger at Onit-
sha, below its confluence with the Benue. This configuration makes a semicircular bulge of forest pro-
jecting into the savanna: at the center of this bulge
lies Ife. This northern bulge of the forest is thus an
area within easy reach of considerable ecological
differentiation: a basically forest environment surrounded on the northern side with forest-savanna
mosaic and full savanna beyond, with riverain environments provided by the great river Niger to the
north and the Ogun and Oshun and other lesser
streams flowing south to the Atlantic, where there
were both lagoon and coastal environments. In all
this area, speakers of Yoruba were intelligible to
each other. In such ecological diversity, there were
opportunities for people to specialize in the products most readily obtained in their own particular
environment, whether in the savanna, the forest,
along the river, around the lagoons, or on the coast.
This opportunity for specialization would not only
have been in food production in the technical
sense, but also in hunting, fishing, and the gathering of local wild products. Other specialist centers
are likely to have arisen concerned with needs and
wants not directly connected with subsistence—
such as iron-smelting where good ore was plentiful,
and pottery where good clay was available; specialist, localized activities in supplying less utilitarian
needs may also have arisen, as in the production of

camwood dye or seashells and beads for personal
adornment. Shea-butter, from the northern savanna tree *Buterospermum parkii*, is still a valued
ingredient in the Yoruba pharmacopoeia in the forest, while kola nuts are exported from the forest to
the northern savannas in vast quantities. Such complementary movements of products have probably
been going on for many centuries.

Such symbiotic interdependence between geographically adjacent segments of the society and
the complementarity of their resources thus favor
specialization and economic interdependence (cf.
R. McC. Adams, 1966: 52). This in turn favors
institutionalization of redistributive arrangements,
whether by barter, by gift and marriage exchange,
or by tributary gifts to maintain the state of agricultural deities and their priests or of village heads
and larger chiefs who hold the political power that
regulates the system.

Another feature of all early agricultural systems enters into the situation. This is the fact that
all settled agricultural populations in prescientific
times have to do something, as part of their agricultural practice, to try to ensure the fertility of their
land and their crops in the face of the vagaries of
the weather, the exhaustion of soils, and the incidence of pests and disease. The occurrence at any
given time of favorable or unfavorable circumstances for agricultural production is attributed to supernatural powers; it therefore becomes of vital
importance to manipulate such powers in the best
interests of agricultural production. Ordinary folk
may feel confident that they know how to handle
these supernatural powers or may be afraid to do
so; they are thus happy to delegate the job to specialists who have the necessary confidence and expertise and who are willing, for a suitable consideration, to carry out these functions. In any case, it is
a matter of community concern, not one just for the
individual farmer.

Now put these two things together—the need
for specialists in supernatural farm management
and the need for redistributive arrangements for
local products—and you are well on the way to the
ceremonial center. The priestly function *can* be
performed at the village level and probably continues to be, so far as the localized earth-spirits are
concerned, but where there is a build-up toward

exchange systems, such specialists may tend more and more to become located at the nodes of the system and be concerned with larger supernatural issues. Similarly, the redistributive need *can* be met by a system of market exchange only, but where there is a priestly functionary mediating supernatural goodwill to secure the fertility of the land and the welfare of the people, he will demand a price for his services, sometimes directly, sometimes in the form of sacrificial offerings to the divine powers, most commonly a recognized mixture of both in which the distinction is blurred. In any case, many of the contributions are redistributed in the form of sacrificial feasts—or, as the institution becomes more politicized, in the form of gifts and privileged access to resources for members of an élite who in turn support the institution.

It is in circumstances such as these that the ceremonial center grows up, in which the coordinated institutions of temple and palace emerge as the effective redistributive institutions. Perhaps something of this sort was happening at Ife by the second half of the first millennium A.D. (Wheatley, 1970; 1971: 238–40). It flowed directly from centuries of food production in an area of ecological diversity. It meant that Ife was exceptionally well situated to take advantage of the benefits of long-distance trade when this began to finger down into the forest from the Islamic world toward the end of the millennium. The developments that flowed from that, in the first four centuries of the second millennium A.D., constitute another story (T. Shaw, 1973b; 1978: 158–160).

16

Early Iron Age Economy in the Inland Niger Delta (Mali)

RODERICK J. MCINTOSH AND
SUSAN KEECH MCINTOSH

In 1977 we conducted a seven-month program of exploratory excavation and extensive site survey in the western Inland Niger Delta of Mali (McIntosh and McIntosh, 1980). This area has figured prominently in reconstructions of West African prehistory. Various scholars have hypothesized that the easily navigable Middle Niger region, including the Inland Delta, functioned as a natural corridor along which innovations passed southward from the Sahara to the savanna: innovations transmitted via the Middle Niger are thought to include plant domestication (Munson, 1976: 205), aspects of the Kintampo "Neolithic" (O. Davies, 1961; 1967:

This article is an amplification of parts of an earlier article, "Initial perspectives on prehistoric subsistence in the Inland Niger Delta (Mali)," *World Archaeology* 11: 227–243. Several sections have been reproduced here, with amendments, by permission of Routledge and Kegan Paul, Ltd. The authors wish to express their deep gratitude to the many people, particularly those in Mali, who encouraged or otherwise contributed to this research. Funding was generously provided by the National Science Foundation, the American Association of University Women, and the Crowther-Benyon Fund of Cambridge University.

222; Goody, 1966), iron technology (O. Davies, 1966; T. Shaw, 1969a: 228), and painted pottery (O. Davies, 1964; Mathewson, 1968; Posnansky, 1975: 28). The Inland Niger Delta has also been cited as the possible locus of indigenous domestication of African rice (*Oryza glaberrima*) and fonio (*Digitaria exilis*) (Portères, 1976: 424, 445). We were initially attracted to the Inland Delta as a research area precisely because so many claims have been advanced for its role in West African prehistory in the virtual absence of relevant archaeological data.

Examination of published reports on archaeological research prior to 1977 revealed that controlled excavation and systematic regional survey in the Inland Delta were nonexistent.[1] This is not to say that archaeological investigation had never been conducted. A number of large pits were dug at several sites in the Delta during the 1950s by G. Szumowski (Szumowski, 1954, 1955, 1956). Absent from Szumowski's reports, however, are maps and sections drawn to scale, full discussion of stratigraphy, and rigorous description of pottery and other artifacts, even to the limited extent of drawing them and indicating the relative frequency of various types. As a result, a basic framework for the prehistory of the Inland Niger Delta remained very much out of reach in 1977. The fundamental questions requiring answers included: (1) Is there any evidence for Later Stone Age occupation in the Inland Delta? (2) How early are domesticated cereals? (3) Is there any evidence for change in subsistence economy through time? (4) When was iron technology accepted? (5) What are the major characteristics of material culture in the Inland Delta, and how did they change through time? Our program of regional survey and excavation was specifically designed to answer these questions as reli-

1. In 1975, R. M. A. Bedaux investigated two sites in the Inland Niger Delta during a two-month period. Much of the work focused on cleaning stratigraphic sections already exposed by local quarrying for mud bricks and by river downcutting; vertical control was therefore maintained. The results were published in early 1980, after this paper was written: R. M. A. Bedaux, T. S. Constandse-Westermann, L. Hacquebord, A. G. Lange, and J. D. van der Waals, 1980, "Recherches archéologiques dans le Delta Intérieur du Niger,' *Palaeohistoria* 20: 91–200.

ably as was possible in one field season. This paper reports some of the results of the investigation, focusing particularly on the issue of plant domestication and subsistence economy.

The Inland Niger Delta and Cereal Domestication

The Inland Niger Delta (Fig. 1) is a vast interior region of swamps and standing waters that crosscuts savanna grasslands and Sahel scrub vegetation belts. Its false-deltaic hydrology is fed by the Niger and Bani rivers, which contribute to the annual flooding of an 80,000 sq. km area for six to nine months of the year. Agricultural systems today are finely tuned to take maximum advantage of the cyclical rise and fall of floodwaters. African rice is the dominant flood crop, sown before the waters rise in late August or September on low floodplain soils moistened by summer rains. Various millets and sorghums are cultivated as *décrue* (French for "recession of floodwaters") crops planted in the moist soils exposed as the waters recede (Galloy et al., 1963; Harlan and Pasquereau, 1969; Harlan et al., 1976b: 15). Cultivation technology in the Inland Delta has remained at the level of simple hoe agriculture: deliberate irrigation, plowing, and manuring apparently played no part in the indigenous cultivation system (Harlan et al., 1976b: 16). The seeming simplicity and primitiveness of Inland Delta agricultural technology led D. R. Harris (1976: 342) to suggest that the existing system of *crue* and *décrue* cultivation in the region may be "essentially unchanged from the earliest period of rice cultivation." Useful as it would be to have such a perfectly preserved, living laboratory of the past, available information indicates that the *crue/décrue* system, which is in reality a remarkably sophisticated response to a high-risk agricultural situation, probably reached its present state only after a considerable period of experimentation and development. Agriculture in the Inland Delta is a high-risk proposition because crop growth is critically dependent on the arrival date, height, and duration of the annual floods and the arrival date and duration of summer rainfall, all of which are enormously variable. The potentially disastrous effects of

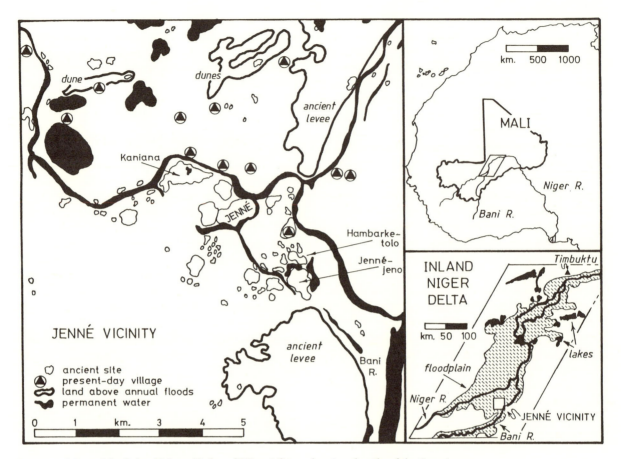

Figure 1. Map of the Inland Niger Delta of West Africa, showing details of the Jenné area.

floods and rains that arrive too early or too late or floods that are too high or too low have been documented (Galloy et al., 1963: 67–76; Gallais, 1967: 221). Farmers can exercise a large number of options to adjust to different annual hydraulic situations and thereby minimize losses. These options include: planting fields located at varying heights above the floodplain; sowing early or late; transplanting seedlings; and mixing crops or varietals having different growth rates in the same field. With reference to the last point, it is relevant to note that forty-one varieties of *Oryza glaberrima* have been counted in the Inland Niger Delta, with maturation rates ranging from 90 to 210 days (Gallais, 1967: 199–200). Several varieties of sorghum are also planted in the delta (Harlan and Pasquer-

eau, 1969: 72). We may suspect, then, that this complex system evolved over a substantial period of time, during which new varieties were selected and new crops may have been introduced, adding increased flexibility to the system. Evidence of this may be detectable archaeologically.

For the past three decades, Portères has maintained that the cultivation of various Sudanic cereals, such as fonio (*Digitaria exilis*), bulrush millet (*Pennisetum americanum*), and African rice (*Oryza glaberrima*) in the Inland Niger Delta is of considerable antiquity. He has identified the Inland Delta as a center of primary variation in *Oryza glaberrima*, "where only forms with genetically dominant characteristics are found" (Portères, 1976: 445). In Portères's opinion, this delta center of primary varietal diversification corresponds to the area where African rice was indigenously domesticated from wild *Oryza breviligulata* (= *O. barthii*, ibid.: 441). He dates this event to sometime before 1500 B.C., based on the assumptions that the builders of the Senegambian megaliths were rice cultivators and that megalithic construction began ca. 1500 B.C. (ibid.: 445). Unfortunately, recent radiocarbon dates for megalithic circles in the Senegambia, indicating that their construction dates to the first millennium A.D., invalidate Portères's chronology for rice domestication (Posnansky and McIntosh, 1976: 185).

The only other author to offer a time frame for the origins of rice domestication in the Western Sudan was Murdock, who believed that the domestication of a constellation of food and fiber plants, including rice, bulrush millet, sorghum, and fonio, had been indigenously initiated in the upper Niger region prior to 4500 B.C. (Murdock, 1959: 66–73). Murdock's logic for this chronology was that Sudanic cereals must have been in cultivation by 4500 B.C. or else they would have been forestalled by wheat and barley diffusing from Egypt. The ecological impossibility of Eurasian winter-rainfall cereal crops penetrating cultivation systems lacking irrigation in the summer-rainfall zone of the Western Sudan clearly invalidates Murdock's argument (Oliver and Fagan, 1975: 12). Numerous aspects of the "Murdockian hypothesis" have drawn fire from botanists and archaeologists (Wrigley, 1960; Baker, 1962; J. D. Clark, 1962), although Munson (1976: 188) has accurately pointed out that the counter arguments shared one basic weakness with Murdock's position: they were all based primarily on studies of modern botanical distributions and, to a lesser extent, on ethnographic use, rather than on direct archaeological data, which has remained virtually nonexistent until the present. Of the more than two dozen domesticates which are believed to have first been brought under cultivation in West Africa (Table 1), direct

TABLE 1. **Cultigens Originating in West Africa according to Various Authors**

	Oryza glaberrima (African rice)	*Pennisetum americanum* (bulrush millet)	*Digitaria exilis* (fonio)	*Brachiaria deflexa* (Guinea millet)	*Voandzeia subterranea* (Bambara nut)	*Kerstingiella geocarpa* (Groundnut)	*Polygala butyracea* (Black beniseed)	*Elaeis guineensis* (Oil palm)	*Butyrospermum paradoxum* (Shea-butter tree)	*Dioscorea cayenensis* (Yellow yam)	*Dioscorea rotundata* (White yam)	several *Coffea* spp.	*Cola* spp. (Kola)	*Ceiba pentandra* (Kapok)	*Parkia filicoidea* (Locust bean)	*Blighea sapida* (Akee)	*Afromomum maligueta* (Grains of paradise)	*Raphea* spp. (Raffia)	*Vigna unguiculata* (Cowpea)	*Sphenostylis stenocarpa* (Yampea)	*Digitaria iburua* (Black fonio)	*Coleus dazo* (Hausa potato)	*Abelmoschus esculentis* (Okra)	*Telfairia occidentalis* (a gourd)
Purseglove (1976)	●	●	●	●	●	●	●	●	●	●	●	●	●	●	●	●	●	●						
Harlan (1971)	●	●	●	●	●	●		●	●	●	●								●	●	●	●	●	●
Portères (1970)	●	●	●	●	●	●	●	●	●	●	●	●												●
Baker (1962)	●			●			●	●	●	●		●				●								
D. R. Harris (1976)	●		●	●	●			●	●	●		●				●	●				●	●	●	
Murdock (1959)	●	●	●		●	●		●	●	●	●				●				●	●		●		●

TABLE 2. **Direct Evidence for Plant Cultigens in West Africa**

Site	Date	Genus, Species
Amekni	6100–4850 B.C.	*Pennisetum* sp. (2 pollen grains)[1]
Meniet	mid-fourth millennium B.C.	cultivated grass (pollen)[2]
Adrar Bous	4000 B.C.	*Brachiaria* (single pottery impression)[3]
Adrar Bous	2000 B.C.	*Sorghum* (single pottery impression)[4]
*Tichitt	1000–900 B.C.	*Pennisetum* sp.[5]
Kintampo (K6)	1400–1250 B.C.	*Elaeis guineensis*[6]
Kintampo (K6)	1400–1250 B.C.	*Vigna unguiculata*
*Niani	A.D. 700–900	*Sorghum bicolor*
*Daima	A.D. 800–900	*Sorghum bicolor*

*plant remains were definitely identified as cultigens.

[1]Camps (1969) claims the pollen comes from a cultigen; T. Shaw (1977: 112) cautions that pollen identification of Graminae is notoriously difficult in this respect. It seems best to hold this piece of data in a "suspense account" for the present. (See also Livingstone, this volume).

[2]H. J. Hugot (1968: 485) interpreted this as pollen from a cultivated grass because of its large size. T. Shaw (1976: 113) reports that wild grasses have subsequently been found in the Sahara with as large or larger pollen grains.

[3]Now thought to be wild (T. Shaw, 1977: 102).

[4]At first thought to be cultivated, latest opinion is that it is wild (T. Shaw, 1977: 99).

[5]*Pennisetum* and *Brachiaria deflexa* are both documented in small amounts in the earlier Naghez phase, but an argument for their domestication has not been advanced.

[6]Neither species at Kintampo could be identified as a cultigen on morphological grounds.

evidence[2] for cultigens of putative West African origin is limited to three species: *Pennisetum* sp., *Elaeis guineensis*, and *Vigna unguiculata* (Table 2). *Sorghum bicolor* (recovered at Niani and Daima) was probably an introduction from East Africa, where it appears to have been originally domesticated (de Wet and Harlan, 1971; Harlan and Stemler, 1976). The need for direct evidence of domesticated food plants from West African sites is imperative. We agree with Shaw's conclusion, in his excellent article reviewing the evidence for early crops in Africa, that we cannot "confine ourselves to the minimum firm ground" provided by direct archaeological evidence for domesticated plants (T. Shaw, 1976: 139). This is particularly true for the "vegecultural" areas of the Guinea savanna and forest. Nevertheless, it does seem reasonable to

2. By *direct evidence* is meant "the recovery from datable archaeological contexts of the actual remains of seed, fruit, root, or tree crops, their pollen, or impressions of them in such material as pottery" (T. Shaw, 1976: 112).

expect that in the cereal-growing regions of the drier Sudanic savanna, Sahel, and southern Sahara, consistent efforts to look for botanical remains, including flotation and screening whenever possible, will inevitably result in a substantial amount of hitherto unavailable direct evidence.

Prior to commencing the 1977 fieldwork, we believed that a committed attempt to recover botanical data during excavation would almost certainly shed some light on the chronology of domesticated African rice in the Inland Delta. Although there have been conflicting opinions about the domestication of crops such as fonio and Guinea millet (*Brachiaria deflexa*), rice domestication in the Inland Niger Delta is widely accepted in the literature (O. Davies, 1967: 149; Harlan, 1971: 471; J. D. Clark, 1976a: 81; 1976b: 69; D. R. Harris, 1976: 342). Despite the lack of a convincingly argued chronology for this process, it is probably fair to say that most researchers would fully expect to find semisedentary Later Stone Age populations in the Inland Delta experimenting with rice cultivation by the late third or early second millennium B.C. However, the first direct archaeological evidence relevant to this problem, resulting from the 1977 research, indicates that permanent settlement in the western Inland Niger Delta may not antedate the Iron Age and that rice cultivation may not have been practiced in the delta until late in the first millennium B.C.

The 1977 Research Project

The first phase of the research consisted of test excavations undertaken from February through May, 1977, at the site of Jenné-jeno, a large mound located 3 km southeast of the present city of Jenné and claimed by oral tradition to be the ancestral settlement. Like Jenné, the site rests on an ancient bed of the Bani River close to its confluence with the Niger. Within easy access of the site are rich fishing grounds, large depressions supporting dry-season pasturage, and thousands of hectares of floodplain soils well suited for rice cultivation.

Due to funding, time, and manpower limitations, it was possible to sink only four vertical excavation units, each measuring 3 × 3 m, into the vastness of this mound (over 331,000 sq. m, or 33 hectares in area) during the four-month excavation period. These excavation units are labeled as Mnd (Mound) 1, Mnd 2, JF (Jar Field) 1, and JF 2 on Figure 2. The goals of these exploratory excavations were threefold: to establish a gross chronology of the site by means of both radiocarbon dating and ceramic analysis; to investigate the specific economic issue of possible local domestication of African rice and millets; and to examine the possible early emergence of urbanism in the Inland Niger Delta. In view of the kind of information we hoped to extract from the site, stratigraphic control was rigorously maintained, at the expense of time. It is unfortunate, given that the recovery of subsistence information was of major interest, that the highly compacted clays prevalent in the deposits made screening impractical. Equally unfortunately, systematic on-site flotation of soils was impossible, as the only available water was remnant pools on

the floodplain that were choked with graminaceous vegetation. As a compromise solution, bags of soil were periodically taken to the town of Jenné for flotation. Additionally, soil samples were collected at the site whenever botanical material appeared to be present.

Excavation revealed five meters of well-stratified, apparently continuous deposits above sterile floodplain alluvium, confirming our initial impression that Jenné-jeno is a true *tell*. The presence of iron and slag and the concomitant absence of chipped- or ground-stone tools throughout the deposits were noted. An internally consistent series of radiocarbon dates places the occupation of the site between ca. 250 B.C. and A.D. 1400. Systematic description and analysis of the excavated pottery by means of attribute seriation revealed that the relative frequencies of certain attributes display a consistent pattern of unimodal change through time (S. McIntosh, n.d.: 198–201). In this manner a preliminary pottery sequence for Jenné-jeno has been established. The temporal relationship among various strata in the different excavation units which we initially inferred using the pottery sequence were confirmed with remarkable consistency by radiocarbon determinations.

We defined four occupation phases at Jenné-jeno, based on identification of discrete series of related stratigraphic events as well as on significant changes in pottery or other cultural characteristics. The chronological framework for these four phases is illustrated in Figure 3.

PHASE I (CA. 250 B.C. TO A.D. 50)

Phase I deposits in central excavation units Mnd 1 and Mnd 2 were identical in color and texture and remained markedly uniform throughout their vertical extent of 1.2 m in Mnd 1 and 0.5 m in Mnd 2. The deposits were somewhat friable, dark khaki-green, heavy loam in platy structure, grading to a firm clay with increasing depth (soil categories from Ahn, 1970: 19–26). Up to 20 percent of the volume was white ash containing panicoid grasses and dispersed wood charcoal; the ash occurred in several extensive lenses three to five centimeters thick. These ash lenses may be the

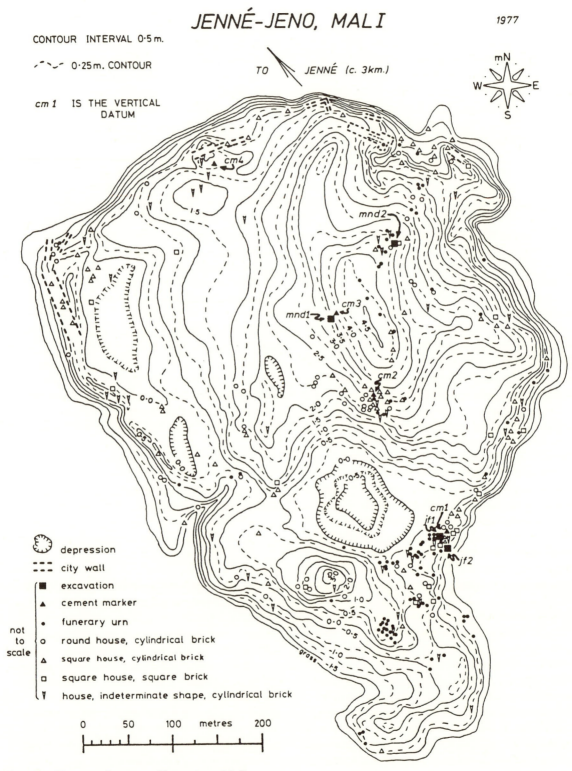

JENNÉ-JENO, MALI   1977

CONTOUR INTERVAL 0·5 m.

⌢⌣⌢⌣ 0·25m. CONTOUR

cm 1   IS THE VERTICAL
         DATUM

TO ⟋ JENNÉ (c. 3km.)

mN
W ✴ E
S

mnd2

cm3
mnd1

cm2

cm1
jf1
jf2

🌀 depression
- - - city wall
■ excavation
▲ cement marker
• funerary urn
○ round house, cylindrical brick
△ square house, cylindrical brick
▢ square house, square brick
⩔ house, indeterminate shape, cylindrical brick

not
to
scale

0   50   100   metres   200
|ᴵᴵᴵᴵ|ᴵᴵᴵᴵ|ᴵᴵᴵᴵ|ᴵᴵᴵᴵ|

Figure 2. Topographic map of Jenné-jeno, Mali.

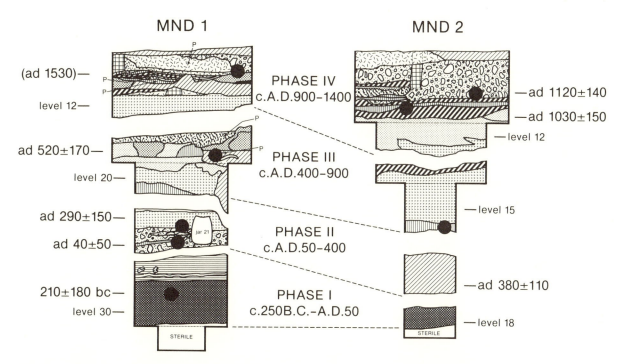

Figure 3. Phases of occupation at Jenné-jeno illustrated by stratigraphic sections from Mnd 1 and Mnd 2. Numbered levels indicate deposits formed contemporaneously under similar or identical conditions (bench levels). Depths of radiocarbon samples are indicated by circles; the uncalibrated dates are listed to the side.

remains of burnt grass huts, fish-smoking activities, or the firing of grass cover. In both excavation units, Phase I material was deposited directly upon the sterile floodplain clay, forming a sharp interface. The occurrence of Phase I deposits in both Mnd 1 and Mnd 2, located 110 m apart, indicates that this was the minimum linear extent of the site at that time.

A radiocarbon sample (RL-807) taken from a large pocket of wood charcoal at a point 60 cm above the interface with sterile alluvium in Mnd 1 yielded a radiocarbon date of 210 ± 180 B.C. (although B.C. and/or A.D. are in small capitals, all radiocarbon dates are given in uncalibrated form and are based on a half-life of 5,568 years). This is the earliest date known for an Iron Age industry in sub-Saharan Africa outside the "Nok Culture" area of Nigeria. Iron and slag are present in the lowest levels stratified directly above floodplain alluvium, indicating that fully iron-using peoples were the first occupants of Jenné-jeno.

The economy at Jenné-jeno can only be partially reconstructed, due to the high degree of postdepositional fragmentation of bone as well as to sampling factors. As previously mentioned, screening was attempted but ultimately abandoned owing to the high degree of compaction of the indurated loam and clay deposits. This may mean that the bones of small fish, small mammals, and birds are under-represented in the sample.[3] Decalcification had taken its toll in post-depositional damage to bone; however, Figure 4 illustrates that the ratio by weight of identifiable to unidentifiable bone does not systematically decrease with depth of deposit. Bones of catfish (*Clarias* and *Synodontis*) and Nile

3. A potential candidate for under-representation is the oil-rich *Alestes* sp., whose soft skeleton and small teeth would render these tiny fish almost invisible archaeologically. Fishing for *Alestes* and boiling them down for oil is a highly specialized and important industry of the Bozo fishermen in the Jenné region today (Gallais, 1967: 414, 421).

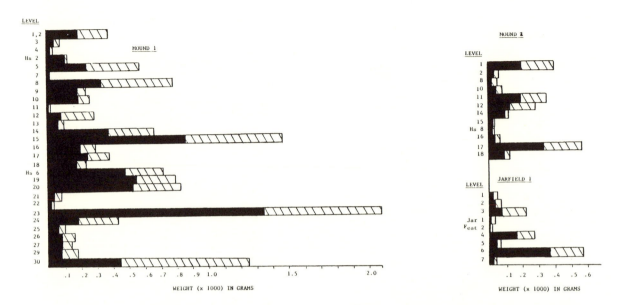

Figure 4. Total non-human bone from Jenné-jeno; weight of potentially identifiable (black) and unidentifiable (diagonal shading) components.

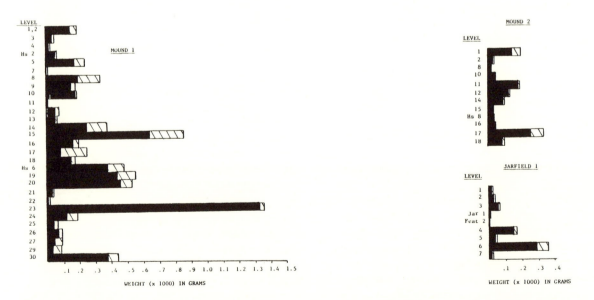

Figure 5. Identifiable bone from Jenné-jeno: weight of mammal (black) and fish (diagonal shading) components.

TABLE 3. **Faunal Remains from Jenné-jeno***

	Phase I				Phase II					Phase III												Phase IV																
Unit, Level	Mnd 1, 30	Mnd 2, 18	Mnd 1, 29–27	Mnd 1, 26–25	Mnd 1, 24–23	Mnd 2, 17	JF 1, 6–5	Mnd 1, 22–21	JF 1, 4	Mnd 1, 20	Mnd 2, 16–15	JF 1, 3	Mnd 1, 19	Mnd 1, 16	Mnd 1, Hs 6	Mnd 1, 15	Mnd 2, 14	Mnd 1, 18–17	Mnd 1, 14–13	JF 1, 2	JF 1, 1	Mnd 1, 12–11	Mnd 2, 13–12	Mnd 2, 11	Mnd 1, 10–9	Mnd 2, Hs 8/10	Mnd 2, 9–8	Mnd 2, Hs 7/7	Mnd 2, Hs 4/4	Mnd 1, 8	Mnd 2, 6	Mnd 2, 5/2	Mnd 1, 5	Mnd 2, Hs 3/3	Mnd 2, 1	Mnd 1, Hs 2/7–6	Mnd 1, 4–3	Mnd 1, 2–1
Bovidae (genus unidentifiable)																																						
Small Bovidae (e.g., *Ourebia oribi*)										×	×																				×						×	
Small Medium Bovidae (e.g., *Redunca redunca*)	×		×	×	×	×	×	×	×	×			×	×	×	×	×	×	×				×								×					×	×	×
Large Medium Bovidae (e.g., *Hippotragus equinus*)	×	×		×	×		×		×	×		×				×			×			×	×	×		×			×		×		×		×	×		
Large Bovidae (e.g., *Bos taurus, Syncerus*)	×	×		×	×	×		×			×	×	×			×			×	×		×	×								×		×				×	×
Bovidae (identifiable)																																						
Small Bovine (*Bos taurus/Syncerus caffer*)	×	×			×	×					×		×	×		×	×					×		×														
Eland (*Taurotragus oryx*)																						×																
Reedbuck (*Redunca redunca*)	×			×	×		×		×					×		×	×	×															×					
Caprine (*Ovis aries/Capra hircus*)																								×														
Warthog (*Phacochoerus aethiopicus*)					×																																	
Carnivora: Wildcat size																	×																					
Jackal size											×		×	×																	×		×					
Viverridae																														×	×							
Common Genet (*Genetta genetta*)																														×								
Tortoise	×				×														×		×																×	
Bird	×						×											×		×											×			×			×	×

*Excavated levels are arranged in most probable chronological order. Bracketed mounds are probably contemporaneous.

perch (*Lates niloticus*) are very common in all four occupation phases at Jenné-jeno; indeed, they still constitute a major part of the fish diet of people in Jenné today (Daget, 1954). Figure 5 shows that in a number of stratigraphic levels, fish bone accounts for between 20 and 50 percent by weight of all identifiable bone. However, the majority of the identifiable faunal material in all phases comes from bovids of various sizes, of which only the reedbuck,

Redunca redunca, could be definitely identified (Table 3). A small bovine—most likely *Bos taurus* (domestic cattle) (R. G. Klein, 1978; pers. comm.) or possibly *Syncerus caffer* (African buffalo)—was also present throughout the deposits. Additionally, remains of tortoise and bird were present in all phases, and crocodile epidermic plates were recovered from Phase I deposits. In summary, major components of the Phase I economy at Jenné-jeno, as it can be reconstructed from the available archaeological evidence, include catfish and Nile perch, a small bovine (very likely domesticated cattle), reedbuck, and possibly a number of other wild bovids such as African buffalo (*Syncerus caffer*), roan (*Hippotragus equinus*), waterbuck (*Kobus defassa*), and topi (*Damaliscus korrigum*) (based on geographical details in Dekeyser, 1955). Despite the consistent presence of African rice in most levels from Phase II on, no evidence of rice or any other cereal remains was recovered from Phase I. Once again, however, the possibility of sampling error must not be overlooked.

PHASE II (CA. A.D. 50 TO 400)

The Phase II deposits are the first in which remains of mud architecture are well preserved. Several distinct hearths and fire-oxidized bits of solid mud walling surround a possible wall stump, also of solid mud, in the central excavation units. The lower boundary in Mnd 1 is provided by a mass of mud-wall collapse; a substantial sample of well-preserved chaff from *Oryza glaberrima* was taken from this level. Associated charcoal yielded a radiocarbon date of A.D. 40 ± 50 (P-2742). Major economic elements show a great deal of continuity with Phase I. Catfish and Nile perch are abundant; Phase II levels yielded iron fishhooks and clay net sinkers. Two clay cattle figurines (and several more in later Phases) resembling those made today by Fulani pastoralists as children's toys may provide additional evidence that the abundant small-bovine remains are those of *Bos taurus* rather than *Syncerus caffer*. Similar clay animal figurines made by Later Stone Age pastoralists were found at Karkarichin-kat in central Mali and at Daima in eastern Nigeria (A. B. Smith, n.d.; Connah, 1976). A warthog tusk with two biconical perforations was also recovered. Two other radiocarbon dates came from Phase II deposits: A.D. 290 ± 150 and A.D. 380 ± 110, which is taken as the upper boundary of Phase II.

Phase II deposits were present in all three excavation units, separated by a maximum distance of 400 m. Again, this may be considered to be the minimum linear extent of the site at that time. If it is reasonable to think that the Phase II site was at least three-quarters as wide as it was long—i.e., 300 m—then the minimum areal extent of Jenné-jeno by A.D. 400 would have been 120,000 sq. m (12 hectares, or ca. 29 acres). By analogy with presently occupied sites on artificial mounds in the Inland Niger Delta, at which settlement tends to be very dense, a site of this size could potentially support a population of up to 4,000. Of course, this extremely tentative estimate is based on the assumptions that settlement was dense in Phase II and that the deposits in the three excavation units were part of a single mound during Phase II, as stratigraphical evidence indicates, and not two different mounds separated by a short stretch of floodplain. Both these assumptions need to be investigated in the course of the next excavation season. Also to be clarified by future excavation is the rate of physical expansion of Jenné-jeno in Phase I and the areal extent of the mound at the beginning of Phase II. Based on present evidence, however, it is probable that Jenné-jeno was a site of considerable dimensions, possibly measuring a half-kilometer or more along its main axis, by A.D. 200.

PHASES III AND IV (CA. A.D. 400 TO 1400)

The third occupation phase dates from approximately A.D. 400 to 900. An increasing number of wall stumps are visible in section and the stratigraphy is noticeably more complex. Wall stumps tend to be associated with fairly deep deposits, suggesting that occupation of a house during Phase III could span an appreciable time period—possibly two or more centuries. These are indications that occupation was becoming increasingly intensive.

The appearance of crowded cemeteries in Phase III may be further evidence of population growth and intensified site occupation. Four inhumations and seven of the nine urn burials found in JF 1 all appear to have been interred during Phase III, based on the ceramic material contained in the cemetery deposits. There are no Phase IV (tenth to fourteenth century A.D.) deposits in JF 1. It is possible, therefore, that Jenné-jeno reached its maximum areal extent in Phase III; by the end of the Phase, the site was apparently linked by a causeway to a site to the north, Hambarketolo, giving the urban complex a combined area of 42 hectares by A.D. 1000. After this point the population began to decline. Abandonment of the site seems to have been a slow process, completed by ca. A.D. 1400, according to the seventeenth-century native chronicler as-Sa'di, who reports that the already abandoned Jenné-jeno was garrisoned by the Songhai conquerer Sonni Ali during his siege of Jenné in ca. 1468 (as-Sa'di, 1900: 26–28).

Throughout Phases III and IV, the subsistence complex continues to be based on rice, fish, and bovids. Wild plants are represented for the first time by remains of *Portulaca oleracea* (common purslane) and *Setaria pallidifusca* (foxtail millet) recovered from the bottom of intact pots in Phase III deposits. The succulent leaves of purslane are used today throughout West Africa as a stew ingredient (Busson et al., 1965: 153); foxtail millet is a common weed widespread in West Africa which was cultivated in the past and is occasionally harvested today (Harlan, 1977; pers. comm.).

The most significant points to emerge from the excavation phase of the research include the absence of Later Stone Age material, direct evidence for rice cultivation by the early first century A.D., and the evidence for rapid growth of Jenné-jeno during Phase II into a town of substantial proportions by late Phase III. We were especially surprised by the lack of evidence for Later Stone Age occupation, as well as for other cereal crops such as fonio and bulrush millet at Jenné-jeno. Like most West African researchers, we had assumed that permanent settlement, based on food production, in the Inland Niger Delta began in the Later Stone Age. Also, the presence of domesticated bulrush millet at Tichitt by 900 B.C. (Munson, 1976) led us to believe that cultivation of *Pennisetum* was at least as early, if not earlier, in the Inland Niger Delta. Neither assumption was supported by the excavation data from Jenné-jeno. Results of the second phase of the research program, a two-month regional site survey covering a 1,100 sq. km area to the north and west of Jenné-jeno, indicate that this situation is by no means unusual; it appears that neither early millet cultivation nor permanent Later Stone Age occupation is to be found in the western Inland Niger Delta.

The survey area illustrated in Figure 6 was chosen for investigation because it includes a representative cross-section of Jenné-jeno's rural hinterland, with a wide diversity of landforms and vegetation. Within this area, six seasonally inundated floodplain soils (soil categories are defined on the basis of constituent grain size and relative depth of flooding) and four landforms permanently above flood level (including artificial mounds on the floodplain) were recognized and mapped. We undertook the survey in order to document the nature of permanent rural settlements in Jenné-jeno's traditional supporting hinterland. Because of time and financial limitations, the survey proceeded on an explicit sampling basis by which we hoped to lay the groundwork for quantitative and qualitative estimates of the character of the archaeological sites in Jenné-jeno's hinterland.

All permanent sites in the floodplain are *tells* visible in aerial photographs; these were numbered individually and a 20 percent sample was selected, with the use of a random number table, for recording surface features and collection of surface pottery. Other upland areas (i.e., dunes and levees in Figure 6) were gridded into consecutively numbered transects measuring 2 by ½ km; 20 percent of these were systematically chosen for careful on-foot investigation. In addition to the sample survey, we covered 100 percent of all land (both floodplain and upland areas) within a 4 km radius of Jenné on foot, recording all sites and finds of archaeological interest. Over 20 km of stream and river channels incised into the floodplain were also carefully searched for traces of Later Stone Age occupation obscured by recent alluviation. No flaked stone was noted at any time during the survey.

Another point emerged as the survey sites were arranged in tentative chronological order; occupation sites on the sandy upland soils favored by millet and sorghum cultivators today all appear to post-date Phase IV. The currently heavy occupation of these light soils can in most cases be attributed to the historically documented penetration of the area by Bambara millet farmers. This migration may have begun as early as the thirteenth century A.D.; it reached its maximum impact from A.D. 1500 to 1800 (Delafosse, 1912: 283–289; as-Sa'di, 1900: 171–172). The overwhelming predominance of archaeological sites earlier than Phase IV on low

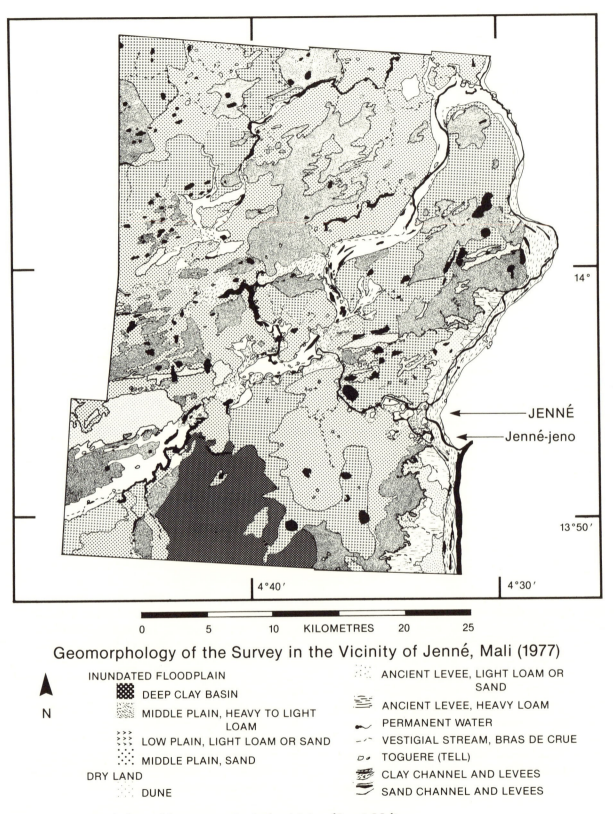

Geomorphology of the Survey in the Vicinity of Jenné, Mali (1977)

N

INUNDATED FLOODPLAIN

DEEP CLAY BASIN

MIDDLE PLAIN, HEAVY TO LIGHT LOAM

LOW PLAIN, LIGHT LOAM OR SAND

MIDDLE PLAIN, SAND

DRY LAND

DUNE

ANCIENT LEVEE, LIGHT LOAM OR SAND

ANCIENT LEVEE, HEAVY LOAM

PERMANENT WATER

VESTIGIAL STREAM, BRAS DE CRUE

TOGUERE (TELL)

CLAY CHANNEL AND LEVEES

SAND CHANNEL AND LEVEES

Figure 6. Geomorphology of the survey region in the vicinity of Jenné, Mali.

floodplain soils suitable only for rice suggests to us that millet cultivation was not introduced into the western Delta until the late first millennium or early second millennium A.D.

Conclusions

Various widely held ideas concerning the antiquity of permanent settlement and cereal domestication in the Inland Niger Delta require substantial modification in light of the 1977 research in the Jenné area. Based on the results of excavation and extensive, systematic regional survey, it does not appear possible, at this time, to see an *in situ* development in the western Inland Niger Delta from Later Stone Age to Iron Age. The Jenné-jeno excavation data suggest that permanent settlement, resulting in *tell* formation, was initiated by fully iron-using peoples who entered the Delta in the last half of the first millennium B.C. The Saharan affinities of the earliest Jenné-jeno pottery point to an origin to the north or northwest.

It is reasonable to ask why Later Stone Age pastoralists/collectors apparently avoided the Inland Niger Delta when similar environments in the Sahara were drying up after ca. 2000 B.C., presumably causing population movement to better-watered areas to the south. Two plausible explanations present themselves. It is entirely possible that there was Later Stone Age occupation in the Inland Delta that was seasonally concentrated in low-lying areas during the driest months of the year (a pattern not unlike that of the Fulani pastoralists in the area today). In this case, evidence of Later Stone Age presence would be buried under a considerable amount of alluvium. Alternatively, it has been suggested on analogy with Lake Chad that the present Inland Niger Delta may have been a slowly desiccating lake or a high-floodwater area during the second or first millennium B.C. Nicholson (n.d.: 72–97) reports evidence of higher water levels in the Niger lakes during the period 1300–500 B.C., which presumably implies a more active flood regime at that time in the upstream Inland Delta region feeding the lakes of the Niger Bend. From 500 B.C. to A.D. 700–800 there is evidence for a

markedly drier period in the Western Sudan (Nicholson, n.d.: 75–97; Rognon, 1976: 272–277; R. McIntosh, n.d.: 110–157). Reduction of rainfall near the southern highland source of the Niger probably had the effect of reducing the height and period of the annual floods, opening to permanent settlement areas that had hitherto remained flooded for all but a few months of the year. Given such a situation, a site such as Kobadi (15°22′ N, 5°28′ W) may be an example of the kind of Later Stone Age site that was located adjacent to the Inland Niger Delta during the second/early first millennium period of high floodwaters. Mauny reports that the surface of Kobadi is "jonché d'ossements humains, d'animaux et de poissons, de fragments de poterie, et de pierres taillées. . . . Il y fut trouvé aussi deux harpons en os" (Mauny, 1972: 76, 78). A radiocarbon date of 713 ± 145 B.C. is available for the site (Posnansky and McIntosh, 1976: 192). Although further work needs to be done before the issue of initial settlement in the Inland Niger Delta can be adequately assessed, it is reasonable to think that the Early Iron Age culture at Jenné-jeno developed out of the Later Stone Age culture of sites like Kobadi. Even if it is not possible to see an *in situ* development from Later Stone Age to Early Iron Age in the Inland Niger Delta, there is no reason to believe that the cultural elements of Phase I occupation at Jenné-jeno were transported from points much more distant than the northern and western periphery of the delta.

The similarity of the Phase I economy at Jenné-jeno to that of earlier sites along the southern Sahara fringe indicates that penetration of the delta was probably part of the southward movement of Saharan pastoralists/collectors that began in response to accelerating desiccation ca. 2000 B.C. (J. D. Clark, 1976a: 80). Between 2000 and 1000 B.C., southern Saharan sites like Tichitt and Karkarichinkat were established on seasonal lakes and stream-courses; their economy was heavily reliant on cattle-herding and seasonal aquatic resources, especially fish (Munson, 1976; A. B. Smith, n.d.). It appears that these herding/fishing/collecting groups responded to the disappearance of aquatic resources that accompanied Saharan desiccation in two ways: by increased reliance upon cereal cultivation (domestic *Pennisetum* at Tichitt); or by southward migration. Settlement during the first millennium B.C. on seasonally inundated flood-plains to the south permitted continuation of the older Saharan herding-and-fishing way of life. Daima, Kobadi, and Jenné-jeno may be examples of this pattern. Domestic cereals appear to have been adopted at Daima, Jenné-jeno, and Tichitt at widely different times, however. More intriguing yet is the current evidence that entirely different cereal crops were adopted at these three sites. Domesticated bulrush millet appears at Tichitt between 1000 and 900 B.C.; at Daima, there is no sign of cereal cultivation before the fifth or sixth century A.D., when sorghum appears to have been introduced (Connah, 1976). African rice is present at Jenné-jeno from the first century A.D., and analysis of prehistoric and historic settlement patterns in the western Inland Niger Delta indicates that millets and sorghums may not have been introduced until the late first millennium or early second millennium A.D. Ultimately, our ability to understand the process of plant domestication in West Africa must take into account the factor of significant

regional differences both in the chronology of cultivation and in the crops cultivated. Traditional "advancing front" models for the spread of farming in West Africa, in which domesticated species or knowledge of them is thought to move outward like ripples in water from an area of origin, are seen increasingly to be counterproductive.

Unfortunately, we do not now know whether rice cultivation was practiced by the earliest occupants of Jenné-jeno. Although it is probable that domesticated rice was introduced from outside the delta, either at the beginning of Phase I or slightly later, the possibility that local manipulation of wild rice was taking place over a wide area of the Inland Delta—including Jenné-jeno—during Phase I should not be rejected out of hand. Whatever the ultimate origins of *Oryza glaberrima* in the western Inland Delta, it is clear that rice cultivation was well established by the first century A.D. as part of a remarkably stable and enduring subsistence complex. This rice/fish/cattle complex remains dominant in the delta today.

17

New Perspectives on the Origins of Food Production in Ethiopia

STEVEN A. BRANDT

As in other parts of the Old and New World, many of the plants and animals that are cultivated and raised in Ethiopia today are derived from the Near Eastern complex of domesticates that include wheat, barley, sheep, and goats. However, the majority of the Ethiopian population depends not upon wheat and barley for their daily bread but upon a group of cultigens that were probably locally domesticated. These include: *teff* (*Eragrostis teff*), the national cereal of Ethiopia, which is grown over more acreage than any other crop (and is made into a pancake-like unleavened bread); *noog* (*Guizotia abyssinica*), a flowering plant which supplies much of Ethiopia's edible cooking oil; *ensete* (*Ensete ventricosum*), a bananalike plant, parts of which are made into a bread; and a wide range of other crops, including perhaps finger millet (*Eleusine coracana*), largely used today for the brewing of

The author would like to thank Stanley Ambrose, J. Desmond Clark, and Glynn L. Issac for their helpful comments and constructive criticisms. Betty Clark helped with the editing, and Judith Ogden is to be thanked for drawing Figure 1. Research at Lake Besaka was funded by grants from the National Science Foundation to J. Desmond Clark, principal investigator.

beer, *ch'at* (*Catha edulis*), a mild narcotic whose leaves are chewed, and coffee (*Coffea arabica*).

The domesticated plants and animals of Ethiopia have traditionally been associated with five distinct food-producing complexes based largely upon physiographic, environmental, cultural, and technological criteria (Huffnagel, 1961; E. Westphal, 1974). Although there may not always be clear-cut boundaries between these systems, they can be summarized as follows.

1. The "plough and cereal complex" of the temperate Ethiopian Plateau in central and northern Ethiopia (Fig. 1), practiced by Cushitic and Semitic-speaking agriculturalists who cultivate a wide range of cereals including teff, wheat, and barley.

2. The mixed-farming economies of subtropical and lowland western Ethiopia, practiced by Eastern Sudanic- and other Nilo–Saharan-speaking groups who hunt, fish, and herd, and who cultivate sorghum and other Sudanic crops.

3. The "hoe and cereal complex" of the temperate hills and valleys of the eastern part of the Southeastern Plateau: Cushitic-speaking groups who depend upon the hoe and digging stick as aids in the cultivation of such plants as sorghum, coffee, and ch'at.

4. The "hoe and vegeculture complex" of the temperate highlands of the southern Ethiopian plateau and the southern part of the Southeastern Plateau, where the hoe is used almost exclusively by Omotic- and Cushitic-speaking groups to grow ensete and other crops.

5. The "pastoral complex" of semiarid northern Eritrea, the Ogaden Desert, and the Ethiopian and Afar Rifts: Cushitic-speaking nomads who depend upon herds of camels, goats, sheep, and cattle for their economic livelihood.

J. R. Harlan (1969: 313) has said:

> We have in the Ethiopian center a survival of an entire agricultural system little changed from prehistoric times. Ancient methods of tillage, sowing, reaping, threshing, winnowing, dehulling and processing for consumption, all have been preserved, as have the use and attitudes of these people toward their ancient crops. It is as if a vanished world had been rediscovered by use of a time machine.

Unfortunately, few investigators have climbed aboard this time machine, for we as yet know very little about the origins of these food-producing systems. Therefore, the goal of this paper is to review the current state of knowledge pertaining to early food production in Ethiopia, which, admittedly, is based largely upon indirect archaeological evidence as well as historical, ethnographic, and linguistic data (but also upon some tantalizing bits of recently recovered direct archaeological evidence). This synthesis of diverse resources of information brings problems into sharper focus and indicates the directions future projects might take to clarify the processes involved in development of Ethiopian food production.

Ethiopia as a Center of Origin

After many years of intensive field and laboratory research, the Russian agronomist Nikolai Vavilov proposed Ethiopia to be one of eight world centers of origin for cultivated plants. He included in his list of indigenous Ethiopian domesticates a number of species of wheat, barley, sorghum, millets, lentils and a wide range of other legumes, oil plants, vegetables, spices, and stimulants (Vavilov, 1926, 1951a). Although the geographer Carl Sauer, in his treatise on *Agricultural Origins and Dispersals*, dismissed Ethiopia as a center of origin for wheat, he still considered it to be "one of the world's greatest and oldest centers of domestic seed plants" (Sauer, 1952: 76). Portères (1962) also recognized the highlands of Ethiopia ("Abyssinia") to be one of eight centers of plant domestication in Africa, encompassing such crops as teff, finger millet, and ensete (wheat and barley, on the other hand, were considered to be representative of a secondary center). As a result of these and other studies, Ethiopia soon became firmly entrenched in the literature as a major center of indigenous food production (Simoons, 1960: 125).

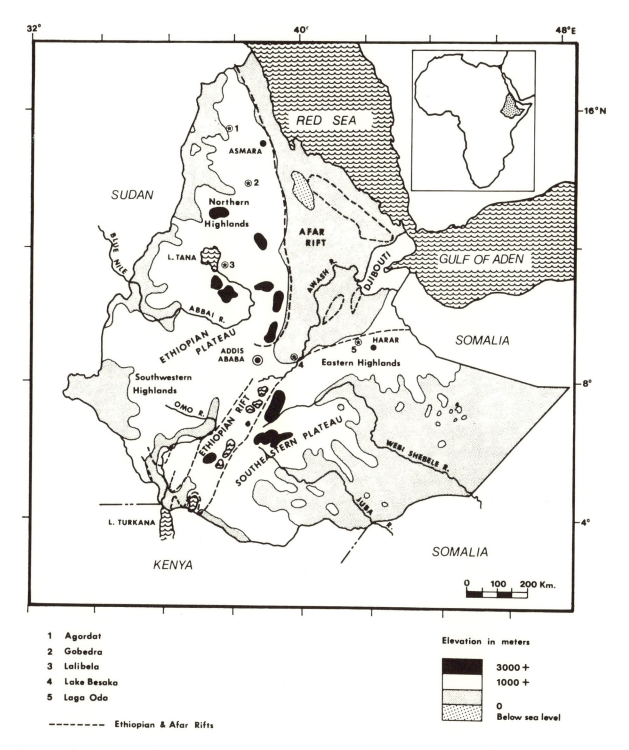

1 Agordat
2 Gobedra
3 Lalibela
4 Lake Besaka
5 Laga Oda

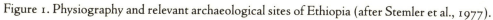 Ethiopian & Afar Rifts

Figure 1. Physiography and relevant archaeological sites of Ethiopia (after Stemler et al., 1977).

The Evidence for Ethiopian Food Production

Before moving to a discussion of the models that have been constructed to account for the origins of Ethiopian food production, it is necessary to conduct a concise but critical examination of the archaeological and historical evidence these models must accommodate.

EXCAVATED SITES

Due to the paucity of Late Quaternary archaeological research in Ethiopia, only a handful of geographically disparate excavations have yielded information relevant to the understanding of the origins of Ethiopian food production. Recent fieldwork by D. W. Phillipson (1977a) at Gobedra rockshelter (elev. 2060 m), situated on a ridge near Axum in Tigre Province, has resulted in the discovery of remarkably fresh-looking uncharred seeds of cultivated finger millet, the single tooth of a domestic camel, and dental fragments which have tentatively been identified as those of domesticated oxen, all of which were recovered from strata containing a ceramic-bearing microlithic industry. The stratum incorporating the possible *Bos* remains has an age of ca. 1000 B.C., while the underlying deposits embodying the finger millet and camel tooth are bracketed between 1000 and 5000 B.C. (although the third millennium B.C. is thought to be the most likely estimate for the age of the lower stratum [Phillipson, 1977a: 68]). The surprisingly fresh condition of the finger millet (see Harlan's comments in Phillipson, 1977a) raises the question of whether these uncarbonized seeds (and, for that matter, the camel tooth) may be intrusive to the stratum in which they were found, particularly since the seeds were recovered only from the square lying outside the shelter's dripline. Given the "extreme dryness of the deposits in which they were preserved" (ibid.: 80), one might expect to find other perishables from the trench, and therefore it would be interesting to know the state of preservation of the other recovered material such as the bones and *Amaranthus* seeds (as well as the possible finger millet seed from Stratum VI). Nevertheless, as

previously mentioned, finger millet may have an Eastern African center of origin and therefore could easily have been domesticated as early as (if not earlier than) the period suggested by the Gobedra dates. If Phillipson (ibid.) is correct in stating that "there is an extremely high probability that the seeds in question were deposited with the layer in which they were found," then these seeds represent the oldest remains of domestic plants (and the *only* remains of African cultigens recovered from a prehistoric archaeological context in Ethiopia) yet known from sub-Saharan Africa (Hilu et al., 1979). The camel tooth, however, remains something of an anomaly.

The earliest evidence of domesticated camel (either dromedary or bactrian) is from southern Turkmenia and eastern Iran and is in the form of bones, dung, and hair dating to between 3500 and 2500 B.C. (Compagnoni and Tosi, 1978). Representations of dromedary camels on tombstones, in addition to osteological remains, have been recovered from the site of Umm an-Nar off the coast of Abu Dhabi and date to 2500 B.C. or earlier (ibid.: 100). The earliest evidence from southern Arabia, however, dates only to ca. 1100 B.C. (van Beek, 1969: 289–290). This latter date, however, is probably only a reflection on the lack of excavated sites, as southern Arabia has long been considered to be an early center of camel domestication (Bulliet, 1975: 36–56; Mikesell, 1955: 244–245).

Although wild camels may have inhabited parts of northern Africa into the Holocene, and pottery figurines and skeletal remains of the dromedary have been recovered from Egyptian sites dating to 2000 B.C. or earlier (Epstein, 1971; Mikesell, 1955), very little can be said about the introduction of this animal into sub-Saharan Africa. Largely on the basis of ecological and ethnographic data, Bulliet (1975: 56) has suggested that camels were first brought into the Horn, "one of the largest and most abundant camel territories in the world, not to mention one of the least known" (ibid.: 40), from southern Arabia sometime between 2500 and 1500 B.C. This range of time is in keeping with the suggested age of the tooth from Gobedra, although it should be kept in mind that the only other remains of camel bones in the Horn recovered from an archaeological context are from Laga Oda Rockshelter in eastern Ethiopia, where the camel-bearing deposits date to ca. A.D. 1300–1600 (Clark and Prince, 1978). Paintings of camels in the Horn are also thought to be relatively late (J. D. Clark, 1976b: 76), but how late is unknown. In any case, one tooth does not make a herd; it is premature to speculate further on camel domestication in the Horn of Africa until additional evidence is forthcoming.

The only other direct evidence for the early cultivation of plants in Ethiopia is restricted to the excavations undertaken by J. C. Dombrowski (n.d.) at Lalibela cave in Begemeder Province, northcentral Ethiopia. Unfortunately, her excavations failed to reveal deposits older than ca. 500 B.C., although domesticated cultigens of the Near Eastern complex, including barley (*Hordeum sp.*), chickpea (*Cicer arietinum*), and unspecified legumes, were recovered from the lowest stratum. Tentative identifications of domestic *Bos* and ovicaprids (sheep and/or goats) have also been made at Lalibela, although they also date to no earlier than 520 B.C. These domesticates are associated with mammal bones, ochre, pottery, worked bone, grindstones, and a nondescript lithic assemblage that includes scrapers and microliths (ibid.: 144).

Possible indications of intensive harvesting of wild grasses as early as 15,000 B.P. have been recovered from Laga Oda, a rockshelter situated in the foothills of the Chercher Mountains in southeastern Ethiopia (Clark and Williams, 1978). "Sickle sheen" gloss and polish have been observed on a wide range of shaped stone tools that were recovered from layers for which C14 dates range between 13,000 B.C. and A.D. 1625. These finds, which include a few microliths with mastic adhering to their surfaces, have led Clark and Prince (1978: 107) to postulate that these tools might indicate "some form of pre-adapted economy making regular use of wild grasses, that later gave rise to cultivation of one or more selected species." Of the combined total of 233 shaped tools recovered from the 1975 test trench at Laga Oda and used in the above analysis, only 3 (one awl, one endscraper, and one curved-backed flake) came from the 80 cm of deposit that underlie the layer dated at 1560 B.C. The endscraper and curved-backed flake revealed signs of polish—which, it should be noted, can be

produced by a wide range of substances (G. Diamond, 1979; Kamminga, 1979)—but none of the three displayed evidence of "sickle sheen" gloss. Although these Laga Oda finds are important and constitute intriguing potential evidence, the sample is extremely small and further excavations will be necessary before the hypothesized existence of a late Pleistocene subsistence economy involving intensive use of wild grasses can be regarded as confirmed.

The abundance of stone tools from Laga Oda displaying "sickle sheen" gloss from levels dating to 1560 B.C., together with the recovery of a few microliths that show evidence of mastic adhering close to the backed edges (Clark and Prince, 1978: 108), strongly suggests, however, that by this time stone tools were being used (probably as components of knives or sickles) to harvest phytolith-producing grasses and other plants. There is no reason why some of these plants could not have been domesticated, but since no botanical evidence of wild or cultivated plants was recovered from Laga Oda, this must remain conjecture until direct evidence is obtained. Domestic cattle, on the other hand, have been identified from faunal remains recovered from strata dating to 1560 B.C., while camel remains, as previously discussed, were recovered from the uppermost deposits, dating to ca. A.D. 1300–1600. The material culture associated with the cattle include a "Somaliland Wilton"-like stone assemblage, ostrich-eggshell beads, decorated and undecorated pottery, and ochre (ibid.).

Further evidence of domesticated cattle may be present at Lake Besaka, a small, graben-enclosed, saline lake in the Ethiopian Rift 200 km east of Addis Ababa, where excavations of open-air sites situated along the western side of the lake have revealed the presence of multiphase Later Stone Age industries, of which the earliest phase dates to ca. 22,000–19,000 years ago and the latest ca. 1500 B.C. (Brandt, 1980, n.d.; Clark and Williams, 1978). One site dating to ca. 1500 B.C. displays a number of characteristics that set it apart from the other sites at Lake Besaka: there is a major shift in artifact composition; fish remains are no longer found in the deposits; cattle (tentatively identified as domesticated) are added to the faunal list; and there is a possible change in settlement location suggesting that the site may be relatively farther away from the lake's shoreline. It has been suggested that these new features represent a shift in subsistence and settlement patterns from one of hunting, gathering, and fishing to an economy based upon pastoralism (Brandt, 1980, n.d.; Clark and Williams, 1978).

ROCK ART

Rock engravings and paintings situated mainly in the caves of northern and eastern Ethiopia often depict scenes of humans and domesticated animals, including humpless cattle with their udders clearly delineated (J. D. Clark, 1954; Drew, 1952; Graziosi, 1964). Unfortunately, there is no way of dating these illustrations chronometrically; however, observed stylistic differences have led some investigators to suggest that the more schematic scenes of people, humpless cattle, and fat-tailed sheep which are often found superimposed over more naturalistic depictions may be later in age, as is the case with the paintings from Laga Oda that reveal sheep, cattle, and stylized human figures (J. D. Clark, 1976b: 77; Clark and Williams, 1978). Although no remains of ovicaprids were found in the archaeological deposits from Laga Oda, it has been suggested that the more schematic illustrations of domestic cattle and fat-tailed sheep from the walls of the rockshelter may equate in age with the strata containing domesticated cattle (i.e., 1560 B.C.). One problem with this associated date is that fat-tailed sheep are not thought to have been domesticated until, at the earliest, 1500 B.C. (in central Arabia: Anati, 1968, II: 38–40; J. D. Clark, 1976b: 76), thereby allowing little time for this animal to have become established in Ethiopia before 1560 B.C.

Similarities between Nubian "C-Group" rock engravings and the stylized cattle paintings from eastern Ethiopia have been noted by J. D. Clark (1980b), while paintings in two caves in Eritrea, northeastern Ethiopia, have provided the only possible evidence for early use of the plow. Clearly depicted on one of the walls of Ba'ati Focada cave is a painting of two humpless cattle pulling a typical Ethiopian-style plow (Drew, 1952, 1954). Although some investigators believe this painting only dates to as early as the Pre-Axumite or Axumite Kingdom, as its rather schematicized style is reminiscent of motifs found at a neighboring site associated with a ca. 200 B.C. southern Arabian inscription (J. D. Clark, 1976b: 78; Mordini, 1947), the only substantiated evidence to indicate that it could not have been painted earlier is that other figures show metal spears and shields. The other possible depiction is from the cave of Zeban Cabessa I, where undated superpositioned motifs including humpless long-bodied cattle (Graziosi, 1964: 188) surround what may be a painting of a plow.

SURFACE OCCURRENCES

It has been suggested (J. D. Clark, 1980b; Phillipson, 1977c: 69–70) that surface finds of ground-stone axes or hoes from southwestern and westcentral Ethiopia (Bailloud, 1959; M. D. Leakey, 1943) may be associated with early ensete cultivation, but this remains to be verified by excavation. Similarly, winged and lugged stone axes, maceheads, grindstones, and a wide range of other ground-stone and ceramic artifacts have been surface-collected from several occupation sites near Agordat in northern Eritrea (Arkell, 1954) and are thought by J. D. Clark (1976b: 86) and Phillipson (1977c: 66) to represent second to first millennium B.C. semipermanent agriculture-based villages, with possible connections with "C-Group" settlements along the Nile in lower Nubia. Mention should also be made of the discovery of an isolated stone bowl of lava recovered from the surface in the spoil of an antbear hole at Lake Besaka (Clark and Williams, 1978). Based on stratigraphic correlation, the sediments from which the stone bowl is believed to have been derived may date to ca. 1500 B.C., while the bowl itself may suggest possible relations with the Neolithic "Stone Bowl" industries of East Africa (ibid.). Unfortunately, further reconnaissance and excavation at Lake Besaka failed to uncover additional bowls either from the surface or *in situ* (Brandt, 1980).

HISTORIC DATA

Dynastic Egyptian writings dating to ca. 2500 B.C. reportedly document the existence of naval trading routes to the land of "Punt," believed by some scholars to have been situated along the Red Sea coast of southeastern Sudan and Eritrea (Kitchen, 1971; J. A. Wilson, 1951). By 1504 B.C., during the reign of King Thutmosis III, both overland and Red Sea trade routes to Punt appear to have been established (Simoons, 1965; Zyhlarz, 1958). On the walls of the temple at Deir el Bahari, which dates to between 1489 and 1469 B.C., Queen Hatshepsut describes in detail the results of her personally sponsored naval expedition to the land of Punt, and it is in these bas-reliefs that we have the first historic illustrations of life in sub-Saharan Africa (Naville, 1898). The bas-reliefs show the native Puntites in possession of domestic animals, including dogs, donkeys, and short- and long-horned humpless cattle, and engaged in trading a wide variety of native goods, including gold rings, wild animals, skins, and incense, in exchange for Egyptian products. Hieroglyphics on the bas-reliefs describe a large banquet given by the Egyptians in the tent of their naval commander, where Puntite chiefs were invited to feast upon Egyptian *haute cuisine*, which included bread, beer, wine, meat, and fruit. Since Egyptian bread was made from wheat and barley, it is possible that the Puntities may at least have known of these Egyptian cereals by this time.

HUMAN SKELETAL EVIDENCE

For many years now, archaeologists as well as ethnographers, historians, and other researchers have attempted to correlate the beginnings of Ethiopian food production with the origins and spread of specific racial, ethnic, or linguistic groups (J. D. Clark, 1962, 1967a, 1976a, 1980b; Ehret, 1974b, 1976, 1979; Honea, 1958; L. S. B. Leakey, 1935; Simoons, 1965—to mention only a few). Murdock (1959: 81) has posited "Bushmanoid" populations occupying southwestern Ethiopia and "Caucasoid Cushites" situated to the north and east of the

"Bushmanoids" as being representative of the indigenous Ethiopian hunters, gatherers, and fisherfolk. With the movement of agriculture-based "Pre-Nilotes" into Ethiopia, Murdock (ibid.) concludes, there was extensive interbreeding with the two indigenous populations, resulting in the supposed present-day situation in which all Ethiopians display "Negro" traits of one form or another. J. D. Clark (1980b) has similarly argued for "Afro-Mediterranean" Cushitic-speaking populations and "Negro" groups as being the aboriginal hunters and gatherers of pre-agricultural Ethiopia, with intrusive populations of Northern Cushites (Bejas) and Eastern Sudanic-speaking "pre-Nilotes" being those responsible for introducing agriculture to the indigenous Ethiopians.

Unfortunately, there is very little empirical data that can be used to verify the existence of such prehistoric Ethiopian populations, for in all of Ethiopia only one prehistoric site (Lake Besaka) has provided reasonably intact and measurable skeletal remains of modern *Homo sapiens*. This skeletal material, which probably dates to ca. 2800 B.C. or earlier, consists of six incomplete individuals from two archaeological localities and is associated with a pre-domestic hunting-and-fishing economy (Brandt, 1980; Clark and Williams, 1978). The results of a preliminary metric analysis of the crania have indicated "Negroid" affinities for these skeletons (McCown, n.d.).

One other line of evidence relating to the racial/ethnic affinities of prehistoric Ethiopian populations is the Deir el Bahari reliefs of the land of "Punt," where two physically distinct types have been depicted (Naville, 1898). J. D. Clark (1976a: 73; 1980b) has suggested that these two groups (Fig. 2) represent Cushitic-speaking "Afro-Mediterraneans" and "Negroids," respectively, and that the reliefs help to substantiate the linguistic evidence for the antiquity of these two physical types in the Horn of Africa. It should be kept in mind, though, that modern systematic anthropometric, genetic, and comparative research of modern (let alone prehistoric) African peoples can only be said to be in its infancy. There is still a heated debate as to what physical characteristics constitute "Negroid" affinities as compared to "Caucasoid" or

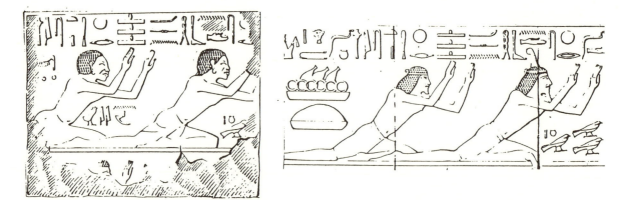

Figure 2. Bas-reliefs of native Puntites as depicted at the temple of Deir el Bahari, Egypt, ca. 1500 B.C. (from Naville, 1898).

"Afro-Mediterranean" (Armelagos and Greene, 1978; Rightmire, 1975a, 1975b; Van Gerven et al., 1973), and speakers of distinct language groups (Greenberg, 1963) cannot as yet be equated on a one-to-one basis with a specific prehistoric physical type (i.e., "Afro-Mediterranean Cushites").

Models for the Origins of Ethiopian Food Production

One can recognize in the current literature five main models pertaining to the origins of Ethiopian food production.

THE MIGRATION MODEL

This model, largely one of primary diffusion, argues that Cushitic-speaking "Caucasoid" agriculturalists migrated into northeast Africa from the Near East or Arabia 5,000 or more years ago, bringing with them their agricultural techniques as well as early forms of wheat and barley. The Ethiopian descendants of these "Caucasoid" migrants, most likely the Central Cushitic Agau people, found wild sorghum growing in their cereal fields, and domesticated the plant by the fourth or third millennium B.C. (Doggett, 1965; 1970: 2–3; Purseglove, 1976: 293).

Some of the problems associated with this model are: (1) It is dependent upon the belief that the Cushitic language and the "Caucasoid" physical type are not in any way indigenous to Africa (Cole, 1963: 334–335; Honea, 1958), a position that is no longer accepted by the majority of linguists (e.g., Bender, 1976; Ehret, 1974b; Greenberg, 1963) or physical anthropologists (e.g., Hiernaux, 1974; Rightmire, 1975a, b). (2) Wild sorghum grows in hot and dry conditions and consequently is found at only low elevations in Ethiopia, *not* in the wheat and barley fields of highland Ethiopia (Stemler et al., 1977). (3) There is no archaeological evidence for either intrusive agricultural populations in Ethiopia or for the growing of domesticated wheat, barley, or sorghum prior to 3000 B.C. And, (4) it does not account for the domestication of local cultigens such as teff, noog, or ensete.

THE PRE-NILOTIC MODEL

George Murdock (1959) may have been the first scholar to suggest that Eastern Sudanic-speaking "Pre-Nilotes" were originally responsible for introducing Sudanic agricultural practices (i.e., a sedentary lifestyle, animal husbandry, and the cultivation of sorghum, cotton, sesame, and other crops by use of the hoe and digging stick) to the indigenous hunting-and-gathering "Bushman-oids" and "Caucasoid Cushites" of the lowlands and bordering hills of western Ethiopia sometime before 3000 B.C. Although the "Bushmanoids" were soon displaced or became totally acculturated by these "Pre-Nilotes," the Cushitic peoples expanded their newly acquired agricultural economy by domesticating some locally available plants and improving upon others, such as sorghum (ibid., pp. 170, 181, 187).

Largely as a result of geographical isolation, it is postulated, three separate centers of Cushitic language, culture, and economy soon developed.

1. A Central Cushitic branch in the highlands of northern and central Ethiopia, where the cultivation of such indigenous cereals as teff and finger millet led Murdock (1959: 182) to consider this "Ethiopian Complex" to be "one of the world's important minor centers of origination of cultivated plants." Cattle, sheep, and goats, Murdock contended, were obtained from ancient Egypt, although the donkey was domesticated locally. Crops of the "Egyptian Complex," which included wheat and barley, may also have diffused from Dynastic Egypt. However, since these crops were rarely grown in Nubia, a more likely explanation would be that they were brought into Ethiopia by southern Arabians during the Semitic migrations of the first millennium B.C.

2. A second Cushitic branch, represented by a diverse group of people collectively referred to as the "Sidamo tribes" of southwestern Ethiopia, who spoke "Western Cushitic" and physically displayed a mixture of "Negroid" (i.e., "Pre-Nilotic") and "Caucasoid" blood (Murdock has argued that the "Pre-Nilotes" "must also have made certain inroads among the Caucasoid Cushites farther east, for all the peoples of Ethiopia today reveal at least a slight admixture of Negro blood" [Murdock, 1959: 181]). Ensete was first brought under domestication by these "Sidamo tribes," while other root crops as well as "Ethiopian" and "Egyptian complex" domesticates were cultivated on terraced fields. As today, animal husbandry remained subordinate to cultivation but was nevertheless vitally important for supplying manure to fertilize the crops.

3. A third branch of Eastern Cushitic-speaking peoples, who were at first largely confined to the Southeastern (Somali) Plateau, where they engaged in farming and animal husbandry in addition to trading. Then, sometime around A.D. 900, large groups of Eastern Cushites, whose modern descendants include the Afar, Oromo, and Somali, took up a pastoral way of life, perhaps as a result of being influenced by pastoral Arabs or Northern Cushitic-speaking Beja people who now occupy the northwestern corner of Eritrea. Subsequent migrations included the Afar, who moved north into the Afar Rift and coastal regions of Eritrea, while the Galla- and (somewhat later) Somali-speaking pastoralists spread into the Ogaden and Somalia (Murdock, 1959: 319–320).

Murdock's model also suffers from a lack of archaeological evidence to substantiate the migration of a new agricultural population into western Ethiopia. Nor is there any skeletal evidence to justify the presence of "Bushmanoids" or "Caucasoid Cushites" or, for that matter, the acquisition of an agricultural economy by Cushitic-speaking hunters and gatherers. However, Murdock's attempt to distinguish three prehistoric centers of Cushitic development, although lacking empirical evidence, does try to deal with the social, geographic, and economic complexities of modern Cushitic-speaking populations in Ethiopia.

THE C-GROUP MODEL

Perhaps best known to archaeologists are J. D. Clark's two models, the earliest of which was formulated in the 1960s (J. D. Clark, 1962, 1967a). Clark argued that cattle pastoralism, and possibly also wheat and barley cultivation, was introduced to the highlands of Ethiopia by "C-Group" immigrants from Nubia some 4,000 years ago. The indigenous crops of Ethiopia, however, were not brought under cultivation until the knowledge of food production had already spread into Ethiopia and surrounding regions (J. D. Clark, 1962: 219).

Hoes and digging sticks were utilized as aids in cultivation, but at some unspecified time these implements were superseded by the plow (J. D.

Clark, 1967a: 615). The main catalyst for C-Group migrations was believed to have been the period of mid-Holocene environmental desiccation in the Sahara and Sahel (Williams and Faure, 1980), which resulted in famine and drought, forcing human communities to search for new pastures and fertile fields such as the temperate Ethiopian plateaux (J. D. Clark, 1967a: 613).

THE DESICCATION MODEL

Clark's second model is similar to his first in that the "C-Group" pastoralists, who originally emigrated to lower Nubia as a result of the late third millennium B.C. Saharan and northeast African drought and famine (J. D. Clark, 1967a: 613; 1976b: 75), were the ones responsible for introducing cattle and a pastoral way of life to the indigenous populations of Ethiopia ("Afro-Mediterranean Cushites" and "Negroids") as they continued to disperse southward into northern Ethiopia, down the Red Sea coast into the Afar Rift and finally up onto the two Ethiopian plateaux (J. D. Clark, 1976b: 71–86; 1980b).

The second model differs from the earlier one by taking Murdock's "Pre-Nilotic" model one step further so that "Pre-Nilotes" occupying the low-lying plains of Sudan and western Ethiopia were also subjected to a long period of climatic deterioration between ca. 2350 and 870 B.C., resulting in "Pre-Nilotic" migrations out of the cattle-disease-ridden plains, east into the more temperate highland regions of the central and northern Ethiopian Plateau. It is from these intrusive populations, then, that knowledge of farming was first introduced to the aboriginal "Afro-Mediterranean" Cushites and "Negro" hunters and gatherers of highland Ethiopia (J. D. Clark, 1976b: 80–81; 1980b). In support of how populations may have migrated in the past, Clark (1976b: 80–81) refers to information supplied by Murdock (1959: 170) in which two "Pre-Nilotic" groups (the Berea and Kunama) were seen by an Arab traveler in A.D. 872 to have been occupying territory near present-day Khartoum but subsequently disappeared from the historical record until the nineteenth century, when these two groups were found to be living in the northern highlands of Eritrea rather than in the Nile Valley.

Following the introduction of pastoral and farming methods into Ethiopia, the aboriginal Ethiopians soon took it upon themselves to raise domesticated animals and, with the aid of hoes and digging sticks, to cultivate such Sudanic crops as sorghum and such indigenous Ethiopian plants as teff, ensete, noog, and perhaps finger millet. Wheat, barley, and other cultigens of the "Near Eastern complex" (and perhaps also durra sorghum) were not grown in Ethiopia until these crops as well as the plow were first brought into Ethiopia by Semitic-speaking southern Arabians who settled in the northeastern part of the country sometime around 500 B.C. (and soon thereafter formed the basis of the Axumite kingdom). It is postulated that indigenous Ethiopian cereals would never have been domesticated if wheat and barley had had a long history of cultivation in Ethiopia (J. D. Clark, 1976b: 78; T. Shaw, 1976: 124).

Clark has also suggested that the general absence of "Pre-Nilotic" populations on the plateaux today is the result of westward pressure from the Galla and Amhara, who may have forced highland "Pre-Nilotic" populations back down into the lowlands of western Ethiopia and eastern Sudan. In this case, present-day "Pre-Nilotic" groups of western Ethiopia (e.g., the Gumuz) "may preserve elements that show the nature of the original system on the Plateau prior to the introduction of plow culture to the Cushites" (J. D. Clark, 1976b: 81).

Although economic systems based upon pastoralism and cultivation were already in full swing in southwestern, central, and northern Ethiopia by the second millennium B.C., those human populations occupying the eastern part of the Southeastern Plateau remained essentially pastoralists, "for agriculture there can be seen to be superimposed on an economy and social organization based on cattle herding with sheep and goats" (J. D. Clark, 1976b: 79). It was not until the ninth century A.D., Clark has maintained, that the main stimulus for farming may have occurred in this area as a direct result of Islamic influence. The modern pastoralists now occupying the arid regions of eastern Ethiopia

and Somalia (e.g., the Afar, Saho, Galla, and Somali) therefore represent descendants of these
early pastoral populations of the Horn, although
camels and Zebu cattle did not become important
components of these pastoral systems until sometime after the first Semitic intrusions into Ethiopia
ca. 500 B.C. (ibid.: 76–78).

Clark's models have the status of hypotheses
that await testing through excavation of appropriate archaeological sites and the recovery of human
skeletal remains from relevant timespans and geographic areas. As far as any connections between
"C-Group" people and Ethiopians are concerned,
it should be noted that other authors have recently
suggested that the "C-Group" culture ("C-Horizon," as it is now called: W. Y. Adams, 1977: 143)
was not a result of population movements into Nubia but instead represents an indigenous development from the earlier A-Horizon populations of
Nubia (ibid.: 143, 152–154; Carlson and Van Gerven, 1979; Trigger, 1976: 52–53). There is also
evidence to indicate that the mid-Holocene period
of climatic amelioration gradually came to a close
toward the end of the fourth millennium B.C., with
more rapid deterioration of the climate at ca.
3000–2800 B.C. (Butzer, 1976: 28, 32).

This might suggest, therefore, that any human
ecological stress resulting from severe climatic
change was already well underway by late A-Horizon times and did not coincide with supposed "C-
Group" movements. In fact, just after the earliest
evidence for C-Horizon Nubian settlements (i.e.,
ca. 2300 B.C.), the upper Nile Valley appears to
have experienced "catastrophically low floods between 2250 and perhaps 1950" (Butzer, 1976: 28,
citing B. Bell, 1971), yet the archaeological evidence from C-Group sites indicates "no recognizable lacunae in the record of occupation at villages
or cemeteries which might point to the temporary
disruption of Nubian society" (W. Y. Adams,
1977: 145). Furthermore, the meager information
that does exist for C-Horizon subsistence patterns
indicates that cattle may not have played a major
role in C-Horizon economics and that sheep and
the cultivation of such crops as wheat, barley, and
legumes could have been just as important, if not
more so, to their economic well-being as cattle

(ibid.: 143, 152–154; Trigger, 1976: 52–53). As
for "Pre-Nilotic" occupation of the Ethiopian Plateau, it should be pointed out that both the Nera
and Kunama people occupy the "Kolla" lowlands
of western Eritrea (<1650 m) and not the Cushi-
tic- and Semitic-occupied highland regions
(Bender, 1975a, 1976; Simoons, 1960: 108).

Although it could be argued that environmental desiccation and diseases of cattle may have
forced Nilo-Saharan populations out of the western lowlands and into the highlands of the Ethiopian Plateau toward 2200 B.C., recent paleoclimatic
evidence lends little credence to the thesis of a
widespread long-term period of climatic deterioration in northeastern Africa between ca. 2350 and
870 B.C. Instead, there appears to have been a distinct interval of wetter conditions (at least in the
upper Nile Valley and Lake Turkana area) at about
1850 B.C. and concluding approximately 500 years
later, in 1200 B.C. (Butzer, 1976: 26–33).

Unfortunately, in view of the fact that past
ecological regimes supportive of fly- and tick-born
cattle diseases are virtually impossible to detect
using modern paleoenvironmental techniques
(D. A. Livingstone, pers. comm.), it will be difficult
to test the hypothesis that diseases of cattle in the
lowlands of the Sudan and western Ethiopia were
an important incentive for people to move up to the
Ethiopian Plateau. Moreover, one could just as
easily argue (although it would be just as difficult to
support) that late Holocene climatic deterioration
would have shifted ecological zones vertically so
that the lowlands would have become disease-free
while the higher zones of the plateau would have
become disease-ridden.

If any ethno/linguistic group can be considered
to have been "displaced" from the highlands of
central and northern Ethiopia, it would have to be
the Central Cushitic-speaking peoples (e.g., the
Agau), who have largely been assimilated by Semitic incursions into their traditional homelands.
Therefore, rather than using the Gumuz as a good
analogical candidate for obtaining insights into agricultural systems on the Ethiopian Plateau prior to
the introduction of the plow, it may be just as rewarding to study those Central Cushitic groups
who have only recently taken up the use of the plow

and who still depend upon the hoe and digging stick as aids in the cultivation of such grains as teff and other crops not grown by Nilo-Saharan cultivators (Simoons, 1960: 20–56).

Given the degree to which those Nilo-Saharan peoples presently occupying the lowlands of western Ethiopia differ socially, economically, politically, technologically, and ecologically from their Cushitic and Semitic neighbors in the highlands to the east (Simoons, 1960), it might be argued that any prehistoric movement into Ethiopia by Nilo-Saharan farmers would have been checked by the unique ecological requirements of the Ethiopian highlands. Those traits shared by Cushitic and Nilo–Saharan-speakers (e.g., cultivation of certain crops and domestication of animals) may therefore be a result of diffusion rather than of large-scale human migrations.

THE AFROASIATIC MODEL

Drawing heavily upon historic linguistic studies and, to a much lesser extent, archaeological evidence, Ehret (1974b, 1976, 1979, 1980c, and this volume) has developed a model for the origins of Ethiopian food production unlike those proposed by other scholars. His main premise is that, toward the end of the Pleistocene, ancestors of northeastern African and Near Eastern peoples who now speak or at one time spoke Afroasiatic languages (i.e., Berber, Chadic, Semitic, Ancient Egyptian, Omotic, and Cushitic), once shared a common homeland in northeastern Africa and a common language, proto-Afroasiatic. They also shared a common subsistence activity, intensive grass-collecting, which was developed as a way in which to deal with a major food crisis affecting large parts of the Old World, including northeastern Africa and the Near East (Ehret, 1979: 166, after Cohen, 1977).

Linguistic evidence suggests that at least by 5000 B.C., Ethiopian proto–Cushitic-speaking peoples were already engaged in the cultivation of such local cereals as teff and finger millet and were raising domestic cattle, donkeys, goats, and sheep, the latter two of which they obtained through secondary diffusion from the Near East via northeastern Africa. Domesticated cattle and donkeys, on the other hand, may have evolved from local northeastern African stock (Ehret, 1979: 163–166).

Ehret (1979: 175; see also Simoons, 1965) has further argued that the linguistic evidence makes a strong case for Ethiopian adoption of the above agricultural items by 4000 B.C., long before the arrival of Semitic-speaking peoples into Ethiopia during the first millennium B.C.

Aside from the general lack of archaeological evidence to support the above hypotheses, the major problem with Ehret's model lies in his attempts to correlate what archaeological information there is with specific linguistic groups. To argue that the later Pleistocene sites of Egyptian Nubia, as well as the Natufian sites of the Levant, represent intensive grass-collectors who spoke a proto-Afroasiatic language, may be stretching the empirical evidence beyond its limit.

In support of the Afroasiatic Model, however, it is interesting to note that "if the Cushitic dating scale proposed here is applied to the percentage of cognation among Ethiosemitic languages (Bender, 1971: 173), the beginnings of Ethiosemitic settlement and expansion can be set in the second half of the last millennium B.C." (Ehret, 1976: 96), a date that is in close accord with archaeological and historic evidence (Hable-Sellasie, 1972).

Discussion

It should by now be clear that the archaeological data-base relevant to an understanding of Ethiopian food production is particularly weak: large areas remain virtually unknown, and there has been only one archaeological project in all of Ethiopia that was specifically concerned with the origins of Ethiopian food production (Dombrowski, n.d.). What little information does exist is largely a by-product of rather disparate excavations with equally disparate goals. All the models constructed to account for the causes and consequences of food production depend to one extent or another upon migration, diffusion, and/or independent invention to explain the origins of Ethiopian food production, while the prime movers are seen to be environmental change and/or demographic pressure.

There is little doubt that these mechanisms of culture change played a profound role in shaping the course of later Ethiopian prehistory, but any introductory textbook in archaeology will tell you that:

> Independent invention, diffusion and migration are studied descriptively by means of the history of individual culture traits in the archaeological record. *A large amount of data* [emphasis added] is needed to establish accurate trait distributions, precise and comprehensive local sequences and the chronological gradients and trait diffusion routers that should stem from these basic descriptive efforts. (Fagan, 1978: 391)

Similarly, a large data-base is necessary before one can invoke environmental change and/or population pressure as unilinear causal factors in the development of Ethiopian food production (Butzer, 1971; Cowgill, 1979). Consequently, those models previously constructed to account for the causes and consequences of food production remain at best untested, and at worst untestable.

There is also a wide range of other questions that need to be considered. With the recent announcement of (domesticated?) wheat and barley from Upper Egypt dating to 17,000 B.P. (but see p. 101), followed by fully agricultural societies dependent upon domesticated wheat, barley, cattle, and sheep by 5000 B.C. (Stemler, this volume; Wendorf and Schild, this volume), is it possible that ecological conditions were such that these "Near Eastern" cereals were growing wild in the highlands of Ethiopia toward the end of the Pleistocene? If so, could these cereals, along with other wild Ethiopian plants, have been brought under domestication by the indigenous populations of Ethiopia? Could this account for the high degree of genetic diversity in some of the modern Ethiopian cereals? If in fact this was the case, why did the knowledge of food production not spread earlier to neighboring countries—or did it? Were human groups domesticating locally available plants as part of a process of adapting to the changing ecological conditions of Late Quaternary Ethiopia? Could economic systems dependent upon domesticated cultigens and hunting and gathering precede the undoubted in-troduction of exogenous domesticated animals? Was the development of pastoral nomadism a relatively late adaptation to changing environmental, cultural, or demographic conditions? Finally, if Ethiopian food-producing systems were found to pre-date the Saharan mid-Holocene period of environmental desiccation, *why* and *how* did people turn to a food-producing economy? Were there earlier periods of environmental change that may have disrupted more traditional foraging strategies, or was it demographic pressure or the result of other social or economic variables that forced people to turn to cultivation and/or herding? These and other questions certainly deserve an answer, but given the state of archaeological research in Ethiopia and the continued dependence upon culture-historically oriented models and research designs, it will be many years before a large enough data-base will be available to answer them.

Perhaps a more desirable avenue of research for the near future, and one that has been proven extremely effective in other areas of the Old and New World, would be to develop research programs designed to investigate the *processes* involved in the transition from hunting/gathering to food production, and the concomitant social, demographic, and ecological effects of such a major economic change. Such programs would not require a vast understanding of Ethiopian culture-history (although they would certainly contribute to it) and could be limited to a geographical area small enough to be archaeologically testable. For example: The most economically important plant of the "hoe and vegeculture complex" of the southern Ethiopian Plateau and the southern part of the Southeastern Plateau is ensete, a large fibrous-leaf plant that closely resembles the banana plant and in fact is sometimes referred to as the "false banana" (Fig. 3). Although wild forms of the plant are found in many parts of southern and eastern Africa, it is only in a relatively small and geographically and environmentally distinct region of Ethiopia, where it is believed to have been first domesticated (Harlan, 1971), that it is grown for food (Fig. 4). Ensete is almost exclusively cultivated by Omotic and Cushitic agriculturalists, with the only significant exception being the Semitic-speaking people of Gurage (Shack, 1963). It can be cared for easily,

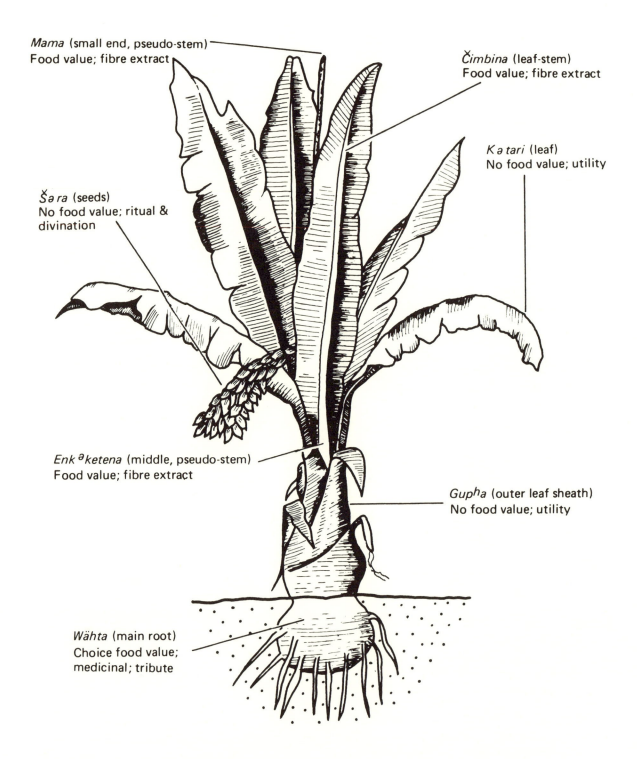

Mama (small end, pseudo-stem)
Food value; fibre extract

Čimbina (leaf-stem)
Food value; fibre extract

Kᵊtari (leaf)
No food value; utility

Šᵊra (seeds)
No food value; ritual &
divination

Enkᵊketena (middle, pseudo-stem)
Food value; fibre extract

Gupʰa (outer leaf sheath)
No food value; utility

Wähta (main root)
Choice food value;
medicinal; tribute

Figure 3. *Ensete ventricosum* and Gurage terms for the edible parts (from T. Shaw, 1977, after Shack, 1966).

Figure 4. Distribution of wild and cultivated ensete (after J. D. Clark, 1980b).

is drought-resistant, and suffers from few diseases or pests. Unlike the banana, the seedy, leathery fruits are not eaten; the main sources of food are the roots, pseudo-stems, and leaf-stems (Fig. 3).

Unfortunately, the biosystematics of *Ensete ventricosum* have never been completely worked out (Baker and Simmonds, 1953a, b; J. R. Harlan, pers. comm.), but over forty different varieties of ensete are said to be present in Ethiopia, including both wild and cultivated forms (Smeds, 1955). To reproduce by seed, as is the case with wild varieties, the ensete plant requires between three and six years of growth before enough carbohydrates can be stored in its leaf-sheaths to permit flowering and fruiting. Seeds reach full maturity and fertility when all the carbohydrates in the plant have been used up, resulting in the plant's death, when the seeds fall to the ground (Shack, 1966: 60–62; Smeds, 1955: 19–22). Cultivated plants, however, are almost always vegetatively propagated by hollowing out a six-year-old corm, filling it with manure and soil, and subsequently transplanting the sprouts (Shack, 1966: 60; Simmonds, 1958: 303; Smeds, 1955: 20). Harvesting of the mature ensete plant is undertaken just after it bears the seedy fruit; otherwise, continued growth of the fruit would deplete the plant's starch reserves, rendering it useless for human consumption.

Shack (1966: 60) has pointed out that seeds from the cultivated ensete are now sterile or only slightly fertile, while Smeds (1955: 26) has argued that cultivated ensete can be reproduced by seed, although with some difficulty. While cultivated ensete can be grown at altitudes greater than 3,100 m, wild plants appear to be restricted to elevations of less than 2,000 m. Plants grown at the uppermost elevation of ensete cultivation rarely flower and are therefore almost totally dependent upon humans for propagation (Smeds, 1955: 21).

There is considerable variation in the way the people of southwestern Ethiopia exploit ensete. The North Omotic-speaking Sheko (Tschako) tribe, for example, occupy the subtropical forests of Kaffa Province and practice a form of shifting cultivation in which ensete, taro, and yams are the most important foods. Neither cattle-herding nor cereal cultivation is of much economic importance (Straube, 1963: 26–33). The ensete is processed

for consumption by simply cutting the roots into pieces and cooking it over hot stones. Population density is low and consists of small settlements of four to six homesteads, each comprising four or so huts. At the other end of the scale are such tribes as the Eastern Cushitic Sidamo, who occupy the highlands bordering the Ethiopian Rift lakes. The Sidamo grow ensete in dense plantations and depend upon it to such an extent that it has developed into a monoculture with a complex social, political, economic, and ritual system centering around the plant. Almost every part of the plant is used, although it is the starchy pseudo-stem which is of utmost dietary importance. In the time-consuming process of preparing ensete for use as food, the pulp of the plant, which is what remains after decortication of the pseudo-stems and leaves, is put into deep earthen pits where it is covered and allowed to ferment for a year or more, thereby allowing for long-term storage (Shack, 1966: 63; Smeds, 1955: 23–24). The resulting paste is then cooked as a porridge or baked into a bread.

The Sidamo are also highly dependent upon sheep, goats, and, in particular, cattle as important sources of manure for fertilizing the soils in which the nutrient-exhausting ensete grows (Smeds, 1955: 32). The animals are pastured during the day in high-altitude grasslands above the cultivation zones and are brought back to the homesteads at night.

Ethnographically and botanically speaking, this fascinating and unusual form of food production is sorely in need of further research. Archaeologically speaking, it offers great potential for studying the causes and effects of food production in Ethiopia and for developing comparable models of prehistoric culture change. The reasons for this are as follows.

1. Unlike the tuberous crops of other vegecultural complexes, which almost always end up archaeologically invisible, the ensete plant is a producer of large, extremely hard, and distinctive seeds which should leave traces in the archaeological record. Furthermore, since there is some evidence to suggest that the cultivated variety is no longer or is hardly capable of fertilizing itself, this could indicate that distinct genetic changes in the plant may have occurred as a result of domestication. Therefore, it *may* be possible to distinguish wild from cultivated varieties by the size and shape of the seeds, which also may have underdone morphological change.

2. It should also be possible to detect in the archaeological record the remains of the deep earthen pits used to ferment and store ensete. Moreover, at a modern homestead "the number of storage pits per land holding, which are spaced between the rows of ensete plants, is determined by the consumption needs of the homestead" (Shack, 1963: 78). Since, on the average, only twelve plants are needed to feed one adult for the whole year (Simmonds, 1958), it should be possible to calculate the population of an active homestead on the basis of number of pits alone. Although some major problems would have to be overcome (some perhaps through ethnoarchaeological research) before one could use this sort of information on an archaeological site, it may very well be possible to determine to some extent the demography of a prehistoric homestead.

3. All ensete-dependent homesteads have distinctive spatial patterns. Many use stone to construct house foundations, walls, terraces, and other structures (Shack, 1966; Straube, 1963: 84–102). Given a reasonable degree of preservation, homesteads may be detectable in the archaeological record.

On the basis of these and other data, processual models for the origins of food production in southwestern Ethiopia can be devised and tested in the field. One testable model could go something like this:

A state of economic and demographic equilibrium existed among Upper Pleistocene hunter/gatherers as they practiced a foraging strategy that made full use of the animal and plant resources found in the ecologically diverse but climatically stable highlands and savannas of southern Ethiopia. This included the gathering of plants from the forest/savanna ecotone and ensete from the highland forests. In general, populations at this time would have been relatively small and residentially mobile (Binford, 1980).

Economic disequilibrium in the form of radical reduction in one or more staple resources, brought about by a combination of factors initiated by more than five thousand years of later Upper Pleistocene (ca. 20,000–12,000 B.P.) hyperaridity (Gasse and Street, 1978; Gasse et al., 1980) would have resulted in severe changes in foraging strategies as the length of the biotic growing season dramatically decreased, the range of environmental zones were substantially reduced (Binford, 1980), and food resources became less predictable (Dyson-Hudson and Smith, 1978). Socioeconomic adaptations to such an environmental change may be postulated to have resulted in a shift from a "normal" residential mobility pattern to one of increased logistic mobility (Binford, 1980) and a change from foraging to the collection and storage of critical resources such as ensete.

The residential base camp would eventually have been moved closer to those resources that proved to be the most dependable, or alternatively, the dependable resource(s) would have been brought closer to the camp. This latter situation might have involved intentional growing of ensete, either by transplanting or by reproduction by seed. Successful growing of ensete near the residential base camp would have resulted in a decrease in the need for logistical mobility and an increase in sedentariness as more time and energy would have been put into the cultivation of this dependable food supply. Experimentation in the vegetative propagation of ensete may also have begun, but to maintain the highly nutritive soils necessary to grow ensete, a system of shifting cultivation would have been required. Populations would have begun to increase as a result of, to name a few factors, reduced female mobility, closer spacing of births, and a decrease in number of miscarriages (D. R. Harris, 1978).

With the return to greater humidity in the Holocene (Gasse et al., 1980), environmental conditions would once again have been amenable to diverse foraging strategies. Those groups who managed to maintain a hunting/gathering way of life throughout the terminal Pleistocene would certainly have taken advantage of the return to more favorable conditions, and it is possible that some incipient farmers would also have returned to this socioeconomic mode. However, the majority of the semisedentary horticulturalists would not have done so, as they would already have been "locked in" to a farming mode supplemented by logistical hunting-and-gathering. Although populations would have continued to increase, undue demographic pressure would have been alleviated by the budding-off of new homesteads and the colonization of new land, thereby increasing the rate of deforestation, which may already have begun to disrupt the foraging strategies of hunting-and-gathering bands.

Sometime during the early to mid-Holocene, domesticated animals and other Ethiopian and non-Ethiopian cultigens diffused into southern Ethiopia. Some of these new cultigens were incorporated into existing horticultural systems, although ensete remained the most important source of food. Perhaps the domesticated animals would at first have been few in number and largely utilized for meat until difficulties with adult lactose intolerance (Simoons, 1973) would have been overcome and a milking industry established. The addition of new crops and domesticated animals would have resulted in a further and relatively rapid expansion of homesteads into new ecological zones. A critical threshold in availability of new farmland may have been reached at this time, resulting in demographic disequilibrium as populations continued to increase and availability of new land decreased. Intensive utilization of manure for fertilizing the ensete fields may have developed as a way in which to maintain the fertility of ensete without having to practice shifting cultivation,, thereby enabling homesteads to become fully sedentary. Since more ensete plants could be grown on a smaller tract of land than ever before, so long as there was a plentiful supply of manure, a positive feedback situation would have been realized as ensete was harvested in ever-increasing amounts and more complex social, economic, technological, and ritual systems necessary for dealing with agriculture-based sedentariness evolved.

The reinforcing effects of a sedentary lifestyle, combined with the need for a large labor force to maintain animals as well as crops, would have resulted in a substantial increase in human populations. The ability to feed this growing population would have been partially solved by the increase in ensete productivity, but ways in which to postpone consumption and prevent spoilage of surplus crops would also have had to be found. This was probably how the present-day methods of storing ensete by fermenting it in deep earthen pits first came to be developed. Eventually, a return to socioeconomic and demographic equilibrium would have been realized and the "hoe and vegeculture" complex of southwestern Ethiopia would have taken its place as one of the most dependable systems of food production the world has yet seen.

Conclusion

Research into the origins of Ethiopian food production remains in its infancy. Archaeological occurrences dating to the period crucial for understanding early Ethiopian agriculture are few and far between, while interdisciplinary projects have yet to be undertaken. Previous models constructed to account for the beginnings of Ethiopian food production, although valid hypotheses, are often culture-historical in orientation and in some instances may prove difficult to test in the archaeological record.

Models designed to examine the *processes* involved in the development of Ethiopian food-producing systems need to be formulated and tested. One such testable model dealing with the evolution of ensete food production has been presented. Although this model remains rather simplistic and is open to criticism, it does serve as an example of how new perspectives may lead to a better understanding of the causes and consequences of food production in Ethiopia and elsewhere in Africa.

18

Human Skeletal Remains from Eastern Africa

G. P. RIGHTMIRE

The oldest farming settlements excavated so far in Africa are located in the Nile Valley and Western Desert of Egypt (Wendorf et al., 1976), where they are somewhat later than comparable sites in the eastern Mediterranean and the Middle East. Clear evidence for the cultivation of emmer wheat and barley and the regular use of sheep/goats and cattle by Neolithic Egyptians dates only to the fifth millennium B.C. (J. D. Clark, 1976a). However, the shift from hunting and gathering to full food-production must have begun long before this time, with the exploitation of a variety of plant and animal resources. Shaped grinding stones found at Tushka and Kom Ombo in southern Egypt date

The author wishes to thank R. E. Leakey and C. B. Stringer for access to skeletal remains in their care. Other colleagues at the Kenya National Museums and the British Museum (Natural History) provided assistance, and J. L. Angel kindly allowed use to be made of his report on the Lothagam material. The work in eastern Africa has been supported by the National Science Foundation and by the Research Foundation of the State University of New York.

from 14,500 to 13,000 B.P. (Wendorf, 1968: 940–946; Butzer and Hansen, 1968: 114). Quite recently, Wendorf et al. (1979) and Wendorf and Schild (this volume) have reported well-preserved, carbonized plant remains identifiable as barley, perhaps in a very early stage of domestication, from a series of sites at Wadi Kubbaniya, just south of Kom Ombo (but see p. 101). These barley grains are associated with late Paleolithic occupations of 18,300 to 17,000 B.P., and it is likely that grain was used subsequently in the Nile Valley for thousands of years without substantial accompanying changes in settlement size, population density, or the conventional hunting/gathering mode of subsistence.

Human skeletal remains have apparently not been found at any of the Wadi Kubbaniya localities, but extensive series of burials have been excavated at Tushka in Upper Egypt, at Sahaba, and at site 6B36 at Wadi Halfa in the northern Sudan. Skeletons from these early cemeteries constitute a valuable source of information about the inhabitants of the Nile Valley during the long period of transition to a settled agricultural way of life (Armelagos et al., this volume). Studies of these and numerous later skeletal remains have documented patterns of pathology, disease, and mortality in Nubian populations. This record stands as a highly useful supplement to evidence of adaptation provided by archaeological fieldwork. Other recent approaches to the skeletons have emphasized changes in the dentition and variations in craniofacial form that can be interpreted in terms of decreasing masticatory stress probably associated with shifting subsistence and diet (Carlson and Van Gerven, 1977, 1979).

Further south in the Sudan and elsewhere in eastern Africa, the inventory of late Upper Pleistocene and Holocene human remains is rather shorter. A few, mostly fragmentary burials can be linked with settlements at Early Khartoum and localities in the Turkana Basin, where bone harpoon-points and stone tools suggest the importance of fishing to a hunter/gatherer economy (Robbins, 1974; Phillipson, 1977b; Barthelme, 1977; Butzer, 1980b). More skeletons are known from Later Stone Age contexts in the central Rift Valley. At some of these early to mid-Holocene sites, pottery is present, along with a variety of lithic artifacts. There is no indication that any form of cultivation

was underway during this period, but steps toward the domestication of livestock in parts of eastern Africa seem to have begun 5,000 years ago or earlier. At least by 3000 B.P., people practicing what has been termed a Pastoral Neolithic way of life were living in the Rift and surrounding highlands (Bower and Nelson, 1978). Relationships among the (several?) pastoralist traditions and ties of these Neolithic groups to preceding hunting/gathering populations are questions that have concerned archaeologists for a long time. Careful study of skeletal remains should help to shed some light on these issues but, unfortunately, human burials excavated in reliable association with pastoralist cultural traces are still few and far between. Large cemeteries such as those of Egypt and Nubia are generally lacking in eastern Africa, and the few burial grounds that have been investigated have contained skeletons in a disappointingly poor state of preservation. However, some useful material is available, and remains from a number of the more important East African localities are reviewed in this paper.

Hominids from the Later Upper Pleistocene

East African populations of the later Upper Pleistocene are not well represented by fossils, although several hominids have come to light since 1924. It was in that year that a cranium was discovered at Singa, on the Blue Nile south of Khartoum in the Sudan. A scattering of stone artifacts from the same horizon but at a different locality from the human bones has been compared with tools of Middle Stone Age manufacture, but neither the implements nor a collection of faunal remains has proved especially informative (Arkell et al., 1951). The date of the Singa assemblage is still uncertain, although a (late?) Upper Pleistocene age seems likely. The cranium was first described as an ancestral Bushman by Sir Arthur Smith Woodward (1938), and a similar conclusion was later reached by Wells (1951). The skull is quite broad, especially across the parietals, which are bossed as in many recent San (Bushman) crania, but Singa shares few other distinctive aspects of San morphology, and the sloping frontal displays a supraorbital torus that is thick and rounded, particularly in its lateral parts. More recently, this individual has been characterized as "Neanderthaloid" rather than Bushman-like (Brothwell, 1974). Stringer (1979) has used measurements to show that Singa is distant from a series of modern crania, and his analysis suggests points of resemblance to archaic *Homo sapiens* of Africa rather than to the Neanderthals of Europe. This last must be broadly correct, although the fossil is clearly not comparable to such other archaic hominids as Broken Hill or even Omo II from Ethiopia. The frontal profile is less flattened, with no signs of sagittal keeling, and the occiput is well filled out. Features of this sort give the Sudan skull a relatively modern appearance, despite the heavy brows.

Another hominid which is more firmly associated with a Middle Stone Age assemblage is the mandible from Porc Epic Cave, near Dire Dawa in eastern Ethiopia. This was picked up during excavations in 1933, and fieldwork has since clarified the stratigraphy of the cave deposits and provided a large collection of stone artifacts (Clark and Williams, 1978). Again, dating is a problem, but a minimum age of ca. 32,000 years obtained by obsidian hydration has been reported (J. Michels, pers. comm.). The mandible itself is broken, and scant attention has been paid to it since Vallois provided an initial description in 1951. Some archaic features of the symphysis and mandibular corpus have been identified, but it is not easy to interpret these without more complete skeletal evidence. Most recently, the Porc Epic jaw has been referred to a modern subspecies of *Homo sapiens* (F. C. Howell, 1978).

These remains do not tell us a great deal about late Pleistocene human evolution in northeastern Africa, but material from Kenya is marginally more helpful. A fragmentary cranium excavated in a rockshelter at Lukenya Hill is less complete than the Singa fossil, but preservation of the remaining bones is excellent. This individual is associated with Later Stone Age flaked stone artifacts, and a date of 17,700 B.P. indicates that the Lukenya Hill assemblage is certainly younger than that at Porc Epic (Gramly and Rightmire, 1973). While the

cranium is heavily built, with well-developed brows and a receding frontal, most of its features can be matched in series of recent East or South African Negro skulls. Characters marking the Lukenya Hill specimen as Bushman-like are lacking. These are useful observations, though the fossil cranium is so fragmentary that measurements which might provide a more definite assessment of its affinities cannot be taken. One point that does emerge from study of both Lukenya Hill and the other remains is that there is now little or no skeletal evidence to support a Pleistocene occurrence of San populations in East Africa. A similar conclusion follows from examination of burials found at early Holocene fishing settlements (described in the next section).

Later Stone Age Settlements of the Holocene

Earlier Holocene sites located in the Nile Valley and in the East African lake basins have frequently been described as "Mesolithic" in economy, as have other similar settlements of the southern Sahara. Many of these sites appear to have been occupied on a semipermanent basis, and adaptation to a waterside way of life is apparent. Pottery is often present, and bone harpoon-points provide a common theme, even where the assemblages are widely dispersed. However, the stone artifacts are quite diverse, consisting of microlithic tools as well as larger blades and scrapers. These lithic traditions seem to defy neat categorization, but all can be termed broadly as late Paleolithic or Later Stone Age.

One well-known fishing settlement is Early Khartoum in the Sudan. Arkell's excavations of this site during 1944–1945 revealed a predominantly microlithic industry with some grooved and bored stones, and also pottery. The bone harpoons found at Early Khartoum are characteristically barbed on one side only, with grooves cut around the base to facilitate binding of the point to a shaft. These harpoon points are similar to others recovered more recently from several sites along the White Nile, south of Khartoum, and occupation of the

TABLE 1. **Selected Holocene Sites in Eastern Africa Yielding Human Skeletal Remains**

Sites	Skeletal remains	Approximate dates, from available radiocarbon determinations
LSA hunting/fishing localities		
Early Khartoum	17 burials (1 individual reconstructed)	uncertain, possibly ~8000 B.P.
Koobi Fora/Ileret	several individuals (work in progress)	10,000–4000 B.P.
Lothagam	13 burials from 3 localities	8500–6000 B.P.
Lowasera	8 burials, all fragmentary	4500–3000 B.P.
Gamble's Cave II	5 skeletons (3 very incomplete)	8500–8000 B.P.(?)
Naivasha Railway Site	1 skeleton	10,850 B.P. (1 date from collagen)
Lake Besaka	6 individuals (4 very incomplete)	4,785 B.P.(?)
Pastoral Neolithic Localities		
Bromhead's Site	~28 individuals, many fragmentary	uncertain: 2500–2000 B.P.(?)
Namoratunga	174 burials at 3 sites; 40 burials have been excavated. Bone poorly preserved.	2285 B.P.
Hyrax Hill	18 burials, mostly fragmentary	uncertain
Njoro River Cave	~80 individuals, mostly fragmentary	2950 B.P.(?)
Laikipia	7 burials from 2 sites	<2150 B.P.
Lukenya Hill	several individuals (work in progress)	in process

latter areas seems to have begun well before 8000 B.P. (Adamson, Clark, and Williams, 1974). While there are no radiocarbon dates for Early Khartoum, it is probably safe to assume that this settlement was in existence at about the same time.

Human remains from the site are generally poorly preserved, and the postcranial parts have never been described. Although a number of burials were discovered, only the skull of one individual was reconstructed by Derry (1949). This cranium is relatively long and narrow, with a large, rugged facial skeleton. The nasal root is wide and flattened, cheek bones are deep, and the upper incisor teeth had been extracted before death. A partial mandible is also present, and this is massive in construction, with everted angles. In his original report, Derry noted that the whole skull is Negroid in appearance, and the published photographs certainly support this conclusion. The Khartoum individual also seems to resemble the ancient Nubians

from Wadi Halfa described by Greene and Armelagos (1972). Remains from the two localities share in a tradition of robusticity that has been documented not only in the Sudan but also in the Sahara (Chamla, 1968), and at several localities in northern Kenya.

Other signs of semipermanent occupation by populations of hunters and fishermen have been found near Lake Turkana. Robbins (1974) has conducted a series of excavations at Lothagam, west of the lake in what is today the Central Turkana Desert. Later Stone Age tools from Robbins's Middle excavation are said to be similar to those of Early Khartoum, and there is a rich bone assemblage containing quantities of unilaterally barbed projectile points. Pottery from Lothagam is undecorated, but sherds from other nearby sites are decorated in the fashion common at Khartoum. Although no human bones were found in this Middle excavation, it is likely that some of the burials from the Lothagam Upper site are approximately contemporary with the artifact horizons.

On the east side of the lake, another settlement at Lowasera has yielded a chipped stone assemblage, fragments of grindstones, and barbed bone-points (Phillipson, 1977b). Pottery is abundant during the later phases of occupation, and several burials associated with the pottery and other artifacts may be 3,500 to 4,500 years old. To the north, near Koobi Fora, more fieldwork has been carried out by Barthelme (1977), and a survey of the Galana Boi beds in this part of the Turkana basin is still underway. The Galana Boi deposits, rich in molluscan fauna, probably represent an early to mid-Holocene transgression of the lake and are dated by radiocarbon to a period between about 10,000 and 4000 B.P. (Butzer et al., 1972; Findlater, 1978). Most of the human skeletons recovered so far are from (earlier) lacustrine-oriented sites, while a few (later) burials may be associated with pastoralist activities.

Descriptions of the Koobi Fora and Ileret remains are being prepared by Karen Bell and are not yet available. However, skeletons from the Lothagam area have been studied by Angel, Phenice, Robbins, and Lynch (1980). Some thirteen rather fragmentary burials are associated with "Mesolithic" occupation at the Lothagam Upper site and at sites Bb-9 and Zu-10 to the west, all of which fall in the interval 8500–6000 B.P. Only adult individuals have been preserved in these sandy deposits, and from them Angel calculates an average life-span of only about thirty years. Some of the cranial bones show signs of porotic hyperostosis or thickening of the diploic marrow space, making it seem likely that the Lothagam people were subject to anemia stemming from infection by a variety of parasites. Of the more complete skeletons, which show considerable variation in form, several are said to be lightly built and are probably female. These have crania that are large but not strongly marked by muscle attachment, and faces are alternately described as massive and flat or as relatively gracile in construction. Glabellar protrusion is minimal, and the nasal root below is generally wide and flattened. Teeth are large, and there is a good deal of alveolar prognathism or forward projection of the lower face and jaws. In both males and females, the mandibles are

often heavy, with strikingly robust bodies and wide ascending rami. Such large jaws are found even with the smaller crania and more slender postcranial remains and seem to provide some contrast to the mandibles of modern Africans. At the same time, these features suggest a resemblance to skeletons of comparable antiquity from the Sudan.

Burials excavated at Lowasera are probably more recent than at Lothagam but merit careful consideration in view of the similarities between the two settlements, both of which were inhabited by Stone Age fishermen. Eight individuals, some very incomplete, have been recovered by Phillipson (1977b). One was buried in a tightly contracted position under a small cairn of loosely piled stones, and the skull and the postcranial parts are badly broken. This is probably a male, and the cranium is relatively long and narrow. The nasal region is flattened, and clearly the nasal aperture itself was very broad. All four upper incisor teeth are in place, and there is some maxillary prognathism. Several of the other teeth are damaged, and the molar crowns show heavy wear, as do these of most of the Lothagam specimens. The mandible exhibits marked eversion of the angle, which is flared laterally to form a prominent shelf. A second individual is represented by a lower jaw which is somewhat heavier and buttressed on both sides of the symphysis so as to present a "square" appearance, which is exaggerated by gonial eversion. Despite these signs of robusticity, there is nothing in the anatomy of either burial to indicate the presence of other than a Negro population (Rightmire, 1977).

Well to the south of Lake Turkana, earlier Holocene artifact assemblages, again including human remains, are known from the central Rift Valley. Gamble's Cave II is one of the more important localities, situated in the Elmenteita-Nakuru lake basin, while Bromhead's Site is close by. The Naivasha Railway Site lies south of Elmenteita, on the east side of the Naivasha basin. All three sites were originally investigated by the Leakeys, beginning in the 1920s (L. S. B. Leakey, 1931). At Gamble's Cave, stone tools recovered in all but the upper levels have been described as "Kenya Capsian" (now Eburran), and a single broken bone-harpoon point was found with these lithic artifacts. Pottery is very rare in the Eburran levels, but one or two sherds appeared in L. S. B. Leakey's excavations, apparently *in situ*. This evidence could suggest parallels with the Turkana settlements, and Gamble's Cave seems to have been occupied at about the same time as Lothagam. Radiocarbon dates of 8540 to 8095 B.P. for charcoal are reported by Isaac (cited in Bower and Nelson, 1978) while Protsch (1978) gives an age of 8,210 years for postcranial bone fragments from one of the human burials found 3 m above the level with the previous dates. A date for the late Eburran (formerly Kenya Capsian C) occurrence at the Naivasha Railway Site is less certain, although human bones from this locality may also be of early Holocene age (Protsch, 1976). However, a date of 2000 ± 135 B.P. has been obtained from Layer 4, with the earliest pottery and domestic animals (Onyango-Abuje, n.d.: 382). This may provide a better indication of the age of the burial, which was associated with potsherds.

At Bromhead's Site more pottery was found, along with artifacts of Neolithic (Elmenteitan Industry) type and domestic animals (L. S. B. Leakey, 1931: 271). Differences between the Elmenteitan and Eburran industries have been recognized, and the Bromhead's assemblage is clearly more recent. A date of 7410 B.P. has been obtained by Protsch (1978) from collagen, but the human bone fragments used in his analysis are derived from several different individuals for which no archaeological provenience is recorded. Another indication that the Elmenteitan materials may in fact be younger is provided by the pottery. This has been identified by Bower and Nelson (1978: 563) as Remnant Ware (now again known as Elmenteitan pottery [Ambrose, this volume]), which is widely distributed on the western side of the Rift. Dates have been obtained at several rockshelters, but even the earliest radiocarbon estimates fall at about 2500 B.P. Most "Elmenteitan" lithic occurrences seem to be no older than this (Ambrose, this volume), so there is reason to believe that the Bromhead's burials are substantially younger than those from Gamble's Cave. It is appropriate, therefore, to group the Elmenteitan people with the pastoralists discussed in the next section rather than with other Later Stone Age hunter/gatherers.

For a long time, human remains from these Rift localities were considered to be representative of a Caucasoid population inhabiting East Africa, as the skeletons were said by L. S. B. Leakey (1935) and others to show a number of non-Negroid characteristics. However, the evidence has never been very solid. Of five burials exhumed at Gamble's Cave, only two have crania that are even partially complete, and neither of these has been reconstructed entirely satisfactorily. Skull number 4 has been warped, and much of the base and part of the face are present in plaster only. Number 5 also lacks most of the occiput, and as a result the facial skeleton has probably been misaligned with the braincase. In any event, both crania are distorted and neither can be measured with much accuracy. The same holds for the one individual found at the Naivasha Railway Site, which is also badly battered.

Fortunately, the material from Bromhead's Site has been better preserved, although some of the specimens were destroyed or damaged by bombing in London during World War II. The skulls are designated by letters; Elmenteita A is the best preserved. Superciliary eminence development gives this individual a male appearance, and the face is broad and robust, with heavy cheekbones. There is definite protrusion of the maxilla below the nose, though the nasal aperture itself is long; this is one reason why the skull has been described as Caucasoid. Elmenteita B is also in good condition, and several of the other crania can be measured.

One way in which the affinities of the more complete individuals can be examined is by means of statistical analysis using cranial measurements. In an earlier study of my own, several of the Bromhead's skulls have been included in a multiple discriminant analysis employing series of San and Khoikhoi crania, South and East African Negroes, and Dynastic Egyptians (Rightmire, 1975b). Results indicate that none of the prehistoric specimens has much chance of belonging in a Bushman or Hottentot population; much firmer ties can be established with one or another of the African Negro groups. Elmenteita A and B are both best assigned as Negroes, though in several analyses skull B seems not quite to fit within the expected distributions of any of the modern populations. Elmenteita D is also placed as Negro, but here, as with F_1, the assignments are not so clear. These latter individuals survive only as casts, and both show signs of considerable reconstructive effort. Skull F_1 has been deformed, especially in its facial parts, so both measurements and discriminant findings are somewhat suspect. However, the bulk of the evidence certainly does not suggest that the central Rift was inhabited by a Caucasoid population in the mid-Holocene. The better Elmenteitan crania here speak rather emphatically, and the fragmentary Gamble's Cave burials do not contradict them.

Burials of the Pastoral Neolithic

In some parts of East Africa, a hunting/gathering mode of subsistence must gradually have given way to greater dependence on domestic stock during the mid-Holocene. How this transition occurred is not well understood, and it is not always clear from archaeological traces whether the people responsible for a given assemblage were actually practicing a pastoral way of life. The East African Pastoral Neolithic has usually been recognized on the basis of domesticated livestock, pottery, and the use of Later Stone Age technology (Bower and Nelson, 1978). However, pastoralist stone artifacts are not much different from those of the earlier Holocene, although ground-stone axes and several varieties of stone bowls or platters make their appearance. Pottery is also known from an early date, especially in the Turkana basin, where it was used by "Mesolithic" fishermen. In the central Rift Valley, pottery has recently been reported from the Salasun site, where two sherds may date to 7255 B.P. (ibid.: 558). But whether the Salasun inhabitants kept cattle is not known, and the extent to which specific ceramic traditions are linked with domestication has not been established. Cattle and sheep or goats are present in the record by at least 4500–4000 B.P. in the Lake Turkana basin (Barthelme, this volume), and the earliest animals from the Kenya Highlands and Rift are at Prospect Farm (2910 B.P.) and Lukenya Hill (3290 B.P.), so it is likely that pastoral societies were well established in East Africa by this time, if not before. After 3000 B.P., microlithic industries with stone bowls, pottery, and livestock occur together at a number of

sites, and stone–tool-using pastoralists then seem to have flourished for more than 1,500 years (Phillipson, 1977c: 76–82; Ambrose, this volume).

Human skeletons thought to be associated with the spread of pastoralism have turned up in cairn burials and rockshelters, but few of these remains have proved to be informative. The burials at Bromhead's Site may be an exception, although these are not accompanied by evidence of domestication. At a few other localities, useful skeletons cannot be tied securely to Stone Age (rather than Iron Age) pastoralism, while in most cases where stone tools and domestic stock are present, human material is badly preserved. In the Turkana area, an example is Namoratunga, consisting of a complex of three sites west of the lake. Each site contains burials and associated rock art (Lynch and Robbins, 1979). At two of these cemeteries near Lokori on the Kerio River, 11 and 162 graves, respectively, have been located, and some 40 burials have been excavated. One skeleton has provided a date of 2285 B.P., and quantities of cattle and sheep/goat tooth fragments were found in grave fill. On the basis of mortuary customs and the rock engravings, Lynch and Robbins argue that the Namoratunga people were pastoralists related to Eastern Cushitic speakers. In view of the difficulty of linking prehistoric assemblages with present-day linguistic groupings, these findings are important, and it is most unfortunate that the skeletal remains are so poorly preserved and fragmentary.

At sites such as Njoro River Cave and Hyrax Hill, near Lake Nakuru, more burials have been excavated by the Leakeys (1950: 41–73). At Hyrax Hill, an undated pastoralist settlement has yielded a stone industry composed predominantly of microliths, along with shallow stone bowls and pottery. A number of skeletons were recovered from low mounds, and the female burials were accompanied by stone platters. All the crania are incomplete, and none has facial parts that can be reconstructed with much confidence. Not a great deal of information can be gleaned from what remains (M. D. Leakey, 1945).

Njoro River Cave also contains stone tools made from obsidian, and the industry has been described as similar to the Elmenteitan at Bromhead's Site and the upper levels at Gamble's Cave.

Stone bowls of various shapes are numerous, as are grindstones, stone beads, and pendants. Pottery is also present, but no bones of domestic animals have been reported. The cave seems to have been used primarily as a burial site, and in it the remains of some 79 human skeletons were found in a mixed and fragmentary state. Many of the bones are warped and shrunk, and some have been reduced to a flaky condition by cremation. As a result, none of the crania can be measured adequately, although steps toward further reconstruction and repair of the Njoro collection have recently been taken at the Kenya National Museum in Nairobi. L. S. B. Leakey has suggested that several of the skulls show definite similarities to individuals recovered at Bromhead's Site, which is probably correct, although the assertion that the Njoro people are "non-Negro" can certainly be questioned.

Questions and Problems

The foregoing brief review necessarily emphasizes the fact that well-preserved human skeletal remains have only infrequently been excavated with Holocene East African artifact assemblages. Questions concerning the identity of populations associated with particular lithic or ceramic traditions are difficult to approach with such limited material, and it is also hard to comment on biological continuity or change through time in a given geographic area. It would be useful, for example, to know more about differences or similarities between "Mesolithic" fishermen of the Turkana basin and later pastoralist people inhabiting the same region, but comparisons of this sort cannot satisfactorily be carried out with present evidence. Current work on skeletons from Koobi Fora should help, but a principal problem is the lack of remains from Pastoral Neolithic localities.

One intriguing possibility is that populations in East Africa may exhibit some of the same morphological trends that have been documented to the north, in Sudanese Nubia. Skeletons from Wadi Halfa and from A- and C-Group cemeteries have been compared with later Meroitic, X-Group, and Christian burials by Carlson and Van Gerven (1977), and this analysis suggests that the faces and

jaws of ancient Nubians show a marked decrease in robusticity through time. Mandibles and teeth of the later groups are smaller, while crania are shorter and higher than those of the A and C peoples. These changes in craniofacial proportions and other related differences in temporomandibular joint size (Hinton and Carlson, 1979) are said to be due to differences in masticatory function resulting from a decrease in stress placed on the bony chewing complex and reduction of the associated musculature. Changes in function of the jaws and chewing muscles may in turn be linked to a gradual shift in subsistence pattern. While Wadi Halfa is a "Mesolithic" settlement, the A- and C-Group sites suggest a transitional way of life and the Meroitic, X-Group, and Christian peoples are fully agricultural. Adoption by hunter/gatherers of an increasingly cereal-based diet is thus an important factor to consider in interpretation of Nubian skeletal remains.

A similar pattern in East Africa cannot be established with much certainty, but some of the "Mesolithic" skeletons from Lake Turkana do have exceptionally large mandibles. Inspection of measurements taken by Angel and Phenice on the Lothagam burials reveals that chin height, corpus height at M_2 and, especially, ramus width are all greater than averages obtained from the Leakeys' (1950) measurements of some 13 of the more complete Njoro River Cave individuals. This is suggestive, and a definite trend toward reduction of the masticatory apparatus of Pastoral Neolithic peoples may become clearer as new studies are undertaken. Whether such changes can exactly parallel the situation in Nubia is doubtful, however, as there is scant indication from Njoro River Cave or other sites that early East African pastoralists were farming on a regular basis. In this region, hunting and gathering seems to have led first to an economy geared to herding rather than toward settled agriculture (Phillipson, 1977c: 56–58).

Relationships among peoples responsible for what may be several distinct Neolithic traditions are again obscure. A better understanding of the anatomy of the Njoro River Cave skeletons is certainly needed, and fresh work on carefully reconstructed specimens may well prove rewarding. Examination of several new Lukenya Hill burials should also tell us more about populations practicing a pastoral way of life in the highlands to the east of the Rift Valley. For the moment, about all that can be said is that some Pastoral Neolithic skeletons are best described as Negroid in morphology. Such is the case for the better crania from Bromhead's Site, although these are not definitely associated with domestic animals. Other prehistoric crania from sites tentatively tied to "stone bowl" industries are also best assigned as Negroes in discriminant analysis (Rightmire, 1975b). These results do not provide any direct insight into the origins of East African herders, and the statistical findings based on skull measurements cannot, of course, be used to sort the specimens according to linguistic criteria, e.g., as speakers of Nilotic or Cushitic languages. Such questions of identification will have to be answered by other routes, as at Namoratunga, where methods of grave construction point to affinities with Eastern Cushites (Lynch and Robbins, 1979). But there is nothing in the skeletal record as read so far to indicate a major influx of new populations into East Africa as hunting and fishing were replaced by pastoralism, especially if earlier dates for the remains from Gamble's Cave, Bromhead's Site, and Naivasha Railway Site can be substantiated. Hypotheses favoring gradual change and local adaptation rather than large-scale movement of peoples are generally consistent with the evidence.

19

Early Evidence for Animal Domestication in Eastern Africa

JOHN W. BARTHELME

Current research in eastern Africa is yielding a wealth of archaeological evidence on the Late Quaternary transition from gathering and hunting to food production. The recent investigations of Bower, Nelson, Wandibba (Bower et al., 1977; Bower and Nelson, 1978), and Onyango-Abuje (1977, n.d.) in the Central Rift of Kenya, Siiriainen (1977) in the Baringo area, and the work of Robbins (1972, 1974), Phillipson (1977b, c) and the present writer (Barthelme, 1977) in the Lake Turkana Basin are examples of this intensification of research activity. While those of us working in eastern Africa are continuing to reconstruct and refine the more traditionally oriented culture-historical successions, study of the cultural processes that shaped and guided the change to food production—this most profound transition in the human

This research has benefited greatly from the logistical support provided by Richard Leakey. Professor Glynn Isaac helped guide much of the work through his continued support and thoughtful criticism. The field and analysis aspects of the project were largely supported by a National Science Foundation grant to the Koobi Fora Research Project.

way of life—is also being pursued. Obviously, the two aspects can and should be complementary.

The present writer's research investigations have been carried out in northern Kenya, along the northeastern shoreline of Lake Turkana (Fig. 1). During initial phases of the research project, little emphasis was placed on investigation of early food-producing settlements. Instead, concern was primarily with reconstruction of land-use patterns for early to mid-Holocene fisher/hunter/gatherers. Previous research in the Lake Turkana area (Robbins, 1974; Phillipson, 1977b) had focused on single, large, shoreline sites and their associated technological and economic remains, including barbed-bone harpoons, microlithic stone tools, pottery, and lacustrine and terrestrial faunal remains. The present research design called for investigation of a larger sample of archaeological sites and examination of interconnecting patterns among a set of variables: aspects of technology, subsistence patterns, settlement features, and Holocene lake-level fluctuations. A second level of inquiry sought to compare the land-use patterns of these anatomically modern but non–food-producing peoples— the early Holocene hunter/gatherer/fishers—with those of the early hominids some 2.5–1.5 million years ago in the same Koobi Fora region (Barthelme, 1977).

During an exploratory survey of some three months' duration, a second set of Holocene archaeological sites was recognized. These occurrences exhibited substantially different economic traditions, new ceramic wares, vessels manufactured from stone, different lithic raw materials, and alternative site-location patterns. Two of the discovered settlements yielded important evidence on the early stages of food production in eastern Africa. Their significance is briefly outlined below.

GaJi 4

The site of GaJi 4 is situated within lacustrine beach sands between 50 and 55 m above the present-day level (April, 1976) of Lake Turkana (Fig. 2). The site was occupied as the expanded lake was undergoing a substantial recession, believed to be in the later stages of the second of three major Holocene transgressive-regressive cycles (Owen et al., 1982). Nderit Ware pottery was recovered in association with a microlithic stone-tool assemblage and faunal remains of domestic ovicaprids and probably domestic cattle (Barthelme, 1977). The bone was well preserved and ovicaprid mandibles with full tooth rows were recovered.

Controversy has surrounded the stratigraphic association and chronological position of Nderit Ware since the early 1930s when L. S. B. Leakey collected examples of a hitherto unknown type of decorated pottery from Nderit Drift, Stable's Drift, and the Makalia Burial Site in the Central Rift of Kenya (L. S. B. Leakey, 1931: 198–199). Leakey named the pottery "Gumban A" after a mythical people known as the Gumba who were thought to have inhabited the Nakura-Elmenteita Basin (Siiriäinen, 1971; Muriuki, 1974: 37–42). Wandibba has recently reexamined Leakey's original collections and proposed that the name "Gumban A" be changed to Nderit Ware (Bower et al., 1977).

Leakey originally believed Nderit Ware sherds to be associated with stone bowls and, by inference, with domestic animals. The stratigraphic provenience of his material was unclear, however, and the pottery's association with domestic stock and stone vessels has remained uncertain until recently. Since the 1930s, surface finds of Nderit Ware sherds have been reported from southwestern Lake Turkana (Robbins, 1972), Nderit Drift (Bower et al., 1977), Lukenya Hill (Gramly, n.d.) and near Rumuruti (Siiriäinen, 1977). A small set of *excavated* sherds has also been reported (Robbins, 1972; Bower, 1973a; Bower et al., 1977). Recently, a claim for possible Nderit Ware pottery at Salasun Rockshelter in central Kenya with a comparatively early C-14 date of 7155 ± 225 B.P. has been made (Bower et al., 1977; Bower and Nelson, 1978). The excavated sample consists of only two weathered sherds, neither of which exhibits internal decoration. While the apparent association of decorated pottery with a radiocarbon age dating to the end of the eighth millennium B.P. is most provocative, given the very small sample, its poor state of preservation, and the absence of diagnostic design features, it seems premature to classify these two sherds as Nderit Ware.

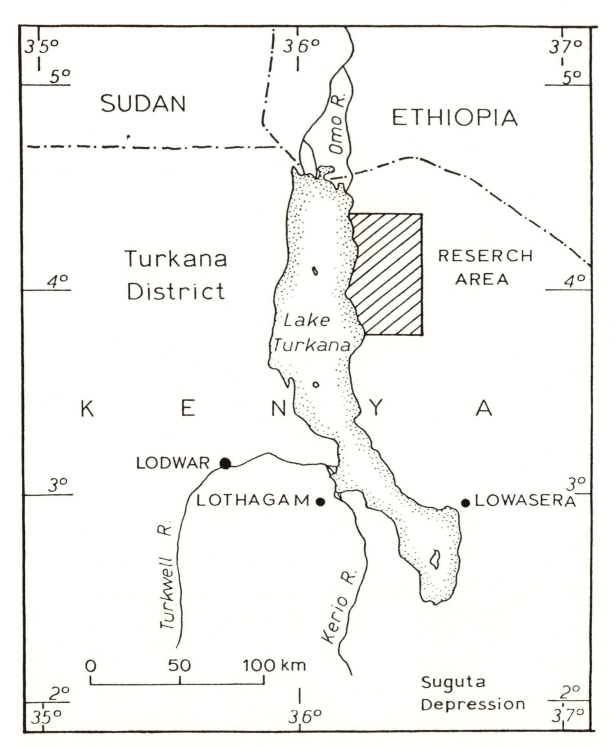

Figure 1. Lake Turkana basin research area.

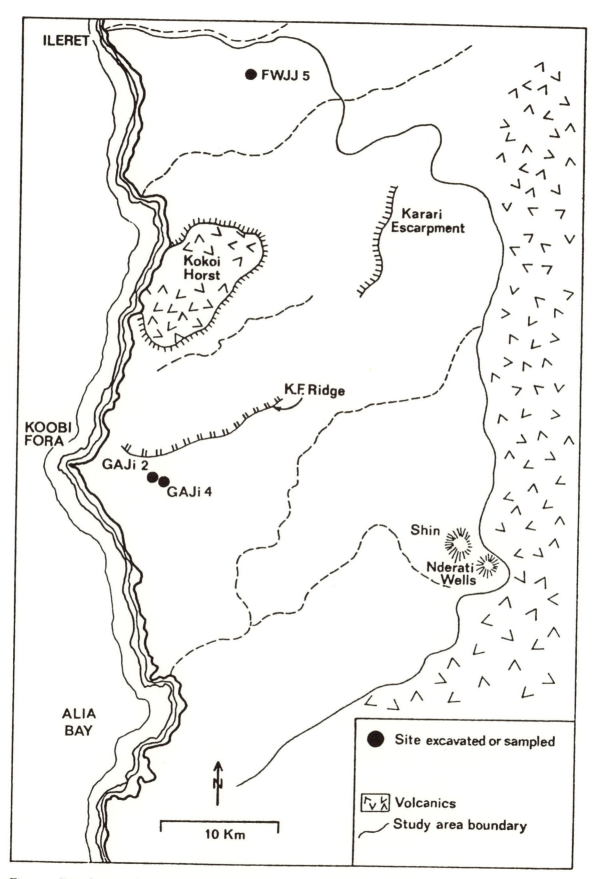

Figure 2. Distribution of excavated sites with domesticated animals.

At GaJi 4, three different organic materials (wood charcoal, mammal bone, and mollusc shell) from the same stratigraphic horizon were selected for radiocarbon analysis. The dating samples were divided into equal portions and shipped to two radiocarbon laboratories. While the mollusc shell and bone dates proved unsatisfactory (Barthelme, n.d.a), two charcoal determinations each yielded dates of ca. 4000 B.P.[1] Their standard deviations overlap at one sigma and hence the dates are interpreted as statistically equivalent.

The site of GaJi 4 is significant for several reasons. First, the recovered material establishes a firm stratigraphic association between Nderit Ware pottery and domestic animals. Second, several C-14 determinations indicate that the site was occupied at least by 4000 B.P. (ca. 4300 MASCA correction).[2] Third, the site of GaJi 4 is close to 1,000 years older than settlements with domestic animals in the Central Rift of Kenya.

The Ileret Stone Bowl Site (FwJj 5)

The Ileret Stone Bowl Site is located in the northernmost sector of the research area (Fig. 2). Abundant archaeological materials were recovered from coarse fluvial sediments that overlie a relatively thick stratigraphic sequence of lacustrine silts and sands. Channel incision of the unconsolidated lake sediments had begun as the lake was undergoing a major, probably second, Holocene regression. Microlithic stone artifacts, stone vessels, abundant potsherds and terrestrial and lacus-

trine faunal remains were recovered. The fragmentary faunal remains include domestic cattle and probably domestic ovicaprids (John Kimengitch of the National Museums of Kenya, pers. comm.). Wild terrestrial mammals were not identified. Fishbone, on the basis of raw counts only, accounted for nearly 40 percent of the faunal remains. Fragments of six stone vessels were collected from the surface within a 100 m radius of the site. While stone vessels were not recovered from the excavation itself, it is assumed that those on the surface were associated with the excavated material. Over 1,700 potsherds were also recovered. The collection exhibits a wide variety of decorative techniques and design features, including a new Pastoral Neolithic pottery type designated as Ileret Ware (Barthelme, n.d.b). Nderit Ware sherds were not recovered.

A single radiocarbon date on bone apatite yielded an age of 4000 ± 140 B.P.[3] This age determination should be viewed with caution, however, as Bower and Nelson (1978) call attention to the susceptibility of hydroxyapatite crystals to various sources of contamination, especially from older dissolved carbonates in aqueous conditions. Sedimentary deposits, including units rich in carbonates, have been accumulating in the Turkana depression since the early to mid-Miocene (Savage and Williamson, 1978), and the C-14 date may well reflect contamination by older carbonates in ground water. Clearly, further radiocarbon samples need to be run before the site is securely dated.

Nevertheless, the Ileret Stone Bowl Site is significant, as it documents both the most northerly distribution of Stone Bowl sites in eastern Africa and the association of stone vessels with domestic stock. Based on preliminary dates and comparison with the nearby, recently excavated occupation at North Horr (Phillipson, 1977c: 71–74), the Ileret Stone Bowl Site may well be 500–1000 years older than the numerous and well-documented Stone Bowl sites in Central Kenya.

---

1. *GaJi 4*

P-2610 (University of Pennsylvania)	Charcoal	3890 ± 60
SUA-637 (University of Sydney)	Charcoal	3945 ± 135

Each determination is reported in years B.P. using the standard Libby half-life. Neither sample was corrected for C-13 fractionation.

2. For a discussion of this issue, see Michael and Ralph (1971: 25–29).

3. *Ileret Stone Bowl Site (FwJj 5)*

Gx-4643-A (Geochron Laboratories)	bone apatite	4000 ± 140

The sample was C-13 corrected.

Summary

Recent investigations in the northeastern sector of the Lake Turkana Basin have documented
the presence of domestic animals—both ovicaprids
and cattle—by the end to middle of the third millennium B.C. No evidence for plant remains, either
wild or domestic, was recovered. Like their immediate predecessors the widespread fisher/hunter/
gatherers, the early pastoral groups took advantage
of the plentiful Holocene fish resources. However,
they apparently made little use of wild terrestrial
animals.

The archaeological evidence from northeastern Lake Turkana appears to provide a geographical and chronological link between the early food-
producing sites along the Sudanese Nile (Krzyzaniak, 1976) and sites later in time located in the
Central Rift of Kenya and farther to the south
(Bower et al., 1977; Sutton, 1974). One factor that
might account for the change, within the Turkana
basin, of economic patterns, technological features,
and settlement location during the third and second
millennia B.C. is small-scale population movements—initially set in motion by climatic deterioration in the Saharan Sahel and savanna zones
(D. A. Livingstone, 1975) resulting in the introduction of new economic and cultural traditions
into the basin from the north. Subsequently, either
due to continued population movements or to diffusion of economic traditions, or both, human
groups with domestic animals occupied the southern areas of Kenya and northern Tanzania. Clearly,
these hypotheses need to be considered and tested
against the growing body of Holocene archaeological evidence in eastern Africa by alternative methodological approaches (see Brandt, this volume)
and theoretical interpretations (Onyango-Abuje,
1976, n.d.). It is to be hoped that continuing research efforts will address the complementary
questions of culture history and culture process.

20

Late Prehistoric Aquatic and Pastoral Adaptations West of Lake Turkana, Kenya

L. H. ROBBINS

Investigations into the later prehistory of the Lake Turkana basin have centered on the early Holocene Later Stone Age fishing communities and also on the earliest evidence for pastoral behavior. Lothagam, Lowasera, and other sites from the Koobi Fora area have demonstrated that Later Stone Age peoples were making pottery and skillfully carved barbed-bone harpoon points as early as 6000–7000 B.P. (Robbins, 1974; Phillipson, 1977b; Barthelme, 1977). These people caught Nile perch sometimes weighing over 45 kg, several varieties of catfish, and in some cases Tilapia. They also hunted animals such as zebra, hartebeeste, warthog, buffalo, hippopotamus, turtle, and crocodile. New sites yielding Nderit Ware pottery have been discovered on the eastern and western sides of the lake, where the available radiocarbon dates suggest an age of between 4000 and 5000 B.P. The recent work of Barthelme (this volume) on the

Thanks are expressed to the National Science Foundation for funding the 1975–1976 research and to the government of Kenya for granting permission to do the fieldwork.

Koobi Fora area has demonstrated that the Nderit Ware pottery (formerly identified as the Gumban A variant of the Stone Bowl Complex) is associated with domesticated sheep or goats and fish in lacustrine beach sands some 50–55 m above the April, 1976, lake level. Barthelme's important discovery indicates that pastoralism was established in northern Kenya at approximately the same time, or only slightly later, than in the Khartoum Neolithic, where sites such as Esh Shaheinab and Kadero have yielded dates of about 5000 B.P. (Haaland, n.d.).

While a growing body of data is available on the Later Stone Age fishing communities and early pastoralists, very little systematic research has been done in the time period that post-dates the early to mid-Holocene high lake-levels of about 9000 to 5000 B.P. For this reason, in 1975–1976, fieldwork was concentrated on the later prehistory in the area and on the question of how human groups exploited the western-lake-edge environment after the establishment of pastoralism and after the recession of the lake from its former high stands.

In the western Lake Turkana basin there is a significant hiatus in the archaeological record between about 3000 and 1000 B.C. Sites have not yet been securely dated to this period, but some of the decorated pottery found in multicomponent, wind-deflated sites overlooking the lake edge may well belong to this time; the styles of decoration could have been derived from earlier wares. In addition, there are numerous Later Stone Age microlithic surface scatters and, while these lack pottery and fauna and have not yet afforded dating evidence, they could belong to this time also. An alternative way of interpreting the gap in the archaeological record is that the area was then only sparsely inhabited, due to deteriorating environmental conditions associated with the retreat of the lake.

Beginning about 300 B.C., the archaeological record becomes much clearer, Our recent research allows us to distinguish at least five ways that the western-lake-edge environment was used between approximately 300 B.C. and A.D. 1888. These adaptations are described below in chronological order.

The first and earliest of these subsistence patterns may be described as a pastoral one, with no use made of fish and little, if any, evidence of exploitation of wild game. The evidence for the exis-

tence of this adaptation along the lake edge is inferred from Lynch's (n.d.) work at the Namoratunga sites (Fig. 1).[1] The Namoratunga I cemetery and rock-art site (335 B.C.) located along the Kerio River Valley in the interior afforded evidence of sheep or goats and domestic cattle, as well as animal brand symbols depicted in rock engravings (Lynch and Robbins, 1977). The Namoratunga II site, located several kilometers from the lake shore near Ferguson's Gulf, revealed similar brand symbols engraved on stone pillars which, it has been suggested, have archaeoastronomical significance (Lynch and Robbins, 1978). This site demonstrates that eastern Cushitic peoples were using the lake edge for ceremonial purposes at about 300 B.C.[2] Whether they also settled along the lakeshore has not yet been demonstrated, but it is likely, given the substantial nature of the archaeological remains. It is significant that Cushitic speakers have a strong customary prohibition against eating fish (Murdock, 1959: 17). For this reason, it is suggested that early Eastern Cushitic speakers who did keep cattle and ovicaprids probably did not fish.

The second subsistence pattern is characterized by temporary visits to the lake edge, probably seasonally, by small groups of pastoralists. These people were exploiting fish and a very little wild game. The most appropriate ethnographic analogy is provided by the Nuer of the Sudan Nilotic pastoralists, who seasonally exploit fish along the Nile (Evans-Pritchard, 1940). (It must be stressed that this is only an analogy; it is not implied that there are direct ethnic relationships to the Nuer.) Sites that belong to this pattern include some of the wind-deflated dune sites that directly overlook the modern lake at various localities situated between Eliye Springs and Ferguson's Gulf (Robbins, 1980). One of the sites, Apeget I, is located in a

1. Both sites are called Namoratunga by the local Turkana inhabitants of the area. According to a Turkana legend, the large standing stones at these sites represent ancient people who were turned to stone by a malevolent spirit. B. M. Lynch has demonstrated that there is a cultural relationship between the sites (see Lynch, n.d.).

2. A discussion of the relationship between the Namoratunga sites and Eastern Cushitic speakers is provided in Lynch and Robbins (1979).

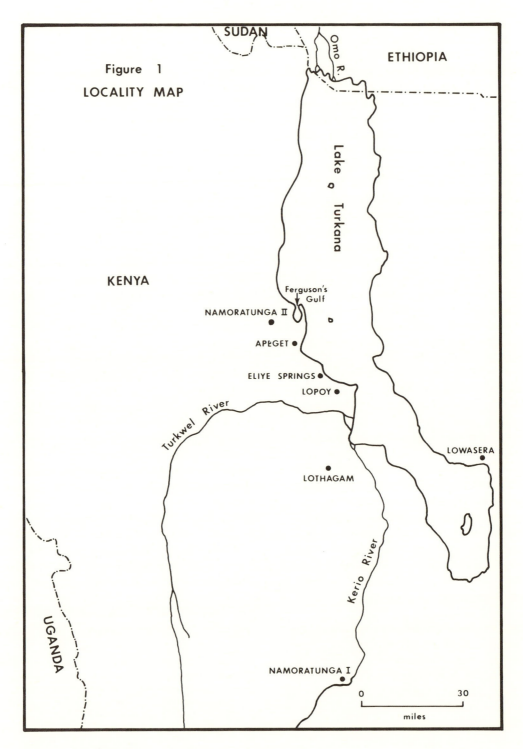

Figure 1. Locality map.

small wind-eroded depression about 9 m above the level of the present lake (Fig. 1). Apeget I was marked by two oval-shaped fish middens. Charcoal from midden 1 was radiocarbon-dated to 1800 ± 300 B.P. (ca. A.D. 150) (UCLA 2124K). Over 95 percent of the bones from this midden were fish, of which 4,637 were identified by S. E. Telengoi of the Lake Turkana Fishermen's Cooperative Society. The remains included 94 percent Tilapia (*Tilapia nilotica*) and 2 percent Nile perch (*Lates niloticus*); the remainder consisted of tiger fish (*Hydrocyon* sp.) and four species of catfish. There are also some turtleshell fragments (*Trionyx* sp.). No wild mammals were evident on this site, but domestic stock was represented by some ovicaprid remains recovered from within Midden 1. This fauna was directly associated with a microlithic quartz industry of poor quality. Apeget I was probably a seasonal camp occupied by pastoralists who were mainly catching Tilapia during their stay at the lake edge. The empasis on Tilapia may well reflect the proximity of shallow water with an abundance of plant growth. Nile perch may not have been abundant in this area. On the other hand, the low frequency of Nile perch in the deposits may be due to the fact that harpoons were not being used. Without harpoons, or possibly hooks and boats, these large fish would have been very difficult to catch. Calculations based on an analysis of the minimum numbers of fish in conjunction with specific ethnographic data concerning the role of Lake Turkana fish in modern diets suggest that the site could have been occupied by about ten people for perhaps as long as three and a half months. Complete data are presented in Robbins (1980). The middens were not large enough to have resulted from a permanent or year-round occupation in the specific site area.

The third subsistence adaptation includes "pastoralists" who hunted much savanna game near the lake edge but who did very little fishing, unless their fish middens occur at undiscovered sites. This probably also represents a short-term occupation which may have been part of a series of repeated visits by relatively small groups to the lake edge. There is no geographically close ethnographic model for this pattern of adaptation unless we are dealing with a small, specialized hunting group or a people similar to the Okiek (Dorobo) of Kenya, who are hunter/collectors who keep domesticated stock in some areas (Blackburn, 1973). The site of Lopoy, located between the Turkwel Delta and Eliye Springs about 3 km from the lakeshore and about 18 m above the lake level, includes the only documented example of this kind of subsistence adaptation (Robbins, 1980) (Fig. 1). The example occurs at the Lopoy microlith area, which is essentially the wind-eroded remains of a hunting and butchering camp radiocarbon-dated to 1100 ± 80 B.P. (A.D. 850) (UCLA 2124H, burned soil sample) (Robbins and Lynch, 1978). An abundance of well-made chert microliths together with pottery similar to Akira Ware (Bower et al., 1977) was found at the microlith area in association with thousands of fragmented mammal bones. A total of nine 2 m squares (all surface collected except for gridsquare I, which was excavated) produced 6,054 bone and tooth fragments. This large sample included only 9 fish bones, the only identifiable species being Silurids (catfish). There were no crocodiles or turtles. The rest of the bone fragments were from mammals, most likely wild bovids and equids. Some domesticated sheep or goat teeth were excavated *in situ*. Elsewhere in the microlith area where more complete bone fragments and teeth were occasionally evident, we identified several zebra, a black rhinoceros, a hippopotamus, and remains of small to medium-sized bovids. Neither zebra nor rhinoceros is found in the Lopoy area today, which is a desert with shifting sand-dunes. Thus, at the Lopoy microlith area we have evidence of a people who relied significantly on wild game and who also kept domestic sheep or goats. This contrasts strongly with the Apeget I site, where there was no evidence of wild game but where Tilapia were of considerable importance to a people who possessed domestic livestock.

The fourth subsistence pattern is also found at Lopoy, where it is associated with a different cultural group identified with the "Turkwel cultural tradition" (Robbins, 1980). (This tradition is characterized by deeply grooved pottery very different from the Akira sherds found on the microlith area.) There is evidence of a large fishing and pastoral

settlement, radiocarbon-dated to about A.D. 1000
(950 ± 80 B.P.) (UCLA 2114J), which was occupied by a relatively large group on a year-round
basis. While there is almost no evidence for the
hunting of wild mammals, there was a major reliance on Nile-perch fishing. This is a lakeside facies
of a much more widespread Eastern Nilotic "para-
nilotic" pastoral adaptation that extends far into
the interior, away from the lake edge (see Lynch
and Robbins, 1979). A general ethnographic analogy would include the modern Turkana, who are
pastoralists maintaining fishing camps along the
lake edge; however, there are no direct ethnic connections between the archaeological evidence and
the modern Turkana. Turkana pottery is completely different and local elders reported that the
Lopoy site was not produced by the Turkana. At
Lopoy, fish middens and large ash areas, which appear to be burned livestock corrals, are the most
noticeable "Turkwel tradition" remains. Eight 2 m
squares were excavated through the largest fish
midden, which was very rich in pottery, fauna, and
microlithic tools made from chalcedony. Several
hundred thousand bone fragments were recovered
from the midden excavations. About 98 percent of
the identifiable bones were from fish, including
(N = 13,894) 52 percent Tilapia, 37 percent catfish, 11 percent Nile perch, and traces of tiger fish.
The catfish group includes *Clarias lazera, Synodontis
schall, Bagrus bayad, Bagrus docmac,* and *Schilbe ura-
nascopus.* Nile perch were actually much more significant than the above percentages indicate. A
live-weight estimate, which is only an approximation, suggests that 75 percent of the fish by weight
were Nile perch. About 41 percent of the Nile
perch were medium-sized (ca. 1.05 m long), 27
percent were small (0.6 m or less) and 25 percent
were large (about 1.5 m). The remainder were very
large (over 1.5 m). Interestingly, at Lopoy were
found several barbed-bone spear or harpoon points
which were probably used to spear Nile perch.
Such artifacts first occur in the Lake Turkana basin
in the Omo area during the early Holocene, nearly
9,000 years ago (K. W. Butzer, pers. comm.), but at
Lopoy they were being used as recently as about
A.D. 1000. The midden also included numerous
bones of Nile crocodiles, mostly medium to large
in size, and turtle fragments (*Trionyx* sp.). Only 971

mammal bones were recovered, and relatively few
were identifiable. All were from domestic ovicaprids, with the possible exception of a reedbuck.
Elsewhere on the site there is further evidence of
ovicaprids and domestic cattle associated with the
Turkwel tradition.

Evidence suggests that the people responsible
for the middens at Lopoy probably occupied the
site year-round (Robbins, 1980). They were attracted specifically to the Lopoy area because of
the rich fishing resources of the former Turkwel
River delta. Even today, the delta area produces
very large Nile perch (occasionally up to 68 kg)
together with concentrations of catfish and Tilapia.

The fifth and most recent kind of subsistence
adaptation includes "pastoralists" who cultivate
sorghum along the Turkwel River floodplains by
exploiting the annual rise and fall of the lake. This
kind of adaptation is not yet known archaeologically but, on the western side of the lake, is represented ethnographically by those Turkana people
who live in the Turkwel delta. They also fish, hunt
crocodile, gather wild plants, and keep large herds
of cattle, sheep, goats, and camels. They were cultivating the delta area at least as early as 1888,
when they were first contacted by the European
explorers Teleki and von Hohnel (von Hohnel,
1894).

Finally, it is interesting to include some ethnoarchaeological observations made on a recently
abandoned fishermen's camp located at the lake
edge south of Eliye Springs (Robbins, 1980). This
camp was inhabited by nine people for a two-year
period. It had been abandoned for about seventeen
months when investigated in 1975 by the present
writer, along with the former headman of the camp.
The bone refuse had been intentionally dumped
around the edges of small groves of *mkoma* palms,
giving a circular pattern to the middens. We sampled a 1 m circular strip around three of the main
dumping areas, recovering 2,538 bones. About 98
percent were from fish, mostly Nile perch but with
Tilapia, various catfish, and other species represented. Crocodiles, turtles, and flamingos were also
found, but only one mammal bone was recovered.
This was from a camel that had been scavenged
from a crocodile kill and had not actually belonged
to the people who lived at the camp. Outside the

main dumping area we found some goat mandibles and associated bone fragments, but they were not abundant. If this site were completely buried by future deposition of windblown sand it would be very likely that an archaeologist's bone sample would reveal that the inhabitants of the site were exclusively fishermen. This observation would be nearly correct based on the composition of the dumps, yet the people who lived at the site owned herds of domestic livestock which were being kept by relatives in an area at least 24 km away, where more favorable grazing and browsing conditions existed. While the above example is not intended to represent an ethnographic model of any particular Pastoral Neolithic adaptation, it adds to the range of available data concerning possible ways of interpreting sites in regional patterns where economic activities may be highly diversified within a single cultural system.

Conclusions

Clearly, the lake edge remained an environment of major importance to Later Stone Age peoples who kept domestic livestock. These peoples continued to make use of microlithic technology until at least A.D. 1000; this is well into Iron Age times further to the south in Kenya. The relatively late survival of Later Stone Age technology is similar to that described by Miller (1969) for the Nachikufan sequence of Zambia.

This paper has illustrated some of the variations in subsistence adaptations to the lake edge environment during the past two and a half millennia. There was a variable emphasis on fishing and hunting and there was even considerable difference in the relative amounts of the fish species caught at the various localities. Although these late prehistoric people for convenience have been described loosely as *pastoralists*, the term may really not be applicable in a strict sense. The term *pastoralism* implies that domestic livestock are the most important economic resource, yet at the Lopoy site we find that fish, associated with the "Turkwel tradition," and wild mammals, linked to the Akira tradition, appear to have been of greater economic significance than domesticated livestock. These diverse late prehistoric adaptations may be explained as having been induced by ecological, chronological, and cultural factors, but the extent of the influence of any one of these is not yet clear. Future fieldwork may be expected to clarify this picture significantly.

21

The Introduction of Pastoral Adaptations to the Highlands of East Africa

STANLEY H. AMBROSE

This assessment of processual and culture-historical models of the introduction of food production to highland East Africa is based on a radically revised understanding of the taxonomic status, chronology, origin, geographic distribution, settlement pattern, economy, and adaptation of several archaeological cultures identified and described by L. S. B. Leakey (1931). This reconstruction and synthesis of the Later Stone Age and Neolithic of the highlands is to serve as the basis for interpretation of the origins of food production in East Africa. For the purposes of this paper the East African highlands are considered to comprise all contiguous regions with elevations over approximately 1,500 m in Kenya and Tanzania (Figs. 1, 2); the Neolithic era, as presently known, dates from 3300 to 1300 B.P. (Figs. 3, 6, Table 1).

A brief summary of the history of the fieldwork reveals why the revision presented below has been so long delayed.

By 1931 Leakey was able to recognize several phases of a supposedly Upper Paleolithic Industry called the Kenya Capsian (originally Kenya Aurignacian, L. S. B. Leakey, 1952). He claimed this

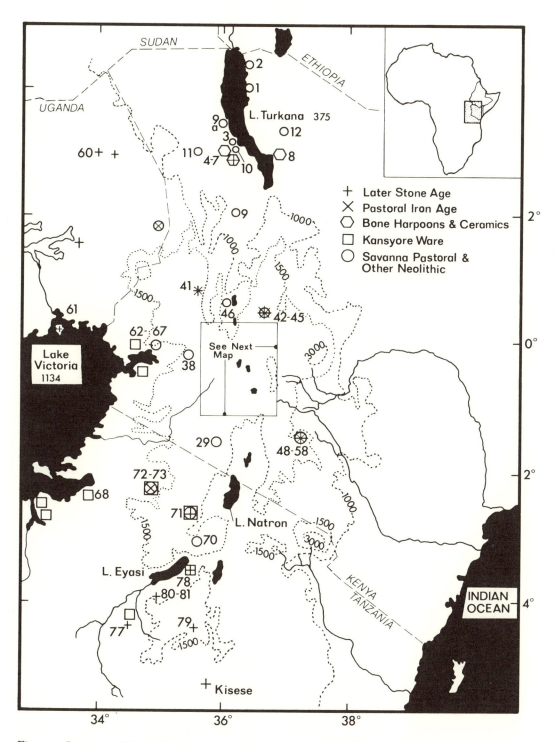

Figure 1. Location of East African archaeological sites listed in Table 1.

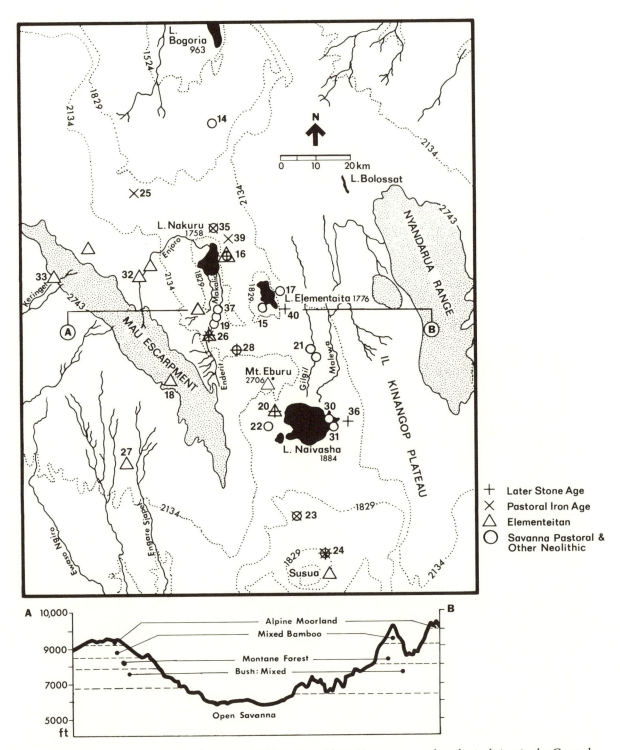

Figure 2. Altitudinal environmental zonation and location of Late Quaternary archaeological sites in the Central Rift Valley, Kenya.

TABLE 1. Radiometric Dates for Later Stone Age Sites in East Africa

1a. Dates for pre-Neolithic sites of northern Kenya:

7 Lothagam	7560 ± 1000 UCLA1247E	LSA Pottery/harpoons (Robbins, 1972)
8 Lowasera	2520 ± 150 GX4345-A	LSA Pottery/harpoons (Phillipson, 1977b)
8 Lowasera	3070 ± 135 GX4347-A	LSA Pottery/harpoons (Phillipson, 1977b)
8 Lowasera	3920 ± 120 GX4348-A	LSA Pottery/harpoons (Phillipson, 1977b)
8 Lowasera	4410 ± 110 GX4349-A	LSA Pottery/harpoons (Phillipson, 1977b)
8 Lowasera	7435 ± 150 GX4346-A	LSA Pottery/harpoons (Phillipson, 1977b)
8 Lowasera	9420 ± 200 HEL867	LSA Pottery/harpoons (Phillipson, 1977b)
6 ZU-10 Turkana	6200 ± 125 N-812	LSA Pottery/harpoons (Robbins, 1972)
5 ZU-4 Turkana	8420 ± 165 N-1100	LSA Pottery/harpoons (Robbins, 1972)
5 ZU-6 Turkana	7960 ± 140 N-813	LSA Pottery/harpoons (Robbins, 1972)

1b. Dates for "Wilton" sites in the Lake Victoria Basin and northern Tanzania:

71 Nasera	8100 ± 120 ISGS427-G	LSA (Mehlman, 1977)
71 Nasera	7100 ± 75 ISGS427	LSA (Mehlman, 1977)
71 Nasera	5400 ± 150	LSA Kansyore (Mehlman, pers. comm.)
71 Nasera	4720 ± 150	LSA Kansyore (Mehlman, pers. comm.)
62 Abindu, Kisumu	1980 ± 240 GX1099	LSA UP (Gabel, 1969)
63 Agoro, Kisumu	2375 ± 320 GX1097	LSA UP (Gabel, 1969)
64 Jawuoyo, Kisumu	2040 ± 110 GX1096	LSA UP (Gabel, 1969)
65 Nyaida, Kisumu	2230 ± 320 GX1098	LSA UP (Gabel, 1969)
66 Randhore, Kisumu	1310 ± 95 GX1152	LSA UP (Gabel, 1969)
67 Rangong, Kisumu	2315 ± 185 GX1100	LSA Kansyore? (Gabel, 1969)
68 Nyang'oma, Mwanza	2640 ± 120 N-493	LSA Kansyore (Soper and Golden, 1969)
77 Lululampembele	3830 ± 180 N-787	LSA (Odner, 1971a)
78 Mumba-Hohle	4890 ± 70 FRA-1-C	LSA Kansyore (Mehlman, pers. comm.)
78 Mumba-Hohle	4860 ± 100 UCLA1913	LSA Kansyore (Mehlman, pers. comm.)
79 Kandaga RS	3375 ± 180 GX3677	LSA (Masao, 1979: 37)
80 Kwa Mwango-Isanzu	3270 ± 110 GX3679	LSA (Masao, 1979: 69)
81 Kirumi Isumbirira	3665 ± 140 GX3681	LSA (Masao, 1979: 80)

1c. Dates for the Lowland and Highland Savanna Pastoral Neolithic:

1 GAJI4 Ileret	3405 ± 130 GX4642-IA	SPN Nderit (Barthelme, this volume)
1 GAJI4 Ileret	4580 ± 170 GX4642IIA	SPN Nderit (Barthelme, this volume)
2 FWJJ5 Ileret	4000 ± 140 GX4643-A	SPN UP (Barthelme, this volume)
10 BB-14 Kangatotha	5020 ± 220 N-814	SPN Nderit? (Robbins, 1972)
12 North Horr I	4405 ± 130 GX3705	SPN Narosura? (Maggs, 1977: 184)
12 North Horr I	3330 ± 130 GX3706	SPN Narosura? (Maggs, 1977: 184)
28 Prospect Farm	2690 ± 80 UCLA1234	SPN UP (Cohen, 1970)
28 Prospect Farm	2910 ± 110 N-651	SPN UP (Cohen, 1970)
19 GSJI2 Nderit Drift	1370 ± 140 GX4320	SPN UP (Bower et al., 1977)
19 GSJI2 Nderit Drift	1925 ± 160 GX4318I-C	SPN UP (Bower et al., 1977)
19 GSJI23 Nderit Drift	2360 ± 155 GX4503-A	SPN Nderit (Bower et al., 1977)
15 GRJI22 L. Elmenteita	1830 ± 130 GX4216	SPN UP (Nelson, pers. comm.)
17 GRJJ5 Cole's Burial	2355 ± 150 GX4714-A	SPN? (Nelson, pers. comm.)
21 GSJJ44 Gil Gil	2200 ± 130 GX4323-C	SPN UP (Bower et al., 1977)
21 GSJJ44 Gil Gil	2040 ± 155 GX4323-A	SPN UP (Bower et al., 1977)
22 GTJ13 Ndabibi	1665 ± 145 GX4463-A	SPN Narosura (Bower et al., 1977)
22 GTJ13 Ndabibi	1815 ± 140 GX4465-A	SPN Narosura (Bower et al., 1977)
22 GTJ13 Ndabibi	1415 ± 150 GX4464-G	SPN Narosura (Bower et al., 1977)
22 GTJ13 Ndabibi	2225 ± 155 GX4465-G	SPN Narosura (Bower et al., 1977)
22 GTJ13 Ndabibi	1255 ± 125 GX4463-G	SPN Narosura (Bower et al., 1977)

22	GTJ13 Ndabibi	410 ± 110 GX4464-A	SPN Narosura (Bower et al., 1977)
23	GUJJ2 Akira	1965 ± 140 GX4386-G	SPN Akira (Bower et al., 1977)
23	GUJJ2 Akira	1255 ± 140 GX4384	SPN Akira (Bower et al., 1977)
23	GUJJ2 Akira	1775 ± 115 GX4385-G	SPN Akira (Bower et al., 1977)
23	GUJJ2 Akira	1440 ± 120 GX4386-A	SPN Akira (Bower et al., 1977)
23	GUJJ2 Akira	1090 ± 150 GX4383-A	SPN Narosura (Bower et al., 1977)
24	GUJJ13 Salasun	1315 ± 135 GX4421-G	SPN UP (Bower et al., 1977)
24	GUJJ13 Salasun	2990 ± 170 GX4468-A	SPN UP (Bower et al., 1977)
24	GUJJ13 Salasun	1110 ± 115 GX4468-G	SPN UP (Bower et al., 1977)
24	GUJJ13 Salasun	2680 ± 150 GX4421-A	SPN Narosura (Bower et al., 1977)
14	GQJI6 Maringishu	1695 ± 105 GX 4466-A	SPN Maringishu (Bower et al., 1977)
30	Crescent Island	2660 ± 120 GX4585-A	SPN Narosura (Onyango-Abuje, 1977)
30	Crescent Island	2405 ± 150 GX4588-A	SPN Narosura (Onyango-Abuje, 1977)
30	Crescent Island	2660 ± 160 GX4589-G	SPN Narosura (Onyango-Abuje, 1977)
30	Crescent Island	2535 ± 140 GX4586-G	SPN Narosura (Onyango-Abuje, 1977)
30	Crescent Island	2795 ± 155 GX4587-G	SPN Narosura (Onyango-Abuje, 1977)
35	GRJI25 Hyrax Hill	1295 ± 105 GX4582-A	SPN Cairn (Onyango-Abuje, n.d.)
35	GRJI25 Hyrax Hill	1955 ± 125 GX4582-G	SPN Cairn (Onyango-Abuje, n.d.)
37	GRJI1 Prolonged Drift	2315 ± 150 GX5735-A	SPN UP and Narosura (Gifford et al., 1980)
37	GRJI1 Prolonged Drift	2530 ± 160 GX5735-G	SPN UP and Narosura (Gifford et al., 1980)
38	Tunnel Rock	2050 ± 60 Y-1397	SPN UP (Sutton, 1966: 54)
38	Tunnel Rock	2730 ± 60 Y-1398	SPN UP (Sutton, 1966: 54)
42	KFR-A4 Terrace RS	530 ± 100 HEL-531	SPN UP? (Siiriainen, 1977)
42	KFR-A4 Terrace RS	2100 ± 110 HEL-530	SPN UP? (Siiriainen, 1977)
42	KFR-A4 Terrace RS	1900 ± 90 HEL-533	SPN UP (Siiriainen, 1977)
43	KFR-A5 Porcupine Cave	2320 ± 160 HEL-852	SPN Akira? (Siiriainen, 1977)
43	KFR-A5 Porcupine Cave	2830 ± 120 HEL-871	SPN Akira? (Siiriainen, 1977)
43	KFR-A5 Porcupine Cave	2490 ± 110 HEL-851	SPN Akira? (Siiriainen, 1977)
44	KFR-A12 River RS	980 ± 100 HEL-532	SPN UP (Siiriainen, 1977)
44	KFR-A12 River RS	1100 ± 120 HEL-534	SPN UP (Siiriainen, 1977)
45	KFR-C4 Kisima Farm	760 ± 90 HEL-853	SPN UP (Siiriainen, 1977)
29	Narosura	2640 ± 115 N-703	SPN Narosura (Odner, 1972)
29	Narosura	2660 ± 115 N-701	SPN Narosura (Odner, 1972)
29	Narosura	2360 ± 110 N-700	SPN Narosura (Odner, 1972)
29	Narosura	2760 ± 115 N-702	SPN Narosura (Odner, 1972)
48	GVJM3 Lukenya	1804 ± 119 GX3539	SPN Nderit (Gramly, n.d.)
48	GVJM3 Lukenya	1501 ± 170 N-1827	SPN Nderit (Gramly, n.d.)
49	GVJM14 Lukenya	1991 ± 133 N-1884	SPN Akira (Gramly, n.d.)
50	GVJM22 Lukenya	1490 ± 131 UCLA1709D	SPN Akira (Gramly, n.d.)
50	GVJM22 Lukenya	2311 ± 127 UCLA1709C	SPN Narosura (Gramly, n.d.)
50	GVJM22 Lukenya	1307 ± 122 N-1076	SPN Akira (Gramly, n.d.)
54	GVJM44 Lukenya	2085 ± 135 GX4160-A	SPN Narosura (Bower and Nelson, 1978)
54	GVJM44 Lukenya	1710 ± 135 GX4160-C	SPN Narosura (Bower and Nelson, 1978)
54	GVJM44 Lukenya	2030 ± 125 GX4507-A	SPN Akira (Bower and Nelson, 1978)
54	GVJM44 Lukenya	2070 ± 155 GX5638-G	SPN Akira (Nelson, pers. comm.)
54	GVJM44 Lukenya	1775 ± 150 GX4507-G	SPN Akira (Bower and Nelson, 1978)
54	GVJM44 Lukenya	2415 ± 155 GX5138	SPN Narosura (Nelson, pers. comm.)
54	GVJM44 Lukenya	3290 ± 145 GX5348	SPN Nderit (Nelson, pers. comm.)
54	GVJM44 Lukenya	1820 ± 200 GX5638-A	SPN Akira (Nelson, pers. comm.)
56	GVJM47 Lukenya	1340 ± 145 GX4161-A	SPN UP (Bower and Nelson, 1978)
56	GVJM47 Lukenya	970 ± 130 GX4161-C	SPN UP (Bower and Nelson, 1978)
57	GVJM48 Lukenya	1810 ± 135 GX5347-G	SPN Narosura (Nelson, pers. comm.)
57	GVJM48 Lukenya	1600 ± 130 GX5347-A	SPN Narosura (Nelson, pers. comm.)
58	GVJM52 Lukenya	1855 ± 180 GX5692-A	SPN Narosura (Nelson, pers. comm.)
58	GVJM52 Lukenya	2050 ± 115 GX5692-G	SPN Narosura (Nelson, pers. comm.)
70	Ngorongoro Burial	2260 ± 180 GX1243	SPN (Sassoon, 1968)
74	HBJD3 Serengeti	3000 ± 140 GX5640	SPN UP (Bower, pers. comm.)
72	SE-3 Seronera	2020 ± 115 N-1067	SPN Nderit (Bower, 1973a)

| 71 | Nasera | 2060 ± 100 ISGS438 | SPN Akira (King and Bada, 1979) |
| 71 | Nasera | 2180 ± 200 ISGS438 | SPN Akira (King and Bada, 1979) |

1d. Dates for the Turkwell Tradition of northern lowland East Africa:

3	Lopoy	1080 ± 80 UCLA2124G	T Turkwell (Lynch and Robbins, 1979: 325)
3	Lopoy	950 ± 80 UCLA2124J	T Turkwell (Lynch and Robbins, 1979: 235)
3	Lopoy	1100 ± 80 UCLA2124H	T Turkwell (Lynch and Robbins, 1979: 325)
3	Lopoy	1375 ± 125 GX5041	T Turkwell (Lynch and Robbins, 1979: 325)
4	Apeget I	1800 ± 300 UCLA2124K	T Turkwell (Lynch and Robbins, 1979: 325)
9	Namoratunga	2285 ± 165 GX5042-A	T Turkwell? (Lynch and Robbins, 1979)
11	Turkwell Scheme	1500 ± 100 N 909	T Turkwell (Robbins, 1972)
12	North Horr II	1525 ± 155 GX3707	T Turkwell? (Maggs, 1977: 184)
12	North Horr II	748 ± 140 GX3708	T Turkwell? (Maggs, 1977: 184)
46	Ngenyn Baringo	2080 ± 130 UCLA1322-C	T Turkwell (Hivernel, n.d.)

1e. Dates for the Eburran (Kenya Capsian) Industry in the central Rift Valley of Kenya:

20	GSJJ25 Masai Gorge RS	2515 ± 140 GX4471-A	Eburran 5a UP (Nelson, pers. comm.)
20	GSJJ25 Masai Gorge RS	2595 ± 135 GX5346	Eburran 5a UP (Nelson, pers. comm.)
20	GSJJ25 Masai Gorge RS	2865 ± 150 GX4462-A	Eburran 5a UP (Ambrose, in press)
33	Keringet Caves	2910 ± 115 N-635	Eburran 5a? UP (Cohen, 1970)
26	GSJI1 Gamble's Cave	8095 ± 190 GX0290	Eburran 3 (Ambrose et al., 1980)
26	GSJI1 Gamble's Cave	8245 ± 175 GX0289	Eburran 3 (Ambrose et al., 1980)
26	GSJI1 Gamble's Cave	8540 ± 180 GX0283	Eburran 3 (Ambrose et al., 1980)
26	GSJI1 Gamble's Cave	7555 ± 190 GX0499	Eburran 3 (Ambrose et al., 1980)
36	GTJK21 Naivasha Rwy	2000 ± 135 GX4583-G	Eburran 5a Narosura, Akira and UP (On-yango-Abuje, n.d.)
31	GTJJ3 Causeway	895 ± 105 GX4319-C	Eburran 5b Narosura (Bower and Nelson, 1978)
31	GTJJ3 Causeway	2380 ± 140 GX5639-A	Eburran 5b Narosura (Bower and Nelson, 1978)
31	GTJJ3 Causeway	2045 ± 125 GX4319-A	Eburran 5b Narosura (Bower and Nelson, 1978)
28	Prospect Farm	10,560 ± 1650 GX0244	Eburran 2/3 (Anthony, 1972)
19	GSJI2 Nderit Drift	7105 ± 180 GX4315	Eburran (Bower et al., 1977)
19	GSJI2 Nderit Drift	7005 ± 175 GX4317	Eburran (Bower et al., 1977)
19	GSJI2 Nderit Drift	10,685 ± 270 GX4214	Eburran 2 (Bower et al., 1977)
19	GSJI2 Nderit Drift	9425 ± 160 GX4313-A	Eburran 2 (Bower and Nelson, 1978)
19	GSJI2 Nderit Drift	9135 ± 235 GX4417	Eburran (Nelson, pers. comm.)
19	GSJI2 Nderit Drift	12,065 ± 365 GX4215	Eburran 2 (Bower et al., 1977)
19	GSJI2 Nderit Drift	10,280 ± 270 GX5136	Eburran 1 (Nelson, pers. comm.)
19	GSJI29 Nderit Drift	7415 ± 200 GX4505-A	Eburran (Bower and Nelson, 1978)

1f. Dates for the Elmenteitan Neolithic and descendant Iron Age variants in the western highlands of Kenya:

16	GRJI60 Lion Hill	1850 ± 130 GX4715	Elmenteitan (Bower and Nelson, 1978)
18	GSJH1 Remnant	1355 ± 145 GX4634	Elmenteitan (Bower et al., 1977)
18	GSJH1 Remnant	2315 ± 150 GX4324	Elmenteitan (Bower et al., 1977)
20	GSJJ25 Masai Gorge RS	1545 ± 135 GX4312	Elmenteitan (Ambrose, 1982)
20	GSJJ25 Masai Gorge RS	1560 ± 135 GX4311-C	Elmenteitan (Ambrose, 1982)
20	GSJJ25 Masai Gorge RS	2325 ± 145 GX5344	Elmenteitan (Nelson, pers. comm.)
20	GSJJ25 Masai Gorge RS	2495 ± 150 GX4345-A	Elmenteitan (Ambrose, 1982)
27	GUJH4 Rotian	2155 ± 140 GX5135-G	Elmenteitan (Ambrose, 1982)
27	GUJH4 Rotian	1965 ± 150 GX5135-A	Elmenteitan (Ambrose, 1982)
32	Njoro River Cave	2920 ± 80 Y-91	Elmenteitan (Cole, 1963: 286)
33	Keringet Caves	2430 ± 110 N-654	Elmenteitan (Cohen, 1970)
33	Keringet Caves	2055 ± 110 N-655	Elmenteitan (Cohen, 1970)
25	Deloraine Farm	1070 ± 110 N-652	IA UP (Cohen, 1970)

25	Deloraine Farm	1150 ± 135 GX5542-A	IA UP (Chittick et al., in press)
25	Deloraine Farm	985 ± 130 GX5542-G	IA UP (Chittick et al., in press)
25	Deloraine Farm	1110 ± 120 GX5541-G	IA UP (Chittick et al., in press)
25	Deloraine Farm	1000 ± 115 GX5541-A	IA UP (Chittick et al., in press)
25	Deloraine Farm	1300 ± 140 GX5543	IA UP (Chittick et al., in press)

1g. Dates for the "Pastoral Iron Age" Lanet Ware Tradition (twisted cord roulette) of the East African highlands:

20	GSJJ25 Masai Gorge RS	1025 ± 130 GX4310	PIA Okiek (Ambrose, 1982)
20	GSJJ25 Masai Gorge RS	405 ± 120 GX4309	PIA Okiek (Ambrose, 1982)
19	GSJI23 Nderit Drift	260 ± 120 GX4504	PIA Lanet (Bower et al., 1977)
19	GSJI23 Nderit Drift	260 ± 105 GX4502-A	PIA Lanet (Bower et al., 1977)
23	GUJJ2 Akira	485 ± 135 GX4382-G	PIA Lanet (Bower et al., 1977)
23	GUJJ2 Akira	445 ± 120 GX4381	PIA Lanet (Bower et al., 1977)
24	GUJJ13 Salasun	1185 ± 140 GX4420-A	PIA Lanet (Bower et al., 1977)
39	Lanet	365 ± 100 Y-570	PIA Lanet (Posnansky, 1967)
41	Muringa	300 ± 80 Y-1395	PIA Lanet (Sutton, 1973)
41	Muringa	300 ± 60 Y-1396	PIA Lanet (Sutton, 1973)
52	GVJM41E Lukenya	1250 ± 115 GX4506-G	PIA Cairn (Bower and Nelson, 1978)
52	GVJM41E Lukenya	1240 ± 145 GX4506-A	PIA Cairn (Bower and Nelson, 1978)
76	HPKD12 Serengeti	260 ± 100 GX5687	PIA? (Bower, pers. comm.)
76	HPKD12 Serengeti	755 ± 135 GX5690	PIA? (Bower, pers. comm.)
76	HPKD12 Serengeti	225 ± 105 GX5688	PIA? (Bower, pers. comm.)
76	HPKD12 Serengeti	205 ± 120 GX5689	PIA? (Bower, pers. comm.)
72	SE-3 Seronera	265 ± 100 N-1068	PIA Lanet (Bower, 1973a)
72	SE-4 Serengeti	250 ± 100 N-1158	PIA Lanet (Bower, 1973a)

1h. Dates for Early Later Stone Age Sites in East Africa:

19	GSJI2 Nderit Drift	13,025 ± 375 GX4467	Early LSA (Bower et al., 1977)
19	GSJI2 Nderit Drift	12,475 ± 320 GX4418	Early LSA (Bower et al., 1977)
19	GSJI2 Nderit Drift	13,485 ± 365 GX4316	Early LSA (Bower et al., 1977)
19	GSJI2 Nderit Drift	13,610 ± 395 GX4321	Early LSA (Bower et al., 1977)
19	GSJI2 Nderit Drift	12,710 ± 310 GX4314	Early LSA (Bower et al., 1977)
19	GSJI2 Nderit Drift	12,935 ± 310 GX4322	Early LSA (Bower et al., 1977)
24	GUJJ13 Salasun	6595 ± 235 GX4469-A	LSA (Bower et al., 1977)
24	GUJJ13 Salasun	7255 ± 225 GX4422-A	LSA ?Pottery? (Bower et al., 1977)
40	GRJI21 Kariandusi	15,990 ± 365 GX4717-A	Early LSA (Nelson, pers. comm.)
50	GVJM16 Lukenya	16,750 ± 200 UCLA 1747D	Early LSA (Merrick, n.d.)
50	GVJM16 Lukenya	13,150 ± 200 UCLA1747B	Early LSA (Merrick, n.d.)
51	GVJM22 Lukenya	17,680 ± 800 UCLA1709A	Early LSA (Gramly, 1976)
51	GVJM22 Lukenya	9910 ± 300 HEL-535	Early LSA (Gramly, 1976)
51	GVJM22 Lukenya	13,730 ± 430 GX3698-A	Early LSA (Gramly, 1976)
51	GVJM22 Lukenya	17,700 ± 760 UCLA1709B	Early LSA (Gramly, 1976)
51	GVJM22 Lukenya	15,320 ± 450 GX3699-A	Early LSA (Gramly, 1976)
55	GVJM46 Lukenya	20,780 ± 920 GX5349-A	Early LSA (Miller, 1979)
55	GVJM46 Lukenya	19,330 ± 1000 GX5350-A	Early LSA (Miller, 1979)
82	Olduvai, Naisiusiu	17,550 ± 1000 UCLA1695	Early LSA (M. D. Leakey et al., 1972)
75	HCJE1 Serengeti	7310 ± 190 GX5642-A	LSA (Bower, pers. comm.)
75	HCJE1 Serengeti	6185 ± 165 GX5641-A	LSA (Bower, pers. comm.)
71	Nasera	22,600 ± 400 ISGS425	MSA/LSA (King and Bada, 1979)
71	Nasera	21,600 ± 400 ISGS445	MSA/LSA (King and Bada, 1979)
71	Nasera	18,000	Early LSA (Mehlman, 1977)
60	Kalokurok	6925 ± 190 GX4218-A	LSA (Nelson, n.d.)
60	Kalokurok	3415 ± 175 GX4218-C	LSA (Nelson, n.d.)

Abbreviations: LSA = Later Stone Age; MSA = Middle Stone Age; SPN = Savanna Pastoral Neolithic; T = Turkwell Neolithic; IA = Iron Age; PIA = Pastoral Iron Age; UP = Unnamed pottery tradition. Number preceding site name refers to sites plotted on Figures 1 and 2.

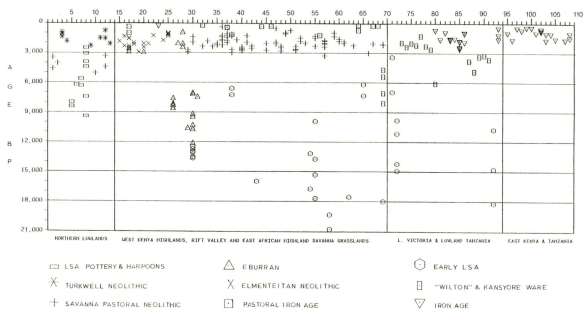

Figure 3. Age and frequency of radiocarbon determinations from East Africa.

bore an antecedent relationship to the Elmenteitan Mesolithic and Gumban A Neolithic cultures. Continuing fieldwork (L. S. B. Leakey, 1942; Leakey and Leakey, 1950; M. D. Leakey, 1945) confirmed the original site-classification framework. Because of inferred genetic relationships these groups were called branches or variants of the Stone Bowl Cultures (M. D. Leakey, 1945). With the advent of radiocarbon dating, the long chronology became foreshortened, and the cultural significance of the original evolutionary model was discounted by some (e.g., Sutton, 1966: 38; 1973: 79–80; Siiriäinen, 1977: 182). The distinctions among industries were further confused by a pottery classification that lumped together wares belonging to different industries (Sutton, 1964; 1973: 146–154).

Despite two decades of research, only one site each of the Neolithic Elmenteitan and Kenya Capsian were described adequately in quantitative terms (Leakey and Leakey, 1950; M. D. Leakey, 1945). The Gumban A Neolithic received little attention in print and only those who had firsthand experience with the type collections were capable of assessing the affinities of new sites.

A more rigorous approach to industry classifi-

cation was attempted by Nelson (n.d.). He used a standardized stone-tool typology which did not adequately account for stylistic differences between industries that shared the same types. Similarities in the relative frequencies of shaped stone tools were the criteria for assessing affinities between sites. By these criteria, with few exceptions, each site in East Africa contained a unique industry. An inadequate sample of each industry and the diversity of industries from different regions, time periods, and environments, with different ecologies, adaptations, and raw materials, precluded recognition of industries with this approach. Other attempts to fit new sites into the original framework focused on the use of *fossils directeurs* such as thumbnail scrapers and backed blades (Gabel, 1969; Sutton, 1973), *outils écaillés* (Odner, 1972: 75), and stone bowls (Cohen, 1970: 37). Since these artifacts are found on some sites of all three archaeological cultures (Table 2), misclassification was inevitable.

An intensive regional survey and excavation project in the Kenya Rift Valley and at Lukenya Hill, directed by Charles Nelson and John Bower in 1975–1976 (Bower et al., 1977) provided further examples of nearly all of the archaeological cultures

TABLE 2. **Key Features of Elmenteitan, Savanna Pastoral Neolithic, and Eburran Phase 5 Industries**

Industry	Elmenteitan Neolithic	Savanna Pastoral Neolithic	Eburran Phase 5
Age	2500?–1300 B.P.	*Lowland*: 5200–3300 B.P. *Highland*: 3300–1300 B.P.	*Phase 5A*: 2900–2000 B.P. *Phase 5B*: 2300–1900 B.P.
Geographic Distribution	West side of Rift Valley, Mau Escarpment, and Loita Plains	*Lowland*: northern Kenya below 1,100 m *Highland*: central Kenya to northern Tanzania above 1,500 m	*Phase 5A*: Naivasha-Nakuru Basin, Rift Valley margins *Phase 5B*: Naivasha-Nakuru Basin, Rift Valley floor
Lithic Industry	Long, broad, punched blades Percussion-segmented blades Bulbar-thinning; small-backed geometrics Very large-backed blades *Burins plans* and burins Heavily utilized, damaged, casually retouched blades Long endscrapers Large sidescrapers *Outils écaillé*s Cores on blade segments	Short, broad blades and flakes Medium-sized geometric microliths and backed blades Short, broad, convex endscrapers Sidescrapers Burins *Outils écaillés* Cores on flakes	Long, narrow blades and flakes Long, narrow geometric microliths and backed blades Narrow endscrapers Sidescrapers Burins *Outils écaillés* only in 5B Cores on flakes Microburins
Pottery Wares	Large and small undecorated, globular vessels with out-turned mouths, occasional milled rims; vertical lug handles, pierced while wet	Up to 3 of the following wares may be found on a single site: Nderit (Gumban A), Narosura, Akira (TIP), Maringishu (trellis motif), herringbone-motif pottery	*Phase 5A*: unique pottery styles, undefinable wares, and Savanna Pastoral Neolithic wares *Phase 5B*: mainly Savanna Pastoral Neolithic wares
Stone Bowls	In burial caves only	In habitation sites and cairns	Only in Phase 5B sites
Mortuary Tradition	Cremation burials in caves with stone bowls, pestle rubbers, ochre palettes, Elmenteitan pottery, and lithic industry; central incisors often removed	Stone cairns, free-standing or in crevices, in shelters, or against walls, with stone bowls, pestle rubbers, ochre palettes; low frequencies of large obsidian blades and other tools; incisors rarely removed	*Phase 5A*: unknown *Phase 5B*: possibly cairn burials with shallow stone bowls or platters
Settlement Location	Savanna/forest ecotone in rockshelters and open sites above 1,900 m, and large settlements above 2,600 m	Open wooded grassland from 1,500 to 2,050 m on well-drained gentle slopes	*Phase 5A*: savanna/forest ecotone in shelters above 1,950 m *Phase 5B*: Open/wooded grassland below 1,950 m
Economy	Ovicaprid-dominated pastoralism, hunting of smaller, closed habitat game ?seed agriculture?	Cattle-dominated pastoralism, hunting of medium and large plains game; lowland savanna pastoralists also fished in Lake Turkana	*Phase 5A*: broad-spectrum hunting and gathering, incipient pastoralism, trade with food-producers *Phase 5B*: hunting large and medium plains game, cattle-dominated pastoralism

previously identified by the Leakeys. These sites were not, however, recognized as such at the time, and most Later Stone Age sites containing pottery were simply classified as Pastoral Neolithic.

In summary, studies of the East African Neolithic era have been hampered by inadequate defini-tion and description of identified archaeological cultures. Reliance on type fossils, type lists, and functional criteria, in isolation, rather than a polythetic set of attributes (Clarke, 1968: 37) derived from all available evidence (i.e., the covariance of a lithic industry, pottery type, mortuary tradition, geographic distribution, settlement pattern, and economy), has effectively precluded cogent regional synthesis.

Comparative metrical studies of the stylistic aspects of the lithic assemblages (Fig. 4), which are just beginning (Ambrose, n.d.a, b; 1980; Ambrose et al., 1980), seem to confirm the basic divisions into Kenya Capsian, Elmenteitan, and Gumban A. However, the recent proliferation of radiocarbon dates has made it clear that the later phases of the Kenya Capsian were contemporary with, rather than antecedent to, both the Elmenteitan and the Gumban A (Fig. 3, Table 1), implying ethnic and economic diversity during the Neolithic era. An explanation of the introduction and development of pastoral and other adaptations to the highlands must, therefore, account for the diversity of coex-

isting industries and economies during the Neolithic era—an exceedingly complex task that requires modeling an interacting series of processes: diffusion, migration, assimilation, interaction, and economic transformation. A combination of archaeological, ecological, and ethnographic evidence will be used as a basis for suggesting models of adaptations and settlement patterns. Current models for the introduction of food production to the highlands can then be reviewed and their viability reassessed from the vantage point of this reconstruction. A refined model for the advent of food production will be proposed that is consistent with evidence from archaeology, physical anthropology, and historical linguistics. In conclusion, speculations will be offered regarding the processes involved in adapting diverse economies to the novel

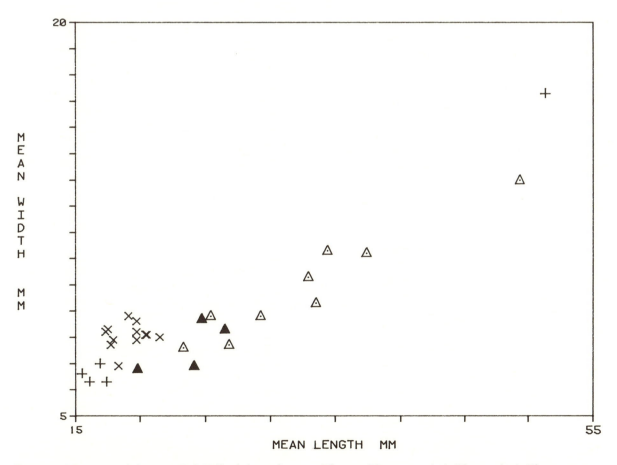

Figure 4. Mean microlith size in Rift Valley lithic industries: Eburran Phases 1–4 (△); Phase 5 (▲); Elmenteitan (+); Savanna Pastoral Neolithic (X).

social and natural environments of the highlands during the Neolithic era.

East African Highland Environments

The high degree of topographic and habitat diversity of the highlands is probably the underlying factor permitting the evolution of the complex prehistoric situation. Precipitation generally increases with elevation; thus, a transect from the middle of the Rift Valley through the adjacent mountains crosses several distinct ecological zones of varying economic potential (Fig. 2):

1. Open to lightly wooded acacia savanna grassland, from 1,500 to 1,980 m (4,900–6,500 ft.), rainfall less than 800 mm.

2. Mixed olive-leleshwa-acacia bush at the montane forest/savanna ecotone, from 1,980 to 2,290 m (6,500–7,500 ft.), rainfall over 600 mm.

3. Closed montane forest, from 2,290 to 2,600 m (7,500–8,500 ft.), with bamboo above 2,440 m, precipitation over 800 mm.

4. Open grassy moorlands with stands of forest and bamboo, above 2,600 m, rainfall over 800 mm (Atlas of Kenya, 1970; Blackburn, 1970, n.d.).

Outside the Rift Valley, topography is more uniform. Acacia/commiphora wooded and open grasslands parallel the Rift Valley from the Leroghi Plateau, Kenya, to the Serengeti Plains, Tanzania, from 1,500 to 2,100 m (4,500–7,000 ft.) (Fig. 1). Below 1,500 m, vegetation is again dominated by bush and thicket, and temperatures and humidity are higher. These factors combined create a prime habitat for tsetse fly (Lambrecht, 1964), an effective barrier to pastoral economies. West of the central Rift Valley, climate is modified by the Lake Victoria weather system. Precipitation is usually higher than 1,200 mm and falls in one long season. In the savanna grasslands, precipitation is usually less than 800 mm, falling in two separate, less predictable seasons. The former region is highly suitable for agriculture, the latter for pastoralism. Where montane forests are still extensive, as in the western highlands, Mau Escarpment, and Nyandarua Mountains, hunter/gatherer groups may still be found.

Prehistoric Climate in the Highlands

The basic climatic sequence of the Late Quaternary is outlined in Figure 6, and can be summarized as follows. The early Holocene, from 12,000 to 8500 B.P., was considerably wetter than more recent periods. Lakes Nakuru, Elmenteita, and Naivasha were at overflow, hundreds of feet above their present levels. The combined lake Nakuru-Elmenteita fell below its overflow level between 8700 and 8500 B.P. Thereafter, a continual decrease in precipitation culminated in the complete desiccation of lakes Naivasha, Nakuru, and Elmenteita prior to 3000 B.P. (Richardson, 1966, 1972). Therefore, conditions much drier than at present probably persisted from 5600 to 3000 B.P. The variable modern precipitation levels were established by approximately 3000 B.P. (Richardson, 1966; Richardson and Richardson, 1972; Coetzee, 1964, 1967). From 3000 to 2500 B.P., the Naivasha core evinces a strongly seasonal pattern of rainfall.

There are no precise indications of the actual changes in the configuration of the floral zones in the area of interest in this paper. One can only infer that during the early Holocene, when precipitation was much greater, that the montane-forest zone would have expanded to higher and lower elevations, and the bush zone at the savanna/forest ecotone would likewise have expanded at the expense of the savanna grasslands. During the subsequent dry phase, an upward shift in vegetation zones may have replaced the savanna grasslands with the tsetse-harboring bush presently found at lower elevations and have pushed the bush and montane forest belt further up the mountains, reducing it to smaller, isolated patches. The profound effects of climate change on prehistoric adaptations will be discussed in a later section.

Neolithic Era Industries of the Highlands of East Africa

The working hypothesis of this paper is that the central Rift Valley functioned as an ecological, physiographic, and cultural boundary region where habitat diversity was great enough to permit coexistence of three distinct lifestyles in close proximity.

For the reader's convenience, a complete list of radiocarbon-dated sites, with an assessment of their cultural affiliations and associated pottery wares, is presented in Table 1 and Figure 3, and a list of the key features of the Neolithic era industries is presented in Table 2. The placement of these industries in their wider geographic, temporal, climatic, and historical context is shown as a graph in Figure 6.

MATERIAL CULTURE, CHRONOLOGY, AND GEOGRAPHIC DISTRIBUTION

Eburran Industry

Only one of the archaeological cultures of the Rift Valley identified by the Leakeys, the Kenya Capsian, can be considered an indigenous development. In accordance with current guidelines for archaeological nomenclature in Africa (Bishop and Clark, 1967: 892–899; Clark et al., 1966), the Kenya Capsian has been renamed the Eburran Industry (Ambrose et al., 1980) after Mount Eburu, located in the center of its confirmed distribution (Fig. 2). Four pre-Neolithic phases have been recognized, roughly corresponding to the Lower Kenya Capsian and the Upper Kenya Capsian Phases A and B. These phases span the late Terminal Pleistocene and early Holocene, from 12,000 to 6000 B.P. (Fig. 3, Table 1e). Despite a reasonable sample of dated occurrences, none falls between 6000 and 3000 B.P. (Figs. 3, 6). There is a progressive stepwise reduction of microlith size from Phase 1 to Phase 2 and from Phase 3 to Phase 4 (Fig. 4).

Phase 5 of the Eburran is divisible into two subphases on the basis of stone-tool typology, settlement patterns, and inferred economic adaptations. However, given the small sample of sites for this phase it is possible that the subphases may reflect two activity facies of a single adaptive system.

Phase 5A comprises the Upper Kenya Capsian Phase C from Layer 12, Gamble's Cave (L. S. B. Leakey, 1931: 109), Lower Stratum 3 at Masai Gorge Rockshelter (Ambrose, n.d.a, b), and the Upper Kenya Capsian Phase D from Strata 1–4 at Naivasha Railway Site (Cole, 1963: 258; L. S. B.

Leakey, 1942; Onyango-Abuje, n.d.; Nelson, n.d.). The undescribed assemblage from the lower horizon at Keringet Caves (Cole, 1963: 292; Cohen, 1970: 35–36) may also belong to Phase 5A. As with earlier phases, 5A sites are located on the Rift Valley margins in the ecotone between savanna grassland and montane forest (Figs. 2, 5).

Dated sites comprising Phase 5A of the Eburran listed in Table 1e show that this phase began before 2900 B.P. and ended well after 2000 B.P. The latter date comes from the lowest of four levels with pottery and domestic animals at Naivasha Railway Site (L. S. B. Leakey, 1942; Onyango-Abuje, n.d.). A skeleton associated with layer 4 has, however, been dated to 10,850 ± 300 B.P. by Protsch (1976: 100). This date is inconsistent with regional evidence for the age of earlier phases of the industry (Ambrose et al., 1980), Holocene sedimentary history (Butzer et al., 1972), and the age of the introduction of pottery and domestic animals (Figs. 3, 6, Table 1). The same reservations apply to Protsch's date of 8020 ± 260 (Protsch, 1978: 103) for the cairn burials overlying the Eburran 5A horizon at Gamble's Cave, as this date is inconsistent with conventional charcoal dates ranging from 8500 to 8000 B.P. on Phase 3 in this site from *4 meters below* this horizon. The Gamble's Cave burials actually overlay the Phase 5A horizon (L. S. B. Leakey, 1931: 117), and are thus later than and unrelated to this horizon, and may not represent the Eburran physical type. The same reservations must also apply to the date of 16,920 ± 920 on Olduvai Hominid 1 (Protsch, 1974), whose association with the Later Stone Age site in the Naisiusiu beds (M. D. Leakey et al., 1972) is not demonstrated. Therefore, conventional dating evidence indicates that the Mediterranean Caucasoid physical type belongs to the Neolithic era.

Phase 5B of the Eburran corresponds to the Upper Kenya Capsian of Neolithic Tradition, known only from Hyrax Hill (M. D. Leakey, 1945) and the Causeway Site (Bower et al., 1977: 134; Onyango-Abuje, n.d.). The lithic industry shows only slight stylistic differences from Phase 5A but contains significant proportions of *outils écaillés* (M. D. Leakey, 1945: 371). Stone bowls are also common. As at 5A sites, the pottery includes a wide variety of Pastoral Neolithic wares.

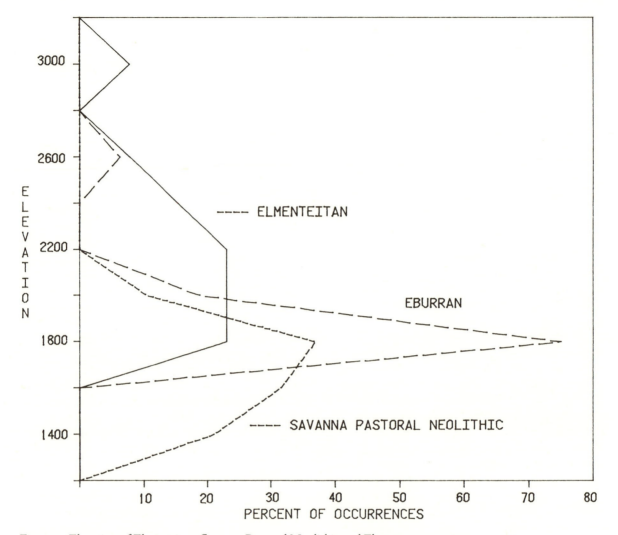

Figure 5. Elevation of Elmenteitan, Savanna Pastoral Neolithic and Eburran occurrences.

Phase 5B sites are located in an open savanna grassland habitat rather than near the savanna/montane-forest ecotone. A date on the Causeway Site of 2380 B.P. and an upper limit of 1955 B.P. on a cairn overlying the Neolithic occupation at Hyrax Hill (Table 1e) demonstrate partial contemporaneity of these subphases.

Elmenteitan Industry

The distribution of Elmenteitan sites is restricted to the western side of the Kenya Rift Valley and the higher reaches of the Mau Escarpment (Figs. 2, 4). The western extent of its distribution is unknown but may include the higher parts of Kisii District, western Kenya (Bower, 1973b; Ambrose, 1982). Unpublished collections from sites on the Loita Plains, south of the Mau Escarpment, also contain typical Elmenteitan pottery (personal observations; Peter Robertshaw, pers. comm.). Low-elevation habitation sites are mainly small rockshelters and caves on the western margin of the Rift Valley in the bush/savanna ecotone, as at Gamble's Cave (L. S. B. Leakey, 1931: 200), Masai

AGE B.P.	CLIMATE IN HIGHLANDS	NORTHERN KENYA LOWLANDS	HIGHLANDS & RIFT VALLEY IN KENYA & TANZANIA	VICTORIA BASIN & LOWLAND TANZANIA	HISTORICAL LINGUISTIC EVIDENCE OF LANGUAGE FAMILY LOCATION	AGE B.P.
0			Pastoral Iron Age (6 3) 1,300-0, Lanet Ware	Carved & plaited roulette wares (7 5)	Western Nilotes at L. Victoria ~400 (7)	0
1,000		Pastoral Iron Age (6 4 3)	Deloraine Farm Pottery 1,300-1,000 (3)		Eastern Nilotes in Highlands by ~1,250 (6)	1,000
1,500			Iron Age, Kwale Ware 1,800-900 (5)			1,500
2,000		Turkwell Ware Neolithic & Namoratunga ~2,300 (4)	Akira Ware ~2,000 (2); Maringishu Ware ~2,000 (2); Narosura Ware ~2,800 (2)	Lelesu Ware 1,800 (5); Urewe Ware ~2,200 (5); Iron Age (5)	Bantu in Victoria Basin by ~2,000 (5)	2,000
2,500	similar to modern ~3,000-0		Elmenteitan Industry 2,500-1,300 (3)		Eastern Cushites in Northern Kenya Lowlands ~2,300 (4)	2,500
		?	Eburran Phase 5 (?1 2 3)		Southern Nilotes in Western Kenya Highlands by ~2,300 (3)	
3,000			Savanna PN Industry 3,300-1,300 (2)		Southern Cushites in Highlands by 3,000-4,000 (2)	3,000
4,000	Drier than modern 5,600-3,000	?	?	Kansyore Ware by ?-4,700 (1)		4,000
5,000		Savanna PN, Nderit & Narosura Wares by ~4,500 (2)	Hiatus ~5,600-3,300		Southern Cushites in Northern Kenya by ~5,000 (2)	5,000
8,000	Gradually drying by ~5,600; Wet ~10,000; Dry ~11,000; Wet ~12,000	Early Ceramics & Bone Harpoons by ~9,000 (?1)	Eburran Phases 1-4 ~12,000-5,600 (?1)	Quartz based Industy ~8,100-~1,000 (1)		8,000
		Later Stone Age		?	Click speakers indigenous to Subsaharan Africa and (?) East African Highlands (1)	
12,000	Hyper-arid 12-17,000	?		Hiatus to ~8,100		12,000
20,000			Later Stone Age by ~21,000	Later Stone Age ~18,000		20,000

Figure 6. Climatic, regional archaeological, and linguistic sequences in East Africa.

Gorge (Ambrose, n.d.a, b) and Lion Hill Cave
(L. S. B. Leakey, 1931: 248; Bower et al., 1977:
121). Burial caves and shelters, most serving as
crematoria, are represented by seven sites at diverse elevations (L. S. B. Leakey, 1931: 175;
Leakey and Leakey, 1950; Cole, 1963: 285–292;
Faugust and Sutton, 1966; Glover et al., 1964;
Cohen, 1970: 35; Bower et al., 1977: 121–122).
Large habitation sites of over ½ km in diameter are
found at higher elevations on the Mau Escarpment
and Mount Eburu (Bower et al., 1977: 131; Ambrose, 1980).

The Elmenteitan lithic industry is characterized by production of very long, broad, punch-
struck blades and smaller blades and flakes, many
of which were systematically broken down into
small rectangular segments on an anvil by direct
percussion on the dorsal face (Nelson, 1980), a
technique used by gunflint knappers but previously
unrecognized in Africa. These blade segments
served as blanks for a variety of tool and core types.
The reduction sequence involving production of
tools on large blades, small blades, and blade segments has resulted in a bimodal size distribution of
some tool classes such as blades and backed pieces
(Fig. 4). Thousands of Elmenteitan sherds were
recovered from Gamble's Cave and the Remnant
Site, but intentionally decorated sherds are extremely rare (L. S. B. Leakey, 1931; Leakey and
Leakey, 1950; Bower et al., 1977: 136–139). The
key features of the pottery are described in Table 2.

Dating evidence from five sites indicates that
the Elmenteitan flourished between 2500 and 1300
B.P. (Fig. 3, Table 1f). The date of 2910 B.P. from
Njoro River Cave is 400 years older than those
more recently obtained. But since this is a single
age determination, run when radiocarbon dating
was in its infancy, it should not be accepted uncriti-
cally. Protsch's (1978: 107) date of 7410 ± 160
B.P. on scattered human bones from Bromhead's
Site, an Elmenteitan burial site, is extremely anom-
alous when compared to the mass of conventional
radiometric dates from other sites. As with other
dates on human skeletons published by Protsch,
this date should either be discarded or a dual chronology must be accepted for the Later Stone Age in
East Africa.

Highland Savanna Pastoral Neolithic Industry

The name Gumban A, like Kenya Capsian, has
misleading connotations (of mythical pit-dwelling
pygmoid forest hunters) and should be abandoned
forthwith. The cursory description and vague definition of the industry provided by L. S. B. Leakey
(1931: 198–200) prevented recognition of the fact
that it is only a small segment of the most widespread and ubiquitous Neolithic industry in the
highlands of Kenya and Tanzania (Fig. 1), albeit
one whose regional and temporal variation defies
simplistic characterization. The original definition
relied heavily on pottery, but since it actually has
five major wares, a suitable replacement name
should not connote a single named pottery ware.
No acceptable name is presently available; in this
paper it will provisionally be referred to as the
Highland Savanna Pastoral Neolithic.

The lithic industry is highly variable, partially a
function of locally available raw materials (J. D.
Clark, 1980c) and regional, temporal, and functional differentiation. In the Rift Valley only obsidian was used, but it was widely traded throughout
the highlands, as a supplement to cherts, quartz,
and lava (Bower, 1973a; Siiriäinen, 1977; Mehlman, 1977; Bower et al., 1977). Ground-stone axes
have been recovered from three habitation sites
(Cohen, 1970; Odner, 1972; Onyango-Abuje, n.d.,
1977). Stone bowls, pestle rubbers, and ochre-
grinding palettes are found on habitation sites and
in cairn burials (L. S. B. Leakey, 1931; M. D.
Leakey, 1966; Sassoon, 1968; Brown, 1966; Bower
et al., 1977: 140).

Five common pottery wares, along with several
minor types, are consistently associated with the
Savanna Pastoral Neolithic industry. Nderit Ware
(Bower et al., 1977: 135) was originally called
Gumban A by L. S. B. Leakey (1931: 199). Narosura Ware (Odner, 1972) seems to be the most
abundantly represented ware in the highlands
(Bower et al., 1977; Mehlman, 1977; Siiriäinen,
1977; Gramly, n.d.). Akira Ware (Bower et al.,
1977: 137), originally named T.I.P. (Thin Incised
Panelled) (Bower, 1973a) dates later than and is
frequently found in direct association with Narosura Ware (Siiriäinen, 1977: 180; Mehlman, 1977:

113; Bower et al., 1977: 140; Gramly, n.d.; Bower, 1973a; Onyango-Abuje, n.d.). Although vessel forms and decorative motifs differ, Narosura and Akira wares share similar techniques of decoration, surface treatment, and firing methods, suggesting close relationships (Siiriäinen, 1977: 180) and differentiation of Narosura Ware into two traditions through time. Maringishu Ware (Bower et al., 1977: 137) is equivalent to the ovoid beaker pottery recovered at Hyrax Hill (M. D. Leakey, 1945: 302–304). It seems to date to later in the Neolithic era (Table 1c), has a localized distribution in the Nakuru-Elmenteita basin (Fig. 2), and may be a late, local derivative of Narosura Ware. The final significant ware is characterized by an incised or impressed herringbone motif. In the absence of a suitable excavated type site this ware remains unnamed, although it is ubiquitous throughout the highlands (L. S. B. Leakey, 1931: 207; Leakey and Leakey, 1950; M. D. Leakey, 1945: 306; Smolla, 1957). Nderit, Narosura, and perhaps the herringbone wares have earlier dates but seem to have persisted until the end of the Neolithic era. Akira and Maringishu appear later but do not totally replace the three earlier wares.

Up to three Savanna Pastoral Neolithic wares may be found in association or stratified at a single site (Bower, 1973a; Bower et al., 1977: 140; Siiriäinen, 1977; Mehlman, 1977). These are rarely associated with Elmenteitan pottery or stone tools. These wares are, however, frequently found on Phase 5A Eburran sites, implying greater interaction between Eburran and Savanna Pastoral Neolithic groups than between Elmenteitan and Eburran groups.

The only glaring exception to the covarying distribution of pottery wares, lithic industries, and site locations is the site of Prolonged Drift (Gifford, this volume), the probable type site for the "Kenya Wilton" Culture identified by L. S. B. Leakey (1931). Although the lithic industry contains an abundance of thumbnail scrapers and small crescents, the "grammar" of the lithic reduction sequence and the resultant morphology of most shaped stone tools and debitage indicate that this is a variant of the Savanna Pastoral Neolithic Industry. The ceramic assemblage is, however, dominated by undecorated Elmenteitan pottery (ibid.: 176), although a few Narosura Ware sherds are also present. It is possible that this site evinces the absorption of Savanna Pastoral Neolithic peoples by Elmenteitan groups or vice versa, or the adoption of Elmenteitan pottery by a Savanna Pastoral Neolithic group.

Nderit Ware and the herringbone-motif pottery are both well represented at earlier dated sites in lowland northern Kenya (Figs. 3, 6, Table 1c) (Robbins, 1972; Barthelme, pers. comm.). The pottery from North Horr, east of Lake Turkana (Phillipson, 1976a; 1977c: 72), is the most likely antecedent of Narosura Ware. These wares date to between 5000 and 3300 B.P. in northern Kenya (Figs. 3, 6, Table 1c), indicating a lowland origin for the Highland Savanna Pastoral Neolithic. The northern sites will thus provisionally be referred to in this paper as the Lowland Savanna Pastoral Neolithic. Dates of 2900 to 3300 B.P. have been obtained throughout the known distribution of highland sites, suggesting an abrupt florescence of Savanna Pastoral Neolithic groups after an 1,800-year tenure in the northern lowlands, rather than a gradual southward diffusion of peoples and/or techniques.

The geographic distribution of the Highland Savanna Pastoral Neolithic is more extensive than that of the other industries of concern here. Sites are found in open and lightly wooded savanna grasslands throughout Kenya and northern Tanzania at elevations over 1,500 m. Surveys conducted in the lowland bush zone east of the savanna grasslands have failed to produce Savanna Pastoral Neolithic sites.

To the south and southwest of the grasslands is found a quartz-based lithic industry associated with Kansyore Ware, and a hunting/gathering economy (Soper and Golden, 1969; Odner, 1971b; Mehlman, 1977, 1979). Sites along this ecological boundary in Tanzania often have Kansyore and Savanna Pastoral Neolithic wares together (Bower, 1973a), indicating interactions between pastoralists and hunters. The displacement of these hunters from the fringe of the grasslands by the pastoralists is evident in the succession at Nasera (Mehlman, 1977), where Kansyore Ware and the quartz industry are replaced by Savanna Pastoral Neolithic pottery with an obsidian industry at 2200 B.P. The quartz-based industry and Kansyore Ware do persist throughout the Neolithic era (Table 1b, Figs. 1, 3) in closed environments below 1,500 m, as at Mumba Hohle and Nyang'oma (Mehlman, 1979; Soper and Golden, 1969), thus defining the southern boundary of the Savanna Pastoral Neolithic.

CLIMATE CHANGE AND THE PATTERN OF RADIOMETRIC DATING

Figure 3 shows that there are few *in situ* radiometric dates between 6000 and 3000 B.P. for the entire highlands of East Africa, although in northern Kenya and in Tanzania below 1,500 m, where less research has been carried out, dates in this period are common. This obvious hiatus in the Later Stone Age succession encompasses the dry phase that began about 5600 B.P. If climate change shifted vegetation toward arid bush, then the gregarious plains game-herd biomass would have been replaced by smaller, solitary species. In the Eburran case, with a lower carrying capacity, the response would be increased mobility and smaller group size (Dyson-Hudson and Smith, 1978): hence, less archaeological visibility. Alternatively, if the ecotonal settlement location pattern was maintained when vegetation zones shifted to higher elevations, then one would expect to find Eburran habitation sites of this period to be clustered at higher elevations along the Rift Valley margins. These elevations are presently poorly surveyed. Thus the apparent hiatus may simply be a function of decreased population densities, site size, and visibility, and/or a shift in preferred settlement location in unsurveyed areas, rather than total abandonment of the region.

The abrupt appearance of pastoral economies in highland East Africa around 3000 B.P., after an 1,800-year tenure in the northern lowlands, suggests that the development of a highland pastoral adaptation may be related to the availability of suitable environments and thus may have been climatically controlled. If the vegetation shifts postulated

above did occur and large areas of the highlands harbored tsetse fly between 5600 and 3000 B.P., then the highlands may have been unsuitable for domestic animals during this period.

The effects of climate change on Elmenteitan chronology are less obvious than for the Eburran and Savanna Pastoral Neolithic. If the recent dates which indicate that the Elmenteitan began at approximately 2500 B.P. are correct, then it is possible that the strongly seasonal environments from 3000 to 2500 B.P. were unsuitable for the Elmenteitan adaptation and may have delayed its appearance. Exactly why a more seasonal climate might have been unsuitable is presently unknown.

SETTLEMENT PATTERNS, ECONOMIES, AND ADAPTATIONS

Savanna Pastoral Neolithic occupations have not been recorded in Rift Valley rockshelters. In fact, if the parameters for intensive shelter utilization are valid, then Savanna Pastoral Neolithic groups did not intensively occupy rockshelters regardless of their location relative to resources (e.g., Bower, this volume). Elmenteitan occupation of rockshelters on the rift margins was intense, resulting in accumulation of copious amounts of ash, artifacts, and midden debris. Eburran 5A occupations in the same shelters were by contrast rather ephemeral, with small impermanent hearths and low densities of fauna and artifacts.

Thus, in the Rift Valley area, site placement and rockshelter utilization patterns suggest that the ecotonal context in which these sites are located was optimal for the adaptation of Elmenteitan groups and only marginal for that of Savanna Pastoral Neolithic and Eburran hunter/gatherer societies. The preferred environment for Savanna Pastoral Neolithic groups was thus savanna grassland and that of Elmenteitan groups was the forest/savanna ecotone and higher montane environments. The few known Eburran 5A sites appear to be sporadically visited way-stations or temporary campsites. The preferred location for Eburran 5A occupation sites may have been within the montane forest, where excavations have yet to be undertaken. Alternatively, the Eburran 5B sites on the open plains may represent the main habitation sites, with the valley margin shelters used as seasonal camps. Differences in habitat preferences among these contemporary cultures may be the key to their stable coexistence during the Neolithic era.

There are few analyzed faunal assemblages for these industries (Gifford et al., 1980; Gifford, this volume, pers. comm.; Onyango-Abuje, n.d.; Gramly, 1972, n.d.). But within each industry, there are regular patterns that are predictable when ecological contexts and adaptations are considered. In Savanna Pastoral Neolithic sites, domestic cattle and ovicaprids account for between 70 and 95 percent of the fauna, with cattle outnumbering ovicaprids by a 2 : 1 margin; the wild fauna is wholly dominated by plains game such as kongoni, wildebeest, impala, and zebra. At Prolonged Drift, domestic stock comprises only 22 percent of the fauna. However, the Savanna Pastoral Neolithic pattern of emphasis on cattle over ovicaprids and grassland over bush game is evident. At contemporary Eburran 5A occurrences such as Naivasha Railway Site, domestic fauna account for only 37 percent of the fauna, with ovicaprids outnumbering cattle by 2.5 : 1. The wild fauna from this site and Masai Gorge Rockshelter both include more small species than in the Savanna Pastoral Neolithic sites. Preliminary observations of the Elmenteitan faunal assemblage from Masai Gorge Rockshelter suggest a 4 : 1 dominance of ovicaprids over cattle. The wild game comprise mainly bovid size 1 and 2 forms, presumably species that prefer more closed habitats.

Independent evidence for the perceived differences in diets may be derived from stable carbon isotope analysis of human and animal bones (J. C. Vogel, 1978; Van der Merwe and Vogel, 1978; Tieszen, Hein, et al., 1979). The central Rift Valley and adjacent highlands are situated on the gradient from isotopically heavy (C4) grasses at 2,000 m to isotopically light (C3) grasses at 3,000 m (Tieszen, Senyimba, et al., 1979). Thus one would predict that there should be detectable differences in the stable carbon isotope ratios of human skeletal material from cultures with different economies and habitat and altitudinal preferences.

MODELS OF ADAPTATIONS AND SETTLEMENT PATTERNS

Elmenteitan

The presently confirmed distribution of the Elmenteitan Industry encompasses a restricted region on the west side of the Kenya Rift Valley and the adjacent Mau Escarpment (Fig. 2). A bimodal pattern of site distribution may be emerging, correlating with high moorland pastures above 2,590 m, and the montane forest/savanna ecotone between 1,920 and 2,380 m (Fig. 4). More complete surveys in the montane forest at intermediate elevations may, however, turn up more sites and erase this emerging pattern.

Elmenteitan territory contains several zones of varying economic potential. The moorlands are excellent pastures for domestic stock, but frequent frosts preclude agriculture based on tropical crops such as sorghum, bulrush millet, and finger millet (Purseglove, 1972: 270). Of these three crops, finger millet is the most tolerant of cold, wet conditions (Purseglove, 1972: 149; Thomas, 1970: 149), and is presently grown at 2,440 m on the western slopes of the Mau Escarpment (R. McGregor, pers. comm.). The forest/savanna ecotone is particularly suited to pastoralism, and grain crops can be grown where precipitation falls in one predictable season, as in the Rift Valley north of Mount Eburu, and in western Kenya (Atlas of Kenya, 1970).

Ecologically oriented ethnographies of several East African food-producing societies provide a ready fund of possible alternative models of Elmenteitan subsistence and settlement patterns.

Assuming Elmenteitan people were purely pastoral, then the Eastern Nilotic-speaking Maasai pastoralists, the present occupants of the Mau moorlands and the adjacent savanna grasslands, provide a good working model for land use and settlement. Some Maasai near the Mau use the high-elevation moorlands as a dry-season grazing reserve, while during the wet season, low-elevation impermanent streams, waterpans, and the surrounding savanna pastures are used (L. M. Talbot, n.d.: 133–140). Okiek hunter/gatherer groups with domestic animals respond in a similar fashion

(Blackburn, 1970). Other Maasai groups occupy the high moorlands permanently. Thus, if Elmenteitan groups were purely pastoral, a pattern of either seasonal transhumance or permanent sedentariness would have been a viable adaptive strategy.

For a mixed pastoral/agricultural model of Elmenteitan subsistence and settlement the Sebei of Mount Elgon provide interesting analogies (Goldschmidt, 1976: 37–50). Groups permanently located in the high moorlands concentrate on pastoralism, those at intermediate altitudes in the lower forest and bush concentrate on mixed farming, and those in the arid savanna concentrate on nomadic pastoralism with supplemental shifting agriculture. This pattern suggests for the Elmenteitan a model of a society internally differentiated in adaptations to different ecological zones, with groups residing in different zones linked by an institutionalized system of exchange.

The adaptation of some Southern Nilotic-speaking Pokot to a similar set of ecological zones along the escarpment at the Kenya-Uganda border (Conant, 1965) suggests a third model of Elmenteitan subsistence and settlement, in which populations practicing agriculture at the savanna/forest ecotone herd surplus stock in the savanna grasslands during the wet season, in the higher moorlands during the dry season.

These models are, of course, highly speculative at this point. There is as yet no direct evidence for agriculture in the form of carbonized remains of domestic plants, nor is there sufficient information about inter-site variation in settlement pattern and material culture to support the model of an internally differentiated economic system. Nonetheless, the pattern of intensive occupation of small shelters on the Rift Valley margins contrasts greatly with the larger settlements to the west, and does suggest an internally differentiated economy, perhaps with seasonal mobility between high- and low-elevation habitats. However, all of the above patterns may have occurred in the Elmenteitan, or other patterns of land use may have existed, and various modes of subsistence and settlement may have been practiced at different times and places or contemporaneously, as Elmenteitan populations developed adaptations to local conditions.

THE HIGHLAND SAVANNA PASTORAL NEOLITHIC INDUSTRY

Highland Savanna Pastoral Neolithic occupation sites such as the middens at Lukenya Hill (Bower et al., 1977) are often situated on gently sloping, well-drained soils. Sites on heavy clay soils have not been reported. Sites are usually roughly elliptical in plan form, ranging from approximately 45 by 90 m to 100 by 300 m. Site boundaries are often readily distinguished because of differences in vegetation on sites: shrubs are usually rare, and grasses, particularly *Themeda triandra* and *Cynodon dactylon*, grow in dense, often pure stands. Midden soils often have a very high organic carbon content and appear to be composed mainly of dung that has been burnt or reworked by termites. Where dung ash is pure and massive it often contains finely comminuted bits of carbonized grass-stems, and the associated bone and artifact refuse is slightly burned. The ash-bed features in Savanna Pastoral Neolithic sites could have originated in several ways, including daily burning of dung and refuse, as among the Dasenech (Gifford, 1978: 88), spontaneous combustion of deep midden accumulations, or burning upon site abandonment, as is done by the Maasai.

The ecological context, topographic placement, size, faunal associations, and distribution of midden debris at Savanna Pastoral Neolithic sites suggest that the settlement strategy and economy of these groups may have been similar to those of modern pastoral societies of the highland savannas such as the Maasai, Barabaig, and Samburu (L. M. Talbot, n.d.; Klima, 1970; Spencer, 1973). Small settlements are established within herding distance of a permanent water-source and may be continuously inhabited for several years. In more arid areas the entire group may move between dry and wet season pastures, as do the Maasai of Amboseli (Western and Dunne, 1979). Where permanent settlements are the rule, the herds, with the exception of a few milking and bleeding cattle and some small stock, are sent to seasonal water-sources where the surrounding pastures can be exploited. Wet-season camps are transient and ephemeral, leaving few visible traces on the landscape. Permanent sites are usually located on higher, gently sloping ground for better drainage, and to avoid the muddy conditions so deleterious to domestic animals (ibid.). These similarities between modern and prehistoric settlement locations and site contents suggest that the Neolithic settlement strategy resembled that of modern pastoralists.

Is it possible that Highland Savanna Pastoral Neolithic groups cultivated domestic plants such as sorghum and finger millet? This is considered, though not impossible, unlikely for several reasons. Stone bowls, pestle rubbers, and grinding palettes have been cited as evidence of grain cultivation (Onyango-Abuje, n.d., 1977). However, bowls are composed of soft, often gritty tuffs, are frequently internally charred, and show no evidence for use as grinders or mortars. Pestle rubbers have an unusual polish not obtained by grinding grain, and the associated stone palettes are too thin to be used for regular food preparation. Moreover, both are often stained with red pigment, suggesting that their primary function was to grind red ochre (Sassoon, 1968: 24).

Climatic factors must also be considered. Throughout most of the high savanna grasslands, rainfall is less than 600 mm and is divided into two seasons, particularly east of the Rift Valley. As a rule, as precipitation decreases, variation from the mean increases. The mean annual rainfall figure is, therefore, often an average of years of drought interspersed with a few years of torrential rains. Since the timing of the onset of the rains and their duration are also unpredictable, a successful crop may rarely be harvested. This rainfall pattern would have made agriculture risky for Savanna Pastoral Neolithic groups except in limited areas where orographic and edaphic factors created locally favorable conditions. There are historical and ideological factors, to be discussed below, that may also support this conclusion.

PHASE 5 OF THE EBURRAN INDUSTRY

Given the similarities between the prehistoric and present social and ecological environment, the modern Okiek adaptation to the Mau Escarpment

(Blackburn, 1970, n.d.) can serve as a good working model for Eburran 5A adaptations to this complex suite of ecological zones and cultures.

The Mau Okiek recognize five distinct ecological zones above 1,980 m on the Mau Escarpment, with different configurations of resources, climatic conditions, and economic potential. The Mau Okiek foraging strategy involves trapping and hunting with dogs in the forest, and hunting alone or in small parties in the bush and savanna fringe, using a bow with poisoned arrows. They also manufacture and maintain beehives, which are strategically placed at lower elevations in individually owned forest sectors. Plant foods are rarely gathered; most of the wild diet is composed of meat and honey.

Trade with surrounding pastoral and agricultural groups is an integral part of the modern Okiek economy. Game skins, horns, honey, and crafted items are exchanged with food-producing groups for grain, domestic stock, and iron. Intertribal alliances are forged, and webs of obligation develop. This may lead to intermarriage, and it facilitates the assimilation of hunters into food-producing tribes and vice versa (Spencer, 1973: appendix).

The preferred Okiek settlement location is at the lower fringe of the montane forest; given the range of environments upon which they depend, this is an optimal location. They must constantly return to the forest to maintain traps and hives, and the bush and savanna fringe are regularly visited in search of natural hives and large game. The higher zones are cold and wet for most of the year, and hives and traps are difficult to maintain. These zones are thus only visited briefly when honey is abundant. Placement of the settlement close to the savanna/montane forest ecotone thus allows them to live a semisedentary existence, since they are within reasonable distance of nearly all the resources they exploit throughout the year.

Eburran 5A occupations in Rift Valley margin rockshelters have small scattered hearths and low densities of lithic, ceramic, and bone debris, indicating low-intensity, occasional occupations. These sites may have seen occasional use as way-stations on hunting expeditions to the plains. The Okiek pattern of land use, settlement location, economy, and intertribal exchange relationships could easily generate this pattern of site utilization and associated remains. If the analogy holds, one would predict Eburran 5A homebase sites would be found at around 2,300 m, the modal elevation of Okiek settlements on the Mau (Blackburn, n.d.).

The location of Eburran 5B sites within a savanna grassland environment (Hyrax Hill and the Causeway site) and the presence of large proportions of domestic stock suggest that some Eburran groups had acquired significant amounts of domestic stock and had made the transition from a hunting to a pastoral mode by 2400 B.P. Again, the Okiek are a source of analogies to interpret the responses during the transition from a hunting to a pastoral lifestyle.

As Okiek increase dependence upon domestic animals, they must spend more time on herd maintenance. Consequently they move out of the forest to the high-elevation pastures of the upper Mau Escarpment and the lower-elevation pastures of the savanna. Okiek groups such as the Omotik and Digiri have recently adopted a Maasai mode of pastoralism (Blackburn, 1976) and have presumably altered their settlement strategy to suit the requirements of domestic animals. This process probably began during the Neolithic era and may account for the presence of an Eburran 5B industry with a savanna settlement location and faunal assemblage dominated by plains game.

Theories of the Advent of Food Production in East Africa

In the previous sections, the rapidly proliferating evidence for dating, economy, and geographic distribution of the Neolithic era industries was resynthesized using the original classification of Louis Leakey, and tentative models of economy, settlement patterns, and adaptations have been proposed. Let us now look at how well previous hypotheses concerning the beginnings of food production in highland East Africa fit the evidence. These hypotheses include:

1. Independent domestication of local animal species (Onyango-Abuje, n.d.).

2. Diffusion of the materials and techniques associated with pastoralism to the indigenous hunter/gatherer populations (J. D. Clark, 1972: 139).

3. Small-scale movement of populations with a food-producing economy into the central highlands, merging with the local hunter/gatherer group who gradually abandoned their old lifestyle (Phillipson, 1977c: 71, 83).

4. Large-scale movements of intrusive populations absorbing the hunter/gatherer groups (Murdock, 1959: 194; Sutton, 1966: 47).

Models 1 and 2 are unsupported by the archaeological evidence outlined above. The hypothesis of independent domestication of local wild species was based upon scattered finds of potsherds from early and mid-Holocene occurrences, with no supporting evidence of domestic fauna (Bower and Nelson, 1978; Onyango-Abuje, n.d.). Potsherds so rare are probably intrusive, particularly in multiple-component sites. Equating pottery with domestic animals is at best an unwarranted assumption. The absence of evidence of hunter/gatherer populations from 6000 to 3000 B.P. throughout the highlands implies extremely low population densities prior to the advent of the Neolithic. Moreover, the abrupt florescence of the Highland Savanna Pastoral Neolithic industry after 3300 B.P. partially supports model 4, large-scale population movements, and is thus the antithesis of model 3, small-scale population movements. The existence of Phase 5B of the Eburran demonstrates that model 2, diffusion, is partially correct, demonstrating that total assimilation of model 4 did not occur.

Continuity of the Eburran Industry through the Neolithic era, the distinctiveness of the Elmenteitan Industry, and the effects of climate on chronologies and subsistence are not accounted for in any of the current models of the advent of food production in the East African highlands. Consideration of these aspects of the archaeological record results in a more complex and accurate model for the beginning of food production and one which agrees with historical linguistic and human skeletal evidence.

The archaeological evidence suggests that small groups of hunter/gatherers were living at low population densities in restricted regions, with territories centered around mountains adjacent to the highland plains, between 6000 and 3300 B.P. They continued their mode of subsistence, with some modifications, after the appearance of Highland Savanna Pastoral Neolithic groups at about 3300 B.P. The abrupt appearance of pastoralists from northern Kenya at this time was probably keyed to shifts in climate and vegetation zones, which made accessible suitable environments for domestic animals. The pastoralists' adaptation to open grasslands did not place them in direct competition with the indigenous hunter/gatherers, allowing stable coexistence and symbiosis. Elmenteitan Neolithic groups entered the highlands from the northwest at about 2500 B.P. Their adaptation was practiced in complementary ecological zones; competition with Savanna Pastoral Neolithic and Eburran 5 groups was minimized. Increases in Elmenteitan population densities may have eventually excluded some Eburran 5A groups from part of their preferred environment, forcing the adoption, by some, of a Savanna Pastoral Neolithic mode of pastoralism, resulting in the appearance of Phase 5B of the Eburran.

The Antecedents of the Highland Neolithic Industries

On the basis of ceramic evidence, obsidian trade, and domestic fauna, one can point to the predecessors of the Highland Savanna Pastoral Neolithic in the Turkana Basin, where Nderit, Narosura, and the herringbone-motif pottery have been found, dating to between 5020 and 3330 B.P. (Barthelme, 1977; this volume; Robbins, 1972; this volume; Phillipson, 1976c, 1977c: 72; Maggs, 1977). There are no reports of an Elmenteitan lithic or ceramic tradition in the northern lowlands of Kenya, although there are no reports of anything like it outside of western Kenya either. However, since it is contemporary with, and is thus unlikely to be an evolutionary development from, the Eburran 5 and the Savanna Pastoral Neolithic, its origins probably lie in the region that is ecologically and climatically most similar to that of the Mau Escarp-

ment and western Kenya. Therefore, applying the principle of least moves, the homeland of the Elmenteitan peoples probably lies to the northwest, in western Kenya and Uganda.

HISTORICAL LINGUISTIC EVIDENCE

Historical linguistic evidence demonstrates the entrance of two food-producing populations to the East African highlands prior to the beginning of the Iron Age (Ehret, 1971, 1974b), suggesting strong correlations with the dating and geographic distribution of the Elmenteitan and Savanna Pastoral Neolithic cultures. Bearing in mind that historical linguistic methods produce only generalized age estimates, they can play no part in the proposed correlations. Rather, the *relative sequence* of prehistoric events reconstructed from linguistic data, independent of the archaeological record, will be compared to the sequence reconstructed from archaeological sources. Correlations are valid only if one is dealing with complete archaeological and linguistic sequences, where correlation of the entire succession, from earliest to latest, should generate the modern distribution of language families and their associated material cultures. If either succession is incomplete, there will be extra archaeological or linguistic entities; congruence between the independent sequences is lost and the entire series of correlations becomes unreliable.

The foremost assumption of this endeavor is that a correlation does exist between a linguistic group and its material culture. Full discussion of the validity of this assumption is beyond the scope of this paper, but maintenance of distinct assemblages of material culture as a means of displaying group identity and reinforcing inter-group boundaries is abundantly evident in East Africa today, as has been well documented by Spencer (1973), Barth (1969), and Hodder (1977, 1978, 1979, 1982). The second important assumption is that all relevant prehistoric archaeological entities and linguistic groups have been documented. This reconstruction of the archaeological record seems to be complete in outline, and further work will no doubt reinforce the perceived patterns. The same confidence is placed in the work of historical linguists.

The relative sequence of population movements reconstructed from linguistic evidence by Ehret (1971, 1974b) is as follows: a Southern Cushitic-speaking population, with domestic stock and possibly a knowledge of agriculture, entered northern Kenya in about the fifth millennium B.P. (Ehret, 1974b: 52). By the third, or possibly as early as the fourth millennium B.P., Southern Cushites spread into central Kenya and northern Tanzania. At a later date, a population probably located near the common border between the Sudan, Uganda, Kenya, and Ethiopia, and speaking a Southern Nilotic language, moved south into the western highlands and Rift Valley regions of Kenya. They arrived in western Kenya shortly before the introduction of iron to East Africa (Ehret, 1971: 32). The Southern Nilotes kept domestic stock and may have cultivated sorghum and finger millet.

The present-day descendants of the Southern Cushites are located in northcentral Tanzania near Lake Eyasi and in a belt to the east, and are far removed from the main body of Cushitic-speakers in northern Kenya, Somalia, and Ethiopia. The past distribution of Southern Cushitic-speakers, as determined by the presence of loan words in other languages, encompasses the known distribution of the Highland Savanna Pastoral Neolithic Industry. Southern Nilotic-speakers are also found in the Lake Eyasi area. However, the main body of this group is presently distributed in the western highlands of Kenya. The past distribution of Southern Nilotic (Kalenjin) speakers, as inferred from place names, loan words, and oral traditions (Ehret, 1971; Sutton, 1973; Blackburn, 1974, 1976) includes the known distribution of Elmenteitan sites.

Considering the relative sequence of the entrance of Southern Cushitic prior to Southern Nilotic groups to highland East Africa, and their past and present geographic distributions, the Savanna Pastoral Neolithic and the Elmenteitan Neolithic most probably correlate with Southern Cushitic- and Southern Nilotic-speaking populations, respectively.

SKELETAL EVIDENCE

Skeletal evidence also supports these correlations. Craniometric studies undertaken by Right-

mire (1975b, this volume) suggest that among the crania from Neolithic burial sites in the Rift Valley were representatives of Nilotic Negroid populations, as well as those whose closest correlates are found among prehistoric Egyptian populations. Rightmire suggests that many of the Rift Valley crania may represent speakers of a Nilotic language (Rightmire, 1974; 1975a, b). One cannot at this point correlate each individual cranium with an individual industry, due to small sample sizes and lack of precise information on artifactual associations. However, we may be dealing with as many as three distinct physical types: a Nilotic Negroid, a Cushitic "Caucasoid," and an indigenous Negroid hunting population (Gramly and Rightmire, 1973). Cushites and Nilotes have a history of several thousand years of contact along a major geographic and ecological boundary that follows the Ethiopia/Sudan and northern Kenya/Uganda border regions (Ehret, 1974b). Archaeological and linguistic evidence demonstrates that the region of contact continued south along the Rift Valley, Kenya, to Lake Eyasi, Tanzania. The Eyasi region is a cul-de-sac where representatives of the four major language phyla of Africa—Khoisan (Hadza and Sandawe), Afro-Asiatic (Southern Cushitic), Nilo-Saharan (Eastern and Southern Nilotic), and Niger-Congo (Bantu)—are spoken today. Racial differences have undoubtedly been minimized by intermarriage during the long period of contact. Thus, although there is strong skeletal evidence for two different Neolithic populations, with Sudanic and Ethiopian origins, respectively, it may never be possible unerringly to correlate skeletal types with industries.

Extraction of the central incisors may prove significant for confirming correlations between modern and prehistoric cultures. Although this is not exclusively a Nilotic practice, it is most common among modern Nilotic populations in Tanzania and Sudan (Klima, 1970: 8; Murdock, 1959: 173). The central incisors were removed from all 79 crania recovered from Njoro River Cave, an Elmenteitan cremation burial cave (Leakey and Leakey, 1950: 76). They may therefore have been of Nilotic origin. This practice is also evident in an early Iron Age context at Wiley's Kopje and the Makalia Burial Site, both located on the western side of the Rift Valley (L. S. B. Leakey, 1935: 95, 107–108). The latter site may represent an Iron

Age expression of the Elmenteitan Industry (Chittick et al., in press).

Many authors have presented selected aspects of these arguments for the hypothesis that food production was introduced to the highlands through the diffusion and migration of Cushitic-speaking populations of Ethiopian origin, rather than the diffusion of innovations (Murdock, 1959; Posnansky, 1967: 641; Sutton, 1966: 47; 1973: 81; Ehret, 1971, 1974b; Fleming, 1969a: 31–33; Odner, 1972: 77–78; Rightmire, 1975b: 368–369; Onyango-Abuje, n.d.; Phillipson, 1977c: 84–85). In the absence of formal definitions of lithic and ceramic industries, the presence of hunters and gatherers contemporary with pastoralists went unrecognized, the distinctiveness of the Elmenteitan Industry was ignored, and the appearance of Southern Nilotic peoples in the highlands was placed in the Iron Age. These misinterpretations obscured the great degree of cultural and economic diversity and complexity that has characterized the highlands of East Africa since the advent of food production.

The Processes of Neolithic Era Adaptations to the Highlands

Taking this resynthesis of the Neolithic era as a basis for discussion, we can now speculate about the processes of adaptation to the new configuration of environments encountered by all three culture groups. At around 3300 B.P. there was clearly no ecological or cultural equilibrium in the highlands. The climatic regime had just changed from very arid to semiarid, and vegetation zones were shifting and adjusting toward modern conditions. As rainfall increased, bush may have been replaced by savanna grassland, ungulate biomass would have increased, and the risk of tsetse-borne tripanosomiasis would have decreased. Clearly, the potentials for hunter/gatherer and food-producer population expansion, and cultural and adaptive change provide interesting cases to which General Systems Theory and Optimal Foraging Strategy models of change and equilibrium can be applied.

DEVELOPMENT OF HIGHLAND SAVANNA PASTORAL NEOLITHIC ADAPTATIONS

To understand the processes of adapting a pastoral economy to the novel highland environment, an attempt must be made to reconstruct prior adaptations to the northern lowlands and the effects that such pre-adaptations may have had on the responses of Savanna Pastoral Neolithic groups to the new environments.

The pattern of radiometric dates in the highlands and surrounding lowlands (Fig. 3, Table 1) shows that Lowland Savanna Pastoral Neolithic groups appeared in northern Kenya between 4500 and 5000 B.P. and did not enter the highlands until 3300 B.P. This discontinuous rate spread of mobile pastoral populations precludes application of linear population-diffusion models for the spread of food production (e.g., Ammerman and Cavalli-Sforza, 1971). More refined models that account for climatic change, topographic and ecological variation, and Pioneer Mode settlement strategies and population dynamics must be generated. This endeavor requires that we take another step back in time and space, to the presumed Ethiopian highland homeland of the Lowland Savanna Pastoral Neolithic populations. The southern Ethiopian archaeological evidence is limited to a few reports of cairns and ground-stone axes (Phillipson, 1977c: 69), so we must rely on historical linguistic evidence, which suggests that domestic plants and animals were present in Ethiopia far earlier than in East Africa (Ehret, 1974b, this volume). If we assume that the highland Ethiopians practiced a mixed pastoral/agricultural mode of subsistence, how and why did they colonize the arid lowlands of northern Kenya?

The general population-pressure model for the evolution of self-sustained pastoral adaptations from farming societies (Spooner, 1973: 5) may apply to this situation. Under increases in population density, successively more marginal zones would have to be exploited by farmers. Maximum productivity in such zones could be achieved by transhumant pastoralism by a section of the economic unit, as among the Eastern Nilotic-speaking groups of Uganda (Deshler, 1965). Eventually, zones totally unsuitable for agriculture would have had to be colonized. Nomadic pastoralism is the only viable option in a semidesert environment like northern Kenya. Thus, as population pressure increased in the Ethiopian highlands, excess populations were probably forced to develop a nomadic pastoral adaptation to the vast, arid lowlands of the Ethiopian Rift and northern Kenya. With the development of a viable pastoral adaptation, dependence on highland groups could have decreased. As time passed and geographic separation increased, tribal division could then occur along economic lines.

If modern lowland adaptations are any indication, it is highly unlikely that agriculture was practiced on a large scale in northern Kenya by Lowland Savanna Pastoral Neolithic groups. At present, crops are grown mainly in receding flood (*décrue*) situations along permanent rivers, such as the Omo and its tributaries, by the Dassenech (Carr, 1977) and the Turkana. The overwhelming majority of lowland pastoralists live by their domestic stock, hunting, gathering, and fishing. Most cultivated grain is obtained in trade from highland agricultural groups.

The arid, semidesert lowlands that separate Ethiopia from the rest of Africa have been an effective biogeographic barrier throughout the Quaternary (D. A. Livingstone, 1975). Presumably, the lowlands were also a barrier to direct transmission of Ethiopian food crops. In a preceding section, the presence of agriculture in the Highland Savanna Pastoral Neolithic was shown to be unlikely on climatic grounds alone. If we accept the working hypothesis that these people originally came from Ethiopia, then if they were cultivators, they probably had crops of Ethiopian origin.

The modern distribution of sorghum races (Harlan and Stemler, 1976) provides a good test of this hypothesis. There are five distinct races of sorghum. *Durra* is almost exclusively associated with Afroasiatic speakers (including Cushitic, Omotic, and Chadic), while *caudatum* is almost exclusively associated with Sudanic speakers (including Nilotic) (Stemler et al., 1975). One would, therefore, expect modern Southern Cushitic farmers in Tanzania (Iraqw) to grow *durra* sorghum. Instead, one finds only *caudatum* sorghum, and in western Kenya and Uganda a rarer *caudatum/durra* hybrid (Harlan and Stemler, 1976: 476). The distribution

of the hybrid variety could be interpreted as evidence of Southern Cushitic farmers in western Kenya who were later displaced by Southern Nilotes, an interpretation for which there is linguistic (Ehret, 1971, 1974b) but not yet archaeological evidence. Alternatively, it is possible that the hybrids developed prior to the occupation of highland East Africa, during the long period of contact between Sudanic and Cushitic groups in southwest Ethiopia, and were then brought south by Southern Nilotic groups. Since *durra* sorghum is not grown by Southern Cushites today, it is unlikely to have been cultivated by Savanna Pastoral Neolithic groups in the past. Therefore, it seems likely that domestic plants were first introduced to the highlands from the northwest, by Southern Nilotic speakers, and were later adopted by Southern Cushitic groups in the highlands.

During their 1,500- to 2,000-year occupation of the lowlands, a tenuous balance must have been maintained among man, domestic animals, and the fragile, arid grassland environment. Population densities would have been rather low, as at present, and settlement strategies would have been dictated by the frequent need to locate fresh pastures and seasonal surface-water. Perhaps, in the process of adapting to these harsh conditions, the ideological passion for domestic animals common to all pastoral nomads, and a disdain for the settled agricultural lifestyle, became ingrained in the Lowland Savanna Pastoral Neolithic self-image.

When the highlands became amenable to pastoral adaptation, the Savanna Pastoral Neolithic groups would have been quick to take advantage of the situation. If highland hunter-gatherer groups were living at low, archaeologically invisible population densities, as suggested by the dearth of archaeological sites between 6000 and 3000 B.P., then pastoral groups were exploiting an essentially unoccupied environment with untapped pastoral resources. In this situation, the Pioneer Mode of population growth (Alexander, 1977) and settlement relocation (Chagnon, 1968), may have operated. In the short term, unrestrained population growth may have continued until the limits of the savanna environment were reached. Population growth rates would then have decreased, but still perhaps have overshot the savanna carrying capacity, in the long run approximating the logistic form.

Settlement relocation in the absence of territorial boundaries may have assumed a linear trajectory (Chagnon, 1968). The high mobility and long-distance travel required by the pastoral nomadic mode would have quickly resulted in an intimate knowledge of the resources over vast regions of the savanna. Thus, in a very short time, Savanna Pastoral Neolithic sites could have been distributed throughout the entire highlands. The difference in age between the northernmost and southernmost sites would only be a few centuries. Therefore, it should come as no surprise that the earliest dates for ceramics and domestic stock cluster closely in time, around 3000 B.P., but widely in space, from the Naivasha/Nakuru basin, Kenya, to the Serengeti Plains, Tanzania (Figs. 1, 3, Table 1).

THE DEVELOPMENT OF ELMENTEITAN ADAPTATIONS

If one accepts the working hypothesis that the Elmenteitan Industry was made by Southern Nilotic-speaking people from the Sudan/Uganda border region, then one would envision a different set of readjustments in adaptations to the highlands from those of Savanna Pastoral Neolithic populations. Climate, precipitation, and vegetation patterns are relatively uniform throughout this broad arc around the eastern side of Lake Victoria. Rainfall is generally higher and more predictable than it is east of the Rift Valley, and it falls in a single long season. Thus, a mixed pastoral/agricultural economy would have been feasible. Unlike the presumed predominantly pastoral Savanna Neolithic groups, only the herding segment of the Elmenteitan population would have been seasonally mobile. Tied to an agricultural system, the frequency of settlement relocations would have been relatively low and the distances moved between settlements would have been less. Knowledge of the resource potential of areas beyond the frontier would have been acquired more slowly.

In Uganda and the western Kenya highlands, Elmenteitan groups may have had exclusive access to the scattered tracts of grassland. Presumably, these habitats would have been exploited by the pastoral section of the mixed economy in a pattern similar to that of the Dodoth, Karamojong, and Kalenjin today. As this population and economy spread south and east within the confines of this ecological zone, they would eventually have reached the Rift Valley, where the extensive pastures of the Rift and adjacent plateaux would already have been occupied by Savanna Pastoral Neolithic groups. As noted previously, the western side of the Rift, south of the Nakuru Basin, marks the boundary between the climatic regimes of a single long wet season and of two short ones. Thus, along a broad front there may have been a twofold barrier to the expansion of the Elmenteitan adaptation—cultural and climatic. Unlike their western and northern antecedents, Rift Valley Elmenteitan groups would have been denied the use of grassland territories by the resident Highland Savanna Pastoral Neolithic groups. Under these competitive conditions, the only option for seasonal grazing may have been the high-elevation moorlands on the Mau Escarpment and the less favorable bush zone at the montane forest/savanna ecotone. Use of these zones may have minimized overt competition between Elmenteitan and Savanna Pastoral Neolithic groups for high-quality grazing resources.

The spread of pastoral Southern Nilotic groups (Barabaig, Datog) to Tanzania implies that displacement and absorption of Southern Cushitic pastoralists did eventually occur. The apparent widespread distribution of Elmenteitan pottery on the Loita Plains, southwest Kenya, may be evidence for the development of a predominantly pastoral Elmenteitan adaptation to the savanna grasslands as a response to increases in population pressure within Elmenteitan territory, by the process of economic differentiation and tribal division described above.

EBURRAN 5 READAPTATIONS

The mid-Holocene Eburran hunter/gatherer adaptation undoubtedly changed with the intrusion of Savanna Pastoral Neolithic groups at 3300 B.P. The pastoralist, pre-adapted to open grasslands, would have avoided savanna/montane forest ecotone settlement locations, because of the danger of tick-borne East Coast fever, until forced there by increases in population density. As this threshold was reached, more marginal zones would have to be occupied.

At the outset, competition between hunters and pastoralists may have been negligible. With population-pressure increases, pastoral groups would become more territorial. Highland Savanna Pastoral Neolithic peoples were avid hunters of plains game, and domestic animals would eventually have displaced wild herbivores. In the absence of domestic stock, East African grasslands support an ungulate biomass of between 12,000 and 17,000 kg/sq. km. With the addition of a pastoral adaptation to the ecosystem, the ungulate biomass is reduced to 6,000–8,000 kg/sq. km, approximately 50 percent of which is domestic stock (Little and Morren, 1976: 55). In the eyes of the hunter, savanna resources would have begun a dramatic decline. Eburran hunters could compensate for a 75 percent reduction in available plains game by the intensification of forest-resource utilization and/or the development of trading relationships with pastoralists and/or assimilation into the food-producing economy. These processes may have been repeated, further restricting the territory and resource base of Eburran groups, when Elmenteitan groups entered from the northwest at about 2500 B.P.

In many ways, the postulated processes of adjustment to a multiethnic regional community in Neolithic East Africa parallel the situation described by Barth (1956) in his study of ethnic groups in Swat, northern Pakistan. In both cases elevation-controlled habitat zonation provided more opportunities for distinctive adaptations than could be exclusively maintained by a single ethnic group.

The diachronic perspective on these areas allows us to draw upon parallels in the way species diversity evolves in nature. In natural communities the species with the most generalized adaptation, i.e., the broadest niche, can tolerate the most competition. Thus, the niche of the generalist can be compressed and partitioned and the remaining niche space can be utilized more intensively. When two narrow-niched specialists are competing for the same essential resources and have a great deal

of overlap in their requirements, one of two things must happen. Competition may intensify, resulting in the extinction of one species, or they may both withdraw to adjacent regions to which they are better adapted. As a rule, the specialist tends to be more competitive than the generalist. This is to be expected, since a specialist has fewer options for survival when the few resources upon which he depends are unavailable. The generalist has many more options for survival but cannot invest as much energy in defending resources which may provide less return than the required costs of defense.

These principles are well documented in the ecological literature (MacArthur, 1972: 71–75) and have been applied to the study of competition between human groups (Barth, 1956). In the East African case, the Eburran hunter/gatherers can be viewed as the generalized species and the Elmenteitan and Highland Savanna Pastoral Neolithic groups as the specialized species. The Eburran use of a broad spectrum of resources accessible from the montane forest/savanna ecotone allowed them to tolerate the reduction in resources that resulted when Highland Savanna Pastoral Neolithic groups modified the grassland ecosystem with domestic animals and, perhaps, fire. The advent of the Elmenteitan adaptation may have further compressed the Eburran niche by grazing stock, and perhaps cutting gardens using swidden methods in the lower forest and ecotone. The hunters probably compensated for the loss of resources by developing symbiotic relationships with both groups. The similarities in the stock-keeping requirements of Elmenteitan and Savanna Pastoral Neolithic economies most likely resulted in their mutually exclusive distribution. Competition would in this case have served to keep them in the regions to which each was best adapted.

Conclusions

In this paper it has been suggested that most of the original industrial classification proposed by L. S. B. Leakey is still valid and accounts for most of the observed variation in Neolithic era assemblages of the highlands of Kenya and Tanzania.

Some of the Neolithic era industries have been renamed and most sites can be classified as Elmenteitan, Eburran (originally Kenya Capsian), or Savanna Pastoral Neolithic (originally Gumban A). Radiometric-dating evidence indicates that these industries were contemporary rather than forming an evolutionary sequence.

Models of adaptation and settlement patterns have been inferred from the actual distribution of sites, faunal analysis, ethnographic analogies, and the economic potentials of the ecological context of the sites. The coexistence of ethnically distinct Eburran hunter/gatherers, Highland Savanna Neolithic pastoralists, and Elmenteitan Neolithic possibly agricultural/pastoral peoples was permitted by the diversity of habitat zones found in the Rift Valley region, a region which functioned as a complex geographical, ecological, and cultural boundary region between two more uniform areas.

The proposed taxonomic framework is consistent with skeletal and historical-linguistic evidence and permits informed speculation about the multiple origins of food production in highland East Africa and the processes of adaptation to highland environments. These lines of evidence, as presently understood, suggest that the beginnings of pastoralism in this region were primarily the result of migrations of Southern Cushitic speakers, originally from Ethiopia (Savanna Pastoral Neolithic), and the beginnings of mixed farming may have been the result of expanding Southern Nilotic speakers (Elmenteitan), originally from southern Sudan. The adoption of food-production techniques by indigenous hunter/gatherer groups is also evident in the archaeological record. Agreement among archaeological, historical-linguistic, and skeletal evidence demonstrates that ethnic diversity in the highlands has a far longer history than was previously realized.

22

Implications of a Faunal Assemblage from a Pastoral Neolithic Site in Kenya: Findings and a Perspective on Research

DIANE P. GIFFORD-GONZALEZ

This paper describes results of the analysis of a large faunal sample from the earliest food-producing period in Kenya and presents a model for the subsistence system it reflects. The faunal assemblage from Prolonged Drift (GrJi 1) constitutes the most exhaustively analyzed sample from an early food-producing site in Kenya, and the implications of patterning in it are of considerable interest to those concerned with the evolution of food production in this area—especially since it apparently reflects an economic system no longer extant in the region (Gifford et al., 1980). However, deri-

Recovery of the Prolonged Drift fauna and the basic research on it was supported by grants to Glynn Isaac from the National Science Foundation and the Wenner-Gren Foundation for Anthropological Research. The writer wishes to thank the trustees and director of the National Museums of Kenya for granting access to reference specimens in the collections. Thanks are also recorded to those friends and colleagues who helped by discussion or in other ways, and to Barbara Isaac and Judith Ogden, who drew the figures. Travel to the symposium for which this paper was originally prepared was provided by the Committee on Research, University of California, Santa Cruz.

vation of inferences from the assemblage and any speculative modeling of subsistence settlement systems in the area are severely handicapped by a lack of parallel or otherwise relevant data from other sites in the region. In part this is due to the relatively recent revival of research into early food production in East Africa. However, it is possibly also the product of continuing problems in research theory and methodology, so that a brief discussion of some of these problems will be included here with substantive suggestions for furthering our understanding of a major economic transformation in East Africa.

Prolonged Drift

The site of Prolonged Drift is located on the floodplain of the Nderit River, southwest of Lake Nakuru in the Central Rift Province of Kenya, about 145 km north of Nairobi (Fig. 1). It was excavated in 1969–1970 by Glynn Isaac and Charles Nelson as part of a major piece of research into the late Pleistocene and Holocene paleogeographic history of the Nakuru-Naivasha region (e.g., Butzer et al., 1972; Isaac et al., 1972). Radiocarbon dates for the site have largely been unsatisfactory, yielding essentially modern determinations, but a recently obtained sample of elephant ivory has yielded a date of 2530 ± 160 B.P. (GX-5753G)

on collagen and 2315 ± 150 B.P. (GX-5753A) on apatite fractions, which is somewhat younger than determinations on other Pastoral Neolithic sites in the Nderit drainage that lie in the 1000 B.C. to A.D. 500 range.

The site, with ground-stone vessels, ceramics, a dominance of microlithic tools in obsidian, and domestic stock, may be referred to what Bower and Nelson have called the Pastoral Neolithic (e.g., Bower et al., 1977). It is, in its placement, site structure, and artifactual content, like other occurrences in savanna environments of northern Tanzania and much of Kenya.

The archaeological sample from the site included about a quarter of a million lithic artifacts and roughly 165,000 pieces of bone, of which some 3,700 were taxonomically identifiable (Table 1). Most of the material was recovered from a dense concentration of stone and bone in an arc about 20 m in area and 20 cm thick, adjacent to a zone nearly entirely free of debris. The concentration is interpreted as a midden. Another similar arc was encountered about 10 m south of the first concentration. No hearths or features were recovered at the site, nor was a clear "floor" discerned. The sample was recovered via a "high-gain," purposive sampling strategy by which the "richest" area was heavily sampled. On the basis of test units around the first concentration, Glynn Isaac and Charles Nelson estimate that over seventy-five percent of that concentration was excavated (Gifford et al.,

TABLE 1. **Summary of the Overall Composition of the Sample of Faunal Remains Analyzed from Prolonged Drift**

Category	Number (%)	Kg Weight (%)	Number burned (%)
Maximally identifiable	3,705 (2.24)	35.13 (26.49)	37 (1.00)
Minimally identifiable:	9,492 (5.74)	15.20 (11.46)	
Tooth fragments	8,760 (5.30)	5.43 (4.10)	
Vertebra fragments	351 (0.21)	3.50 (2.64)	13,261 (8.20)
Appendicular fragments	381 (0.23)	6.26 (4.72)	
Nonidentifiable scrap	152,229 (92.02)	82.25 (62.04)	
TOTAL	165,426 (100)	132.58 (100)	13,298 (8.04)

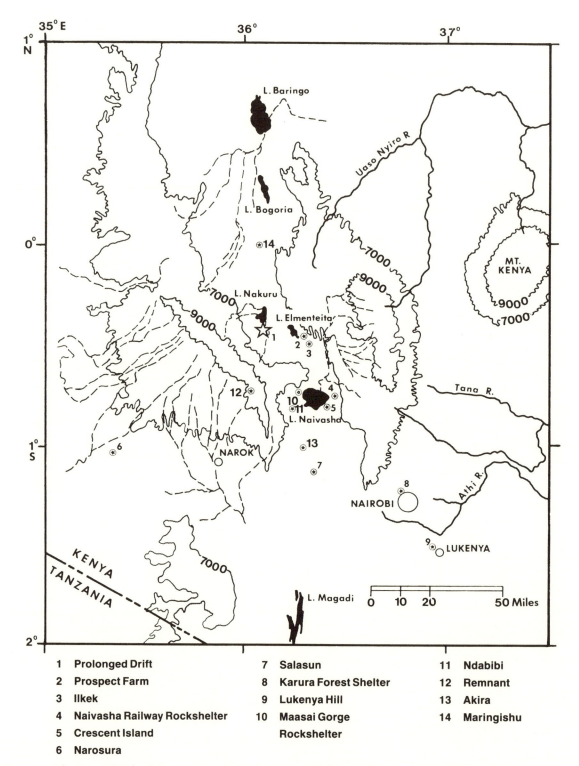

1	**Prolonged Drift**	**7**	**Salasun**
2	**Prospect Farm**	**8**	**Karura Forest Shelter**
3	**Ilkek**	**9**	**Lukenya Hill**
4	**Naivasha Railway Rockshelter**	**10**	**Maasai Gorge**
5	**Crescent Island**		**Rockshelter**
6	**Narosura**		

11	**Ndabibi**
12	**Remnant**
13	**Akira**
14	**Maringishu**

Figure 1. The Central Rift of Kenya, showing the location of Prolonged Drift and other Pastoral Neolithic sites. Contour intervals are in feet.

1980). This fact, with the large absolute size of the sample, gives some confidence in the composition estimates derived from the sample population.

Site Formation

While the spatial aspects indicate consistent patterns of disposal activities on the site, the estimate of the amount of time involved in its formation must be approached through taphonomical analysis. The sediments enclosing the site are poorly sorted alluvial silts and sands, representing overbank phases of the Nderit River. No bedding structures were discernible within the deposits, which have probably undergone considerable subsequent bioturbation. There is no evidence for formation of soil horizons contemporary with the creation of the site. No clear sedimentological evidence exists regarding the length of time over which the midden formed; however, the condition of the bone itself provides an important key to this aspect. Kay Behrensmeyer (1978) and the present writer (1978) have studied the rates of bone-weathering in various modern Kenyan environments and have found broad similarities in the timing of the appearance of certain physical attributes of subaerial bone-weathering. Very little of the bone from Prolonged Drift exhibits the hairline cracking that typifies bone exposed to subaerial weathering for six months. From these facts it can be inferred that the Prolonged Drift assemblage is probably a "single component" occurrence, buried or at least protected from subaerial weathering within a year, possibly less, after its creation.

Species Representation

The relative frequencies of animal species in the Prolonged Drift assemblage are expressed here in terms of minimum number of individuals (MNI). Several points of interest emerge from examining the species structure at the site (Fig. 2). First, the wild component in the assemblage is dominated by migratory herbivores (common zebra, wildebeest, kongoni, Thomson's gazelle). A

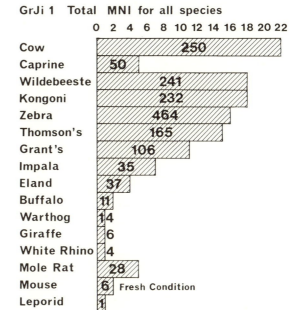

Figure 2. Species representation at Prolonged Drift, as expressed in minimum numbers of individuals (MNI). Numbers in the shaded bars are number of species-diagnostic elements.

few interesting zoogeographic points may be noted, including the presence in the sample of white rhinoceros, a grazer not historically reported in central Kenya or Tanzania, although it is depicted in Later Stone Age paintings in Tanzania (Fosbrooke, 1980). Wildebeest were never reported historically as a numerous species in the Baringo-Naivasha migratory trackway, despite the fact that this was an extremely rich game area when Europeans first entered the Rift. However, they are plentiful in the site sample. Tooth fragments of a giraffe recovered from Prolonged Drift were extremely large, about one third again as large as modern giraffe males, according to Dr. John Harris (until recently of the International Louis Leakey Memorial Institute of African Prehistory, Nairobi). Another very large giraffe element, an astragalus, was recovered from a roughly contemporaneous site on Crescent Island, Lake Naivasha (Onyango-Abuje, n.d.). This may testify to the existence of different size ranges in earlier Holocene giraffe populations.

Evidence for Predation

The overall representation of wild species is much the same as that which Richard Klein (1977) has described for Later Stone Age prey populations in southern Africa, with medium-large individuals most numerous. This pattern of "take," which parallels that of lions in open-country environments, reflects the ability of highly efficient human hunters regularly to capture prey more than twice their body size, which nonetheless fall into a "low risk/high yield per kill" category. Taken overall, the relative frequency of wild species is very close to that of the natural population structure in Nairobi Park, Kenya, with very large and small members of the savanna and savanna-woodland community represented in the assemblage in roughly the same proportions as in the contemporary situation (Fig. 3).

One savanna-woodland browser, the waterbuck (*Kobus defassa*), however, is conspicuous by its absence. Several explanations may be advanced for this phenomenon, including sampling error due either to spatial distribution or recovery bias, but two other alternatives involve some interesting speculations on human predation and husbandry. First, the absence of waterbuck may be due to the hunters' feeding preferences, as the meat of these bovids is known to Africans and Europeans alike as extremely distasteful (e.g., Marks, 1973; Percival, 1924). Another provocative explanation was proposed by Mark Stanley Price, a wildlife ecologist who has compared wild ungulate-species structure in areas near Nairobi with and without domestic stock. He notes that the overall species structure of

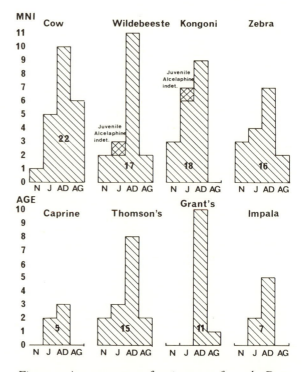

Figure 4. Age structure of various taxa from the Prolonged Drift assemblage, expressed as MNI. N = neonate; J = juvenile; AD = prime adult; AG = aged.

the Prolonged Drift sample, including the domesticates, is virtually identical with his modern samples in the Athi Plains grazing area. Comparison of Athi Plains fauna with that of nearby Nairobi National Park indicates that the waterbuck suffers heavily from the habitat destruction caused by domesticates. Clearly, further elucidation of this interesting situation requires analyses of other reliable and roughly contemporaneous faunal samples.

A crude ranking of dentitions into four age categories indicates that the creators of the midden emphasized capture of large immatures and prime adults (Fig. 4). This would optimize their meat take per kill and again emphasize the hunters' probable effectiveness in obtaining their choice of open-country animals. The presence of neonate dentitions from several species with seasonally restricted birth seasons indicates that at least part of the midden was formed sometime in the first six months of

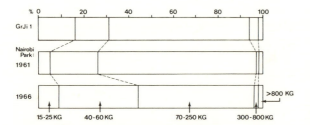

Figure 3. Relative representation of different weight classes of prey species from Prolonged Drift, compared with proportions of those weight classes in Nairobi National Park, in two censuses.

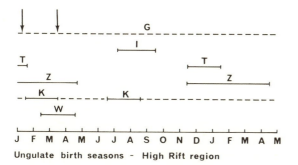

Figure 5. Birth seasons of various species found in the Prolonged Drift assemblage. Note relatively restricted period of overlap among kongoni, wildebeeste, Thomson's gazelle, and zebra, all of which are represented by neonate dentitions in the assemblage.

the calendar year, or in any case after the onset of the heaviest annual rains (Fig. 5).

Historical records indicate that the area bounded by lakes Nakuru, Naivasha, and Elmenteita on the south and lakes Bogoria (formerly Hannington) and Baringo, 100 km to the north, formerly held Kenya's richest concentration of migratory grazers. Huge herds of these animals moved in an annual migratory pattern down into the Nakuru region in the first months of the year, soon after the onset of the spring rains. Arthur Blaney Percival, a European hunter in the area around the turn of the century, notes (1924: 331): "There is a spot between Mount Menengai and the forest where the trek is to be seen at its best, the animals being on their way past Nakuru toward Elmenteita." Thus, Prolonged Drift probably lay in an optimal area for making contact with these migratory herds, minimizing search and stalking time. Its proximity to the Nderit River course, which probably was perennial at that time (G. Isaac, pers. comm.), may reflect the hunters' use of the strategic advantages presented by fording or watering places.

Detailed data on the relative frequencies of body parts and inferences concerning schlepp effect are present in the full report on the assemblage, but it appears that full processing of carcasses, from secondary butchery operations through cooking, consumption, and disposal, occurred on the site. Wild ungulates consumed at this

relatively short-term encampment amount to ninety-two as a minimum number of individuals.

Evidence for Pastoralism

Despite this heavy emphasis on efficient procurement of wild ungulates, the most numerous species, according to MNI figures, is domestic cattle, especially older juveniles and adults (Fig. 2). Caprine remains were present but much less numerous. The question naturally arises as to why, if the creators of the site were such efficient hunters, they were killing large domestic stock in such quantity. Several explanations are possible, some more easily dismissed than others:

1. The creators of the site were treating cattle and wild ungulates in the same manner because they were not themselves pastoralists but were acquiring cattle from pastoralists.

2. The creators of the site consumed numbers of cattle for reasons, such as ritual occasions, that were not directly linked to day-to-day subsistence needs.

3. The creators of the site were practicing a seasonallly variable subsistence economy, of which the site samples two temporally successive phases, one in which cattle and resident wild ungulates formed the protein base and one in which seasonally available nomadic grazers were exploited.

With regard to alternative 1, the relatively high number of older juveniles and younger adults in the cattle segment of the assemblage might be taken to reflect slaughter of a herd of cattle driven off from their owners, rather than patterned culling by stockowners (e.g., Klein, 1978). However, we know relatively little about the culling practices of modern East African pastoralists, and any "logical" inference of rustling based on this age structure is, therefore, not supported by hard facts. One problem to be faced if one wishes to see the creators of the midden as "pure" hunter/gatherers is explaining how they came to share, down to a partially manufactured stone bowl, the typical artifactual trappings of sites, such as Narosura, in which domestic stock predominates (Odner, 1972) and which are accepted as being "Neolithic." If what we are actually interested in is the transformation of subsistence systems in East Africa, the fact that the cows were or were not stolen is probably of less interest than the fact that they were definitely in the area, competing with wild species and being consumed by peoples who also hunted on a substantial scale.

With regard to alternative 2, which may appeal to those familiar with the modern ethnography of the region, increasing evidence indicates that ritual meat-feasting among pastoralists is strongly cyclical and reaches its height in the part of the yearly subsistence cycle when all other foods are at their lowest levels (e.g., Dyson-Hudson and Dyson-Hudson, 1969; Almagor, 1978). Assuming that the cows were eaten at the same time as the wild ungulates, proponents of this use of ethnographic analogy must explain why this ancient system is at variance with modern ones.

With regard to alternative 3, one ideally should demonstrate that the bones of domesticates were mainly deposited at a different time, either earlier or later, than the rest of the assemblage. Chi-square tests of vertical segregation of various species in the midden revealed no discernible pattern as might be expected in a thin deposit lacking apparent limits on lateral expansion (Gifford et al., 1980). However, this finding does not necessarily falsify the hypothesis. A few moderate-sized and moderately well-analyzed faunal assemblages of roughly similar age from open habitats in the same region, such as the Crescent Island sites, appear to exhibit this same combination of wild, nomadic grazers, some resident wild ungulates, and domestic stock (e.g., Onyango-Abuje, n.d.). But other Pastoral Neolithic settlements, such as Narosura, apparently have faunas dominated by domesticates (Gramly, 1972). More faunal samples, from which detailed data on seasonality as well as species representation can be taken, are required in order to test this hypothesis.

It is important to keep in mind that although the migratory grazers of the Central Rift represented an exceedingly large amount of animal biomass for the tapping, they were not, as the Serengeti herds now are not, a stable resource in either time or space. Human hunters, like other predators, must respond to this basic fact. Generally speaking, two alternative predatory strategies are

possible: extreme mobility—the strategy of nomadic lions that follow the Serengeti herds—or a less mobile, more territorially restricted strategy that involves turning to other food resources, such as resident game, when the migratory herds are out of the area—the strategy of pride-living lions. Humans are better suited to the latter strategy than are lions, as their omnivorous habits permit exploitation of local plant as well as animal resources. In his study of contemporary Okiek hunter/gatherers of the Mau Forest, Roderick Blackburn (1974) notes that complete dependence upon wild grazers would necessitate greater mobility than was practiced by historical Okiek peoples. This certainly does not mean that the creators of Prolonged Drift were necessarily nonmobile, as it is conceivable that they could have followed the game through part or all of its migratory cycle. By analogy with modern mobile hunters, one would expect populations following such a strategy to have large home ranges, low population densities, few material effects, and a low expression of territoriality (e.g., H. J. Deacon, 1976; Foley, n.d.). Groups following the less mobile regimen, in which resident wild game and plant resources formed a major part of the diet, might be expected to have smaller home ranges, higher population densities, and greater levels of territoriality, at least with regard to optimal hunting and gathering grounds.

For hunter/gatherers following the second strategy, domestic stock could, by supplementing resident wild game and local plant resources, provide a more reliable food supply. Although herding does demand an energy investment, domesticates offer the advantage of being constantly accessible and may be tapped for animal protein (milk and blood) without diminishing the population. Water appears to be the major limiting factor affecting pastoralist distributions in East Africa (Western, 1975), and the permanent lakes and upland streams of the Rift in the first to the second millennium B.C. would have provided for this need in dry seasons. Altitudinal variations in vegetation are such that dry-season browse and some grazing could be provided for stock driven into the upland forests. Stanley Ambrose (1980) has proposed that the creators of the Elmenteitan industry of the Central Rift were following much this pattern. The question remains as to the relative mobility of the creators of savanna-oriented sites of the Pastoral Neolithic.

There is yet another aspect to the temporal instability of wild nomadic grazers that bears importantly on the question of human subsistence and population levels and the origin of food-producing economies in this period. These species, as noted by Hillman and Hillman (1977) are all "re-selector" taxa, which may lose well over half their numbers in times of ecologic stress and then rebound to their former numbers within a few good years. Stress has been a major factor in the climatic regime of Holocene Africa, and the Pastoral Neolithic sites of Kenya were largely created during a span of increasing aridity, with many short-term fluctuations within the general trend. Since, however, this kind of economic and cultural phenomenon apparently endured in the region for at least 2,500 years, one must assume that the subsistence strategies of these people were, at some level, adjusted to such fluctuations in game availability. Domestic cattle and small stock, while generally following the same patterns of "boom and bust" as wild animals, offer several advantages to their owners, including their relative accessibility as opposed to dispersed game and their role as living protein banks from which withdrawals may be made.

The more stressed the overall ecological situation is, either through lowered plant productivity during drought cycles or through increasingly dense populations of human and domestic stock, the greater the direct competition between domestic and wild grazers (e.g., Western, 1975) and the higher the likelihood of deviation from "traditional" management of wild herds for a major part of the diet. One can conceive of a certain threshold of demographic/environmental stress, considerably different in its details from that described for the Wilton peoples of the southern Cape by Hilary Deacon but similar in its impulse to economic reorganization, occurring in the course of the first millennium B.C., as formerly permanent water sources in the Central Rift were radically reduced.

Turning back to the earlier phases of this adaptation, Figures 6 and 7 present two speculative

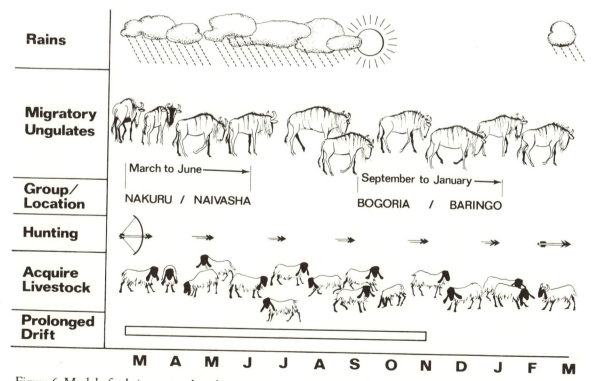

Figure 6. Model of subsistence and settlement pattern of Prolonged Drift creators, assuming high mobility and strong emphasis on hunting of wild ungulates.

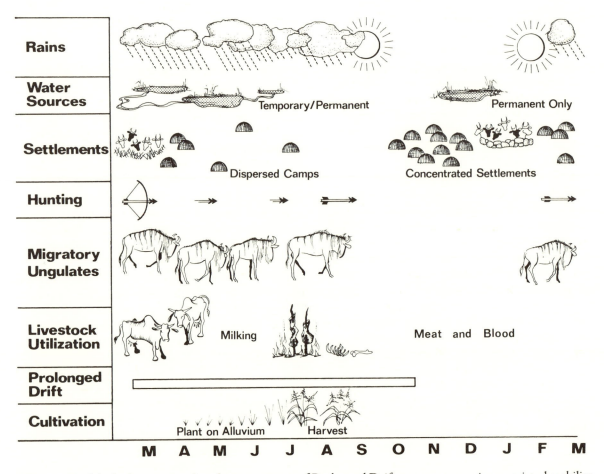

Figure 7. Model of subsistence and settlement patterns of Prolonged Drift creators, assuming restricted mobility and strong reliance on livestock (cultivation of indigenous plants added as a purely speculative component of the model).

models of subsistence and settlement in the Naivasha-Baringo trackway around the time of the formation of Prolonged Drift and other Pastoral Neolithic sites. One model assumes a high-mobility, hunting-dominant strategy (Fig. 6). The other assumes that at that time wild-animal resources were of considerable importance to a substantial segment, if not all, of the human population in the region (Fig. 7). The first model essentially posits that hunting groups followed the same extractive strategies through most of the year, although in different locales. The second posits seasonally variable extractive strategies in the same locale. A number of observational predictions can be drawn

from these models concerning the placement of archaeological sites and the nature of artifactual and biological remains recoverable from such sites. It is hoped that further research in the region will support, falsify, or call for modifications of either or both of these modes. (See also Bower, this volume.)

Some of the questions these predictions should be asking may be phrased as follows.

1. Are ceramics found in the Baringo-Bogoria basin of the migratory trackway made of clay from similar or different sources or do they belong to the same or different stylistic variants as those found in the Nakuru-Naivasha basin at the southern end of the trackway? (Similarity might be taken to support the first model; consistent differences, the second.)

2. Do faunal remains from savanna-oriented sites in these areas display marked variations either in the taxa represented or in the season of death? (If the majority of sites in both areas have a dominance of wild nomadic grazers and if they are temporally complementary, the first model could be supported. If the lake basins displayed an inter-site diversity of species dominance and year-round predation habits, the second model would seem more feasible.)

3. Are faunal remains on sites located close to permanent water-sources dominated by domesticates and resident wild ungulates? (If so, the second model is supported; if not, the first is favored.)

Such questions can only be dealt with when further reliable samples of artifacts and faunal materials are recovered from these regions of the Central Rift.

Most of the foregoing analytic and theoretic exercise is, in isolation, not of much use in helping us to understand the major transformations that occurred in East Africa over the last few millennia B.C. Such faunal analyses must be integrated into a broader framework for conducting research and ordering findings on early food production in the region. To balance the somewhat myopic view of early food production that looking at a single site provides, it is proposed to offer some general reflections and suggestions regarding the appropriate ways to construct such a broad framework.

Wider Issues

Three sets of problems appear for some time to have impeded the integration of research on early food production in East Africa. The first set involves the overall focus of past research. The second involves conceptual problems regarding the nature of sites and site formation. The third concerns the kinds of research in which most energy has been expended. The aim in this discussion is simply to delineate areas in which a shift in emphasis is needed if we are to begin to make headway.

RESEARCH FOCUS

The first set of problems concerns the general focus of research into the development of food production in East Africa. The recent emphasis on culture history, with its attendant use of ethnographic analogy, could fruitfully be supplemented by explicitly economic and ecologic emphasis, with attendant use of generalizations derived from biological and ecological sciences. While reconstruction of the cultural and linguistic history of a region is a valid goal in archaeology, the last twenty years have taught us that this is not the only aim of prehistoric research (e.g., Flannery, 1967). Nor, at a time when static anthropological models of ethnicity are being replaced by processual models in general anthropological theory (e.g., Naroll, 1964) can archaeologists afford to be bound by traditional conceptions of "peoples" in their approach to culture history. Furthermore, description of movements of ethnic or linguistic groups does not itself constitute an explanation of an *economic* transformation which, if our interests are truly "the causes and consequences of food production in Africa," must be our prime concern.

Attendant on continued preoccupation with culture history has been continuing overdependence upon ethnographic analogy as a source of explanation (e.g., Gramly, n.d.). This approach, as was pointed out by Binford (1967) and Freeman (1968) over a decade ago, severely restricts the inferences to be drawn from patterning in the archaeological data. As a case in point, over the past four years the present writer has analyzed two large faunal assemblages from Kenya, each of which apparently represents the debris of subsistence systems no longer extant in East Africa (Gifford et al., 1980; Gifford, n.d.). This might well be expected of a diachronic sequence representing the evolution of subsistence systems in a region; however, it presents real problems to those who try to interpret the data through improper use of modern ethnographic analogues.

SITES AND FORMATION PROCESSES

Archaeologists are sufficiently aware of site formation processes (e.g., Schiffer, 1976), and the vagaries of archaeological sampling in single-component and stratified sites (e.g., J. A. Brown, 1975; Ammerman et al., 1978) to dismiss the notion that an archaeological site is a kind of porthole through which, via cluster sampling of various sorts, we may peer out into a whole prehistoric landscape. Use of stratified sites in ones and twos as witnesses to cultural and economic successions in a region should be replaced by more behaviorally and taphonomically defensible analyses of deposits (e.g., G. A. Clark et al., n.d.). With this in mind, and in an entirely unoriginal vein, it may be suggested that sites such as Prolonged Drift should not serve as the basis for models of economic transformation but, rather, as the data by which models derived from other sources can be tested (e.g., Clarke, 1972; Bower, this volume). The foregoing models of prehistoric subsistence in the Baringo-Naivasha trackway are first attempts in this direction, necessitating specific data from other sites in the region to assess predictions derived from them.

INVESTMENT OF RESEARCH ENERGY

A third area of concern is what seems to be a continued tendency toward misdirection of research energy in analysis of archaeological materials. If discernment of both economic and ethnic processes is our goal, should we not focus our limited resources on those aspects of the archaeological record to which we may be able to ascribe a rough functional context? The word *functional* is here used in its broadest sense, including those aspects of artifactual variation that may, on the basis of analogue models, be assumed to have a social-functional significance. It is imperative that we retrieve and swiftly analyze evidence that can be expected to provide us with some reflection of prehistoric economics. Floral and faunal remains are our major keys to understanding the biological and ecological processes involved in the transition from hunting and gathering to food production. We must now face the fact that our resources for doing any kind of archaeological research in East Africa are destined only to contract in the coming years.

We should also recognize that archaeology can make a considerable contribution to the understanding of human ecology in a region currently undergoing critical transformations in land use. In view of these facts, it behooves us to spend what little human energy and monetary resources we have in the most productive enterprises.

We do have a number of promising ways of proceeding with future research into early food production in East Africa which are even now being initiated by various workers.

There is now a rich, detailed, and even sophisticated body of literature on the operation of natural and human-modified ecosystems in East Africa (e.g., Western, n.d.). The relevance of such materials to the study of a major economic change is obvious. General principles underlying the interactions of floral and faunal components of various communities may be used to construct models for prehistoric subsistence, as they have been used in Europe (Clarke, 1976) and southern Africa (Parkington, 1972; H. J. Deacon, 1976).

These data may also be employed in the design of more appropriate sampling strategies. Robert Foley (1978) has recently suggested that regional sampling schemes should be behavioral in their fundamental principles and design. In concrete terms, this involves some kind of *a priori* assessment of the probable adaptive patterns of prehistoric inhabitants of a region, with a delineation, based on analogue models, of probable range and critical resources and their availability, in order to create a plan for appropriate sampling area, frames, and survey strategies. The recent stratified-ecozone survey of some 22,100 sq. km between Naivasha and Lake Bogoria approaches such a strategy (Bower et al., 1977). Of note to those interested in prehistoric subsistence behavior is the fact that "Stone Age" sites (Middle Stone Age, Later Stone Age, Pastoral Neolithic) are concentrated in the more open habitats of the basin lowlands, while Pastoral Iron Age sites are more evenly distributed through various ecozones. In view of the facts that the lowland ecozones are the normal habitats of open-country grazers and that these species form the optimal suite of prey animals for East African hunters (Foley, n.d.), the strong association of Pastoral Neolithic, as opposed to Pastoral Iron Age, sites with these zones may imply a heavy emphasis on hunting in the former subsistence system. Studies of great potential value include functionally oriented artifact analyses of the sort presented by Hilary Deacon (1976); detailed edge-damage research on suitable raw materials such as has been initiated by students of J. R. Bower (pers. comm.); and the work begun by the Massachusetts group (C. M. Nelson, pers. comm.) in tracing the sources of the obsidian found at the sites. Also highly relevant to a study of cultural dynamics would be trace-element analysis of the clay used in ceramics of similar and different styles and proveniences, to determine the sources of the clay, and thermoluminescent dating of pottery within a given spatial and temporal framework. Naturally, detailed attribute analyses of ceramic styles of the sort undertaken by Wandibba (1980) in Kenya should continue, with greater emphasis on the sociocultural implications of design variation.

Recovering sufficiently large samples of optimally useful materials may involve, one might suggest, excavation of vast numbers of artifacts that will not be subject to detailed analysis, due to their present functionally enigmatic status. While a return to nineteenth century excavation practices is not advocated, a kind of analytical triage is recommended, based on the fact that some archaeological materials are more immediately amenable to analysis than others but cannot, due to the way sites are formed, be separated from those less amenable. It is high time that this critical theoretical and methodological problem be directly addressed, since our time, money, and human resources will probably never be any greater than they are now.

DEMOGRAPHY

One last area of relevance to archaeologists that is almost totally ignored in the East African context is human demography. In positing the expansion of a set or sets of subsistence systems, do we not implicitly assume differential population growth? What *is* the balance of life and death among nomadic pastoralists or primitive horticulturalists of the Sahel-savanna zone? What are natural rates of increase among peoples practicing economies that involve different nutritional bases and mobility requirements? Some data from the Sahel region indicate that nomadic pastoralists have a substantially lower rate of increase than do settled horticulturalists (e.g., Ware, 1977). What was the situation for nomadic pastoralists compared to hunter/gatherers? It is imperative that fecundity, fertility, morbidity, and mortality patterns of modern pastoral nomads be investigated now, since these peoples' demographic structures are our only source of models for the past, and since these aspects of their lives are being transformed, often tragically, by state intervention.

Conclusion

An underlying theme of this paper has been an argument for the validity, importance, and feasibility of an ecological and evolutionary approach to the origins of food production in East Africa. Human adaptation and evolutionary change were reaffirmed as proper fields of prehistoric studies well over fifteen years ago. Biological evidence and biologically based models are essential to our understanding of the shift, in East Africa as elsewhere on the continent, from simple exploitation to the unique forms of mutualism that human propagation of domesticated species represents. But this is more than an argument for scientifically appropriate approaches to a given problem. Since the region in which we work is currently facing a number of crises in human ecology, it behooves us as archaeologists to design our research in such a way that our efforts are neither isolated nor irrelevant utterances but, rather, contributions linked to this theme in useful ways.

23

Settlement Behavior of Pastoral Cultures in East Africa

JOHN R. F. BOWER

Included among the most crucial ecological adaptations of pre-industrial societies are those that relate to the spatiotemporal distribution of basic resources—resources that are essential for maintenance of human life in a given cultural setting. The behavioral systems involved in such adaptations have been called subsistence-settlement systems (Struever, 1968), and they have at least two discrete components:

1. Settlement pattern, which reflects the character of ecological relationships.
2. Settlement technology (Judge and Dawson, 1972), which expresses the means of dealing with resource distribution and its variations.

The meaning of these components can perhaps best be conveyed by offering examples of analytical concepts associated with them. In analyzing or describing settlement patterns, one employs concepts such as concentration/dispersal, mobility/sedentariness, or settlement-size modalities—and, of course, appropriate methods of measuring these. For settlement technology, relevant concepts include site selection, territoriality, seasonal migra-

tion, and so on. If one views settlement as an artifact class, broadly comparable with, e.g., pottery,
stone tools, or descent groups, settlement pattern
and settlement technology can be seen as its structural and functional properties, respectively.

Such a description of settlement behavior is, to
be sure, unoriginal. While other workers might
express their positions differently in detail, it is
clear that generally similar views have channeled
productive research in both ethnography and archaeology (Flannery, 1976; Lee, 1976b; Parkington, 1977, n.d.; Ritchie and Funk, 1973; Yellen,
1976, 1977a). However, the settlement behavior of
Pastoral Neolithic cultures in East Africa (Bower
et al., 1977) has yet to be studied in anything but an
exceedingly vague and general way. This is partly
because, until very recently, few archaeological data
were available to be set against the relatively abundant ethnographic data in, for example, Evans-
Pritchard (1940) and Monod (1975). However,
there has been a major surge in research on Pastoral Neolithic cultures during the past few years
(Onyango-Abuje, n.d.), such that data suitable for
a preliminary inquiry into settlement behavior are
now available. Thus, it is proposed to attempt some
trial formulations concerning the settlement patterns and technologies of Pastoral Neolithic cultures in Kenya and Tanzania. Since some Pastoral
Neolithic pottery traditions, such as Akira and
Narosura wares (Wandibba, n.d.), are more or less
continuously distributed through vast portions of
these countries, ranging through some 800 km on a
north-south axis and perhaps as much as 200 km
east-west, some aspects of the formulations will be
more or less East African in scope. On the other
hand, there is much ecological diversity within East
Africa, and some effort will be directed toward
comparing responses to different micro-environ-
mental configurations by similar cultures.

Settlement Behavior of Contemporary Pastoralists

In this section, certain key aspects of pastoralism as it has been ethnographically recorded in
East Africa will be reviewed, beginning with the

cautionary observation that the subject is one about
which it is difficult to generalize in any but trite
ways. As I. M. Lewis (1975: 431) points out, even
two such closely related cultures as the Boran Galla
and the Somali, occupying essentially the same
habitat, differ markedly in herding practices and,
therefore, settlement behavior. Nevertheless, we
may at least recognize gradients of variability along
two axes: mobility and commitment to livestock.
More descriptive labels for the axes are *nomadism*
and *pastoralism*, and they are obviously directly related to settlement and subsistence, respectively.
The former axis includes two components: range,
and incidence and/or duration of movement. If we
extend our geographic perspective slightly to the
north of Kenya, we may identify three cultures occupying different positions along these axes: Nuer
(Sudan), Kalenjin (Kenya), and Maasai (Kenya and
Tanzania). A brief overview of pastoral and nomadic aspects of these cultures may serve as a comparative framework for studying the subsistence-
settlement systems of prehistoric pastoralists.

With respect to pastoralism, the Maasai (Jacobs, 1975) and the Kalenjin cultures (Sutton,
1973: 13ff.) occupied polar extremes, while the
Nuer (Evans-Pritchard, 1940) were intermediate.
Traditionally, the Maasai subsisted exclusively on
the milk, meat, and blood of their livestock and
even had strong taboos against eating agricultural
and other nonpastoral foods. In contrast, most Ka-
lenjin-speaking peoples subsisted primarily upon
grain (eleusine and sorghum), although milk and
meat from cattle and the meat of sheep and goats
constituted an important component of their diet.
Thus, while Kalenjin folk professed a strong emotional commitment to livestock, from a more practical point of view their subsistence practices could
be described as mixed pastoral-horticultural, with a
bias in the direction of cereal cultivation. As Sutton
(1973: 13ff.) points out, in any given year it was the
failure of crops, rather than loss of livestock, which
threatened famine.

In the case of the Nuer, subsistence seems to
have been based more or less in equal parts on
livestock (milk and meat) and nonpastoral resources (chiefly, millet and fish). However, the variation in subsistence patterns was more or less complementary over the annual cycle, with an emphasis

on grain and meat during much of the wet season (July through November) and fish during the dry season, when milk was also consumed at a slightly higher rate. Furthermore, the Nuer not only attended their cattle with an interest bordering on obsession but were also manifestly incapable of surviving without livestock products. Thus, unlike the Kalenjin, their emotional and practical commitments to livestock were more or less equally intense.

With respect to nomadism, none of the cultures under discussion exhibited much range in their migrations—certainly not by comparison with such West African pastoralists as the Fulani. Moreover, nomadism is not necessarily correlated with pastoralism, for the Maasai, who are probably the most firmly committed to livestock subsistence of all African pastoralists, occupy a very low position on the scale of migratory range (I. M. Lewis, 1975: 432). Nevertheless, some distinctions can be recognized: most Kalenjin (barring those Pokot who have moved onto the plains) were essentially stationary, often occupying a single location for periods in excess of a decade (Sutton, 1973: 140ff.). The Maasai and the Nuer were both transhumant, and though quantitative data are unavailable, one has the impression that they differed little in range of migration. However, there were subtle differences in mobility between the two cultures, and these may perhaps most effectively be revealed by a brief comparison of their settlement patterns.

According to Jacobs (1975), the Maasai settlement and livestock-management unit was the *kraal camp* (*enkang'*), consisting of several families who commonly represented several different descent groups. Such kraal camps moved back and forth between dry-season pastures, with permanent water supplies, and wet-season grazing areas, where water supplies were generally ephemeral. An important point is that the transhumant migration involved repetitious use of pasture areas but not necessarily, or even commonly, settlement sites. In fact, Maasai often burned their settlements, leaving only an ash scar on the landscape, when they moved from one pasture area to another.

Among the Nuer, too, the settlement and stock-management unit, which their ethnographer calls a village (Evans-Pritchard, 1940: 115), was

composed of families representing different kinship units. Permanent village sites were located on high ground away from streams and were occupied during the wet season. Millet gardens were located in and around the villages. During the dry season, there was a gradual migration to the floodplains, starting with young adults and cattle, who settled in small, temporary, dry-season camps. Remaining in the villages in the early stages of the dry season were elderly people, children, and some of the lactating cows. Later in the dry season the villages were abandoned and large groups of people coalesced in more durable dry-season camps, many of which were located in the same spot year after year. With the onset of rains there was an abrupt return to the village site.

In comparing the Maasai and Nuer settlement patterns, one can recognize several conspicuous differences. For one, the Nuer repeatedly reoccupied sites, while the Maasai did not. In addition, the rhythm of Nuer migration was rather more complex, proceeding in stages from wet-season to dry-season settlements, but the geographic distribution of Maasai migrations was greater, having involved more variable ecological factors, such as the presence or absence of tsetse fly and the location of other kraal camps. Moreover, though quantitative data are lacking, it appears likely that the Maasai relocated more frequently over a period of years than did the Nuer.

In concluding this ethnographic review, it is well to remember J. Grahame Clark's oft-quoted caveat (1957: 172): "Existing peoples can only be used as sources for reconstructing the lives of prehistoric peoples with extreme caution and within well-defined limits, since one is otherwise in danger of assuming what one is after all trying to discover."

Pastoral Neolithic Subsistence-Settlement Systems

This is not the place for an extensive review of the evidence for Pastoral Neolithic subsistence and settlement practices. Instead, a synopsis of some of the more informative observations that can be drawn from existing data will be presented:

1. Some sites, such as Narosura (Odner, 1972), contain abundant domestic fauna and sparse wild game, while others, such as Prolonged Drift (Isaac et al., 1972; Gifford, this volume) exhibit a complementary faunal distribution.

2. The material culture of Pastoral Neolithic societies includes many bulky items, such as pottery and stone bowls, which are difficult to transport.

3. In some cases, as on the Mau Escarpment of Kenya (Ambrose, n.d.b, 1980), there are sites that contain only a restricted portion of the total range of pottery vessels known for the culture, while other sites embrace a much wider spectrum of vessel forms.

4. There are some tenuous indications of agriculture (Phillipson, 1977c: 77ff.).

5. There is circumstantial evidence for repetitive and/or prolonged occupation of some sites—profusion of cultural debris, heavy trampling of artifacts, and stone structures (see below) the construction of which involved major expenditures of human energy. In contrast, other sites appear to represent ephemeral occupation, being small and containing only a light scatter of material (Bower, 1977; Bower et al., 1977).

From these observations it is possible to derive models for Pastoral Neolithic subsistence-settlement systems virtually anywhere along the range of variability in pastoralism and nomadism described earlier for contemporary East African herders. There are, for example, observations that suggest a very intense commitment to pastoralism and others suggesting a minimum commitment, observations suggesting sedentary settlements and others implying considerable mobility. Indeed, it is possible to derive models that closely approach the subsistence-settlement systems of specific, contemporary pastoral cultures. For instance, one might construct a model for settlement technology involving seasonally complementary use of wild and domestic resources exploited through transhumant migrations between relatively fixed, seasonal settlements. This is, of course, the Nuer system, and recent archaeological work in the Sudan (Haaland, 1978; Krzyzaniak, 1978) suggests that it may have a long pedigree, having perhaps originated more than 5,000 years ago. But, given the ecological diversity of East Africa and the great chronological depth and cultural diversity of the Pastoral Neolithic (Bower and Nelson, 1978), it seems likely that (1) several different models will be appropriate, and (2) some of them will differ substantially from any ethnographically known system.

Relationships Between Environment and Subsistence-Settlement Systems

How can we begin to construct plausible models for Pastoral Neolithic subsistence-settlement systems from so varied a range of possibilities? Two methods seem promising: comparative studies of Pastoral Neolithic cultures occupying different environments, and application of relevant theory from cultural ecology. In this section these approaches will be combined in an effort to develop some tentative models suitable for testing through existing data and (more effectively) through the results of fieldwork yet to be done.

Two regions with very different environmental structures are the Central Rift Valley of Kenya and the Serengeti National Park, Tanzania. Between August, 1975, and September, 1976, Charles Nelson and the present writer (Bower et al., 1977) conducted a stratified survey and test excavations of Pastoral Neolithic sites in the area indicated in Figure 1. As the map suggests, the region is one of marked geographic heterogeneity, with complex and abrupt environmental changes occurring within a relatively small area. Precipitation, for example, varies over a range of more than 1,000 mm per annum, and differences of up to 700 mm per annum occur over lateral intervals of less than 10 km. In contrast, the Serengeti National Park, where research was carried out on the Pastoral Neolithic in 1977, has about a 600 mm range, and the variability occurs on a gentle gradient from southeast to northwest (Fig. 2), the steepest slope involving differences of less than 100 mm per annum over a lateral distance of 10 km.

The southeastern portion of the park, which is more or less below the 750 mm isohyet, consists of open, short-grass plains—the renowned Serengeti

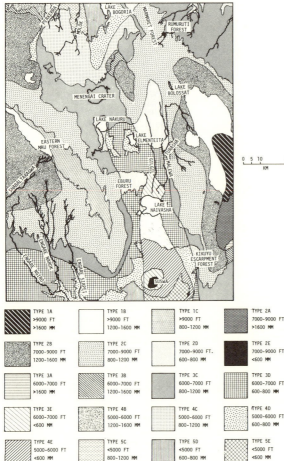

Figure 1. Ecological variability in the Central Rift Valley, Kenya: ecozones defined by elevation and precipitation.

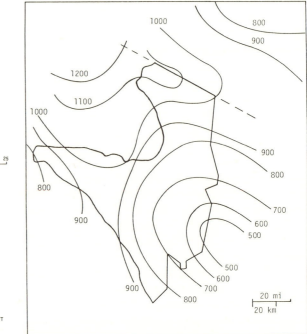

Figure 2. Distribution of average annual precipitation (mm) over the Serengeti National Park.

Plains. Portions of the park between about the 750 and 900 mm isohyets are covered by tall grass and intermittent *Acacia* forest. In the northern part of the park, above the 900 mm isohyet, tree cover is fairly continuous, though not dense. There is a regular annual migration of wildebeest, zebra, and Thomson's gazelle through these regions (R. H. V. Bell, 1971) in the order in which they have been described here. The opening phase of the migration, i.e., the invasion of the short-grass plains, is triggered by the arrival of the "long rains" (January to March), which stimulates a burst of grass growth. (Such a grass flush would, of course, also

be beneficial to domestic livestock, should they have been present.) Although there is no comparable game migration in the modern Rift Valley, historical evidence suggests that in pre-European times substantial migrations occurred annually from north to south in the region of inquiry (Gifford, this volume).

Recently, several authors have attempted to develop ecologically based theories for settlement behavior in pre-industrial societies. Two articles seem particularly relevant: (1) Dyson-Hudson and Smith (1978); and (2) Harpending and Davis (1977). At the risk of oversimplifying it can be said that the central feature of the former is a cost-benefit analysis of territoriality, from which it emerges that, if critical resources are abundant and spatiotemporally predictable, the costs of territorial behavior (defined as the exclusive use and defense of an area) are outweighed by its benefits. Accordingly, Dyson-Hudson and Smith have developed a crudely predictive scheme for aspects of

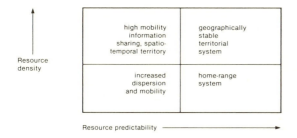

settlement pattern (mobility and dispersion) and technology (territoriality), shown in the accompanying chart.

In using this scheme, one is confronted with the problem of assessing "resource predictability"; the measurement of resource density is, of course, a fairly straightforward matter, at least in modern environments. Harpending and Davis (1977: 283) have provided the basis for a partial measure of predictability; their statement also constitutes an elaboration of the Dyson-Hudson–Smith scheme:

> We expect *maximum range size* in poor environments where there are *few resources*, all of which are *maximally out of phase* with each other over distances of 10 to 100 kilometers. We expect *minimum range size* when resources show very *little spatial variation* or when their *variation is exactly in phase*, so that population and exploitation are concentrated at particularly rich locations. [Emphasis added.]

The variables that could serve as indices of resource predictability are: (1) number of resources; (2) spatial variation in resources; and (3) phase relationships of resources. In addition to measuring resource predictability, the values obtained for these variables in any given environmental setting are supposed to predict range size—another aspect of settlement pattern.

Many difficulties lie in the way of attempting to apply this scheme to Pastoral Neolithic subsistence-settlement systems of the Kenya Rift Valley and the Serengeti Park. To begin with, there are great disparities in the quality and quantity of relevant environmental and archaeological data in the two regions, information on modern Serengeti ecosystems being much superior while the Rift is heav-

ily favored with respect to both archaeological and paleoenvironmental data. Moreover, even if the data were uniformly abundant and reliable, there remain formidable methodological problems—for example, the problem of assessing the mobility and range size of prehistoric communities. Although some solutions have been proposed (e.g., Isaac, 1975: 515) none has been thoroughly tested or widely accepted. However, since we are concerned with *trial* formulations, offered in a heuristic spirit, the reader is asked to make some "leaps of faith" in moving from the predictive scheme to models of Pastoral Neolithic settlement patterns and technology. It is perhaps too early to speak of subsistence-settlement systems, but we are obviously groping in that direction. Regardless of their eventual destiny, the models to be suggested should at least be testable.

The first step toward deriving the models involves an environmental comparison of the two regions of inquiry, focused on resource density and predictability. Specifically, the resources we will consider are grass, wild-game animals, and water, since various combinations of these seem to have been crucial for Pastoral Neolithic cultures (cf. Gifford, this volume). Unfortunately, good comparative data are lacking, so the argument will be based largely on impressions—hence the appeal for "leaps of faith."

Turning first to the density of grass, it is suggested that it is substantially higher on the average in the Serengeti Park than in the surveyed portion of the Kenya Rift. This is largely because of the rugged topography of the latter and its high incidence of lava flows; grass is sparse on many of the steeper slopes of the Rift, where *leleshwa* shrubbery is dominant, and is virtually absent from the lava flows. The density of game is much greater in the Serengeti, but the Park obviously approaches aboriginal conditions much more closely than does the Rift. (For example, the game migrations that have been historically documented in the Rift no longer occur.) Nevertheless, judging from data on large mammal biomasses representing various more or less undisturbed biotopes of tropical Africa (Bourlière, 1963: 50), it seems reasonable to suppose that the aboriginal density of game in the Rift was lower than in the Serengeti.

The density of water (as a resource) is obviously much greater in the Rift than in the Serengeti, but it seems possible that this observation is ecologically trivial in the context of the present discussion. The most important distinction in water resources between the two regions is probably not relative abundance but, rather, the form of water sources. In the Rift, water bodies are predominantly either areal (lakes) or linear (rivers), whereas, in the Serengeti, areal bodies are scarce and ephemeral while linear ones are common, as are point sources (springs and wells).

Of the three variables mentioned earlier as possible indicators of resource reliability, only one will be considered here: spatial variation. Certainly, as far as grass is concerned, spatial variability is much greater in most parts of the Rift than in the Serengeti. This is largely because of the kaleidoscopic heterogeneity of elevation and rainfall in the former (Figs. 1, 2). Although it is not possible to observe the aboriginal distributions of game animals in the Rift, it seems reasonable to suppose that they, too, might have exhibited more spatial variability there than in the Serengeti. As for spatial variations in the density of water resources, no useful comparison can be offered.

Recognizing that there are major gaps in the environmental data and that in any case they may not accurately reflect paleoenvironmental conditions, we may summarize as follows.

1. Resource density (grass and game animals) was probably higher in the Serengeti than in the Rift.

2. Resource reliability was also probably higher in the Serengeti, at least insofar as it was determined by low spatial variation in grass and game animals.

This suggests that markedly different models for settlement pattern and technology might be derived for Pastoral Neolithic cultures in each region—a particularly interesting prospect in view of the evidence for cultural continuity mentioned earlier.

What might be predicted from the environmental data is that settlement behavior in the Serengeti would tend toward geographical stability, territoriality, and a limited range, while in the Rift it would tend toward dispersion, mobility, a large range, and the absence of territoriality. Two models

are suggested reflecting these opposing tendencies; the one for the Serengeti will be called the Transhumant Pastoralist model, and the one for the Kenya Rift, the Peripatetic Pastoralist model. They bear close resemblances to the subsistence-settlement models proposed by Gifford (this volume), which is the more interesting since we arrived at our models independently and from different approaches and largely independent data.

The two models share a subsistence pattern in which both domestic livestock and wild game play important roles, although the relative contributions of game and livestock differ. As earlier sections of this paper suggest, this assumption concerning subsistence is reasonably well documented at a number of sites. The settlement technology in the Transhumant Pastoralist model closely resembles that of the Nuer (see above), except that the pursuit of wild game substitutes for fishing as a dry-season source of protein. Thus, we may summarize the Transhumant Pastoralist model as follows:

1. Small, stable territories.

2. Annual migration within the territory between fixed wet-season and dry-season settlements—large villages in the open, short-grass plains and small camps in tall grass and woodlands, respectively.

3. A core social unit (such as a lineage) uniquely and persistently identified with each village.

4. Wet-season subsistence focused on livestock products (meat, milk, blood) and agriculture.

5. Dry-season subsistence focused on wild game.

The Peripatetic Pastoralist model has no specific ethnographic analogue among pastoralists, though it does broadly resemble the settlement pattern and technology of East African hunter/gatherers such as the Hadza (Woodburn, 1968b, 1972; see also J. Deacon, 1978: 107). It may be summarized as follows:

1. Large, amorphous ranges lacking boundary definition (i.e., nonterritorial).

2. Sporadic or, more likely, seasonal movement with infrequent and unscheduled revisitation of sites; perhaps broadly comparable with the transhumance of the Maasai.

3. Unstable social aggregates, subject to fissioning when the number of members approached a threshold value (perhaps around 50).

4. Subsistence pattern in which wild game was generally prominent and livestock products played a lesser role; no agriculture.

There is a small and rather tenuous body of data which lends limited substance to these models. For example, in the open, short-grass plains of the Serengeti, which could have supported substantial populations of humans and livestock only during the wet season, the Pastoral Neolithic sites tend to be large and sometimes include extensive and complex lines of boulders (Bower, 1977) whose function remains enigmatic but which may represent some form of territorial demarcation (cf. Tringham, 1972: 466) and which clearly involved a major investment of labor. In contrast, the sites of the tall-grass and woodland regions are generally smaller and lack boulder structures. While there is no direct evidence of seasonality at such sites, one of them—Seronera Game Lodge kopje (Bower, 1973a)—exhibited a concentration of debris in open areas and very little material inside a rockshelter, which suggests dry-season occupation.

The Kenya Rift sites have so far failed to yield data on seasonality; however, barring sampling error (and the sampling fraction in the Rift survey was substantially greater than in the Serengeti), there are no sites in the Rift with structures comparable to those of the Serengeti Plain. Furthermore, the size of sites in the Rift does not appear to correlate with environment in any obvious way.

Figure 3 shows rank-size curves on a log-log plot for Pastoral Neolithic sites of the Kenya Rift

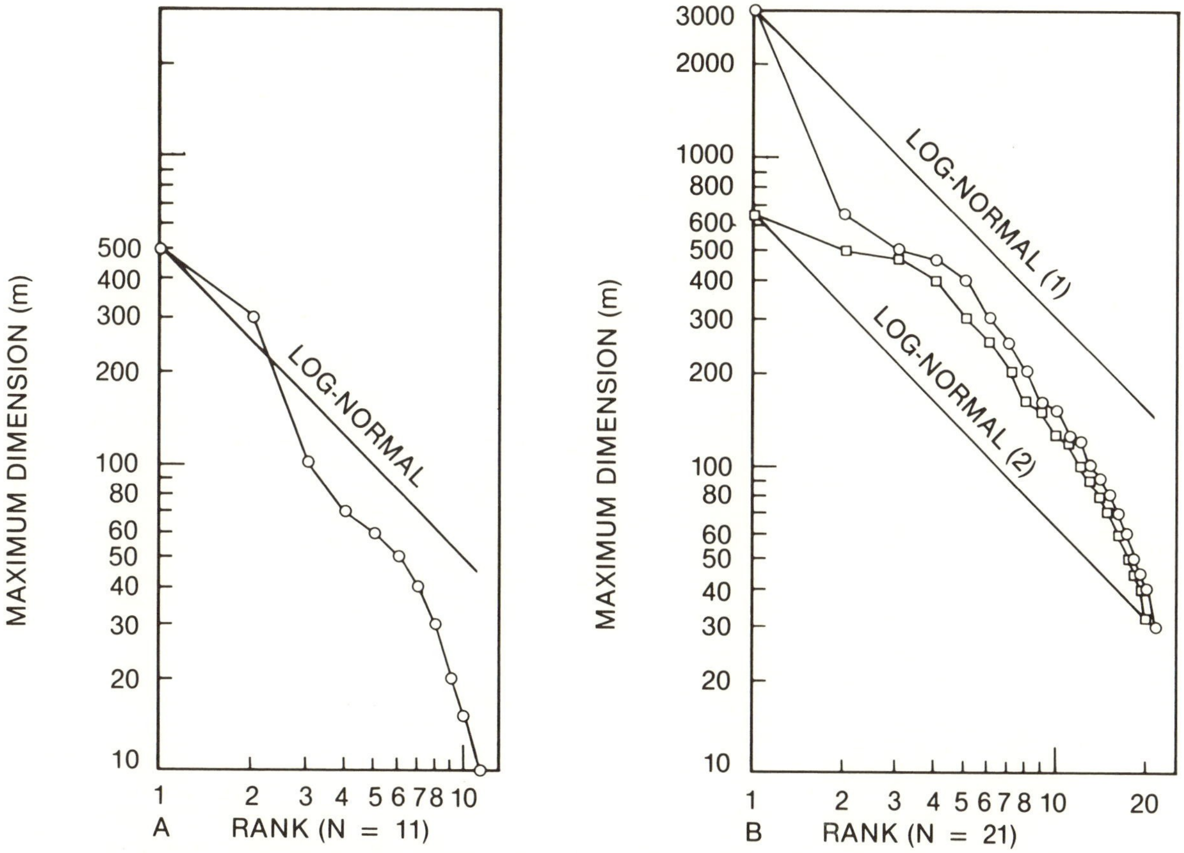

Figure 3. Rank-size distribution of Pastoral Neolithic sites: (A) Serengeti; (B) Central Rift Valley, Kenya ([1] includes all sites; [2] excludes one exceptionally large site).

and the Serengeti. The value of these data is impaired by many things, including differences in sampling strategy in the respective surveys, differences in sample size, assumptions in determining the size (maximum dimension) of sites, and the fact that the Kenya sample includes occurrences from the Rift margin that may fit the Transhumant Pastoralist model (Ambrose, n.d.b, 1980). Nevertheless, it seems clear that the curve for the Kenya Rift sites approaches the "rank-size rule" (settlement of rank r has a size equal to $1/r$ that of the largest settlement in the system), while the Serengeti curve shows a markedly "primate" distribution, meaning that large settlements are larger than expected and small ones smaller than expected (Johnson, 1977). The former curve suggests that settlement size may have varied stochastically, while the latter may imply management of a territory so as to exclude competition.

Although there are theoretical difficulties in the interpretation of major differences of some sort in settlement pattern, it is possible that such differences are related, at least in part, to the kinds of variance in water sources discussed earlier.

There are many archaeologically testable predictions that emerge from the models discussed above. They include most, if not all, of the predictions from Gifford's models (this volume), plus the following:

1. Sites in the Peripatetic Pastoralist model were occupied at different seasons and exhibit differences in resource utilization from time to time, while Transhumant Pastoralist sites were always occupied during the same season and do not exhibit much variation in resource utilization. (This prediction would, of course, differ if one assumed a Maasai-like pattern of transhumance for the Peripatetic Pastoralist model.)

2. The "functional size" (i.e., number of activ-

ities; Johnson, 1977) at Peripatetic Pastoralist sites is more or less invariant, but varies with site area in the Transhumant Pastoralist model.

3. Activity areas of Peripatetic Pastoralist sites vary in lateral position from occupation to occupation, but are more or less fixed over time at Transhumant Pastoralist sites.

4. Microstylistic features of pottery vary from occupation to occupation at Peripatetic Pastoralist sites but are more or less stable at Transhumant Pastoralist sites.

5. The spatial distribution of any given microstylistic tradition is broad and discontinuous in the Peripatetic Pastoralist model but occurs as a small, discrete area in the Transhumant Pastoralist model.

Another approach to testing the models would be to examine Pastoral Neolithic settlement behavior in regions where the environmental structure parallels that of either the Kenya Rift or the Serengeti. A particularly promising area in this connection is Lukenya Hill, overlooking the Athi-Kapiti Plain east of Nairobi—a region which in many respects compares closely with the Serengeti and where substantial research has been conducted on Pastoral Neolithic cultures (Bower et al., 1977). Although the data needed to determine whether or not the model applies at Lukenya Hill are not presently available, they could undoubtedly be obtained. Other important requirements for understanding the settlement behavior of Pastoral Neolithic cultures, regardless of the utility of the models described here, are data on plant foods (if any), on the aboriginal character of the Rift Valley's flora and fauna, and on paleoenvironments throughout the region. Evidently we still have a long way to go in seeking to understand the consequences, for settlement behavior, of early food production in East Africa.

24

Holocene Human Evolution in Southern Africa

ALICE J. HAUSMAN

Changes in economic systems can generate multi-level evolutionary consequences for human populations. Changes in economic conditions that affect the health environment will generate new patterns of individual growth and development. Changes in individual survival and reproductive success will effect new mortality and fertility profiles within a population. Shifts in population size and settlement patterns related to the requirements of new subsistence patterns can influence mating systems and patterns of gene exchange between populations, altering gene frequencies over time.

Recognition of these processes has generated new perspectives on the origins of modern human biological variation. Rather than seeking purely genetic explanations for observed patterns of variation,

I would like to thank Drs. Q. B. Hendey, P. V. Tobias, E. N. Keen, P. Beaumont, N. J. van der Merwe, and P. T. Robertshaw, and Mr. J. J. Oberholzer for access to material and facilities. I thank Dr. J. C. Vogel for radiocarbon dates, and Dr. G. P. Rightmire for guidance and support. Ms. L. Wiseman aided in the preparation of the text. This work was supported by the National Science Foundation, the Pitt Rivers Museum, Oxford, and Sigma Xi.

more attention is being paid to the interaction of cultural and biological processes and their influence on evolutionary trajectories of human populations.

This shift in perspective can be seen in the different ideas concerning the origins of biological variability among Khoisan peoples of southern Africa. Early ideas on Khoisan evolution relied upon scattered subfossil and fossil remains to support models of massive immigrations and complex processes of interbreeding, isolation, and separate development of different "strains" (Dreyer and Meiring, 1952; Tobias, 1955; Louw, 1960). Recent archaeological, ethnohistorical, and biomedical research has shown that there was not a great deal of external influence on either the cultural or biological diversification of the Khoisan. Modern Khoisan cultural variability is now viewed in terms of a local process of economic development involving the shift from hunting and gathering to nomadic pastoralism about 2,000 years ago. The nature of the economic changes and their impact on human biological systems make it likely that the biological variability of the Khoisan is related to this episode of cultural change.

The research presented here addresses the issue of Khoisan evolution through morphometric analysis of Khoisan crania from different geographic regions and time periods of southern African prehistory. When this sample of archaeologically derived remains is combined with the more famous subfossil remains from the Cape Province, South Africa, and the collection of historically documented skeletons, a skeletal record of the last 9,000 years in southern Africa is available. This record, spanning the critical time of the economic transition from hunting and gathering to food production, permits the testing of hypotheses of biological change suggested by models of cultural change during this time. In this manner, Khoisan variation may be better understood in terms of the population dynamics involved in the introduction and spread of pastoralism in southern Africa.

Background

There are two major population groupings in southern Africa: the Bantu-speaking negroid peo-

ples and the Khoisan. Bantu-speakers are generally characterized by medium height, dark skin, a broad nasal bridge, prognathic facial profile, and a long ovoid skull (Villiers, 1968; Tobias, 1978b). They practice a mixed farming and herding economy and have been associated with the Iron Age cultural era. Skeletons from the Iron Age sites of Phalaborwa, Bambandyanalo, Leopard's Kopje, and Ingombe Ilede have been firmly classified as negroid (Rightmire, 1970a; Rightmire and van der Merwe, 1976).

The Khoisan are characterized by lighter skin color, smaller stature, a flat facial profile with concave nasal bridge, "pentagonoid"-shaped skulls, and epicanthic eyefolds (Nurse and Jenkins, 1977: 15–16). In recent prehistory, the Khoisan inhabited most of South Africa, Namibia, and Botswana. They were the sole inhabitants of the Cape Province until the European settlement there in the 1600s.

Variation among the Khoisan has provoked much discussion, part of which implicates the introduction of food production as a major stimulus for diversity. The early settlers of southern Africa described at least two distinct groups of Khoisan (e.g., Thom, 1952–1958: 305ff.). The "Bushmen" (today known as San) were the small, pedomorphic hunter-gatherers who lived in small migratory bands. The "Hottentots" (Khoi) were the taller, more robust herders of sheep and cattle. They were distributed along the coastal regions of southern Africa and along some of the major rivers of the interior (Dreyer and Meiring, 1937; Humphreys and Maggs, 1970; Denbow et al., n.d.).

Later Stone Age archaeological materials in southern Africa are often attributed to ancestors of modern San. The Later Stone Age is distributed over most of southern Africa, its beginnings dated to about 20,000 years ago (Parkington, 1972; H. J. Deacon, 1976: 6). San morphology has been firmly linked with fossil remains such as the Fish Hoek cranium, which is at least 15,000 years old (Howells, 1973; Rightmire, 1974), and other subfossil remains from the last 10,000 years of southern African prehistory fall into modern ranges of San variation (Rightmire, 1970b, 1978b). The San are clearly long-term residents of southern Africa.

The origins of Khoi culture are not as clear. The earliest evidence of Khoi pastoralism comes from Die Kelders, a site on the Cape coast, where sheep remains have been radiometrically dated to 1950 B.P. (Schweitzer, 1974). Early ideas on the origins of the Khoi suggested that they migrated en masse from northeastern Africa (Dreyer and Meiring, 1952). This implied that they were biologically very different from their San neighbors and that their pastoral culture developed outside of southern Africa. New biomedical information has shown that although Khoi do demonstrate some serological and morphological differences from San, they are enough alike to be grouped together as Khoisan and together distinguished from their negroid neighbors (Rightmire, 1970b; Harpending and Jenkins, 1973; Nurse and Jenkins, 1977: 16; Tobias, 1978b). Growing archaeological information makes it increasingly apparent that although domesticated animals were introduced from elsewhere, Khoi pastoralism developed locally in southern Africa (H. J. Deacon, 1976: 9; H. J. Deacon et al., 1978; Robertshaw, n.d.; Klein, this volume).

The current model of the introduction and spread of pastoralism throughout southern Africa suggests that Khoi pastoralism had an important center of development in Botswana, where aboriginal Khoisan contacted immigrating pastoralists (Elphick, 1977: 11; Robertshaw, n.d.; Denbow et al., n.d.). The route by which Khoi pastoralism spread throughout southern Africa is somewhat debated, but it is likely that the western central corridor of Namibia was the major route (Stow, 1905: 236; Cooke, 1965; H. J. Deacon et al., 1978; Robertshaw, n.d.). Auxiliary routes have been suggested, but their confirmation awaits further data (Elphick, 1977: 17).

There are three main gaps of knowledge within this model: (1) the identity of the people from whom Khoi derived their pastoral economy; (2) the degree of impact on the biology of the populations involved; and (3) how pastoralism spread throughout southern Africa.

The most obvious candidate for the identity of the contacting pastoralists is the Iron Age people who entered Botswana and Namibia as part of the great Bantu-speakers expansion throughout Africa. They had cattle and sheep, knowledge of pottery manufacture, and their distribution in southern Africa is compatible with that of the Khoisan. Phillipson (1977c: 206, 223, 259) suggests that the

reason Iron Age peoples did not occupy the southwestern parts of southern Africa was because the dry desert environment could not support their mixed farming economy. Because Khoi pastoralists supplemented their diet with gathered wild foods, they were, presumably, able to expand into these areas and avoid competition with the Iron Age herders (Elphick, 1977: 22).

Several problems surround this suggestion. Mixed farming agriculture is currently practiced in the Kalahari today (Wilmsen, 1978). Linguistic anomalies, such as the non-Bantu words for cattle, sheep, and milk used by some Bantu-speaking herders, contribute to the confusion by suggesting that the Bantu-speakers got domestic animals from the Khoisan (Ehret, 1967).

At present, the most damaging argument against this idea is found in the distribution of known dates for pottery and sheep in southern Africa. The earliest dates for Khoi pastoralism are on the coast, and these pre-date the earliest known Iron Age dates by almost 1,000 years (Klein, 1979). Furthermore, analysis of Khoisan pottery styles indicates only minimal influence from Iron Age pottery-manufacturing techniques. Some Bantu-style elements have been recognized in Khoi pottery (Rudner, 1968; Phillipson, 1977c: 248); however, the distinctiveness of Cape coastal pottery suggests some independent development of pottery manufacture there (Sampson, 1974: 409; Robertshaw, n.d.). Cultural connections between Khoi pastoralism and other pastoralist cultures of different parts of Africa have been made, but few have suggested the actual movement of people from those areas (J. D. Clark, 1959; Robertshaw, n.d.). Although continued archaeological investigations reveal increasingly early dates for the Iron Age in Botswana and Namibia, the archaeological link between Later Stone Age Khoisan and the first immigrant pastoralists has yet to be made.

There is very little information about the nature of the contact situation. Continued archaeological investigations must be relied upon to provide better data. However, the maintenance of distinct Khoisan populations today indicates that complete assimilation of contacted populations did not occur. While modern groups are known to intermarry, there is not enough genetic evidence of admixture to suggest 2,000 years of free mating between aboriginal and foreign populations (Harpending and Jenkins, 1973).

The third area of disagreement concerns the way in which Khoi pastoralism spread through the Cape Province. Some suggest the movement of Khoi pastoralists from Botswana through Namibia and around the Cape coast (J. Deacon, 1972; Elphick, 1977: 17). The flood of immigrating pastoralists generated radical changes in patterns of resource exploitation and probably forced hunter-gatherers to move elsewhere (J. Deacon, 1972). An alternative model suggests that pastoralism spread by the diffusion of cultural traits, with only minimal population movement. Robertshaw (n.d.) notes the rapid spread of pottery throughout the southern Cape and suggests the simultaneous and independent invention of pottery manufacture. H. J. Deacon et al. (1978) cite the *in situ* evolutionary sequence of hunting and gathering to full-time pastoralism at Boomplaas Cave as evidence of the local nature of economic development. While competition between herders and hunters is envisioned by these authors, the assumption is of strictly local influences.

Current Research

Patterns of spatial and temporal variation within the skeletal record of this time period can test some of these ideas of the consequences of the adoption of food production in southern Africa. For example, if the initial split between hunters and herders occurred in Botswana, then inland populations should reflect some differentiation as the result either of differential interbreeding with contacted pastoralists or of local microevolution. Coastal populations should demonstrate different patterns of variation before and after the arrival of pastoralism in that area if the spread of the Khoi culture involved massive population movements to the coast.

A comparative structure of skeletal populations was formulated from the Holocene skeletal record in order to test these ideas. Five test groups were formed. The first and second are comprised of remains from the interior regions of southern Africa that are culturally recognizable as hunter-gath-

erers. Some individuals were known in life to be San; others have archaeological contexts characteristic of hunter-gatherers. Group 1 is comprised of thirty male specimens, and Group 2 has twenty-four females. Group 3 contains twenty-four individuals from interior regions that are recognized as pastoralist. Seventeen are historically known Khoi, and the rest were found in burials characteristic of the "Hottentots." There were not enough female Khoi remains to form a separate test group. The striped area of Figure 1 shows the general geographic distribution of these remains.

Documentation of historical individuals only securely identifies the cultural affiliation at time of death. Admixture among modern populations and the resettlement of people during recent historic times make some of these specimens unreliable. However, they have figured in previous studies of Khoisan variation and are considered to represent traditional groups of southern African populations (Stern and Singer, 1967; Rightmire, 1970b; Howells, 1973). Furthermore, the addition of the archaeological specimens enlarges the sample to include prehistoric populations.

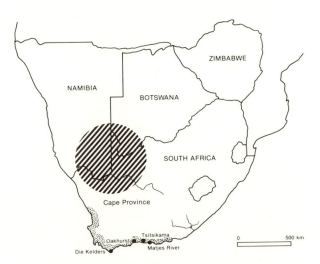

Figure 1. Distribution of skeletal remains and of archaeological sites mentioned in the text. The striped area marks the distribution of groups 1 (San hunter/gatherer males), 2 (San hunter/gatherer females) and 3 (Khoikhoi herder males). The stippled area shows the distribution of groups 4 (coastal males) and 5 (coastal females).

The fourth and fifth groups consist of males (34) and females (21) from coastal regions of the Cape Province. These specimens are derived from dune shell-midden Later Stone Age contexts and from rockshelters in shoreline cliff-faces. Radiometric dating by collagen extraction dates some of these individuals to between 200 and 4445 years B.P. (J. Vogel, pers. comm.). The distribution of these remains is represented by the dotted area of Figure 1.

A sixth group of seventeen South African Negro males was included to provide a non-Khoisan comparative sample.

The continuous cranial traits used in this study are listed and described elsewhere (Hausman, 1982, n.d.). The analytic procedure used is discriminant analysis. Distance relationships among groups can be evaluated in the reduced dimensional space generated by discriminant functions. Individual specimens can be reevaluated in terms of their relation to all the groups, and group overlap can be determined by the proportion of misclassified individuals. Ungrouped individuals can be classified into one of the groups according to the distance from the group centroid, or multivariate means. Two probability statements are provided to evaluate this classification procedure. P(G/X) is the posterior probability that the individual actually belongs to the group to which it is closest in the discriminant space. P (X/G) is the likelihood that a known member of a group would have the same distance from the centroid as the unknown individual who is placed into that group by the analysis. This latter probability is equivalent to a chi-squared test of the distance of the individual from the group centroid (Nie et al., 1975).

Results

The generalized D^2 distances between group centroids are listed in Table 1. The values were tested according to the procedure suggested by Sjovold (1975) and found to be significant at the .05 level.

Two patterns are clear in the distances among the five Khoisan groups. The general similarity between San and Khoi is confirmed in the greater distance from the South African Negro group to either Khoisan group than among Khoisan themselves. Yet, the significant distance between the inland male hunter-gatherers and the inland herder males supports the traditional San-Khoi division. The validity of this division for the archaeological specimens extends the distinction back to prehistoric times, supporting the idea of minimal influence

TABLE 1. **Generalized squared distances between group centroids. All distances are significant at the .05 probability level, using Sjovold's Formula 3 for F tests of significance (1975).**

	San Males	San Females	Khoi Males	Coastal Males	Coastal Females	South African Negro Males
San Males	0	11.13	4.97	3.30	9.83	26.71
San Females		0	12.07	11.36	6.72	31.04
Khoi Males			0	3.80	9.63	14.62
Coastal Males				0	5.72	24.63
Coastal Females					0	32.25
South African Negro Males						0

of interbreeding on the historic populations. This suggests that morphological differentiation may be associated with the arrival of pastoralism 2,000 years ago rather than with more recent processes of population admixture. More prehistoric remains from these inland regions will permit further testing of this suggestion.

A different pattern of variation occurring on the coast is indicated by the separation of the male and female coastal groups from their inland counterparts. If they were of the same biological population, one would expect complete overlap of the groups and no significant distance separating the centroids. The almost equal distance of the coastal male group could be the result of sampling error. However, if the group contained a mixture of San and Khoi individuals, greater overlap among these groups would be expected. The results of more indepth comparisons between coastal and inland males done elsewhere (Hausman, 1982, n.d.) showed that although the coastal males were more similar to the inland San males than to the Khoi, significant distances among the groups were maintained. This indicates that sampling error may be minimal and that the traditional San-Khoi distinction made for inland peoples may not apply to coastal inhabitants.

In order to test for population movement associated with the spread of pastoralism in the Cape, the subfossil remains from the Cape coast were separated into temporally distinct groups and compared individually with the test groups. The division was based on available stratigraphical information and radiocarbon dates.

The remains that pre-date the appearance of pastoralism on the coast include the following: two undisturbed burials, numbers 3 and 15, in the Wilton/Smithfield levels of the Oakhurst Rock Shelter (Goodwin, 1938); two disturbed graves from the Wilton levels of Oakhurst, numbers 2 and 8b; MRB 1, 2, and 3 from Level B of Matjes River Rock Shelter, dated to between 5000 and 7000 B.P. (Vogel, 1970; Protsch and Oberholzer, 1975); and W2, W3, W4, W7, and W8 from Level C of Matjes River, dated to 7000–9000 B.P. (Protsch and Oberholzer, 1975).

The remains that date to after the arrival of pastoralism on the coast include 7 individuals from the Tsitsikamma Forest area, and burials 1 and 13 from the upper levels of Oakhurst (Goodwin, 1938).

The group assignments and probability levels are listed in Table 2. Several issues should be clear before these results are interpreted. There are problems with the stratigraphical provenience of the burials. There are no radiocarbon dates for the Oakhurst burials, and some confusion in the Matjes River dates. Louw (1960) places Level C between 5000 and 7000 B.P. and notes that pottery was found with a Level B burial. Also, the association of the dated samples with the skeletons is very vague. In both sites, interment was intentional, so determining provenience is a tricky matter. The Tsitsikamma remains are even more problematical, for there is no record of which cave or stratigraphical level each individual came from (Turner, 1970). The individuals used here have figured in other studies of Khoisan evolution and are considered to be of relatively recent age (Wells, 1929).

A second problem concerns the condition of the remains. Much of the postcranial skeletal material has disappeared, making confirmation of the sex assignments given at the time of excavation impossible. Sex designations are accepted as given, although not given much weight in the interpretations. Finally, plaster reconstructions of the crania, particularly the Matjes River material, confound any final conclusion of group assignment due to cranial deformation (Rightmire, 1978b).

Oakhurst 3 and 15, the lower-level undisturbed graves, classify as inland San, although they are probably quite distant from the centroid, as is indicated by the low $P(X/G)$ value. The two disturbed graves, 2 and 8b, that are presumed to be fairly old are firmly classified as coastal individuals. Oakhurst 13, the individual found on the shell midden, and Oakhurst 1 from the upper level also classify as coastal males with strong probabilities of correct classification.

The Level B individuals of Matjes River associated with the shell-midden deposits fall well within the range of coastal males. W7 from the lower Level C approaches the coastal male centroid, while W2 and W4 classify as Khoi males. W3 and W8 classify as San males, but with only moderate significance.

TABLE 2. Classification results and probability statements for individual subfossil remains. P (X/G) is the equivalent of a chi-squared significance test of the distance; P (G/X) is the posterior probability of correct classification. The material from Oakhurst is housed in the University of Cape Town Medical School, and the material from Matjes River and Tsitsikamma are in the University of Witwatersrand Medical School, Johannesburg.

Individual	Sex	Assigned Group	P (X/G)	P (G/X)
Oakhurst:				
1	male	coastal male	.86	.75
2	male	coastal female	.66	.46
3	female	San male	.001	.90
8b	male	coastal male	.82	.57
13	female(?)	coastal male	.31	.66
15	female	San female	.05	.50
Matjes River:				
Level C:				
W2	female(?)	Khoi male	.35	.83
W3	male	San male	.27	.56
W4	male	Khoi male	.67	.65
W7	?	coastal male	.33	.49
W8	female(?)	San male	.39	.68
Level B:				
MRB1	male	coastal male	.40	.49
MRB2	male	coastal male	.89	.53
MRB3	female(?)	coastal male	.62	.64
Tsitsikamma:				
KO7	male	Khoi male	.15	.67
KO3	female	Khoi male	.45	.65
QO4	?	San female	.02	.82
Za1	male	Khoi male	.18	.42
Za2	female	San male	.49	.78
Za3	male	coastal male	.16	.80
PE1	female	coastal female	.85	.98

The Tsitsikamma remains are a varied group. Laing and Gear (1929) originally considered Za1 and Za2 to be "typical" Bushmen, while Za3 was more "primitive" and PE1 lay somewhere in between. In this comparison, Za1 classifies as a Khoi male, and the Za2 female falls near the San male centroid. The classification of Za3 as a coastal male confirms its difference from the other two individuals, but the only indication of a more primitive status is the low probability of its actual membership in this group. PE1 is firmly classified as a coastal female. Individuals KO7, KO3, and QO4 are presumably from Whitcher's Cave in the Tsitsikamma Forest, although this cave has not been relocated since FitzSimons' original excavations in the 1920s (Turner, 1970). KO3 and KO7 classify as Khoi males, although KO3 is catalogued as a female.

The mixture of Khoi and San classifications among the coastal remains may reflect some population movement associated with the spread of pastoralism. Since domesticated stock cannot migrate on their own, some population influx accompanying stock may be expected. However, the assignment of both pre-and post-pastoralism remains as "coastal" and the relatively small number of Khoi individuals indicate that no major population succession took place on the coast with the arrival of pastoralism.

Discussion

The analysis of the Holocene remains from southern Africa presents several points for discussion.

First, the traditional distinction made between San-Bushmen and Khoi-Hottentots is upheld for recent and prehistoric inland populations. The overall similarity of the groups reflects their close biological relationship and common origin. Furthermore, their mutual distance from the South African Negro group suggests there has been no major interbreeding between them. The most reasonable remaining explanation for the observed morphological/biological differences between Khoi and San is that the adoption of a new economic system by part of the aboriginal population stimu-lated changes in population parameters that contributed to the biological separation of the groups. By focusing on the known differences of the two ethnic groups, it is possible to outline the processes by which their differences could have arisen.

The shift from hunting and gathering to nomadic pastoralism involved relatively few changes. Khoi continued to rely on gathered foodstuffs and wild game when stock was low (Elphick, 1977: 31, 38). The only major dietary changes were the improved access to milk and the potential for a more constant food supply. Yet, these differences alone could have stimulated improved growth and health conditions for the Khoi and generated some of the morphological features that distinguish them from San.

The suggestion that milk enhanced the nutritional environment of the Khoisan is problematical, due to the high rate of lactose intolerance found among them (Jenkins et al., 1974; Nurse and Jenkins, 1974). Recently, however, Johnson et al. (1981) have argued that lactose intolerance and malabsorption of lactose are two related but separate phenotypes. Intolerance, manifested by diarrhea and stomach cramping, can be overcome with continued use of milk and milk products (Kretchmer, 1972). Fermentation of milk can also improve tolerance among adults, and ingestion of small quantities can habituate the individual toward tolerance. Malabsorption does limit the nutritional impact of milk, but reaction to lactose does not inhibit the absorption and use of the other nutritional elements of milk (Johnson et al., 1981). Vitamins, minerals, and other carbohydrates are available to the malabsorber who has improved tolerance. San have been noted to use the milk products of their Bantu-speaking pastoral neighbors whenever available (Nurse and Jenkins, 1974; Wilmsen, 1978). If the supply were more regular, as it would be for those who kept domesticated stock, it is possible that the added nutrients would improve the growth conditions and permit greater skeletal growth.

The sensitivity of San to seasonal food stress has been demonstrated in several studies. Truswell and Hansen (1976) concluded that seasonal or chronic caloric deficit during the growth period of San children accounts for the lower adult stature. Wilmsen (1978, in press b) noted that San who supplement their diets with domesticated foods are heavier than more traditional San and do not regulate their births to specific seasons of the year. Tobias (1975) noted a secular trend of increased height among San who had adopted an agricultural lifestyle. Thus, San have been shown to be very sensitive to the marked seasonality of their food resources and quick to respond to any improvement in the constancy of food supply.

The greater stature of the Khoi (Wells, 1960) can easily be seen as a response to improved nutritional conditions. Some aspects of cranial morphology may also be related to differential growth between Khoi and San. Stern and Singer (1967) note size as a major distinguishing feature between Khoi and San skulls. Rightmire (1970b) noted certain features of facial rugosity distinguishing Khoi and San crania, and this too could be related to growth differences. Closer inspection of the variables that distinguish Khoi and San in the study presented here may reveal additional growth-related differences.

Experimental studies have shown that some dimensions of the cranium are more sensitive to malnutrition than others (Pucciarelli, 1980; Corruccini and Whitley, 1981). Malnourished individuals tend to be shorter and narrower in certain facial lengths and maxillary breadths. Preliminary investigation of some of these dimensions among the Khoisan crania shows that San are smaller than Khoi (Hausman, 1982). Further investigation of these nutritionally related variables is required, but growth-related differences are indicated.

Subsistence changes could also be responsible for some of the populational differences between Khoi and San. Khoi tribes were much larger than San bands. This size difference could be related to the labor needs of the pastoral economy and the ability to support greater numbers of people. However, population growth may have been stimulated by improved nutritional conditions.

Demographic studies on the San indicate that nutrition does play a role in population regulation. N. Howell (1979: 190–211) suggests that a critical fat level is affecting birth spacing in San populations. Wilmsen's comparative study provides further support for the role of nutrition in affecting San population parameters (1978, in press b). He

found that San women who supplemented their diets with domesticated foods were heavier and had higher levels of serum cholesterol and gonadal steroids than San women who relied solely on traditional bush foods (Van der Walt et al., 1977; Wilmsen, 1978, in press b).

Lee (1979: 328), on the other hand, believes that breast-feeding is a more important factor in birth spacing. Konner and Worthman (1980) provide data showing that frequency of breast-feeding is the critical aspect of lactation that prolongs postpartum amenorrhea. It is likely that the most effective force in regulating these populations is the dynamic between the energy cost of breast-feeding, the constancy of prolactin secretion, and the slow restoration of critical fat levels among San women due to their dietary regimen. Amelioration of the nutritional environment could speed fat recovery and reduce the spacing between births. Changed fertility profiles, such as have been noted by Wilmsen among modern San, could contribute to population growth and larger population sizes.

Changes in population parameters can influence marriage systems and marriage distances, that is, the geographic distance between the residences of prospective spouses (Wobst, 1974; Hammel et al., 1979). Since these features directly influence the role of drift and gene flow, new systems generate opportunities for change in gene frequencies and genetic differentiation among sympatric populations (Schull, 1972; Spuhler, 1972).

The differences between San and Khoi marriage and kinship systems could have contributed to the biological differentiation of the groups. The large distances between place of birth and residence and the high mobility of the San influence the low degree of endogamy that has been noted for the Kalahari populations (Harpending and Jenkins, 1973; Harpending, 1976). However, since most marriages occur within a specified territory (M. Wilson, 1969), there is some variation among geographically separate groups. Within broad geographic boundaries, San are fairly homogeneous, but some north-south clinal variation occurs between territories (Harpending, 1976; Nurse and Jenkins, 1977: 36).

Historic records indicate that Khoi were organized into tribes made up of exogamous patrilineal clans (M. Wilson, 1969: 59; Elphick, 1977: 44). While settlements varied in size and composition, marriage partners often resided in the same tribal territory or cluster of villages (Theal, 1882: 76; Schapera and Farrington, 1933: vii–viii, 23; Elphick, 1977: 44). Cross-cousin marriages were allowed, and this system can increase the level of inbreeding and the level of homozygosity within a population (Schull, 1972; Spuhler, 1972). It is difficult to predict the effects of this marriage system on the intrapopulation variation among Khoi, because there are so few living today. However, if the amount of inbreeding among social groups is related to nucleation, as Yellen and Harpending suggest (1972), then it is possible that Khoi were more nucleated than the San. Increased nucleation could strengthen social boundaries between groups and social bonds within groups and contribute to the separation of Khoi pastoralists from San hunter-gatherers. This separation would inhibit interbreeding between the groups and encourage genetic separation.

Competition between domesticated herds and wild game for sparse Kalahari grasses would add to this separation of the economically different groups. Unfriendly encounters between San and Khoi are noted in historical records (e.g., Thom, 1952–1958: 313).

The second issue to which the Cape skeletons draw attention is the possibility that a biologically distinct San population occupied the coast both before and after the arrival of pastoralism. This idea of a separate coastal population is not new, for "Strandlopers" were often distinguished by early settlers and scholars (Shrubsall, 1907; FitzSimons, 1926; Thom, 1952–1958). Support for this idea is derived from a variety of sources other than craniometrics. Linguistic data suggest tremendous variation among San throughout southern Africa. The large number of dialects indicates a long period of settlement and enough separation of the groups to generate this variability (E. O. J. Westphal, 1963). If there was enough time for linguistic divergence, biological differentiation may also have been possible. As noted above, geographic variation in certain allelic frequencies currently distinguishes San populations, for example, north-south gradients of the A_1 and D_1 alleles (Nurse and Jenkins, 1977: 36, 51).

Patterns of artifact variation also support differences between geographically distant populations. Rudner (1968) characterizes a particular coastal Strandlooper pottery type, and Robertshaw (n.d.) also distinguishes coastal ware from inland ware. Sampson (1974: 409) suggests that the simple scraper technology of the coastal midden sites represents a different cultural tradition from that of the interior. Many deny the distinctiveness of coastal remains, claiming that they merely represent the coastal phase of migrations between the mountains and the coast of the resident hunter-gatherers (Parkington, 1972, 1980). However, there is growing evidence that year-round occupation of the coast was possible (Buchanan et al., 1978). Furthermore, there is no clear relationship between the occupants of the coastal plains and those who lived in the Karoo and the Kalahari beyond the mountains. Thus, it is quite possible that a somewhat biologically and culturally different population of San lived on the coast of southern Africa during the later Holocene.

The third issue raised by the Cape crania is the lack of great morphological change on the coast before and after the arrival of pastoralism there. There may have been some overall increase in numbers of people living on the coast, as evidenced by the increased exploitation of marine resources (Avery, 1975) and the exploitation of new resources in other ecozones (J. Deacon, 1978). The small number of remains studied here may not be sufficient to draw firm conclusions. However, the persistence of a distinct morphological pattern on the coast during the transition from hunting and gathering to pastoralism strongly suggests that complete population succession did not occur.

This phenomenon may indicate that the development of pastoralism on the coast occurred differently from that in inland areas. The abundance and flexibility of coastal resources may not have generated the competitive boundaries between herders and non-herders. Thus, forces that may have stimulated genetic differentiation among inland populations may not have occurred on the coast. Acceptance of pastoralism by resident hunter-gatherers may not have required major shifts in subsistence; likewise, immigrant herders could exploit marine resources in the same manner as the aboriginal inhabitants. Thus, economic practices among hunters and herders could have been very similar, making cultural assimilation of local inhabitants easy. Also, the lack of dietary differences between the groups would mean that the growth-related differences noted for inland groups should not be evident in coastal groups. Although more work is needed here, this pattern has been suggested in the analyses above. Thus, while some population movement into coastal regions is evidenced by the presence of recognizably Khoi individuals there, the persistence of the distinctive coastal morphology into pastoralist times indicates no radical population succession.

Summary

Geographic and temporal patterns of variation among Khoisan of the Holocene indicate that the introduction of pastoralism played an important role in generating observed differences among modern populations. Much more work is needed to determine the exact process of differentiation, but the existing differences point to areas of inquiry. By focusing on known events of culture change and on the interaction between biological and cultural processes, a more dynamic model of Khoisan evolution can be presented.

25

Early Food-Production in Central and Southern Africa

DAVID W. PHILLIPSON

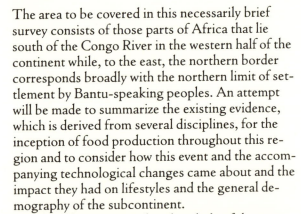

The area to be covered in this necessarily brief survey consists of those parts of Africa that lie south of the Congo River in the western half of the continent while, to the east, the northern border corresponds broadly with the northern limit of settlement by Bantu-speaking peoples. An attempt will be made to summarize the existing evidence, which is derived from several disciplines, for the inception of food production throughout this region and to consider how this event and the accompanying technological changes came about and the impact they had on lifestyles and the general demography of the subcontinent.

It will be apparent that the whole of the area here discussed, except the extreme south and southwest, has been occupied within the recent past by people speaking languages of the closely interrelated Bantu type. It has for some time been generally believed that there is a demonstrable correlation between the local advent of food production and the spread of people speaking Bantu lan-

This chapter was written in 1979; additional data that have come to light since are not reflected here.

guages. This view will be discussed and evaluated below.

The term *advent* of food production is used advisedly. There can be little reasonable doubt from the steadily growing body of archaeological evidence that techniques of food production were introduced from elsewhere into the area described in this chapter. Such a conclusion receives some support from linguistic studies and from botanical and faunal investigations. The major domestic animals of the subcontinent in historical times have been cattle, sheep, and goats: for none of these is a local wild ancestor attested. Likewise, the indigenous food crops grown in Africa south of the equator prior to the introduction of New World species seem, mostly if not exclusively, to have been introduced from beyond the Indian Ocean or to have been of types whose wild progenitors are found, and which appear first to have been brought under cultivation, in the savanna country that lies to the north of the equatorial forest.

The Archaeology

It is first of all necessary to summarize the archaeological sequence for the period that saw the local inception of food production. Domestic animals and cultivated crops are, in the Bantu-speaking regions of this part of Africa, first attested in Early Iron Age contexts dated to the first millennium A.D. In the extreme south, beyond the limits of Bantu settlement, the earliest remains of domestic animals are associated with sites of stone–tool-using peoples dating to the earliest centuries of the Christian era. Prior to this, it seems that virtually the whole of the area here described was occupied by hunter/gatherers who practiced an aceramic, stone-tool technology. The only firmly attested exception to this generalization was in the area immediately to the south of the lower Congo where, during the last few centuries B.C., a pre-metallurgical industry of ground- and chipped-stone artifacts—the so-called "Leopoldian Neolithic" (De Maret et al., 1977)—is associated with pottery but, as yet, not with any firm evidence for food production.

The present writer has recently published a detailed synthesis (Phillipson, 1977c) of the archaeological and linguistic evidence for the spread of the Early Iron Age industrial complex in Bantu-speaking Africa, so only a brief summary need be presented here.

Archaeologically, the most striking features of the earliest Iron Age manifestations throughout the area here considered are their very marked similarity and near-contemporaneous occurrence. The earliest evidence for Iron Age occupation comes from the interlacustrine region of East Africa. In the Haya country of Tanzania, on the western side of Lake Victoria, extensive settlements and iron-smelting sites such as Katuruka (Schmidt, 1978) certainly date to the very beginning of the Christian era and may be several centuries older yet. The characteristic pottery of these sites approximates to that known elsewhere as Urewe ware, which is of widespread distribution from eastern Zaire to southwestern Kenya. In the latter area its appearance around the Winam (Kavirondo) Gulf may have been somewhat later than the corresponding event further to the west (Soper, 1969).

So far there is only indirect evidence that the makers of Urewe ware practiced any form of food production. Bones of domestic cattle recovered from rockshelter sites near the northern shore of the Winam Gulf (Gabel, 1969) may be associated with an Early Iron Age presence, but the recorded stratigraphic data are inadequate to demonstrate their precise associations or date. Sediment cores raised from the bed of Lake Victoria have revealed pollen spectra that suggest that a pronounced reduction in forest vegetation took place around the middle of the last millennium B.C. This could, of course, be linked with extensive deforestation caused by charcoal-burning for iron-smelting rather than by agricultural clearance. There is as yet no convincing evidence that the stone–tool-using pastoralists of the Rift Valley highlands ever penetrated so far to the west as the country bordering on Lake Victoria. Indeed, the Rift Valley territory of the pastoralists is remarkable for the near-total lack of any Early Iron Age material in the many archaeological assemblages of the relevant period that have now been investigated. It may be surmised that the relatively arid pastoralist territory was unsuited to settlement by the Early Iron Age folk and/or that the well-established pastoralist population was able effectively to discourage incursion by the Early Iron Age peoples who settled in the better-watered lands both to the west and to the east.

In the subsequent spread of the Early Iron Age industrial complex into the more southerly parts of Africa two distinct streams may be recognized. Of these, the eastern stream seems clearly to have been derived from the Urewe settlements of the interlacustrine region, while the western stream apparently combined Urewe-derived elements with local traits of the western Zaire/northern Angola region.

The eastern stream may be shown to have spread, by about the second century A.D., to the coastal regions of southeastern Kenya and to adjacent parts of northeastern Tanzania, where it is represented by sites yielding the highly characteristic type of pottery known as Kwale ware (Soper, 1967a, 1967b). Early Iron Age settlement seems here to have been restricted to the relatively well-watered hilly country where the villages of the region's present Bantu-speaking mixed-farming communities are still concentrated. Early Iron Age penetration further inland, to the eastern highlands of Kenya, appears to have taken place at a later date and from an easterly direction. It is known that cattle and small stock were being herded, and cereals possibly cultivated, in the North Pare and adjacent hill areas of eastern Kenya and Tanzania by the close of the first millennium A.D. (Odner, 1971a).

During the fourth century A.D., there is attested an extremely rapid dispersal of Early Iron Age culture attributed to the eastern stream through a wide area extending south through Malawi, eastern Zambia, and Zimbabwe into the eastern Transvaal and Swaziland (Phillipson, 1975). Two distinct manifestations may be recognized in the eastern stream, one of which is restricted to the coastal lowlands while the other has a more general distribution inland. The coastal variant clearly sprang from the Kwale-ware settlements of East Africa and penetrated as far to the south as Tzaneen, in the eastern Transvaal, and the lowlands of northernmost Natal. More than 2,400 km appear to have been covered in only two centuries. Known

sites of the eastern stream are far more numerous in the inland regions and here, as will be shown below, some data are also forthcoming concerning the food-producing economy of their inhabitants.

The archaeology of the western stream areas has been much less intensively investigated, being well known only in the valley of the upper Lualaba and in central Zambia, where its inception is not demonstrable before the fifth century A.D. In the former area, furthermore, our knowledge is virtually restricted to excavated cemetery sites such as Sanga (Nenquin, 1963; De Maret, 1977) and Katoto (Hiernaux et al., 1973). Despite the apparently late advent of the Early Iron Age in central Zambia (Phillipson, 1968, 1972), there are some indications both from northern Angola and from the valley of the upper Zambezi that this material may belong to a relatively late phase in the development of the western stream. An early date—perhaps in the last century B.C. or thereabouts—for the initial southward spread of the western stream would, as will be shown below, provide an excellent fit with what is currently known about the earliest beginnings of pastoralism in southwesternmost Africa, and with certain linguistic evidence.

The sites in the southern and western Transvaal and in Natal that form the southernmost manifestations of the Early Iron Age industrial complex have only recently been investigated (e.g., Maggs and Michael, 1975; Mason, 1974a). The earliest sites probably belong to the fourth century A.D. It seems probable that their affinities will prove to be with the western rather than with the eastern stream.

Detailed evidence for the food-producing economies of the Early Iron Age communities, with information relating to the plant and animal species on which they were based, has only rarely been recovered. A settlement pattern based on large semipermanent villages of up to several hectares in extent in areas that lack concentrated non-seasonal potential food-resources such as fish is, of course, strongly suggestive of an economy based to a substantial extent on some sort of food production. While the presence of iron hoes and of numerous grindstones may be indicative of agricultural practices, conclusive proof of this in the form of specifically identifiable remains of the cultigens and do-

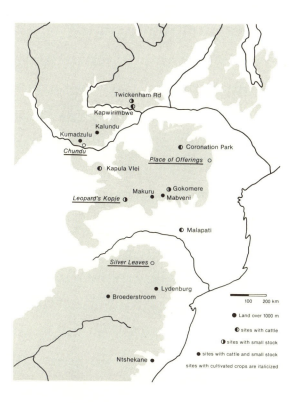

Figure 1. Sites of the Early Iron Age industrial complex that have yielded remains of cultivated plants and/or domestic animals.

Cultivated plants
> Chundu (J. O. Vogel, 1969)
> Leopard's Kopje (Huffman, 1971, 1974)
> "Place of Offerings" (Summers, 1958)
> Silver Leaves (Klapwijk, 1974)

Sheep/goats
> Broederstroom (Mason, 1974a)
> Gokomere (Robinson, 1963)
> Kalundu (Fagan, 1967)
> Kumadzulo (J. O. Vogel, 1971)
> Leopard's Kopje (Huffman, 1971, 1974)
> Lydenburg (Evers, 1975)
> Mabveni (Huffman, 1975)
> Makuru (Huffman, 1973)
> Ntshekane (Maggs and Michael, 1975)
> Twickenham Road (Phillipson, 1970)

Cattle
> Broederstroom (Mason, 1974a)
> Coronation Park (Huffman, 1973)
> Lydenburg (Evers, 1975)
> Kalundu (Fagan, 1967)
> Kapula Vlei (Huffman, 1973)
> Kapwirimbwe (Phillipson, 1968)
> Kumadzulo (J. O. Vogel, 1971)
> Mabveni (Huffman, 1975)
> Makuru (Huffman, 1973)
> Malapati (Huffman, 1973)
> Ntshekane (Maggs and Michael, 1975)

mesticates that were exploited has been recovered from disappointingly few sites.

Virtually all the detailed information so far available concerning the Early Iron Age food-producing economy of Bantu Africa comes from Zambia, Zimbabwe, and South Africa. The cultivated crops for which there is detailed evidence comprise sorghum, cowpeas (*Vigna cf. unguiculata*), and unidentified squash and beans (Fig. 1). To date, all these occurrences are on sites that are attributed to the eastern stream. It is unfortunate that more detailed botanical descriptions of this material are not yet available, for until they are, no comparisons can be made with the crops that were grown in more northerly regions that would throw light on the manner in which their cultivation was begun in southcentral Africa.

The evidence for domestic livestock is some-what more comprehensive. Cattle may at first have been largely restricted to the areas settled by the western stream of the Early Iron Age in southcentral Zambia, parts of the Transvaal, and Natal and, presumably—although tangible evidence for this is so far lacking—to the regions further to the west and northwest. They appear to have been rare or absent in other, eastern, stream areas until around the seventh or eighth century A.D. Small stock were, in contrast, common in the territory of both the eastern and the western streams, on sites that cover the whole period of the Early Iron Age in their respective regions.

Throughout the duration of the Early Iron Age the hunting of wild animals maintained considerable economic importance. Iron arrowheads and spearpoints (which need not, of course, have been used exclusively for hunting) have been recovered from many sites and are significantly more common than hoes. Early Iron Age sites from which bones of wild animals have been recovered are appreciably more numerous than those that have yielded remains of domestic stock. At the western stream site of Kalundu in southern Zambia (Fagan, 1967: 69ff.), the faunal remains from successive layers show a gradual replacement of wild by domestic species. The wild animals represented in Early Iron Age faunal assemblages include wildebeest and buffalo, as well as many of the lesser antelope. Fish bones are rarely preserved but are recorded from Early Iron Age contexts in Malawi, notably at Nkope (Robinson, 1970).

The Linguistic Evidence

In order that maximum use may be made of the evidence afforded by linguistic studies, it is necessary to evaluate the possibility of a correlation between the archaeological picture described above and the processes of dispersal of the Bantu languages. The geographical distribution of the Early Iron Age industrial complex is almost identical with the area occupied in more recent times by peoples speaking languages of the closely interrelated Bantu type; and this observation has lent support to the widely held belief that this complex represents the archaeological manifestation of an initial southward spread of the Bantu-speakers. The Bantu languages, which are today spoken by more than 130 million people spread over an area of nearly nine million square kilometers, show a remarkable degree of inter-comprehensibility; and there can be no reasonable doubt that they have attained their present wide distribution as a result of dispersal from a common localized ancestral language within the comparatively recent past—certainly within the last 3,000 or 4,000 years. Linguists are virtually unanimous in the belief that this ancestral Bantu language was spoken close to the northwestern border of the present Bantu-speaking area, in what is now Cameroon and eastern Nigeria (B. Heine, 1979).

To the south and east of the equatorial forest, in the areas where the Early Iron Age complex is attested in the archaeological record, the modern Bantu languages fall into two major groups (Dalby, 1975a; Heine et al., 1977). These have been designated the Western Highland group, which is centered in Angola and northern Namibia, and the Eastern Highland group, which covers almost all the eastern half of the subcontinent. Of these two groups, the Western Highland languages show appreciably more internal diversity than do their Eastern Highland counterparts, and the dispersal of the Eastern Highland group may thus be assumed to have been significantly later in date than that of the Western Highland group. The boundary between these two language groups does not, it must be emphasized, coincide with that between the eastern and western streams of the Early Iron Age; but the general picture that emerges from linguistic studies is nevertheless strikingly similar in several ways to that deduced from the archaeological evidence.

The consensus of linguistic opinion suggests that the dispersal of the Bantu languages from their northwestern homeland took roughly the following course. From the Cameroon area, expansion initially took place both eastward along the northern fringes of the equatorial forest toward the interlacustrine region and southward to the country to the north of the Congo River. In this latter area a second dispersal took place that gave rise to the Western Highland languages. Subsequently, and from a westerly source, the Eastern Highland languages were dispersed—most probably from somewhere in the vicinity of the Zambia/Shaba Copperbelt. It is from this third dispersal that virtually all the Bantu languages spoken today in the eastern half of the subcontinent are derived. The Western Highland Bantu languages may have developed in an Early Iron Age context, eventually giving rise to the Eastern Highland languages whose dispersal may have coincided with the advent of the later Iron Age in the eastern regions (Phillipson, 1977c: 226). This assumption involves acceptance of the view that there must have been a previous, Early Iron Age, Bantu speech in eastern Africa, spoken by the bearers of the eastern stream industries and derived from the northwest via the interlacustrine region.

There is thus a remarkably close fit between the archaeological picture of the spread of Iron Age industries and that independently derived from linguistic data for dispersal of the Bantu languages. This will have a major bearing on the overall picture that is now emerging of the inception of food production in Bantu Africa; meanwhile, it allows a more detailed examination of the archaeological and linguistic evidence.

Pre-Iron Age Food-Production?

Throughout the area of its distribution the Early Iron Age industrial complex makes a pronounced contrast with the industries that preceded it. Not only was a microlithic technology replaced by a metallurgical one and techniques of food production introduced to areas where they had apparently been previously unknown, but the Early Iron Age also saw the first pottery and, it appears, the first settled village life in at least the greater part of the area under review.

Two problems here require consideration before we turn to a discussion of the processes by which food production was begun in this part of Africa. The first is to ascertain whether there is in fact any possible indication in this region for any form of pre-Iron Age food-production, and the second is to examine the evidence for interaction between the earliest farmers and their predecessors.

The enormous rapidity of the initial dispersal of the Early Iron Age industries into subequatorial Africa and the apparent completeness of the contrast between their bearers and the preexisting populations have led several scholars to inquire whether the Early Iron Age folk were indeed the first food-producers to inhabit these regions. Several candidates have been proposed for this pre-Iron Age farming status, but in no case is the evidence conclusive or even convincing. It has been suggested that similarities between stone bowls in Namibia and those in East Africa could indicate an early southwestward penetration of pre-Iron Age pastoralists (J. D. Clark, 1964a), but the two groups are not demonstrably contemporary nor are the associated artifacts comparable. Further to the east, comparisons have been proposed between some East African pottery types and certain wares from Malawi and Natal: these have been interpreted as representing possible pre-Iron Age pastoral influences, but subsequent clarification of the relevant chronologies effectively disproves this possibility. Bambata ware in Zimbabwe has also been proposed as the archaeological manifestation of a pre-Iron Age food-producing society (cf. Garlake, 1979), but it cannot in fact be demonstrated that this material is not contemporary with the local Early Iron Age. (Huffman [1978] has recently reapplied the term *Bambata ware* to certain Early Iron Age material in what appears to be an inadequately defined extension of the original usage.) It also cannot be shown that Bambata ware, as originally defined, was not the work of hunter/gatherers.

The other argument that has been propounded in favor of pre-Iron Age food-production in this part of Africa is a linguistic one. Ehret (1974a) has drawn attention to the presence in widely distributed recent Bantu languages of vocabulary, relating inter alia to food production, that appears to be derived from languages of the Central Sudanic type now spoken near the northeastern fringes of the equatorial forest. He has argued that these words indicate that Central Sudanic-speaking food-producers must have been present in these southerly latitudes before the arrival of Bantu-speaking people. It may, however, be argued with at least equal plausibility that the Sudanic loanwords were borrowed into Bantu far to the north, near the present Central Sudanic-speaking areas, and that they were subsequently transmitted southward with the Bantu speech in which they had become incorporated.

It may be concluded that the only part of the Bantu-speaking territory here considered where there is any convincing evidence, either archeological or linguistic, for the possible practice of food production prior to the advent of the Iron Age is lower Zaire. Here, as noted above, the so-called "Leopoldian Neolithic" industry dates from the last few centuries B.C. and may (although it must be emphasized that the evidence for this remains entirely circumstantial) have been based upon some form of food production.

The Coming of the Iron Age

Despite the novelty of the Iron Age lifestyle, economy, and technology, it is clear that these did not rapidly or totally replace those of the indigenous populations. In several areas, indeed, there is plentiful evidence both from archaeology and from oral tradition for the survival of a microlithic technology long after the appearance of metallurgy. In some parts of southcentral Africa this continued until only two or three centuries ago, although the degree of this survival obviously varied according to the intensity of Early Iron Age settlement in the various areas. The best-studied of these very late microlithic industries are those of northern and eastern Zambia, where detailed analyses of industrial successions covering the last three millennia, such as those from Nakapapula, Thandwe, and Makwe (Phillipson, 1969; 1976b: 186–196), indicate no significant discernible typological changes such as would be expected had there been any major change in the hunter/gatherer economy and lifestyle of the stone–tool-makers as a result of cultural contact with their Iron Age contemporaries. That some form of contact did in fact take place between the indigenes and the immigrant food-producers is indicated by the presence in nearly all the microlithic assemblages of this period of varying numbers of sherds of characteristic Early Iron Age pottery. The steady continuation of the microlithic industries, showing only gradual typological development following trends that were already apparent before any contact had been established with the Early Iron Age folk, suggests that such contact between the two groups was probably minimal. By contrast, in areas where Early Iron Age settlement at an early date was relatively dense, there seems to have been fairly rapid displacement of the hunter/gatherer populations. Such appears to have been the situation in much of southern Zambia, for example.

The most satisfactory interpretation of the interactions that must undoubtedly have taken place between the stone–tool-using hunter/gatherers and the Iron Age food-producers is that of a temporary client relationship such as has been recorded in recent times both in southern Africa and further to the north. The upper Zambezi valley has within the last few decades provided a clear illustration of the processes involved. It must be admitted that virtually all our present evidence for interaction between Early Iron Age peoples and indigenous populations comes from the territory of the eastern stream of the Early Iron Age; we have as yet no reliable means of knowing whether the processes were similar in western stream-areas.

The final absorption of the stone–tool-using hunting peoples in southcentral Africa may be attributed to the expanding population of the later Iron Age, with its increased emphasis on the herding of domestic animals, notably cattle. With the passage of time, these factors would have restricted the ability of the stone–tool-users to follow their traditional lifestyle. Client relationships would have become more permanent, resulting in disruption of the social and economic distinctions between the two populations. This in turn would have brought about the absorption of the last of the stone–tool-using hunter/gatherers into the societies of the Iron Age farmers.

From the data that have been summarized above, it will be seen that there can be little doubt that the Early Iron Age industrial complex was introduced into subequatorial Africa as a result of a substantial and rapid movement of population. The whole culture represented on sites of that complex can be shown to be foreign to the area of its distribution, and most of its constituent traits may be traced archaeologically to a source in the northern savanna. The large number of available radiocarbon dates is concordant with this hypothesis; and the consensus interpretation of Bantu linguistic data also lends it a considerable degree of support.

It is much more difficult to put forward a plausible explanation of how and why this population movement took place. Although the numbers of people involved need not have been at all large, they were evidently sufficient to sustain the migrants' self-sufficient lifestyle and technology, and it would also seem reasonable to suppose that whole family groups must have been involved.

Another largely unexplained factor is the great speed that the radiocarbon dates indicate for the main southward expansion of the Early Iron Age migrants. On the scale here proposed and over the huge and sparsely populated area that was involved, population pressure clearly cannot have been a major contributing factor. (It may, however, plausibly be put forward as at least a partial explanation for the initial expansion of Bantu speakers southward and eastward from Cameroon.) "Superior" metallurgical technology and the high status accorded to agriculture may have facilitated the expansion but are inadequate as factors of prime motivation. Food production in the African southern savanna is not a strikingly superior means of exploitation.

It is useful to speculate on the reasons why the Early Iron Age expansion, which proceeded with such remarkable rapidity as far to the south as the Transvaal and Natal, was there arrested so abruptly. Although the Early Iron Age site distribution remains very imperfectly known, especially in the west, it is nevertheless reasonably clear that its southern limit broadly coincides with the northern edge of the southwest African zone of desert vegetation and that of the long-grass veld of the Orange Free State. On the eastern side of the continent the southernmost extent of the Early Iron Age complex is restricted to the west by the Drakensberg and to the south by the Cape winter-rainfall zone. Recent societies have demonstrated that this border presents no barrier to pastoralist communities: it is, however, an effective southern limit for the cultivation of traditional African cereals and other food crops. It seems reasonable to suppose, therefore, that agricultural potential was a major limiting factor in the initial phases of Iron Age expansion. It was not until the development of the more pastorally oriented societies of the later Iron Age that further southward expansion took place, resulting in settlement by Bantu-speaking peoples of such marginal lands as those of the Orange Free State and parts of Namibia.

During the first millennium A.D., however, stone–tool-using people of more southerly latitudes are now known to have obtained domestic sheep and, probably, cattle (fig. 2). Domestic animal bones make their appearance on sites in the southwestern Cape dated to around the second century A.D.—broadly contemporary with the earliest local occurrence of pottery (Schweitzer, 1974) (see also Klein, this volume—Eds.). The characteristic Cape coastal pottery seems, however, to have been produced (or at least used) by many communities who did not have access to domestic stock and who continued their traditional reliance

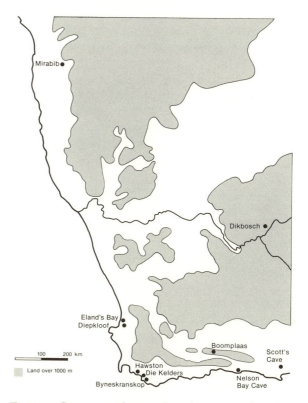

Figure 2. Sites in southern and southwestern Africa that have yielded remains of domestic sheep in contexts dated to the first millennium A.D.

Boomplaas (Deacon et al., 1978)
Byneskranskop (Schweitzer and Wilson, 1978; Schweitzer, 1979)
Die Kelders (Schweitzer, 1974)
Dikbosch (Humphreys, 1974)
Diepkloof (Parkington, n.d.)
Eland's Bay (Parkington, n.d.)
Hawston (Avery, 1975)
Mirabib (Sandelowsky et al., 1979)
Nelson Bay Cave (Klein, 1977)
Scott's Cave (Klein and Scott, 1974)

on wild vegetable foods, shellfish-collecting, fishing, and hunting.

Recent archaeological research in the southwestern Cape has revealed a complicated pattern of local seasonal resource-exploitation. At least in some areas, such as the west coast north of the Cape of Good Hope, this seems to have involved movement of population between, on the one hand, the inland regions where wild vegetable foods were plentiful during the summer and where the diet could then readily be supplemented by the meat of small animals and, on the other hand, the caves and open sites near the coast where shellfish and fish were exploited during the winter (Parkington, 1972). This appears to have been the main regimen of life during the centuries that preceded the advent of food production. It also seems to be a lifestyle that continued into relatively recent centuries without discernible modification.

The extent to which sheep-herding was adopted by these seasonally migrating groups cannot yet be determined. It is possible that the herders formed a distinct population element whose sites have not yet been located or differentiated in the archaeological record. It is not yet possible to determine with any confidence whether the sheep bones that have been recovered represent animals that were herded by the inhabitants of the sites on which the bones were found, or ones that were obtained by raiding from elsewhere.

In the absence of any local, wild, possible ancestor in the relatively well-studied South Afri-can faunal assemblages of the last millennium B.C., there can be no reasonable doubt that the first domestic animals in southernmost Africa were introduced into the region from more northerly latitudes. The archaeological picture at present available reveals no potential source for these animals other than the Early Iron Age complex. It has been pointed out that the first appearance of domestic stock in the southwestern Cape precedes by two centuries or so the earliest manifestations of the Early Iron Age industrial complex yet known in South Africa—those of the Transvaal and Natal. However, it must be emphasized that, while virtually nothing is definitely known concerning the chronology of the western stream in southern Angola and northern Namibia, there are good grounds (as has been indicated above) for supposing that the Early Iron Age was introduced there significantly earlier than it was further to the east. The western stream of the Early Iron Age thus stands as the most likely source of the domestic stock adopted by the stone–tool-using inhabitants of the Cape during the first centuries of the Christian era.

26

The Prehistory of Stone Age Herders in South Africa

RICHARD G. KLEIN

At the time of the first European contact, from the end of the fifteenth through the mid-nineteenth century, the indigenous population of South Africa comprised three basic kinds of people. On the northeast and east, in what is today the northernmost Cape Province, the eastern Orange Free State, the Transvaal, Natal, and the southeasternmost Cape Province, Europeans encountered Bantu-speaking Iron Age farmers. In the central and northcentral Cape and the western Orange Free State they found Stone Age hunter/gatherers (loosely referred to as Bushmen or San), while in the western and southern Cape they found Stone Age pastoralists (loosely called Hottentots or Khoikhoi) (Fig. 1). Hunter/gatherers existed in close contact with and, in part, among the pastoralists and even to some extent among the Iron Age farmers, especially on the edges of the farmers' distribution.

For allowing him to analyze relevant faunal samples, the writer wishes to thank P. B. Beaumont, H. J. Deacon, A. J. B. Humphreys, R. R. Inskeep, C. G. Sampson, and F. R. Schweitzer. Funding for the research was provided by the National Science Foundation and the South African Museum.

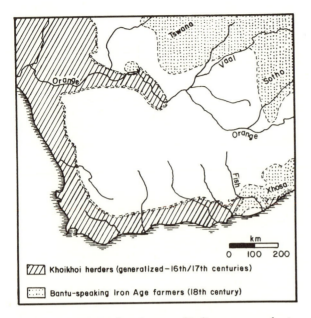

Figure 1. Historic distribution of indigenous peoples in the western part of South Africa (modified from Butzer et al., 1979). Hunter/gatherers (San or Bushmen) occupied the area not occupied by herders or farmers and were also found living among the herders and farmers.

For the most part, the farmers were very dark-skinned compared to the hunter/gatherers and the pastoralists and contrasted with them in other important physical traits, as has been confirmed by modern biological anthropology (Tobias, 1978a with references). The hunter/gatherers and pastoralists were physically very similar and it was believed initially that they spoke very closely related languages. These languages (and often the hunter/gatherers and pastoralists themselves) have frequently been lumped together as Khoisan, though it is now recognized that this term masks an extraordinary amount of linguistic diversity (Traill, 1978).

The languages of the pastoralists were in fact for the most part reasonably similar to one another, but those of the hunter/gatherers often differed remarkably. Some hunter/gatherer linguistic variation perhaps resulted from different degrees of contact and acculturation with pastoralists or Iron Age farmers, but most of it probably reflected the very considerable antiquity of the hunter/gatherer

way of life in South Africa. The hunter/gatherers contacted by Europeans were in fact probably the direct lineal descendants of people who had lived in South Africa for tens if not hundreds of thousands of years. During this time, people living hundreds or even only scores of kilometers apart probably had very little contact with each other, and substantial linguistic divergence resulted.

In contrast, both linguistic data and more general considerations may be used to argue conclusively that both Iron Age farming and Stone Age pastoralism had been present in South Africa for a relatively short time. A combination of linguistic, biological, and archaeological evidence suggests that the farmers were basically the descendants of immigrants from the north and east who probably first arrived on the northern periphery of South Africa in the early centuries of the Christian era. Thereafter, they rapidly colonized the eastern quarter of the country, where environmental conditions were most appropriate for their mixed farming economy. Recent archaeological discoveries indicate that they had spread through Natal to their historic limit in the eastern Cape before the end of the first millennium A.D. (Maggs, 1977). The last part of their historic distribution area to be colonized—perhaps only in the fourteenth or fifteenth century—was the southern highveld (eastern Orange Free State and adjacent Lesotho), in which environmental conditions were least suited for the Iron Age mode of mixed farming.

Relative to the histories of the hunter/gatherers and the Iron Age farmers, the history of the Stone Age pastoralists of South Africa remains especially obscure, and it is only very recently that pertinent archaeological evidence has begun to accumulate. The purpose of this paper is to summarize this evidence and to discuss its implications for the antiquity of Stone Age pastoralism in South Africa, the route(s) by which domesticated stock was introduced to the country, and the way of life of the pastoralists.

The Antiquity of Stone Age Pastoralism in South Africa

There is no archaeological or historical evidence that any of the indigenous ungulates of

South Africa were domesticated prehistorically. The Stone Age pastoralists encountered by Europeans herded only cattle (*Bos taurus*), sheep (*Ovis aries*), and/or goats (*Capra hircus*), none of which has wild antecedents in the local fauna. The earliest appearance of cattle, sheep, or goats in the South African archaeological record would therefore constitute the most direct evidence for the antiquity of Stone Age pastoralism.

There are two problems with documenting the earliest appearance of the herded species. First is the difficulty of distinguishing their bones from those of their indigenous relatives—various species of wild bovids. This is particularly a problem with regard to cattle, whose bones are remarkably similar to those of their fairly close and widespread indigenous relative, the Cape buffalo (*Syncerus caffer*). Reliable, systematic differences between homologous cattle and buffalo bones have yet to be documented in detail, and only horncores are probably foolproof evidence for differentiating the two species at present. Sheep and goats, though generally difficult to tell from one another in the absence of horncores, are less of a problem, since their dentitions are very different from those of any indigenous species. Their phalanges are usually also very distinctive, and it is likely that most of their other skeletal elements could also be distinguished from those of native bovids. However, a comparative study to establish differences would be difficult, because postcranial skeletons of several relevant native species are still in very short supply in local museums. Furthermore, reliable systematic postcranial differences could probably only be established on fairly complete bones. In most South African archaeological faunas, including ones potentially relevant to the origins of Stone Age pastoralism, the bones are highly fragmented.

The second problem with establishing the earliest appearance of domesticated species concerns sampling. Most archaeological faunal samples from South Africa are relatively small, consisting of no more than a few hundred taxonomically identifiable bones that need represent no more than a few dozen individual animals. In small samples, the likelihood that a species will be absent by pure chance is obviously fairly strong. This is particularly a problem for domesticated animals, since both ethnohistoric and archaeological observations indicate that

Stone Age herders in South Africa continued to make substantial use of wild animals whose bones dominate, often heavily, even those samples in which the bones of domestic species are clearly present.

The largest available faunal samples from sites spanning the late Holocene period when it is likely that domesticated animals were introduced to South Africa come from the cave sites of Die Kelders 1, Byneskranskop 1, Boomplaas A, and Nelson Bay in the southern Cape Province (Fig. 2). At all four sites, sheep horncores or dentitions or both have been identified from deposits that are radiocarbon-dated to between 2000 and 1700 B.P. (Table 1). Relatively large faunal samples from deposits that are only slightly older than this at Byneskranskop, Boomplaas, Nelson Bay, and other southern Cape sites lack sheep bones, and it seems reasonable to conclude that sheep first appeared locally between 2000 and 1700 B.P., the exact time perhaps depending on the place. Sheep bones of comparable antiquity have also been documented in the relatively small faunal sample from an open-air shell-midden at Hawston and are further known in the relatively small samples from somewhat later deposits at Scott's Cave in the southern cape and at Elands Bay and Diepkloof Caves in the adjacent western Cape (Table 1, Fig. 2).

Since the present writer is unable to distinguish the dentitions of sheep from those of goats and since the sheep dentitions and horncores found at southern and western Cape sites are no longer connected to one another by intermediate cranial bones, the possibility cannot be discounted that some of the dentitions derive from goats. This seems unlikely, however, partly because no goat horncores have been found and partly because southern and western Cape herders do not seem to have possessed goats at the time of first European contact (M. Wilson, 1969; Schweitzer, 1974). However, in addition to sheep they did have cattle, and it is necessary to consider the possibility that sheep and cattle were introduced at different times.

Inskeep (1969) suggested that cattle may have been introduced to South Africa more recently than sheep, since depictions of cattle in local rock-art are both less numerous and less widely distributed than those of sheep. Additionally, sheep are the only domestic stock depicted in the rock art of

TABLE 1. The Principal Radiocarbon-Dated Stone Age Southern Africa Sites with Remains of Sheep and/or Potsherds

Sites	C-14 dates associated with sheep remains (in stratigraphic order from top to bottom where this information is available)	C-14 dates associated with potsherds (in stratigraphic order from top to bottom where this information is available)	Sources
Namibia			
Eros Shelter	No reported sheep remains	1745 ± 35 (GrN–5297)	J. C. Vogel (1970)
Mirabib Rockshelter	No reported sheep remains, but sheep hair and dung present: 1550 ± 50 (Pta-1535)	1550 ± 50 (Pta-1535)	Sandelowsky et al. (1979)
Apollo 11 Rockshelter	No reported sheep remains	1460 ± 55 (KN-I 846) 1670 ± 55 (KN-I 870) 1960 ± 45 (Pta-1918)	Wendt (1976); Sandelowsky et al. (1979); Thackeray (1979)
Western Cape			
Elands Bay Cave	1120 ± 85 (GaK-4335)	1120 ± 85 (GaK-4335) 1520 ± 80 (GaK-4337)	Parkington (n.d.)
Diepkloof Cave	1590 ± 85 (GaK-4595)	1590 ± 85 (GaK-4595)	Parkington (n.d.)
Southern Cape			
Hawston	1860 ± 60 (Pta-834) 1900 ± 40 (Pta-835)	1860 ± 60 (Pta-834) 1900 ± 40 (Pta-835)	Avery (1975)
Die Kelders	1465 ± 100 (GX-1685) 1600 ± 120 (GaK3955) 1590 ± 80 (GaK-3956) 2020 ± 95 (GX-1686) 1960 ± 95 (GX-1687)	1465 ± 100 (GaK-3955) 1600 ± 120 (GaK-3955) 1590 ± 80 (GaK-3956) 2020 ± 95 (GX-1686) 1960 ± 95 (GX-1687) 1960 ± 85 (GX-1688)	Schweitzer (1979)
Byneskranskop 1	535 ± 50 (Pta-1866) 1880 ± 50 (Pta-1865)	535 ± 50 (Pta-1866) 1880 ± 50 (Pta-1865)	Schweitzer and Wilson (1978); Klein (1981)
Boomplaas A	1630 ± 50 (UW-337) 1510 ± 75 (UW-307) 1700 ± 55 (UW-338)	1630 ± 50 (UW-337) 1510 ± 75 (UW-307) 1700 ± 55 (UW-338)	Deacon et al. (1978); Klein (1978)
Nelson Bay Cave	1930 ± 60 (GrN-5703)	1930 ± 60 (GrN-5703)	J. C. Vogel (1970); Inskeep and Klein (unpubl.)
Scott's Cave	360 ± 80 (Y-1425) 1190 ± 100 (SR-82)	360 ± 80 (Y-1425) 1190 ± 100 (SR-82)	H. J. Deacon (1967); Klein and Scott (1974)
Northern Cape			
Klein Witkrans	Sheep remains tentatively identified below a date of 1490 ± 40 (Pta-2447)	1490 ± 40 (Pta-2447)	Beaumont and Klein (unpubl.)
Limerock 1	1620 ± 50 (Pta-1621)	1620 ± 50 (Pta-1621)	Klein (1979)
Limerock 2	No reported sheep remains	1430 ± 50 (Pta-1759)	Klein (1979)
Dikbosch 1	3060 ± 60 (Pta-1065)	3060 ± 60 (Pta-1065)	Humphreys (1974); Klein (1979)
Zaayfontein	No reported sheep remains	430 ± 95 (SR-133)	Sampson (1967a, 1970); Klein (1979)
Riversmead	No reported sheep remains	2645 ± 95 (GX-723)	Sampson and Sampson (1967); Klein (1979)
Glen Elliott Shelter	No reported sheep remains	Potsherds at and below a date of 235 ± 80 (GX-1295)	Sampson (1967b, 1970); Klein (1979)

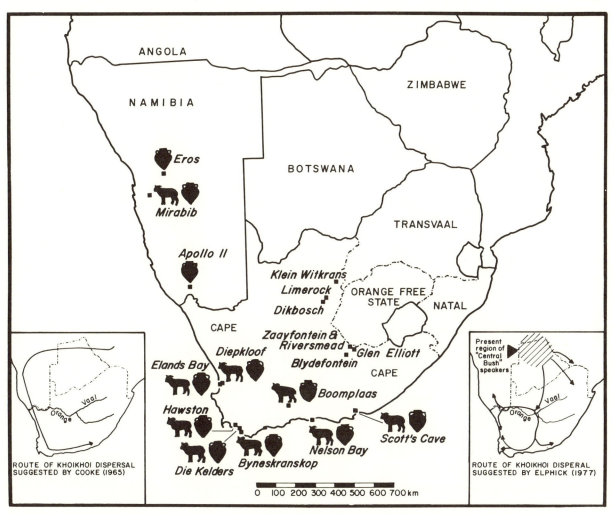

Figure 2. Approximate locations of the principal sites mentioned in the text. The sheep and pot symbols indicate the presence of sheep remains or potsherds in a reasonably well-documented, radiocarbon-dated Stone Age context. The insets show the routes of herder (Khoikhoi) movement into South Africa suggested by Cooke (1965) and Elphick (1977).

the southwestern Cape, which suggested to Inskeep that cattle were only introduced after the local artistic tradition had gone into a decline in the very late prehistoric period. Archaeological resolution of this problem is complicated by the difficulty of separating cattle from buffalo on osteological criteria, but it is possible that some large bovid phalanges (first isolated by K. Scott: Klein and Scott, 1974) found in the same levels as bones of early sheep at Die Kelders may belong to cattle. If future research shows they do derive from cattle, they would constitute evidence that sheep and cattle were introduced more or less simultaneously, at least to the extreme southern part of South Africa.

In sum, then, we have evidence that people herding sheep and perhaps also cattle first appeared in the southern Cape Province between 2000 and 1700 B.P. The situation elsewhere in South Africa is much less clearly established. Stone Age deposits of appropriate late Holocene age with good faunal preservation have been excavated at several rock-shelters along the Gaap Escarpment and in the upper Orange River drainage in the northcentral Cape (Klein, 1979 with references), but the evidence they provide is ambiguous. Sites in the Orange River drainage have supplied the largest faunal samples, roughly comparable in size to some of the like-aged southern Cape samples that contain sheep bones. However, none of the Orange River samples contains bones that unquestionably derive from domestic animals.

Two of the sites along the Gaap Escarpment—Limerock 1 and Dikbosch 1—have each provided a single tooth that has been identified as sheep or goat, but in each case context is a problem. At Limerock 1, the tooth involved is associated with a radiocarbon date of approximately 1600 B.P., while at Dikbosch 1, the tooth underlies a level that has been dated to more than 3000 B.P. (Table 1). The difficulty is that neither site possessed clear-cut stratigraphy, so the excavations in each case proceeded according to arbitrary levels or spits. The homogeneity of the deposits made it impossible to isolate disturbances which may have caused objects to move vertically within the site, and there is the further possibility that the spits crosscut the natural stratigraphy, so that items such as dated charcoal and teeth found in the same spit may not really be contemporaneous.

At a third Gaap site, Klein (= Little) Witkrans, recent excavations provided dental fragments that have been tentatively assigned to sheep or goat in a level below a radiocarbon date of approximately 1500 B.P. Once again, however, the site was excavated in arbitrary spits, and the tentative nature of the identification must be emphasized.

In sum, the evidence for domesticated animals in a Stone Age context in the South African interior is nebulous at present; any reasonably firm statement on the antiquity of herding there is impossible. In the southern and western Cape, there appears to be a close coincidence between the first appearance of sheep and the first appearance of pottery (Table 1), raising the possibility that the appearance of pottery could be used as proxy evidence for the existence of herders in the interior even if the people who used or made pots at a particular site remained hunter/gatherers. Unfor-

tunately, establishing a date for the first appearance of pottery in the interior is complicated by the same problems of sampling, homogeneous deposits, and excavations according to arbitrary spits that complicate establishment of the first appearance of domestic stock. On present evidence, it is possible to argue that pottery appeared in the interior as long ago as 3000 or as recently as 500–600 B.P. Some indication of where the truth may lie here is perhaps to be found in the nature of early pottery in the interior, which Humphreys (pers. comm.) believes has more in common with Iron Age pottery than with the pottery found in southern and western Cape sites in association with early sheep. Present evidence suggests that Iron Age peoples only appeared in South Africa within the last 2,000 years, and they perhaps only penetrated the vicinity of the Gaap Escarpment and the upper Orange River drainage within the past 1,000 years. In other words, using pottery as proxy evidence for the appearance of herders (or its absence as evidence for their absence) may ultimately suggest that herders appeared in the southern and western Cape a millennium or more before they appeared in the interior.

Route(s) by Which Domestic Stock Were Introduced to South Africa

Linguistic research summarized by Elphick (1977: 6–7) has shown that the Khoikhoi dialects widely spoken by herders in South Africa at the time of historic contact are very similar to the Central Bush family of languages spoken by hunter/gatherers living in northern Botswana. This may be used to argue that the ultimate origin of the herders in South Africa, or at least of their way of life, was in or near northern Botswana. It does not, of course, follow that the introduction of herding to South Africa involved large-scale or long-distance movements of former hunter/gatherers driving stock from northern Botswana. Although substantial population movements cannot be ruled out, it is at least equally possible that resident hunter/gatherers with whom the earliest herders came into contact were often assimilated by them or acculturated to them, and that stock-herding and associated cultural traits spread into South Africa as much or more by diffusion as by the physical movements of people. Diffusion would perhaps have been facilitated by the fact that the earliest herders were probably very similar physically to the hunter/gatherers they encountered and probably shared a great deal of culture with them, including the manufacture of stone artifacts and a considerable reliance on hunted and gathered foods.

Assuming a northern Botswana origin for the herders to the south, there remain several important questions. Where did the domestic stock in northern Botswana originate? What was responsible for the movement of people or stock from northern Botswana southward? What route(s) did the movement take? The first two questions are especially difficult to answer, but it seems likely that the immediate source of the domestic stock was East Africa, where domestic animals in association with pottery and stone tools (but not agriculture) have been found in sites that may be as much as 5,500 years old (Bower and Nelson, 1978). By 3000 B.P., Stone Age herders with pottery were widespread in East Africa (Bower and Nelson, 1978; Phillipson, 1977c: 71–85 and references). The reasons for the movement of people, stock, or both southward from Botswana are probably complex, perhaps involving both the herders' search for new pastures and the pressures placed on them by expanding Iron Age farmers. Pressure on Stone Age pastoralists from Iron Age farmers has not yet been documented archaeologically, but it seems likely to be more than coincidence that domestic stock appears in Stone Age contexts in the western and southern parts of South Africa at virtually the same time that Iron Age farmers appear in the northern and eastern parts of the country.

Among the questions posed above, the one that archaeology is most likely to answer in the near future concerns the route(s) by which domestic stock were introduced to Stone Age South Africa. Linguistic evidence presented by Westphal (1963), supported by ethnohistoric observations summarized by Elphick (1977: 14–22), may be used to argue that the original route out of Botswana was south to the Orange River, then along the eastern margin of the Karoo to the eastern Cape coast

(Fig. 2). Movement east along the coast may have been essentially blocked by unsuitable environmental conditions or by the presence of Iron Age farmers. Movement west, however, would have encountered both favorable environmental conditions and human populations consisting only of relatively sparsely distributed hunter/gatherers. Elphick (1977: 18–19) additionally postulates a later movement of herders west along the Orange River to the Atlantic Coast and thence south and north into Namaqualand and Namibia (Fig. 2).

Considering the environmental zones through which early herders or stock would have had to move in southcentral Africa, as well as the distribution of sheep paintings and figurines and rock paintings of people who may have been early sheep herders in Zimbabwe, Cooke (1965) has proposed an alternative route, broadly similar to one proposed by Stow (1905), mainly on the basis of oral traditions. Cooke's route would have the initial movement from northern Botswana east across northern Namibia, then south to the Cape of Good Hope, and finally east to the eastern Cape (Fig. 2). This route finds some support in the historic distribution of Khoikhoi herders (Fig. 1), particularly if historical evidence is accepted that no Khoikhoi peoples were living as far east as the Orange/Vaal confluence prior to the European contact period (Elphick, 1977: 19).

If the route through the interior proposed by Elphick is correct, then we would expect to find domestic stock in northern Cape archaeological sites at least as early as in southern and western Cape ones. The archaeological evidence summarized in the last section is inconclusive on the question of the antiquity of stock in the northern Cape, but it is perhaps significant that bones of domestic animals are absent in the faunal assemblages from Zaayfontein, Riversmead, Blydefontein, and Glen Elliott in the upper Orange drainage (Klein, 1979 with references; Table 1 and Fig. 2 here). The faunal assemblages from these sites are roughly comparable in size to some of the broadly contemporaneous ones in the southern and western Cape that have provided well-documented sheep bones.

Very tentatively, the absence of sheep in the upper Orange sites, located in or near the area through which herders would have passed following

Elphick's proposed route, suggests that the initial movement may in fact have been along the coast rather than through the interior. This is perhaps further suggested by a C-14 date of approximately 1600 B.P. on a Stone Age level with sheep dung and hair at Mirabib Rockshelter in Namibia and more indirectly by dates of between 2000 and 1500 B.P. on pottery at Mirabib and at Eros and Apollo 11 shelters, also in Namibia (Table 1, Fig. 2). It is of course entirely possible that both interior and coastal routes were used to introduce stock to South Africa, and this question can probably be resolved by careful excavation of large faunal samples from pertinent sites in the South African interior, in Namibia and, if possible, also in Botswana.

Way of Life of Prehistoric Herders in South Africa

The Khoikhoi (Hottentot) herders encountered by early European travelers and colonists in the southern and western Cape were nomadic, moving about the countryside with their herds and flocks and living in temporary open-air encampments. Their herds and flocks sometimes numbered hundreds of head, while cohabiting groups of herders sometimes included dozens of people (M. Wilson, 1969). If any of the herder encampments have left archaeological traces, they have yet to be discovered and published, and the prehistory of indigenous herders in South Africa must be written entirely on finds from rockshelters, with the relatively minor exception of discoveries in open-air shell-middens like the one at Hawston. It seems likely that the ancestors of the historic herders also camped mainly in open-air sites, which means that the archaeological record as we know it must be highly biased.

The potential of the existing record for shedding light on the way of life of prehistoric herders is further limited by the possibility that the rockshelters containing bones of prehistoric stock were occupied by hunter/gatherer thieves rather than by herders. Even at the time of historic contact, hunter/gatherers continued to exist in the more re-

mote and mountainous portions of the herder landscape, and contacts between the two kinds of people were reasonably frequent, including raids by hunter/gatherers on domestic stock. At only three of the known shelter sites containing early sheep remains is there reasonable evidence that the occupants were actually herders. These sites are Mirabib and Boomplaas, where the sedimentary matrix enclosing the sheep remains is mainly calcined sheep dung, suggesting that the sites were used as kraals, and Die Kelders, where the age-sex profile of the subfossil sheep appears more likely to reflect rational flock management than indiscriminate plundering by raiders (Schweitzer, 1974). It should be added that Die Kelders is the only site where the sheep bones are well enough preserved and the sample is large enough for construction of a meaningful age-sex profile.

Among the three sites where actual herder occupation seems reasonably well demonstrated, Boomplaas is the most informative on the prehistoric-herder way of life (Deacon et al., 1978). The laminated nature of the calcined dung matrix suggests that use of the cave as a kraal was intermittent, perhaps confined to spring or autumn, when local pastures would have been at their best. It is not clear why the occupants of Boomplaas used a cave rather than a more conventional thornbush enclosure for kraaling their sheep; it may have afforded better protection from hunter/gatherer raids. The Boomplaas C-14 dates support this idea, insofar as they suggest that use as a kraal occurred for no more than a century or two shortly after the initial introduction of sheep, by which time local hunter/gatherers perhaps posed a comparatively minor threat to the now well-established herders.

Although the introduction of pottery at the same time as sheep is an obvious indication of change in material culture at Boomplaas and other southern and western Cape sites, the stone artifacts associated with the sheep remains at Boomplaas and other sites are essentially similar to those found in pre-sheep levels, suggesting some measure of cultural and economic continuity. This may be taken as evidence for the possible or probable complexity of the introduction of the herding way of life, involving a mix of population replacement, assimilation, and acculturation. With regard to the pottery, it is interesting that there appears to have been a change through time at Boomplaas and, more certainly, at Die Kelders, from an emphasis on bowl shapes earlier on to necked pots later. The broader cultural significance of this, however, remains obscure.

The historic Khoikhoi herders of South Africa often relied heavily on hunted and gathered foods in addition to those supplied by their stock, and analysis of the faunal remains from Boomplaas and Die Kelders suggests a similar subsistence pattern for the early herders. However, the variety of well-represented indigenous mammal species in the sheep levels is smaller than in pre-sheep ones (this is also true at Byneskranskop and Nelson Bay), suggesting that the herders may have been more casual in their hunting or that they often restricted themselves to the creatures that could be found within relatively easy reach of campsites or kraals. It is difficult to assess the long-term impact of the herders and their stock on the indigenous fauna, but it is perhaps no coincidence that two endemic southern Cape antelope—the blue antelope (*Hippotragus leucophaeus*) and the bontebok (*Damaliscus dorcas dorcas*)—had become extremely rare by the time of first European contact. Both would have competed with stock for grass in an environment in which grass was not especially plentiful, and it is possible that this led to their exclusion from the best pastures, or to persecution at the hands of the herders, or both. If so, the advent of Europeans, who were probably responsible for the final extinction of the blue antelope about A.D. 1800, was only the culmination of a process of faunal impoverishment that had begun more than a thousand years before.

Summary and Conclusions

The archaeological record of indigenous (Khoikhoi or "Hottentot") pastoralists whom Europeans encountered in the western and southern parts of South Africa is very sketchy, largely because their principal sites, open-air encampments and kraals, apparently have very limited archaeological visibility in the present landscape. Recent research in rockshelters has made it clear that sheep-herding, probably accompanied by pottery-making and possibly by cattle-herding, reached the southern and western Cape Province shortly after the time of Christ, but it remains highly uncertain whether stock-raising has a comparable antiquity in the interior. The same evidence bearing on the antiquity of Stone Age pastoralism may be used to argue that it was introduced to South Africa by a route paralleling the west coast, though an alternative or additional route through the interior cannot yet be ruled out. The only major change in material culture apparent at or immediately after the introduction of herding is the use and manufacture of pottery, and the herders made stone tools that are very similar to the ones manufactured by the hunter/gatherers who preceded them and continued to exist alongside them. The limited archaeological record indicates that, like their historic descendants, early herders in South Africa relied heavily on nondomestic foods for subsistence. A more detailed understanding of the relationship between prehistoric herders and their environment will only be possible with fuller materials from future excavations, but it seems likely that the herders were directly or indirectly responsible for a decline in the numbers of at least two indigenous ungulates.

III

**The Transition from
Hunting/Gathering
to Food Production:
The Evidence
from the San**

INTRODUCTION

This section, which describes the effects of incipient agricultural and herding practices on three groups of predominantly hunting-and-gathering San still living in the Kalahari today, is of particular importance for interpreting the evidence revealed in the archaeological record. We have here studies dealing specifically with actual, present-day reactions to contact between hunter/gatherers and food-producing groups, and the authors examine both the effects of these interactions on the hunter/gatherers and the success or otherwise of their attempts at incipient agriculture or stock-keeping. Some of the results strike one as surprising; for example, that hunter/gatherers often produce more successful crops in the semiarid Kalahari environment than do their village farming neighbors, and that the herding of goats and donkeys by the //Gana adds to their well-being by reducing the number of moves they need to make to subsist in the dry season.

These studies are not only of considerable intrinsic interest but are also of great value for the insights they provide into the possible variations in adaptations which must have taken place among prehistoric hunter/gatherer groups beginning to make the change to food production.

27

Food Production and Culture Change among the !Kung San: Implications for Prehistoric Research

ALISON S. BROOKS,

DIANE E. GELBURD, AND

JOHN E. YELLEN

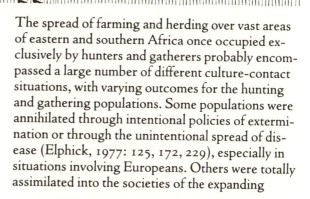

The spread of farming and herding over vast areas of eastern and southern Africa once occupied exclusively by hunters and gatherers probably encompassed a large number of different culture-contact situations, with varying outcomes for the hunting and gathering populations. Some populations were annihilated through intentional policies of extermination or through the unintentional spread of disease (Elphick, 1977: 125, 172, 229), especially in situations involving Europeans. Others were totally assimilated into the societies of the expanding

The research on which this paper is based was supported in large part by the National Science Foundation (SOC75-14227, BNS 76-19633). Earlier work was funded by the National Institutes of Mental Health, the Wenner Gren Foundation, and the National Geographic Society. For all this support, we express our gratitude. We would also like to acknowledge our deep appreciation to the government of Botswana, which permitted us to work in the Dobe region, to Alec Campbell, Aron L. Crowell, Robert K. Hitchcock, and Pauline Wiessner for ideas and assistance, and to our informants, especially the people of Dobe. We owe a particular debt to Thomas Hargrove, whose Master's thesis provides part of the underlying data for this paper.

farmer/herders, leaving no living traces of their existence other than in the gene pools (e.g., Zulus) or languages (e.g., !Xhosa) of the assimilators (Bleek, 1927; Elphick, 1977: 199–200; Harpending and Jenkins, 1973; Jenkins, n.d.). Particularly in areas less desirable for farming and herding, a small minority of hunting-and-gathering populations preserved a distinct identity through many years of contact, often relating to farmer/herder societies as a distinct caste of traders, hunters, or smiths or as a lower class of permanent or intermittent serfs or servants. Indeed, the existence of this lower class may have been crucial to the survival of farmer/herder societies in marginal lands, consuming surplus production and providing additional labor in good times when the herds or fields were expanding, and allowing a rapid reduction of both dependents and the labor force when surplus food was not available.

The contact situation was certainly complicated by the potential for marginal farmer/herders themselves to lose their herds or fields through disease, environmental fluctuation, conquest, or raiding, and to move into a serf or servant status vis-à-vis other farmer/herders. Most recently, in southern Africa, the Herero, who were driven from their lands and deprived of their cattle by the Germans in 1904–1906, became servants to the dominant Tswana groups of Botswana. Through the *mafisa*, or cattle-loaning system, they were able to rebuild their herds and regain their independent status. With dates in the second century A.D. (Deacon et al., 1976) for domesticated sheep at Boomplaas Cave at the southern tip of the continent, the shifting interrelationships of hunter/gatherers and farmer/herders may be assumed to have had a considerable antiquity over the entire continent.

The remaining hunting and gathering societies of Africa, largely concentrated in southern Africa and in the Congo Basin, may be of questionable relevance to specific reconstructions of the past. This has been pointed out at some length in the recent literature (Wobst, 1978; Binford, 1968a; Freeman, 1968; Schrire, n.d.). It is debatable to what extent the northern San ("Bushmen"), in particular, may be regarded as pristine or "uncontaminated" by contact with more technologically advanced societies. Although the linguistic evidence

suggests that the Khoikhoi herders of the early European contact period in the Cape were derived from central Bush speakers who border the !Kung San to the south, archaeological, linguistic, ethnohistorical, and genetic data imply a relatively slight degree of subsequent contact between the !Kung and the later migrations of Bantu populations to the east and the west. The southeastern part of the !Kung area is characterized by low and variable rainfall and by few permanent water sources. It is surrounded by large areas with no permanent water sources and thus is at best a marginal environment for livestock-herding or cultivation. As a result, the major migration routes of both the Khoi and the western and eastern Bantu may have skirted this region (Elphick, 1977: 14–22). With the exception of a possible *Bos taurus* radius and four maxillary bone fragments of indeterminate date 63 cm below the present surface at /Ai/ai (Wilmsen, 1979), no archaeological evidence of domestic stock or settled villages in the Dobe–/Ai/ai[1] area prior to the ethnographic and ethnohistoric present has been uncovered, despite extensive surveys and excavations in the area by Yellen and then by Wilmsen (1979). At the stratified Later Stone Age/Middle Stone Age site of ≠ Gi, 7 km south of Dobe, Botswana, very limited contact with technologically more advanced people is suggested by the presence of iron beads in the topmost level (Brooks and Yellen, 1977; Brooks et al., 1980). This level is probably less than 500 years old, and contains a mixture from the ethnographic present. Although Wilmsen's /Ai/ai survey recovered small amounts of both pottery and metal from depths of up to one meter below the surface in a loose, sandy matrix, he also concludes that "there is no evidence . . . to suggest that pastoralism was the principal subsistence mode at any time until the present" (1979: 19). Certainly the trade goods suggest at least a

1. The Dobe–/Ai/ai area is located in Botswana at latitude 19°20' to 20°30' S and 20°45' to 21°20' E longitude on the border with Namibia and about 100 miles south of the Caprivi Strip. It is classed as semiarid and is surrounded by broad areas with heavy sand-cover and no permanent water points. Today, livestock may enter or leave the area only during the height of the rainy season, and even then the journey can be hazardous for both people and animals.

remote contact with farmer/herders over 500 years ago.

Even if the Dobe area !Kung San survived as a relict population that had somehow been bypassed by the movements of more technologically advanced Khoi and Bantu speakers, one may question the value of this limited ethnographic example in providing direct analogies for interpretation of Stone Age archaeological remains in the more varied and complex environments utilized by hunters and gatherers in the past.

A different approach to the utility of hunter/gatherer studies in archaeology involves the testing of dynamic models of cultural systems that are equally applicable across a wide range of technological levels, social organizations, and ecological situations. The study of cultural dynamics is increasingly possible in view of the changes observed during the expanded period of the ethnographic present, which now, in the case of many hunter/gatherer groups, spans thirty or more years. If hunters and gatherers of today are poor examples of Stone Age hunters, they are excellent examples of functioning cultural systems that are changing from a way of life, however ancient, based exclusively on hunting and gathering to one based on other technoeconomic states. While these changes have been discussed at great length in the theoretical literature (e.g., Binford, 1968b; Flannery, 1968, 1969, 1972, 1973; Redman, 1978; White, 1959: 286), we have rarely had a chance to observe them in action over a considerable period of time. The record of the Dobe area !Kung, from the mid-1940s to the mid-1970s, affords just such an opportunity.

Theoretical Models

Whether the change is pristine or secondary, most present and past theories that view culture as a dynamic system postulate the existence of a prime mover that initiates the transition to a new cultural state marked by dependence on domesticated foods. Candidates for the position of prime mover within or outside the cultural system include: environmental change (Childe, 1951a, b; Kenyon,

1956, 1959); technological invention or diffusion (Braidwood, 1952, 1960; White, 1959); a change in values or religion (G. L. Isaac, 1978); and new social or organizational developments such as demographic change (Smith and Young, 1972), political pressure from a neighboring or conquering society, or population shifts resulting from sedentariness, environmental variation, or population increase (Binford, 1968b). The vitalistic theories of cultural evolution prevalent in the nineteenth century have largely been rejected in favor of either continuous feedback models of gradual change set in motion long ago as part of the fundamental human adaptive system (e.g., Higgs and Jarman, 1972), or stepwise models of punctuated equilibrium or abrupt change in which each stage is initiated by a new prime mover and is characterized by eventual achievement of a new and stable equilibrium state.

Once the system has been set in motion, change proceeds through the interrelationship of various cultural subsystems. In the materialist models of change (e.g., White, 1959: 286; Sahlins and Service, 1960; Binford, 1968b; Cohen, 1977: 279; M. Harris, 1979: 333), changes in the sociological or ideological subsystems of culture are seen as secondary to or dependent upon changes in the amount of energy extracted from the environment through the technoeconomic subsystems of culture. Although a shift in values has been seen as fundamental to the *beginning* of the human hunting and gathering way of life (G. L. Isaac, 1978; Lancaster, 1975: 4), the role of a similar shift in the transition from hunting and gathering to another way of life has been largely ignored by archaeologists, for whom ideologically based theories present the problem of non-testability.

Finally, few theories attempting to explain the spread of domestication have dealt with the reversibility of a shift from hunting and gathering to agriculture or herding (but see Ingold, 1980). Complex models of positive feedback, where each change requires a shift in other cultural subsystems, do not encompass the mechanisms for a return to an earlier state. In addition, punctuated equilibrium models imply that intermediate states are inherently unstable and that a society must either be based primarily upon hunting and gathering or

upon domestication, since each requires proper socialization, the acquisition of appropriate knowledge, and a specific social organization and value
system. On the analogy of an intermediate stage
between bipedalism and quadrupedalism, the long-
term viability of a society that oscillates between
hunting and gathering and farming is in some
doubt.

In the body of this paper, we present three
main arguments against the above characteristics of
traditional models. First, we suggest that the cause
of a shift to a domesticated economy is inherently
multifactorial and that it is the exigencies of the
archaeological record which have favored materi-
alistic, environmental, or demographic explanations. When such shifts are observed by anthropologists rather than deduced from the archaeological
record, the shift is rarely attributable to a single
cause, even in cases of direct intervention by an
outside agency of change. Second, we emphasize
the importance of a shift in values in this transition,
as in other major transitions or revolutions in human history and prehistory. Finally, we argue, from
the ethnographic and ethnohistoric record of Africa, against the idea of punctuated equilibrium and
the existence, after the introduction of domestication, of stable adaptations totally dependent on
either hunting and gathering or domestication.

We shall also examine, for the !Kung data, the
validity of two hypotheses drawn from the theoretical literature. The first hypothesis, derived from
models of the operation of *cultural* systems, suggests that a change in the technoeconomic base
from hunting and gathering to mixed pastoralism
should be associated with rapid shifts in other cultural subsystems such as material culture and patterns of differential access to goods, settlement
patterns, social structure, socialization patterns,
and values or ideals. The second hypothesis is derived from certain classes of models of the operation of *biological* systems (biogeography), and argues that, due to the regional, seasonal, short- and
long-term variability and unpredictability of the
Dobe environment, the optimum subsistence strategy for both pastoralists and hunter/gatherers is a
generalist strategy rather than a specialist one
(J. M. Diamond, 1977; Slobodkin and Sanders,
1969; Yellen, 1977a).

The Changing Economy of the Dobe
!Kung San

As was suggested in the introduction to this
paper, the archaeological and linguistic evidence
suggests that the !Kung are long-term residents of
the Dobe area, broadly defined, and have not migrated there in the recent past as refugees from less
"marginal" habitats. The presence of iron beads
and coarse, poorly fired pottery in the upper deposits of several Later Stone Age sites suggests pre-
twentieth-century direct or indirect contact with
technologically more advanced peoples. At this
time we cannot place an absolute date on the antiquity of this trade, except to suggest that at $\neq$ Gi,
evidence of iron and pottery is limited to a dark
upper level, provisionally dated to 110 ± 50 B.P.
(SI-4098, charcoal). Although no one at Dobe has
any knowledge of chipped-stone tools, most men in
the 1960s still made bone arrowheads of the type
found at $\neq$ Gi, and one older man remembers the
manufacture of stone axes (now entirely replaced
by metal ones). The fact that the middle-aged sons
of this man had never before heard their father
mention or describe this technology indicates the
rapidity with which technological knowledge, as
opposed to environmental knowledge, may pass out
of the cultural inventory. That the contact with
Bantu, Khoikhoi, or Europeans was limited to a
sporadic exchange of trade goods is suggested by
the absence of strong evidence of either domesticated stock or village settlement in the Dobe area
prior to the ethnographic or ethnohistoric present.

Lee (1979: 76–87) has described in some detail the increasing contacts between Bantu groups
and the Dobe San, beginning about 1870. This
relationship proceeded rapidly from an initial trading relationship to one in which Dobe area San
worked as servants on seasonally occupied Tswana
cattle-posts. Since, according to Lee's description,
San servants did not acquire rights in the offspring
of the cattle they tended, the relationship was not a
mafisa relationship in the traditional sense and
would not have led to the acquisition of livestock by
the San.

The Hereros passed through the Dobe area in
large numbers during the German-Herero wars of
1905–1906 but did not return to establish perma-

nent villages until the mid-1920s. By the mid-1930s, several permanent Herero villages with live-stock and small fields were established throughout the Dobe area, although not at Dobe itself. In the 1940s, when our ethnographic record begins, a small group of San at Dobe subsisted entirely by hunting and gathering. During the subsequent decade, all these individuals moved to Bantu (Herero and Tswana) villages a few kilometers to the east (especially Mahopa and !Kabe) to work as herders. During this period, they lived primarily on food provided by their employers. The establishment of a permanent Tswana headman resident in 1948 and a major influx of Hereros from the Okavango Delta region in the 1950s may have been instrumental in this shift. In 1963, a group that included most of the original Dobe inhabitants from the 1940s returned to Dobe, where it has formed the core of the Dobe group in the 1970s. A second large group of San, distantly related to the original group, moved to Dobe in the early 1970s. The population rose from 35 in 1964 (Lee, 1979: 53) to ca. 125 in 1976, and from one group in 1963 to four in 1976.

In 1963 and 1964, when Lee carried out his initial study of the Dobe San, he described them as living exclusively by hunting and gathering. Despite the fact that all the adults involved had spent much of the previous decade in herding cattle and consuming domesticated foods, the pattern of individual movement, of fluid band composition, of daily foraging, of house construction, of ownership and sharing of material goods, of socialization, and of values described by Lee were seen as highly logical and adaptive for a hunting and gathering way of life and not related to a way of life based on pastoralism. By 1967, the Dobe San had begun to accumulate a small herd of goats, partly from their exchange or *hxaro* networks with Bantu or with San servants in Bantu villages and partly from anthropologists, who themselves were drawn into exchange networks with the Bantu involving goats and medicine, clothing, and other Western amenities.

During the rains of early 1968 and early 1969, about half the Dobe families attempted to establish fields, which they cleared, fenced with thornbrush, and planted with maize, melons, sorghum, tobacco, cucurbits, beans, and sugarcane (Lee, 1979: 409–412). Lee estimates only a 10 to 40 percent success rate for these years. As of the early 1970s, no Dobe resident had been an established farmer or livestock owner. The number of animals and the intensity of agricultural effort continued to increase throughout the early 1970s, aided by very heavy rainfall from 1973 to 1977, so that by 1976 most Dobe San had access to domesticated foods produced by themselves well into the hot dry season (September).

Outside Influences

The role of outsiders to the Dobe area in promoting the change now taking place is certainly part of the answer to the question of why this transition had not taken place earlier. Since independence in 1966, the government of Botswana has taken an increasingly active role in the lives of rural and extra-rural dwellers. Seed for San agricultural experiments was provided by the government as early as 1967, and a resident Botswana agricultural officer has been assisting the San of the area since 1976. A school was opened 40 km east of Dobe in 1973, and another school was opened ca. 40 km to the south in 1977. A parastatal organization for the international marketing of native crafts began sending a regular buyer to the area in 1974, creating a cash influx and stimulating a market economy in both livestock and consumer goods. This market was also stimulated by the opening in 1967 of a store 40 km to the east of Dobe. In 1975 a Catholic missionary began working in the area to help the San dig wells and claim legal rights to their traditional land under the new tribal land-use policies being promulgated by the government. In 1977 the government sent a group of adult men from Dobe to the government agricultural school near Maun, 210 km to the east, for a three-week crash course in modern agricultural methods. The Kalahari People's Fund, working in cooperation with the government, sponsored development initiatives to send children to school, register land, and make a successful transition to peasant farming in a modern state. Finally, the Dobe area is strongly influenced by the policies and practices of South Africa in the administration of Namibia, whose border with Botswana is only 1 km west of Dobe. In order to keep track of "nationalist" movements into and out of Namibia across the sparsely populated border, the South African administration built higher and higher fences along the border, dug boreholes along the border in the traditional rainy-season camping areas of the Dobe group (see Yellen, 1977b), and established permanent camps of San derived from elsewhere in Namibia to watch over the border area and report the movements of strangers. The individuals in these camps are not closely related to the Dobe people (Lee, 1979: 430–431), and their presence in these areas strongly inhibits traditional land-utilization patterns of the Dobe residents. The Dobe group, swollen to record numbers due to in-migration, is thus experiencing a de facto crowding as they are forced to draw their livelihood from decreasing amounts of land.

The most striking characteristic from the history of contacts between the Dobe San and more technologically advanced peoples is that until very recently, members of industrial societies (Europeans) have had little or no influence on the process of economic transition. Even today, the change is taking place largely under pressures imposed by an independent black African government. The history of contact and the observed changes, therefore, are much closer to proposed reconstructions of the spread of agriculture in African prehistory than is the case for Inuit or Australian aborigines, whose transition from hunting and gathering to other economic states was largely brought about through European contact.

The model that we propose in order to describe the economic shifts in the Dobe area takes the form of a triangle within which individual !Kung families can be placed as points in one moment in time and within which these individual points shift through time. One corner of the triangle represents a 100 percent independent hunting/gathering way of life. Another corner represents a 100 percent independent mixed-pastoral existence, and the apex represents a way of life based on economic dependence and a master-servant relationship with local Bantu groups (Fig. 1).

For our purposes, the 100 percent independent

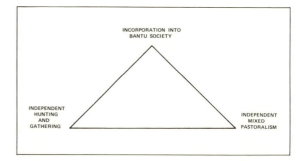

Figure 1. Dynamics of culture contact and change.

hunting/gathering way of life is defined according to Lee and DeVore (1968a: 11–12) and others (for example, Yellen, 1977b: 46–48; Wilmsen, 1973; Friedl, 1975: 38–39; Flannery, 1972; Draper, 1975). Lee and DeVore's basic hunter/gatherer model includes the following characteristics:

1. . . . the amount of personal property has to be kept at a very low level. Constraints on the possession of personal property also serve to keep wealth differences between individuals to a minimum and we postulate a general egalitarian system for the hunters. . . .

2. . . . the nature of the food supply keeps the living groups small, usually under fifty people. . . .

3. . . . the local groups as groups do not ordinarily maintain exclusive rights to resources. . . .

4. . . . food surpluses are not a prominent feature of the small-scale society. . . .

5. . . . frequent visiting between resource areas prevents any one group from becoming too strongly attached to any single area. . . . Individuals and groups can change residence without relinquishing vital interests in lands or goods. (Lee and DeVore, 1968a: 11–12)

In addition, specific correlates of this general model that relate to settlement patterns, social structure, and ideology are:

1. Houses tend to be relatively impermanent: they are easily erected and often leave little evidence behind after their collapse or removal.

2. Camp plans tend to be relatively intimate, roughly circular in shape (Flannery, 1972) and flexible in the addition or modification of house structures (Turnbull, 1963).

3. The camp tends to be composed of consanguinal and affinal kin (Lee, 1968). While strictly lineal inheritance may operate in the acquisition of rights and affiliations, it would not maintain optimum flexibility for such ties to determine the *economic* unit (local residence group) at any particular time.

4. Storage structures are minimal.

5. Child-rearing is egalitarian with regard to family and sex differences (Draper, 1975, 1976).

6. The status of women is relatively high, especially in those groups where the basic food supply is controlled by women (Friedl, 1975: 39).

7. Formal political and legal structures are minimal. Disputes are usually settled by fission, and egalitarianism is strongly supported by the economic system (Lee, 1972c).

8. Sharing and generosity are strongly encouraged values which serve to reduce tension (Marshall, 1961, 1976) and to strengthen the network of ties which ensure survival in difficult times (Wiessner, n.d.). Differential accumulation of wealth is discouraged by these values and by the restrictions that accumulated wealth of any sort places on individual mobility in the absence of domesticated animals.

9. Demographic and epidemiological correlates include a low birthrate and long birth-spacing (N. Howell, 1979: 133), and low rates of microbial diseases (Nurse and Jenkins, 1977) such as tuberculosis and of some parasitic diseases such as malaria.

The characteristics of a society whose economy is based entirely on mixed pastoralism should include:

1. Greater expenditure of energy on house construction and the use of sturdier building materials and/or fencing to discourage damage to the house by livestock.

2. Longer occupation times and fewer changes in intra-camp patterning during a particular occupation. These follow from the greater labor involved in the construction of more durable housing.

Camp plans would be expanded to accommodate livestock.

3. Cooperative herding of animals or even corporate ownership and lineal inheritance because of a need to maintain optimum herd size (Spooner, 1973) and to care for and protect the herd.

4. Accumulation and storage of agricultural products, following a limited growth season, to cushion the stresses of the dry or non-growing season for both animals and humans.

5. Increased value of children's labor as herders, fieldworkers, baby-sitters, and food-processors.

6. A reduction in free access to particular areas, since many resources now derive from human improvements to the land such as wells and cleared fields (Meillassoux, 1972, 1973; Ingold, 1980).

7. Formal political and legal mechanisms for the resolution of conflict and for governing the pooling or sharing of group resources, since individuals would no longer be free to shift their group affiliations from year to year (Lee, 1973).

8. The emergence of material accumulation and differential wealth, together with values that favor this accumulation, even if only in the form of livestock and seed grains.

9. An increased birthrate and increased rates of infectious diseases (Lee, 1972b; N. Howell, 1979: 363).

It is logical to suggest that the third corner of the triangle, which involves living with mixed pastoralists in a dependent master-servant relationship, does not impose the same stresses on hunters and gatherers as owning their own fields and herds. Our observations have shown that traditional settlement patterns are less changed and that traditional patterns of mobility are maintained to a greater degree among these dependent !Kung groups. These groups also readily set their disputes and disagreements before Bantu headmen for arbitration, so that they do not experience a pressing need to develop internal mechanisms of formal political control. The master-servant corner of the model, therefore, should be characterized by:

1. Settlement of hunters and gatherers within or adjacent to the mixed-pastoralist camp, with

maximum choice in both house form and camp plan, including maintenance of the traditional ones.

2. Incorporation into the economic unit of the employer, with subsistence provided in direct or indirect exchange for labor.

3. The possible retention of most organizational and ideological features of the traditional hunter/gatherer culture, although hunter/gatherers do have the opportunity, under many variants of this arrangement, to acquire livestock and material goods and/or to marry into the families of the employers, thereby moving toward a different corner of the triangle.

1975–1976 Study of the Dobe !Kung

During a total of twelve months in 1975–1976, we attempted to describe and measure the effects of some of the changes that had been observed by us and others since the first study of the Dobe group in 1963. In the course of this study, we collected data on the changing settlement plan and archaeologically recoverable remains from a series of dry-season camps at Dobe occupied from ca. 1947 to 1976. We also made an inventory of the material goods owned in 1976 by a representative group (Gelburd, n.d., 1978), together with data on the economic practices of the Dobe group in terms of traditional versus modern subsistence practices (Hargrove, n.d.) and in terms of sources of outside income and of the ownership of fields and livestock (Gelburd, n.d., 1978). In addition, by means of information gathered through interviews and questionnaires, we attempted to correlate these changes with degree of exposure to the outside world and changes in traditional values and cultural practices (Gelburd, n.d., 1978).

SETTLEMENT PATTERNS

During 1976, Yellen located, mapped, and excavated a number of old Dobe campsites dating from the late 1940s to the present and interviewed informants about the activities that occurred at

those camps. He analyzed the changes over time by comparing camp arrangements and the percentage of wild/domestic faunal remains. He found that hunting and gathering camps were characterized by a roughly circular camp-plan and little evidence of any of the following: (1) houses, except for the hearth area; (2) kraals; (3) storage structures; or (4) domesticated faunal remains.

Settlement-pattern changes due to domesticated livestock subsistence are characterized by increasing similarities to modern local Bantu villages (Fig. 2). Increased dependency on domesticated animals correlates with: (1) permanent houses; (2) fences around the houses; (3) a kraal within the camp circle; (4) storage structures; and (5) a large percentage of domesticated faunal remains.

The changing settlement patterns can be illustrated by five camps. In the 1947 camp (Fig. 3), huts were constructed of grass and arranged in a circle. Excavations yielded faunal remains of wild species only. The plan of a 1963/64 camp (Fig. 4) is similar to that of the 1947 camp except that 17 percent of the faunal remains were of domesticated species. Goats were first herded in 1968/69, an activity that is indicated in the camp plan by a kraal off to one side (Fig. 5). A 1970/71 excavated camp had a kraal and fences (Fig. 6) and 70 percent of the faunal remains were of domesticated species. From the most recent camp plan, mapped while the site was still occupied in 1975/76 (Fig. 7), it can be seen for the first time that the kraal is included within the camp circle. Semipermanent mud huts and storage facilities were also built. At this camp, occupied over four months, the same people built a series of sequentially occupied houses within the camp area. This indication of increased sedentariness probably would not have been revealed by excavation but, rather, would have led archaeologists greatly to overestimate the population. Only 16 percent of the bones from this camp are from wild animals. Between 1968 and 1969 the Dobe population had a turnover of about 50 percent; between 1975 and 1976 the population turnover was only about four percent.

The study of camp plans documented the following Dobe San settlement pattern changes that had occurred since the 1940s: (1) a change in

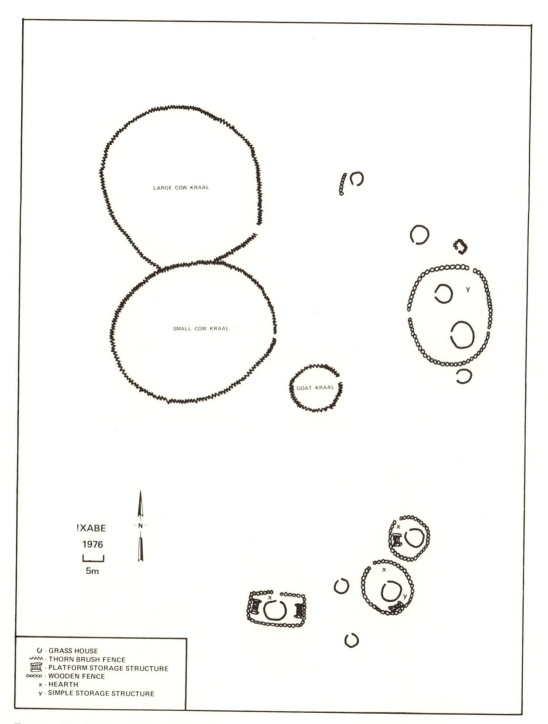

LARGE COW KRAAL

SMALL COW KRAAL

GOAT KRAAL

y

x

x

x

y

!XABE

1976

N

5m

∪ - GRASS HOUSE
∧∧∧ - THORN BRUSH FENCE
▥ - PLATFORM STORAGE STRUCTURE
∞∞∞ - WOODEN FENCE
x - HEARTH
y - SIMPLE STORAGE STRUCTURE

Figure 2. Modern local Bantu village plan.

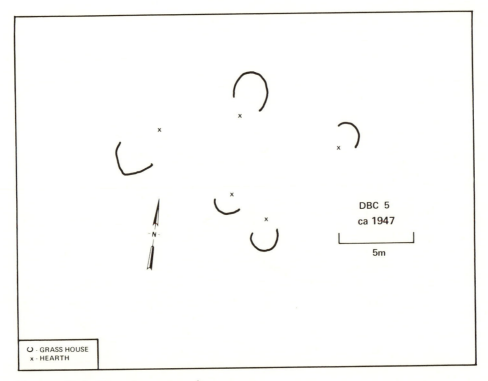

Figure 3. Dobe !Kung base-camp plan, 1947.

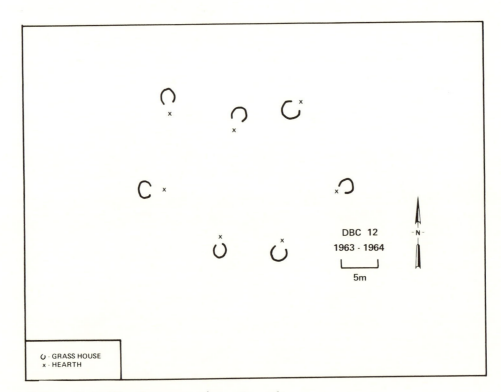

Figure 4. Dobe !Kung base-camp plan, 1963–1964.

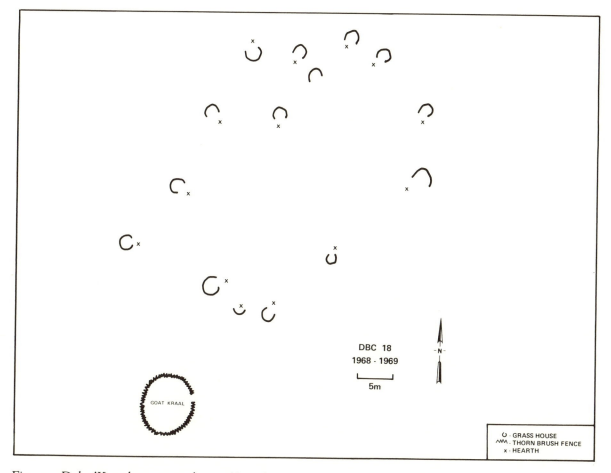

Figure 5. Dobe !Kung base-camp plan, 1968–1969.

camp-plan layout to accommodate domesticated animals; (2) a change in house architecture to accommodate increased storage and longer occupation times, and to protect against destruction by livestock; (3) the addition of fencing and doors to increase private space; (4) the use of separate storage structures; and (5) more permanent residences (camps established on a yearly or multiyear basis rather than a temporary seasonal one).

ECONOMIC CHANGE

Economic change was measured in four ways: (1) daily interviews to determine the types of food consumed by basically the same group of people studied by Lee (1968, 1979) in 1963; (2) excavated samples of bone remains from all dry-season camps occupied by the Dobe group between 1962 and 1976; (3) interviews and questionnaires concerning individual participation in various economic activities and employment histories; and (4) determination of degree of participation in a cash economy and accumulation of wealth, as measured by material culture.

In the subsistence study (Hargrove, n.d.) we tried to replicate the qualitative results of Lee's 1968 food-study with the same people. Lee recorded the types of food consumed by the Dobe group during a four-week study in June and July of 1964. He found that over 99 percent of the foods consumed by the Dobe group were derived from

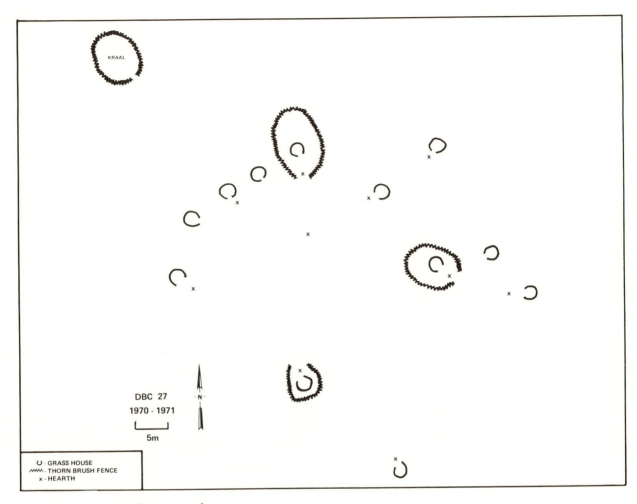

Figure 6. Dobe !Kung base-camp plan, 1970–1971.

wild sources: 60–80 percent vegetable foods and the remainder hunted, snared, or captured game. Less than 1 percent of the meat and less than 0.03 percent of the total calories were derived from domesticated foods acquired through gift exchanges (Lee, 1979: 250–280). In June and July of 1976, 13 adults (5 families) from Lee's original group of 28 individuals were interviewed over a six-week period. Even though 3 of the families had fields and 4 owned livestock, slightly over half of their food was still derived from wild sources. Vegetable foods were particularly important, especially the mangetti (mongongo) nut. Even families who owned livestock and had successfully cultivated fields that

year continued to depend on gathered foods for daily subsistence. Wild foods included many species of roots and berries, mangetti nuts, baobab fruits, and some wild meat (gemsbok, duiker, kudu, porcupine, and guineafowl). The domesticated foods were acquired through self-production, *hxaro* (gift) exchanges, or purchases using wages. Purchases could be made at a store in Tsum!kwe, Namibia, 60 km west of Dobe, or a store at !Kangwa, 40 km to the east. Food purchases, carried back to Dobe on donkeys or on passing trucks, included maize, maize meal, melons, cucurbits, sugar, tea, beer, soured cow's milk, goat's milk, beef, and goat meat. Maize, melon, sorghum, millet, cucurbits,

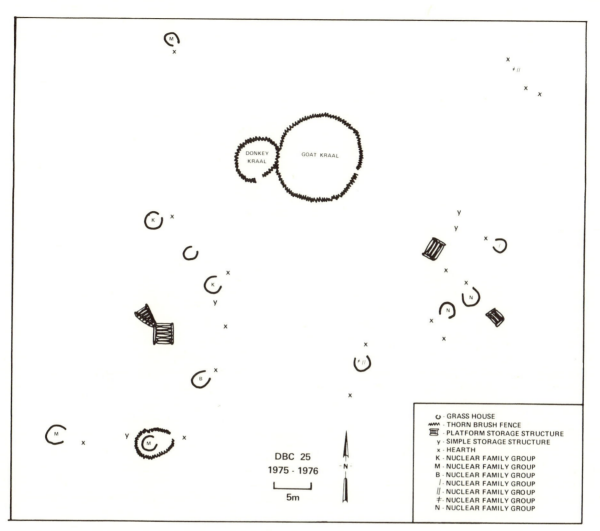

Figure 7. Dobe !Kung base-camp plan, 1975–1976.

and goats were also raised both by San and by their Herero neighbors. Beer was occasionally made by the San, using brown sugar, *grewia* spp. berries or grain, and other ingredients such as hops, honey, and spices. Beef, beer, and soured cow's milk were purchased from Hereros. The increasing dependence on domesticated foods correlated with the results of the camp-plan study, where the excavated domesticated faunal remains increased from none in 1947 to 84 percent in 1976.

Also in 1976, interviews and questionnaires were used in a study of the culture-change pro-

cesses of the Dobe !Kung San (Gelburd, 1978, n.d.) to determine the extent to which changes in Dobe San material culture could be used as indicators of change in other !Kung San cultural subsystems. Initial hypotheses were: (1) that a change in subsistence techniques (economic subsystem) would be correlated with changes of other kinds; (2) that the most obvious indicator of change would be the presence of a conspicuous level of material wealth (especially non-traditional San items) in a household, and that this would be interrelated with culture change, broader economic access, and a high level of exposure beyond the community; and (3) that there would be a positive correlation between cultural and material modernity among the younger San population and that this correlation would prove less strong among the older San age-groups. The hypotheses were derived, in part, from a similar study of the relationship between artifactual and cultural modernity among the Buganda (Robbins and Pollnac, 1977).

In 1976, the Dobe population consisted of about 125 individuals organized into twenty-three households in four "villages," or camps. The population had almost quadrupled from the 1968 population of 35 individuals in twelve households of one village. This increase was mainly due to the influx of San from nearby Bantu villages. The study involved 65 individuals, comprising all the members of fifteen households and three villages. All the adults who had lived at Dobe in 1963 and in 1968 were included in the study in order that information on material wealth and subsistence could be compared. Inventories were compiled of the material possessions of 52 individuals; 22 of these people were also interviewed extensively concerning their economic practices, employment histories, exposure beyond their community, and attitudes toward social practices, traditional rituals, and beliefs. Individuals were tested on their knowledge of languages other than Zu/wasi (Herero, Setswana, Afrikaans, English), on their perceptions of the nation and the outside world, and on their ability to recognize pictures of common, nontraditional objects. In addition, lengthy interviews were conducted with informants concerning their present adherence to traditional values and practices in the areas of socialization, ritual, and medical practices. A total of 38 individual cases were used in the final analysis, consisting of all individuals who had agreed to the inventory of their material possessions and who had also completed at least one of the other three types of interviews. These cases represented a good cross-section of the community in terms of age, sex, and levels of material wealth.

The results of the study showed a correlation between nontraditional subsistence pursuits and accumulation of material wealth (especially of non-traditional San items), indicating that many Dobe San were beginning to move toward a mixed-pastoralist lifestyle. For example, in 1963 no Dobe San owned livestock or cultivated fields. In 1976, 12 people cultivated fields and 24 people owned livestock. The total number of animals owned by the sample population was 9 cows, 113 goats, 10 chickens, 9 donkeys, and 4 horses. Of the people who practiced agriculture, 83.3 percent of them also owned livestock, 91.7 percent had previous employment experience, and 83.3 percent were presently employed. Only people who had fields, livestock, and employment experience owned large trunks (5 individuals, 13.21 percent of the sample population) in which to store possessions, and only these individuals had built storage structures.

Greater material wealth was definitely evident in the possessions of those individuals involved in nontraditional San subsistence pursuits. This was especially significant among San who were cultivating fields and had employment experience. People who had fields had, on the average, 1.5 times as many total manufactured (European) possessions as those who did not own fields (26.5 for field owners; 17.96 for non-field owners). Livestock owners also averaged 1.5 times as many European possessions as non-livestock owners (24.21 for livestock owners; 16.71 for non-livestock owners). Those people who were employed during the time of the study averaged 26.48 European possessions, while people not employed averaged 15.24 European possessions. People with previous work experience owned an average of 1.7 times the number of European possessions as those who had no previous work experience.

An increasing amount of differential wealth with economic modernization was also evident. In almost all cases, the range of material wealth was much greater for those people with fields, livestock, and work experience, and in some cases the range was almost twice as great. The range for those people not exhibiting these characteristics is much more restrictive. For example, the range of European possessions owned by the 21 people (presently) employed was 7 to 50, while for those 17 people not (presently) employed it was 0 to 30.

As the San move toward a mixed-pastoralist lifestyle, the emphasis on traditional subsistence pursuits has decreased. No women went on *overnight* gathering trips during 1976, and few men hunted successfully. This interview data correlates with the results of the subsistence study, which showed no overnight gathering trips and only about a dozen wild animals killed, over half of them guineafowl caught in snares. Only one large game animal, an oryx, was recorded (Hargrove, n.d.). Despite increasing dependence on domesticated foods, however, the Dobe San are actively pursuing a number of different subsistence techniques rather than specializing in one.

Further analysis of the data suggested that one effect of economic change among the Dobe !Kung is the emergence of a large and growing inequality between men and women, as well as among different age groups. Ownership, mobility, and knowledge of the outside world is concentrated among the men. Men in the 30–50 age group own most of the wealth, and these goods are not being exchanged through the *hxaro* system to the same extent as before (Wiessner, n.d.). Out of a sample population of 20 men and 18 women (ranging in age from 15 to 65 years), 85 percent (17) of the men but only 38.9 percent (7) of the women owned livestock.

The sexual differences in the extent of economic (subsistence) cultural change are very significant and will probably lead to an eventual modification of sexual roles that could have a major impact on the Dobe !Kung San culture. As hunter/gatherers, the !Kung San are basically egalitarian (Lee and DeVore, 1968a: 12). The women have an important economic role, providing 60 to 80 percent of the subsistence base. But the women appear to have a very minor economic role in Dobe San mixed-pastoralist society.

Women also have much more limited access to wage employment than men. Selling crafts is the only opportunity open to men and women equally. It is not a reliable means of obtaining cash, since it is totally dependent on the sporadic visits of a crafts buyer. Men have almost sole access to employment by the Namibian and Botswana governments. Since women have little access to wage employment, they have difficulty buying livestock. Thus, most women have only obtained livestock

and other forms of material wealth as gifts.

It is interesting to note, however, that while female hunter/gatherers provided the gathered vegetable foods, women do not seem to be turning to agriculture. Only 2, or 11.1 percent, of the women had fields, while 10, or 50 percent, of the men did. Perhaps this is due to the specific organization of both Tswana and Herero mixed pastoralism, in which women do not usually work in the fields or herd cattle. It is significant that five times as many men as women have fields, more than twice as many men as women own livestock, and the average number of work experiences is 3.05 for men but only 0.89 for women.

The study also revealed changing correlations between cultural and material modernity among different age groups, in contrast to the correlations suggested by Robbins and Pollnac's study (1977). San between the ages of 30 and 50 are the most heavily involved in nontraditional subsistence pursuits: the age category 30–50 consistently had the highest percentage of people practicing agriculture, owning livestock, and involved in wage employment. The people in this age group also had the highest average number of material items (except for clothing) and the widest range. The youngest (15–20) and the oldest (over 50) age categories had the smallest percentages of people owning livestock or practicing agriculture. In most cases they also owned the smallest percentage of material items. Although no one in the youngest age category had a field, 50 percent of them owned livestock and 33.3 percent were presently employed. It is significant that the highest percentage of nontraditional subsistence pursuits and material wealth is among those people between the ages of 30 and 50. In traditional !Kung society (Lee, 1979; Wiessner, n.d.) this is the age group most involved in the subsistence support of the youngest and oldest age groups and is therefore most economically important. The Dobe results are in contrast with Robbins and Pollnac's study, which found the material wealth concentrated in Buganda's ruling elders.

Although people between the ages of 30 and 50 averaged 35 percent more European possessions than any other age group, and were the only ones owning large trunks and storage structures, they also owned the highest average number of traditional items and maintained a more traditional ideology than the younger age groups. This indicates a developing conflict between the values and the economic imperatives of those men who have most of the goods but are also the most conservative. They still profess beliefs and behave in the traditional ways, especially in gift-giving (*hxaro*) and exchange. This conflict creates problems that this most influential decision-making part of the group cannot solve.

While the younger San (15 to 20 years old) expressed the strongest nontraditional ideology and reflected a greater exposure to the world outside Dobe, they had little material wealth. This is probably due to the fact that they have not yet had the opportunities that would allow them to accumulate material possessions. There will probably be a significant increase in the positive correlation between cultural and material modernity as the young San assume an adult role in Dobe !Kung San society.

Discussion

The observed change in the Dobe group from subsistence based on hunting and gathering to a combination of hunting and gathering with independent mixed-pastoralism is an extremely unusual occurrence in the ethnographic present. While many San in Botswana are being drawn into the modern state, virtually all of them are entering the economy as a permanent underclass of servants with no independent rights in land or livestock (Hitchcock, in press; Hitchcock and Ebert, this volume). The owners of these resources are most often Bantu but also include Europeans (in the case of the farms at Ghanzi). The few settlement schemes for San that exist in southern Africa are inherently fragile and would most certainly collapse if the government involved withdrew its direct support and intervention. It is this pattern of an underclass ultimately assimilated into the overlord society through intermarriage which probably characterized most of the prehistoric contact situa-

tions between African hunter/gatherers and Bantu pastoralists and farmers. Only rarely has a hunter/gatherer society moved toward the other corner of the triangle in our model.

Even though the changes at Dobe have been continuously observed by anthropologists, no single factor can be considered responsible for the economic and other changes. The existence of an extremely strong-willed and individualistic group of interrelated families, political pressures from outside causing increasing population concentration and limited mobility, the greater willingness of Bantu groups to sell or dispose of their cattle in exchange for cash or labor, the influence of a growing cash economy, and extensive support from the government and outside groups are all important factors, as is the favorable rainfall of the 1970s. As a result, *all* the causes usually given as prime movers in the development of or transition to domestication, i.e., environment, technology, demography, social organization, and ideology, are operating in this situation. If single-factor explanations do not work in the ethnographic present, how likely is it that they operated in the archaeological past? Perhaps it is only this combination of many factors which is finally tipping the balance away from an independent hunting/gathering way of life. Hargrove (n.d.) compared the San transition at Dobe to that described for the Sandawe of Tanzania by Newman (1970). Like the San, the Sandawe were in contact with the Bantu farmers over a long period but have only become food producers themselves within the last century.

A second major point of this paper concerns the observation that, in the Dobe case, changes in values are occurring last and are most crucial to the success of the new adaptation. There is currently among the Dobe !Kung a notable lack of fit between differential wealth and year-round fixed residence, on the one hand, and, on the other hand, the continuing stated emphasis on *hxaro* (gift-giving, egalitarian relationships) and refusal to accept one person as leader and arbiter. The system as it now stands is fragile. It could easily disintegrate, given its inherent internal contradictions and the pressures thus generated. If such a possibility comes to pass, the most likely result is that the Dobe group will throw in the towel, so to speak, and cast their lot with the Bantu in what might roughly be described as a master-servant relationship; in other words, they will be assimilated. When one looks at the original movement of Bantu peoples over much of sub-Saharan Africa, it is clear that this original expansion was relatively rapid and the subsequent cultural domination nearly complete. One need only point to a linguistic map to underline this fact. What happened to all those hunters and gatherers? By what mechanism or process did their culture, in most instances, dissolve? This question has long interested students of African prehistory and is reflected, for example, in the 1950s and 1960s by the argument that iron spears made effective weapons for subjugation. We would tentatively speculate that what provided a major, if not the most important, factor in the rapid assimilation of hunting and gathering populations was a form of "cultural dissolution," if one wants to call it that. It was caused not so much by forces external to the group but, rather, by internal stresses that led eventually to increased dependence and assimilation to dominant groups that followed an agricultural or mixed-pastoral way of life—in terms of the triangle model proposed earlier, groups would move rapidly toward the apex.

Further examples of the strain that old values can impose on a new economic venture are provided by Lee (1979: 413) and by M. Biesele (pers. comm.). Lee describes one individual who had acquired a substantial herd of goats through *hxaro* and who husbanded this reserve carefully. In economic terms he was very successful. His sons, however, were unable to acquire or maintain wives, because their father was not perceived as adequately generous to his in-laws in proportion to his wealth. In social terms, therefore, the man was a failure. He eventually gave away his herd and moved to a settlement where he became dependent on government handouts. In a second example, Biesele became involved in a San agricultural experiment on the edge of the Okavango delta. San who were living on the periphery of the grazing territory of a Bantu village were encouraged to plant fields. The experiment foundered, owing to the inability of the group to appoint and accept the judgments of a leader as settlement of disputes over allocation of scarce resources such as a plow. In

both cases, the individuals involved moved into a dependent relationship with more technologically advanced peoples rather than back to independent hunting and gathering.

Our third point concerns the fluidity of groups within the triangular model in the arid and semiarid regions of southern and, perhaps, eastern Africa. At first we had to assume that as we followed the Dobe group through their changes, they would eventually come to lie almost completely at the mixed-pastoralist end of the scale and that as of 1977 they simply had not had the time to reach that point. Now we are not so sure. Given the extremely variable and unpredictable nature of the northern Kalahari Desert rainfall—and this is typical of semiarid regions—a "generalist strategy" (as a biogeographer would term it) makes a good deal of sense. In effect, one would want to maintain a broad subsistence base and not put all one's eggs in a single basket. Therefore, we suggest that the process of subsistence change may have almost played itself through and that the balance, in which women still invest a good deal of effort in gathering and men in hunting, may have been struck.

The question that then arises is why Bantu groups who live in the same environment do not adopt the same approach. The answer is that in fact they do. Data on the Hereros indicate that a substantial portion of their diet consists of hunted and gathered food (Murdock, 1967: 62). For eastern Botswana, Grivetti (1979) published a study showing that the Tlokwa, a Tswana group in southeastern Botswana, the most densely populated and overgrazed part of the country, utilized 126 species of wild plant food and 100 different categories of wild animal foods. This is considerably in excess of the similar figures of the !Kung, which are 105 and 54, respectively. Similarly high figures for wild food usage by farmer/herders in Africa have been published for the Lamba (84 plants, 145 animals [Doke, 1931]), the Bemba (98 plants, 131 animals [Richards, 1939]), the Ila (46 plants, 115 animals [Smith and Dale, 1920]), the Pedi (50 plants, 95 animals [Quin, 1959]), the Lovedu (145 + plants, no data on animals [Krige and Krige, 1943]) and the Tonga (139 plants, no data on animals [Scudder, 1962]). Among the Natal Zulu, twelve wild plants are used to supplement the basic cornmeal diet, thereby supplying essential niacin and increasing the amount of available protein (Shanley and Lewis, 1969: 256; Hennessey and Lewis, 1971). In Zambia, Marks (1976) has described the economic pursuits of the Valley Bisa who, although farmers, rely extensively on hunted game meat, spending much time at this activity. For East Africa, Fleuret has described the considerable reliance on plant foods as a supplement to a monotonous starchy diet among the Shambaa of Tanzania (1979: 89). Her research suggests that this practice is widespread in East Africa.

In this paper, we have documented the close relationship between changes in the technoeconomic subsystem and changes in other cultural subsystems. The Dobe !Kung example also supports our hypothesis (Yellen, 1977a) that in a variable and unpredictable environment, narrowly defined equilibrium states based on a narrow range of resources will be less successful in the long run than broadly based adaptations that depend on the widest possible range of resources. In this sense, the technology of domestication may be an addition, rather than an alternative, to hunting and gathering. Yet the evidence also suggests that once the

technology is introduced, it is rare for a group to return exclusively to hunting and gathering.[2] The more common occurrence, for a group that does not succeed in becoming an independent food-producing community, is a shift toward a master-servant relationship and, ultimately, assimilation.

2. One factor we have not considered here is the role of environmental degradation resulting from the introduction of foreign domesticates into a fragile environment. While we have anecdotal evidence to confirm the hypothesis that this introduction restricts hunting and gathering, our observations are qualitative rather than quantitative. Wilmsen (pers. comm.) has suggested that the overgrazing evident at /Ai/ai, 50 km south of Dobe, has suppressed the growth of new mongongo trees from young shoots and is in the process of eliminating this major wild food staple from the area's resources. This process was evident long before the establishment of a borehole at /Ai/ai in 1977 (see also Lee, 1979). Just to the south of Dobe, in areas that are accessible to Herero cattle and goats, a clear difference may be observed between the vegetation on the Botswana side of the border fence and that on the Namibian side, where livestock are prohibited. In particular, the overgrazed side has more acacia at the expense of open, grassy areas. The effect of this difference on San wild food species other than the mongongo has not been measured.

28

The Effects of
Food Production
on Mobility in
the Central Kalahari

ELIZABETH A. CASHDAN

The adoption of food production by hunter/gatherers is usually accompanied by increased sedentariness, but the relationship between these two variables is complex. Because they collect needed resources in one place, agriculture and husbandry can be expected to be associated with an increase in settlement permanence. When food production is not the main basis of the economy, however, but is part of a hunting and gathering adaptation, interesting indirect effects on mobility can result from the interaction of food-production and food-gathering strategies. Two of these indirect effects will be discussed in this paper, one dealing with agriculture and the other with husbandry. It will be shown

This paper was written before the monographs of Tanaka (1980) and Silberbauer (1981) were published, so earlier works by these authors were drawn upon in the discussion of G/wi mobility. However, these later works do not invalidate the statements made here.

The fieldwork on which this paper is based was sponsored by National Science Foundation Grant No. SOC 75-02253 to Henry Harpending and Patricia Draper. The writer is also indebted to Patricia Draper for her helpful criticism and advice on the paper and to William J. Chasko, Jr., for his help and encouragement during the fieldwork.

that where agriculture permits sufficient permanence of settlement to make a home base feasible, the existence of the home base can in turn increase settlement permanence by making it practicable to store bush foods and other nonagricultural items. A second type of indirect effect to be considered concerns the ways in which certain kinds of domestic animals affect hunting and gathering by acting as transport for game and bush foods. By enabling hunter/gatherers to forage more efficiently, this transport allows the population to make fewer residential moves while at the same time making it possible for them to remain in large groups throughout the year.

These and other arguments relating to food production and mobility will be developed through analysis of the mobility patterns of a little-known group—the //Gana Bushmen of the Central Kalahari Game Reserve.[1] The //Gana live in essentially the same environment as the G/wi Bushmen but have incorporated a small amount of food production into their economy. It will be of interest, therefore, to use the published information on the hunting/gathering G/wi as a baseline against which to measure the effects on mobility of these differences in subsistence. The G/wi have been well described in the literature (Silberbauer, 1965, 1972, 1978, 1981; Tanaka, 1969, 1976), but there is as yet only one publication dealing specifically with the //Gana (Cashdan, 1980). However, three (unpublished)

1. The term //Gana is applied to all inhabitants of the central and northeastern parts of the Central Kalahari Game Reserve, although this embraces both cultivating and noncultivating peoples. Those discussed here are cultivating //Gana, a group whose physical and cultural origins derive both from the aboriginal residents of the Reserve and from the Bakgalagadi of Botswana's Kweneng region. These people have lived in the Reserve for at least 150 years, practicing essentially the same mode of subsistence as they do today. All the members of this group speak the //Gana language, which is closely related to G/wi, but many also speak the Bantu language of the Bakgalagadi. The data presented here were collected as part of a regional study on mobility and food exchange that encompassed not only the //Gana but also other ethnic groups living along the Botletle River; among the //Gana, the research emphasized space use rather than subsistence per se. Because of the regional nature of the project, the data collection depended more heavily on interviews than is usually the case in ethnographic work.

reports to the government of Botswana (Murray, n.d.; Sheller, n.d.; Cashdan, n.d.) contain recent material on both G/wi and //Gana, as does J. Tanaka's recent publication (1980).

By subsistence differences is meant the variation in reliance on cultivation, domestic-animal management, and interactions with groups living outside the region. All these factors act directly or indirectly to reduce the impact of resource variability for the //Gana and, as such, have important implications for mobility. The effects of these subsistence variables will be considered on two aspects of mobility: the number of residential moves in a year, and the distances between residential locations.

While interactions between these subsistence variables make their effects complex, each one tends to be most significant during a particular season of the year. For example, cultivation is most important for //Gana mobility during and immediately following the rains, whereas the significance of husbandry for mobility is greatest in the early dry season. Interactions with external groups, on the other hand, are particularly important for mobility during the very late dry season, when water in the //Gana region is extremely scarce. Discussion of these subsistence variables and their effects on mobility, therefore, provides at the same time a picture of //Gana mobility throughout the year. We shall follow the //Gana through their seasonal round as we consider how the factors under consideration affect mobility. Each section will begin with a brief description of G/wi mobility during the relevant season in order to provide a standard for comparison. Before discussing //Gana mobility, it will be useful to give a brief description of the //Gana and their environment.

The //Gana and Their Environment

The //Gana are a population of some 800 people who live in the eastern and northeastern parts of the Central Kalahari Game Reserve in central Botswana (Figure 1). The //Gana with whom we are concerned are a subgroup consisting of 209 people living in the northeastern part of this region near

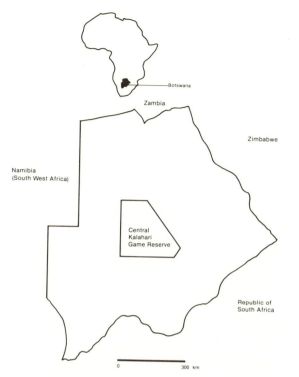

Figure 1. Botswana, including the Central Kalahari Game Reserve.

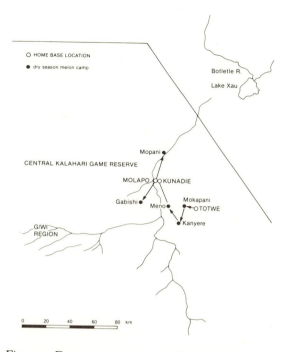

Figure 2. Dry-season moves to wild melon areas.

the Molapo and Totwe pans (Fig. 2).[2] Although the range of the //Gana population as a whole overlaps with that of the G/wi, who live in the western part of the Central Reserve, the Molapo and Totwe people to be discussed in this paper are located approximately 95 km from the principal G/wi loca-

2. For the benefit of readers unfamiliar with Khoisan pronunciation, the marks for the "click" consonants have been eliminated in the text except for names that have already appeared in the literature (G/wi, //Gana, ≠Kade); these have been left in their published forms. The following list provides the correct pronunciation: / indicates the dental click, ≠ the alveolar click, and // the lateral click; a "g" indicates voicing.

Name in text	Correct spelling
Totwe	/"o ≠ we
Gabishi	/Gabishi
Kunadie	Kun//adie
Kanyere	//K'anyere
Gage	/Ga/ge
Xau	//Gau ("Xau" is the spelling on Botswana maps)

The other names are pronounced as spelled.

tion of ≠ Kade, and direct ties between them and the G/wi are few. The Molapo area supports 151 //Gana in several bands and the Totwe area supports a single large band of 58 (Table 1). The //Gana at Molapo and Totwe practice essentially the same mode of subsistence, and the discussion that follows applies to them both.

During the period of fieldwork in 1976, Molapo had a good year with abundant rain and a bountiful harvest, while Totwe had a bad year with little rain and few or no crops. This situation, a chance result of the unpredictable nature of rainfall in the Kalahari, revealed the responses of the people to different environmental conditions, and Molapo and Totwe will therefore be contrasted in the discussion that follows. Because Totwe had a year of little rain and few crops in 1976, the group there approached the G/wi to some extent in their reliance on wild plant foods and hence also, to a slight degree, in their amount of mobility. It should be stressed, however, that this divergence is only part of the behavioral differences that can always be observed among these people due to the extreme variability of their Kalahari environment.

Residence in a game reserve has protected both the G/wi and the //Gana from hunters with firearms and the encroachment of Bantu cattle-herders, both of which have affected the way of life of traditional hunter/gatherers elsewhere in Botswana. Cattle have been kept out, however, not only by the laws of the game reserve but also by the total lack of any permanent standing water in the region.[3] In spite of the official ban on domestic animals in the Reserve, the //Gana do in fact keep goats and the government so far has been willing to overlook the infraction. Goats, unlike cattle, can obtain all their moisture requirements from wild plants, whereas cattle must have a great deal of water. The absence of firearms and cattle has no doubt had the effect of keeping this area rich in game, which is hunted regularly by both //Gana and G/wi. The absence of Bantu cattle-herders has also protected the area from the serious overgrazing so common elsewhere in Botswana.

Water is the crucial factor affecting plant resources and human and animal movement in this region. Mean annual rainfall, low everywhere in the Kalahari, is somewhat lower for the G/wi and //Gana (300–400 mm per year) than it is for the !Kung (400–450 mm per year). Since hunter/gatherers must adapt to the whole range and not simply to the average rainfall, the variation in rainfall is even more significant than is the low yearly mean. The importance of temporal and spatial variability in rainfall has been emphasized for the !Kung (Lee, 1972d) but it is even more severe for the G/wi and //Gana. Pike (1971) has computed the coefficient of variation (standard deviation/mean) to measure the percentage deviation from the mean annual rainfall, and his data indicate a figure of between 50 and 60 percent for the G/wi and //Gana compared to only 25 to 30 percent for the !Kung region. The absence of permanent standing water is particularly critical in the area inhabited by the G/wi and the //Gana. Unlike the !Kung region, where even temporary pans may hold water for months, none of the

pans in this area holds water for more than about two weeks after a heavy rain. Several generations ago the G/wi and //Gana had access to sip wells in certain parts of the region, but a gradual lowering of the watertable has now eliminated this source of water also.

The //Gana depend heavily on wild plant foods for the approximately five to seven months of the year when they are in dry-season bush camps. These resources are important at other times of the year also, but at the home-base camps they also have cultivated crops and are often able to obtain water from local pools. The absence of permanent standing water in the Central Reserve means that both //Gana and G/wi must obtain a large part of their moisture from wild melons and roots. The *mokate* (tsama) melon, which appears around February and remains available for most of the dry season, is particularly valued for its high moisture content and pleasant taste and is the chief source of moisture for the //Gana and their livestock during the dry months of the year.[4] The //Gana tsama collection strategy differs from that of other Central Reserve residents in that the women customarily gather using donkeys and are thereby able to carry a much larger load of melons back to camp each trip. (The implications of this for mobility will be discussed later.) The //Gana also increase the crop of the wild melons by systematic burning, a practice that takes place about every third year in the late dry season. The //Gana recognize that the melons do not grow well when the grass is tall, and they speak of the practice of burning as "plowing the grass." A second incentive for the practice is that the new, tender green shoots of the grass attract wild game.

Water roots (*lerushwa, tobokwe, serowa*), a reliable year-round source of moisture, are used only as

---

3. A borehole was recently drilled at !'wi !um (at the G/wi location of ≠Kade); with this exception, there are no wells or boreholes in any part of the Central Reserve. At the time of Silberbauer's studies in the 1960s this borehole did not exist, and as it is only very rarely used as a source of water by the Molapo and Totwe //Gana it need not be considered in the account that follows.

4. The plant species mentioned in the text are given in Setswana; their botanical names are as follows:

mokate (tsama)	*Citrullus lanatus*
mokapani	*Citrullus naudinianus*
lerushwa	*Strophantus* spp.
tobokwe	*Eriosema cordatum* or *Rhaphionacme burkei*
serowa	*Brachystelma* spp.
mogwana	*Grewia bicolor*
motsotsojane	*Grewia retinervis*
moretwa	*Grewia flava*
lekonkoto	not identified

TABLE 1. Population by Home-Base Location

Camp number	Location	Adults	Children*	Total
1	Molapo	26	17	43
2	Molapo	23	20	43
3	Molapo	11	7	18
4	Molapo	6	8	14
5	Molapo	4	5	9
6	Totwe	32	26	58
7	Kunadie†	13	11	24
	Total	115	94	209

*Distinction between adults and children is only approximate, as age estimates were based on visual inspection. Children include all those judged to be 16 years or younger.
†The settlement from Kunadie moved its home base to Meno in the beginning of the 1976/77 rainy season.

a last resort when the tsama melons are gone or have become rotten; hence they are widely used only at the end of the dry season. If tsama melons are available throughout the dry season, as they were in 1976, most species of water root are seldom used.

Although the //Gana use a wide array of other wild plant foods (see lists by Silberbauer, 1972: 282; Tanaka, 1976: 117–119), the siting of their settlements is determined chiefly by the location of tsama melons; people do not normally make a change of camp simply to exploit other resources. A case in point is the wild bean, *Bauhinia* spp.; this high-protein staple of the G/wi diet is not found in all parts of the //Gana area, but residents indicated unwillingness to travel long distances simply to collect it. This is probably due in part to the fact that they are able to substitute cultivated crops (in this case, cultivated beans) for wild ones, and perhaps also to their ability to store selected wild foods, which are then available throughout the year. The various species of grewia berries (*mogwana*, *motsotsojane*, and *moretwa*) are particularly suitable for storage, and large quantities of dried grewia berries are regularly kept at the home-base, rainy-season camps. This year-round use makes grewia a highly important part of the //Gana diet. Although melons

are the most important resource for a dry-season camp, grewia berries are also highly valued, and each of the tsama-melon camps used in 1976 was also a source of at least one species of grewia.

Game meat is of great importance to the //Gana diet at all times of the year. Whereas agricultural crops substitute for wild plant foods to some degree, domestic animals do not appear to substitute for game meat to the same extent. Domestic animals (in this case, goats) are eaten on certain ritual occasions and also when they die of natural causes, but only occasionally are they killed solely for food. This does not mean that goats are not an important resource to fall back upon when supplies of game are low, but in 1976 game meat was abundant and goats were seldom killed for food.

The //Gana, unlike the G/wi, do not hunt with bows and poisoned arrows. Instead, they use spears as their principal hunting weapon, aided by the use of horses and dogs. Horses are not commonly owned by the //Gana (105 adults surveyed owned a total of 8 horses), but when available they enable hunters to run down large game such as eland or gemsbok. Birds and smaller game (including duiker and steenbok) are normally taken with snares, and predators are sometimes caught in steel traps.

Data were not collected on the number of game animals taken, but it appears that the //Gana are killing considerably more eland than are reported as being taken by the G/wi (Silberbauer, 1972: 286; Tanaka, 1976: 111). It is possible that the //Gana hunting methods, which include use of horses, enable them to kill a greater number of individuals of these preferred species than can be taken with the bow-and-arrow methods of the G/wi. On the other hand, the numbers of certain animals in the Central Reserve have fluctuated considerably in recent years (Biesele, 1971: 66) and differences in the percentage of species taken, including the differences between Silberbauer's and Tanaka's reports, may simply be due to yearly fluctuations in available game.

Cultivation and Rainy-Season Mobility

As we have seen, the environments of G/wi and //Gana are similar as regards rainfall, standing water, and the absence of cattle-herding neighbors. They are also similar in plant and animal resources, although differences in subsistence strategies between the two groups may affect the range of species commonly procured. A comparison of G/wi and //Gana, therefore, holds constant the major environmental factors affecting mobility and allows us to explore the effects of the subsistence differences between the two groups. In the discussion of //Gana rainy-season mobility that follows, the mobility patterns of the noncultivating G/wi will first be briefly summarized in order to provide a point of contrast.

G/WI RAINY-SEASON MOBILITY

Even during the rainy season, moisture is a critical resource governing G/wi mobility. Water in the pans of this region lasts only one or two weeks after a heavy rain; hence even in the rainy season there are inevitably periods between showers during which a particular pan will be dry. The G/wi have no means of storing water and must therefore move frequently even during the rainy season, either to different rain-filled pans or to patches of the wild melons that supply their moisture when there is no available water.

Although the timing of onset and ending of the rainy season is highly variable, the rains usually begin around December and end around April or May. Silberbauer (1972) indicates that in a good year of abundant tsama melon, a "synoecious" band (which he defines as the largest aggregate of people, approximately 50 or 60 individuals) moved six times in the rainy season between November and April/May. In a bad year the pattern was similar, with the same band moving five times between December and May. In the period immediately following the rains, although the G/wi must obtain their moisture from wild melons, plant resources are plentiful. The G/wi are thus able to remain in large groups through July. The frequency of residential moves during this period appears to be similar to that during the rainy season, with the G/wi moving three times between May and July in a year of plentiful tsama melon, and twice in this period during a year when the melons were scarce (Silberbauer, 1972).

On the average, then, the G/wi move about once a month during and immediately after the rainy season, their pattern of movement being determined both by water and plant resources. As these plant resources are, in large part, used as a source of moisture, we should expect sedentariness to be impossible without some means of collecting and storing moisture. For the //Gana this need is filled by cultivation, which provides moisture as well as food, and so enables them to remain virtually sedentary throughout the rainy season.

//GANA CULTIVATION

It has been argued that agriculture requires a degree of sedentariness that is not possible in this region, due to the scarcity and dispersion of resources (Silberbauer, 1965: 39). One of the most significant features of agriculture, however, is that it stores needed resources; hence it would appear to be more fruitful to consider how agriculture makes permanent settlement possible. By collecting resources together, agriculture may make it possible to be sufficiently sedentary to make feasible a home-base strategy and the construction of permanent facilities. The existence of such facilities permits, in addition, the storage of noncultivated foods and other items, which may allow still greater permanence of habitation.

As we have seen, wild melons, particularly the tsama melon, are an important source of moisture for both G/wi and //Gana. The //Gana, however, also cultivate a domestic melon called *marotsi* that is similar to the tsama but considerably larger. In cultivating marotsi melons they are, in effect, growing a water supply for dry periods both during and after the rains. Normally, when one thinks of agriculture one thinks of *food* resources, but in the Central Kalahari Game Reserve, where the dominant factor governing mobility is the availability of moisture, it is appropriate that agriculture should be used to produce a naturally storable form of moisture. Unlike the G/wi, who do not cultivate marotsi and must move from pan to pan during the rainy season, the //Gana use the moisture from their cultivated melons when there is no water in nearby pans. This water supply allows them to remain sedentary during the rainy season (after the marotsi have become ripe) and, if the crop has been good, for some months after the rains have ended.

//Gana cultivation takes place in fields at the home-base settlement, which is reoccupied each rainy season. While cultivation of marotsi helps make semipermanent settlement possible, the settlements themselves also make it more practicable to cultivate other crops, in particular maize and beans, which must be processed and stored if they are grown in any quantity. Foodstuffs are stored in conical, grass-covered "storage houses" that are identical in size and form to the living houses of the camp (which are similar to !Kung rainy-season huts but are somewhat larger) and are located near the dwellings inside the clearing of each camp.

The importance of agriculture in this region, however, must be seen from the perspective of the frequent crop failures that are the inevitable result of extremely sparse and unpredictable rainfall. In a year of good crops, agriculture provides both food and moisture and so permits the people to remain somewhat sedentary, but the //Gana must always be prepared, in the not unlikely event of crop failure, to resort to a more mobile strategy of total dependence on wild foods. Agriculture for the //Gana, in other words, is a provision against short-term scarcity (particularly week-to-week variability in water supplies) but not against long-term (yearly) variations in the availability of food or water.

Because rainfall varies not only from one year to the next but from place to place within the region at any one time, it is possible to see the response to drought conditions and to a bountiful "water" harvest simultaneously. The following comparison of the two //Gana settlements in the study area illustrates the consequences of differences in agricultural production; it will be seen that the response to a bad crop is for the group to increase mobility by leaving the home base immediately after the rains, and to make less use of it during the following dry season. In 1976 a total of seven groups were surveyed in this region; five had their home-base camp at the large Molapo pan, an additional camp was located at the nearby Kunadie pan, and a single large camp was located at Totwe, some 40 km southeast of Molapo (Fig. 2). In the 1975/76 rainy season, the camps at Molapo were favored with

good rains and a plentiful harvest while the people at Totwe had a very poor crop and virtually no marotsi melon. The people from Totwe consequently left their camp for wild-melon locations immediately after the rains, and when the Totwe home-base was visited in July no one was there and no marotsi were stored there. At Molapo, by contrast, people did not start to leave the main camp in significant numbers until August, and even in September—the height of the dry season—there were still some marotsi melons stored at the camp for the few who chose to remain.

USE OF THE HOME BASE

After their poor 1976 harvest, the people from Totwe essentially abandoned their home-base camp until the following rainy season. The more fortunate Molapo people, however, continued to use their main camp as a home base throughout the year, even while most of them were at the wild-melon locations, and generally a few people were there even in the dry season. Those at the wild-melon camps would periodically bring in a donkey-load of game meat and bush foods (chiefly grewia berries) and take back a load of cultivated marotsi for their moisture needs.

The degree to which the //Gana use their home-base camp during the dry season is dependent on three factors: the presence of sufficient donkeys for transport of melons and bush foods, the proximity of the wild-melon sites to the home-base camp, and the size of the marotsi harvest. These factors vary from camp to camp and from year to year, and the use made of the home base varies in consequence. The Totwe people, whose marotsi harvest had been poor, did not remain at their home base during the dry season and no regular transport between home base and dry-season camp took place (Fig. 3).

Both bush foods (including game meat) and cultivated crops are stored at the home-base camp during the dry season (Table 2). Although some stored food is used by the few people staying at the home base during the dry season, it appears that much of it is consumed early in the following rainy season when the group returns en masse to the

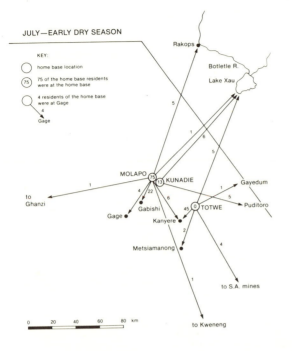

JULY—EARLY DRY SEASON

KEY:

⬭ home base location

㊵ 75 of the home base residents
were at the home base

◯ 4 residents of the home base
were at Gage
|
4
Gage

Figure 3. Seasonal mobility, early dry season. Figures 3, 4, and 5 are based on censuses taken at three times during the year. The figures indicate: (1) numbers of individuals at the dry-season camps at various times of the year; (2) numbers of individuals visiting at the Botletle River and elsewhere; and (3) areas along the river and within the region visited from each home base. A home-base camp is always the rainy-season camp and is distinguished from a dry-season camp by the presence of fields and more permanent structures. Skins, drums, and other material items not needed during the dry season are kept at these home-base camps. These criteria, rather than the number of people at the camp, distinguish the home base from other camps.

It can be assumed that where the number of people associated with the mobility arrow is 8 or less, the mobility is due to social and/or "business" reasons. Larger numbers indicate band moves to dry-season melon camps (in July and September) or visiting provoked by lack of local water during the early rainy season (in January). Places indicated without a dot or circle are approximations.

camp; a similar inventory made in January showed a considerably smaller amount of food in storage.

These home-base camps, made possible in the first instance by the cultivation of marotsi melons, also permit use of other buffers against scarcity, for example, storage of nonagricultural items. Material items, the most important of which are water containers, are stored at the camps. Most //Gana camps have at least a few 55-gallon metal drums, the range for the five camps surveyed being from 2 to 9 drums per camp. These drums, as well as plastic containers, are filled from the pans to provide a supply of water when the pans become dry between rains and for a short period after the rains have ended. The marotsi melons allow the //Gana to remain sedentary at the home-base camp during the latter part of the rainy season, and the drums provide water from the first good rains even before the marotsi are ripe. At the home-base camps the //Gana also store large quantities of skins, furs, and skin mats, which they sell and trade to people living outside the Central Reserve (see Table 2). The trade in skins is also, indirectly, important for mo-

bility in that money and goods received in exchange provide the means to purchase such things as drums and other water containers, and it is the presence of a home base in which to store the skins that makes the trade possible on anything other than a very small scale.

Even in a bad year with a poor harvest, therefore, these other safeguards against shortages enable the //Gana to remain sedentary during the rainy season in a way that is impossible for the G/wi. While the cultivation of their water supply enables the //Gana to be more sedentary, the home base itself provides the means, through storage of bush foods and material items, to make this home-base sedentariness more reliable. The positive feedback between agriculture and permanent settlement is limited for the //Gana by environmental conditions that make total dependence on food production impossible. In spite of this, however, the //Gana are considerably more sedentary during the rainy season (and during the early months of the dry season, if the crop has been successful) than are the noncultivating G/wi.

TABLE 2. **Commonly Stored Items, Dry Season** (Based on an inventory of food items and skins stored at one Molapo home-base camp. Each house belongs to an individual man or woman rather than to a family. An "X" indicates the presence of an item in the house; a number indicates the quantity. A similar inventory made in the rainy season showed far fewer food items stored.)

	House Numbers											Outside
	1	2	3	4	5	6	7	8	9	10	11	
marotsi melon	144	30	200	46	20	100	100	120	268	220	24	
tsama melon					30		18					
grewia berry	X	X			X		X		X	X		
marotsi seeds	X				X	X			X	X		
maize (field)	X				X	X	X		X			
maize (river)*	X								X			
beans (field)	X	X	X	X	X		X		X	X	X	
meat (dried)	X						X					
skins, goat			1	5	2		6		2	4		8
skins, small fur†				20			1				6	17
skins, lion, leopard												5
skins, other‡			7	2	5			1	3	2		1

*Maize from the river (as opposed to maize from the //Gana fields) was purchased at the Botletle River in exchange for meat and skins.
†Jackal, wildcat, genet, etc.
‡Steenbok (12), gemsbok (2), wildebeeste (1), cow (1), kudu (1), duiker (4).

Husbandry and Dry-Season Mobility

Let us now consider how the use of domestic stock can enable the //Gana to minimize moves during the dry season. We shall first consider G/wi dry-season mobility, then take a look at the impact of goats and donkeys on the dry-season mobility of the //Gana, and conclude with some general remarks on the interaction of husbandry and foraging.

G/WI DRY-SEASON MOBILITY

The pattern of G/wi rainy-season mobility described above changes markedly as the dry season progresses. After July, as resources decrease, the band of 50 to 60 people splits into small family groups, each moving to a separate part of the band's territory and remaining there until the rains begin (Silberbauer, 1972, 1978). Silberbauer states that the "band responds [to the decrease in resources] by splitting up into units which are small enough to remain sedentary during the period of food scarcity" (Silberbauer, 1972: 297) and that "as a rule the isolated household occupies only one camp for the duration of the period of separation" (Silberbauer, 1978: 115). Tanaka, who studied the same group four years later, also reports that the G/wi split up into small family groups during the middle to late dry season. Unlike Silberbauer, however, he indicates the possibility of considerable mobility during this period; he reports that one

G/wi extended family group moved eleven times between September and February, although he notes that this group moved more frequently than did the others in the ≠Kade area (Tanaka, 1969: 9). The first half of this period is in the late dry season, but the latter half, December through February, would normally be the beginning of the rainy season. The fact that Tanaka is referring to the movements of a family group suggests that the rains were probably sparse or nonexistent during this entire time and that the people were, therefore, prevented from reforming into a large group. If this interpretation is correct, it implies that this was an extremely harsh year, during which one might expect to find greater mobility than usual.

Although the evidence we have does not allow generalizations to be made about the number of residential moves made by the G/wi during the dry season, the data on group size presented by Silberbauer and Tanaka are unambiguous. A decrease in group size and an increase in mobility are two ways of dealing with diminishing resources, and it appears certain that the G/wi split up into small, scattered groups during the dry season to avoid increasing their mobility. In this regard it is significant that the //Gana are able to remain at least as sedentary as the G/wi during the dry season while, at the same time, remaining in large groups. The role of husbandry in bringing this about will be discussed below.

GOATS

We have already noted that the //Gana do not often kill their goats solely for food, although they do eat them on certain ritual occasions, and they eat those that have died from natural causes.[5] Goats are useful as a source of milk in the rainy season, for the supply of skins for mats and clothing, and, presumably, as an addition to the meat supply when game is scarce.

The //Gana goats impose few constraints on

the mobility required for hunting and gathering. During the rainy season they are often kept a short distance away from the settlement, and many camps have a rainy-season *moraka* ("goat post") one or two kilometers away, where the goats are kept while the crops are growing. This affects labor strategies to some extent but has no significant effect on residential mobility, since the morakas are near the home-base camp. The dry-season pattern is for the goats to move with the band to various wild-melon areas where, in addition to what the goats forage for themselves, the //Gana give them tsama melons and rinds for moisture. If these are not available, the people collect *lekonkoto*, a water root reserved solely for livestock, since it is considered to be inedible by humans. Cultivated marotsi melons are never fed to the animals, as the people prefer them to the wild tsama. Goats are never taken to sources of permanent water outside the Central Reserve; rather, they move with the people inside the Reserve to the wild-melon locations the //Gana use for their own food and moisture needs.

This pattern of movement is made possible by the fact that goats are not dependent on standing water, and they are thus easily incorporated into a mobile hunting-and-gathering subsistence strategy. A significant implication is that either large or small herds of goats can be kept without the necessity for major organizational change should the size of the herd drop below a certain level. An indication of this is the considerable range in the numbers of goats kept by the //Gana, a wealthy band having about 150 goats and a poor one having only about 20.[6]

While they do not occasion major changes in mobility, goats do affect the speed of travel to some degree—a trip that would take a man one day on foot was estimated to take between two and three days if he was traveling with a herd of goats. Husbandry of a large herd also involves some labor investment in structures at the dry-season camp, and this is probably an added incentive to move less frequently. If the herds are large, brush kraals must

---

5. The number of goats killed solely for food depends upon the size of the herd. Over a four-month period, one band with a large herd killed four goats for food, another band with many goats killed two for food, and two bands with few goats did not kill any for food.

6. The numbers are based on observations of goats kept in kraals and close to camps. The actual range of ownership is probably greater than this, due to the practice whereby people with few or no goats care for those of wealthier individuals.

be constructed for them at the dry-season camps, and a large brush enclosure must be erected to protect the piles of tsama melons that are gathered and kept at these camps. Goat management, then, while compatible with human foraging and mobility, is a force for decreasing the number of residential moves—but, as will be suggested below, it is the transport provided by the //Gana donkeys that makes this reduced mobility a practical possibility.

DONKEYS

Donkeys, unlike goats, appear to have a significant effect on mobility because of their use as transport. As has been mentioned above, donkeys contribute to more extended use of the home base by carrying cultivated melons from it to a dry-season camp as well as by conveying bush foods and game meat back to the home base. The use of donkeys as transport also has a direct effect on hunting-and-gathering strategies. Donkeys have the potential to extend the foraging radius around a residential camp, and they increase procurement efficiency by allowing a larger quantity of melons to be carried back to camp in a shorter period. This second point is important, because wild animals compete with the //Gana for tsama melons. The use of donkeys in gathering has the effect of increasing the resources at the dry-season camp, which can thus be expected to support a larger band, probably over a longer period of time.

On the average, the //Gana have one donkey for every two adults, but as with other livestock, ownership is not distributed evenly among the population. Nearly three-fourths of the adults (75/105) own no donkeys at all, while 11 adults out of 105 each own two or more. However, the effects of this uneven distribution appear to be somewhat mitigated by sharing. Donkeys were frequently not with their owners, and it appears that access to them for plowing and other purposes is widely shared, even between individuals of different camps. The donkeys obtain moisture in the dry season from tsama melons that the people collect for them, and when the people leave the Central Reserve they often do so on donkeyback, so the donkeys then have access to water.

The //Gana transport game, wild and cultivated plants, and skins on their donkeys, but the transport of wild tsamas is of particular importance in its effects on dry-season mobility. The dry-season camps of the //Gana are distinguishable from those of other Bushman groups by the presence of enormous piles of tsama melons, brought there on donkeyback and protected in large shelters made of brush and branches. The explicit aim of collecting such large quantities early in the season—rather than simply gathering them as they are needed—is to prevent them from being eaten by wild animals; it is also probable that the shade of a brush shelter helps to prevent the melons from rotting. No attempt was made to count the tsama melons in the shelters around the camp, but it is estimated that they numbered well over 1,000. We once attempted to help the Totwe band by transporting in our vehicles some of the tsamas they had collected; filling two one-ton pickup trucks full of melons had no noticeable effect on the remaining pile. This took place shortly after the Totwe group had moved to the site, and the entire pile of melons had been collected in approximately a week. Collection of such large quantities in so short a time would clearly be impossible without some form of transport to carry the load, and, indeed, groups in the Central Reserve with few or no donkeys do not have large piles of melons at their camps.[7]

It was suggested earlier that one motivation for reducing the number of residential moves through efficient melon collection is the greater labor investment in structures required by a large herd of goats. An additional motive for the //Gana melon-collecting strategy is the undesirability of water roots as compared with melons; such roots are widely available throughout the year, but both the G/wi and the //Gana prefer not to use them for moisture so long as tsama are available. This is due

---

7. Although all //Gana bands use donkeys when gathering, it appears that in highly favorable circumstances they may not bother to collect the melons into large piles at the dry-season camps. In 1976 it was chiefly the Totwe and Kunadie bands that engaged in this practice, perhaps because those from Molapo were able to depend to a large extent on their abundant marotsi harvest; even the Kunadie people said that they would not collect melons in this fashion if they were extremely plentiful.

to the superior taste and moisture content of the
melons and to the comparative ease with which they
can be obtained (the roots must be dug, while the
melons can simply be picked). It is also possible
that the distribution of melons in largish patches
makes them easier to collect than the roots, although this was not put forward by informants as a
reason for their preference. By amassing large piles
of tsama, therefore, the people can reduce the
length of time they are forced to subsist on water
roots. This point was never reached in 1976, a year
of abundance in which the supply of tsama lasted
until the rains returned.

//GANA VERSUS G/WI DRY-SEASON MOBILITY

Figure 2 shows the wild-melon areas in the
region that were used by //Gana bands in 1976.
The people from Molapo left for the tsama areas of
either Gabishi or Mopani in August and remained
there until the rains began. The people from Totwe
made a total of three residential moves before re-
turning to their home base. They moved first,
shortly after the rains, to a Mokapani melon area,
then, in July, to the tsama area at Kanyere, and
from there, in September, to the tsama area at
Meno, where they remained for the rest of the dry
season. The greater number of moves made by the
Totwe band appears to have been occasioned by
their poor marotsi harvest, which forced them to
begin moving earlier in the dry season.

It is difficult to compare G/wi and //Gana mobility during the dry season, because of the problem
of evaluating the existing data about the G/wi. Silberbauer's reports appear to indicate that the family camps formed in the dry season between August
and November/December are sedentary, while
Tanaka found that at least one G/wi family was
quite mobile during this period (see above). If this
interpretation of Silberbauer's remarks is correct,
then G/wi and //Gana are similar in the number of
moves they make between August and December;
they do, however, differ strikingly in group size.

Generally, all the //Gana from one home-base
camp will move to the same melon area and will not
split up into smaller groups as the dry season progresses as do the G/wi. Indeed, in September the

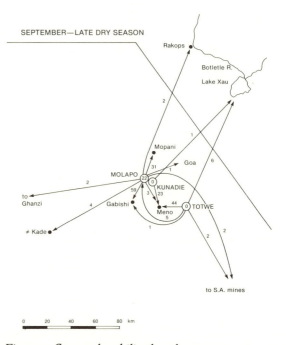

Figure 4. Seasonal mobility, late dry season.

//Gana were still in large groups with an average
band size of 34. The number of people supported
by the resources of a given area is even larger than
this would indicate, because at some locations (e.g.,
Meno) there were two entire bands camped approximately one kilometer apart. If we disregard
camp divisions, therefore, we can see from Figure 4
that in September, the height of the dry season,
there were an average of 53 //Gana camped at each
of the three melon locations (Gabishi, Mopani, and
Meno) being used at the time.

A qualification should be added to these conclusions based on data gathered in a year of abundant tsama melon. There is little doubt that in a
year of little tsama and/or late rains, the //Gana,
like the G/wi, would be forced to scatter into
smaller groups and subsist on water roots; indeed,
in December, 1975, informants at the Botletle
River reported that the //Gana in the Reserve were
doing exactly that. This necessity apparently comes
later for them than for the G/wi, however, and in
some years is avoided entirely.

A second point to note is that in the late dry

season some //Gana avail themselves of an option (to be discussed below) to leave the Reserve for permanent water at the Botletle River. This may reduce the population of //Gana in the Reserve by as much as one-third or one-half toward the end of the dry season. In September, 1976, however, only 4 percent of the //Gana were at the Botletle River, and their large group size and relatively sedentary camps at this time must therefore have resulted from their use of donkey transport for efficient melon collection and, for the Molapo groups, from their partial reliance on cultivated marotsi.

DISTANCE BETWEEN CAMPS (RANGE SIZE)

The tsama-melon locations being used in 1976, like most such localities reportedly used in the last three years, are approximately 20 km from the home bases of the groups exploiting them. This compares closely with Silberbauer's maps of residential site locations, which show a radius of about 24 km for the ≠Kade band in both good and bad years.[8] This suggests that cultivation and husbandry, although they affect the number of moves made in a year and the size of the dry-season camps, may have little or no effect on range size as measured by the distance *between* such camps. This is not surprising, because although the //Gana have incentives to reduce the number of times they move camp they apparently do not have any motivation to reduce the distance between camps. Reasons for reducing the number of residential moves, which include the labor investment in kraals and other structures required by a large herd of goats, are reinforced by a strong emotional preference not to move camp frequently. The //Gana of this area speak disparagingly of residents of the Central Reserve who have no fixed home base as "moving around like animals," an attitude which may stem partly from their interactions with wealthier Bantu peoples outside the Reserve. Emulation of these higher-status groups may have contributed to the feeling that "proper" people live in villages. There

is, however, no motive for reducing the distance *between* camps, and the extra labor expended in moving an additional few kilometers each time appears not to be significant to the //Gana. It might be expected, therefore, that they would prefer to move to the most abundant, rather than the closest, tsama-melon locations within their territory, since this would enable the group to remain in one place for the longest possible time. Moving to the most abundant melon locations, which may be farther away, would result in a reduction of moves per year but not in a reduction in range size as measured by the maximum distance between camps.

It is of interest that density pressure is not a factor in inducing the //Gana to reduce their range size. Some recent models for the origins of agriculture hold that food production is a response to pressure on resources arising from increased population density, and this would ordinarily lead one to expect that food production would act to decrease range size. This does not, however, appear to apply to the //Gana, who are at a very low density, even lower than that of the noncultivating G/wi.[9]

Husbandry in a Foraging Subsistence

We have seen how the use of animal transport, added to a foraging subsistence pattern, can reduce mobility by affecting the strategy and logistics of gathering. Even where husbandry is chiefly important in providing a source of food, there may be situations where interaction with hunting and gathering will affect the organization of food procurement and, as a consequence, mobility patterns. A case in point is that of llamas in northern Chile; these animals may have been domesticated chiefly as a source of meat, but their potential as transport may have affected gathering strategies in a manner

8. According to a researcher for the Botswana government, the hunting ranges for //Gana and G/wi are also similar—approximately a day and a half's walk in all directions (Sheller, pers. comm.).

9. Silberbauer gives the density of G/wi bands as from 4 to 8 sq. mi. per person ($10.4–20.7$ km²), with a mode of 6 square miles (15.5 km²) (Silberbauer, 1972: 295), while this writer estimates the //Gana of the Molapo and Totwe areas to be at a density of about 23 km² per person. Density figures depend on how one draws boundaries around the population, however, so comparisons between the figures of different observers must be treated with caution.

analogous to that of the //Gana donkeys. It would not be unreasonable to suppose that llama transport may have been one of the causes of the increased home-base sedentariness that occurred with their domestication during the Vega Alta II phase in the Atacama desert, where domestication of these animals apparently took place before the cultivation of food crops (Pollard and Drew, 1975).

The ease with which animal husbandry is incorporated into the hunter/gatherer economy of the //Gana is due to the mobility of the livestock. Not only do the livestock move to the gathering locations visited by the people (since both use wild plants for moisture), but their mobility apparently prevents them from taking over the area from the wild game. Goat husbandry has thus been able to coexist with hunting and gathering for a long time in the Central Kalahari, whereas, elsewhere in Botswana, cattle-keeping has caused irreversible environmental changes that have made inevitable the final supplanting of hunting by husbandry. Since cattle need a great deal of standing water, which is scarce in Botswana, they remain close to the available water sources. As "sedentary herd animals," cattle have successfully competed with wild ungulates in these areas and have made significant changes in the vegetation. The //Gana goats, by reason of their mobility, are akin to wild herd animals, and as a result their effect on the environment appears to be slight.

Long-Distance Moves in the Late Dry Season

We have seen how food production reduces the number of residential moves for the //Gana without causing a similar reduction in range size as measured by the distance between camps. These two aspects of mobility appear to have quite separate determinants, a fact that is not surprising but is often overlooked by those who speak of "mobility" and "sedentariness" as opposite ends of a single continuous variable. The importance of the distinction between these two mobility variables will become more apparent in the discussion to follow, which considers the effects on //Gana mobility of their relations with groups outside the local region. These interactions constitute an additional force

for reducing the number of residential moves, but they do this by facilitating an increase in range size.

The external groups in question here are //Gana and non-//Gana who live at the Botletle River, a permanent water source located some 115 km from Molapo, just north of the Central Reserve boundary (Fig. 2). The Central Reserve //Gana have intermarried with these river Bushmen, and when water resources in the Reserve become scarce late in the dry season some //Gana visit their relatives and friends at the Botletle River and remain with them until the rains return. The number who do this varies from year to year depending on the amount of tsama melon remaining in the local area. This helps to adjust the population density in the Reserve to the dwindling resources and keeps the quantity of resources more nearly constant for those who remain within the Reserve. At the same time, it permits those who have moved to the river to remain sedentary at a place with abundant water for the remainder of the dry season.

The G/wi also have ties to individuals living at permanent water sources outside the region but these ties do not appear to play a large role in their dry-season mobility. The nearest source of water for the G/wi is at the Ghanzi farms, and Silberbauer indicates that the "nearer Reserve" G/wi maintain contact with relatives who live at Ghanzi and may visit them in years of bad drought (Silberbauer, 1972: 274). It is not clear whether these "nearer Reserve" G/wi include the bands in ≠Kade territory (those studied by him and described here), but in his discussions of mobility within ≠Kade territory Silberbauer does not suggest that moves to Ghanzi are common in either good or bad years. If, as appears likely, the ≠Kade G/wi do not go to the permanent water at Ghanzi to the same extent that the Molapo //Gana go to the Botletle River, the reason is probably simply one of distance—the G/wi settlement at ≠Kade is 240 km from Ghanzi whereas the //Gana settlement at Molapo is only 115 km from the Botletle River.

RELATIONSHIPS WITH BUSHMEN AT THE BOTLETLE RIVER

A network of kinship ties links the //Gana to Bushman groups living at Bantu cattle-posts along

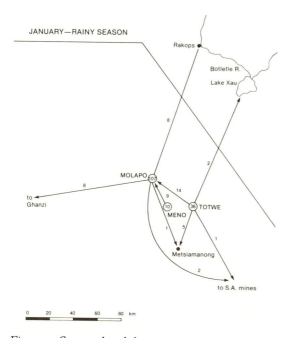

JANUARY—RAINY SEASON

Figure 5. Seasonal mobility, rainy season.

Lake Xau is roughly 50 km southeast of Rakops, so this pattern of alliances and mobility is one of groups moving north in parallel paths, each going to the part of the river closest to its home base.[10]

LATE DRY-SEASON MOVES TO THE RIVER

The importance of these long-distance moves as a buffer when resources are scarce in the Central Reserve is shown by the fact that the number of people who move to the river in the dry season varies considerably depending on the degree of drought. In 1976 there was abundant tsama melon, and comparatively few people left the Reserve for water. In 1975, on the other hand, there was a scarcity of tsama in the Totwe area and the new rains did not begin until quite late. This combination of sparse tsama and late rains resulted in many more people leaving the Reserve (at least from the Totwe area) in that dry season than in the dry season of 1976. The data illustrating the difference between the 1975 and 1976 river moves, derived from interviews rather than censuses, are shown in Table 3. Most of the people from Totwe were questioned in July, 1976, about their movements to the Botletle River in the late dry season of 1975, and many of these people were also seen at the river in December of 1975. To compare the moves made in 1976, most of the residents of both Totwe and Molapo were interviewed in January, 1977, about their movements during the previous year. Over twice as many people left for the river at some time during the late dry season of 1975 (57 percent) than left in the same season of 1976 (22 percent).

It is clear, then, that access to the Botletle River adjusts the population density in the Reserve to changes in local water and melon resources. Access to the river means that a single long-distance move allows those who make it to remain sedentary throughout the drought months, and at the same time lessens the pressure on resources for those

the Botletle River and at nearby Lake Xau. Most of these people are non-//Gana who have traditionally lived along the river, but some of them are //Gana who came originally from the Central Reserve. Sometimes these //Gana stay for a year or two at the river and then return to the Central Reserve (residents of this type formed a new camp in the Reserve during the 1976/77 rainy season) and sometimes they remain more or less permanently at the river, often entering into work relationships with cattle-owners there. In either case, the //Gana living along the river maintain their ties with the people in the Reserve and provide a place for visiting relatives to stay; the Central Reserve residents also intermarry with the non-//Gana Bushmen who have traditionally lived along the river. Owing to the large numbers of cattle, there is relatively little game at the Botletle River; hence, alliances with people from the game-rich Central Reserve are beneficial to these river residents as well.

The //Gana from Molapo have most of their ties with people at the western river cattle-posts near Rakops, while those from Totwe have ties at the eastern cattle-posts around Lake Xau (Figs. 3–5). Totwe is some 40 km southeast of Molapo, and

10. Although the Kunadie people have their home base near Molapo, their ties are with people at the Lake Xau area; they came originally from Totwe, and lived at Lake Xau for several years before moving to Kunadie five years ago. Their *lefatshe* (territory) is still the Totwe region, and they have close relatives living at the Lake Xau cattle-posts.

TABLE 3. **Moves to the Botletle River in the Late Dry Season, 1975 and 1976**

	Totwe, 1975	Molapo and Totwe, 1976 (combined sample)	Totwe, 1976
Pop. sampled/total adult population	23/29	71/121	27/32
No. of adults at Botletle River	13	23	6
Percent of sample at Botletle River	57	32	22

remaining in the Reserve. The people in the Reserve are thus better able to exploit the available resources without having to split up into small, scattered mobile groups. These moves to the river, therefore, reduce the number of residential moves in the drought periods both for those who go to the river and, presumably, for those who stay behind in the Reserve.[11]

It is often impossible to make a clear distinction between social visits and moves prompted by scarcity; at any time of the year, ostensibly social visiting may in fact be prompted by resource scarcity. For example, in mid-January, 1977, rain was still extremely sparse in the Totwe area, and about a third of the group was away "visiting" relatives at Molapo where there had been a great deal of rain (Fig. 5). Visits such as this serve the same purpose as the late dry-season moves to the Botletle River in that they permit people to remain at a place of abundant resources outside the local region.

It is not possible to make comparisons between the //Gana and the G/wi with respect to this type of mobility, as there are no comparable published

11. This discussion is chiefly concerned with late dry-season moves made for the purpose of obtaining water, but visits to the river also take place at other times of the year. While water is the chief motive for visits made in the late dry season, social visits and trading trips are often made in the early dry season. This business, which is usually conducted by the men, includes the sale of skins, game meat, and sewn skin articles, and the buying of tobacco and other goods. Visits to the Botletle River in the early dry season were commonly two to four weeks in duration, whereas virtually all who left in the late dry season remained away from one to several months and did not return until the beginning of the rains.

data. It is possible that the G/wi make less use of visits to relatives at permanent water sources outside the region because of the greater distances involved, but it is not yet known whether they depend to the same extent as the //Gana on long-distance moves within the Central Kalahari Game Reserve itself.

It would seem likely, however, that an increase in food production would be associated with a decreasing reliance on long-distance visits to relatives outside the local region. In the general case where food production is initially adopted by mobile foragers, it could be expected that hunter/gatherers would respond to increasing pressure on resources by denying people in other areas access to these scarce resources. This closing-off of ties would make it necessary to depend to a greater extent on storage as the primary means of dealing with local resource scarcity. Even where the context for adoption of food production is somewhat different, the permanence of settlement associated with it should decrease the cost of storage as a buffer while at the same time increasing the cost of long-distance mobility.

Although there are no comparable data on this long-distance type of mobility among the different groups, it is of interest that the //Gana do not appear to rely on the various cultural means of strengthening and extending kin ties that are found among some other Bushman groups (e.g., the name relationship of the !Kung, the *hxaro* system of delayed reciprocity, and so on). The long-distance visits that this writer observed among the //Gana nearly always involved real kin relationships based on close blood ties or marriage. This may indicate that they are less dependent on a widespread network of social ties for dealing with the risks of scarce resources. There is also an apparent trend toward endogamy in recent years, which may be associated with an increase in property. If one compares the birthplaces of husbands and wives for three age groups, one finds that, for the younger couples, 63 percent of husbands and wives were born in the same location, whereas this is true for only 18 percent of middle-aged couples and only 11 percent of older ones. The numbers here are quite small (complete data were available for only 39 marriages), but as marriages are a prime way of forming ties with people in other areas, these figures may be an indication that a greater dependence on storage and property (including drums and livestock) is associated with a decrease in the need for widespread marriage partnerships. These conclusions are highly speculative, however; comparable data on G/wi and //Gana with respect to social networks and the visiting that is based on them would help in understanding the effects of food production on this type of mobility.

Conclusion

This paper has considered the impact of food production on hunter/gatherer mobility, using data from the //Gana of the Central Kalahari Game Reserve and making comparisons, where possible, with the published material on the G/wi Bushmen, also of the Central Reserve. Small-scale cultivation and husbandry were shown to reduce the number of residential moves made by the //Gana while permitting the population to remain in large groups. There appears to be little or no effect on range size, however, as measured by the distance between residential camps. The discussions of cultivation and husbandry suggest that the mobility of hunter/gatherers who are also marginal food-producers is affected not only by the fact that food production aggregates resources but also by interactions between food production and hunting/gathering. For example, the transport provided by the //Gana don-

keys affects the logistics of gathering, and as such is an important intervening variable in reducing their residential mobility. The paper concludes with a discussion of long-distance visits to relatives living outside the region and shows how a single long-distance move to the Botletle River allows the //Gana to remain relatively sedentary during times of drought. Although comparable data on long-distance visiting among the G/wi are not available, it was suggested that an increase in food production should be associated with a decrease in reliance on this type of mobility together with substitution of storage as the primary means of buffering local resource scarcity.

Although the G/wi have survived successfully in their arid environment for many generations without food production, it is of interest that the //Gana, with their limited cultivation and animal husbandry, appear to be more successful competitors than the original hunter/gatherers of the region. The //Gana camps include a number of people who formerly depended solely on hunting and gathering, some of whom came into the polygynous //Gana society through intermarriage. The only other hunter/gatherers in the //Gana region today are a band of some 53 people, and this group is also beginning to adopt food production by caring for the goats of the //Gana from Totwe.[12] While both hunting/gathering and food production are successful in this area in the absence of competition, therefore, it appears that when the two are competing for the same resources, those who produce food have the advantage over those who are restricted to hunting and gathering. This may be one reason why incipient agriculture and domestic animals were originally adopted by hunting and gathering communities in southern Africa.

12. These nonagricultural hunter/gatherers, who call themselves "Thumkhwe," resemble the G/wi physically and are similar to them in that they have no home base, plant no crops, and use bows and arrows as their principal hunting weapon. They live in the Totwe region and their territory extends eastward a short distance beyond the Central Reserve border.

29

Foraging and Food Production among Kalahari Hunter/Gatherers

ROBERT K. HITCHCOCK AND
JAMES I. EBERT

Though the origins of agriculture have been a major focus of anthropological inquiry for decades, many of the processes involved in the shift from foraging to food production are still unclear. Relatively few contemporary groups have been well documented both as foragers and food producers. Detailed records on a wide range of topics are, however, available for the Basarwa (San, Bushmen) of southern Africa, many of whom live in the Kalahari Desert of Botswana and adjacent countries (Fig. 1).

The primary reason the Basarwa have drawn so much anthropological attention is that many of them still practice a way of life that characterized

The research on which this paper is based was supported by U.S. National Science Foundation Grants No. SOC75-02253 and No. BNS76-20373, and by a grant to the Remote Area Development Program, Ministry of Local Government and Lands, Botswana. We would like to thank the residents of the Kalahari for the information presented here and to express our gratitude to those of our colleagues who kindly shared with us their data and their ideas.

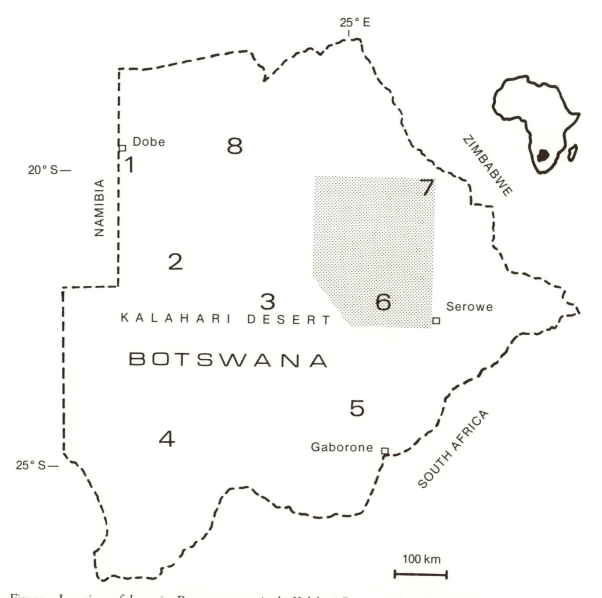

Figure 1. Locations of the major Basarwa groups in the Kalahari, Botswana. (1) !Kung; (2) Nharo and other Ghanzi Farms groups; (3) G/wi and G//ana; (4) !Xō; (5) Kūa (southeastern Kalahari); (6) Kūa (eastern Kalahari); (7) /Aise and other Nata River groups; (8) Bugakwe and other Okavango Swamps and river Basarwa groups.

most of human history (Lee and DeVore, 1968a: 3). In 1965 Richard Lee estimated that of the 24,000 Basarwa in Botswana, 16,300 worked on farms or cattle-posts and 2,000 were practicing a mixed agricultural and hunting strategy, but the remaining 6,100 were traditional hunter/gatherers (Lee, n.d.: 13, 20). A decade later, Lee (1976a: 8) revised his estimate, saying that less than 5 percent of Basarwa were then hunting and gathering for a living.

The purpose of this paper is to discuss some of the ways in which agriculture has come about among foraging populations in the Kalahari Desert of Botswana and to show some of the reasons for the fact that few groups in the Kalahari today are completely dependent on domesticated foods.

Contact and the Origins of Food Production

Most of the discussions of the origins of food production in southern Africa have stressed the significance of incursions of Bantu-speaking populations, saying that the beginnings of agriculture are directly related to the presence of new ethnic groups (Seddon, 1968: 490; Fagan, 1973: 159, 165; Phillipson, 1977c: 145-147; J. D. Clark, 1962: 219–220, 222–223; 1972: 128). However, archeological evidence of sheep in Namibia and the Cape indicates the possibility that domesticated stock existed in southern Africa prior to the incursions of Bantu-speaking groups (Klein, this volume).

One oft-cited reason for the lack of agriculture among Kalahari populations is their lack of contact with outside groups. Archaeological evidence tends to belie this notion. Artifacts found in both Later Stone Age and Iron Age sites reveal that there must have been at least a certain amount of contact between foraging and food-producing populations in the Kalahari that may date back over 1,500 years. At first, contacts may have been sporadic, usually in the form of occasional hunting parties taking on local guides. Later, these contacts would have become more frequent, as trading parties went into remote areas in search of skins and other local goods. The major Tswana towns attracted itinerant Basarwa traders, who brought firewood, wild plant foods (e.g., mogorogorowana [*Strychnos cocculoides*] and mmilo [*Vangueria infausta*]), skins, and handicrafts for sale or exchange. Some Basarwa groups even cultivated domesticated plants, particularly tobacco (*Nicotiana tabacum*) and marijuana (*Cannabis sativa*), which they exchanged with other groups for food and material goods.

By the second half of the nineteenth century, trade had become increasingly institutionalized, particularly after Shoshong, the Bamangwato tribal capital, became a major commercial center (Parsons, 1974: 655). As hunters, traders, and travelers poured into the Kalahari after Livingstone and Oswell's trip across the eastern Kalahari in 1849, ivory, ostrich feathers, and skins were procured in massive amounts for markets in the Cape. Basarwa groups were able to obtain firearms, making them more effective hunters. Many of the larger game species that were once found in abundance in the eastern Kalahari in particular were increasingly restricted both in numbers and distribution by the end of the nineteenth century, a process which was exacerbated by habitat deterioration (Campbell and Child, 1971).

As populations expanded and the market for livestock products opened up, cattle became increasingly important as a source of both labor and food for groups seeking opportunities other than hunting and gathering. Some Basarwa groups began to settle around the peripheries of cattle-posts in order to gain access to livestock products. At first, cattle were taken into the waterless Kalahari only seasonally, primarily to pans where water was available for short periods during the rainy season. As well-digging increased and, later, when boreholes began to be drilled, the availability of permanent water meant that cattle could be kept in the new grazing areas year-round (Devitt, 1977; Hitchcock, 1978a, n.d; Vierich, n.d.a). Although the first boreholes were drilled in Botswana around the turn of the century, it was not until the 1930s and 1940s that drilling of water wells was done systematically. The numbers of water sources expanded in the 1950s and especially during the 1960s drought (Hitchcock, 1978a, b). With the rising numbers of water points, stock rates went up and the chance for obtaining employment as a herder increased. It must be stressed, however, that cattle-posts existed in the Kalahari long before the advent of the borehole, and Basarwa presumably had had access to livestock employment and livestock products for centuries.

Many of the Basarwa groups that settled on wells and boreholes began to be incorporated into a system of serfdom or patron-clientage (Silberbauer and Kuper, 1966; Tlou, 1977; Vierich, n.d.a, n.d.b; Hitchcock, 1978a). In exchange for their labor as herders or domestic servants, Basarwa were given in-kind payment, usually in the form of clothes, food, and tobacco. Specific families of Basarwa began to be identified with individual families, particularly chiefly families in the Bamangwato and Batawana tribes (Hitchcock, 1978a; Tlou, 1977). Basarwa serfs were passed from one generation to the next, often being inherited patrilineally. Although we have no idea how old the institution of serfdom is, it has been suggested that "clientship has been a central feature of inter-ethnic relations in Botswana for at least two centuries and probably much longer" (Russell and Russell, 1979: 82).

Whereas at first the relationship between the foragers and farmers could be said to be a symbiotic one, with benefits accruing to both sides, elements of competition soon began to be seen. There are numerous reports of cattle-owners seeking retribution for livestock that had mysteriously disappeared. On the other hand, Basarwa were known to voice their dissatisfaction over the fact that livestock were eating melons they themselves needed (Russell and Russell, 1979: 83). Hunting laws were instituted by chiefs, and violators of those laws were often punished. Basarwa frequently decried what they felt to be laws passed expressly to prevent them from eating. Setting bush fires, a common practice of both foragers and pastoralists in Botswana, was another source of contention.

Simple contact with crop- and livestock-raising populations, however, did not result in the adoption of food-production techniques by the Basarwa. It was only when forced to do so, either as a result of demographic or environmental pressures, that Kalahari foraging populations began to raise their own food.

Foraging in the Kalahari Ecosystem

A second major reason frequently cited for the lack of food production in the Kalahari is the marginal nature of the ecosystem itself, which is a vast tableland consisting of rolling tree-bush savanna dotted with pans and dissected by fossil drainages in some areas. Soils are primarily unconsolidated sands, through which rain-water percolates quickly, a feature that is in part responsible for relatively low crop yields. Because these sands are also deficient in certain minerals, notably phosphate, unless they are fed salt and bonemeal, domestic ungulates often contract diseases such as aphosphorosis.

The interior basin of southern Africa is characterized by a semiarid climate, with rainfall varying from approximately 200 to 700 mm annually

along a southwest-to-northeast axis in Botswana. The Kalahari fits the criteria used to define a desert, in that water is the crucial limiting factor for production and water inputs are largely random both in space and time (Noy-Meir, 1973). Unlike some deserts, however, the Kalahari is relatively thickly vegetated, which has led some researchers to suggest that it should more properly be termed a "thirstland." Droughts are common in Botswana and, as a consequence, populations inhabiting the Kalahari and adjacent areas have developed a variety of strategies to deal with stress periods (Devitt, 1977, 1978; Silberbauer, 1978; Hitchcock, 1978b); two of the most effective of these strategies are small group size and flexibility in group composition (Lee and DeVore, 1968a: 7, 9, 11).

Group sizes tend to fluctuate, depending, at least in part, on resource availability. Patterns of aggregation and dispersal also vary in the Kalahari, with !Kung, for example, collecting around water sources in the dry season and dispersing into smaller groups in the wet season, while G/wi do just the opposite (Barnard, 1979).

The determinants of mobility patterning also vary. Yellen and Lee (1976: 43) note that scarcity of water is the most crucial limiting factor for the !Kung, and Marshall (1976: 76) says that "if they have to choose between lack of food and lack of water, they stay by the water and leave the food." In the central and eastern Kalahari, on the other hand, surface water is only available seasonally; consequently, the crucial determinants of mobility patterning are the distribution and abundance of water-bearing plant species, particularly melons (e.g., *Citrullus vulgaris*) (Tanaka, 1971, 1976; Cashdan, n.d.; Silberbauer, 1965, 1972, n.d.). In the southwest Kalahari, water is obtained from sip-wells, and the size of the group and its mobility are determined by the yield of these sip-wells and their distribution, respectively.

The most critical period of the year for Kalahari foragers is the late winter and early spring, when resource abundance is at its lowest point and the rains have not yet begun. The groups adapt by shifting not only their population size and composition but also their spatial location. Before the onset of winter, each group assesses the whereabouts of resources and then breaks down into minimal units, spreading out across the landscape in such a way as not to conflict with other groups.

Patterns of year-round land use in the Kalahari are far from random. The landscape is divided systematically, which serves both to spread groups spatially and to provide information on the whereabouts of other groups (Wiessner, n.d.: 54). While some Kalahari researchers maintain that these land divisions are "territories" (e.g., Heinz, 1972), this term implies defense of space (Pianka, 1974: 105). Perhaps a better way of looking at these divisions is to see them as "ranges," areas over which humans and animals move for subsistence procurement and other purposes. Essential to these ranges is a variety of resources in sufficient amounts to support a group over the course of a year (Silberbauer, n.d.: 208; Yellen, 1976: 54; Hitchcock, 1978a: 243; Marshall, 1976: 71).

Lee (1968) made a significant contribution to the study of hunter/gatherers when he noted that their work effort was generally low, ranging from 12 to 19 hours per week. Again, there is regional variation even among !Kung, with Draper (n.d.) pointing out that work effort among groups occupying the southern portion of the !Kung range involved more time and labor than among Dobe groups. Another important feature of work effort among foragers is that by and large it is continuous throughout the year, primarily because of the lack of surpluses. In general, Kalahari foragers do not store food for any length of time, since, as Lee and DeVore (1968a: 12) put it, "The environment itself is the storehouse." Most of the work is carried out by adults, with children contributing little, if any, labor (Draper, 1975).

Another characteristic feature for foraging societies is their emphasis on the sharing of resources (Lee and DeVore, 1968a: 11). Given the variation in success rates in food procurement, foragers require social mechanisms that act to ensure the equitable distribution of resources. Links between groups in a region are maintained not only in terms of kinship and affinal ties but also in terms of a network of exchange and trading (Silberbauer, 1972: 273–274). The egalitarian nature of Kalahari foragers is maintained in part by public criticism of stingy individuals, which acts as a kind of leveling mechanism (Marshall, 1961; Draper, pers.

comm.). Wiessner (n.d.) has described in careful detail a system of delayed reciprocity known as *hxaro* found among !Kung groups. This system, combined with the patterns of land division and ties among groups through kinship and marriage, acts to provide reciprocal access to resource areas in the Kalahari.

The diet of arid land foragers is a very generalized one, consisting of what Flannery (1969) calls a "broad spectrum" exploitative pattern. Kalahari foragers have a wide knowledge of both plants and animals; they know where they can be found and how they reproduce. They tend to be selective about the species they exploit at various times during the year (Lee, n.d., 1968, 1969; Silberbauer, 1972; Tanaka, 1969, 1971, 1976; Yellen and Lee, 1976). During times of abundance, groups usually exploit a restricted range of species, broadening their diet in periods of less abundance.

A feature of Basarwa diet that has received wide comment is the degree of dependence on plants as opposed to animals (Lee, n.d., 1968, 1969; Silberbauer, 1965, 1972; Tanaka, 1971, 1976). Marshall (1976: 92) estimates that 75 percent of the diet is comprised of plant foods, while the balance is of animal foods; Tanaka (1976: 116) estimates that 80 percent of the diet is from vegetal sources. Once again, there is a range of variation to be found in the Kalahari.

A great deal of attention has been paid to the fact that a single Kalahari plant-food, the mongongo (*Ricinodendron rautanenii*), comprises a significant portion of the diet of !Kung populations (Lee, n.d.; 1968; 1969; 1972a; 1973; 1979: 182–204). This nut species has been described by Lee (n.d.: 192; 1968: 33) as being both abundant and predictable. The fact that the !Kung have what has been termed a "superabundant" resource, combined with the wide variety of other plant and animal foods available, has served to underscore arguments about the security of the hunting and gathering way of life and to supply another explanation for why food production has not come about.

Ardrey (1976: 60) has attacked Lee's findings, saying that the !Kung case is not representative, but anthropologists working among !Kung have stressed that they were chosen for study specifically because they were atypical (Lee, n.d.: 32; 1976a: 3;

N. Howell, 1979: 4). It has been stressed that foragers do sometimes experience periods of difficulty (Sahlins, 1972: 36; Marshall, 1976: 62). It is interesting to note that although /Aise and other Basarwa in the Nata River region have access to mongongos, they do not exploit them in any quantity, ostensibly because "they do not taste good" (Hitchcock, field notes). Thus, the simple presence of an abundant resource does not guarantee its exploitation. Wiessner (n.d.: xxxi, 154) points out that in 1974, because of intense convective thunderstorms, the mongongo crop in the /Ai/ai area was almost completely destroyed, causing widespread hunger among !Kung populations living there. Nata River Basarwa groups also informed us that mongongo nuts were available in greater quantity in dry years than in wet ones. Other kinds of problems can affect the availability of mongongos: Wiessner (n.d.: 27) and Lee (1973: 312) both mention, for instance, the damage caused by elephants in mongongo groves.

Origins of Food Production in the Kalahari

Given the emphasis on the foraging way of life in the Kalahari it is perhaps not surprising that food production there has received relatively little attention from anthropologists. However, Kalahari populations have engaged in food production, some of them for a substantial period of time. Table 1 contains a listing of a number of Basarwa (San, Bushmen) groups in various areas of the Kalahari, with the types of domestic plants they cultivate and animals they raise, as gleaned from reports of anthropologists, development workers, and others. It can be seen that food production is practiced in almost every part of the desert and that many groups participate in both agricultural production and animal husbandry, if only to a limited extent.

Food production may have come about in the Kalahari as a result of contact with food-producing populations, or it may have begun locally, without other groups having provided either the methods or the domestic plants and animals.

D. R. Harris (1972: 183) points out that agriculture may have been preceded for a substantial

period of time by what he calls a "manipulation strategy," involving transformation of selected parts of the environment so as either to stimulate the natural ecosystem or to reduce the diversity only slightly (D. R. Harris, 1969: 6). Perhaps the most important of the strategies in the Kalahari is controlled burning. Reports of use of fire by Kalahari foragers are found in many nineteenth-century explorers' journals; Schapera (1929: 140) says that veld-burning is the closest Basarwa had got to practicing agriculture by the early twentieth century. Bleek (1928: 17) says that burning was done at the end of winter in order to encourage bulb growth. It is also used to encourage the growth of new shoots to attract game (Hitchcock, 1978a), for signaling, and to eliminate pests such as snakes and ticks, as well as to protect humans from large predators (M. L. Murray, n.d.; E. Wily, B. Clauss, pers. comm.). Murray summarizes:

> Fire eliminates competition from undesirable plant species on potentially productive melon sites or gathering areas and apparently promotes reproduction and growth of tsama melon (*Citrullus vulgaris*), gemsbok cucumber (*C. naudinianus*), sour berry (*Grewia* spp.) and *Cucumis* spp. during the wet season. Used in this manner, fire is referred to as a type of "ploughing." (n.d.: 27)

Groups do not usually return to burned areas until the third year. Timing of the burns is critical, since burning at the wrong time of year, such as during the mid-to-late rainy season, may tend to harm the plants. Burning, therefore, is usually done carefully, as an integral part of the overall subsistence system.

Other environmental manipulation strategies that have been observed in the Kalahari include intentional protection of important food-plant species, replanting of certain species in areas near base camps, and intentional cultivation of at least one species of wild melon. Kūa foragers in the eastern Kalahari practice a kind of protection strategy for groves of trees bearing hard-shelled fruits known as *d//ao'a* or *mogorogorowana* (*Strychnos cocculoides*). Since this species is subject to damage by fire, fire breaks are cleared around the groves. In the southeastern portion of the Central Kalahari Game Reserve a camp was found with a number of *bai* plants

TABLE 1. **Domesticated Animals Owned and Crops Cultivated among a Sample of Kalahari Foragers and Food Producers**

Area	Group name	Crops cultivated	Animals owned	Reference
Southwest Kalahari	!Xõ (Hukuntsi,etc.)	melons, beans, maize	donkeys, goats, dogs, chickens	Thoma (n.d.; pers. comm.)
Southwest Kalahari	!Xõ (Takatshwane, etc.)	melons, beans, maize	cattle, goats, dogs, donkeys, horses	Heinz (n.d.; 1979: 243–245); Wily (pers. comm.)
Western Kalahari	Ghanzi groups (Nharo, ≠Xau//ei, ≠Kaba, G/wi, etc.)	melons, beans, maize, tobacco	cattle, horses, dogs, donkeys, goats, chickens	Childers (1976: 58–63); Guenther (1975/76: 46; 1977: 198–199); Bleek (1928: 17); Silberbauer (1965: 127ff.)
Central Kalahari	G/wi, G//ana (!Xade)	melons, beans, squash	donkeys, goats, horses, dogs	Jeffers and Childers (n.d.: 5, 11–13, 18); Sheller (n.d.); Tanaka (1976: 100)
Central Kalahari	G/wi, G//ana, etc. (Central Reserve groups)	melons, beans, maize	donkeys, horses, goats, chickens, dogs	M. L. Murray (n.d.); Sheller (n.d.); Cashdan (n.d., this volume); Vierich (pers. comm.)
Northwest Kalahari	!Kung (Dobe, etc.)	melons, beans, maize, sorghum, tobacco	cattle, donkeys, goats, horses, chickens, dogs	Wiessner (n.d.); N. Howell (1979); Brooks et al. (this volume); Lee (1976a, 1979); Gelburd (n.d.: 56–59, 64); Draper et al. (n.d.) Hargrove (pers. comm.)
Eastern Kalahari	Kūa	melons, beans, sorghum, maize, tobacco, pumpkins, cowpeas, sweet reed, groundnuts, marijuana	cattle, horses, goats, sheep, chickens, dogs, donkeys, cats	Hitchcock (field notes); Ebert et al. (n.d.)
Southeast Kalahari	Kūa, Tsassi, etc.	melons, beans, maize, sorghum, groundnuts	cattle, goats, donkeys, chickens, horses, dogs, cats	Vierich, Copperman (pers. comm.); Hitchcock (field notes)
Northeast Kalahari	/Aise, Ganade, //Owochu, etc. (Nata groups)	melons, maize, sorghum, millet, groundnuts, beans, sweet reed, tobacco, marijuana, squash, pumpkins, gourds, calabashes, tomatoes, cabbage, sunflowers	cattle, donkeys, horses, goats, sheep, chickens, dogs, cats	Hitchcock (field notes); Cashdan and Chasko (n.d.); Filteau, J. Ebert, M. Ebert (pers. comm.)
Northern Kalahari Okavango Delta, Mababe Depression	Bugakwe, /Tannekwe, Tzexa, Goekwe, !Garikwe, Hukwe, etc.	millet, pumpkins, beans, maize, sorghum	goats, cattle, donkeys, dogs, chickens	Heinz (1969: 746–747, 750); Seiner (1977: 32–35); Campbell (1976 and pers. comm.)

(*Raphionacme burkei*) growing next to the abandoned huts. Subsequent interviews with Kūa revealed that such transplanting was not uncommon and that root and melon plants were sometimes taken from their native habitats and replanted closer to residential locations. One problem with this transplantation strategy was noted, however: often the plants became even more bitter than they were originally.

Story (1958: 7; 1964), among others, has emphasized the detailed botanical knowledge possessed by Basarwa. One species with which they are extremely familiar, and which plays an important role in their economy, is the tsama melon (*Citrullus vulgaris*); crucial to foragers who occupy waterless areas such as those in the Central Kalahari (Story, 1958; Tanaka, 1969, 1971, 1976; Silberbauer, 1965, 1972, n.d., 1978; Cashdan, n.d., this volume). The melons are raised not only to provide moisture for humans but also for the livestock and the small stock they sometimes possess; however, Cashdan (n.d.: 32) notes that the cultivated variety of melon is generally reserved for human consumption, only the rinds being fed to animals. Although we do not know the length of time that melons have been intentionally planted in the Kalahari, it is possible that they have been grown for hundreds of years.

The traditional anthropological view of foraging societies is that they have relatively little impact on their physical environment. Some researchers attribute this limited environmental impact to their inherently conservationist attitude (e.g., Campbell, 1977). A more likely explanation is that forager groups are often characterized by low population density and a wide-ranging mobility that allows resource areas to recover from periods of exploitation.

There is a growing argument in the biological field over the causes of what has been termed "desertification," the process of environmental degradation that was seen most recently in the Sahel zone of Africa. Some scientists attribute this process to climatic factors, noting the frequent droughts that occur in savanna ecosystems; other scientists see man and his domestic animals as the major causes of environmental change. This argument has continued among researchers working in Botswana, with some people holding that habitat deterioration is due primarily to the effects of burning, cutting of trees, overhunting, and, especially, the grazing of domestic herbivores (e.g., Campbell and Child, 1971; Child, 1971; Parris and Child, 1973; Child et al., 1971). Cole and Brown (1976: 195) point out, however, that population density in the Kalahari is generally too low for cutting, at least, to have had much effect. There is no question that human settlement in limited areas has had significant impact (see, for example, the discussion of Parris and Child, 1973: 4, 7), but it is not clear whether the effects are long-term or merely short-term.

Cycles in the Kalahari environment have been documented, both in ancient and more recent times, though plant and animal species respond differentially to these cycles. While Walter (1973: 86–87) has noted that production in arid ecosystems is related linearly to rainfall, he also points out that there is less year-to-year variation in perennial species than in annuals, suggesting that there may be a lag in the response time of perennials (Walter, 1971: 277). Droughts, therefore, pose serious threats to foragers, particularly since they adversely affect the availability of moisture-bearing plants, such as melons, which are annuals.

Changes in the Kalahari have come about as the result of a number of different processes, some of them climatic, others biotic, and still others technological and even political.

The increased densities of livestock in particular have led to significant changes in the environment, but it is our belief that the processes of change began long before cattle and other domestic stock existed in the Kalahari in sufficient numbers to affect the distribution and abundance of resources.

A major factor that brought about changes in adaptive strategies in the Kalahari was the increasing sedentariness of human groups, caused in part by demographic pressures and in part by technological and environmental change (Hitchcock, n.d.). Increases in population density, such as along rivers in eastern and northeastern Botswana, resulted in competition for residential space. The numbers of residential moves of foraging groups

TABLE 2. **Range Size for a Sample of Kalahari Foragers and Food Producers**

Location	Number of ranges	Range size (km²)	Population size	Population density*	Reference
Central Kalahari	6	457–1,036	21–85	0.046–0.097	Silberbauer (1981)
Central Kalahari	11	505–4,323	41–167	0.02–0.3	Sheller (n.d.)
Central Kalahari	?	4,000	229	0.03	Tanaka (1971; 1976: 100)
Southwest Kalahari	5	1,000–2,200	80–315	0.041–0.247	Thoma (pers. comm.)
Northwest Kalahari	9	300–600	9–52	0.154	Lee (n.d.: 47, 199–200; 1979)
Northwest Kalahari	?	1,000–3,000	?	?	Yellen and Harpending (1972: 245); Harpending (pers. comm.)
Eastern Kalahari	7	675–1,370	19–42	0.021–0.039	Hitchcock (1978a: 259; field notes)
Northeast Kalahari	5	195–400	14–88	0.072–0.27	Hitchcock (field notes)

*Calculated as number of persons per sq. km.

were reduced, and groups settled in areas where they had access to bulk resources, the most important of which was permanent water. As competition increased, so, too, did the degree of territoriality, and range sizes were increasingly restricted. Table 2 contains data on range sizes, population sizes, and population density for a number of Kalahari Basarwa populations. It can be seen that there is wide variation in range size, but, in general, ranges in waterless areas such as the central Kalahari are greater than those in the northwest (the Dobe region) or the northeast (the Nata region.)

When groups spend increasing lengths of time in specific locations the resources there become depleted, necessitating a number of shifts in adaptive strategies. Lee (n.d.: 111) notes the two possible strategies employed by Basarwa when foods are scarce: they can travel farther in order to continue to exploit more desirable species, or they can remain closer to camp and exploit less desirable food species. This latter alternative occurs seasonally as well, with !Kung diet becoming "more eclectic" in the latter part of winter (ibid.: 172).

One major shift that occurs among foragers living in an area for an extended period of time is in the body-size classes of prey exploited (cf. Pyke et al., 1977: 142), a shift known as prey-switching. Yellen and Lee (1976: 39) note that although depletion of larger game has occurred in the north-

west Kalahari, the hunting-and-gathering way of life has not collapsed, since groups have developed methods for procuring smaller game species. In several parts of the Kalahari, technological changes such as the erection of veterinary cordon fences have disrupted the migration patterns of large game and sometimes have led directly to a reduction in their numbers (Silberbauer, 1965). Another major change that has directly affected the availability of large game is the introduction of the borehole. With the resulting greater numbers of permanent water sources has come an increase in the numbers and density of domestic livestock, a factor which, perhaps more than any other in recent decades, has resulted in the decrease of hunting and gathering. Cattle require water fairly often and so must stay close to water sources, in contrast to wild Kalahari species which move according to the distribution of rainfall or of the plants that provide both water and food. Being less mobile than wild species, cattle are apt to graze and browse out certain local plants. One result of this has been the replacement of perennial grasses by annuals, and another has been the increase in shrubs. Cattle also eat some of the species favored by foragers, such as *Grewia flava* (Cole and Brown, 1976: 195), as well as competing successfully with wild game, for the food plants and aerial censuses in Botswana have revealed that densities of large wild mammal species are much lower in ranching areas than elsewhere. On the other hand, the bush encroachment that occurs when cattle overgraze an area may have positive effects for some game species (e.g., small antelopes like duiker and steenbok). Thus, the prey-switching seen among human foragers may be due not solely to resource depletion but also to an increase in the abundance of smaller prey.

While it has been suggested by some researchers that overhunting among foragers is not uncommon and may even account for the widespread extinctions at the end of the Pleistocene, there is no evidence from the Kalahari, at least, that this has occurred; game depletion there is more likely the result of habitat deterioration (Campbell and Child, 1971) or climatic change. Wild animals still exist in substantial numbers in the Kalahari, but they tend to stay away from ranching and residential areas. In the Nata River region large die-offs of wildebeest and buffalo, as well as other species, occurred during major droughts in 1933, 1947, and the early 1960s. Correlated with these die-offs were changes in hunting strategies (Crowell, field notes) and shifts to alternative resources, including aquatic species, especially fish (Hitchcock, n.d.).

One major response to drought among agricultural populations in southern Africa was to fall back on hunted and gathered foods (Scudder, 1971, 1976; Grivetti, 1978, 1979). In drought periods the Kalahari foragers expand the numbers of species they exploit, often including bitter roots, leaves, and barks they might otherwise ignore. J. D. Clark (1976a: 83) points out that a study of the ethnographic literature, particularly that which deals with human behavior in times of food scarcity, may throw light on the processes involved in the beginnings of domestication. Table 3 contains a listing of the numbers and kinds of plant species exploited by a sample of southern African foragers and food producers. The agricultural groups are seen to exploit an even wider array of plant species than do the foragers, and they use somewhat different parts of the plants. Foragers often focus on the reproductive parts—the roots, fruits, and nuts—while agriculturalists often utilize growing tissue, including stems, bark, and leaves. This difference is due in part to the fact that agriculturalists often exploit plants in stress periods, when they are not reproducing, but they also tend to select parts, such as leaves, that can be used as relishes. Agriculturalists such as the Gwembe Tonga of the Middle Zambezi in Zambia also utilize grasses (Scudder, 1971, 1976). In the Near East this tendency may well be related to the trend toward exploitation of

TABLE 3. **Comparative Data on Wild Edible Plant Species Utilized by Foragers and Food Producers in Southern Africa (adapted from Grivetti, 1979: 251, with additions).** *

Food plant category	Dobe !Kung	Nyae Nyae !Kung	G/wi	G//ana	Moshaweng Tlokwa	Gwembe Tonga
tubers, roots, bulbs	4	27	6	14	22	17
fruits, nuts, berries, seeds	31	30	8	34	31	53
leaves, stalks	34	4	20	20	47	58
barks, flowers, gums	16	11		9	23	3
grasses						9
mushrooms				1	3	"several"
TOTALS	85	72	34	78	126	140 +

*The sources from which these figures are derived are as follows. Dobe !Kung: Lee (n.d.); Nyae Nyae !Kung: Marshall (1976: 109–123); G/wi: Silberbauer (1965); G//ana: Tanaka (1976); Moshaweng Tlokwa (located in southeastern Botswana near Gaborone): Grivetti (1979); Gwembe Tonga (located in the middle Zambezi Valley of Zambia): Scudder (1971: 39–45; 1976: 374–380). It should be pointed out that some of these plants may overlap in use; in the list provided by Marshall (1976), for example, some plants used as tubers are also utilized as nuts or fruits, and the leaves of fruit-bearing plants are also utilized.

TABLE 4. **Daily Foraging-Trip Distances for a Sample of Kalahari Foragers and Food Producers**

Location	Group	Foraging trip distance	Comments	Reference
Central Kalahari (!Xade)	G//ana	10 km	movement determined by availability of plants, not by hunting; water critical only part of year (p. 113)	Tanaka (1976: 116)
Central Kalahari	G/wi	8 km 6–7 km (Dec.–May) 0.414 km²/person/day (winter)	year-to-year variation in amount of tsama melons available and amount of territory necessary to exploit them (1972: 300)	Silberbauer (1972: 287; 1978: 115, 116)
Northwest Kalahari (Dobe)	!Kung	10 km radius	day's round trip of 20 km serves to define a "core" area 10 km in radius . . . except for a few weeks each year (Lee, 1968: 35); June: 10–15 km round trip, August: 20 km (Lee, n.d.: 107); 32 km. av. max. distance (Lee, n.d.: 144); rarely more than 15 km (on straight line) from camp and generally no more than 10 km (Yellen and Lee, 1976: 43)	Lee (1968: 35; 1969: 57; n.d.: 107, 143–145, 150–151); Yellen and Lee (1976: 43)
Northwest Kalahari (Nyae Nyae)	!Kung	13–20 km round trip	within area women zigzag another km or so looking for roots to dig	Marshall (1976: 106)
Eastern Kalahari (Ramokgophane)	Kūa	4–20 km round trip	av. approx. 12 km	Hitchcock (1978a: 237; field notes)
Eastern Kalahari (Mmasana)	Kūa	7–46 km round trip	group mostly sedentary; long-distance gathering trips undertaken with donkeys	Hitchcock (1978a: 237; field notes)
Northeast Kalahari (Man/otai)	/Aise	2–60 km round trip; 20 km average	group sedentary and produces food; gathering trips include salt and palm leaves procurement	Hitchcock (field notes)

wheat, barley, and other grains toward the end of the Pleistocene (Flannery, 1969, 1973), when foragers may have had to increase their utilization of less desirable foods, including grasses, thus setting the stage for manipulation and intentional cultivation of such plants.

Table 4 presents a record of daily foraging-trip distances for Kalahari groups. Distances covered in a day generally average up to approximately 20 km. As groups become increasingly sedentary, the daily foraging-trip distances may well increase. There are also changes in the frequency and in the length of trips, measured in terms of number of days' duration. Whereas foragers rarely go on overnight gathering trips, such trips are not uncommon among sedentary groups. Long-distance gathering trips of a few days to a few weeks in duration have

been noted in the Ghanzi Farms area of western Botswana (Guenther, 1976: 125) and in the borehole area of the eastern Kalahari (Hitchcock, 1978a: 237). The same is true for hunting trips. Long-distance hunts, often involving several men, are not characteristic of mobile foragers, whereas they are quite common among settled groups such as those in the Nata River region (Hitchcock, n.d.), the eastern Kalahari (Hitchcock, 1978a: 236), and the Ghanzi Farms region (Guenther, 1976: 125). In this sense, Grivetti's (1979: 245, 251) statement that the Tlokwa "regularly" exploit more wild food resources than do hunter/gatherers is incorrect.

With reduced residential mobility, many groups no longer have access to areas where resources may be seasonally available. As a result,

TABLE 5. **Wild Edible Plant Species Found Stored in Households of Eastern and Northeastern Kalahari Foragers and Food Producers (adapted from Vierich and Hitchcock, 1978).**

Scientific name	Common names	Description and uses	Seasonality	Reference
Bauhinia macrantha Oliv.	coffee bean, machancha (Setswana), ≠en≠e (Kūa), /en (G/wi)	60–90 cm high shrub, with long pods containing 4–8 beans; roasted and ground, or brewed like coffee	ripens January–June; found stored 1 year after harvesting	Marshall (1976: 114); Silberbauer (n.d.: 47, 301); Tanaka (1971: 17, 36; 1976: 117); Clauss (n.d.: 3a)
Citrullus vulgaris Schrad. (or *Colocynthus citrullus*)	tsama melon, d/un (Kūa), n≠a (g/wi), n//an (G//ana), mokate (Setswana)	melons growing 2–3.5m runners attached to deep mass of roots; annual plant similar to the cultivated melon grown by Kalahari groups; cut into strips and dried for storage	ripens April–June, stored through August but sometimes longer	Marshall (1976: 120); Silberbauer (1972: 283; n.d.: 48, 301); Story (1958: 48–49); Tanaka (1971: 17)
Grewia flava	raisin berry; moretlwa (Setswana), kxum (Kūa), kxam (G/wi)	woody shrub with small berries; eaten raw, sometimes pounded and mixed with meat or porridge	ripens November–March, stored year-round	Marshall (1976: 113); Silberbauer (n.d.: 303); Story (1958: 33–34); Clauss (n.d.: 3a)
Raphionacme burkei	water root, leditsa (Setswana), bai (Kūa), //an (!Xō), bi (G/wi)	small, woody, slender-leaved plant with tuber	year-round; sometimes transported to camp and replanted	Marshall (1976: 122); Story (1958: 38–39); Clauss (n.d.: 3c); Tanaka (1976: 117)
Ricinodendron rautanenii Schinz	mongongo nut, mokongwa (Setswana), /um (/Aise)	tall tree growing on dune crests; nut has outer fruit cover, boiled, nut roasted and broken	fruit ripens April–November, nut available all year	Marshall (1976: 114–116); Lee (1973); Yellen and Lee (1976: 40–41)
Tylosema esculenta Burch (or *Bauhinia esculenta*)	tsin bean, morama (Setswana), //odu (Kūa), /oi (G//ana)	large underground storage organ with long vines attached; bean grows on vine; both beans and tuber consumed	ripens November–May, bean found stored year-round	Cole and Brown (1976: 180): Marshall (1976: 109, 113–114); Story (1958: 26); Clauss (n.d.: 3d)
Vangueria infausta Burch	wild medlar, mmilo (Setswana), /duru (!Kung)	2.5–3.0m tree with small round yellow fruits, either eaten raw or boiled	fruit ripens in rainy season (November–April)	Lee (n.d.: 109; 1979: 472); Grivetti (1979: 249)

they must develop a means for extending the use-life of the resources they exploit; Binford (n.d.) has described these methods as a way of gaining "time utility" from resources. Whereas foragers consume foods immediately, sedentary groups are forced either to trade for them or to develop storage methods so as to have the resources on hand in periods of scarcity. Table 5 contains a listing of some of the edible plant species stored by eastern and northeastern Kalahari Basarwa households. Some of these plants had to be specially processed for storage—mmilo (*Vangueria infausta*), for example, had to be pounded in wooden mortars and then formed into cakes which were kept in baskets in people's houses.

Animal foods obtained in quantity were also processed for storage by sedentary groups. In the winter, Nata River groups sometimes went on expedition hunts during which large game was killed, sometimes in substantial numbers. Runners were then sent back to the residential locations and groups of men, women, and children came out to the kill sites. Animals were cut up by special butchering parties: the meat was cut into strips and hung to dry on trees or on racks built for the purpose. (In the rainy season the meat was smoked, since drying was then relatively ineffective.) The processed meat was taken back to the camps and shared among those who had stayed behind, any left-over meat being placed in the eaves of houses or on racks in the compounds. However, food storage not only necessitates an increase in procurement time but also, in some cases, specialized processing and preserving. The processed food also requires the development of protective facilities such as storage baskets or even storehouses. Many Nata River compounds contain drying racks and

mud storehouses in which both wild and domestic foods are kept. As groups become more residentially stationary, therefore, work effort tends to increase. Table 6 sets out data on work effort for a number of Kalahari groups. It has already been pointed out that Lee's (1968) research emphasized that labor time of !Kung was relatively low, ranging from 12 to 19 hours per week. Draper's (n.d.) data, also collected among !Kung but in a region ecologically somewhat different from Dobe, reveal that foragers under certain conditions do expend a fairly substantial amount of time in subsistence work. It is interesting to compare the work effort of !Kung with that of the Nata groups, who are engaged in food production. It is clear that work effort for Nata groups is higher than that of foragers in either the northwest or the eastern Kalahari region. However, the data for the Nata groups were obtained during the rainy season (February) and dur-

TABLE 6. **Subsistence Work Effort for a Sample of Kalahari Foragers and Food Producers**

Area	Observation period	Group size	Total days	Number of work days	Percentage of days worked	Number of days worked per week
Foragers:						
Dobe[1]	1 (7/6–7/12, '64)	25.6 (23–29)	114	37	.32	2.3
	2 (7/20–7/26, '64)	34.3 (29–40)	156	42	.27	1.9
	3 (7/27–8/2, '64)	35.6 (32–40)	167	77	.46	3.2
/Du/Da[2]	1 (2/27–3/4, '69)	25.3 (16–29)	74	42	.57	3.99
	2 (3/27–4/1, '69)	32.0 (29–35)	142	62	.44	3.1
	3 (5/15–5/21, '69)	41.0 (34–43)	187	55	.29	2.0
	4 (6/1–6/6, '69)	54.6 (51–56)	173	35	.20	1.4
	5 (7/15–7/18, '69)	19.0 (19)	48	4	.08	0.6
	6 (8/15–8/25, '69)	56.5 (44–69)	439	142	.32	2.2
	7 (10/5–10/9, '69)	50.8 (44–59)	205	68	.33	2.3
Food Producers:						
Khwee[3]	1 (1/28–1/30, '78)	28.5 (24–33)	57	29	.51	3.6
Uwe-Abo[3]	1 (2/14–2/17, '78)	26.5 (23–30)	44	21	.48	3.3
Bae[3]	1 (1/9–3/9, '78)	15.0 (11–19)	24	9	.38	2.6
Nata[4]	1 (2/3–2/6, '76)	7.0 (5–9)	32	24	.75	5.3
	2 (2/21–2/25, '76)	9.5 (9–10)	48	40	.83	5.8
	3 (8/2–8/6, '76)	6.0 (5–7)	37	25	.68	4.8

[1] Lee (1968)
[2] Draper (n.d.)
[3] Hitchcock (field notes, eastern Kalahari groups)
[4] Hitchcock (field notes, northeastern Kalahari groups)

ing the latter part of the harvest season (August). There are other periods when agriculturalists do little, if any, work related directly to food procurement, living instead on stores from the previous harvest. Overall, though, the amount of labor expended by agriculturalists is higher than that of foragers. This is one reason why eastern Kalahari Kūa told us they did not want to grow food. As they put it, "It's too damned much work."

Changes in work effort are correlated with changes in the organization of labor. Organizing trips to collect wild plant and animal foods in the rainy season tends to conflict with activities closer to home, particularly that of food production. To facilitate the work, children are increasingly being brought into the labor force (Draper, 1975; Hitchcock, n.d.), and tasks become increasingly differentiated, with young boys and girls taught to do separate kinds of things.

It should be emphasized that stress on groups due to food scarcity does not necessarily lead to intensification of effort. Marshall (1976: 107) notes that in the late dry season, when resources are at their lowest ebb, women tend to work less than in periods of abundance. People may opt for any one of an array of different strategies, including becoming dependents, going to visit relatives who have sufficient resources to share, trading, doing specialized work for others such as healing (Guenther, 1975/76; J. B. Wright, 1971: 9), raiding (M. Wilson, 1969: 64), or simply making do with less food. The important point is that people choose what they perceive to be the most secure strategy. Agriculture is in many ways less efficient than foraging, since it involves a greater expenditure of time and effort. It is also less secure, crop failures being frequent in the Kalahari (Schapera, 1943: 17) necessitating returns to hunting and gathering (Scudder, 1971, 1976; Grivetti, 1978, 1979; Devitt, 1977, 1978; Hitchcock, 1978b).

At some point in the intensification of foraging strategies a threshold must have been reached where the benefits derived from increasing labor time, distances covered, and bulk resources procured, and developing processing and maintenance strategies resulted in diminishing returns. Although it is difficult to pinpoint the exact threshold, there is no doubt that at some point foragers began

to intensify local exploitation, manipulating their environment to increase productivity. It is very likely that it was in this way that the tsama melon began to be intentionally cultivated by Basarwa. Other less desirable foods, particularly grasses and herbaceous plants, would also have received increasing attention, as noted by Scudder (1971, 1976).

The model that has been presented for the changes in foraging strategies and the beginnings of environmental manipulation is by no means simple, nor is it a one-way process. Cashdan (this volume) has pointed out that food production may have come about in the absence of range restriction. It is also clear that groups may not opt for food production but instead trade for the domestic food products they want—as, for example, at Nata. Foragers in this way may receive from the food producers not techniques of food production but, rather, the domestic foods themselves, thus reducing their need for growing their own food. They may also work in the fields of other groups, getting a portion of the crop produced in exchange for their labor. Agriculture was not so much a revolutionary phenomenon as it was an evolutionary one. Food production began simply as a buffer against scarcity; it was only after a substantial period of time that domestic foods became the staples and wild foods the buffering resources.

Strategies of Agricultural Production in the Kalahari

Guenther (1975/76: 45–46, 52; 1977: 196) has described the Basarwa of the Ghanzi Farms as "marginal herders and cultivators." Many other groups in the Kalahari would fit this description, since they do on occasion raise crops and care for domestic stock. Nonetheless, few Basarwa groups depend completely on domesticated foods. Lee (1976a: 8–9) notes that hunting and gathering plays an important role in the economy of the !Kung, and he goes on to imply that wild foods continue to be significant in the diet of even the most acculturated of Basarwa communities. Although nearly 40 percent of the Ghanzi Farms Basarwa were involved in agricultural production in

1975, domestic food crops made up only 6 percent of their subsistence (Childers, 1976: 62). Sheller (n.d.: 20) estimates that 5 to 20 percent of the diet of the G//anakwe of the Central Kalahari is made up of what he describes as "supplemental" agriculture and stock-raising. Even the Bakgalagadi, a Bantu-speaking group of Sotho stock who are related to the Tswana, have a diet which comprises only 15 to 35 percent domestic foods, according to Sheller's (ibid.: 30) investigation for the Central Kalahari Game Reserve survey of 1976.

The agricultural techniques used by food producers in the Kalahari are almost exactly the same as those used by foragers. Nearly all the agriculture can be described as a kind of swidden system. Small areas are cleared, either by hand or with cutting implements such as knives and axes. The debris is then piled up and burned, a process that not only rids the area of unwanted material but also adds nutrients to the soil. Small holes are dug in the ground with digging sticks and seeds are dropped in and covered with soil.

Crops are grown either in gardens near the houses, or in fields (*masimo*), agricultural areas usually some distance from people's homes. The gardens are small and are cultivated with the aid of either a digging stick or a hoe. Most Kalahari foragers and part-time food producers grow crops in gardens rather than fields. By contrast, the more sedentary populations usually plant fields, which they cultivate with ploughs. One advantage of having the gardens close to the houses is that potential competitors such as baboons or antelopes probably stay away from the crops when people are living there; D. R. Harris (1976: 338–340) has suggested that the tending of gardens near people's homes is probably the earliest system of cultivation in the tropics.

Planting is done in the early part of the rainy season, which usually begins in November. After that the groups may leave the area, continuing on their annual rounds. Occasionally they protect their small gardens with low thorn fences, but more often than not they leave them unenclosed. Sometimes individuals or small foraging parties will check on the progress of the crops if they happen to be in the area, but generally the gardens are forgotten until the group returns to the rainy-season camp the

following year. If they are lucky, if the seeds have sprouted and no animals or birds have eaten the crop, they are able to harvest some melons, beans, or whatever else they may have planted. If the group remains in camp they usually weed only once, often in mid-February or early March. Crops that ripen early, such as green maize, sweet reed, and melons, may be harvested in late March or April. An important crop, sorghum (*Sorghum vulgare* or *S. bicolor*), begins to seed in April or May, and then it is necessary for people to keep birds away from the crops. We observed as many as fifty people involved in bird-scaring in field areas in the eastern Kalahari in 1978. In some areas whole crops of maize, sorghum, and millet were destroyed by depredations of Quelea finches and other birds. Harvesting of crops is carried out from June through July and sometimes into August, depending on field size and yield.

Following harvest, there is a period of processing in which crops are threshed on mud and cow dung threshing-floors known as *diboa*. The grains are winnowed to get rid of the chaff, and the processed material is put into bags, often mixed with burned dung and ash to protect it from insects. The bagged material is then placed in houses or in special compartmentalized storehouses. In some cases, expecially when yields are low, crops are processed and then simply kept in baskets or stored in the eaves of houses. Once the harvest is over, cattle are frequently allowed to graze on the stubble, thus increasing soil nutrients through the addition of manure. However, they also harden the ground surface by trampling, as well as spreading weeds.

Crop failures are common in the Kalahari, and food-producing groups have developed a number of different strategies to deal with problems incurred by low or poorly timed rainfall and destruction by insects, birds, and animals: (1) spatial diversification; (2) temporal diversification; and (3) crop or product diversification. Some Kūa groups in the eastern Kalahari were observed to have planted crops in several different places, thus increasing the chances that at least one of them would receive sufficient rain or would not be preyed upon by competing animals. A kind of temporal diversification strategy was also observed. Groups of !Xō in the southwest Kalahari, for example, stagger their planting, cultivating one patch of about 10 by 10 m each week for five to six weeks (A. Thoma, pers. comm.). This strategy increases the chance that at least one patch will receive rainfall at the correct time. Finally, a variety of crops are planted in the hope that at least some of them will grow. A combination of melons, beans, maize, sorghum, pumpkins, and millet is sown. Since the crops have different degrees of drought-resistance and different soil and moisture requirements, some of them may grow while others will not. It is significant that foragers in the eastern Kalahari who used these strategies had fewer unsuccessful plantings than did plow agriculturalists, who, theoretically, are far more familiar with crop-production techniques (Hitchcock, 1978a: 352).

Table 2 lists the domesticated plants grown by foragers and food producers in the Kalahari. Not all of these plants are grown for food. Bottle gourd and calabashes (*Lagenaria* spp.), for example, are used as scoops and containers; also, tobacco and marijuana are often cultivated not so much for home consumption as for exchange. Some groups in the Kalahari were observed to exchange smoking products for food and sometimes for cash.

The most popular crop among Kalahari groups was melons. Several reasons were offered for their popularity: first, they provided a source of water; second, they were relatively drought-resistant, especially when compared to seed crops like sorghum and maize; and, third, dried melons are an article of food for both humans and livestock and, after they have been cut into strips and hung on thorn trees to dry, they are easy to store. The second most popular plant was beans (*Phaseolus* spp.). Although sorghum and maize were well liked by Kalahari groups, success in growing them was not as high. It is interesting to note that, overall, groups that only recently began planting crops tended to have greater success than food-producing populations such as the Bakgalagadi and Bamangwato, the reasons being that they selected crops specifically for their ability to withstand drought and that they used the diversification strategies mentioned previously. In addition, the Tswana sow by throwing a mixture of seeds by hand, or broadcast, as the earth is turned over by the plow. Foragers and part-time food producers preferred instead to make a hole

with a digging stick and drop a single seed into it; this far more efficient method resulted in higher yields in terms of return per unit of seed planted.

In the Kalahari, groups do not have to be sedentary in order to practice food production, nor does it necessarily lead to people becoming sedentary. Some of the groups at Khwee in the eastern Kalahari made as many as nine residential moves a year, and they had gardens at several of their campsites. They returned to harvest the crops in April and May of 1978, going from one abandoned campsite to another collecting the melons and maize and taking them back to their dry-season camp on donkeys.

It is difficult to obtain data on yields in the Kalahari because the growers frequently consume the crops immediately after harvest. In a few cases, however, it was possible to get rough estimates of how much food was obtained by a given household. Hitchcock (1978a: 351, table 12.7) was able to collect data on yields of 45 households in the eastern Kalahari. Of those households 14 (31 percent) got nothing whatsoever, 22 (49 percent) got melons only, and the remainder got relatively small amounts of sorghum, maize, millet, beans, cowpeas, and a few other crops. Data obtained in the 1977/78 agricultural season revealed that three of the twelve groups of independent or "intact" foragers planted gardens, but in the previous year nine of the twelve had done so. Comparison with part-time food producers residing on cattle-posts revealed that the success rate was higher among mobile foragers than among sedentary groups.

Field sizes of food-producing groups in the Kalahari vary tremendously, but in general the Basarwa have relatively small fields. This is due at least in part to the fact that the vast majority of the Basarwa use either digging sticks or hoes in cultivation, as opposed to other groups, which mainly use single-furrow plows drawn by oxen or donkeys. Table 7 presents data on field sizes among Basarwa populations in the Kalahari, as reported by anthropologists and development workers. It can be seen that the average field size is small—about one-half hectare, when the entire data set is considered. Fields in the southeast Kalahari and those at Nata, which tend to be larger than other fields, were cultivated with plows. The introduction of the plow in

TABLE 7. **Comparative Data on Field Sizes of Bushman Populations in Botswana**

Location	Group	Size in hectares (1 ha = 2.471 acres)	No. of fields	Reference
I. Southwest Kalahari				
a. N!haite/Hukuntsi	!Xō	0.2–1.0 ha	7	Thoma (n.d.)
b. Pepane/Lehututu	!Xō	0.2–0.6 ha	10	Thoma (n.d.)
c. Monong	!Xō	0.5–0.6 ha	2	Thoma (n.d.)
d. Ngwatle	!Xō	0.3–0.4 ha	2	Thoma (n.d.)
e. Kwakai	!Xō	0.2–0.3 ha	2	Thoma (n.d.)
f. Tshotswa	!Xō	4.5 ha	1 (communal)	Thoma (n.d.)
Subtotal		average = 0.5166 ha	24	
II. Southeast Kalahari				
a. Thotayamarula	Kūa	5.875 ha	1	Vierich (n.d.b)
b. Mazane	Kūa	0.62–8.4 ha	3	Vierich (n.d.b)
Subtotal		average = 3.2 ha	4	
III. Southern Kalahari				
a. Molopo Farms	Balala	average = 0.027 ha	30	Lawry (1978: 23)
IV. Northwest Kalahari				
a. Dobe, etc.	!Kung	0.532 ha	64	Matlhare (1978)
V. Northeast Kalahari				
a. Nata River region	/Aise, etc.	average = 1.146 ha	12	Cashdan and Chasko (n.d.: 28)
VI. Eastern Kalahari				
a. Western Sandveld region	Kūa, etc.	0.01–1.1 ha average = 0.14 ha	18	Hitchcock (1978a: 350)
TOTAL		0.501 ha average	152	

the nineteenth century led to an increase in field sizes and yields and also had implications for the division of labor in agriculture. Among the Tswana, hoe agriculture was done mainly by women, men taking little part, but once the plow came into use men were needed to control the oxen that pulled them. Among the Basarwa, on the other hand, men were observed taking part in food-production activities nearly as often as the women, both mainly using digging sticks and hoes.

We have stressed repeatedly that the Kalahari is subject to cycles of wet and dry years, and rainfall frequently comes at the wrong time of the year for good crop-production. The result is crop failure, which forces people to rely on hunting and gathering. Among the !Kung, for example, Lee (1976a: 19) mentions that they planted gardens in the good rainfall years of 1967 to 1970 but fell back on foraging in 1972/73, a drought year in the north-

west Kalahari. By 1975/76, many of the same people were again cultivating crops in the Dobe area (Gelburd, n.d.; T. H. Hargrove, pers. comm.).

Another constraint on agriculture is lack of access to seeds, implements, oxen to use for drawing the plows, and labor. A characteristic feature of foraging societies is their emphasis on immediate consumption of food; frequently they do not even save seeds for the next year's planting (Reid, n.d.: 12). Competition from both wild and domestic species also results in crop failures, particularly in areas near villages, where there are large numbers of domestic animals. Building of thorn fences and close herding of cows and smallstock will help to protect the crops, but destruction of crops is still an all-too-frequent occurrence. The emphasis on sharing among Kalahari foragers also militates against agricultural production. Guenther (1977: 200) mentions that individuals owning livestock are

TABLE 8. **Estimated Percentages of Kalahari Populations Engaged in Agricultural Production**

Location	Group	Size of population	No. doing agriculture	Percentage	Reference
Northwest Kalahari	!Kung	38	12	31.6	Gelburd (n.d.: 79–82, table 8)
Northwest Kalahari	!Kung	?	?	7.0	Wiessner (n.d.: 85, table 3)
Western Kalahari	Nharo, G/wi, etc.	4,512	?	nearly 40	Childers (1976: 62)
Southeast Kalahari (Kgatleng)	Tsassi, etc.	52	23	44.2	Caye and Koitsiwe (n.d.: 26)
Southeast Kalahari (Kweneng)	Kūa, etc.	136 hh's	66 hh's	48.5	Vierich (pers. comm.)
Eastern Kalahari	Kūa, etc.	666 hh's	147 hh's	22.1	Hitchcock (1978a: 339)

often asked to slaughter their animals and share the meat. Wiessner (n.d.: 370) notes that in order for people to become successful agriculturalists they must take certain items, such as agricultural implements, out of the sharing network. These must begin to be seen as the personal property of their possessors, a fact that is anathema to egalitarian-minded foragers. Sometimes there is social pressure not to farm. Wiessner (n.d.: 151) mentions a !Kung man who was heavily criticized for his agricultural and livestock-raising activities, the reason being that his friends and relatives were afraid he would cease foraging, which would have had adverse effects on the group as a whole.

Estimated percentages of Kalahari groups engaged in agricultural production are set out in Table 8. It is apparent that the numbers range from very few among some !Kung groups to nearly half the households in the Kweneng District area. Two other areas, not shown in this table, are the Nata River region and the eastern hardveld region, e.g., along the Motloutse River in the Central District. Basarwa in these areas are engaged in agriculture to a greater extent than they are in other parts of Botswana. However, in virtually all these areas people still derive a substantial portion of their diet from foraging.

If we accept the diffusionist model of the spread of agriculture, we would expect those groups in closest proximity to food-producing people such as the Tswana to be the ones most involved

in agriculture. Just the opposite is the case. Those groups which live on the peripheries of the major Tswana towns tend to be least involved in agriculture. The reason is twofold: first, these people have access to alternative ways of obtaining domestic products, through trade or employment; second, near towns, the crop damage by livestock is the highest, so people have less success in raising crops. The result is that the Basarwa groups most involved in agriculture are usually those in marginal areas, away from food producers. It is also interesting that the areas with the greatest diversity of resources are not usually those where food producers are found.

Consequences of Food Production in the Kalahari

While food production clearly did not at first substantially alter the subsistence, mobility, and social systems of Kalahari populations, it did eventually lead to some important changes among those groups that began to depend on domestic foods. These changes are perhaps most marked in the nutritional state of those using domestic foods for a large proprotion of their subsistence.

Grivetti (1978, 1979) maintains that nutritional stress is not a characteristic feature of most Kalahari groups even during drought periods, but

there are signs of at least a certain amount of malnutrition among cattle-post populations (H. Vierich, pers. comm.; Hitchcock, field notes). The major foods of most Botswana groups—maize meal
and sorghum porridge—are high in carbohydrates,
and substantial amounts are usually consumed at
each sitting. Obesity is, therefore, more often
found among agriculturalists than among foragers.
Also, vitamin and protein deficiency is more common among groups using domestic foods than
among foragers, whose diet is more mixed and reasonably well-balanced nutritionally. Another problem, far more common among agriculturalists than
among foragers (Scudder, 1971: 6), is seasonal
hunger. Under these circumstances it is not surprising that foragers are loath to take up agriculture as a way of life.

Lee (1972b) has suggested that the availability
of soft foods, especially porridge made of grains,
may have implications for rising fertility levels
among Kalahari populations. He argues that the
earlier weaning such foods allow would mean that
lactation would no longer be a factor in suppressing
ovulation, thus decreasing the interval between
births. Binford and Chasko (1976) have examined
this hypothesis as well as several others and have
concluded that although lactation may indeed be a
factor, it is less important than dietary changes,
especially increased carbohydrate intake, among
sedentary populations. The three most important
variables causing changes in conception frequencies among Nunamiut Eskimo were: (1) changes in
miscarriage rate; (2) changes in male absenteeism;
and (3) dietary changes, with the latter variable
accounting for over 87 percent of the observed
patterning (ibid.: 130). The findings of Wilmsen
(1978) tend to corroborate those of Binford and
Chasko. Working among !Kung populations,
Wilmsen found that foragers dependent upon wild
foods were subject to annual periods of nutritional
stress, resulting in seasonal fluctuations in conception frequency. Populations dependent upon milk
and grain products, on the other hand, tended to
have less fluctuation in weight and larger numbers
of births. Wilmsen attributes these differences to
varying hormonal levels in females. N. Howell
(1979), basing her arguments on the ideas of demographer Frisch (e.g., Frisch, 1975), notes that

women must achieve a critical level of fatness in
order to ovulate. The increased availability of domestic products would facilitate the maintenance of
appropriate body-fat levels, making the women
more prone to become pregnant. Thus, fertility
levels are said to increase as groups have greater
access to domestic foods. However, Harpending
(1976: 160) disagrees, noting that fertility has not
increased among !Kung to any great extent. Rather
than an increase in fertility levels, Harpending
(ibid.: 165) favors the idea of a drop in mortality
levels, a suggestion in accordance with traditional
Malthusian demographic theory.

A number of other changes have occurred as a
result of increased dependence on domestic foods.
As Hitchcock (n.d.) has pointed out, increased investment in land and facilities leads to the emergence of inheritance patterns and to greater inequality in the distribution of wealth as sharing begins to
break down and individuals and families accumulate property for themselves. This means that food
production, in the long run, leads to hereditary
inequality, though among most Kalahari groups the
process has not yet gone far enough to occasion
such organizational changes.

Conclusions

Study of the emergence of food production
among Kalahari foraging populations reveals that
many of the assumptions about how agriculture
evolved in southern Africa need to be reexamined.
The suggestion that this evolution was the result of
contact with immigrating Bantu-speaking agriculturalists is now open to doubt. Information on the
distribution of food-producing Basarwa groups
shows, on the contrary, that the closer they are in
space to food producers the less likely they are to
take to raising their own food. Ethnohistoric and
ethnographic data on forager/farmer contacts reveal that foragers will trade with farmers, work for
them, and even become their dependents, and so
gain access to non-local goods, including domestic
foods, without resorting to food production
themselves.

A second major conclusion is that foragers may

not immediately opt for food production, because they do not necessarily perceive it to be a more secure or more efficient strategy. Stress on foragers, brought about as a result of either environmental or demographic change, causes them to employ a number of responses, ranging from doing nothing at all to intensifying their foraging activities by increasing trip distances, expending more time and effort in food procurement, accumulating resources in bulk for storage purposes, and investing greater amounts of energy in the manufacture and maintenance of storage facilities. A major response is broadening of the diet to include new plants and aquatic species.

Kalahari foragers also employ a number of environmental-manipulation strategies to enhance the productivity of wild resources, the most important being the use of controlled burning and special treatment of favored plant species through protection, transplanting, and even a degree of cultivation. Increasing attention paid to specific plants such as melons, in the local area, may have led to intentional cultivation in gardens around residential camps; thus, there is no clear dividing line between environmental manipulation and food production.

While some (e.g., Phillipson, 1977c: 56) have argued that food production "secured man's vegetable diet," thus allowing him to become sedentary, data on Kalahari foragers reveal that some groups are sedentary in the absence of food production and others are food producers while still remaining mobile; the two are not necessarily correlated. The security of agriculture as a way of life may also be questioned in the light of Kalahari data. Most domesticated plants are annuals, highly responsive to rainfall variations, which in the Kalahari are extreme both in space and time, so that it is not uncommon to find localized crop failures. Foragers, who often depend on perennial species such as mongongo and morama nuts and fall back on roots in times of severe stress, are not as subject to environmental fluctuations and seasonal hunger as are agriculturalists.

By itself, therefore, agriculture is not a secure strategy in the Kalahari, but when combined with foraging and other kinds of strategies (e.g., trading or working for others), it provides a much-needed buffer against resource scarcity.

Lack of familiarity with agricultural techniques is also not the reason that people in the Kalahari have not begun to produce food in quantity. In fact, examination of the agricultural methods of foragers and part-time food producers reveals that their techniques are often more effective than those employed by groups with a long history of food production. Kalahari groups tend to choose their crops carefully and to try a number of different methods to ensure success.

The transition to food production in human society probably did not occur just once but many times. There is abundant evidence in the Kalahari that groups fall back on foraging in drought years, while in years of higher rainfall they may plant some crops. Even their domestic animals are said to cycle directly with rainfall, with higher calving rates among cattle in wet years. There may also be an inverse relationship between rainfall and high productivity among, say, sheep and goats, which tend to do poorly in heavy rainfall years, possibly because of increased numbers of intestinal parasites. The relationship between rainfall and food production in the Kalahari is thus not a simple and direct one, though there is no question that food production is becoming increasingly important among the populations there. One reason for this is the decrease in the availability of wild foods. Game has been reduced, partly by habitat deterioration and partly by overhunting, as well as by modern technological change (as we have seen above).

It should be stressed, however, that environmental degradation and population pressure alone may not account for the decreasing reliance on hunted and gathered foods in the Kalahari. Availability of manpower may also be a factor. As wage-labor opportunities increase, there is a decrease in the labor available for either foraging or food production. Also, the introduction and strict enforcement of game laws in remote areas has made many Basarwa afraid to hunt. Even prestige sometimes plays a part; many people in the eastern Kalahari told us they did not like to hunt and gather because "some people might think we are animals." Another change that should be mentioned is the effort on the part of governments and people interested in development to introduce agriculture to Kalahari groups. Three major examples of this are: (1) the

South African settlement scheme at Tsumkwe in eastern Namibia; (2) Bere, a settlement in the western Kalahari where H. J. Heinz and others have worked; and (3) the development work undertaken by the Remote Area Development Program, especially in the western parts of Botswana.

However, the success of such schemes has not as yet been very marked and, although self-help input is now increasing among Kalahari groups, none of them is yet able to depend totally on the products of their fields. There is no doubt, however, that Basarwa groups would like to produce their own food, and they are openly appreciative of the efforts being made on their behalf.

Food production did not come about because people were suddenly exposed to a new way of making a living: it was a gradual process and one that was by no means unidirectional. It began as a buffer in times of resource depletion and, even to-

day, forms only a part of the total subsistence system of the Kalahari groups. The main determining factor was competition for increasingly scarce resources, exacerbated by increase in livestock and human populations and by competition from more highly organized groups. Before other groups had become an important factor, the processes leading to food production had already been set in motion; indeed, for a long time it was one of the several strategies employed to overcome increasing resource scarcity. In many ways it was a last resort undertaken with great misgiving by foragers in whose eyes it appeared a far from secure way of life. It was only when it became painfully apparent that foraging activities would no longer support the group that the Kalahari peoples began to relinquish their time-tested hunting and gathering in order to become food producers.

IV

Epilogue:
Perspectives and Prospects

30

Perspectives and Prospects for Understanding the Effects of Population on the Causes and Consequences of Food Production in Africa

NANCY HOWELL

Prominent among the causes and consequences of the initiation of food production in Africa considered by the authors of this volume are population growth and population dynamics. This paper is a demographer's attempt to organize the questions about population processes raised by various authors into a single set and to evaluate the evidence available for forming solid answers to these questions: the evidence available here in this volume, that not here which is potentially available, and that which is likely to be perpetually elusive. Some of what follows will be discouraging to those committed to empirical resolution of these theoretical questions, but what we can do is piece together models of how the "first demographic transition," that between hunting/gathering and food production, must have occurred. These models can be refined and tested by evidence from archaeology, from ethnographic analogies, and from the study of the processes of population among contemporary peoples.

We can start by considering two versions of the

relationship between food production and population. One might be called the "invention model": pre–food-producers are seen as living a hand-to-mouth existence, with low population densities maintained by scarcity of food or other vital resources. The starting point for this model is the Hobbesian view of life in a state of nature—"nasty, brutish, and short." Some Mesolithic genius thinks to try domestication of plants and animals, and suddenly life is easier. Productivity per worker increases; the need for constant movement is eliminated; a settled life permits accumulation of possessions, storage of food, and increased leisure; and population starts to grow absolutely and density increases as a result of the better life. New ways of life spread until large sections of humanity are food producers rather than hunter/gatherers. None of the authors in this volume evokes this model directly, but it underlies much of the speculation.

At the other extreme is the model associated with Boserup (1965), whose argument (pp. 38–39) is focused primarily on the relations between population growth and continued intensification of agriculture in modern Africa. The point she makes about relative costs and benefits of food production has stimulated many scholars (Spooner, 1972; Higgs, 1972) to reevaluate the sequence of events in the change from hunting/gathering to food production. In this model, hunter/gatherers do not "invent" agriculture during the Mesolithic; rather, they have known about it as an unattractive strategy of food-getting over a long period of time, and they adopt it only when forced to by events. Population growth forces the use of food production; this growth is caused by environmental variation or random fluctuations in population size. When population is high relative to hunting and gathering resources, the argument goes, parents adopt agriculture in preference to letting their children starve.

These two models, deliberately oversimplified, can be seen as the alternative answers to the question posed by the subtitle "Causes and Consequences of Food Production in Africa." Is population growth a cause of food production, as the Boserup model suggests, or is it merely a consequence? We do not need to choose between these simple models, as each of them includes a number of assumptions and propositions about events which might be better considered separately. It is entirely possible that the sequences of events that led to food production were different on the various occasions at which humans adopted food production around the world. The models are useful as polar types, directing our attention to more refined and more readily answerable questions.

These more answerable questions can be clearly specified even if the data with which to answer them are not, and maybe cannot be, available. We divide the questions into the stages of the process of change that we want to understand, starting with stable hunter/gatherer societies, "hunters in a world of hunters" (Sahlins, 1968); then the incipient food-producing situation, those societies in which horticulture and herding were invented, developed, and exported; and, finally, the food-producing simple societies.

The strictly demographic facts we need to know about each of these stages of human society can be reduced, at a minimum, to (1) age-sex specific probability schedules of birth and death, and (2) the processes of maintenance of population boundaries or borders, enclosing groups of a certain size, capable of splitting into two when the group outgrows its permitted limits or coalescing, two into one, when groups decline in size. In addition, we cannot feel we understand the process until we know (3) the proximate variables that produce the probability schedules and their causal connections to other variables such as diet, work, and economic organization.

We need to know the determinants of the age-sex probabilities of birth and death, such as the ages of entrance and exit from the childbearing population for women, the length of birth intervals, and rates of infecundity. We need not only the central tendency but the variances of these distributions. Most importantly, we need to know how each of these is related to resource fluctuations, so that we can specify not only the annual fluctuations in fertility, for example, in the hunting/gathering societies, but precisely how these are related to environmental and economic conditions. What resources were the people harvesting? How many workers and dependents were there? How far did people have to travel to collect their food supplies? How frequently did they have to move their home base? How much energy, time, and work did it cost them every time they did so? How much fluctuation in food supplies and other crucial resources (such as water and firewood) was there from season to season, from year to year, and over longer periods? Relative to resources, we need to know the minimum required calories per person for subsistence, and how much of the potentially harvestable surplus over this amount was consumed as extra food, how much as leisure, and how much as increases in the standard of living through artistic expression, religion, and entertainment. Obtaining answers to these detailed questions for even one prehistoric society would be a great help in resolving the theoretical issues at stake, and information on a few societies will go a long way toward acceptance of the unfortunate truth that it is never going to be possible to draw a random sample of prehistoric time segments and geographical areas.

We have been discussing the detailed dynamics of small populations, even though such populations are subject to a great deal of stochastic fluctuation and unpredictability (see N. Howell, 1979: 100–121). It might be objected that for the purposes of archaeological theory it is not necessary to know the specific dynamics of particular populations but merely to know what the overall trends are. We need to be suspicious of the accuracy of generalizations that are not based upon specified particular cases. It is true, of course, that there is a macro-level of analysis of these questions, exemplified by the work of Cohen (1977), who has a real gift for setting out the complex questions of population dynamics and interrelated variables that need to be clarified. The macro-questions apply to the classes of hunting/gathering and food-producing societies, and result from our current understanding, tentative as it is, of the population dynamics of the two kinds of groups. We think we know that hunting/ gathering populations were uniformly small in size (less than 1,000 members in cross-section), low in density, and very low in mean population growth rate overall, although particular populations may have alternately grown and contracted over time. And we believe that it is a fact that food-producing populations were frequently much larger in size,

were much more dense in living arrangements, and had higher sustained population growth rates such that populations doubled and redoubled over centuries of food production. The macro-questions, therefore, ask for identification of mechanisms of ceilings on total population size, density, and growth among the hunter/gatherers and of mechanisms for loss of those ceilings with food production.

The Evidence from Archaeology

The discouraging conclusion, mentioned before, is that it is not going to be possible to produce a full, empirically based set of answers to the questions we pursue from even one archaeological site, let alone a reasonable sample of them. Archaeologists simply cannot recover the detailed data on mortality, fertility, migration, and population-boundary maintenance that we demographers need to construct a fully satisfactory model of population change in the "first demographic transition."

Gifford (this volume) indicates that archaeologists are aware of the problems of inference:

> Archaeologists are sufficiently aware of site formation processes and the vagaries of archaeological sampling in single-component and in stratified sites to dismiss the notion that an archaeological site is a kind of porthole through which we may peer out into a whole prehistoric landscape. Thus sites such as Prolonged Drift should not serve as the basis for models of economic transformation but as the data with which models derived from other sources can be tested.

Certainly we have, in this volume, parts of the total data base which we need to test good models. Lubell, for example, provides information on the environments and food supply of the Magreb, and Posnansky provides that information for the early agricultural societies in Ghana, Shaw for Nigeria, and Hays and Hassan for Egypt. We get dates for the persistence of hunting/gathering in various localities, and dates for the earliest evidence of domesticated plants and/or animals. Wendorf and

Schild's announcement (this volume) of apparently domesticated barley some 7,000 to 8,000 years earlier than was previously documented from Egypt (but see p. 101) is an example of evidence from dates and locales that causes reevaluation of the overall model of process; it also serves as an example of the kind of unexpectedly vivid evidence from prehistory that occasionally survives, despite low probabilities of preservation.

Evidence on food (Brandt, Gifford), on climate (Lubell, Butzer), and on technology and culture is plentifully available from this volume, although it may be that there are not enough rich data from any single site for a short enough period of time that we could answer all the questions we would like to pose about the "carrying capacity" of the environment for a given population. For one thing, it is hard to detect missing information from the study of available information, however rich. For another thing, it is often difficult to interpret the meaning for ancient populations of observations about the environment: for example, Shaw (this volume) suggests that the best-watered areas in Nigeria were very likely reservoirs of onchocerciasis, "river blindness" transmitted by flies. The cultivation and consumption of palm oil as a source of vitamin A gives some protection from this disease, and populations with the ability to use palm oil were free to use ecological zones previously impossible for them. Harpending (1976) has noted a similar effect in northern Botswana, on the boundaries of the !Kung range, where there is more water and the plant growth is lush and thick. The population density of !Kung thins out in this apparently richer environment, as malaria takes its toll of the local residents. Archaeologically one could, no doubt, detect the richer plant growth (although Livingstone warns of the difficulties of pollen analysis in Africa, this volume), and one could probably detect the absence of human occupation (although it is always tricky to interpret absence of preserved remains as absence of occupation). It would require an extremely clever design to demonstrate any causal connections among these factors. It is hard to imagine how such a connection could be detected in archaeological evidence.

Where the archaeological data are strongest and most illuminating to a demographer is on the question of population boundaries. The volume here shows the linguistic evidence (Ehret), the pottery evidence (Clark), the cultigen evidence (Stemler), and the physical anthropological evidence (Rightmire et al.) for the proposition that these populations were at least slightly open so that genes, goods, and ideas could be transmitted among them. In the study of contemporary populations it is rare that we find a group which has any resemblance to closure at all: indeed, the most useful definition of a population or breeding group currently in use is that group (whatever its size) within which 80 percent of mating choices take place (Adams and Kasakoff, 1975). In modern industrial societies, the size of the 80 percent breeding group is likely to be on the order of 50,000; in agricultural populations, it is likely to be about 5,000. Such studies have not been done on a statistically substantial sample of hunter/gatherer and horticultural and herding societies, but we can probably be confident that the group size will be an order of magnitude smaller. Even more important, the "tail" of the distribution will be steeper in the simpler societies, so that the 98 percent breeding group will be closer in size to the 80 percent cutoff level. But the relatively greater boundedness of the simple societies must not be allowed to blind us to the extremely important difference between a truly bounded society, in which new genetic material can arise only by mutation and new artifacts and ideas only by independent invention, and the open society, in which genes, goods, diseases, and ideas are transmitted by contact with outsiders. The powerful consequences of even a very small rate of contact are explored for the general case among the !Kung by N. Howell (1979: 333–358). This is not to say, of course, that there are never fully bounded "island" populations: there are several well-documented cases of small populations that admitted no outside members for a period of centuries (Benoist, 1973), and such populations may have been extremely important in the evolutionary history of the species. But the probability of obtaining direct archaeological evidence on such a small and rare phenomenon is infinitesimally small. The evidence of contact and diffusion across Africa is clear from the archaeological evidence.

On the evidence of the age-specific probabilities of birth and death among the prehistoric populations before, during, and after the transition from hunting/gathering to food production, the archaeological evidence is much less satisfactory. Direct evidence for the fertility level of the group is not available. While there has been considerable interest in a method of counting the pitting of the pelvic cavity in the hopes that it correlates strongly with the number of children born, the method has been shown to be highly inaccurate among contemporary women whose childbearing histories are known (Suchey et al., 1979; Kelley, 1979). The most usual method of estimation of fertility in prehistoric populations is merely calculating the death rates from skeletal collections and then setting the fertility rate as that which would produce a stationary population. Since the growth rate of these populations is precisely the subject we wish to establish empirically, assuming a growth rate to estimate a fertility rate cannot be a satisfactory method.

Estimating mortality rates for prehistoric populations from direct evidence is somewhat more satisfactory. To do so, we must find collections of skeletons large enough for statistical analysis. For the earlier periods and the simpler societies, this is extremely difficult to do. Armelagos et al. (this volume), for instance, report on 39 crania of Nubians for the Mesolithic period and 12 for the next thousand-year period. Armelagos et al. show that a great deal can be learned from a few crania that are not necessarily a representative sample of the population of the period. We cannot, however, derive a useful life-table for the population from those numbers. Even for the later period, when the number of skeletons and skeletal fragments is greatly increased, and even if we are willing to make the strong assumptions that the skeletons recovered are a random sample of the people who lived at the site and that we can ascertain with a small error the age and sex of the skeletons we find, we cannot resolve the questions empirically. Butzer (this volume) mentions in passing that the life expectancy (the expectation of life at birth column calculated by a life table) dropped from 36 in late prehistoric times to 30 during early historical times (citing Masali and Chiarelli, 1972), without pausing to discuss the problems of making such an analysis.

The analytic problems would be daunting even

if the data problems happened to be solved. Imagine, for a moment, an extremely well-preserved site, which we know to have been occupied for a fixed portion of every year over a long period of time spanning the food-production revolution. Everyone who dies in the group during the occupancy is buried there and we have a foolproof method of dating, aging, and sexing the skeletons. An enormous amount of valuable data could be derived from excavation of such a site but we could not, unfortunately, interpret the demographic results unambiguously, due to three stubborn problems.

The first of these is unpredictability. The annual numbers of births and deaths in a small population are expected to vary to some extent even when the probabilities of these events for individuals remain constant from time to time. Worse, this continuous randomly generated variance in numbers of births and deaths has consequences for the future of the population through the interaction of generations. This "noise," inherently uninteresting, continually threatens to overwhelm the interesting changes in the underlying probabilities of birth and death as related to resource fluctuations. Only combining large numbers of data or plotting changes in population and resources over long periods of time permits one to distinguish stochastic fluctuation from meaningful patterns. A single observation, in itself, can never be interpreted clearly.

The second problem in interpretation of data is rooted in the speed of population adjustments to environmental changes. If there are density-dependent biological mechanisms in humans, it is likely that population adjustments to resource fluctuations are plentiful, mortality rates may decline and fertility rates increase in the short run, leaving the population with more dependents per worker. In periods of scarcity, fertility rates decline and mortality, primarily of children and old people, increases, leaving the population with an age distribution best adapted to support the survivors and resume population growth when the scarcity is past. Developing food production as an alternative to hunting and gathering is too slow a process to be a realistic alternative to short-run resource fluctuations. For the empirical exploration of our ideal data base, rapid changes in demographic rates complicate the problem of small sample sizes. We need to have at least a few hundred deaths in order to tell anything about the population structure of the living group from which the deaths were drawn. In the small communities of the early period, this means that for statistical analysis we have to lump together deaths that occurred over a period of time. For example, if we found about five deaths per year deposited, we would have to collect data for something like fifty-year periods to obtain stable and reliable results. But this period of time could easily include several "booms and busts" in population growth and decline. We cannot detect population structure changes, therefore, over any period of time shorter than that required to collect a statistically adequate sample.

Finally, our data, unrealistically ideal as they are, do not permit us to distinguish among population changes caused by fertility, mortality, and migration, or to take account of population growth in the analysis. If we have more deaths in one period than another, we know at least that those numbers of people were at risk of death at the time, but we cannot know whether apparent population growth was caused by a reduction in mortality, while fertility remained constant; an increase in fertility while mortality remained constant; an increase in migration from outside the group; or some complex combination of all three factors. Paleodemographers conventionally compute the life tables for the population on the assumption that the population is stationary, a powerful assumption which allows us to know the age distribution and the fertility rate of the living population from which the deaths were drawn. But we cannot be satisfied with this assumption when population growth is precisely the subject we are trying to investigate and to correlate with changes in resource availability. And much as the paleodemographers would like to ignore it, the fact remains that the rate of population growth in the living population is a crucial determinant, along with the age-specific mortality rates, of the age composition of a skeletal collection.

All of which does not mean that we cannot hope to understand the relationships between population growth and calories and work in the "first demographic transition," that associated with the origins of food production. Research currently underway on the physiology of survival and reproduc-

tion under varying dietary and activity regimes will contribute much to that understanding, as will archaeological studies that help to clarify the changes in diet and activity patterns associated with food production. The point of this discussion is that it is unreasonable to expect to be able to construct models of those changes inductively, from prehistoric evidence discovered, or even rigorously to test deductive models from those data.

The Evidence from Ethnographic Analogy

Ethnographic analogy allows us the opportunity to ask and answer the whole range of demographic questions that we wish to investigate by focusing attention on functioning contemporary societies with some of the characteristics of the prehistoric populations of interest. The relevant characteristics for these purposes are economic: we seek hunting/gathering, horticultural, and herding societies not too disturbed by or involved in the industrialized societies.

Having located such a society, the task is merely to describe its demographic processes accurately. The only real difference between "anthropological demography" and the conventional sort is that the numbers of people available for study are frequently small in the anthropological populations. This requires calculation of standard errors of measures that demographers usually do not present, since standard errors are so very small in large populations. The tendency of anthropologists to organize the observations into "culturally specific categories" or to invent new concepts and measures for their data is, of course, counterproductive even (or especially) when it is highly original. Conventional counts of the population at risk and the incidence of births and deaths are needed if we are to use the data comparatively and in models.

Having described such groups, there are still problems of interpretation of the evidence we find. We need to study such societies over a sufficiently long period of time that information about the range of variation in demographic variables becomes apparent. When the goal is to generalize to prehistoric populations, we need to study not just one but a range of such societies, ideally a random sample but more realistically a selection of convenient groups that encompasses geographical, climatic, and economic variation. Even with a random sample of contemporary simple societies, we would still fear that the surviving groups are a biased sample of those that existed in prehistory, which, after all, included groups not merely in the marginal environments used in the twentieth century, but all over the world.

Still, ethnographic analogy permits us a kind of detailed information about a total ecological/economic niche, and the way that people exploit their resources. Brandt (this volume, quoting Harlan, 1969: 313) states the grounds for the power of the ethnographic analogy in terms that all of us who do this kind of work devoutly hope are true: "We have in the Ethiopian center a survival of an entire agricultural system little changed from prehistoric times. . . . It is as if a vanished world had been rediscovered by the use of a time machine."

With the combination of direct observation of the contemporary "relic" side by side with the excavated remains of the early period, we have a hypothesis to test: that the archaeological remains are survivals from an ongoing society just like the contemporary one. The interpretation of the prehistoric remains then proceeds by attempting to try to reject that hypothesis.

The society examined most closely in this book is the !Kung San—this writer's and everybody's favorite ethnographic analogy for the hunting/gathering way of life and for the transition to horticulture and stock-keeping. One of the lessons of the !Kung studies for archaeologists is probably the warning not to underestimate the scientific investment required to cover all the various aspects of even the simplest society. In the !Kung case there have been some 25 researchers involved over a period of more than 20 years, and we are far from confident that we yet have all the relevant information and have asked all the important questions about their adaptation.

Brooks et al. (this volume) review the issues of the history of the !Kung, for the purpose of making sure that we have the crucial facts about the !Kung themselves, and for the purpose of constructing models of the general sequence of events in the transition from hunting and gathering to food production. She and her colleagues, Yellen and Gelburd, document change over time in camp size, duration of stay in camps, and changes in food remains deposited, and lay out a set of characteristic features of the transition which can, in principle, be tested. The main thrust of their article from the point of view of this set of considerations is the argument that the shift in economic form is not simply caused by demographic change but is a multifactorial process. Surely it would not be a gain in understanding, even if it is strictly speaking true, to say that there are a variety of causes and consequences of food production, giving up on the attempt to specify exactly what the causes and consequences are and to measure them one at a time, "all other things being equal."

The demographic study of the !Kung has uncovered some unexpected features of the population, primarily in the area of low fertility and little need for contraception or deliberate birth limitation. It has been rather a large task merely to establish that this is the case for the few hundreds of !Kung living in the 1960s and 1970s. Two distinctive tasks must be undertaken before we can take the !Kung as a model of demographic functioning during the food-production revolution, each an order of magnitude larger than the other. The first of these tasks is to establish that the population trends hold true and cover the range of expected variation over periods of centuries rather than just years. The second is to investigate the range of demographic models that characterize distinctive populations at the same level of economic development.

The question of fluctuation over time has led to the construction of computer models which can take information collected over a period of months or years and examine the implications of those processes over periods of centuries, from the point of view of long-run implications and from the point of view of expected stochastic variability (Howell and Lehotay, 1978). A number of processes look quite different from a longer time perspective. The population limits, for instance, may easily appear to the field investigator to be tightly bounded, with the occasional appearance of an outsider over the period of those hard-earned months in the field seen as a rare exception to the rule of isolation. From the point of view of centuries, however, it becomes clear that an outside visitor to a small group once or twice a year is sufficient to prevent genetic random drift and technological and ideological isolation. It seems likely that Schrire (1980), who stresses the amount of contact, and Lee (1979) and other fieldworkers, who stress the isolation of the !Kung, are describing the same reality—Schrire from the archaeologists' perspective of centuries, the cultural anthropologists from the perspectives of months or years in the field.

The larger task remaining is the need for equally detailed studies of more small societies at various points on the transition from hunting/gathering to food production, in Africa and elsewhere. Some of this is being done, in the studies of Woodburn on the Hadza (1968a), Turnbull (1965), Bailey and others currently in the field on the Pygmies of the Ituri forest. There is a strong need for a range of representatives of these types of societies to introduce whatever variability exists within the populations of hunter/gatherers, horticulturalists, etc. The !Kung studies, as the most readily available and most fully researched ethnographic analogy, are made to stand for what should be an elaborated and detailed inventory of knowledge of small societies. As a result, prehistoric data, which require an ethnographic analogy for interpretation, lean on the !Kung studies to what is sometimes an exaggerated extent (Speth and Davis, 1976).

The Evidence from Processual Models of Modern Peoples

We remind ourselves that if we know the causal relations of variables, it may be possible to put fragments of knowledge of prehistory to work to explain large amounts of unknown data. We do not need to know the details of mortality in prehistory, for instance, if it can be clearly established what the limits of the age-specific mortality rates are and how they respond to changes in diet. There are several areas of research currently underway, the results of which will have important consequences for our understanding of the causes and consequences of food production, which we will mention

here. The first of these is research into human mortality. From the study of contemporary peoples it seems that there is invariance in the age-sex probabilities of death (N. Howell, 1976a). If this generalization holds true for prehistory, we already know quite a lot about the demographic functioning of the prehistoric populations and about the composition of the living groups: hence it is important to know whether the prehistoric groups followed the same pattern of age-sex probabilities of death as contemporary groups. The evidence from paleodemography contradicts the generalization by pointing to a pattern that involves good survivorship in infancy and childhood and much worse survivorship in young adulthood than is ever seen today (Weiss, 1973). It is possible that the apparent discrepancy could be due to systematic errors in estimation of the age at death of the skeletons, differential preservation of skeletons, or other biases in the data. On the other hand it could be that the generalization of a common human pattern of death is simply incorrect and that that of prehistoric people was entirely different. The question cannot be resolved by further study of the prehistoric skeletal evidence itself, but will probably come from one of two avenues of research on contemporary peoples.

One of these is the studies in cell biology of the mechanisms of aging and genetic repair—research that has great potential importance for archaeology. The second promising direction of research is the study of skeletal aging, a subject popular among those who study prehistoric skeletons, none of which are of known age, but very unpopular among those who study skeletons of modern peoples, where the age of the deceased person can be ascertained with accuracy. As Washburn (1976) has pointed out, the age standards in general use among physical anthropologists have been constructed on a highly unusual population of victims of violent death and, in old age, indigent persons who were often long-time alcoholics. The lack of a representative sample of deceased persons of known age is only a part of the problem of standards, however. A full-scale multivariate statistical analysis of a range of skeletons of known age, of varying ages, social classes, racial and ethnic groups, diets, and morbidity histories is urgently needed to form an adequate basis for the estimation of age at death in populations of unknown age, along with not just the estimated age but some measure of the expected error of estimate. The diagnosis of age and sex from skeletal evidence seems to be treated more as an art than as a science by the highly skilled practitioners, who seem to find it gratifying to spend their time with the ancient bones but not with modern bones of known age. Until the two sets of evidence are brought together into a single framework, we cannot evaluate the claim of distinctively different mortality schedules in prehistory.

On the area of fertility dynamics and particularly the physiological correlates of fertility, research is being actively pursued, particularly on the hormonal correlates of lactation and the mechanism of suppression of ovulation by circulating prolactin (Wilmsen, 1982) and the possibility that a minimal level of fatness is needed in the female to permit ovulation (Frisch and McArthur, 1974). We know in great detail the proximate variables of fertility (exposure to risk, monthly probabilities of conception, dynamics of interbirth intervals) and how these interact, but much less about the determinants of the proximate variables, especially diet and health. Progress in this research will permit improvements in the models of fertility process in prehistoric societies.

One major question is that of the extent to which our models must incorporate conscious and deliberate population control, either through the fertility variables (late marriage and reduced fertility in marriage) or the mortality variables: infanticide, murder, warfare, and senilicide (M. Harris, 1975). The !Kung studies seem to suggest that populations in simple societies had no need for deliberate control of their population growth, as their moderate mortality and low natural fertility led to something close to a balance, at least in the long run. It is not as yet at all clear whether the !Kung model should be interpreted as a common pattern or as a rarely achieved balance between growth and the limitations of growth in a marginal environment. If there are natural density-dependent population-growth rate limits in hunting/gathering populations, they must have mechanisms in either the fertility process, the mortality process, or both, and these mechanisms must somehow incorporate information from the environment in diet, health, work loads, age composition of the population, or some other factor in order to stop growth when some sort of ceiling is reached and start growth again when the population dips below that ceiling.

Whatever the mechanism is, it must somehow have been removed in the complex process of instituting food production, whether it stems from greater caloric intake, more or different carbohydrates in the diet, less frequent moves, less work, changes in health, or some other factor. The interrelations of these variables are complex, and correlational analyses of known societies, small and nonrandomly selected as they are, are unlikely to reveal the mechanism of population-growth limitation even if it is clearly happening. As Gifford (this volume) suggests, such data can most usefully serve as tests of models constructed by an understanding of causal relationships established by the study of contemporary events.

Prospects for the eventual clarification of the causes of population growth and its effects on the process of food production in prehistory would seem to be good, but unpredictable in detail. The contributions to a satisfactory solution are likely to come from a wide range of disciplines and may well emerge as unexpected by-products of research on topics of human growth and reproduction, ecology, climate, and disease, as well as the more obvious continued research in archaeology itself.

Contributors

Stanley H. Ambrose
Department of Anthropology
University of California
Berkeley, California 94720

Prof. George J. Armelagos
Department of Anthropology
University of Massachusetts
Amherst, Massachusetts
    01003

Dr. John W. Barthelme
Department of Sociology and
    Anthropology
St. Lawrence University
Canton, New York 13617

Dr. John R. F. Bower
Department of Sociology and
    Anthropology
Iowa State University
Ames, Iowa 50011

Dr. Steven A. Brandt
Department of Anthropology
University of Georgia
Athens, Georgia 30602

Dr. Alison S. Brooks
Department of Anthropology
George Washington
    University
Washington, D.C. 20052

Prof. Karl W. Butzer
Departments of Geography
    and Anthropology
University of Chicago
Chicago, Illinois 60637

Dr. Elizabeth A. Cashdan
Department of Anthropology
University of Pittsburgh
Pittsburgh, Pennsylvania
    15260

Prof. J. Desmond Clark
Department of Anthropology
University of California
Berkeley, California 94720

James I. Ebert
Southwest Cultural Resources
    Center
Division of Remote Sensing
National Park Service
Box 26176
Albuquerque, New Mexico
    87125

Dr. Christopher Ehret
Department of History
University of California
Los Angeles, California 90024

Diane E. Gelburd
Department of Agriculture
Soil Conservation Service
Washington, D.C. 20013

Dr. Diane P. Gifford-
    Gonzalez
Anthropology Board of
    Studies
University of California
Santa Cruz, California 95064

Dr. Fekri A. Hassan
Department of Anthropology
Washington State University
Pullman, Washington 99164

Dr. Alice J. Hausman
Boston University
African Studies Center
125 Bay State Road
Boston, Massachusetts 02215

Dr. Thomas R. Hays
Institute of Applied Sciences
North Texas State University
Denton, Texas 76203

Robert K. Hitchcock
Department of Anthropology
University of New Mexico
Albuquerque, New Mexico
    87131

Dr. Nancy Howell
Department of Sociology
University of Toronto
Toronto, Ontario M5S 1A1
    CANADA

Rebecca Huss-Ashmore
Department of Anthropology
University of Massachusetts
Amherst, Massachusetts
        01003

Prof. Richard G. Klein
Department of Anthropology
University of Chicago
Chicago, Illinois 60637

Prof. Daniel A. Livingstone
Department of Zoology
Duke University
Durham, North Carolina
        27706

Dr. David Lubell
Department of Anthropology
University of Alberta
Edmonton, Alberta T6G 2H4
CANADA

Debra L. Martin
Department of Anthropology
University of Massachusetts
Amherst, Massachusetts
        01003

**Drs. Roderick J. and Susan
      K. McIntosh**
Department of Anthropology
Rice University
Houston, Texas 77001

Dr. David W. Phillipson
University Museum of
      Archaeology and
      Ethnography
Downing Street, Cambridge
      CB2 3D2
ENGLAND

Dr. Merrick Posnansky
Department of History
University of California
Los Angeles, California 90024

Dr. G. P. Rightmire
Department of Anthropology
State University of New York
Binghamton, New York 13901

Dr. L. H. Robbins
Department of Anthropology
Michigan State University
East Lansing, Michigan 48823

Dr. Romuald Schild
Institute for the History of
      Material Culture
National Academy of Sciences
Warsaw, POLAND

Prof. Thurstan Shaw
Professor Emeritus
University of Ibadan, Nigeria
37 Hawthorne Road
Stapleford, Cambridge
      CB2 5DU
UNITED KINGDOM

Dr. Andrew B. Smith
Department of Archaeology
University of Capetown,
      Private Bag
Rondebosch, Cape 7700
      SOUTH AFRICA

Ann Brower Stahl
Department of Anthropology
University of California
Berkeley, California 94720

Dr. Ann Stemler
Biology Department
De Anza College
Cupertino, California 95014

Dr. Dennis P. Van Gerven
Department of Anthropology
University of Colorado
Boulder, Colorado 80309

Prof. Fred Wendorf
Department of Anthropology
Southern Methodist
      University
Dallas, Texas 75275

Dr. Martin A.J. Williams
School of Earth Sciences
Macquarie University
North Ryde, N.S.W. 2113
AUSTRALIA

Dr. John E. Yellen
Program Director for
      Anthropology
National Science Foundation
Washington, D.C. 20050

Bibliography

Adams, J. W., and A. B. Kasakoff
1975 Factors underlying endogamous group size. In M. Nag, ed., *Population and Social Organization*: 147–174. The Hague: Mouton.

Adams, R. McC.
1966 *The Evolution of Urban Society*. Chicago: Aldine.
1978 Strategies of maximization, stability, and resilience in Mesopotamian society, settlement, and agriculture. *Proceedings of the American Philosophical Society* 122: 329–335.

Adams, W. Y.
1967 Continuity and change in Nubian culture history. *Sudan Notes and Records* 48: 1–32.
1970 A reappraisal of Nubian culture history. *Orientalia* 39: 269–279.
1977 *Nubia: Corridor to Africa*. Princeton: Princeton University Press.

Adamson, D. A., J. D. Clark, and M. A. J. Williams
1974 Barbed bone points from Central Sudan and the age of the "Early Khartoum" tradition. *Nature* 249: 120–123.

Adamson, D. A., F. Gasse, F. A. Street, and M. A. J. Williams
1980 Late Quaternary history of the Nile. *Nature* 287: 50–55.

Addison, F.
1942 *Wellcome Excavations in the Sudan*. Vol. I: *Jebel Moya*. London: Oxford University Press.

Agorsah, E. K.
n.d. Some considerations on the archaeology and traditional history of the Begho area. M.A. thesis, University of Ghana, Legon (1976).

Ahn, P.
1970 *West African Soils*. London: Oxford University Press.

Albanese, A. A.
1977 *Bone Loss: Causes, Detection, and Therapy*. New York: Alan R. Liss.

Aldred, C.
1975 Egypt: the Amarna period and the end of the Eighteenth Dynasty. *Cambridge Ancient History*. 3rd ed., Vol. 2, pt. 2: 49–97.

Alexander, J.
1977 The "frontier" concept in prehistory: the end of the moving frontier. In J. V. S. Megaw, ed., *Hunters, Gatherers and First Farmers beyond Europe*: 25–40. Surrey: Leicester University Press.

Alexander, J., and D. G. Coursey
1969 The origins of yam cultivation. In P. J. Ucko and G. W. Dimbleby, eds., *The Domestication and Exploitation of Plants and Animals*: 405–425. Chicago: Aldine.

Ali, A. M.
1972 Meroitic settlement of the Butana (central Sudan). In P. J. Ucko, R. Tringham, and G. W. Dimbleby, eds., *Man, Settlement, and Urbanism*: 639–646. London: Duckworth.

Almagor, U.
1978   *Pastoral Partners—Affinity and Bond Partnership among the Dassanetch of South-West Ethiopia.* Manchester: University of Massachusetts Press.

Ambrose, S. H.
1980   Elmenteitan and other late Pastoral Neolithic adaptations in the central highlands of East Africa. In R. E. Leakey and B. A. Ogot, eds., *Proceedings of the Eighth Panafrican Congress of Prehistory and Quaternary Studies*: 279–282. Nairobi: The International Louis Leakey Memorial Institute for African Prehistory.
1982   Archaeological and linguistic reconstructions of history in East Africa. In C. Ehret and M. Posnansky, eds., *The Archaeological and Linguistic Reconstruction of African History*: 104–157. Berkeley: University of California Press.
n.d.a   Masai Gorge Rock Shelter: The significance for central Kenya prehistory. B.A. Honors thesis, Department of Anthropology, University of Massachusetts/Boston (1977).
n.d.b   The archaeology of Masai Gorge Rock Shelter: implications for the recent prehistory of central Kenya. Paper presented at the 4th biennial meeting of the Society of Africanist Archaeologists in America, New Orleans (1977).

Ambrose, S. H., F. Hivernel, and C. M. Nelson
1980   The taxonomic status of the Kenya Capsian. In R. E. Leakey and B. A. Ogot, eds., *Proceedings of the Eighth Panafrican Congress of Prehistory and Quaternary Studies*: 248–252. Nairobi: The International Louis Leakey Memorial Institute for African Prehistory.

Ammerman, A. J., and L. L. Cavalli-Sforza
1971   Measuring the rate of spread of early farming in Europe. *Man* 6: 674–688.

Ammerman, A. J., D. P. Gifford, and A. Voorrips
1978   Toward an evaluation of sampling strategies: simulated excavation of a Kenyan pastoralist site. In I. Hodder, ed., *Simulation Studies in Archaeology*: 123–136. Cambridge: Cambridge University Press.

Anati, E.
1968   *Rock Art in Central Arabia.* Vol. 2. Louvain: Institut Orientaliste, Bibliothèque de l'Université.

Anderson, E.
1960   The evolution of domestication. In Sol Tax, ed., *Evolution after Darwin* (Vol. 2): 67–84. Chicago: University of Chicago Press.
1967   The bearings of botanical evidence on African culture history. In C. Gabel and N. R. Bennett, eds., *Reconstructing African Culture History*: 169–180. Boston: Boston University Press.

Angel, J. L., T. W. Phenice, L. H. Robbins, and B. M. Lynch
1980   *Late Stone Age Fishermen of Lothagam, Kenya.* East Lansing: Michigan State University, Museum Anthropological Series, Vol. 3, No. 2.

Anquandah, J. R.
1965   Ghana's terracotta cigars. *Ghana Notes and Queries* 7: 26.
1976   Boyasi Hill, a Kintampo "Neolithic" village site in the forest of Ghana. *Sankofa* 2: 92.

Anthony, B.
1972   The Stillbay question. In H. Hugot, ed., *Proceedings of the Sixth Panafrican Congress of Prehistory, Dakar*: 80–82. Paris: Chambéry.

Ardrey, R.
1976   *The Hunting Hypothesis: A Personal Conclusion Concerning the Evolutionary Nature of Man.* New York: Athenaeum.

Arkell, A. J.
1949   *Early Khartoum.* London: Oxford University Press.
1953   *Shaheinab.* London: Oxford University Press.

1954 Four occupation sites at Agordat. *Kush* 2: 33–62.

1975 The prehistory of the Nile Valley. In B. Spuler et al., eds. *Handbuch der Orientalistik*. 7. *Kunst und Archäologie*, 1A, pp. 1–55. Leiden/Köln: E. J. Brill.

Arkell, A. J., D. M. A. Bate, L. H. Wells, and A. D. Lacaille
1951 *The Pleistocene Fauna of Two Blue Nile Sites*. Fossil Mammals of Africa No. 2. London: British Museum (Nat. Hist.).

Arkell, A. J., and P. J. Ucko
1965 Review of Predynastic development in the Nile Valley. *Current Anthropology* 6(2): 145–166.

Armelagos, G. J., and D. L. Greene
1978 Racial and demographic interpretation of the Kadero (Sudan) Neolithic. *Current Anthropology* 19: 411–412.

Armelagos, G. J., and A. McArdle
1975 Population, disease and evolution. In A. C. Swedlund, ed., *Population Studies in Archaeology and Biological Anthropology: A Symposium*, *American Antiquity* 40(2): 1–10.

Armelagos, G. J., J. H. Mielke, K. H. Owen, D. P. Van Gerven, J. R. Dewey, and P. E. Mahler
1972 Bone growth and development in prehistoric populations from Sudanese Nubia. *Journal of Human Evolution* 1: 89–119.

Armstrong, R. C.
1964 *The Study of West African Languages*. Ibadan: Institute of African Studies.

Arnold, D.
1977 Fajjum. *Lexikon Ägyptologie* 2: 87–93.

Arnold, T. R., and W. F. Libby
1951 Radiocarbon dates. *Science* 113L: 111–120.

Aschmann, H.
1968 Comment on "The origins of agriculture." *Current Anthropology* 9: 494–495.

Atlas of Kenya
1970 Survey of Kenya. Nairobi: Government Printer.

Attia, M. I.
1954 *Deposit in the Nile Valley and the Delta*. Cairo: Geological Survey of Egypt, Government Press.

Audebeau, M. C.
1919 L'agriculture égyptienne à la fin du XVIII siècle. *L'Egypte contemporaine* 10: 132–169.

Aumassip, G.
1979 Les problèmes climatiques posés par l'archéologie préhistorique. *Bulletin de l'Association Sénégalaise pour l'étude du Quaternaire de l'Ouest africain* 56–57: 86–89.

Avery, G.
1974 Open station shell midden sites and associated features from the Pearly Beach area, Southwestern Cape. *South African Archaeological Bulletin* 29: 104–114.

1975 Discussion on the age and use of tidal fish-traps (viswywers). *South African Archaeological Bulletin* 30: 105–113.

Baer, G.
1969 *Studies in the Social History of Modern Egypt*. Chicago: University of Chicago Press.

Baer, K.
1960 *Rank and Title in the Old Kingdom: The Structure of the Egyptian Administration in the 5th and 6th Dynasties*. Chicago: University of Chicago Press.

1963 An 11th-Dynasty farmer's letters to his family. *Journal of the American Oriental Society* 83: 1–19.

n.d. Egyptian Chronology. Unpublished manuscript.

Bailloud, G.
1959 La préhistoire de l'Ethiopie. *Cahiers de l'Afrique et de l'Asie* 5: 15–43.

Baker, H. G.
1962 Comments on the thesis that there was a major centre of plant domestication near

the headwaters of the river Niger. *Journal of African History* 3: 229–233.

Baker, R. E. D., and N. W. Simmonds
1953a   The genus Ensete in Africa. *Kew Bulletin* 3: 405–416.
1953b   The genus Ensete in Africa: a correction. *Kew Bulletin* 4: 574.

Ball, J.
1939   *Contributions to the Geography of Egypt.* Cairo: Survey of Egypt, Government Press.

Ballais, J. L.
1976   Morphogenèse holocène dans la région de Chéria (Nementchas-Algérie). *Actes du symposium sur les versants en pays méditerranéens, Aix-en-Provence*, 1975. CEGERM Vol. 5: 127–130.

Balout, L.
1955   *Préhistoire de l'Afrique du Nord.* Paris: Arts et Métiers Graphiques.

Barich, B. E.
1978   Recenti risultati della Missione Paletnologica italiana nel Sahara Libico. La facies a microliti del Ti-n-Torha. *Quaderni de "La Ricerca Scientifica"* 100, 1: 153–172. Roma: Consiglio Nazionale delle Ricerche.
n.d.   With regard to a North African and Saharan Neolithic. Abstract of Paper for Eighth Panafrican Congress on Prehistory, Nairobi (1977).

Barnard, A.
1979   Kalahari Bushman settlement patterns. In P. Burnham and R. F. Ellen, eds., *Social and Ecological Systems*: 131–144. London: Academic Press.

Barth, F.
1956   Ecologic relations of ethnic groups in Swat, north Pakistan. *American Anthropologist* 58(5): 1079–1089.
1969   (ed.) *Ethnic Groups and Boundaries—The Social Organization of Culture Difference.* Boston: Little, Brown.

Barthelme, J. W.
1977   Holocene sites north-east of Lake Turkana: a preliminary report. *Azania* 12: 33–41.
n.d.a   Radiocarbon dates from Lake Turkana: Summary and appraisal. In preparation.
n.d.b   Late Pleistocene-Holocene Prehistory Northeast of Lake Turkana, Kenya. Ph.D. dissertation,, University of California, Berkeley (1982).

Bascom, W. R.
1955   Urbanization among the Yoruba. *American Journal of Sociology* 60(5): 446–454.

Baumgartel, E. J.
1955   *The Cultures of Predynastic Egypt.* London: Oxford University Press.
1960   *The Cultures of Prehistoric Egypt.* London: Oxford University Press.
1965   *Predynastic Egypt.* Cambridge: Cambridge University Press.

Beaudet, G., P. Michel, D. Nahon, P. Oliva, J. Riser, and A. Ruellan
1976   Formes, formations superficielles et variations climatiques récentes du Sahara occidental. *Revue de géographie physique et de géologie dynamique* 18(2): 157–174.

Behrensmeyer, A. K.
1978   Taphonomic and ecological information from bone weathering. *Paleobiology* 4: 150–167.

Beliquini, H. M.
1946   *Cultivation of Egyptian Crops* (in Arabic), pt. 1. Cairo: Matba't el'Oloum.

Bell, B.
1970   The oldest records of the Nile floods. *Geographical Journal* 136: 569–573.
1971   The Dark Ages in ancient history. I. The first Dark Age in Egypt. *American Journal of Archaeology* 75: 1–26.
1975   Climate and the history of Egypt: the Middle Kingdom. *American Journal of Archaeology* 79: 223–269.

Bell, R. H. V.
1971   A grazing ecosystem in the Serengeti. *Scientific American* 225: 86–93.

Bender, M. L.
1971   The languages of Ethiopia: a new lexicostatistic classification and some problems of diffusion. *Anthropological Linguistics* 13: 165–288.
1975a   *The Ethiopian Nilo-Saharans.* Addis Ababa.
1975b   *Omotic: A New Afroasiatic Language Family.* Carbondale: Southern Illinois University Museum.
1976   (ed.) *The Non-Semitic Languages of Ethiopia.* East Lansing: Michigan State University Press.

Benoist, J.
1973   Genetics of isolate populations. In M. Crawford and P. Workman, eds., *Methods and Theories of Anthropological Genetics*: 67–81. Albuquerque: University of New Mexico Press.

Berry, A. C., R. J. Berry and P. J. Ucko
1967   Genetical change in ancient Egypt. *Man* 2: 551–568.

Berry, L.
1960   Large-scale alluvial islands in the White Nile. *Hydrobiological Research Unit, University of Khartoum*: 14–19.

Biesele, M.
1971   Hunting in semi-arid areas: the Kalahari Bushmen today. *Botswana Notes and Records*, special ed. 1: 62–67.

Bietak, M.
1975   Tell el-Daba II: der Fundort im Rahmen einer archäologisch-geographischen Untersuchung über das ägyptische Ostdelta. *Denkschriften der Akademie der Wissenschaften, Wien* 4: 1–236.

Billy, G.
1976   La population de la forteresse de Mirgissa: Mirgissa III. *Etudes anthropologiques*: 7–55, 97–140. Paris: Geuther.

Binford, L. R.
1967   Reply to Chang: major aspects of the interrelationship between archaeology and ethnology. *Current Anthropology* 8: 227–243.

1968a   Methodological considerations of the archaeological use of ethnographic data. In R. B. Lee and I. DeVore, eds., *Man the Hunter*: 268–273. Chicago: Aldine.
1968b   Post-Pleistocene adaptations. In L. Binford and S. Binford, eds., *New Perspectives in Archaeology*: 313–341. Chicago: Aldine.
1980   Willow smoke and dogs' tails: hunter-gatherer settlement systems and archaeological site formation. *American Antiquity* 45: 4–20.
n.d.   The subsistence ecology of hunters and gatherers. In preparation.

Binford, L. R., and W. J. Chasko, Jr.
1976   Nunamiut demographic history: a provocative case. In E. B. W. Zubrow, ed., *Demographic Anthropology: Quantitative Approaches*: 63–143. Albuquerque: University of New Mexico Press.

Bishop, W. W., and J. D. Clark
1967   (eds.) *Background to Evolution in Africa*: Recommendations, sections L, M, N, O: 892–899. Chicago: University of Chicago Press.

Blackburn, R. H.
1970   A preliminary report of research on the Ogiek tribe of Kenya. Institute for Developmental Studies, Discussion Paper no. 89, University of Nairobi, Kenya.
1973   Okiek ceramics: evidence for central Kenya prehistory. *Azania* 8: 55–70.
1974   The Okiek and their history. *Azania* 9: 139–158.
1976   Okiek history. In B. A. Ogot, ed., *Kenya before 1900*: 53–83. Nairobi: East African Publishing House.
n.d.   Honey in Okiek personality, culture, and society. Ph.D. dissertation, Michigan State University (1971).

Bleek, D. F.
1927   The distribution of Bushmen languages in South Africa. *Festschrift Meinhof: Sprachwissenschaftliche und andere Studien.* Hamburg, Austria: L. Friederichsen.
1928   *The Naron: A Bushman Tribe of the Central*

Kalahari. London: Cambridge University Press.

Blong, R. J., and R. Gillespie
1978   Fluvially transported charcoal gives erroneous 14 C ages for recent deposits. *Nature* 271: 739–741.

Bolick, M.
n.d.   A vegetational history of the Mt. Meru Lahar, Tanzania. M.S. thesis, Duke University (1974).

Bonnefille, R.
1968   Contribution à l'étude de la flore d'un niveau pléistocène de la haute vallée de l'Aouache (Ethiopie). *Compte rendu hebdomadaire des séances de l'Académie des Sciences*: 266 (D): 1229–1232.
1969   Indication sur la paléoflore d'un niveau du Quaternaire moyen du site de Melka Kontouré (Ethiopie). *Comptes rendus sommaires des séances de la Société Géologique de France* 270(D): 2430–2433.
1970   Premiers résultats concernant l'analyse pollinique d'échantillons du Pléistocène inférieur de l'Omo (Ethiopie). *Compte rendu hebdomadaire des séances de l'Académie des Sciences* 7: 238.
1973   Nouvelles recherches en Ethiopie: recherches sur le Quaternaire en Afrique. In *Le Quaternaire géodynamique, stratigraphie et environnement*: 182–187. Paris: Comité National Français de l'INQUA.
1976a   Implications of pollen assemblage from the Koobi Fora Formation, East Rudolf, Kenya. *Nature* 264: 403–407.
1976b   Palynological evidence for an important change in the vegetation of the Omo Basin between 2.5 and 2 million years ago. In Y. Coppens, F. C. Howell, G. Ll. Isaac, and R. E. F. Leakey, eds., *Earliest Man and Environments in the Lake Rudolf Basin*: 421–423. Chicago: University of Chicago Press.
n.d.   Associations polliniques actuelles et quaternaires en Ethiopie (Vallées de l'Awash et de l'Omo). Ph.D. dissertation, University of Paris, France (1972).

Boserup, E.
1965   *The Conditions of Agricultural Growth: The Economies of Agrarian Change under Population Pressure.* Chicago: Aldine.

Bouchud, J.
1975   La faune de Medjez II. In H. Camps-Fabrer, *Un gisement capsien de faciès sétifien: Medjez II, El Eulma (Algérie)*: 377–391. Paris: CNRS.

Bourlière, F.
1963   Observations on the ecology of some large mammals. In F. C. Howell and F. Bourlière, eds., *African Ecology and Human Evolution*: 43–54. Chicago: Aldine.

Bower, J. R. F.
1973a   Seronera: excavations at a stone bowl site in the Serengeti National Park, Tanzania. *Azania* 8: 71–104.
1973b   Early pottery and other finds from Kisii district, western Kenya. *Azania* 8: 131–140.
1977   Preliminary report of a study of prehistoric cultures of the Serengeti National Park. *Nyame Akuma* 11: 20–27.

Bower, J. R. F., and C. M. Nelson
1978   Early pottery and pastoral cultures of the Central Rift Valley, Kenya. *Man* n.s. 13: 554–566.

Bower, J. R. F., C. M. Nelson, A. F. Waibel, and S. Wandibba
1977   The University of Massachusetts' Later Stone Age/Pastoral Neolithic comparative study in central Kenya. *Azania* 12: 119–146.

Boyé, M., F. Marnier, C. Nesson, and G. Trécolle
1978   Les dépôts de la Sebka Mellala (Ouargla, Sahara algérien). *Revue de géomorphologie dynamique* 28: 49–62.

Braidwood, R. J.
1952   *The Near East and the Foundations of*

Civilization. Eugene: Oregon State System of Higher Education.

1960   The agricultural revolution. *Scientific American* 203(3): 130–148.

Brandt, S. A.

1980   Investigation of late Stone Age occurrences at Lake Besaka, Ethiopia. In R. E. Leakey and B. A. Ogot, eds., *Proceedings of the Eighth Panafrican Congress of Prehistory and Quaternary Studies*: 239–243. Nairobi: The International Louis Leakey Memorial Institute for African Prehistory.

n.d.   A late Quaternary cultural/environmental sequence from Lake Besaka, Southern Afar, Ethiopia. Ph.D. dissertation, University of California, Berkeley (1982).

Brentjes, B.

1968   Comments on "The origins of agriculture." *Current Anthropology* 9: 495.

Broeker, W. S., M. Ewing, and B. C. Heezen

1960   Evidence for abrupt change in climate close to 11,000 years ago. *American Journal of Science* 258: 429–448.

Bronson, B.

1972   Farm labour and the evolution of food production. In B. Spooner, ed., *Population Growth: Anthropological Implications*: 190–218. Cambridge, Mass.: MIT Press.

1975   The earliest farming: demography as cause and consequence. In S. Polgar, ed., *Population, Ecology, and Social Evolution*: 33–78. The Hague: Mouton.

Brooks, A. S., A. L. Crowell, and J. E. Yellen

1980   ≠ Gi: a StoneAge archaeological site in western Ngamiland, Botswana. In R. E. Leakey and B. A. Ogot, eds., *Proceedings of the Eighth Panafrican Congress of Prehistory and Quaternary Studies*: 304–309. Nairobi: The International Louis Leakey Memorial Institute for African Prehistory.

Brooks, A. S., and J. E. Yellen

1977   Archaeological excavations at ≠ Gi (western Ngamiland, Botswana): a report on the first two field seasons. *Botswana Notes and Records* 9: 21–30.

Brothwell, D. R.

1974   The Upper Pleistocene Singa skull, a problem in paleontological interpretation. In W. Bernhard and A. Kandler, eds., *Bevölkerungsbiologie*: 534–545. Stuttgart: G. Fischer–Verlag.

1975   Salvaging the term "domestication" for certain types of man-animal relationship: the possible value of an eight-point scoring system. *Journal of Archaeological Science* 2(3): 397–400.

Brower, A. M.

n.d.   African agricultural origins: a perspective. M.A. thesis, University of Calgary, Alberta, Canada (1978).

Brown, J.

1966   The excavation of a group of burial mounds at Ilkek, near Gilgil, Kenya. *Azania* 1: 59–78.

Brown, J. A.

1975   Deepsite excavation strategy as a sampling problem. In J. W. Mueller, ed., *Sampling in Archaeology*. Tucson: University of Arizona Press.

Brunken, J., J. M. J. de Wet, and J. R. Harlan

1977   The morphology and domestication of pearl millet. *Economic Botany* 31(2): 163–174.

Brunton, G.

1937   *Mostagedda and the Tasian Culture*. London: Bernard Quaritch.

Brunton, G., and G. Caton-Thompson

1928   *The Badarian Civilization*. London: British School of Archaeology in Egypt.

Brunton, G., E. W. Gardner, and W. M. F. Petrie

1927–   *Qua and Badari* (3 parts). London: British
1930   School of Archaeology in Egypt.

Buchanan, W. F., S. L. Hall, J. Henderson, A. Olivier, J. M. Pettigrew, J. E. Parkington, and P. T. Robertshaw

1978   Coastal shell middens in the Paternoster area, southwestern Cape. *South African Archaeological Bulletin* 33: 89–93.

Buckland, A. W.
1878   Primitive agriculture. *Journal of the Anthropological Institute* 7: 2–18.

Budge, E. A. W.
1928   *A History of Ethiopia, Nubia and Abyssinia.* (2 vols.) London: Methuen.

Bulliet, R. W.
1975   *The Camel and the Wheel.* Cambridge, Mass.: Harvard University Press.

Burnor, D. R., and J. E. Harris
1968   Racial continuity in lower Nubia: 12,000 to the present. *Proceedings of the Indiana Academy of Science 1967* 77: 113–121.

Busson, F., P. Jaeger, P. Lunven, and M. Pinta
1965   *Plantes alimentaires de l'ouest africain: étude botanique, biologique et chimique.* Marseilles: Leconte.

Butzer, K. W.
1959a   Environment and human ecology in Egypt during Predynastic and early Dynastic times. *Bulletin de la Société de géographie d'Egypte* 32: 43–87.
1959b   Some recent geological deposits in the Egyptian Nile Valley. *Geographical Journal* 125: 75–79.
1960   Archaeology and geology in ancient Egypt. *Science* 132: 1617–1624.
1971   *Environment and Archaeology.* Chicago: Aldine.
1976   *Early Hydraulic Civilization in Egypt: A Study in Cultural Ecology.* Chicago: University of Chicago Press.
1979   Climate patterns in an un-glaciated continent. *Geographical Magazine* 51(3): 201–208.
1980a   Pleistocene history of the Nile Valley in Egypt and Lower Nubia. In M. A. J.

Williams and H. Faure, eds., *The Sahara and the Nile*: 248–276. Rotterdam: Balkema.
1980b   The Holocene lake plain of North Rudolf, East Africa. *Physical Geography* 1: 42–58.
1980c   Civilizations: organisms or systems? *American Scientist* 68: 517–523.

Butzer, K. W., G. J. Fock, L. Scott, and R. Stuckenrath
1979   Dating and context of rock engravings in Southern Africa. *Science* 203: 1201–1214.

Butzer, K. W., and C. L. Hansen
1968   *Desert and River in Nubia: Geomorphology and Prehistoric Environments at the Aswan Reservoir.* Madison: University of Wisconsin Press.

Butzer, K. W., G. L. Isaac, J. L. Richardson, and C. Washbourn-Kamau
1972   Radiocarbon dating of East African lake levels. *Science* 175: 1069–1076.

Caminos, R. A.
1954   *Late Egyptian Miscellanies.* London: Oxford University Press.
1977   *A Tale of Woe.* Oxford: Griffith Institute, Ashmolean Museum.

Campbell, A. C.
1976   Traditional utilization of the Okavango delta. In *Proceedings of the Symposium on the Okavango Delta and Its Future Utilization*: 163–173. Gaborone, Botswana: Botswana Society.
1977   Conservationist par excellence. *Botswana Magazine* 2(3): 40–45.

Campbell, A. C., and G. Child
1971   The impact of man on the environment of Botswana. *Botswana Notes and Records* 3: 91–110.

Camps, G.
1969   *Amekni: Néolithique ancien du Hoggar.* Centre de Recherches Anthropologiques, Préhistoriques et Ethnographiques, Mémoire 10. Paris: Arts et Métiers Graphiques.
1974   *Les civilisations préhistoriques de l'Afrique du Nord et du Sahara.* Paris: Doin.

1975   The prehistoric cultures of North Africa:
        radiocarbon chronology. In F. Wendorf
        and A. E. Marks, eds., *Problems in
        Prehistory: North Africa and the Levant*: 181–
        192. Dallas: Southern Methodist
        University Press.
1979   Twelve years of prehistoric research in the
        Sahara. *Research* 9: 40–48.

Camps, G., and H. Camps-Fabrer
1972   L'Epipaléolithique récent et le passage au
        Néolithique dans le nord de l'Afrique. In
        J. Lüning, ed., *Die Anfänge des Neolithikums
        vom Orient bis Nordeuropa* 7: 19–59.
        Westliches Mittelmeergebiet und britische
        Inseln. Köln: Böhlau.

Camps-Fabrer, H.
1966   *Matière et art mobilier dans la préhistoire
        nord-africaine et saharienne.* CRAPE Mém.
        5. Paris: Arts et Métiers Graphiques.
1970   Différents faciès céramiques du
        Néolithique saharien. In *Acts of the 7th
        International Congress of Prehistoric and
        Protohistoric Sciences, Prague, 1966*: 166–
        172.
1975   *Un gisement capsien de faciès sétifien: Medjez
        II, El-Eulma (Algérie).* Paris: CNRS.

Caneva, I.
n.d.   Unpublished paper on a Neolithic site at
        Geili (Khartoum) presented at the Eighth
        Panafrican Congress on Prehistory and
        Quaternary Studies, Nairobi (1977).

Carlson, D. S.
1976a   Temporal variation in prehistoric Nubian
        crania. *American Journal of Physical
        Anthropology* 45: 467–484.
1976b   Patterns of morphological variation in the
        human midface and upper face. In J. A.
        McNamara, Jr., ed., *Factors Affecting the
        Growth of the Midface*: 277–299.
        Craniofacial Growth Series Monograph
        No. 6. Ann Arbor: Center for Human
        Growth and Development.
n.d.   Temporal Variation in Prehistoric Nubian
        Crania. Ph.D. dissertation, University of
        Massachusetts, Amherst (1974).

**Carlson, D. S., G. J. Armelagos, and D. P.
Van Gerven**
1974   Factors influencing the etiology of cribra
        orbitalia in prehistoric Nubia. *Journal of
        Human Evolution* 3: 405–410.
1976   Patterns of age-related cortical bone loss
        (osteoporosis) within the femoral
        diaphysis. *Human Biology* 48(2): 295–314.

Carlson, D. S., and D. P. Van Gerven
1977   Masticatory function and post-Pleistocene
        evolution in Nubia. *American Journal of
        Physical Anthropology* 46: 495–506.
1979   Diffusion, biological determinism, and
        biocultural adaptation in the Nubian
        corridor. *American Anthropologist* 81: 561–
        580.

Carr, C. J.
1977   *Pastoralism in Crisis: The Dassenech and
        Their Ethiopian Lands.* University of
        Chicago, Department of Geography
        Research Paper No. 180.

Carter, G.
1977   A hypothesis suggesting a single origin of
        agriculture. In C. A. Reed, ed., *Origins of
        Agriculture*: 89–133. The Hague: Mouton.

Carter, P. L., and C. Flight
1972   A report on the fauna from the sites of
        Ntereso and Kintampo Rock Shelter Six in
        Ghana with evidence for the practice of
        animal husbandry during the second
        millennium B.C. *Man* 7: 277–282.

Cashdan, E. A.
1980   Egalitarianism among hunters and
        gatherers. *American Anthropologist* 82(1):
        116–120.
n.d.   Subsistence, mobility, and territorial
        organization among the //Ganakwe of the
        northeastern Central Kalahari Game
        Reserve. Report to the Ministry of Local
        Government and Lands, Gaborone,
        Botswana (1977).

Cashdan, E. A., and W. J. Chasko, Jr.
n.d.   People of the middle and upper Nata River
        area: origins, population, economics, and
        health. Report to the Ministry of Local

Government and Lands, Gaborone,
Botswana (1977).

Caton-Thompson, G.
1952   *Kharga Oasis in Prehistory.* London:
         Athlone.

Caton-Thompson, G., and E. W. Gardner
1934   *The Desert Fayum.* (2 vols.) London: Royal
         Anthropological Institute of Great Britain
         and Ireland.

Caton-Thompson, G., and E. Whittle
1975   Thermoluminescence dating of the
         Badarian. *Antiquity* 49: 89–97.

Caye, V. M., and S. R. Koitsiwe
n.d.   Report on a survey of Basarwa in Western
         Kgatleng District. Report to the Ministry
         of Local Government and Lands,
         Gaborone, Botswana (1976).

Černý, J.
1933   Fluctuations in grain prices during the
         20th Egyptian Dynasty. *Archiv Orientalní*
         6: 173–178.
1975   Egypt from the death of Ramses III to the
         end of the Twenty-First Dynasty. In
         Cambridge Ancient History (3rd ed.): Vol. 2,
         pt. 2, 606–657.

Chagnon, N.
1968   The culture-ecology of shifting
         (pioneering) cultivation among the
         Yanomamo Indians. *International Congress
         of Anthropological and Ethnological Sciences*
         8(3): 249–255.

Chamard, P. C.
1973   Monographie d'une sebkha continentale
         du Sud-Ouest Saharien: la sebkha de
         Chemchane (Adrar de Mauritanie).
         *Bulletin de l'Institut fondamental d'Afrique
         Noire* 35A: 207–243.

Chamla, M.-C.
1968   Les populations anciennes du Sahara et
         des régions limitrophes: étude des restes
         osseux humains néolithiques et proto-
         historiques. *Mémoires du Centre de
         recherches anthropologiques, préhistoriques et
         ethnographiques* 9: 1–249.

1978   Le peuplement de l'Afrique du Nord de
         l'Epipaléolithique à l'époque actuelle.
         Anthropologie 82(3): 385–430.

Chevalier, A.
1938   Le Sahara, centre d'origine des plantes
         cultivées. *Société de biogéographie, Mémoires*
         6: 307–322.

Child, G.
1971   Ecological constraints on rural
         development in Botswana. *Botswana Notes
         and Records* 3: 157–164.

Child, G., R. Parris, and R. LeRiche
1971   Use of mineralized water by Kalahari
         wildlife and its effects on habitats. *East
         African Journal of Wildlife* 9: 125–144.

Childe, V. G.
1936   *Man Makes Himself.* London: Watts.
1951a   *Man Makes Himself* (3rd ed.). London:
         Watts.
1951b   *Social Evolution.* World: Cleveland.

Childers, G. W.
1976   *Report on the Survey/Investigation of the
         Ghanzi Farm Basarwa Situation.* Gaborone,
         Botswana: Government Printer.

**Chittick, H. N., S. H. Ambrose, and D. P.
Collett**
in press Excavations at Deloraine, Rongai, 1978.
         Azania 18.

**Clark, G. A., L. G. Straus, J. Altuna, and D.
Young**
n.d.   The La Riera Paleoecological Project
         (Asturias, Spain): aims and preliminary
         results. Paper presented at the forty-third
         annual meeting of the Society for
         American Archaeology, Tucson (1977).

Clark, J. D.
1954   *The Prehistoric Cultures of the Horn of
         Africa.* Cambridge: Cambridge University
         Press.
1959   *The Prehistory of Southern Africa.*
         Harmondsworth: Penguin.
1962   The spread of food production in sub-
         Saharan Africa. *Journal of African History*
         3: 211–228.

1964a Stone vessels from northern Rhodesia. *Man* 64: 69–73.
1964b The prehistoric origins of African culture. *Journal of African History* 5: 161–183.
1967a The problem of Neolithic culture in sub-Saharan Africa. In W. W. Bishop and J. D. Clark, eds., *Background to Evolution in Africa*: 601–627. Chicago: University of Chicago Press.
1967b A record of early agriculture and metallurgy in Africa from archaeological sources. In C. Gabel and N. R. Bennett, eds., *Reconstructing African Culture History*: 3–24. Boston: Boston University Press.
1970 *The Prehistory of Africa*. New York: Praeger.
1971 A re-examination of the evidence for agricultural origins in the Nile Valley. *Proceedings of the Prehistoric Society* 37: 34–79.
1972 Mobility and settlement patterns in sub-Saharan Africa: a comparison of late prehistoric hunter-gatherers and early agricultural occupation units. In P. J. Ucko, R. Tringham, and G. W. Dimbleby, eds., *Man, Settlement, and Urbanism*: 127–148. London: Duckworth.
1973 The University of California, Berkeley, expedition to the central Sudan. *Nyame Akuma* 3: 56–64.
1976a Prehistoric populations and pressures favoring plant domestication in Africa. In J. R. Harlan, J. M. J. de Wet, and A. B. L. Stemler, eds., *Origins of African Plant Domestication*: 67–105. The Hague: Mouton.
1976b The domestication process in sub-Saharan Africa with special reference to Ethiopia. In *Origine de l'élevage et de la domestication*: 56–115. Nice: Union International des Sciences Préhistoriques et Protohistoriques.
1980a Human populations and cultural adaptations in the Sahara and Nile during prehistoric times. In M. A. J. Williams and H. Faure, eds., *The Sahara and the Nile*: 527–582. Rotterdam: Balkema.
1980b The origins of domestication in Ethiopia.

In R. E. Leakey and B. A. Ogot, eds., *Proceedings of the Eighth Panafrican Congress of Prehistory and Quaternary Studies*: 268–270. Nairobi: The International Louis Leakey Memorial Institute for African Prehistory.
1980c Raw material and African lithic technology. *Man and Environment* 4: 44–55.

Clark, J. D., G. H. Cole, G. L. Isaac, and M. R. Kleindienst
1966 Precision and definition in African archaeology. *South African Archaeological Bulletin* 21: 114–121.

Clark, J. D., and G. R. Prince
1978 Use-wear on later Stone Age microliths from Laga Oda, Haraghi, Ethiopia and possible functional interpretations. *Azania* 13: 101–110.

Clark, J. D., and A. Stemler
1975 Early domesticated sorghum from central Sudan. *Nature* 254: 588–591.

Clark, J. D., and M. A. J. Williams
1978 Recent archaeological research in southeastern Ethiopia (1974–1975): some preliminary results. *Annales d'Ethiopie* 11: 19–44.

Clark, J. D., M. A. J. Williams, and A. B. Smith
1973 The geomorphology and archaeology of Adrar Bous, central Sahara: a preliminary report. *Quaternaria* 17: 245–297.

Clark, J. G. D.
1957 *Archaeology and Society*. London: Methuen.
1961 *World Prehistory, an Outline*. Cambridge: Cambridge University Press.

Clarke, D. L.
1968 *Analytical Archaeology*. London: Methuen.
1972 Models and paradigms in contemporary archaeology. In D. L. Clarke, ed., *Models in Archaeology*: 9–10. London: Methuen.
1976 Mesolithic Europe: the economic basis? In G. de G. Sieveking, I. H. Longworth, and K. E. Wilson, eds., *Problems in*

Economic and Social Archaeology: 449–481. London: Duckworth.

Clauss, B.
n.d.   Some comments on possibilities of agricultural research of veld foods ("traditional foods") in the central Kalahari. Report to the Ministry of Agriculture, Gaborone, Botswana (1979).

CLIMAP Project Members
1976   The surface of the ice-age earth. *Science* 191: 1131–1137.

Close, A. E.
1974   The lithic artifacts from Tamar Hat. In E. A. Saxon, A. E. Close, C. Cluzel, V. Morse, and N. J. Shackleton, Results of recent investigations at Tamar Hat. *Libyca* 22: 58–66.
1977   *The Identification of Style in Lithic Artefacts from Northeast Africa.* Mémoire de L'Institut d'Egypte, Tome 61. Cairo.

Coetzee, J. A.
1964   Evidence for a considerable depression of the vegetation belts during the Upper Pleistocene on the East African mountains. *Nature* 204: 564–566.
1967   Pollen analytical studies in eastern and southern Africa. *Palaeoecology of Africa* 3: 1–146.

Cohen, M. N.
1970   A reassessment of the Stone Bowl cultures of the Rift Valley, Kenya. *Azania* 5: 27–38.
1975   Population pressure and the origins of agriculture: an archaeological example from the coast of Peru. In S. Polgar, ed., *Population, Ecology and Social Evolution*: 79–122. The Hague: Mouton.
1977   *The Food Crisis in Prehistory.* New Haven: Yale University Press.

Cole, M. M., and R. C. Brown
1976   The vegetation of the Ghanzi area of western Botswana. *Journal of Biogeography* 3(3): 169–196.

Cole, S.
1963   *The Prehistory of East Africa.* New York: MacMillan.

Commelin, D., and N. Petit-Maire
1980   Chronologie isotopique saharienne pour les derniers 10.000 ans—essai d'interprétation: migrations humaines et paléoclimatologie. *Bulletin du Musée anthropologique préhistorique de Monaco* 23: 37–88.

Compagnoni, B., and M. Tosi
1978   The camel: its distribution and state of domestication in the Middle East during the third millennium B.C. in light of finds from Shar-I-Sokhta. In R. H. Meadow and M. A. Zeder, eds., *Approaches to Faunal Analysis in the Middle East*, Bulletin 2: 91–103. Cambridge, Mass.: Peabody Museum.

Conant, F. P.
1965   Korok: a variable unit of physical and social space among the Pokot of East Africa. *American Anthropologist* 67(2): 429–434.

Connah, G.
1976   The Daima sequence and the prehistoric chronology of the Lake Chad region of Nigeria. *Journal of African History* 17: 321–352.

Conrad, G.
1969   *L'évolution continentale post-hercynienne du Sahara algérien.* Paris: CNRS.

Cooke, C. K.
1965   Evidence of human migrations from the rock art of Southern Rhodesia. *Africa* 35: 263–285.

Coque, R.
1962   *La Tunisie présaharienne: étude géomorphologique.* Paris: Armand Colin.

Corruccini, R. S., and D. Whitley
1981   Occlusal variability in a rural Kentucky community. *American Journal of Orthodontics* 79: 250–262.

Cour, P., and D. Duzer
1976   Persistance d'un climat hyperaride au Sahara central et méridional au cours de

l'Holocène. *Revue de géographie physique et de géologie dynamique* 18: 175–198.

Coursey, D. G.
1967   *Yams*. London: Longmans.
1972   The civilizations of the yam: interrelationships of man and yams in Africa and the Indo-Pacific region. *Archaeology and Physical Anthropology in Oceania* 7: 215–233.
1976   The origins and domestication of yams in Africa. In J. R. Harlan, J. M. J. de Wet, and A. B. L. Stemler, eds., *Origins of African Plant Domestication*: 384–408. The Hague: Mouton.

Coursey, D. G., and J. Alexander
1968   African agricultural patterns and the sickle cell. *Science* 160: 1474–1475.

Coursey, D. G., and C. K. Coursey
1971   The new yam festivals of West Africa. *Anthropos* 66: 444–484.

Couvert, M.
1972   Variations paléoclimatiques en Algérie. *Libyca* 20: 45–48.
1976   Traduction des éléments de la flore préhistorique en facteurs climatiques. *Libyca* 24: 9–20.

Cowgill, G. L.
1975   On causes and consequences of ancient and modern population change. *American Anthropologist* 77(3): 505–525.
1979   Review of *The Food Crisis in Prehistory* by M. N. Cohen. *American Anthropologist* 81: 658–660.

Crichton, J. M.
1966   A multiple discriminant analysis of Egyptian and African Negro crania. *Papers of the Peabody Museum of Archaeology and Ethnology* 57: 43–67.

Curwen, E.
1946   *Plough and Pasture*. London: Cobbett Press.

Daget, J.
1954   *Les poissons du Niger supérieur*. Mémoire No. 36. Dakar: Institut Français d'Afrique Noire.

Dalby, D.
1975   The prehistorical implications of Guthrie's *Comparative Bantu*—I: problems of internal relationship. *Journal of African History* 16: 481–501.
1976   The prehistorical implications of Guthrie's *Comparative Bantu*—II: interpretation of cultural vocabulary. *Journal of African History* 17: 1–27.

Dalziel, J. M.
1955   *The Useful Plants of West Tropical Africa*. London. The Crown Agents for the Colonies.

Damon, P. E., C. W. Ferguson, A. Long, and E. T. Wallick
1974   Dendrochronologic calibration of the radiocarbon time scale. *American Antiquity* 39: 350–366.

Darby, W. J., P. Ghalioungui, and L. Grivetti
1977   *Food: The Gift of Osiris*. (2 vols.) London: Academic Press.

Daveau, S.
1977   L'évolution géomorphologique quaternaire au Portugal. *Supplément du Bulletin de l'Association française d'études quaternaires* 50: 11–21.

David, N.
1976   History of crops and peoples in North Cameroon to A.D. 1900. In J. R. Harlan, J. M. J. de Wet, and A. B. L. Stemler, eds., *Origins of African Plant Domestication*: 223–267. The Hague: Mouton.
n.d.a   Rop Rock Shelter revisited. Unpublished.
n.d.b   Lecture to Cambridge University Archaeological Field Club, October 25, 1978.

Davies, N. de G.
1929   The graphic work of the expedition. *Bulletin of the Metropolitan Museum of Art* 24 (November): sect. II, 1–29.

Davies, O.

1960   The Neolithic revolution in tropical
         Africa. *Transactions of the Historical Society
         of Ghana* 4(2): 14–20.
1961   The invaders of northern Ghana.
         Universitas 4: 134–136.
1962   Neolithic cultures of Ghana. In G.
         Mortelmans and J. Nenquin, eds., *Actes du
         quatrième Congrès de préhistoire et de l'étude
         du Quaternaire*: 291–302. Tervuren: Musée
         Royal de l'Afrique Centrale.
1964   Gonja painted pottery. *Transactions of the
         Historical Society of Ghana* 7: 4–11.
1966   The invasion of Ghana from the Sahara in
         the Early Iron Age. In L. D. Cuscoy, ed.,
         *Actas del Quinto Congreso Panafricano de
         Prehistoria y de Estudio del Cuaternaria* 2:
         27–42. Tenerife.
1967   *West Africa before the Europeans*. London:
         Methuen.
1968   The origins of agriculture in West Africa.
         Current Anthropology 9: 479–482.

Deacon, H. J.

1967   Two radiocarbon dates from Scott's Cave,
         Gamtoos Valley. *South African
         Archaeological Bulletin* 22: 51–52.
1976   *Where Hunters Gathered*. Monograph
         Series No. 1. Claremont: South African
         Archaeological Society.

Deacon, H. J., J. Deacon, and M. Brooker

1976   Four painted stones from Boomplaas
         Cave, Oudtshoorn District. *South African
         Archaeological Bulletin* 31: 141–145.

**Deacon, H. J., J. Deacon, M. Brooker, and
M. L. Wilson**

1978   The evidence for herding at Boomplaas
         Cave in the southern Cape, South Africa.
         South African Archaeological Bulletin 33:
         39–65.

Deacon, J.

1972   Wilton: an assessment after 50 years.
         South African Archaeological Bulletin 27:
         10–45.
1974   Patterning in the radiocarbon dates for the
         Wilton/Smithfield complex in southern

Africa. *South African Archaeological Bulletin*
         29: 3–18.
1978   Changing patterns in the Late Pleistocene/
         Early Holocene prehistory of Southern
         Africa as seen from the Nelson Bay Cave
         stone artifact sequence. *Quaternary
         Research* 10: 84–111.

Debono, F.

1956   La civilisation prédynastique d'El Omari
         (Nord d'Helouan): nouvelles données.
         Bulletin de l'Institut d'Egypte 37: 329–339.

Dekeyser, P.-L.

1955   *Les mammifères de l'Afrique Noire française*.
         (2nd ed.) Initiations et Etudes Africaines
         No. 1. Dakar: Institut Français d'Afrique
         Noire.

Delafosse, M.

1912   *Haut-Sénégal-Niger*. (3 vols.) Paris:
         Larose.

Delibrias, G., M. T. Guillier, and J. Labeyrie

1974   Gif natural radiocarbon measurement
         VIII. *Radiocarbon* 16(1): 15–94.

De Maret, P.

1977   Sanga: new excavations, more data, and
         some related problems. *Journal of African
         History* 18: 321–337.

De Maret, P., and F. Nsuka

1977   History of Bantu metallurgy: some
         linguistic aspects. *History in Africa* 4: 43–
         65.

De Maret, P., F. Van Noten, and D. Cahen

1977   Radiocarbon dates from West Central
         Africa: a synthesis. *Journal of African
         History* 18: 481–505.

**Denbow, J., D. Mulindwa, and E. N.
Wilmsen**

n.d.   Prehistoric hunters and herders of the
         Kalahari. Unpublished manuscript.

Derricourt, R. M.

1976   The origins of the South African Iron
         Age. In B. Abebe, J. Chavaillon and
         J. E. G. Sutton, eds., *Proceedings of the
         Seventh Panafrican Congress of Prehistory and*

Quaternary Studies: 215–220. Addis Ababa.

Derry, D. E.
1949   Report on the human remains. In A. J. Arkell, *Early Khartoum*: 31–36. London: Oxford University Press.

Deshler, W. W.
1965   Native cattle keeping in Eastern Africa. In A. Leeds and A. P. Vayda, eds., *Man, Culture and Animals*: 153–168. Publication no. 78. Washington, D.C.: American Association for the Advancement of Science.

Devitt, P.
1977   Coping with drought in the Kalahari. In D. Dalby, R. J. H. Church, and F. Bezaz, eds., *Drought in Africa* 2: 186–200. London: International African Institute.
1978   Drought and poverty. In M. T. Hinchey, ed., *Proceedings of the Symposium on Drought in Botswana*: 121–127. Gaborone, Botswana: Botswana Society.

De Wet, J. M. J., and J. R. Harlan
1971   The origin and domestication of *Sorghum bicolor*. *Economic Botany* 25: 128–135.

Dewey, J. R., G. J. Armelagos, and M. H. Bartley
1969   Femoral cortical involution in three archaeological populations. *Human Biology* 41: 13–28.

Diamond, G.
1979   The nature of so-called polished surfaces on stone artifacts. In B. Hayden, ed., *Lithic Use-Wear Analysis*: 143–157. New York: Academic Press.

Diamond, J. M.
1977   Colonization cycles: man and beast. *World Archaeology* 8(3): 249–261.

Dickerson, J. W. T., and R. A. McCance
1961   Severe undernutrition in growing and adult animals. 8: The dimensions and chemistry of the long bones. *British Journal of Nutrition* 15: 567–576.

Diester-Haass, L.
1980   Upwelling and climate off northwest Africa during the Late Quaternary. *Palaeoecology of Africa* 12: 229–238.

Doggett, H.
1965   The development of the cultivated sorghums. In J. Hutchinson, ed., *Essays on Crop Plant Evolution*: 50–69. Cambridge: Cambridge University Press.
1970   *Sorghum*. London: Longmans.

Doke, C. M.
1931   *The Lambas of Northern Rhodesia: A Study in Their Customs and Beliefs*. London: George G. Harrap.

Dolphyne, F. A.
1979   The Brong dialect of Akan. In K. Arhin, ed., *Brong Kyempim*: 88–118. Accra: Afram Publications.

Dombrowski, J. C.
1970   Preliminary report on excavations in Lalibela and Natchabiet Caves, Begemeder. *Annales d'Ethiopie* 8: 21–29.
1976   Mumute and Bonoase—two sites of the Kintampo Industry. *Sankofa* 2: 64–71.
n.d.   Excavations in Ethiopia: Lalibela and Natchabiet Caves, Begemeder Province. Ph.D. dissertation, Boston University (1971).

Doran, J. E., and F. R. Hodson
1975   *Mathematics and Computers in Archaeology*. Cambridge, Mass.: Harvard University Press.

Draper, P.
1975   !Kung women: contrasts in sexual egalitarianism in the foraging and sedentary contexts. In R. Reiter, ed., *Towards an Anthropology of Women*: 77–109. New York: Monthly Review Press.
1976   Social and economic constraints of childlife among the !Kung. In R. B. Lee and I. DeVore, eds., *Kalahari Hunter-Gatherers: Studies of the !Kung San and Their Neighbors*: 199–217. Cambridge, Mass.: Harvard University Press.
n.d.   Regional variation in hunter-gatherer work

effort: comparisons among Kalahari
!Kung. In preparation.

Draper, P., J. Marshall, and H. C. Harpending

n.d.   Biosocial consequences of culture change among the !Kung. Grant proposal to the National Science Foundation, Washington, D.C. (1978).

Drew, S. F.

1952   The mysterious rock carvings of the Eritrean Highlands. *Illustrated London News* (August 9): 225–227.

1954   Notes from the Red Sea hills. *South African Archaeological Bulletin* 9: 101–102.

Dreyer, T. F., and A. J. D. Meiring

1937   A preliminary report on an expedition to collect Hottentot skulls. *Researches of the National Museum of Bloemfontein* pt. 1, no. 7: 81–88.

1952   The Hottentot. *Researches of the National Museum of Bloemfontein* 1: 19–22.

Dunham, D.

1938   The biographical inscriptions of Nebhebu in Boston and Cairo. *Journal of Egyptian Archaeology* 24: 1–8.

Dyson-Hudson, R., and N. Dyson-Hudson

1969   Subsistence herding in Uganda. *Scientific American* 220: 76–89.

Dyson-Hudson, R., and E. A. Smith

1978   Human territoriality: an ecological reassessment. *American Anthropologist* 80: 21–41.

Dzierzykray-Rogalski, T.

1977   Neolithic skeletons from Kadero, Sudan. *Current Anthropology* 18(3): 585–586.

Ebert, J. I., A. Thoma, M. C. Ebert, R. K. Hitchcock, and M. Oabile

n.d.   Report and recommendations for land allocations and Basarwa development in the sandveld region of Central District, Botswana. Report to the Ministry of Local Government and Lands, Gaborone (1976).

Edmunds, W. M., and E. P. Wright

1979   Groundwater recharge and palaeoclimate in the Sirte and Kufra basins, Libya. *Journal of Hydrology* 40: 215–241.

Effah-Gyamfi, E.

1974   Aspects of the archaeology and oral tradition of the Bono State. *Transactions of the Historical Society of Ghana* 15: 217–227.

Ehret, C.

1967   Cattle-keeping and milking in eastern and southern Africa history: the linguistic evidence. *Journal of African History* 8: 1–17.

1968a   Sheep and central Sudanic peoples in southern Africa. *Journal of African History* 9: 213–221.

1968b   Cushites and the Highland and Plains Nilotes. In B. A. Ogot and J. A. Kieran, eds., *Zamani: A Survey of East African History*: 158–176. New York: Humanities Press.

1971   *Southern Nilotic History*. Evanston: Northwestern University Press.

1972   Bantu origins: critique and interpretation. *Transafrican Journal of History* 2: 1–9.

1973   Patterns of Bantu and central Sudanic settlement in central and southern Africa. *Transafrican Journal of History* 3: 1–71.

1974a   Agricultural history in central and southern Africa. *Transafrican Journal of History* 4: 1–25.

1974b   *Ethiopians and East Africans: The Problem of Contacts*. Nairobi: East African Publishing House.

1976   Cushitic prehistory. In M. L. Bender, ed., *The Non-Semitic Languages of Ethiopia*: 85–96. East Lansing: Michigan State University Press.

1979   On the antiquity of agriculture in Ethiopia. *Journal of African History* 20: 161–177.

1980a   Historical inference from transformations in culture vocabularies. *Sprache und Geschichte in Afrika* 2: 189–218.

1980b   *The Historical Reconstruction of Southern Cushitic Phonology and Vocabulary*. Köln: Beiträge, Institut für Afrikanistik, Universität zu Köln.

1980c   The Nilotic languages of Tanzania. In E. Polome, ed., *Language in Tanzania*: 68–78. London: Oxford University Press.

1980d   Omotic and the subclassification of the
        Afroasiatic language family. In *Proceedings
        of the Fifth International Congress of
        Ethiopian Studies*, pt. 2: 51–62.

1980e   Review of D. W. Phillipson, *The Later
        Prehistory of Eastern and Southern Africa*.
        ASA Review of Books 6: 123–125.

1981   Shona subclassification and its
        implications for Iron Age history in
        southern Africa. *International Journal of
        African Historical Studies* 14: 401–444.

1982   The first spread of food production to
        southern Africa. In C. Ehret and M.
        Posnansky, eds., *The Archaeological and
        Linguistic Reconstruction of African History*:
        158–181. Berkeley: University of
        California Press.

in press East African words and things:
        agricultural aspects of economic
        transformation in the nineteenth century.
        In B. A. Ogot, ed., *Kenya in the Nineteenth
        Century*.

n.d.   The southern Nilotes to 1600 A.D.: a
        linguistic approach to East African
        history. Ph.D dissertation, Northwestern
        University (1969).

**Ehret, C., M. Bink, T. Ginindza, E.
Gotschall, B. Hall, M. Hlatshwayo, D.
Johnson, and R. Pouwels**

1972   Outlining southern African history: a
        reconsideration, A.D. 100–1500. *Ufahamu*
        3(1): 9–27.

**Ehret, C., T. Coffman, L. Fliegelman, A.
Gold, M. Hubbard, D. Johnson, and D. E.
Saxon**

1974   Some thoughts on the early history of the
        Nile-Congo watershed. *Ufahamu* 5(2):
        85–112.

Ehret, C., and D. E. Saxon

n.d.   The central Sudanic peoples: linguistic
        reconstruction and ethnohistory.
        Unpublished.

**El-Najjar, M. Y., D. J. Ryan, C. G. Turner
II, and B. Lozoff**

1976   The etiology of porotic hyperostosis
        among the prehistoric and historical

Anasazi Indians of the southwestern
        United States. *American Journal of Physical
        Anthropology* 44: 477–488.

Elphick, R.

1977   *Kraal and Castle*. Miscellany No. 116. New
        Haven: Yale Historical Publications.

Emery, W. B.

1961 *Archaic Egypt*. Harmondsworth: Penguin.

Endesfelder, E.

1979   Zur Frage der Bewässerung im
        pharaonischen Ägypten. *Zeitschrift für
        ägyptische Sprache und Altertumskunde* 106:
        37–51.

Eng, L. L.

1958   Chronic iron deficiency anemia with bone
        changes resembling Cooley's anemia. *Acta
        haematologica* 19: 263–268.

Epstein, H.

1971   *The Origin of the Domestic Animals of
        Africa*. New York: Africana Publishing
        Co.

Erickson, M. F.

1976   Cortical bone loss with age in three native
        American populations. *American Journal of
        Physical Anthropology* 45: 443–452.

Erman, A.

1971   *Life in Ancient Egypt*. Trans. H. M. Tirard.
        New York: Dover. (Original publ.
        London: Macmillan, 1894.)

Estorges, P., G. Aumassip, and A. Dagorne

1969   El Haouita, un exemple de remblaiement
        fini-würmien. *Libyca* 17: 53–91.

Evans-Pritchard, E. E.

1940   *The Nuer*. Oxford: Clarendon Press.

Evers, T. M.

1975   Recent Iron Age research in the eastern
        Transvaal, South Africa. *South African
        Archaeological Bulletin* 30: 71–83.

Eyo, E.

1972   Rop Rock Shelter excavations 1964. *West
        African Journal of Archaeology* 2: 13–16.

Faegri, K., and J. Iversen
1964   *Textbook of Pollen Analysis*. New York: Hafner.

Fagan, B. M.
1965   *Southern Africa during the Iron Age*. New York: Praeger.
1967   *Iron Age Cultures in Zambia—I*. London: Chatto and Windus.
1968   Comment on "The origins of agriculture." *Current Anthropology* 9: 496.
1973   Early food production in southern Africa. In D. W. Lathrap and J. Douglas, eds., *Variations in Anthropology: Essays in Honor of John C. MacGregor*: 155–169. Urbana: Illinois Archaeological Survey.
1978   *In the Beginning: An Introduction to Archaeology*. New York: Little, Brown.
n.d.   Mammalian remains from Daima, northern Nigeria. Unpublished.

Fage, J. D.
1961   Anthropology, botany, and the history of Africa. *Journal of African History* 2: 299–309.

Fagg, B. E. B.
1944   Preliminary report on a microlithic industry at Rop Rock Shelter, Northern Nigeria. *Proceedings of the Prehistoric Society* 10: 68–69.
1965   Carbon dates for Nigeria. *Man* 65: 22–23.
1972   Rop Rock Shelter excavations 1944. *West African Journal of Archaeology* 2: 1–12.

Farris, J. C.
1975   Social evolution, population, and production. In S. Polgar, ed., *Population, Ecology and Social Evolution*: 101–142. The Hague: Mouton.

Faugust, P. M., and J. E. G. Sutton
1966   The Egerton Cave on the Njoro River. *Azania* 1: 149–175.

Faulkner, R. O.
1975   Egypt from the inception of the Nineteenth Dynasty to the death of Ramesses III. In *Cambridge Ancient History* (3rd ed.): Vol. II, pt. 2, 217–251.

Faure, H.
1966   Evolution des grands lacs sahariens à l'Holocène. *Quaternaria* 8: 167–175.

Faure, H., E. Manguin, and R. Nydal
1963   Formations lacustres du Quaternaire supérieur du Niger oriental: diatomites et âges absolus. *Bulletin du Bureau de recherches géologiques et minières (Dakar)* 3: 41–63.

Fecht, G.
1972   Der Vorwurf an Gott in den "Mahnworten des Ipu-wer." *Abhandlungen der Heidelberger Akademie der Wissenschaften (Philosophisch-Historische Klasse)* 1: 1–240.

Findlater, I. C.
1978   Stratigraphy. In M. G. Leakey and R. E. Leakey, eds., *Koobi Fora Research Project: The Fossil Hominids and an Introduction to Their Context, 1968–1974*: 14–31. Oxford: Clarendon Press.

FitzSimons, W.
1926   Cliff dwellers of Zitzikama: results of recent excavations. *South African Journal of Science* 23: 813–817.

Flannery, K. V.
1967   Culture history vs. culture process: a debate in American archaeology. *Scientific American* 217: 119–122.
1968   Archaeological systems theory and early Mesoamerica. In B. Meggers, ed., *Anthropological Archaeology in the Americas*: 67–87. Washington, D.C.: Anthropological Society of Washington.
1969   Origins and ecological effects of early domestication in Iran and the Near East. In P. J. Ucko and G. W. Dimbleby, eds., *The Domestication and Exploitation of Plants and Animals*: 73–100. Chicago: Aldine.
1972   The origins of the village as a settlement type in Mesoamerica and the Near East: a comparative study. In P. J. Ucko, R. Tringham, and G. W. Dimbleby, eds., *Man, Settlement and Urbanism*: 23–53. London: Duckworth.
1973   The origins of agriculture. *Annual Review of Anthropology* 2: 271–310.

1976   (ed.) *The Early Mesoamerican Village*. New
        York: Academic Press.

Fleming, H. C.
1969a   Asa and Aramanik: Cushitic hunters in
        Masai-land. *Ethnology* 8: 1–36.
1969b   The classification of West Cushitic within
        Hamito-Semitic. In D. McCall, M. R.
        Bennett, and J. Butler, eds., *Eastern African
        History*. Boston University Studies in
        African History, No. 3. New York:
        Praeger.
1974   Omotic as an Afroasiatic family. *Studies in
        African Linguistics* suppl. 5: 81–94.
1976   Omotic overview. In M. L. Bender, ed.,
        The Non-Semitic Languages of Ethiopia:
        308. East Lansing: Michigan State
        University Press.

Fleuret, A.
1979   The role of wild foliage plants in the diet: a
        case study from Lushoto, Tanzania.
        Ecology of Food and Nutrition 8: 87–93.

Flight, C.
1973   A survey of recent results in the
        radiocarbon chronology of northern and
        western Africa. *Journal of African History*
        14(4): 531–554.
1976a   Diffusionism and later African prehistory.
        In B. Abebe, J. Chavaillon, and J. E. G.
        Sutton, eds., *Proceedings of the Seventh
        Panafrican Congress of Prehistory and
        Quaternary Studies*: 321–323. Addis Ababa.
1976b   The Kintampo culture and its place in the
        economic prehistory of West Africa. In
        J. R. Harlan, J. M. J. de Wet, and A. B. L.
        Stemler, eds., *Origins of African Plant
        Domestication*: 211–221. The Hague:
        Mouton.

Flohn, H., and S. Nicholson
1980   Climatic fluctuations in the arid belt of the
        "Old World" since the last glacial
        maximum: possible causes and future
        implications. *Palaeoecology of Africa* 12: 3–
        21.

Foaden, A. P., and F. Fletcher
1910   *Text-Book on Egyptian Agriculture*. Cairo: F.
        Eimer.

Foley, R. A.
1978   Incorporating sampling into initial
        research design: some aspects of spatial
        archaeology. In J.-F. Cherry, C. Gamble,
        and S. Shennan, eds., *Sampling in
        Contemporary British Archaeology*. Oxford:
        British Archaeological Research Series
        No. 50: 49–65.
n.d.   Inferring predatory behavior from prey
        attributes. Unpublished.

Fosbrooke, H. A.
1980   The socio-economic life of the rock
        painters. In R. E. Leakey and B. A. Ogot,
        eds., *Proceedings of the Eighth Panafrican
        Congress of Prehistory and Quaternary
        Studies*: 344–347. Nairobi: The
        International Louis Leakey Memorial
        Institute for African Prehistory.

**Frandson, A. M., M. M. Nelson, E. Sulon,
H. Becks, and H. M. Evans**
1954   The effects of various levels of dietary
        protein on skeletal growth and enchondral
        ossification in young rats. *Anatomical
        Record* 119: 247–261.

Frankfort, H.
1948   *Kingship and the Gods*. Chicago: University
        of Chicago Press.

Fredoux, A., and J. P. Tastet
1976   Apport de la palynologue à la
        connaissance paléogéographique du
        littoral ivoirien entre 8000 et 12000 ans
        B.P. Seventh African
        Micropaleontological Colloquium, Ile-Ife,
        Nigeria. 7pp. mimeo.

Freeman, L. G., Jr.
1968   A theoretical framework for interpreting
        archaeological materials. In R. B. Lee and
        I. DeVore, eds., *Man the Hunter*: 262–267.
        Chicago: Aldine.

Friedl, E.
1975   *Women and Men: An Anthropologist's View*.
        New York: Holt, Rinehart and Winston.

Frisch, R. E.
1975   Demographic implications of the

biological determinants of female fecundity. *Social Biology* 22(1): 17–22.

Frisch, R. E., and J. W. McArthur
1974   Menstrual cycles: fatness as a determinant of minimum weight for height necessary for their maintenance or onset. *Science* 185: 949–951.

Frost, H. M.
1966   Morphometry of bone in paleopathology. In S. Jarcho, ed., *Human Paleopathology*: 131–150. New Haven: Yale University Press.

Fryberger, S. G.
1980   Dune forms and wind regime, Mauritania, West Africa: implications for past climate. *Palaeoecology of Africa* 12: 79–96.

Gabel, C.
1969   Six rock shelters on the northern Kavirondo shore of Lake Victoria. *Journal of African Historical Studies* 2(2): 205–254.

Gabriel, B.
1977   Zum ökologischen Wandel im Neolithikum der östlichen Zentralsahara. *Berliner geographische Abhandlungen* 27. Institut für Physische Geographie der Freien Universität Berlin.

Gabus, J.
1952   Contribution à l'étude des Nemadi, chasseurs archaïques du Djouf. *Bulletin der Schweizerischen Gesellschaft für Anthropologie und Ethnologie* 28: 49–83.

Gaherty, G.
1968   The human skeleton from Rop Rock Shelter, Nigeria. *West African Archaeological Newsletter* 9: 18–19.

Gallais, A.
1967   *La delta intérieur du Niger.* (2 vols.) Mémoire No. 79. Dakar: Institut Fondamental de l'Afrique Noire.

Galloway, A.
1937   Man in Africa in the light of recent discoveries. *South African Journal of Science* 34: 89–120.

Galloy, P., Y. Vincent, and M. Forget
1963   *Nomades et paysans d'Afrique Noire occidentale.* Mémoire No. 23. Paris: Annales de l'Est.

Garlake, P. S.
1979   Review of Phillipson, 1977c. *Journal of African History* 20: 457–459.

Garn, S. M.
1970   *The Earlier Gain and Later Loss of Cortical Bone in Nutritional Perspective.* Springfield, Illinois: C. C. Thomas.

Garn, S. M., C. G. Rohmann, and M. A. Guzman
1966   Malnutrition and skeletal development in the preschool child. In *Preschool Child Malnutrition*: 43–62. Washington, D.C.: National Academy of Sciences–National Research Council.

Gasse, F.
1977   Evolution of Lake Abhe (Ethiopia and T.F.A.I.) from 70,000 B.P. *Nature* 265: 42–45.
n.d.   L'évolution des lacs de l'Afar central (Ethiopie et T.F.A.I.) du Plio-Pléistocène à l'actuel. Thèse, Docteur ès Sciences Naturelles, l'Université de Paris (1975).

Gasse, F., J. C. Fontes, and P. Rognon
1974   Variations hydrologiques et extension des lacs holocènes du désert Danakil. *Palaeogeography, Palaeoclimatology, Palaeoecology* 15: 109–148.

Gasse, F., P. Rognon, and F. A. Street
1980   Quaternary history of the Afar and Ethiopian Rift lakes. In M. A. J. Williams and H. Faure, eds., *The Sahara and the Nile*: 361–400. Rotterdam: Balkema.

Gasse, F., and F. A. Street
1978   Late Quaternary lake level fluctuations and environments of the northern Rift Valley and Afar region (Ethiopia and Djibouti). *Palaeogeography, Palaeoclimatology, Palaeoecology* 24: 279–325.

Gates, W. L.
1976   Modeling the ice-age climate. *Science* 191: 1138–1144.

Gautier, A.
1976   Animal remains from archaeological sites of terminal Paleolithic to Old Kingdom in the Fayum. In F. Wendorf and R. Schild, eds., *Prehistory of the Nile Valley*: 369–381. New York: Academic Press.

Gelburd, D. E.
1978   Indicators of culture change among the Dobe !Kung San. *Botswana Notes and Records* 10: 27–36.
n.d.   Indicators of culture change among the Dobe !Kung San. Master's thesis, George Washington University, Washington, D.C. (1978).

Geyh, M. A., and D. Jäkel
1974   Spätpleistozäne und holozäne Klimageschichte der Sahara aufgrund zugänglicher 14-C Daten. *Zeitschrift für Geomorphologie* N.F. 18: 82–98.

Ghorbal, M. S.
n.d.   *Tarikh al-Haddarah al-Misriyia* (History of Egyptian Civilization) Vol. 1, no. 1. Cairo: Matetabet al-Nahda al-Misriyia.

Gifford, D. P.
1978   Ethnoarchaeological observation of natural processes affecting cultural materials. In R. A. Gould, ed., *Explorations in Ethnoarchaeology*: 77–101. Albuquerque: University of New Mexico Press.
n.d.   The fauna from Eli Bor: cultivators without livestock? In preparation.

Gifford, D. P., G. L. Isaac, and C. M. Nelson
1980   Evidence for predation and pastoralism at Prolonged Drift: a Pastoral Neolithic site in Kenya. *Azania* 15: 57–108.

Gilman, A.
1976   A later prehistory of Tangier, Morocco. *American School of Prehistoric Research, Bulletin 29*. Cambridge, Mass.: Peabody Museum, Harvard University.

Glover, P. E., E. C. Glover, E. C. Trump, and L. E. D. Wateridge
1964   The lava caves of Mt. Suswa. *Studies on Speleology* 1(1): 51–66.

Gobert, E. G.
1938   Les escargotières: le mot et la chose. *Revue Africaine* 81: 631–645.

Goedicke, H.
1960   Die Stellung des Königs im Alten Reich. *Ägyptologische Abhandlungen* 2: 1–95.
1967   Dokumente aus dem Alten Reich. *Ägyptologische Abhandlungen* 14: 1–256.

Goldschmidt, W.
1976   *Culture and Behavior of the Sebei.* Berkeley: University of California Press.

Goodman, A. A., G. J. Armelagos, and J. C. Rose
1980   Enamel hypoplasias as indicators of stress in three prehistoric populations from Illinois. *Human Biology* 52: 515–528.

Goodwin, A. J. H.
1938   Archaeology of the Oakhurst Shelter, George. Part V: Disposition of the skeletal remains. *Transactions of the Royal Society of South Africa* 25: 247–258.

Goody, J.
1966   The Akan and the north. *Ghana Notes and Queries* 9: 18–24.

Goodyear, F. H.
1971   *Archaeological Site Science* (London).

Gramly, R. M.
1972   Report on the teeth from Narosura. *Azania* 7: 87–91.
1976   Upper Pleistocene archaeological occurrences at site GvJm/22, Lukenya Hill, Kenya. *Man* n.s. 11(3): 319–344.
n.d.   Pastoralists and hunters: recent prehistory in southern Kenya and northern Tanzania. Ph.D. dissertation, Harvard University (1975).

Gramly, R. M., and G. P. Rightmire
1973   A fragmentary cranium and dated Later Stone Age assemblage from Lukenya Hill, Kenya. *Man* n.s. 8: 571–579.

Graziosi, P.
1964 New discoveries of rock paintings in Ethiopia. *Antiquity* 38: 91–101 (pt. I) and 187–193 (pt. II).

Grébénart, D.
1976 Le Capsien des régions de Tébessa et d'Ouled Djellal (Algérie). *Etudes Méditerranéennes 1*. Aix-en-Provence: Université de Provence.
1978 Une civilisation d'Afrique du Nord: le Capsien. *Recherche* 9(86): 138–145.

Greenberg, J. H.
1949– Studies in African Linguistic
1951 Classification. *Southwestern Journal of Anthropology* 5: 79–100, 190–198, 309–317; 6: 47–63, 143–160, 223–237, 388–398; 10: 405–415.
1963 *The Languages of Africa*. Bloomington: Indiana University Research Center in Anthropology, Folklore, and Linguistics.
1964 Historical inferences from linguistic research in sub-Saharan Africa. In J. Butler, ed., *Boston University Papers in African History* 1: 1–15.

Greene, D. L.
1966 Dentition and the biological relationships of some Meroitic, X-Group and Christian populations from Wadi Halfa, Sudan. *Kush* 14: 285–288.
1972 Dental anthropology of early Egypt and Nubia. *Journal of Human Evolution* 1: 315–324.
n.d. A critique of methods used to reconstruct racial and population affinity in the Nile Valley. Paper presented at the Second International Congress of Egyptologists. Grenoble, France (1979).

Greene, D. L., and G. J. Armelagos
1972 *The Wadi Halfa Mesolithic Population*. Research Report No. 11. Amherst: Department of Anthropology, University of Massachusetts.

Greene, D. L., G. Ewing, and G. J. Armelagos
1967 Dentition of a Mesolithic population from Wadi Halfa, Sudan. *American Journal of Physical Anthropology* 27: 41–56.

Grivetti, L. E.
1978 Nutritional success in a semi-arid land: examination of Tswana agro-pastoralists of the eastern Kalahari, Botswana. *American Journal of Clinical Nutrition* 31: 1204–1220.
1979 Kalahari agro-pastoralist hunter-gatherers: the Tswana example. *Ecology of Food and Nutrition* 7: 235–256.

Guenther, M. G.
1975– The San trance dance: ritual and
1976 revitalization among the Ghanzi Farm Bushmen. *Journal of the South West Africa Scientific Society* 20: 45–53.
1976 From hunters to squatters: social and cultural change among the Farm San of Ghanzi, Botswana. In R. B. Lee and I. DeVore, eds., *Kalahari Hunter-Gatherers: Studies of the !Kung San and Their Neighbors*: 120–133. Cambridge, Mass.: Harvard University Press.
1977 Bushman hunters as farm labourers. *Canadian Journal of African Studies* 11(2): 195–203.

Guglielmi, W.
1977 Hunger. *Lexikon Ägyptologie* 2: 82–84.

Guiraud, R.
n.d. Evolution post-triasique de l'Avant-Pays de la Chaîne alpine en Algérie d'après l'étude du Bassin du Hodna et des régions voisines. Ph.D. dissertation, University of Nice (1973).

Gundlach, R.
1977a Expedition(en). *Lexikon Ägyptologie* 2: 55–59.
1977b Goldminen. *Lexikon Ägyptologie* 2: 740–751.

Haaland, R.
1978 The seasonal interconnection between Zakiab and Kadero: two Neolithic sites in the central Sudan. *Nyame Akuma* 13: 31–35.

1979a Report on the 1979 season in the Sudan. *Nyame Akuma* 14: 62.

1979b Some new C-14 dates from central Sudan. *Nyame Akuma* 15: 56–57.

n.d. Pastoral adaptations in the central Nile Valley of Sudan 5000 years ago. Paper presented at meeting of Society of Africanist Archaeologists in America, Calgary, Canada (1979).

Habachi, L.
1974 A high inundation mark in the temple of Amenre at Karnak in the 13th Dynasty. *Studien Altägyptischer Kultur* 1: 207–214.

Hable-Sallasie, S.
1972 *Ancient and Medieval Ethiopian History to 1270.* Addis Ababa: United Printers.

Hagedorn, H.
1980 Fluvial processes in the Sahara. *Palaeoecology of Africa* 12: 115–123.

Hall, J. B., M. D. Swaine, and M. R. Talbot
1978 An Early Holocene leaf flora from Lake Bosumtwi, Ghana. *Palaeogeography, Palaeoclimatology, Palaeoecology* 24: 247–261.

Hamilton, A.
1972 The interpretation of pollen diagrams from highland Uganda. *Palaeoecology of Africa* 7: 45–149.

1976 The significance of patterns of distribution shown by forest plants and animals in tropical Africa for the reconstruction of Upper Pleistocene paleoenvironments: a review. *Palaeoecology of Africa* 9: 63–67.

Hammel, E. A., C. K. McDaniel, and K. W. Wachter
1979 Demographic consequences of incest taboos: a microsimulation analysis. *Science* 205: 972–977.

Hargrove, T. H.
n.d. Food production and culture change among hunter-gatherers of southern Africa. Master's thesis, George Washington University, Washington, D.C. (1980).

Harlan, J. R.
1969 Ethiopia: a center of diversity. *Economic Botany* 23: 309–314.

1971 Agricultural origins: centers and noncenters. *Science* 174: 468–474.

1975 *Crops and Man.* Madison, Wisconsin: American Society of Agronomy, Crop Science Society of America.

1976 Plant and animal distribution in relation to domestication. *Philosophical Transactions of the Royal Society of London B.* 275: 13–25.

Harlan, J. R., and J. Pasquereau
1969 *Décrue* agriculture in Mali. *Economic Botany* 23: 70–74.

Harlan, J. R., and A. B. L. Stemler
1976 The races of sorghum in Africa. In J. R. Harlan, J. M. J. de Wet, and A. B. L. Stemler, eds., *Origins of African Plant Domestication*: 465–478. The Hague: Mouton.

Harlan, J. R., J. M. J. de Wet, and A. B. L. Stemler
1976a (eds.) *Origins of African Plant Domestication.* The Hague: Mouton.

1976b Plant domestication and indigenous African agriculture. In J. R. Harlan, J. M. J. de Wet, and A. B. L. Stemler, eds., *Origins of African Plant Domestication*: 3–19. The Hague: Mouton.

Harlan, J. R., and D. Zohary
1966 Distribution of wild wheats and barley. *Science* 153: 1074–1080.

Harpending, H. C.
1976 Regional variation in !Kung populations. In R. B. Lee and I. DeVore, eds., *Kalahari Hunter-Gatherers: Studies of the !Kung San and Their Neighbors*: 152–165. Cambridge, Mass.: Harvard University Press.

Harpending, H. C., and H. Davis
1977 Some implications for hunter-gatherer ecology derived from the spatial structure of resources. *World Archaeology* 8: 275–286.

Harpending, H. C., and T. Jenkins
1973 Genetic distance among southern African

populations. In M. Crawford and P. Workman, eds., *Methods and Theories of Anthropological Genetics*: 177–199. Albuquerque: University of New Mexico Press.

Harris, D. R.
1967 New light on plant domestication. *Geographical Review* 57(1): 90–107.

1969 Agricultural systems, ecosystems, and the origins of agriculture. In P. J. Ucko and G. W. Dimbleby, eds., *The Domestication and Exploitation of Plants and Animals*: 3–15. London: Duckworth.

1972 The origins of agriculture in the tropics. *American Scientist* 60: 180–193.

1976 Traditional systems of plant food production and the origins of agriculture in West Africa. In J. R. Harlan, J. M. J. de Wet, and A. B. L. Stemler, eds., *Origins of African Plant Domestication*: 311–356. The Hague: Mouton.

1977 Alternative pathways toward agriculture. In C. A. Reed, ed., *Origins of Agriculture*: 179–243. The Hague: Mouton.

1978 Settling down: an evolutionary model for the transformation of mobile bands into sedentary communities. In J. Friedman and M. J. Rowlands, eds., *Evolution of Social Systems*: 401–417. Pittsburgh: University of Pittsburgh Press.

Harris, M.
1975 *Culture, People, Nature*. New York: Crowell.

1978a *Cannibals and Kings*. London and New York: Random House.

1978b The origins of agriculture. In M. Harris, *Cannibals and Kings*: 19–30. London and New York: Random House.

1979 *Cultural Materialism: The Struggle for a Science of Culture*. New York: Random House.

Harvey, T. J.
n.d. The paleolimnology of Lake Mobutu Sese Seko, Uganda-Zaire: the last 28,000 years. Ph.D. dissertation, Duke University (1976).

Hassan, F. A.
1974 The archaeology of the Dishna Plain, Egypt: a study of a late Palaeolithic settlement. *Paper No. 59, Geological Survey of Egypt*. Cairo.

1979 Demography and archaeology. *Annual Review of Anthropology* 8: 137–160.

1980 Prehistoric settlements along the main Nile. In M. A. J. Williams and H. Faure, eds., *The Sahara and the Nile*: 421–450. Rotterdam: Balkema.

1981 *Demographic Archaeology*. New York: Academic Press.

Hassan, F. A., T. R. Hays, and J. C. Shepard
n.d. Chronology of Predynastic Egypt. Unpublished.

Hausman, A. J.
1982 The biocultural evolution of Khoisan populations of southern Africa. *American Journal of Physical Anthropology* 58: 315–330.

n.d. Holocene human evolution in southern Africa: The biocultural development of the Khoisan. Ph.D. dissertation, State University of New York, Binghamton (1980).

Haynes, C. V., P. J. Mehringer, and E. S. A. Zaghloul
1979 Pluvial lakes of north-western Sudan. *Geographical Journal* 145: 439–445.

Hays, T. R.
1974 "Wavy Line" pottery: an element of Nilotic diffusion. *South African Archaeological Bulletin* 29: 27–32.

1975 Neolithic settlement of the Sahara as it relates to the Nile Valley. In F. Wendorf and A. E. Marks, eds., *Problems in Prehistory: North Africa and the Levant*: 193–204. Dallas: Southern Methodist University Press.

1976 Predynastic Egypt: recent field research. *Current Anthropology* 17: 552–554.

n.d. The Karmakol industry: part of the "Khartoum horizon-style." In J. L. Shiner, ed., The prehistory and geology of the northern Sudan: pts. 1 and 2, 84–153.

Report to the National Science
Foundation (1971).

Hays, T. R., and F. A. Hassan
n.d.   Neolithic economy at El Khattara.
         Technical report to the National Science
         Foundation (1976).

Hedberg, O.
1954   A pollen-analytical reconnaissance in
         tropical East Africa. *Oikos* 5: 137–166.

Heine, B.
1979   Some linguistic observations on the early
         history of Africa. *Sugia* 1: 37–54.

Heine, B., H. Hoff, and R. Vossen
1977   Neuere Ergebnisse zur
         Territorialgeschichte der Bantu. In W. J.
         Mohlig, F. Rottland and B. Heine, eds.,
         *Zur Sprachgeschichte und Ethnohistorie in
         Afrika*: 57–72. Berlin: Reiner.

Heine, H.
1963   Solanaceae. In F. N. Hepper, ed., *Flora of
         West Tropical Africa* (2nd ed.): Vol. 2, 325–
         335. London: Crown Agents for Overseas
         Governments and Administrations.

Heinz, H. J.
1969   Search for Bushman tribes of the
         Okavango. *Geographical Magazine* 41(10):
         742–750.
1972   Territoriality among the Bushmen in
         general and the !Ko in particular.
         Anthropos 67: 405–416.
1979   *Namkwa: Life among the Bushmen*. Boston:
         Houghton Mifflin.
n.d.   Experiences gained in a Bushman pilot
         settlement scheme. Department of
         Pathology, Witwatersrand University,
         Johannesburg, South Africa (1970).

Heinzelin, J. de
1964   Le sous-sol du temple d'Aksha. *Kush* 12:
         102–110.
1968   Geological history of the Nile Valley. In F.
         Wendorf, ed., *The Prehistory of Nubia*: Vol.
         1, 19–55. Dallas: Southern Methodist
         University Press.

**Heinzelin, J. de, P. Haesarts, and F. Van
Noten**
1969   Géologie récente et préhistoire au Jebel
         Uweinat. *Africa-Tervuren* 15: 120–125.

Helbaek, H.
1959   How farming began in the Old World.
         Archaeology 12: 183–189.

Helck, W.
1954   Untersuchungen zu den Beamtentiteln des
         ägyptischen alten Rieches. *Ägyptologische
         Abhandlung* 18: 1–146.
1956   Untersuchungen zu Manetho und den
         ägyptischen konigslisten. *Untersuchungen
         zur Geschichte und Altertumskunde Ägyptens*
         18: 1–91.
1966   Nilhöhe und Jubiläumsfest. *Zeitschrift für
         Ägyptische Sprache und Altertumskunde* 93:
         74–79.
1974   Bermerkungen zum Analenstein.
         *Mitteilungen des Deutschen Archäologischen
         Instituts, Abteilung Kairo* 30: 31–35.
1975a   Domänen. *Lexikon Ägytologie* 1: 1117–
         1120.
1975b   Abgaben und Steuern. *Lexikon Ägyptologie*
         1: 3–12.
1975c   Dienstanweisung für den Wesir. *Lexikon
         Ägyptologie* 1: 1084.

Hengen, O. P.
1971   Cribra orbitalia: pathogenesis and
         probable etiology. *Homo* 22: 57–75.

Hennessey, E., and O. Lewis
1971   Anti-pellagragenic properties of wild
         plants used as dietary supplements in
         Natal (South Africa). *Plant Foods in
         Human Nutrition* 2: 75–78.

Hiernaux, J.
1974   *The People of Africa*. New York: Charles
         Scribner's Sons.

Hiernaux, J., E. Maquet, and J. de Buyst
1973   Le cimetière protohistorique de Katoto,
         vallée du Lualaba, Congo-Kinshasa. In H.
         Hugot, ed., *Actes du sixième Congrès
         panafricain de préhistoire*: 148–158. Paris:
         Chambéry.

Higgs, E. S.

1967a   Environment and chronology: evidence
from mammalian fauna. In C. M.
McBurney, *The Haua Fteah (Cyrenaica)
and the Stone Age of the South-East
Mediterranean*: 16–44. Cambridge:
Cambridge University Press.

1967b   Domestic animals. In C. M. McBurney,
*The Haua Fteah (Cyrenaica) and the Stone
Age of the South-East Mediterranean*: 313–
319. Cambridge: Cambridge University
Press.

1972   (ed.) *Papers in Economic Prehistory.*
Cambridge: Cambridge University Press.

1976   Archaeology and domestication. In J. R.
Harlan, J. R. J. de Wet, and A. B. L.
Stemler, eds., *Origins of African Plant
Domestication*: 29–39. The Hague:
Mouton.

Higgs, E. S., and M. R. Jarman

1972   The origins of plant and animal husbandry.
In E. S. Higgs, ed., *Papers in Economic
Prehistory*: 3–13. Cambridge: Cambridge
University Press.

Hill, M. H.

1978   Dating of Senegambian megaliths: a
correction. *Current Anthropology* 19: 604–
605.

Hillaire-Marcel, C.

1979   Les teneurs en isotopes stables des faunes
pléistocènes en milieu continental pour les
reconstitutions paléoclimatiques. Premiers
commentaires après une étude
préliminaire de faunes à *Cerastoderma
glaucum* et à *Melania tuberculata* du Wadi
Shati (Libye). *Bulletin de l'Association
sénégalaise pour l'étude du Quaternaire de
l'Ouest africain* 56–57: 79–85.

Hillman, J. C., and A. K. K. Hillman

1977   Mortality of wildlife in Nairobi National
Park, during the drought of 1973–74. *East
African Wildlife Journal* 15: 1–18.

**Hilu, K. W., J. M. J. de Wet, and J. R.
Harlan**

1979   Archaeobotanical studies of *E. Coracana*
ssp. *coracana* (finger millet). *American
Journal of Botany* 66(3): 330–343.

Hinton, R. J., and D. S. Carlson

1979   Temporal changes in human
temporomandibular joint size and shape.
American Journal of Physical Anthropology
50: 325–333.

Hitchcock, R. K.

1978a   *Kalahari Cattle Posts: A Regional Study of
Hunter-Gatherers, Pastoralists, and
Agriculturalists in the Western Sandveld
Region, Central District, Botswana.*
Gaborone, Botswana: Government
Printer.

1978b   The traditional response to drought in
Botswana. In M. T. Hinchey, ed.,
*Proceedings of the Symposium on Drought in
Botswana*: 91–97. Gaborone, Botswana:
Botswana Society.

in press   Traditional systems of land tenure and
agrarian reform in Botswana. In R. P.
Werbner, ed., *African Agrarian Structures:
Transformations in Botswana.*

n.d.   Patterns of sedentism among hunters and
gatherers in eastern Botswana. Paper
presented at the conference on Hunter-
Gatherer Societies, Maison des Sciences
de l'Homme, Paris, France (1978).

Hivernel, F. M. M.

n.d.   An ethnoarchaeological study of
environmental use in the Kenya highlands.
Ph.D. dissertation, University of London
(1978).

Hobler, P. M., and J. J. Hester

1969   Prehistory and environment in the Libyan
Desert. *South African Archaeological
Bulletin* 23: 120–130.

Hodder, I.

1977   The distribution of material culture items
in the Baringo district, western Kenya.
Man 12(2): 239–269.

1978   The maintenance of group identities in the
Baringo district, w. Kenya. In D. Green, C.
Haselgrove, and M. Spriggs, eds., *Social
Organization and Settlement*. British

Archaeological Reports International Series 47(1): 47–73.

1979   Economic stress and material culture patterning. *American Antiquity* 44(3): 446–454.

1982   *Symbols in Action*. Cambridge: Cambridge University Press.

Holdship, S. A.
n.d.   The paleolimnology of Lake Manyara, Tanzania: a diatom analysis of a 56-meter sediment core. Ph.D. dissertation, Duke University (1976).

Honea, K. A.
1958   *A Contribution to the History of the Hamitic Peoples of Africa*. Acta Ethnologica et Linguistica 5.

Howell, F. C.
1978   Hominidae. In V. J. Maglio and H. B. S. Cook, eds., *Evolution of African Mammals*: 154–248. Cambridge, Mass.: Harvard University Press.

Howell, N.
1976a   Toward a uniformitarian theory of human paleodemography. In R. H. Ward and K. M. Weiss, eds., *Demographic Evolution of Human Populations*: 25–40. London: Academic Press.

1976b   The population of the Dobe area !Kung. In R. B. Lee and I. DeVore, eds., *Kalahari Hunter-Gatherers: Studies of the !Kung San and Their Neighbors*: 138–151. Cambridge, Mass.: Harvard University Press.

1979   *Demography of the Dobe !Kung*. New York: Academic Press.

1980   Demographic behavior of hunter-gatherers: evidence for density-dependent population control. In T. Burch, ed., *Demographic Behavior: An AAAS Selected Symposium, Vol. 45*. Boulder: Westview.

Howell, N., and V. Lehotay
1978   AMBUSH: a computer program for stochastic microsimulation of small human populations. *American Anthropologist* 80: 905–922.

Howells, W. W.
1973   *Cranial Variation in Man*. Papers of the Peabody Museum. Cambridge, Mass.: Harvard University Press.

Huffman, T. N.
1971   Excavations at Leopard's Kopje main Kraal: a preliminary report. *South African Archaeological Bulletin* 26: 85–89.

1973   Test excavations at Makuru, Rhodesia. *Arnoldia* 5: 39.

1974   *The Leopard's Kopje Tradition*. Museum Memoir No. 6. Salisbury, Rhodesia: National Museums and Monuments of Rhodesia.

1975   Cattle from Mabveni. *South African Archaeological Bulletin* 30: 23–24.

1978   The origins of Leopard's Kopje: an 11th century *difaqane*. *Arnoldia* 8: 23.

Huffnagel, H. P.
1961   (ed.) *Agriculture in Ethiopia*. Rome: Food and Agriculture Organisation.

Hugot, G.
n.d.   Un secteur du Quaternaire lacustre mauritanien—Tichitt: (Aouker) éléments pour servir à une étude géomorphologique. Thesis, Paris (1977).

Hugot, H. J.
1957   Essai sur les armatures de pointes de flèches du Sahara. *Libyca* 5: 89–236.

1968   The origins of agriculture: Sahara. *Current Anthropology* 9: 483–489.

Humphreys, A. J. B.
1974   A preliminary report on test excavations at Dikbosch Shelter 1, Herbert District, northern Cape. *South African Archaeological Bulletin* 29: 115–119.

Humphreys, A. J. B., and T. Maggs
1970   Further graves and cultural material from the banks of the Riet River. *South African Archaeological Bulletin* 25: 116–126.

Hunter, J. M.
1966   River blindness in Nangodi, N. Ghana. *Geographical Review* 56: 398–416.

Huss-Ashmore, R.
1978   Nutritional determination in a Nubian skeletal population (abstract). *American Journal of Physical Anthropology* 28(3): 407.

Huss-Ashmore, R., L. H. Goodman, and G. J. Armelagos
1982   Nutritional inference from paleopathology. In M. B. Schiffer, ed., *Advances in Archaeological Method and Theory*: Vol. 5, 395–474. New York: Academic Press.

Ingold, T.
1980   *Hunters, Pastoralists and Ranchers*. Cambridge: Cambridge University Press.

Inskeep, R. R.
1969   The archaeological background. In M. Wilson and L. Thompson, eds., *The Oxford History of South Africa*: Vol. 1, 1–39. New York and Oxford: Oxford University Press.

Isaac, E.
1971   On the domestication of cattle. In S. Struever, ed., *Prehistoric Agriculture*: 451–470. New York: American Museum of Natural History.

Isaac, G. L.
1975   Stratigraphy and cultural patterns in East Africa during the middle ranges of Pleistocene time. In K. W. Butzer and G. L. Isaac, eds., *After the Australopithecines*: 495–542. The Hague: Mouton.
1978   The food-sharing behavior of protohuman hominids. *Scientific American* 238(4): 90–108.

Isaac, G. L., H. V. Merrick, and C. M. Nelson
1972   Stratigraphic and archaeological studies in the Lake Nakuru Basin, Kenya. *Palaeoecology of Africa* 6: 225–232.

Iversen, J.
1941   Landnam i Danmarks Stenalder. *Danmarks geologiske undersögelse* 2, rk. 66.

Jacobs, A. H.
1975   Maasai pastoralism in historical perspective. In T. Monod, ed., *Pastoralism in Tropical Africa*: 406–425. London: Oxford University Press.

Jacques-Félix, H.
n.d.   Grain impressions. In P. J. Munson, The Tichitt tradition: a late prehistoric occupation of the southwestern Sahara: Appendix K. Ph.D. diss., University of Illinois, Urbana-Champaign (1971).

Jäkel, D.
1979   Run-off and fluvial formation processes in the Tibesti Mountains as indicators of climatic history in the central Sahara during the late Pleistocene and Holocene. *Palaeoecology of Africa* 11: 13–44.

Janssen, J. J.
1975   *Commodity Prices from the Ramessid Period: An Economic Study of the Village of Necropolis Workmen at Thebes*. Leiden: E. J. Brill.

Jardin, C.
1967   *List of Foods Used in Africa*. Rome: Food and Agriculture Organisation.

Jaritz, H., and M. Bietak
1977   Zweierlei Pegeleichungen zum Messen der Nilfluthohen im alten Ägypten. *Mitteilungen des deutschen archäologischen Instituts-Abteilung Kairo* 33: 47–62.

Jeffers, B., and G. Childers
n.d.   First report on the !Xade area of the Central Kalahari Game Reserve. Report to the Ministry of Local Government and Lands, Gaborone, Botswana (1976).

Jenkins, T.
n.d.   Genetic polymorphisms of man in southern Africa. M.D. thesis, University of London (1972).

Jenkins, T., H. Lehmann, and G. T. Nurse
1974   Public health and genetic constitution of the San ("Bushmen"): carbohydrate metabolism and acelylator status of the

!Kung of Tsumkwe in the north-western Kalahari. *British Medical Journal* 2: 23–26.

Jochim, M. A.
1976   *Hunter-Gatherer Subsistence and Settlement: A Predictive Model.* New York: Academic Press.

Johnson, G. A.
1977   Aspects of regional analysis in archaeology. *Annual Review of Anthropology* 6: 479–508.

Johnson, R. C., R. E. Cole, and F. M. Ahern
1981   Genetic interpretation of racial/ethnic differences in lactose absorption and tolerance: a review. *Human Biology* 53: 1–13.

Johnston, F. E.
1962   Growth of the long bones of infants and young children at Indian Knoll. *American Journal of Physical Anthropology* 20: 249–254.
1968   Growth of the skeleton in earlier peoples. In D. R. Brothwell, ed., *The Skeletal Biology of Earlier Populations*: 57–66. New York: Pergamon.

Jowsey, J.
1963   Microradiography of bone resorption. In R. F. Sognnaes, ed., *Mechanisms of Hard Tissue Destruction.* Publication 75. Washington, D.C.: American Association for the Advancement of Science.

Judge, W. J., and J. Dawson
1972   Paleoindian settlement technology in New Mexico. *Science* 176: 1210–1216.

Junker, H.
1929–   Vorläufiger Bericht über die Grabung der
1940   Akademie der Wissenschaften in Wien auf der neolithischen Siedelung von Merimde-Benisalama (Westdelta). Vienna: Denkschriften der (Kaiserl.) Akademie der Wissenschaften.

Kadish, G. E.
1973   The complaints of Kha-kheper-Re-senebu. *Journal of Egyptian Archaeology* 59: 77–90.

Kaiser, W.
1957   Zur inneren Chronologie der Naqadakultur. *Archaeologia Geographica* 6: 69–77.

Kamau, C. K.
1967   Lake levels and Quaternary climates in the eastern Rift Valley of Kenya. *Nature* 216: 672–673.

Kamminga, J.
1979   The nature of use-polish and abrasive smoothing on stone tools. In B. Hayden, ed., *Lithic Use-Wear Analysis*: 143: 157. New York: Academic Press.

Kanawati, N.
1977   *The Egyptian Administration in the Old Kingdom: Evidence on Its Economic Decline.* Warminster: Aris and Phillips.

Kantor, H. J.
1965   The relative chronology of Egypt and its foreign correlations before the Late Bronze Age. In R. W. Ehrich, ed., *Chronologies in Old World Archaeology*: 1–46. Chicago: University of Chicago Press.

Kaplony, P.
1965   Bemerkungen zu einigen Steingefässen mit archäischen Königsnamen. *Mitteilungen des deutschen archäologischen Instituts-Abteilung Kairo* 20: 1–46.
1975   Chasechem(ui). *Lexikon Ägyptologie* 1: 910–912.

Kees, H.
1961   *Ancient Egypt: A Cultural Topography.* (Ed. T. G. H. James and trans. from German by I. F. D. Morros.) Chicago: University of Chicago Press.

Kelley, M. A.
1979   Parturition and pelvic changes. *American Journal of Physical Anthropology* 51: 541–546.

Kendall, R. L.
1969   An ecological history of the Lake Victoria basin. *Ecological Monographs* 39: 121–176.

Kenyon, K.
1956   Jericho and its setting in Near Eastern history. *Antiquity* 30: 184–194.
1959   Some observations on the beginning of settlement in the Near East. *Journal of the Royal Anthropological Institute* 89: 35–44.

King, K., Jr., and J. L. Bada
1979   Effects of *in-situ* leaching on amino acid racemization rates in fossil bone. *Nature* 281: 135–137.

Kitchen, K. A.
1971   Punt and how to get there. *Orientalia* 40: 184–207.

Klapwijk, M.
1974   A preliminary report on pottery from the north-eastern Transvaal. *South African Archaeological Bulletin* 29: 19–23.

Klaus, D.
1980   Climatological aspects of the spatial and temporal variations of the Southern Sahara margin. *Palaeoecology of Africa* 12: 315–331.

Klein, R. G.
1977   The ecology of early man in Southern Africa. *Science* 197: 115–126.
1978   A preliminary report on the larger mammals from the Boomplaas Stone Age cave site, Cango valley, Oudtshoorn District, South Africa. *South African Archaeological Bulletin* 33: 66–75.
1979   Palaeoenvironmental and cultural implications of late Holocene archaeological faunas from the Orange Free State and north-central Cape Province, South Africa. *South African Archaeological Bulletin* 34: 34–49.
1981   Archaeological implications of the mammalian fauna from the later Stone Age cave site of Byneskranskop 1, southern Cape Province, South Africa. In R. S. O. Harding and G. Teleki, eds., *Omnivorous Primates: Gathering and Hunting in Human Evolution*: 166–190. New York: Columbia University Press.

Klein, R. G., and K. Scott
1974   The fauna of Scott's Cave, Gamtoos Valley, south-eastern Cape Province. *South African Journal of Science* 70: 186–187.

Klichowska, M.
1978   Preliminary results of palaeoethnobotanical studies of plant impressions on potsherds from the Neolithic settlement of Kadero. *Nyame Akuma* 12: 42–43.

Klima, G.
1970   *The Barabaig: East African Cattle Herders.* New York: Holt, Rinehart and Winston.

Klitsch, E., C. Sonntag, K. Weistroffer, and E. M. El-Shazly
1976   Grundwasser der Zentralsahara: Fossile Vorräte. *Geologische Rundschau* 65: 264–287.

Kolla, V., P. Biscaye, and A. Hanley
1979   Distribution of quartz in Late Quaternary Atlantic sediments in relation to climate. *Quaternary Research* 11: 261–277.

Konner, M., and C. Worthman
1980   Nursing frequency, gonadal function, and birth spacing among !Kung hunter-gatherers. *Science* 207: 788–791.

Krapf-Askari, E.
1969   *Yoruba Towns and Cities.* London: Oxford University Press.

Kraybill, N.
1977   Pre-agricultural tools for the preparation of foods in the Old World. In C. A. Reed, ed., *Origins of Agriculture*: 485–521. The Hague: Mouton.

Kretchmer, N.
1972   Lactose and lactase. *Scientific American* 227: 70–78.

Krige, E. G., and J. D. Krige
1943   *The Realm of a Rain-Queen: A Study of the Patterns of Lovedu Society.* London: Oxford University Press.

Krueger, H. W., and C. F. Weeks
1965   Geochron Laboratories, Inc. Radiocarbon measurements I. *Radiocarbon* 7: 47–53.

Krzyzaniak, L.
1976   Note on Kadero. *Nyame Akuma* 9: 41.
1977   *Early Farming-Cultures on the Lower Nile:
        The Predynastic Period in Egypt.* Warsaw:
        Polish Academy of Sciences.
1978   New light on early food production in the
        central Sudan. *Journal of African History* 19:
        159–172.
1980   The origin of pastoral adaptation in the
        Nilotic savanna. In R. E. Leakey and B. A.
        Ogot, eds., *Proceedings of the Eighth
        Panafrican Congress of Prehistory and
        Quaternary Studies*: 265–267. Nairobi: The
        International Louis Leakey Memorial
        Institute for African Prehistory.

Laing, G. D., and J. H. Gear
1929   A final report on the Strandlooper skulls
        found at Zitzikama. *South African Journal of
        Science* 26: 575–601.

**Lallo, J. W., G. J. Armelagos, and R. P.
Mensforth**
1977   The role of diet, disease, and physiology in
        the origin of porotic hyperostosis. *Human
        Biology* 49(3): 471–483.

Lallo, J. W., J. C. Rose, and G. J. Armelagos
1978   Paleoepidemiology of infectious disease in
        Dickson Mounds population. *Medical
        College of Virginia Quarterly* 14(1): 17–23.

Lambrecht, F. L.
1964   Aspects of the evolution and ecology of
        tsetse flies and trypanosomiasis in the
        prehistoric African environment. *Journal of
        African History* 5(1): 1–24.

Lancaster, J. B.
1975   *Primate Behavior and the Emergence of
        Human Culture.* New York: Holt, Rinehart
        and Winston.

Lathrap, D. W.
1970   *The Upper Amazon.* London: Thames and
        Hudson.
1977   Our father the cayman, our mother the
        gourd: Spinden revisited, or a unitary
        model for the emergence of agriculture in
        the New World. In C. A. Reed, ed.,
        Origins of Agriculture: 711–751. The
        Hague: Mouton.

Lawry, S.
1978   *An Integrated Development Plan for the
        Malopo Farms, Kgalagadi District.*
        Gaborone, Botswana: Ministry of Local
        Government and Lands.

Leakey, L. S. B.
1931   *The Stone Age Cultures of Kenya Colony.*
        London: Cambridge University Press.
1935   *The Stone Age Races of Kenya.* London:
        Oxford University Press.
1942   The Naivasha fossil skull and skeleton.
        *Journal of the East African Natural History
        Society* 16: 169–177.
1952   Capsian or Aurignacian—which term
        should be used in Africa? *Proceedings of the
        First Panafrican Congress of Prehistory,
        Nairobi* (1947): 205–206.

Leakey, M. D.
1943   Notes on the ground and polished stone
        axes of East Africa. *Journal of the East
        African Natural History Society* 17: 182–
        195.
1945   Report on the excavations at Hyrax Hill,
        Nakuru, Kenya Colony 1937–38.
        *Transactions of the Royal Society of South
        Africa* 30(4): 271–409.
1966   Excavation of burial mounds in
        Ngorongoro Crater. *Tanzania Notes and
        Records* 66: 123–125.

**Leakey, M. D., R. L. Hay, D. L. Thurber,
R. Protsch, and R. Berger**
1972   Stratigraphy, archaeology and age of the
        Ndutu and Naisiusiu Beds, Olduvai
        Gorge, Tanzania. *World Archaeology* 3:
        328–341.

Leakey, M. D., and L. S. B. Leakey
1950   *Excavations at the Njoro River Cave.*
        Oxford: Clarendon.

Lee, R. B.
1968   What hunters do for a living, or how to
        make out on scarce resources. In R. B. Lee
        and I. DeVore, eds., *Man the Hunter*: 30–
        48. Chicago: Aldine.

1969   !Kung Bushman subsistence: an input-output analysis. In A. P. Vayda, ed., *Environment and Cultural Behavior: Ecological Studies in Cultural Anthropology*: 47–79. New York: Natural History Press.

1972a   The !Kung Bushmen of Botswana. In M. G. Bicchieri, ed., *Hunters and Gatherers Today*: 327–368. New York: Holt, Rinehart, and Winston.

1972b   Population growth and the beginnings of sedentary life among the !Kung Bushmen. In B. Spooner, ed., *Population Growth: Anthropological Implications*: 329–342. Cambridge, Mass.: MIT Press.

1972c   The intensification of social life among the !Kung Bushmen. In B. Spooner, ed., *Population Growth: Anthropological Implications*: 343–350. Cambridge, Mass.: MIT Press.

1972d   !Kung spatial organization: an ecological and historical perspective. *Human Ecology* 1: 125–247.

1973   Mongongo: the ethnography of a major wild food resource. *Ecology of Food and Nutrition* 2: 307–321.

1976a   Introduction. In R. B. Lee and I. DeVore, eds., *Kalahari Hunter-Gatherers: Studies of the !Kung San and Their Neighbors*: 3–24. Cambridge, Mass.: Harvard University Press.

1976b   !Kung spatial organization: an ecological and historical perspective. In R. B. Lee and I. DeVore, eds., *Kalahari Hunter-Gatherers: Studies of the !Kung San and Their Neighbors*: 73–97. Cambridge, Mass.: Harvard University Press.

1979   *The !Kung San: Men, Women, and Work in a Foraging Society*. New York: Cambridge University Press.

n.d.   Subsistence ecology of !Kung Bushmen. Ph.D. dissertation, University of California, Berkeley (1965).

Lee, R. B., and I DeVore

1968a   Problems in the study of hunters and gatherers. In R. B. Lee and I. DeVore, eds., *Man the Hunter*: 3–12. Chicago: Aldine.

1968b   (eds.) *Man the Hunter*. Chicago: Aldine.

Le Houerou, H. N.

1970   North Africa: past, present, future. In H. E. Dregne, ed., *Arid Lands in Transition*: 227–278. Washington, D.C.: American Association for the Advancement of Science.

Leroi-Gourhan, A.

1969   Pollen grains of Gramineae and Cerealia from Shanidar and Zawi Chemi. In P. J. Ucko and D. W. Dimbleby, eds., *The Domestication and Exploitation of Plants and Animals*: 143–148. Chicago: Aldine.

Leveau, P.

1978   Une vallée agricole des Némenchas dans l'Antiquité romaine: l'oued Hallaïl entre Djeurf et Ain Mdila. *Bulletin Archéologique du CTHS*, n.s., fasc. 10–11b: 103–121.

Lewis, H. T.

1972   The role of fire in the domestication of plants and animals in Southwest Asia: a hypothesis. *Man* 7: 195–222.

Lewis, I. M.

1975   The dynamics of nomadism: prospects for sedentarization and social change. In T. Monod, ed., *Pastoralism in Tropical Africa*: 426–442. London: Oxford University Press.

Lhote, H.

1944   *Les Touaregs du Hoggar*. Paris: Payot.

1958   *A la découverte des fresques du Tassili*. Grenoble: Arthaud.

Libby, W. F.

1955   *Radiocarbon Dating*. (2nd ed.) Chicago: University of Chicago Press.

Lichtheim, M.

1973   *Ancient Egyptian Literature*. I: *The Old and Middle Kingdoms*. Berkeley: University of California Press.

Ligers, Z.

1966   *Les Sorko (Bozo): Maîtres du Niger*. (4 vols.) Paris: Librairie des Cinq Continents.

Little, M. A., and G. E. B. Morren, Jr.
1976   *Ecology, Energetics, and Human Variability.*
        Dubuque: Wm. C. Brown.

Livingstone, D. A.
1967   Postglacial vegetation of the Ruwenzori
        Mountains in equatorial Africa. *Ecological
        Monographs* 37: 25–52.
1971   A 22,000-year pollen record from the
        plateau of Zambia. *Limnology and
        Oceanography* 16: 349–356.
1975   Late Quaternary climatic change in Africa.
        Annual Review of Ecology and Systematics 6:
        249–280.
1980   Environmental changes in the Nile
        headwaters. In M. A. J. Williams and H.
        Faure, eds., *The Sahara and the Nile*: 335–
        355. Rotterdam: Balkema.
in press Quaternary geography of Africa and the
        theory of rainforest refugia. In G. T.
        Prance, ed., *Association for Tropical Biology
        Fifth International Symposium on the
        Biological Model of Diversification in the
        Tropics.* New York: Columbia University
        Press.

Livingstone, D. A., and T. van der Hammen
1978   Palaeogeography and palaeoclimatology.
        In *Tropical Forest Ecosystems*: 61–90. Paris:
        UNESCO.

Livingstone, F. B.
1958   Anthropological implications of sickle cell
        gene distribution in West Africa. *American
        Anthropologist* 60(3): 533–562.

Long, R. D.
1976   Ancient Egyptian chronology, radiocarbon
        dating and calibration. *Zeitschrift für
        Ägyptische Sprache und Altertumskunde* 103:
        30–48.

Louw, J. T.
1960   *The Prehistory of the Matjes River Rock
        Shelter.* Memoir No. 1. Bloemfontein:
        Researches of the National Museum.

Lubell, D.
1974   The Fakhurian: a late palaeolithic industry
        from Upper Egypt. *Paper No. 58,
        Geological Survey of Egypt.* Cairo.

**Lubell, D., J. L. Ballais, A. Gautier, and
F. A. Hassan**
1975   The prehistoric cultural ecology of
        Capsian escargotières. *Libyca* 23: 43–121.

Lubell, D., and A. Gautier
1979   Holocene environment and Capsian
        subsistence in Algeria. *Palaeoecology of
        Africa* 11: 171–178.
in press The prehistoric cultural ecology of
        Capsian escargotières. II: The 1976 field
        season. *Libyca.*

**Lubell, D., F. A. Hassan, A. Gautier, and
J. L. Ballais**
1976   The Capsian escargotières. *Science* 191:
        910–920.

Lwanga-Lunyiigo, S.
1976   The Bantu problem reconsidered. *Current
        Anthropology* 17: 282–286.

Lynch, B. M.
n.d.   The Namoratunga cemetery and rock art
        sites of N.W. Kenya: a study of early
        pastoralist social organization. Ph.D.
        dissertation, Michigan State University
        (1978).

Lynch, B. M., and L. H. Robbins
1977   Animal brands and the interpretation of
        rock art in East Africa. *Current
        Anthropology* 18: 538–539.
1978   Namoratunga: the first archaeo-
        astronomical evidence in sub-Saharan
        Africa. *Science* 200: 766–768.
1979   Cushitic and Nilotic prehistory: new
        archaeological evidence from northwest
        Kenya. *Journal of African History* 20: 319–
        328.

Mabogunje, A.
1968   *Urbanisation in Nigeria.* London and New
        York: Africana Publishing Co.

MacArthur, R. H.
1972   *Geographical Ecology.* New York: Harper
        and Row.

Maggs, T. M. O'C.
1977   Some recent radiocarbon dates from

eastern and southern Africa. *Journal of African History* 18: 161–191.

Maggs, T. M. O'C., and M. A. Michael
1975   Ntshekane: an Early Iron Age site in the Tugela basin, Natal. *Annals Natal Museum* 22: 705–740.

Mahler, P. E.
n.d.   Growth of the long bones in prehistoric population from Sudanese Nubia. Master's thesis, University of Massachusetts, Amherst (1968).

Maingard, L. F.
1931   The lost tribes of the Cape. *South African Journal of Science* 28: 487–504.

Maley, J.
1972   La sédimentation pollinique actuelle dans la zone du lac Tchad (Afrique Centrale). *Pollen et Spores* 3: 253–307.
1973   Mécanisme des changements climatiques aux basses latitudes. *Palaeogeography, Palaeoclimatology, Palaeoecology* 3: 193–227.
1977a   Palaeoclimates of central Sahara during the early Holocene. *Nature* 269: 573–577. 573–577.
1977b   Analyses polliniques et paléoclimatologie des douze derniers millénaires du bassin du Tchad (Afrique Centrale). *Supplément Bulletin de l'Association française d'études quaternaires* 50: 187–197.

Maley, J., J. Cohen, H. Faure, P. Rognon, and P. M. Vincent
1970   Quelques formations lacustres et fluviatiles associées à différentes phases du volcanisme au Tibesti (Nord du Tchad). *Cahiers ORSTOM Séries Géologie* 2: 127–152.

Maquirizi, A.
1854   *Al-Khitat*. Cairo: Dar il-Tahrir lil Tiba' w' Nashr. (From the 1854 edition of Bulaq. Original manuscript completed A.D. 1436.)

Maresh, M. M.
1955   Linear growth of long bones of extremities

from infancy through adolescence. *American Journal of Diseases of Children* 89: 725–742.

Marks, A. E., and C. R. Ferring
n.d.   The Karat Group: an early ceramic-bearing occupation of the Dongola Reach, Sudan. In J. L. Shiner, ed., *The Prehistory and Geology of the Northern Sudan*: pts. 1 and 2, 335–394. Report to the National Science Foundation (1971).

Marks, S. A.
1973   Prey selection and annual harvest of game in a rural Zambian community. *East African Wildlife Journal* 11: 113–138.
1976   *Large Mammals and a Brave People: Subsistence Hunters in Zambia*. Seattle: University of Washington Press.

Marshall, L.
1961   Sharing, talking, and giving: relief of social tensions among !Kung Bushmen. *Africa* 31: 231–249.
1976   *The !Kung of Nyae Nyae*. Cambridge, Mass.: Harvard University Press.

Martin, A. R. H.
1968   Pollen analysis of Groenvlei Lake sediments, Knysna (South Africa). *Review of Paleobotany and Palynology* 7: 107–144.

Martin, D. L., and G. J. Armelagos
1979   Morphometrics of compact bone: an example from Sudanese Nubia. *American Journal of Physical Anthropology* 51: 571–578.

Martin-Pardey, E.
1976   Untersuchungen zur ägyptischen Provinzialverwaltung bis zum Ende des alten Reiches. *Hildesheimer ägyptologische Beiträge* 1: 1–246.

Martins, R. de C.
n.d.   New archaeological techniques for the study of ancient root crops in Peru. Unpublished Ph.D. thesis (1976) University of Birmingham.

Masali, M., and B. Chiarelli
1972   Demographic data on the remains of

ancient Egyptians. *Journal of Human Evolution* 1: 161–169.

Masao, F. T.
1979   *The Later Stone Age and the Rock Paintings of Central Tanzania.* Studien zur Kulturkunde 48. Wiesbaden: Steiner.

Mason, R. J.
1974a   Background to the Transvaal Iron Age—discoveries at Olifantspoort and Broederstroom. *Journal of the South African Institute of Metallurgy* 74: 211–216.
1974b   The last Stone Age San (Bushman) of the Vaal-Limpopo Basin. *South African Journal of Science* 70: 375.

Mathewson, D.
1968   The painted pottery sequence in the Volta Basin. *West African Archaeological Newsletter* 8: 24–30.

Matlhare, L.
1978   Report on agriculture in remote areas of North West District. In E. Wily, ed., *Minutes of Remote Area Development Workshop.* Gaborone, Botswana: Ministry of Local Government and Lands.

Mauny, R.
1967   Comment on Clark's "A record of early agriculture and metallurgy in Africa from archaeological sources." In C. Gable and N. R. Bennett, eds., *Reconstructing African Culture History*: 626. Boston: Boston University Press.
1972   Contribution à l'inventaire de la céramique néolithique d'Afrique occidentale. In H. Hugot, ed., *Actes du sixième congrès panafrican de préhistoire*: 72–79. Paris: Chambéry.

McBurney, C. B. M.
1967   *The Haua Fteah (Cyrenaica) and the Stone Age of the Southeast Mediterranean.* Cambridge: Cambridge University Press.
1975   The archaeological context of the Hamitic languages in northern Africa. In J. Bynon and T. Bynon, eds., *Hamito-Semitica*: 495–506. The Hague: Mouton.

McCown, E. R.
n.d.   Human skeletal remains from Lake Besaka. Unpublished.

McIntosh, R.
n.d.   The development of urbanism in West Africa: the example of Jenné, Mali. Ph.D. dissertation, Cambridge University (1979).

McIntosh, S.
n.d.   Archaeological explorations in Terra Incognita: the excavations at Jenné-jeno (Mali). Ph.D. dissertation, University of California, Santa Barbara (1979).

McIntosh, S. K., and R. J. McIntosh
1980   *Prehistoric Investigations at Jenné, Mali.* Oxford: BAR International Series 89 (ii).

McIntyre, A., and CLIMAP project members
1976a   The surface of the Ice-Age earth. *Science* 191: 1131–1144.
1976b   Glacial North Atlantic 18,000 years ago: a CLIMAP reconstruction. *Geological Society of America Memoirs* 145: 43–76.

McMaster, D. N.
1962   Speculations on the coming of the banana to Uganda. *Journal of Tropical Geography* 16: 57–69.

Meeussen, A.
1956   Statistique lexicographique en Bantu: Bobangi et Zulu. *Kongo-Overzee* 22: 86–89.

Mehlman, M. J.
1977   Excavations at Nasera Rock. *Azania* 12: 111–118.
1979   Mumba-Hohle revisited: the relevance of a forgotten excavation to some current issues in East African prehistory. *World Archaeology* 11(1): 80–94.

Meiklejohn, C., and G. Molgat
n.d.   Cluster analysis of North African Epipalaeolithic crania. Manuscript on file at Department of Anthropology, University of Winnipeg, Canada.

Meillassoux, Claude
1972   From Reproduction to Production. *Economy and Society* 1: 93–105.
1973   On the mode of production of the hunting band. In P. Alexander, ed., *French Perspectives in African Studies*: 187–203. London: Oxford University Press.

Menghin, O., and M. Amer
1932   *The Excavations of the Egyptian University in the Neolithic Site at Maadi*. Part I. Cairo: Egyptian University, Faculty of Arts.
1936   *The Excavations of the Egyptian University in the Neolithic Site at Maadi*. Part II. Cairo: Egyptian University, Faculty of Arts.

Mensforth, R. P., C. O. Lovejoy, J. W. Lallo, and G. J. Armelagos
1978   The role of constitutional factors, diet, and infectious disease in the etiology of porotic hyperostosis and periosteal reactions in prehistoric infants and children. *Medical Anthropology* 1: 1–57.

Merrick, H. V.
n.d.   Change in later Pleistocene lithic industries in eastern Africa. Ph.D. dissertation, University of California, Berkeley (1975).

Messerli, B., and M. Winiger
1980   The Saharan and East African uplands during the Quaternary. In M. A. J. Williams and H. Faure, eds., *The Sahara and the Nile*: 87–118. Rotterdam: Balkema.

Michael, H. N., and E. K. Ralph
1971   (eds.) *Dating Techniques for the Archaeologist*. Cambridge, Mass.: MIT Press.

Michel, P.
1973   *Les bassins des fleuves Sénégal et Gambie: étude géomorphologique*. (3 vols.) Mémoires ORSTOM 63.
1980   The southwestern Sahara margin: sediments and climatic changes during the recent Quaternary. *Palaeoecology of Africa* 12: 297–306.

Mikesell, M. W.
1955   Notes on the dispersal of the dromedary.

Southwestern Journal of Anthropology 9: 231–245.

Miller, S. F.
1969   Contacts between the Later Stone Age and the early Iron Age in southern central Africa. *Azania* 4: 81–90.
1979   Lukenya Hill: GvJm46 excavation report. *Nyame Akuma* 14: 31–34.

Monod, T.
1963   The Late Tertiary and Pleistocene in the Sahara. In F. C. Howell and F. Bourlière, eds., *African Ecology and Human Evolution*: 117–229. Chicago: Aldine.
1975   (ed.) *Pastoralism in Tropical Africa*. London: Oxford University Press.

Morant, G. M.
1925   A study of Egyptian craniology from prehistoric to Roman times. *Biometrika* 17: 1–52.
1935   A study of pre-dynastic Egyptian skulls from Badari based on measurements taken by Miss B. N. Stoessiger and Professor D. F. Derry. *Biometrika* 27: 293–308.

Mordini, A.
1947   Le incisioni rupestri de Gazien (Medri Senofe nell' Enderta (Ethiopia)). *Rivista di Scienze preistoriche* 21: 321–323.

Morel, J.
1974   La faune de l'escargotière de Dra-Mta-El-Ma-El-Abiod (sud-Algérien). *Anthropologie* 78(2): 299–320.
1978a   L'industrie lithique de l'escargotière de Dra-Mta-El-Ma-El-Abiod dans le sud-est Algérien: sa composition, son évolution. *Anthropologie* 82(3): 335–372.
1978b   Les sources d'alimentation des épipaléolithiques de Tamar Hat et le problème des origines de la domestication en Afrique du Nord. *Bulletin du Musée d'anthropologie préhistorique de Monaco* 22: 72–78.
n.d.   Sur certains aspects de la vie des populations capsiennes (épipaléolithiques nord-africain). Communication given at Ninth U.I.S.P.P. Congress, Nice (1976).

Morgan, W. B.
1962   The forest and agriculture in West Africa. *Journal of African History* 3: 235–239.

Mori, F.
1965   *Tadrart Acacus.* Turin: Einaudi.
1974   The earliest Saharan rock-engravings. *Antiquity* 48: 87–92.
1978   Zur Chronologie der Sahara—Felsbilder. In *Sahara*, ed. P. Stehli: 253–261. Köln: Museen Köln.

Morrison, M. E. S.
1961   Pollen analysis in Uganda. *Nature* 190: 483–486.
1966   Low-latitude vegetation history with special reference to Africa. In *Proceedings of the Royal Meteorological Society International Symposium on World Climate from 800 to 0 B.C.*: 142–148.
1968   Vegetation and climate in the uplands of southwestern Uganda during the later Pleistocene period—I: Muchoya Swamp, Kigezi District. *Journal of Ecology* 56: 363–384.

Morrison, M. E. S., and A. C. Hamilton
1974   Vegetation and climate in the uplands of south-western Uganda during the later Pleistocene period—II: forest clearance and other vegetational changes in the Rukiga highlands during the past 8000 years. *Journal of Ecology* 62: 1–32.

Moseley, J. E.
1965   The paleopathologic riddle of "symmetrical osteoporosis." *American Journal of Roentgenology* 95: 135–142.
1966   Radiographic studies in haematologic bone disease. In S. A. Jarcho, ed., *Human Paleopathology*: 121–130. New Haven: Yale University Press.

Muhkerjee, R., C. R. Rao, and J. C. Trevor
1955   *The Ancient Inhabitants of Jebel Moya.* Cambridge: Cambridge University Press.

Munson, P. J.
1976   Archaeological data on the origins of cultivation in the southwestern Sahara and their implications for West Africa. In J. R.
        Harlan, J. M. J de Wet, and A. B. L. Stemler, eds., *Origins of African Plant Domestication*: 187–210. The Hague: Mouton.
1977   Africa's prehistoric past. In P. M. Martin and P. O'Meara, eds., *Africa*: 62–82. Bloomington: Indiana University Press.
n.d.   The Tichitt tradition: a late prehistoric occupation of the southwestern Sahara. Ph.D. dissertation, University of Illinois, Urbana-Champaign (1971).

Murdock, G. P.
1959   *Africa: Its Peoples and Their Culture History.* New York: McGraw-Hill.
1967   *Ethnographic Atlas.* Pittsburgh: University of Pittsburgh Press.

Muriuki, G.
1974   *A History of the Kikuyu 1500–1900.* Nairobi: Oxford University Press.

Murray, G. W.
1947   A note on the Sadd el-Kafara: the ancient dam in the Wadi Garawi. *Bulletin de l'Institut d'Egypte* 28: 33–43.

Murray, M. L.
n.d.   Present wildlife utilization in the Central Kalahari Game Reserve, Botswana: a report on the Central Kalahari Game Reserve reconnaissance. Report to the Department of Wildlife, Tourism, and National Parks, Gaborone, Botswana (1976).

Musonda, F.
n.d.   The Later Stone Age of the Volta Scarp. M.A. thesis, University of Ghana, Legon (1976).

Naroll, R.
1964   On ethnic unit classification. *Current Anthropology* 5: 283–312.

Naveh, Z., and J. Dan
1973   The human degradation of Mediterranean landscapes in Israel. In F. di Castri and H. A. Mooney, eds., *Mediterranean Type Ecosystems: Origin and Structure*: 373–390. New York: Springer-Verlag.

Naville, E.
1898   *The Temple of Deir el Bahari*. Vol. III. London: Egypt Exploration Fund.

Nelson, C. M.
1980   The Elmenteitan lithic industry. In R. E. Leakey and B. A. Ogot, eds., *Proceedings of the Eighth Panafrican Congress of Prehistory and Quaternary Studies*: 275–278. Nairobi: The International Louis Leakey Memorial Institute for African Prehistory.
n.d.   A comparative analysis of 29 Later Stone Age occurrences from East Africa. Ph.D. dissertation, University of California, Berkeley (1973).

Nenquin, J.
1963   *Excavations at Sanga, 1957*. Tervuren: Musée Royal de l'Afrique Centrale.

Newman, J. L.
1970   *The Ecological Basis for Subsistence Change among the Sandawe of Tanzania*. Washington, D.C.: National Academy of Sciences.

Newman, P.
1977   Chadic classification and reconstructions. *Afroasiatic Linguistics* 5: 1–42.

Nicholson, S. E.
n.d.   A climatic chronology for Africa: synthesis of geological, historical and meteorological information and data. Ph.D. dissertation, University of Wisconsin (1976).

Nicholson, S. E., and H. Flohn
1980   African environmental and climatic changes and the general atmospheric circulation in the late Pleistocene and Holocene. *Climatic Change* 2: 313–348.

Nicolaisen, J.
1963   *Ecology and Culture of the Pastoral Tuareg*. Ethnografisk Raekke 9. Copenhagen: National Museum.

Nie, N. H., C. H. Hull, J. G. Jenkins, K. Steinbrenner, and D. H. Brent
1975   *Statistical Package for the Social Sciences*. New York: McGraw-Hill.

Nordström, H. A.
1972   Neolithic and A-Group sites. In T. Säve-Soderbergh, ed., *Scandinavian Joint Expedition to Sudanese Nubia*: Vol. 3, pts. 1 and 2. Stockholm: Scandinavian University Press.

Noy-Meir, I.
1973   Desert ecosystems: environment and procedures. *Annual Review of Ecology and Systematics* 4: 25–51.

Nurse, G. T., and T. Jenkins
1974   Lactose intolerance in San populations. *British Medical Journal* 3: 809.
1977   *Health and the Hunter-Gatherer: Biomedical Studies on the Hunting and Gathering Populations of Southern Africa*. Monographs in Human Genetics 8. Basel: S. Karger.

Nzewunwa, N.
n.d.   Aspects of economy and culture in the prehistory of the Niger Delta. Ph.D. dissertation, Cambridge University (1979).

O'Connor, D.
1972   The geography of settlement in ancient Egypt. In P. J. Ucko, R. Tringham, and G. W. Dimbleby, eds., *Man, Settlement, and Urbanism*: 681–698. London: Duckworth.
1974   Political systems and archaeological data in Egypt: 2600–1780 B.C. *World Archaeology* 6: 15–38.

Odner, K.
1971a   Usangi Hospital and other archaeological sites in the North Pare mountains, northeastern Tanzania. *Azania* 6: 89–130.
1971b   An archaeological survey of the Iramba Plateau, Tanzania. *Azania* 6: 151–198.
1972   Excavations at Narosura, a Stone Bowl site in the southern Kenya highlands. *Azania* 7: 25–92.

Oliver, R. A.
1966   The problem of the Bantu expansion. *Journal of African History* 7: 361–376.
1979   Cameroun—the Bantu cradleland? *Sprache und Geschichte in Afrika* 1: 7–20.

Oliver, R. A., and B. M. Fagan
1975   *Africa in the Iron Age*. Cambridge: Cambridge University Press.

Olsson, I.
1959   Uppsala national radiocarbon measurements I. *Radiocarbon* 1: 87–102.

Onyango-Abuje, J. C.
1976   Reflections on culture change and distribution during the Neolithic period in East Africa. In B. A. Ogot, ed., *History and Social Change in East Africa*: 14–30. *Hadith* 6, Nairobi: East African Literature Bureau.
1977   Crescent Island. *Azania* 12: 147–160.
n.d.   A contribution to the study of the Neolithic in East Africa with particular reference to the Naivasha-Nakuru Basin. Ph.D. dissertation, University of California, Berkeley (1977).

Ortner, D. J.
1975   Aging effects on osteon remodeling. *Calcified Tissue Research* 18: 27–36.

Osmaston, H. A.
1958   Pollen analysis in the study of the past vegetation and climate of Ruwenzori and its neighborhood. B.Sc. thesis, Oxford. Entebbe: Uganda Forest Dept.
n.d.   The past and present climate and vegetation of Ruwenzori and its neighborhood. D. Phil. thesis, Oxford University (1965).

Otto, K. H.
1963   Shaqadud: a new Khartoum Neolithic site outside the Nile Valley. *Kush* 11: 108–115.

Owen, R. B., J. W. Barthelme, R. W. Renaut, and A. Vincens
1982   Palaeolimnology and archaeology of Holocene deposits north-east of Lake Turkana, Kenya. *Nature* 298: 523–529.

Pachur, H.
1975   Zur spätpleistozanen und holozänen Formung auf der Nordabdachung des Tibestigebirges. *Die Erde* 106: 21–46.

Pachur, H. J., and G. Braun
1980   The paleoclimate of the central Sahara, Libya, and the Libyan desert. *Palaeoecology of Africa* 12: 351–363.

Palmer, P. G.
1976   Grass cuticles: a new paleoecological tool for East African lake sediments. *Canadian Journal of Botany* 54: 1725–1734.

Parkin, D. W.
1974   Trade-winds during the glacial cycles. *Proceedings of the Royal Society, London A.* 337: 73–100.

Parkin, D. W., and N. J. Shackleton
1973   Trade wind and temperature correlations down a deep-sea core off the Sahara coast. *Nature* 245: 455–457.

Parkington, J. E.
1972   Seasonal mobility in the Later Stone Age. *African Studies* 31: 223–243.
1977   Soaqua: hunter-fisher gatherers of the Olifants River Valley, western Cape. *South African Archaeological Bulletin* 32: 150–157.
1980   Time and place: some observations on spatial and temporal patterning in the Later Stone Age. *South African Archaeological Bulletin* 35(132): 73–83.
n.d.   Follow the San: an analysis of seasonality in the prehistory of the western Cape, South Africa. Ph.D. dissertation, Cambridge University (1975).

Parris, R., and G. Child
1973   The importance of pans to wildlife in the Kalahari and the effects of human settlement on these areas. *Journal of the South African Wildlife Management Association* 3: 1–8.

Parsons, Q. N.
1974   The economic history of Khama's Country in southern Africa. *African Social Research* 18: 643–675.

Pastouret, L., H. Chamley, G. Delibrias, J. C. Duplessy, and J. Thiede
1978   Late Quaternary climatic changes in

western tropical Africa deduced from deep-sea sedimentation off the Niger delta. *Oceanologica Acta* 1: 217–232.

Peake, H. J. E.
1927   The beginnings and the early spread of agriculture. *Nature* 119: 894–896.
1928   *The Origins of Agriculture*. London: Ernest Benn.

Pearsall, D. M.
1978   Phytolith analysis of archaeological soils: evidence for maize cultivation in formative Ecuador. *Science* 199: 177–178.

Percival, A. B.
1924   *A Game Ranger's Notebook*. London: Nisbet.

Perzigian, A. J.
1973   Osteoporotic bone loss in two prehistoric Indian populations. *American Journal of Physical Anthropology* 39: 87–96.

Peterson, G. M., T. Webb, J. E. Kutzbach, T. van der Hammen, T. A. Wijmstra, and F. A. Street
1979   The continental record of environmental conditions at 18,000 yr. B.P.: an initial evaluation. *Quaternary Research* 12: 47–82.

Petit-Maire, N.
1979a   Prehistoric paleoecology of the Sahara Atlantic Coast in the last 10,000 years: a synthesis. *Journal of Arid Environments* 2(1): 85–88.
1979b   *Le Sahara atlantique à l'Holocène*. Mémoires 28. Algiers: CRAPE.

Petit-Maire, N., G. Delibrias, and C. Gaven
1980   Pleistocene lakes in the Shati area, Fezzan (27°30′N). *Palaeoecology of Africa* 12: 288–295.

Petrie, W. M. F.
1895   *Nagada and Ballas*. London: Quartich.

Pflaumann, U.
1980   Variations of the surface water temperatures along the eastern North Atlantic continental margin (sediment surface samples, Holocene climatic

optimum and last glacial maximum). *Palaeoecology of Africa* 12: 191–212.

Phillipson, D. W.
1968   The Early Iron Age site at Kapwirimbwe, Lusaka. *Azania* 3: 87–105.
1969   The prehistoric sequence at Nakapapula Rockshelter, Zambia. *Proceedings of the Prehistoric Society* 35: 172–202.
1970   Excavations at Twickenham Road, Lusaka. *Azania* 5: 77–118.
1972   Early Iron Age sites on the Zambian Copperbelt. *Azania* 7: 93–128.
1975   The chronology of the Iron Age in Bantu Africa. *Journal of African History* 16: 321–342.
1976a   The Early Iron Age in Eastern and Southern Africa: a critical re-appraisal. *Azania* 11: 1–23.
1976b   *The Prehistory of Eastern Zambia*. Memoir 6. Nairobi: British Institute in Eastern Africa.
1976c   Fishermen and the beginnings of East African farming: new light from northern Kenya. *Kenya Past and Present* 7: 2–9.
1977a   The excavation of Gobedra Rock-Shelter, Axum: an early occurrence of cultivated finger millet in northern Ethiopia. *Azania* 12: 53–82.
1977b   Lowasera. *Azania* 12: 1–32.
1977c   *The Later Prehistory of Eastern and Southern Africa*. New York: Africana.

Pianka, E. R.
1974   *Evolutionary Ecology*. New York: Harper and Row.

Piccione, P. A.
n.d.   The historical effects of the levels of the Nile inundation on the Second Dynasty. M.A. thesis, University of Chicago (1976).

Pierre, M. C. de
1977   *Tébessa, notice écrite*. Algiers: Ministère de l'Information et de la Culture, Direction des Beaux-Arts.

Pike, J. G.
1971   Rainfall over Botswana. *Botswana Notes and Records* spec. ed. 1: 69–76.

Polgar, S.
1975   Population evolution and theoretical paradigm. In S. Polgar, ed., *Population, Ecology and Social Evolution*: 1–25. The Hague: Mouton.

Pollard, G. C., and I. M. Drew
1975   Llama herding and settlement in prehistoric northern Chile: application of an analysis for determining domestication. *American Antiquity* 40: 296–304.

Pollard, M.
1968   Floods according to an ancient Egyptian scientific chronicle. *Journal of Geophysical Research* 13(22): 7158.

Pond, A. W., L. Chapuis, A. Romer, and F. C. Baker
1938   *Prehistoric Habitation Sites in the Sahara and North Africa*. Logan Museum Bulletin 5. Beloit: Beloit College.

Portères, R.
1950   Vieilles agricultures de l'Afrique intertropicale. *Agronomie tropicale* 5: 489–507.
1962   Berceaux agricoles primaires sur le continent africain. *Journal of African History* 3: 195–210.
1970   Primary cradles of agriculture in the African continent. In J. D. Fage and R. A. Oliver, eds., *Papers in African Prehistory*: 43–58. Cambridge: Cambridge University Press.
1976   African cereals: eleusine, fonio, black fonio, teff, *Brachiaria*, *paspalum*, *Pennisetum*, and African rice. In J. R. Harlan, J. R. J. de Wet, and A. B. L. Stemler, eds., *Origins of African Plant Domestication*: 409–452. The Hague: Mouton.

Posener-Kriéger, P., and J. L. de Cenival
1968   *Hieratic Papyri in the British Museum: The Abu Sir Papyri*. London: British Museum.

Posnansky, M.
1966   The origins of agriculture and iron working in southern Africa. In M. Posnansky, ed., *Prelude to East African History*: 82–94. London: Oxford University Press.
1967   The Iron Age in East Africa. In W. W. Bishop and J. D. Clark, eds., *Background to Evolution in Africa*: 629–649. Chicago: University of Chicago Press.
1969   Yams and the origins of West African agriculture. *Odu* 1: 101–107.
1975   Archaeology, technology, and Akan civilization. *Journal of African Studies* 2: 25–38.
1976   New radiocarbon dates from Ghana. *Sankofa* 2: 60–71.
1979   Dating Ghana's earliest art. *African Arts* 13: 52–53.
in press The agriculturalist as hunter-gatherer: a case study from Hani, Ghana. In *Essays in Memoriam to C. B. M. McBurney*.

Posnansky, M., and R. McIntosh
1976   New radiocarbon dates for northern and western Africa. *Journal of African History* 17: 161–195.

Protsch, R.
1974   The age and stratigraphic position of Olduvai Hominid 1. *Journal of Human Evolution* 3(5): 379–385.
1976   The Naivasha hominid and its confirmed later Upper Pleistocene age. *Anthropologischer Anzeiger* 35: 97–102.
1978   The chronological position of Gamble's Cave II and Bromhead's Site (Elmenteita) of the Rift Valley, Kenya. *Journal of Human Evolution* 7: 101–109.

Protsch, R., and J. J. Oberholzer
1975   Paleoanthropology, chronology and archaeology of the Matjes River Rock Shelter. *Zeitschrift für Morphologie und Anthropologie* 67(1): 32–43.

Pucciarelli, H. M.
1980   The effects of race, sex and nutrition on craniofacial differentiation in rats: a multivariate analysis. *American Journal of Physical Anthropology* 53: 359–368.

Purseglove, J. W.
1972   *Tropical Crops: Monocotyledons*. Vol. 1. New York: Wiley.

1976   The origins and migrations of crops in
          tropical Africa. In J. R. Harlan, J. M. J. de
          Wet, and A. B. L. Stemler, eds., *Origins of
          African Plant Domestication*: 291–310. The
          Hague: Mouton.

**Pyke, G. H., H. R. Pulliam, and E. L.
Charnov**
1977   Optimal foraging: a selective review of
          theory and tests. *Quarterly Review of Biology*
          52(2): 137–154.

Quézel, P.
1978   Analysis of the flora of Mediterranean and
          Saharan Africa. *Annals of the Missouri
          Botanical Gardens* 65: 479–534.

Quézel, P., and S. Santa
1962   *Nouvelle flore de l'Algérie et des régions
          désertiques méridionales.* Paris: CNRS.

Quin, P. J.
1959   *Food and Feeding Habits of the Pedi.*
          Johannesburg: Witwatersrand University
          Press.

Rabin, C.
1975   Lexicostatistics and the internal division of
          Semitic. In J. Bynon and T. Bynon, eds.,
          Hamito-Semitica: 85–99. The Hague:
          Mouton.

Rattray, R. S.
1923   *Ashanti.* London: Oxford University Press.

Redman, C. L.
1978   *The Rise of Civilization: From Early Farmers
          to Urban Society in the Near East.* San
          Francisco: W. H. Freeman.

Reed, C. A.
1977   A model for the origin of agriculture in the
          Near East. In C. A. Reed, ed., *Origins of
          Agriculture*: 543–567. The Hague:
          Mouton.

Reid, N.
n.d.   A report on Basarwa living in Kang village,
          Kgalagadi District, Botswana. Report to
          the Ministry of Local Government and
          Lands, Gaborone, Botswana (1977).

Reille, M.
1976   Analyse pollinique de sédiments

          postglaciaires dans le Moyen Atlas et le
          Haut Atlas marocains: premiers résultats.
          Ecologia Méditerranéenne 2: 153–170.
1977   Contribution pollenanalytique à l'histoire
          holocène de la végétation des montagnes
          du Rif (Maroc séptentrional). Rècherches
          Françaises sur le Quaternaire, INQUA
          1977, *Supplément au Bulletin de l'Association
          française d'études quaternaires 1977-1* 50:
          55–76.

Richards, A.
1939   *Land, Labor and Diet in Northern Rhodesia:
          An Economic Study of the Bemba Tribe.*
          London: International Institute of African
          Languages and Cultures.

Richardson, J. L.
1966   Changes in the level of Lake Naivasha,
          Kenya during post-glacial times. *Nature*
          209–291.
1972   Paleolimnological records from rift lakes
          in central Kenya. *Palaeoecology of Africa* 6:
          131–136.

**Richardson, J. L., T. J. Harvey, and S. A.
Holdship**
1978   Diatom in the history of shallow East
          African lakes. *Polski Archivum
          Hydrobiologii* 25: 341–353.

Richardson, J. L., and A. E. Richardson
1972   The history of an East African rift lake
          and its climatic implications. *Ecological
          Monographs* 42: 499–534.

Rightmire, G. P.
1970a   Iron age skulls from southern Africa re-
          assessed by multiple discriminant analysis.
          American Journal of Physical Anthropology
          33: 147–168.
1970b   Bushman, Hottentot, and South African
          Negro crania studied by distance and
          discrimination. *American Journal of Physical
          Anthropology* 33: 169–196.
1974   *The Later Pleistocene and Recent Evolution of
          Man in Africa.* MSS Module No. 27. New
          York: MSS Module Publications.
1975a   Problems in the study of later Pleistocene
          man in Africa. *American Anthropologist* 77:
          28–51.

1975b New studies of post-Pleistocene human skeletal remains from the Rift Valley, Kenya. *American Journal of Physical Anthropology* 42: 351–369.

1977 Notes on the human burials from Lowasera. In D. W. Phillipson, *Lowasera*. *Azania* 12: 30–32.

1978a Florisbad and human population succession in southern Africa. *American Journal of Physical Anthropology* 48: 475–486.

1978b Human skeletal remains from the southern Cape Province and their bearing on the Stone Age prehistory of South Africa. *Quaternary Research* 9: 219–230.

1979 Implications of Border Cave skeletal remains for later Pleistocene human evolution. *Current Anthropology* 20(1): 23–35.

Rightmire, G. P., and N. J. van der Merwe
1976 Two burials from Phalaborwa and the association of race and culture in the Iron Age of southern Africa. *South African Archaeological Bulletin* 31: 147–152.

Ritchie, W. A., and R. E. Funk
1973 *Aboriginal Settlement Patterns in the Northeast.* Memoir No. 20. Albany: New York State Museum and Science Service.

Robbins, L. H.
1972 Archaeology in Turkana District, Kenya. *Science* 176: 359–366.

1974 *The Lothagam Site: A Later Stone Age Fishing Settlement in the Lake Rudolf Basin, Kenya.* East Lansing: Michigan State University Museum Anthropological Series, Vol. 1, no. 2.

1980 *Lopoy: A Late Stone Age Fishing and Pastoralist Settlement West of Lake Turkana, Kenya.* East Lansing: Michigan State University Museum Anthropological Series, Vol. 3, no. 1.

Robbins, L. H., and B. M. Lynch
1978 New evidence on the use of microliths from the Lake Turkana Basin, East Africa. *Current Anthropology* 19(3): 619–620.

Robbins, M. C., and R. B. Pollnac
1977 A multivariate analysis of the relationship of artifactual to cultural modernity in rural Buganda. In D. Ingersol, J. E. Yellen, and W. MacDonald, eds., *Experimental Archaeology*: 332–351. New York: Columbia University Press.

Robertshaw, P. T.
n.d. Khoi and San: aspects of the later prehistory of the western Cape, South Africa. Ph.D. dissertation, Cambridge University (1978).

Robinson, K. R.
1963 Further excavations in the Iron Age deposits at the Tunnel Site, Gokomere Hill, Southern Rhodesia. *South African Archaeological Bulletin* 18: 155–171.

1970 *The Iron Age in the Southern Lake Area of Malawi.* Blantyre: Department of Antiquities.

Rodale, J. I.
1959 (ed.)*The Health Builder.* London: Rodale.

Rognon, P.
1967 *Le massif de l'Atakor et ses bordures: étude géomorphologique.* Paris: CNRS.

1976 Essai d'interprétation des variations climatiques au Sahara depuis 40,000 ans. *Revue de géographie physique et de géologie dynamique* 18: 251–282.

1979 Evolution du relief et paléoclimats depuis 40,000 ans sur la bordure nord du Sahara. *Bulletin de l'Association des géographes français* 463: 205–214.

Rognon, P., and M. A. J. Williams
1977 Late Quaternary climatic changes in Australia and North Africa: a preliminary interpretation. *Palaeogeography, Palaeoclimatology, Palaeoecology* 21: 285–327.

Rohdenburg, H., and U. Sabelberg
1980 Northwestern Sahara margin: terrestrial stratigraphy of the Upper Quaternary and some palaeoclimatic implications. *Palaeoecology of Africa* 12: 267–275.

Romer, A. S.
1938   Mammalian remains from some paleolithic stations in Algeria. In A. W. Pond et al., eds., *Prehistoric Habitation Sites in the Sahara and North Africa*: 165–184. Logan Museum Bulletin 2. Beloit: Beloit College.

Rose, J. C., G. J. Armelagos, and J. W. Lallo
1978   Histological indicator of childhood stress in prehistoric skeletal samples. *American Journal of Physical Anthropology* 49: 511–516.

Roth, H. L.
1886   On the origin of agriculture. *Journal of the Anthropological Institute* 16: 102–136.

Roubet, C.
1971   Sur la définition et la chronologie du Néolithique de tradition capsienne. *Anthropologie* 75(7–8): 553–574.
1978   Une économie pastorale pré-agricole en Algérie orientale: le Néolithique de tradition capsienne. *Anthropologie* 82(4): 583–586.

Rudner, J.
1968   Strandlooper pottery from the coasts of South and South West Africa. *Annals of the South African Museum* 49(2): 441–663.

Rudney, J. D.
1979   An evaluation of pathological bands in tooth enamel as indicators of developmental stress (abstract). *American Journal of Physical Anthropology* 50: 477.

Russell, Margo, and M. Russell
1979   *Afrikaners of the Kalahari: White Minority in a Black State*. Cambridge: Cambridge University Press.

Sadek, S.
1916   *Ancient Egyptian Agriculture* (in Arabic). Cairo: Matba'et al-Maref.

as-Sa'di, A.
1900   *Ta'rikh es-Sudan*. Trans. O. Houdas. Paris: Leroux.

Saffirio, L.
1975   L'alimentazione umana nell'antico Egitto V. *Aegyptus* 55: 14–46.

Sahlins, M. D.
1968   Notes on the original affluent society. In R. B. Lee and I. DeVore, eds. *Man the Hunter*: 85–89. Chicago: Aldine.
1972   *Stone Age Economics*. Chicago: Aldine-Atherton.

Sahlins, M. D., and E. R. Service
1960   (eds.) *Evolution and Culture*. Ann Arbor: University of Michigan Press.

Salonen, A.
1968   Agricultura Mesopotamica nach sumerisch-akkadischen Quellen. *Annales Academiae Scientiarum Fennicae* B-149: 1–502.

Sampson, C. G.
1967a   Excavations at Zaayfontaein Shelter, Norvalspont, northern Cape. *Navorsinge van die Nasionale Museum (Bloemfontein)* 2: 41–124.
1967b   Excavations at Glen Elliott Shelter, Colesberg District, northern Cape. *Navorsinge van die Nasionale Museum (Bloemfontein)* 2: 125–210.
1970   The Smithfield Industrial Complex: further field results. *National Museum (Bloemfontein) Memoir* 5: 1–172.
1974   *The Stone Age Archaeology of Southern Africa*. New York: Academic Press.

Sampson, C. G., and M. Sampson
1967   Riversmead Shelter: excavations and analysis. *National Museum (Bloemfontein) Memoir* 3: 1–111.

Sandelowsky, B. H., J. H. van Rooyen, and J. C. Vogel
1979   Early evidence for herders in the Namib. *South African Archaeological Bulletin* 34: 50–51.

Sarnthein, M.
1978   Sand deserts during glacial maximum and climatic optimum. *Nature* 272: 43–46.

Sarnthein, M., and B. Koopman
1980   Late Quaternary deep-sea record on northwest African dust supply and wind circulation. *Palaeoecology of Africa* 12: 239–253.

Sassoon, H.

1968   Excavation of a burial mound in
Ngorongoro Crater, Tanzania. *Tanzania
Notes and Records* 69: 15–32.

Sauer, C. O.

1952   *Agricultural Origins and Dispersals.* New
York: American Geographic Society.

1969   *Seeds, Spades, Hearths and Herds.* (Reprint
of 1952 ed.) Cambridge, Mass.: MIT
Press.

Savage, R. J. G., and P. G. Williamson

1978   The early history of the Turkana
depression. In W. W. Bishop, ed.,
Geological Background to Fossil Man: 375–
394. Edinburgh: Scottish Academic Press.

Saxon, D.

n.d.   A lexicostatistical classification of the
Chadic languages. Seminar paper,
University of California at Los Angeles
(1975).

Saxon, E. C.

1976   The evolution of domestication: a
reappraisal of the Near Eastern and North
African evidence. In E. S. Higgs, ed.,
Origine de l'élevage et de la domestication.
*Colloque 20, Ninth UISPP Congress
(Nice)*: 180–226.

**Saxon, E. C., A. E. Close, C. Cluzel,
V. Morse, and N. J. Shackleton**

1974   Results of recent investigations at Tamar
Hat. *Libyca* 22: 49–91.

Schalke, H. J. W. G

1973   The Upper Quaternary of the Cape Flats
Area (Cape Province, South Africa).
Scripta Geologica 15: 1–57.

Schapera, I.

1929   *The Khoisan Peoples of South Africa:
Bushmen and Hottentots.* London:
Routledge and Kegan Paul.

1943   *Native Land Tenure in the Bechuanaland
Protectorate.* Lovedale, South Africa:
Lovedale Press.

Schapera, I., and E. Farrington

1933   *The Early Cape Hottentots.* Westport:
Negro University Press (reprint 1970).

Schenkel, W.

1965   Memphis-Herakleopolis-Theben: die
epigraphischen Zeugnisse der 7–11.
Dynastie Ägyptens. *Ägyptologische
Abhandlungen* 12: 1–306.

1978   *Die Bewässerungs Revolution im alten
Ägypten.* Mainz: P. v. Zabern.

Schiegl, W. E.

n.d.   Natural deuterium in biogenic materials:
influence of environment and geophysical
applications. Thesis, University of South
Africa, Pretoria (1970).

Schiffer, M. B.

1976   *Behavioral Archaeology.* New York:
Academic Press.

Schmidt, P. R.

1978   *Historical Archaeology.* Westport:
Greenwood Press.

Schneider, J. L.

1967   Evolution du dernier lacustre et
peuplements préhistoriques au Pays-Bas
du Tchad. *Bulletin de l'Association
sénégalaise pour l'étude du Quaternaire de
l'Ouest africain* 14–15: 18–23.

Schrire, C.

1980   Identity enquiry of San hunter-gatherers.
Human Ecology 8: 9–32.

n.d.   Hunter-gatherer studies and interpreting
paleolithic data: how far we have come.
Paper delivered at the Symposium on
Contemporary Theory and Paleolithic
Data, SUNY, Binghamton, New York,
March 5, 1977.

Schull, W. J.

1972   Genetic implications of population
breeding structure. In G. W. Harrison and
A. J. Boyce, eds., *The Structure of Human
Populations.* Oxford: Clarendon Press.

Schulz, P. D., and H. McHenry

1975   Age distribution of enamel hypoplasia in

prehistoric California Indians. *Journal of Dental Research* 54(4): 913.

Schweitzer, F. R.
1974   Archaeological evidence for sheep at the Cape. *South African Archaeological Bulletin* 29: 75–82.
1979   Excavations at Die Kelders, Cape Province, South Africa: the Holocene deposits. *Annals of the South African Museum* 78: 101–233.

Schweitzer, F. R., and M. L. Wilson
1978   A preliminary report on excavations at Byneskranskop, Bredasdorp District, Cape. *South African Archaeological Bulletin* 33: 134–140.

Scudder, T.
1962   *The Ecology of the Gwembe Tonga.* Kariba Studies Vol. 2, Rhodes-Livingstone Institute. Manchester: Manchester University Press.
1971   *Gathering among African Woodland Savannah Cultivators: A Case Study—the Gwembe Tonga.* Zambian Papers No. 5. Lusaka: Institute for African Studies, University of Zambia.
1976   Social anthropology and the reconstruction of prehistoric land use systems in tropical Africa: a cautionary case study from Zambia. In J. R. Harlan, J. M. J. de Wet, and A. B. L. Stemler, eds., *Origins of African Plant Domestication*: 357–381. The Hague: Mouton.

Seddon, J. D.
1968   The origins and development of agriculture in east and southern Africa. *Current Anthropology* 9: 489–494.

Seiner, F.
1977   Die Buschmänner des Okavango und Sambesigebietes der Nord-Kalahari. *Botswana Notes and Records* 9: 31–36.

Servant, M.
1974   Les variations climatiques des régions intertropicales du continent africain depuis la fin du Pléistocène. *Treizièmes Journées Hydrologiques Paris* Qu. 1, rap. 8.

n.d.   Séquences continentales et variations climatiques: évolution du bassin du Tchad au Cénozoïque supérieur. Thesis, University of Paris (1973).

Servant, M., P. Ergenzinger, and Y. Coppens
1969   Datations absolues sur un delta lacustre quaternaire au Sud du Tibesti (Angamma). *Compte rendu sommaire des séances de la Société géologique de France* 8: 313–314.

Servant, M., and S. Servant-Vildary
1970   Les formations lacustres et les diatomées du Quaternaire récent du fond de la cuvette tchadienne. *Revue de géographie physique et de géologie dynamique* 12(1): 63–76.
1980   L'environnement quaternaire du bassin du Tchad. In M. A. J. Williams and H. Faure, eds., *The Sahara and the Nile*: 133–162. Rotterdam: Balkema.

Servant-Vildary, S.
1970   Répartition des diatomées dans les séquences lacustres holocènes au nord-est du Lac Tchad. *Cahiers ORSTROM série géologie II*: 115–126.
1978   *Evolution des diatomées et paléolimnologie du bassin tchadien au Cénozoïque supérieur.* (2 vols.) Paris: ORSTOM.
n.d.   Evolution des diatomées et paléolimnologie du bassin tchadien au Cénozoïque supérieur. Thèse de Doctorat d'Etat es-Sciences Naturelles, l'Université de Paris (1977).

Shack, W. A.
1963   Some aspects of ecology and social structure in the Ensete Complex in southwestern Ethiopia. *Journal of the Royal Anthropological Institute of Great Britain and Ireland* 93, 1: 72–79.
1966   *The Gurage: A People of the Ensete Culture.* London: Oxford University Press.

Shackleton, N. J.
1974   Oxygen isotopic demonstration of winter seasonal occupation. In E. Saxon, A. E. Close, C. Cluzel, V. Morse, and N. J.

Shackleton, Results of recent investigations at Tamar Hat, *Libyca* 22: 49–91.

Shanley, B. M. G., and O. A. M. Lewis
1969   The protein nutritional value of wild plants used as dietary supplements in Natal (South Africa). *Plant Foods in Human Nutrition* 1: 253–258.

Shaw, B. D.
1976   Climate, environment and prehistory in the Sahara. *World Archaeology* 8(2): 133–149.

Shaw, T.
1968   Comment on "The origins of agriculture." *Current Anthropology* 9: 500–501.
1969a   On radiocarbon chronology of the Iron Age in sub-Saharan Africa. *Current Anthropology* 10(2–3): 226–231.
1969b   The late Stone Age in the Nigerian forest. *Actes du premier colloque international d'archéologie africaine, Fort Lamy*: 364–373.
1973a   Finds at the Iwo Eleru Rock Shelter, western Nigeria. *Actes du sixième congrès panafricain de préhistoire et de l'étude du Quaternaire*: 190–192. Paris: Chambéry.
1973b   A note on trade and the Tsoede bronzes. *West African Journal of Archaeology* 3: 233–238.
1976   Early crops in Africa: a review of the evidence. In J. R. Harlan, J. M. J. de Wet, and A. B. L. Stemler, eds., *Origins of African Plant Domestication*: 107–153. The Hague: Mouton.
1977   Hunters, gatherers and first farmers in West Africa. In J. V. S. Megaw, ed., *Hunters, Gatherers and First Farmers beyond Europe*: 69–126. Surrey: Leicester University Press.
1978   *Nigeria: Its Archaeology and Early History.* London: Thames and Hudson.

Sheller, P.
n.d.   The people of the Central Kalahari Game Reserve: a report on the reconnaissance of the Reserve, July-September 1976. Report to the Government of Botswana, Gaborone (1977).

Shiner, J. L.
1968   The Khartoum Variant Industry. In F. Wendorf, ed., *The Prehistory of Nubia*: Vol. 20, 768–790. Dallas: Southern Methodist University Press.
1973   Wear patterns on stone tools. *Nyame Akuma* 3: 32.
n.d.   (ed.) *The Prehistory and Geology of the Northern Sudan*, pts. 1 and 2. Report to the National Science Foundation (1971).

Shrubsall, F. C.
1907   Notes on some Bushmen crania and bones from the South African Museum. *Annals of the South African Museum* 5: 227–266.

Siiriäinen, A.
1971   The Iron Age site at Gatung'ang'a, central Kenya: contributions to the Gumba problem. *Azania* 6: 199–232.
1977   Later Stone Age investigations in the Laikipia highlands, Kenya: a preliminary report. *Azania* 12: 161–186.

Silberbauer, G. B.
1965   *Report to the Government of Bechuanaland on the Bushman Survey.* Gaborone, Botswana: Bechuanaland Government Printer.
1972   The G/wi Bushmen. In M. G. Bicchieri, ed., *Hunters and Gatherers Today*: 271–326. New York: Holt, Rinehart and Winston.
1978   Social hibernation: the response of the G/wi band to seasonal drought. In M. T. Hinchey, ed., *Proceedings of the Symposium on Drought in Botswana*: 112–120. Gaborone, Botswana: Botswana Society.
1981   Hunter-gatherers of the central Kalahari. In R. S. O. Harding and G. Teleki, eds., *Omnivorous Primates: Gathering and Hunting in Human Evolution*: 455–498. New York: Columbia University Press.
n.d.   Socio-ecology of the G/wi Bushmen. Ph.D. dissertation, Monash University, Clayton, Victoria, Australia (1973).

Silberbauer, G. B., and A. J. Kuper
1966   Kgalagari masters and Bushman serfs: some observations. *African Studies* 25(4): 171–179.

Simmonds, N. W.
1958   Ensete cultivation in the southern highlands of Ethiopia: a review. *Tropical Agriculture* 35: 307.

Simon, H. A.
1969   *The Sciences of the Artificial.* Cambridge, Mass.: MIT Press.

Simoons, F. D.
1960   *Northwest Ethiopia: Peoples and Economy.* Madison: University of Wisconsin Press.
1965   Some questions on the ecomic prehistory of Ethiopia. *Journal of African History* 6: 1–13.
1973   The determinants of dairying and milk use in the Old World: ecological, physiological, and cultural. *Ecology of Food and Nutrition* 2: 83–90.

Simpson, W. K.
1973   (ed.) *The Literature of Ancient Egypt.* (2nd ed.) New Haven: Yale University Press.

Singer, R.
1958   The Boskop "race" problem. *Man* 58: 173–178.

Sjovold, T.
1975   Some notes on the distribution and certain modifications of Malhalanobis' generalized distance. *Journal of Human Evolution* 4: 549–558.

Slobodkin, L. B., and H. L. Sanders
1969   On the contribution of environmental predictability to species diversity. *Diversity and Stability in Ecological Systems.* Brookhaven, N.Y.: Brookhaven Symposium in Biology No. 22.

Smeds, H.
1955   The Ensete planting culture of eastern Sidamo. *Acta Geographica* 13(4): 34.

Smith, A. B.
1974   Preliminary report of excavations at Karkarichinkat Nord and Sud, Tilemsi Valley, Mali, spring 1972. *West African Journal of Archaeology* 4: 33–55.
1975a   Problems of pastoralism in the West African Sahel: an archaeological perspective. *Sankofa* 1: 41–44.
1975b   Radiocarbon dates from Bosumpra cave, Abetifi, Ghana. *Proceedings of the Prehistoric Society* 41: 179–182.
1975c   A note on the flora and fauna from the post-Palaeolithic sites of Karkarichinkat Nord and Sud. *West African Journal of Archaeology* 5: 201–204.
1976   A microlithic industry from Adrar Bous, Ténéré Desert, Niger. In B. Abebe, J. Chavaillon, and J. E. G. Sutton, eds., *Actes du septième congrès panafricain de préhistoire*: 181–196. Addis Ababa.
1979   Biogeographical considerations of colonization of the lower Tilemsi valley in the second millennium B.C. *Journal of Arid Environments* 2: 355–361.
1980a   Domesticated cattle in the Sahara, and their introduction into West Africa. In M. A. J. Williams and H. Faure, eds., *The Sahara and the Nile*: 489–500. Rotterdam: Balkema.
1980b   The Neolithic tradition in the Sahara. In M. A. J. Williams and H. Faure, eds., *The Sahara and the Nile*: 451–465. Rotterdam: Balkema.
n.d.   Adrar Bous and Karkarichinkat: examples of post-Palaeolithic human adaptation in the Saharan and Sahel zones of West Africa. Ph.D. dissertation, University of California, Berkeley (1974).

Smith, C. E.
1969   From Vavilov to the present: a review *Economic Botany* 23(1): 2–19.

Smith, E. W., and A. M. Dale
1920   *The Ila-Speaking Peoples of Northern Rhodesia.* (2 vols.) London: Macmillan.

Smith, H. S.
1964   Egypt and C^{14} dating. *Antiquity* 38: 32–37.

Smith, J.
1949   *Distribution of Tree Species in the Sudan in Relation to Rainfall and Soil Texture.* Bulletin No. 4. Khartoum, Republic of the Sudan: Ministry of Agriculture.

Smith, P. E. L.
1972   Changes in population pressure in archaeological explanation. *World Archaeology* 4: 5–18.
1976   Early food production in northern Africa as seen from southwestern Asia. In J. R. Harlan, J. M. J. de Wet, and A. B. L. Stemler, eds., *Origins of African Plant Domestication*: 155–183. The Hague: Mouton.

Smith, P. E. L., and T. C. Young
1972   The evolution of early agriculture and culture in Greater Mesopotamia: a trial model. In B. J. Spooner, ed., *Population Growth: Anthropological Implications*: 1–59. Cambridge, Mass.: MIT Press.

Smith, S. E.
1980   The environmental adaptation of nomads in the West African Sahel: a key to understanding prehistoric pastoralists. In M. A. J. Williams and H. Faure, eds., *The Sahara and the Nile*: 467–487. Rotterdam: Balkema.

Smolla, G.
1957   Prähistorische Keramik aus Ostafrika. *Tribus* 6: 35–64.

Sonntag, C., U. Thorweihe, J. Rudolph, E. P. Löhnert, C. Junghaus, K. O. Münnich, E. Klitsch, E. M. El-Shazly, and F. M. Swailem
1980   Isotopic identification of Saharan groundwaters, groundwater formation in the past. *Palaeoecology of Africa* 12: 159–171.

Soper, R. C.
1967a   Kwale, an Early Iron Age site in south-eastern Kenya. *Azania* 2: 1–17.
1967b   Iron Age sites in north-eastern Tanzania. *Azania* 2: 19–36.
1969   Radiocarbon dating of "dimple-based ware" in western Kenya. *Azania* 4: 148–153.

Soper, R. C., and B. Golden
1969   An archaeological survey of the Mwanza region, Tanzania. *Azania* 4: 15–80.

Sparks, B. W., and A. T. Grove
1961   Some Quaternary fossil non-marine molluscs from the central Sahara. *Journal of the Linnean Society–London Zoology* 44: 355–364.

Spencer, P.
1973   *Nomads in Alliance: Symbiosis and Growth among the Rendille and Samburu of Kenya.* London: Oxford University Press.

Speth, J., and D. Davis
1976   Seasonal variability in early hominid predation. *Science* 192: 441–445.

Spiegel, J.
1975   Admonitions. *Lexikon Ägyptologie* 1: 65–66.

Spooner, B. J.
1972   (ed.) *Population Growth: Anthropological Implications.* Cambridge, Mass.: MIT Press.
1973   *The Cultural Ecology of Pastoral Nomads.* Modules in Anthropology No. 45. Reading, Mass.: Addison-Wesley.

Spuhler, J. N.
1972   Behavior and mating patterns in human populations. In G. W. Harrison and A. J. Boyce, eds., *The Structure of Human Populations.* Oxford: Clarendon Press.

Stanton, W. R.
1962   The analysis of the present distribution of varietal variation in maize, sorghum, and cowpea in Nigeria as an aid to the study of tribal movements. *Journal of African History* 3: 251–262.

Steinbock, R. T.
1976   *Paleopathological Diagnosis and Interpretation: Bone Disease in Ancient Human Populations.* Springfield, Ill.: C. C. Thomas.

Stemler, A. B. L.
1980   Origins of plant domestication in the Sahara and the Nile. In M. A. J. Williams and H. Faure, eds., *The Sahara and the Nile*: 503–526. Rotterdam: Balkema.

Stemler, A. B. L., and R. H. Falk
1980   A scanning electron microscopic study of cereal grains from Wadi Kubbaniya. In F. Wendorf, R. Schild, and A. E. Close, *Loaves and Fishes: The Prehistory of Wadi Kubbaniya*: 299–306. Dallas: Department of Anthropology, Institute for the Study of Earth and Man, Southern Methodist University.

Stemler, A. B. L., J. R. Harlan, and J. M. J. de Wet
1975   Caudatum sorghums and speakers of Chari-Nile languages in Africa. *Journal of African History* 16(2): 161–183.
1977   The sorghums of Ethiopia. *Economic Botany* 31: 446–460.

Stenning, D. J.
1959   *Savannah Nomads*. London: Oxford University Press.

Stern, J. T., and R. Singer
1967   Quantitative morphological distinctions between Bushman and Hottentot skulls: a preliminary report. *South African Archaeological Bulletin* 22: 103–111.

Stern, L.
1873   Die Nilstele von Gebel Silsileh. *Zeitschrift für ägyptische Sprache und Altertumskunde* 1: 129–135.

Story, R.
1958   *Some Plants Used by the Bushmen in Obtaining Food and Water*. Memoir No. 30. Pretoria: Botanical Survey of South Africa.
1964   Plant lore of the Bushmen. In D. H. S. Davis, ed., *Ecological Studies in Southern Africa*: 87–99. The Hague: W. Junk.

Stout, S. D.
1979   Use of histology in ancient bone research. *Yearbook of Physical Anthropology* 22: 228–249.

Stout, S. D., and S. L. Teitelbaum
1976a Histomorphometric determination of formation rates of archaeological bone. *Calcified Tissue Research* 21: 163–169.

1976b Histological analysis of undecalcified thin sections of archaeological bone. *American Journal of Physical Anthropology* 44: 263–270.

Stow, G. W.
1905   *Native Races of South Africa*. Ed. G. Theal. New York: MacMillan.

Straube, H.
1963   *Westkuschitische Völker Süd-Äthiopiens*. Stuttgart: W. Kohlhammer.

Street, F. A., and A. T. Grove
1976   Environmental and climatic implications of Late Quaternary lake-level fluctuations in Africa. *Nature* 261: 385–390.

Stringer, C. B.
1979   A re-evaluation of the fossil human calvaria from Singa, Sudan. *Bulletin of the British Museum of Natural History* 32: 77–83.

Strouhal, E.
1968   Une contribution à la question du caractère de la population préhistorique de la Haute-Egypte. *Anthropologie* (Brno) 6: 19–22.
1971a Anthropometric and functional evidence of heterosis from Egyptian Nubia. *Human Biology* 43: 271–287.
1971b A contribution to the anthropology of the Nubian X-Group. *Anthropological Congress Dedicated to Ales Hrdlicka*: 541–547. Prague: Humpolec.
1971c Evidence of the early penetration of Negroes into prehistoric Egypt. *Journal of African History* 12: 1–9.

Strowbridge, N.
n.d.   Linguistic evidence for Berber history. Seminar paper, University of California, Los Angeles (1975).

Struever, S.
1968   Woodland subsistence-settlement systems in the Lower Illinois Valley. In S. Binford and L. Binford, eds., *New Perspectives in Archaeology*: 285–312. Chicago: Aldine.

Suchey, J. M., D. V. Wiseley, R. F. Green, and T. T. Noguchi
1979   Analysis of dorsal pitting in the *os pubis* in an extensive sample of modern American females. *American Journal of Physical Anthropology* 51: 517–523.

Summers, R.
1958   *Inyanga*. Cambridge: Cambridge University Press.

Sundick, R. I.
n.d.   Human skeletal growth and dental development as observed in the Indian Knoll population. Ph.D. dissertation, University of Toronto (1979).

Sutton, J. E. G.
1964   A review of the pottery from the Kenya highlands. *South African Archaeological Bulletin* 19(74:2): 27–35.
1966   The archaeology and early peoples of the highlands of Kenya and northern Tanzania. *Azania* 1: 37–58.
1967   The East African "Neolithic." In H. J. Hugot, ed., *Actes du sixième congrès panafricain de préhistoire*: 88–90. Paris: Chambéry.
1968   The settlement of East Africa. In B. A. Ogot and J. A. Kieran, eds., *Zamani: A Survey of East African History*: 69–99. New York: Humanities Press.
1969   "Ancient civilizations" and modern agricultural systems in the southern highlands of Tanzania. *Azania* 4: 1–13.
1971   The interior of East Africa. In P. L. Shinnie, ed., *The African Iron Age*: 142–182. Oxford: Clarendon.
1973   *The Archaeology of the Western Highlands of Kenya*. Memoir No. 3. Nairobi: British Institute in East Africa.
1974   The aquatic civilization of middle Africa. *Journal of African History* 15: 527–546.
1977   The African Aqualithic. *Antiquity* 51: 25–34.

Swärdstedt, T.
1966   *Odontological Aspects of a Medieval Population in the Province of Jamtland/Mid-Sweden*. Stockholm: Tiden-Barnangen Tryckerier.

Szumowski, G.
1954   Fouilles à Fatoma (région de Mopti, Soudan). *Notes africaines* 64: 102–108.
1955   Fouilles à Kami et découvertes dans la région de Mopti (Soudan). *Notes africaines* 67: 65–69.
1956   Fouilles à Nantaka et Kélébéré (région de Mopti, Soudan). *Notes africaines* 70: 33–38.

Täckholm, V.
1941   Flora of Egypt I. *Bulletin of the Faculty of Science* 17. Cairo: Egyptian University.

Talbot, L. M.
n.d.   The Ecology of Western Masailand. Ph.D. dissertation, University of California, Berkeley (1963).

Talbot, M. R.
1980   Environmental responses to climatic change in the West African Sahel over the past 20,000 years. In M. A. J. Williams and H. Faure, eds., *The Sahara and the Nile*: 37–62. Rotterdam: Balkema.

Tanaka, J.
1969   The ecology and the social structure of central Kalahari Bushmen: a preliminary report. *Kyoto University African Studies* 3: 1–26.
1971   *The Bushmen*. Tokyo: Shisakusha.
1976   Subsistence ecology of the central Kalahari San. In R. B. Lee and I. DeVore, eds., *Kalahari Hunter-Gatherers: Studies of the !Kung San and Their Neighbors*: 98–119. Cambridge, Mass.: Harvard University Press.
1980   *The San, Hunter-Gatherers of the Kalahari*. Tokyo: University of Tokyo Press.

Terell, J.
1977   Biology, biogeography of man. *World Archaeology* 8(3): 237–248.

Thackeray, J. F.
1979   An analysis of faunal remains from archaeological sites in southern South

West Africa (Namibia). *South African Archaeological Bulletin* 34: 18–33.

Theal, G. M.
1882   *Chronicles of the Cape Commanders.* Cape Town: W. A. Richards and Sons.

Thiede, J.
1978   A glacial Mediterranean. *Nature* 276: 680–683.
1980   The Late Quaternary marine paleoenvironments between Europe and Africa. *Palaeoecology of Africa* 12: 213–225.

Thom, H. B.
1952–   *Journal of van Riebeeck.* (Trans. from
1958   Dutch, 3 vols.) Cape Town: Van Riebeeck Society.

Thoma, A.
n.d.   Arable land development by Basarwa. Report to the Kgalagadi District Council, Tsabong, Botswana (1978).

Thoma, D. G.
1970   Finger millet (*Eleusine coracana* (L.) Gaertn). In J. D. Jameson, ed., *Agriculture in Uganda*: 145–153. London: Oxford University Press.

Thunell, R. C.
1979   Eastern Mediterranean sea during the Last Glacial maximum: an 18,000 years B.P. reconstruction. *Quaternary Research* 11(3): 353–372.

Tieszen, L. L., D. Hein, S. A. Qvortrup, J. H. Troughton, and S. K. Imbamba
1979   Use of $\delta^{13}C$ values to determine vegetation selectivity in East African herbivores. *Oecologia* 37(3): 351–359.

Tieszen, L. L., M. M. Senyimba, S. K. Imbamba, and J. H. Troughton
1979   The distribution of C3 and C4 grasses and carbon isotope discrimination along an altitudinal and moisture gradient in Kenya. *Oecologia* 37(3): 337–350.

Tigani el Mahi, A.
1979   Preliminary analysis of the osteological

remains from 4 sq. m. excavated from Shaheinab site. *Nyame Akuma* 15: 57–60.

Tixier, J.
1954   Le gisement préhistorique d'El-Hamel. *Libyca* 2: 78–120.
1963   *Typologie de l'Epipaléolithique du Maghreb.* Mémoires du CRAPE 2. Paris: Arts et Métiers Graphiques.
1976   L'industrie lithique capsienne de l'Aïn Dokkara. *Libyca* 24: 21–54.

Tlou, T.
1977   Servility and political control: Batlhanka among the Batawana of northwestern Botswana, ca. 1750–1906. In S. Miers and I. Kopytoff, eds., *Slavery in Africa: Historical and Anthropological Perspectives*: 367–390. Madison: University of Wisconsin Press.

Tobias, P. V.
1955   Physical anthropology and somatic origins of the Hottentots. *African Studies* 14(1): 1–15.
1975   Anthropometry among disadvantaged peoples: studies in southern Africa. In E. S. Watts, F. E. Johnston, and G. W. Lasker, eds., *Biosocial Interrelations in Population Adaptations*. Paris: Mouton.
1978a   Introduction to the Bushmen or San. In P. V. Tobias, ed., *The Bushmen*: 1–15. Cape Town and Pretoria: Human and Rousseau.
1978b   The San: An Evolutionary Perspective. In P. V. Tobias, ed., *The Bushmen*: 16–32. Cape Town and Pretoria: Human and Rousseau.

Tosi, M.
1973   Early urban evolution and settlement patterns in the Indo-Iranian borderland. In C. Renfrew, ed., *The Explanation of Culture Change*: 42–46. London: Duckworth.

Traill, A.
1978   The languages of the Bushmen. In P. V. Tobias, ed., *The Bushmen*: 137–147. Cape Town and Pretoria: Human and Rousseau.

Trigger, B. G.
1965   History and settlement in lower Nubia. *Yale University Publications in Anthropology* 69: 1–224.
1968   *Beyond History: The Methods of Prehistory.* New York: Holt, Rinehart and Winston.
1976   *Nubia under the Pharaohs.* Boulder: Westview.

Tringham, R.
1972   Territorial demarcation of prehistoric settlements. In P. J. Ucko, R. Tringham, and G. W. Dimbleby, eds., *Man, Settlement and Urbanism*: 463–475. London: Duckworth.

Tringham, R., G. Cooper, G. Odell, B. Voytek, and A. Whitman
1974   Experimentation in the formation of edge damage: a new approach to lithic analysis. *Journal of Field Archaeology* 1: 171–196.

Truswell, A. S., and J. D. L. Hansen
1976   Medical research among the !Kung. In R. B. Lee and I. DeVore, eds., *Kalahari Hunter-Gatherers: Studies of the !Kung San and Their Neighbors*: 156–194. Cambridge, Mass.: Harvard University Press.

Turnbull, C. M.
1963   The lesson of the Pygmies. *Scientific American* 208: 1.
1965   *Wayward Servants: Two Worlds of the African Pygmies.* New York: Natural History Press.

Turner, M.
1970   A search for the Tsitsikama shelters. *South African Archaeological Bulletin* 25: 67–70.

Ubelaker, D. H.
1978   *Human Skeletal Remains.* Chicago: Aldine.

Vallois, H. V.
1951   La mandibule humaine fossile de la grotte du Porc Epic, près Diré-Daoua (Abyssinie). *Anthropologie* 55: 231–238.

Van Beek, G. W.
1969   *Hajar bin Humeid.* Baltimore: Johns Hopkins.

Van der Merwe, N. J., and J. C. Vogel
1978   13C content of human collagen as a measure of prehistoric diet in woodland North America. *Nature* 276: 815–816.

Van der Walt, L. A., E. N. Wilmsen, J. Levin, and T. Jenkins
1977   Studies on the San ("Bushmen") of Botswana. *South African Journal of Medicine* 52: 230–232.

Vandier, J.
1936   *La famine dans l'Egypte ancienne.* Cairo: Institut Français d'Archéologie Orientale.

Van Gerven, D. P., G. J. Armelagos, and A. Rohr
1977   Continuity and change in cranial morphology of three Nubian archaeological populations. *Man* n.s. 12: 270–277.

Van Gerven, D. P., D. S. Carlson, and G. J. Armelagos
1973   Racial history and bio-cultural adaptation of Nubian archaeological populations. *Journal of African History* 14: 555–564.

Van Zinderen Bakker, E. M.
1962   A late-glacial and post-glacial climatic correlation between East Africa and Europe. *Nature* 194: 201–203.
1964   A pollen diagram from Equatorial Africa–Cherangani, Kenya. *Geologie en Mijnbouw* 43: 123–128.

Van Zinderen Bakker, E. M., and Coetzee, J. A.
1972   A re-appraisal of Late-Quaternary climatic evidence from tropical Africa. *Palaeoecology of Africa* 7: 151–181.

Vaufrey, R.
1955   *Préhistoire de l'Afrique I: Le Maghreb.* Paris: Masson.

Vavilov, N. I.
1926   *Studies on the Origin of Cultivated Plants.* (Russian and English.) Leningrad: Institute of Applied Botanical Plant Breeding.
1951a   The origin, variation, immunity and

breeding of cultivated plants. *Chronica Botanica* 13: 1–364.

1951b   *Phytogeographic Basis of Plant Breeding of Cultivated Plants*. (Reprint of 1926 ed.) New York: Ronald Press.

Vermeersch, P. M.
1970   L'Elkabien, une nouvelle industrie Epipaléolithique à Elkab en Haute Egypte: sa stratigraphie, sa typologie. *Chronique d'Egypte* 45: 42–67.

Vierich, H. I. D.
n.d.a   Interim report on Basarwa and related poor Bakgalagadi in Kweneng District. Report to the Ministry of Local Government and Lands, Gaborone, Botswana (1977).

n.d.b   The parameters of hunting and gathering in a multi-ethnic setting: adaptive flexibility in the southeast Kalahari. Paper presented at the Conference on Hunter-Gatherer Societies, Maison de Sciences de l'Homme, Paris, France (1978).

Vierich, H. I. D., and R. K. Hitchcock
1978   Some economically important plant species in the Kalahari: description and uses. In R. K. Hitchcock, ed., *Kalahari Cattle Posts*: II, pp. 42–54. Gaborone: Botswana Government Printer.

Villiers, H. de
1968   *The Skull of the South African Negro: A Biometrical and Morphological Study*. Johannesburg: University of Witwatersrand Press.

Vita-Finzi, C.
1967   Late Quaternary alluvial chronology of northern Algeria. *Man* 2(2): 205–215.
1976   Diachronism in Old World alluvial sequences. *Nature* 263: 218–219.

Vita-Finzi, C., and E. S. Higgs
1970   Prehistoric economy in the Mount Carmel area of Palestine: site catchment analysis. *Proceedings of the Prehistoric Society* 36: 1–37.

Vogel, J. C.
1970   Groningen radiocarbon dates IX. *Radiocarbon* 12: 444–471.
1978   Isotopic assessment of the dietary habits of ungulates. *South African Journal of Science* 74: 298–301.

Vogel, J. O.
1969   On early evidence of agriculture in southern Zambia. *Current Anthropology* 10: 524.
1971   *Kumadzulo*. Lusaka: Oxford University Press.

Von Hohnel, L.
1894   *Discovery by Count Teleki of Lakes Rudolf and Stefanie*. London: Longmans, Green.

Wagner, P. L.
1977   The concept of environmental determinism in cultural evolution. In C. A. Reed, ed., *Origins of Agriculture*: 49–74. The Hague: Mouton.

Walker, A., H. W. Hoeck, and L. Perez
1978   Microwear of mammalian teeth as an indicator of diet. *Science* 201: 908–910.

Walter, H.
1971   *Ecology of Tropical and Subtropical Vegetation*. Edinburgh: Oliver and Boyd.
1973   *Vegetation of the Earth (in Relation to Climate and the Ecophysiological Conditions)*. New York: Springer-Verlag.

Wandibba, S.
1980   The application of attribute analysis to the study of later Stone Age/Neolithic ceramics in Kenya—a summary of conclusions. In R. E. Leakey and B. A. Ogot, eds., *Proceedings of the Eighth Panafrican Congress of Prehistory and Quaternary Studies*: 283–285. Nairobi: The International Louis Leakey Memorial Institute for African Prehistory.

n.d.   An attribute analysis of the ceramics of the early pastoralist period from the southern Rift Valley, Kenya. M.S. thesis, University of Nairobi (1977).

Ward, F. K.
1940   Plant hunting through the centuries. *Nature* 145: 574–576.

Ware, H.
1977   Desertification and population: sub-Saharan Africa. In M. H. Glantz, ed., *Desertification*. Boulder: Westview.

Warren, A.
1970   Dune trends and their implications in the central Sudan. *Zeitschrift für Geomorphologie* n.f. Suppl. 10: 154–180.
1972   Observations on dunes and bi-modal sand in the Ténéré Desert. *Sedimentology* 19: 37–44.

Washburn, S. L.
1976   Foreword. In R. B. Lee and I. DeVore, eds., *Kalahari Hunter-Gatherers: Studies of the !Kung San and Their Neighbors*: xv–xvii. Cambridge, Mass.: Harvard University Press.

Weisrock, A., and P. Rognon
1977   Evolution morphologique des basses vallées de l'Atlas atlantique marocain. *Géologie méditerranéenne* 4: 313–334.

Weiss, K.
1973   Demographic models for anthropology. *American Antiquity* 38(2) (pt. II): 1–186.

Wells, L. H.
1929   Fossil Bushmen from the Zuurberg. *South African Journal of Science* 55: 806–834.
1951   The fossil human skull from Singa. *Fossil Mammals of Africa* 2: 29–42.
1960   Bushmen and Hottentot statures: a review of the evidence. *South African Journal of Science* 56: 277–281.

Welmers, W.
1973   *African Language Structures*. Berkeley: University of California Press.

Wendorf, F.
1968   (ed.) *The Prehistory of Nubia*. (2 vols. and atlas.) Dallas: Fort Burgwin Research Center and Southern Methodist University Press.

Wendorf, F., and F. A. Hassan
1980   Holocene ecology and prehistory in the Egyptian Sahara. In M. A. J. Williams and H. Faure, eds., *The Sahara and the Nile*: 407–419. Rotterdam: Balkema.

Wendorf, F., R. Said, and R. Schild
1970   Egyptian prehistory: some new concepts. *Science* 169: 1161–1171.

Wendorf, F., and R. Schild
1976a   *Prehistory of the Nile Valley*. New York: Academic Press.
1976b   The use of ground grain during the late Palaeolithic of the lower Nile Valley, Egypt. In J. R. Harlan, J. M. J. de Wet, and A. B. L. Stemler, eds., *Origins of African Plant Domestication*: 269–288. The Hague: Mouton.
1980   *Prehistory of the Eastern Sahara*. New York: Academic Press.

Wendorf, F., R. Schild, N. El Hadidi, A. E. Close, M. Kobusiewicz, H. Wieckowska, B. Issawi, and H. Haas
1979   The use of barley in the Egyptian late Palaeolithic. *Science* 205: 1341–1347.

Wendorf, F., R. Schild, and R. Said
1970   Problems of dating the late Paleolithic age in Egypt. In I. U. Olsson, ed., *Radiocarbon Variations and Absolute Chronology*: 57–79. Stockholm: Almqvist and Wiksell.

Wendorf, F., R. Schild, R. Said, C. V. Haynes, A. Gautier, and M. Kobusiewicz
1976   The prehistory of the Egyptian Sahara. *Science* 193: 103–114.
1977   Late Pleistocene and Recent climatic changes in the Egyptian Sahara. *Geographical Journal* 143: 211–234.

Wendt, W. E.
1966   Two prehistoric archaeological sites in Egyptian Nubia. *Postilla* 102: 1–46.
1976   "Art mobilier" from the Apollo 11 Cave, South West Africa: Africa's oldest dated works of art. *South African Archaeological Bulletin* 31: 5–11.

Wente, E. F., and C. C. Van Siclen
1977   A chronology of the New Kingdom.

Studies in Ancient Oriental Civilization 39: 217–261.

Westermann, D.
1927   *Die westlichen Sudan-Sprachen und ihre Beziehungen zum Bantu.* Supplement to *Mitteilungen des Seminars für orientalischen Sprachen.* Berlin: W. de Gruyter.

Western, D.
1975   Water availability and its influence on the structure and dynamics of a savannah large mammal community. *East African Wildlife Journal* 13: 265–286.
n.d.   The structure, dynamics and changes of the Amboseli ecosystem. Ph.D. dissertation, University of Nairobi (1973).

Western, D., and T. Dunne
1979   Environmental aspects of settlement site decisions among pastoral Maasai. *Human Ecology* 7(1): 75–98.

Westphal, E.
1974   *Pulses in Ethiopia, their taxonomy and agricultural significance.* Wageningen: Centre for Agricultural Publishing and Documentation.

Westphal, E. O. J.
1963   The linguistic prehistory of southern Africa: Bush, Kwadi, Hottentot and Bantu linguistic relationships. *Africa* 33: 237–265.

Wheatley, P.
1970   The significance of traditional Yoruba urbanism. *Comparative Studies in Society and History* 12: 393–423.
1971   *The Pivot of the Four Quarters.* Chicago: Aldine.

White, L. A.
1959   *The Evolution of Culture.* New York: McGraw-Hill.

Whittle, E. H.
1975   Thermoluminescent dating of Egyptian Predynastic pottery from Hemamieh and Qurna-tarif. *Archaeometry* 17: 1.

Wickens, G. E.
1976   *The Flora of Jebel Marra (Sudan Republic)*

and Its Geographical Affinities. Kew Bulletin Additional Series. London: Her Majesty's Stationery Office.

Wiesenfeld, S. L.
1967   Sickle-cell trait in human biological and cultural evolution. *Science* 157: 1134–1140.

Wiessner, P.
n.d.   Hxaro: a regional system of reciprocity for reducing risk among the !Kung San. Ph.D. dissertation, University of Michigan (1977).

Wildung, D.
1969   Die Rolle ägyptischer Könige im Bewusstsein ihrer Nachwelt. *Münchener ägyptologische Studien* 17: 1–265.

Wilke, P. J., R. Bettinger, T. F. King, and J. F. O'Connell
1972   Harvest selection and domestication in seed plants. *Antiquity* 46: 203–208.

Willcocks, W.
1889   *Egyptian Irrigation.* London: Spon.
1904   *The Nile in 1904.* London: Spon.

Willcocks, W., and J. I. Craig
1913   *Egyptian Irrigation.* (3rd ed., 2 vols.) London: Spon.

Willett, F.
1962   The microlithic industry from Old Oyo, Western Nigeria. *Actes du quatrième congrès panafricain de préhistoire et de l'étude du Quaternaire*: 261–271. Tervuren.
1971   A survey of recent results in the radiocarbon chronology of western and northern Africa. *Journal of African History* 12(3): 339–370.

Williams, G. E.
1970   Piedmont sedimentation and Late Quaternary chronology in the Biskra region of the northern Sahara. *Zeitschrift für Geomorphologie N.F. Suppl.* 10: 40–63.

Williams, M. A. J.
1971   Geomorphology and Quaternary geology of Adrar Bous. *Geographical Journal* 137: 450–455.

1975   Late Pleistocene tropical aridity synchronous in both hemispheres? *Nature* 253: 617–618.

1976a   Upper Quaternary stratigraphy of Adrar Bous (Republic of Niger, south-central Sahara). *Actes du septième congrès panafricain de préhistoire et de l'étude du Quaternaire*: 435–441. Addis Ababa.

1976b   Radiocarbon dating and Saharan palaeoclimates: a discussion. *Zeitschrift für Geomorphologie* n.f. 20: 361–362.

Williams, M. A. J., and D. A. Adamson

1974   Late Pleistocene desiccation along the White Nile. *Nature* 248: 584–586.

1980   Late Quaternary depositional history of the Blue and White Nile rivers in central Sudan. In M. A. J. Williams and H. Faure, eds., *The Sahara and the Nile*: 281–304. Rotterdam: Balkema.

Williams, M. A. J., D. A. Adamson, F. M. Williams, W. H. Morton, and D. E. Parry

1980   Jebel Marra volcano: a link between the Nile Valley, the Sahara and Central Africa. In M. A. J. Williams and H. Faure, eds., *The Sahara and the Nile*: 305–337. Rotterdam: Balkema.

Williams, M. A. J., and H. Faure

1980   (eds.) *The Sahara and the Nile*. Rotterdam: Balkema.

Williams, M. A. J., A. H. Medani, J. A. Talent, and R. Mawson

1974   A note on Upper Quaternary mollusca west of Jebel Aulia. *Sudan Notes and Records* 54: 168–172.

Wilmsen, E. N.

1973   Interaction, spacing behavior and the organization of hunting bands. *Journal of Anthropological Research* 29(1): 1–31.

1978   Seasonal effects of dietary intake on Kalahari San. *Federation of American Societies for Experimental Biology Proceedings* 37(1): 65–72.

1979   Prehistoric and historic antecedents of a contemporary Ngamiland community.

Working Paper No. 12. Boston: African Studies Center, Boston University.

1982   Studies in diet, nutrition and fertility among a group of Kalahari Bushmen in Botswana. *Social Science Information* 21: 95–125.

in press   Underlying variables in hunter and herder fertility performance. In P. Handwerker, ed., *Culture and Reproduction*. Academic Press.

Wilson, J. A.

1946   Egypt. In H. Frankfort, H. A. Frankfort, J. A. Wilson, T. Jacobsen, and W. A. Irwin, eds., *The Intellectual Adventure of Ancient Man*: 31–122. Chicago: University of Chicago Press.

1951   *The Burden of Egypt*. Chicago: University of Chicago Press.

1963   *The Culture of Ancient Egypt*. (9th impression.) Chicago: University of Chicago Press.

Wilson, L. E.

n.d.   The evolution of Krobo society: a history from c. 1400–1892. Ph.D. dissertation, University of California, Los Angeles (1980).

Wilson, M.

1969   The hunters and herders. In M. Wilson and L. Thompson, eds., *The Oxford History of South Africa*: Vol. 1, 40–84. London: Oxford University Press.

Wishart, D.

1978   *CLUSTAN User Manual*. Edinburgh: Edinburgh University.

Wittfogel, K.

1938   Die Theorie der orientalischen Gesellschaft. *Zeitschrift für Sozialforschung* 7: 90–122.

Wobst, H.

1974   Boundary conditions for Paleolithic social systems: a simulation approach. *American Antiquity* 39: 147–178.

1978   The archaeo-ethnology of hunter-gatherers, or the tyranny of the ethnographic record in archaeology. *American Antiquity* 43(2): 303–309.

Woodburn, J.
1968a Stability and flexibility in Hadza residential groupings. In R. B. Lee and I. DeVore, eds., *Man the Hunter*: 103–110. Chicago: Aldine.
1968b An introduction to Hadza ecology. In R. B. Lee and I. DeVore, eds., *Man the Hunter*: 49–55. Chicago: Aldine.
1972 Ecology, nomadic movement and the composition of the local group among hunters and gatherers: an East African example and its implications. In P. J. Ucko, R. Tringham, and G. W. Dimbleby, eds., *Man, Settlement and Urbanism*: 193–206. London: Duckworth.

Woodel, S. R. J., and L. E. Newton
1975 A Standard-winged Night-jar breeding in the forest zone of Ghana. *Nigeria Field* 40: 169–171.

Woodward, A. S.
1938 A fossil skull of an ancestral Bushman from the Anglo-Egyptian Sudan. *Antiquity* 12: 193–195.

Worthington, B. S., J. Vermeersch, and S. R. Williams
1977 *Nutrition in Pregnancy and Lactation.* St. Louis: C. V. Mosby.

Wright, H. E., Jr.
1976 The environmental setting for plant domestication in the Near East. *Science* 194: 385–389.

Wright, J. B.
1971 *Bushman Raiders of the Drakensberg 1840–1870.* Pietermaritzburg: University of Natal Press.

Wrigley, C.
1960 Speculations on the economic prehistory of Africa. *Journal of African History* 1: 189–203.

Yellen, J. E.
1976 Settlement pattern of the !Kung Bushmen: an archaeological perspective. In R. B. Lee and I. DeVore, eds., *Kalahari Hunter-Gatherers: Studies of the !Kung San and Their Neighbors*: 47–72. Cambridge, Mass.: Harvard University Press.
1977a Long-term hunter-gatherer adaptation to desert environments: a biogeographic perspective. *World Archaeology* 8(3): 264–274.
1977b *Archaeological Approaches to the Present.* New York: Academic Press.

Yellen, J. E., and H. C. Harpending
1972 Hunter-gatherer populations and archaeological inference. *World Archaeology* 4(4): 244–253.

Yellen, J. E., and R. B. Lee
1976 The Dobe-/Du/Da environment: background to a hunting and gathering way of life. In R. B. Lee and I. DeVore, eds., *Kalahari Hunter-Gatherers: Studies of the !Kung San and Their Neighbors*: 27–46. Cambridge, Mass.: Harvard University Press.

York, R. N.
1974 Excavations at Dutsen Kongba near Jos, Nigeria (preliminary notice). *Nyame Akuma* 4: 17–20.

Zyhlarz, E.
1958 The countries of the Ethiopian empire of Kash (Kush) and Egyptian Old Ethiopia in the New Kingdom. *Kush* 6: 7–38.

Index

Designer: Randall Goodall
Compositor: Wilsted & Taylor
Printer: Malloy Lithographing, Inc.
Binder: John H. Dekker & Sons
Text: 12/12 Cloister
Display: Cloister and Palatino